DATE DUE

Printed
in USA

The Mexican American Experience

AN ENCYCLOPEDIA

MATT S. MEIER AND MARGO GUTIÉRREZ

GREENWOOD PRESS
Westport, Connecticut • London

Library of Congress Cataloging-in-Publication Data

Meier, Matt S.
   The Mexican American experience : an encyclopedia / Matt S. Meier and Margo Gutiérrez.
      p. cm.
   Includes bibliographical references and index.
   ISBN 0–313–31643–0 (alk. paper)
   1. Mexican Americans—Encyclopedias.   2. Mexican Americans—Southwest, New—Encyclopedias.   I. Gutiérrez, Margo.   II. Title.
E184.M5M4535   2003
973′.046872′003—dc21   2003052845

British Library Cataloguing in Publication Data is available.

Library of Congress Catalog Card Number: 2003052845
ISBN: 0–313–31643–0

First published in 2003

Greenwood Press, 88 Post Road West, Westport, CT 06881
An imprint of Greenwood Publishing Group, Inc.
www.greenwood.com

Printed in the United States of America

The paper used in this book complies with the Permanent Paper Standard issued by the National Information Standards Organization (Z39.48–1984).

10 9 8 7 6 5 4 3 2 1

Contents

Guide to Selected Related Entries

The following list is intended to provide the reader with a guide to inter-related entries by topics. The entries are subsumed under the following topics:

Administration, Academic
Administration, Government
Agriculture
Bilingualism
Border
Business/Commerce
Civic Leadership
Civil Rights
Community
Discrimination
Education, Classroom
Education, Scholarship
Engineering
Finance
Fine Arts
Immigration
Journalism/Publishing
Labor
Land Grant Issues
Law/Legal Cases
Legislation
Literature, Poetry
Literature, Prose
Medicine
Migration
Military
Movimiento

Guide to Selected Related Entries

ADMINISTRATION, ACADEMIC

ADMINISTRATION, GOVERNMENT

TELLES, RAYMOND L.
TORRES, ESTEBAN E.
VALLEJO, MARIANO GUADALUPE
VILLALPANDO, CATHI
VILLARAIGOSA, ANTONIO R.
XIMENES, VICENTE TREVÍNO

AGRICULTURE

AGRICULTURE, SOUTHWESTERN
AUSTIN MARCH
LABOR, AGRICULTURAL
LETTUCE STRIKE, SALINAS
NATIONAL FARM LABOR UNION

BILINGUALISM

BILINGUALISM EQUAL EDUCATIONAL OPPORTUNITY ACT

BORDER

BANDITRY, SOCIAL
BORDER CONFLICT
BORDER CULTURE
BORDER PATROL
COMMUTER
GADSDEN PURCHASE TREATY
GUADALUPE HIDALGO, TREATY OF
LIGHT UP THE BORDER
OPEN BORDER
PLAN DE SAN DIEGO
RIO GRANDE
SALT WAR
SAN ANTONIO
TEXAS
TUCSON
UNDOCUMENTED

BUSINESS/COMMERCE

ÁLVAREZ, MANUEL
APODACA, JERRY
ARMIJO, MANUEL
BAÑUELOS, ROMANA ACOSTA
BARELA, CASIMIRO
BEAUBIEN, CARLOS
BENAVIDES, SANTOS
BONILLA, TONY

CIVIC LEADERSHIP

CIVIL RIGHTS

COMMUNITY

COLEGIO CÉSAR CHÁVEZ
CORTÉS, CARLOS E.
COTERA, MARTHA P.
EDUCATION
ESPINOSA, AURELIO M.
GILBERT, FABIOLA CABEZA DE BACA
GUZMÁN, RALPH C.
HEAD START
JARAMILLO, MARÍ-LUCI
JUÁREZ- LINCOLN UNIVERSITY
MONTOYA, JOSÉ
PALOMINO, ERNIE
PAREDES, AMÉRICO
ROMANO, OCTAVIO I.
SAMORA, JULIÁN
SÁNCHEZ, GEORGE I.
ULIBARRÍ, SABINE R.
UNZUETA, MANUEL

EDUCATION, SCHOLARSHIP

ACUÑA, RODOLFO F.
BOGARDUS, EMORY S.
CAMPA, ARTHUR LEÓN
CASTAÑEDA, CARLOS E.
CHÁVEZ, ANGÉLICO
CORTÉS, CARLOS E.
ESPINOSA, AURELIO M.
GALARZA, ERNESTO
GÓMEZ-QUIÑONES, JUAN
GONZALES, SYLVIA ALICIA
GUZMÁN, RALPH C.
LOPEZ, LINO M.
MANUEL, HERSCHEL THURMAN
McWILLIAMS, CAREY
NAVA, JULIAN
PAREDES, AMÉRICO
PAZ, OCTAVIO
SAMORA, JULIAN
SÁNCHEZ, GEORGE I.
TYLOR, PAUL
TIREMAN, LOYD

ENGINEERING

COLMENARES, MARGARITA H.
OCHOA, ELLEN

FINANCE

BAÑUELOS, ROMANA ACOSTA
BRAVO, FRANCISCO

FINE ARTS

ARREGUÍN, ALFREDO MENDOZA
ARTS AND ARTISTS
BARELA, PATROCINIO
BURCIAGA, JOSÉ ANTONIO
GARZA, CARMEN LOMAS
GONZALEZ AMEZCUA, CHELO
JIMÉNEZ, LUIS A.
MARTÍNEZ Y OROZCO, XAVIER T.
MONTOYA, JOSÉ
NAVA, GREGORY
NEW MEXICO
PALOMINO, ERNIE
PONCE DE LEÓN, MICHAEL
RODRÍGUEZ, PETER
SALINAS, PORFIRIO, JR.
UNZUETA, MANUEL

IMMIGRATION

AGRICULTURE, SOUTHWESTERN
ASSIMILATION
GAMIO, MANUEL
GREENCARDER
IMMIGRATION
IMMIGRATION LEGISLATION
IMMIGRATION REFORM AND CONTROL ACT
LOS ANGELES
MCCARRAN-WALTER IMMIGRATION AND NATIONALITY ACT
MEXICAN REVOLUTION

JOURNALISM/PUBLISHING

BARRIO, RAYMOND
CABEZA DE BACA, EZEQUIEL
CHACÓN, FELIPE MAXIMILIANO
CON SAFOS
EL CLAMOR PÚBLICO
EL GRITO: A JOURNAL OF CONTEMPORARY MEXICAN AMERICAN THOUGHT
EL GRITO DEL NORTE
GARZA, CATARINO ERASMO
LÓPEZ, IGNACIO L.

LOZANO, IGNACIO E., JR.
LOZANO, IGNACIO E., SR.
MARTÍNEZ, FÉLIX T., JR.
MORTON, CARLOS
ORTEGA Y GASCA, FELIPE D.
QUINTO SOL
RAMÍREZ, SARA ESTELA
RODRÍGUEZ, RICHARD
ROMANO, OCTAVIO I.
SALAZAR, RUBÉN
VELASCO, CARLOS I.

LABOR

AUSTIN MARCH
BISBEE "DEPORTATIONS," 1917
BOYCOTT, GRAPE
BOYLE, EUGENE J.
BRACERO PROGRAM
CANNERY AND AGRICULTURAL WORKERS INDUSTRIAL UNION
CHÁVEZ, CÉSAR ESTRADA
COMMUNIST PARTY
CONFEDERACIÓN DE UNIONES DE CAMPESINOS Y OBREROS MEXICANOS
CONFEDERACIÓN DE UNIONES OBRERAS MEXICANAS
CORONA, BERT N.
COTTON STRIKE, SAN JOAQUIN
DELANO GRAPE STRIKE
DI GIORGIO CORPORATION
EL MONTE BERRY STRIKE
EL PASO INCIDENT
EMIGRANT AGENCY LAW
ENGANCHADOR
EQUAL EMPLOYMENT OPPORTUNITY COMMISSION
FAIR EMPLOYMENT PRACTICES COMMITTEE
FARAH STRIKE
FARM LABOR ORGANIZING COMMITTEE
GALARZA, ERNESTO
GALLUP INCIDENT
GREAT DEPRESSION
HUELGA
HUERTA, DOLORES FERNÁNDEZ
LABOR, AGRICULTURAL
LABOR CONTRACTOR
LABOR ORGANIZATION
LUDLOW MASSACRE
MORENO, LUISA
ORENDAIN, ANTONIO
PARSONS, LUCY GONZÁLEZ

LAND GRANT ISSUES

LAW/LEGAL CASES

LAU v. NICHOLS
LEMON GROVE INCIDENT
MARTÍNEZ, VILMA SOCORRO
MEDINA, HAROLD R.
MEDRANO ET AL. v. ALLEE ET AL.
MÉNDEZ ET AL. v. WESTMINSTER SCHOOL DISTRICT ET AL.
MORENO, CARLOS R.
OLIVÁREZ, GRACIELA
PLESSY v. FERGUSON
PLYLER v. DOE
REYNOSO, CRUZ
SALVATIERRA v. DEL RIO INDEPENDENT SCHOOL DISTRICT
SERRANO v. PRIEST

LEGISLATION

BAKKE SUIT
BILINGUAL LEGISLATION
BOX BILL
CALIFORNIA AGRICULTURAL LABOR RELATIONS ACT
CALIFORNIA ANTI-VAGRANCY ACT
ECONOMIC OPPORTUNITY ACT
EMIGRANT AGENCY LAW
EQUAL EDUCATIONAL OPPORTUNITY ACT
FOREIGN MINERS LICENSE TAX LAW
HARRIS BILL
IMMIGRATION LEGISLATION
IMMIGRATION REFORM AND CONTROL ACT
MCCARRAN-WALTER IMMIGRATION AND NATIONALITY ACT
MIGRANT HEALTH ACT

LITERATURE, POETRY

ABELARDO
ALURISTA (URISTA, ALBERTO B.)
BURCIAGA, JOSÉ ANTONIO
CERVANTES, LORNA DEE
CHACÓN, EUSEBIO
CHÁVEZ, DENISE
DE LEÓN, NEPHTALÍ
GONZÁLEZ AMEZCUA, CHELO
HOYOS, ANGELA DE
I AM JOAQUÍN
LITERATURE, CHICANO
MORTON, CARLOS
SÁNCHEZ, RICARDO
VILLANUEVA, TINO
ZAMORA, BERNICE

ÁLVAREZ, EVERETT, JR.
ARCHULETA, DIEGO
BEAR FLAG REVOLT
BORDER CONFLICT
CARBAJAL, JOSÉ M. J.
CÁRDENAS, ROBERTO L.
CHAVES, MANUEL ANTONIO
CIVIL WAR
FRÉMONT, JOHN CHARLES
GLORIETA PASS, BATTLE OF
LONGORIA, FÉLIX
PICO, ANDRÉS
SANTA ANNA, ANTONIO LÓPEZ DE
TAOS REBELLION
U.S.-MEXICAN WAR
VIETNAM CONFLICT
WORLD WAR I
WORLD WAR II
ZARAGOZA SEGUIN, IGNATIO

MOVIMIENTO

CUAUHTÉMOC
MOVIMIENTO, EL
MOVIMIENTO ESTUDIANTIL CHICANO DE AZTLÁN (MEChA)
NATIONAL CHICANO MORATORIUM
NATIONALISM, CHICANO
PLAN DE SANTA BARBARA
PLAN DEL BARRIO
PLAN ESPIRITUAL DE AZTLÁN
RAZA UNIDA PARTY, LA
VIETNAM CONFLICT
VILLA, PANCHO
ZAPATA, EMILIANO

ORGANIZATIONS

ALIANZA FEDERAL DE PUEBLOS LIBRES
ALIANZA HISPANO-AMERICANA
ALINSKY, SAUL
AMERICAN COORDINATING COUNCIL OF POLITICAL EDUCATION
AMERICAN COUNCIL OF SPANISH-SPEAKING PEOPLE
AMERICAN G. I. FORUM
ASOCIACIÓN DE JORNALEROS
ASOCIACIÓN NACIONAL MÉXICO-AMERICANA
ASSOCIATED FARMERS OF CALIFORNIA, INC.
BARAJAS, GLORIA
BLACK BERETS

PERFORMING ARTS

MUSIC, CHICANO
NOVARRO, RAMÓN
OLMOS, EDWARD JAMES
QUINN, ANTHONY
RODRÍGUEZ, PAUL
ROLAND, GILBERT
RONSTADT, LINDA
SELENA
TEATRO CAMPESINO
VALDEZ, LUIS
ZAPATA, CARMEN

POLITICS/GOVERNMENT

ALATORRE, RICHARD
ALDRETE, CRIS(TÓBAL)
ALVARADO, JUAN BAUTISTA
ANAYA, TONEY L.
APODACA, JERRY
ARCHULETA, DIEGO
ARMIJO, MANUEL
AUSTIN, STEPHEN FULLER
BACA, ELFEGO
BACA, POLLY B.
BARELA, CASIMIRO
BARRERA, ROY R.
BENAVIDES, SANTOS
BERNAL, JOE J.
BONILLA, TONY
CANALES, J. T. (JOSÉ TOMÁS)
CASTRO, RAÚL
CENSUS, 2000
CENSUS DATA
CHAVES, JOSÉ FRANCISCO
CHÁVEZ, DENNIS (DIONISIO)
CISNEROS, HENRY GABRIEL
CONGRESSIONAL HISPANIC CAUCUS
CUTTING, BRONSON
DE LA GARZA, KIKA (ELIGIO)
GALLEGOS, JOSÉ MANUEL
GARZA, REYNALDO G.
GONZÁLEZ, HENRY BARBOSA
GUTIÉRREZ, JOSÉ ANGEL
HERNÁNDEZ, ALFRED J.
HOUSTON, SAM(UEL)
INTER-AGENCY COMMITTEE ON MEXICAN AMERICAN AFFAIRS
LARRAZOLO, OCTAVIANO A.
LUJÁN, MANUEL, JR.

MOLINA, GLORIA
MONDRAGÓN, ROBERTO A.
MONTOYA, JOSEPH M.
OFFICE OF ECONOMIC OPPORTUNITY
OFFICE OF INTER-AMERICAN AFFAIRS
ORTEGA, KATHERINE D.
ORTIZ Y PINO DE KLEVEN, CONCHA
OTERO, MIGUEL ANTONIO, JR.
OTERO, MIGUEL ANTONIO, SR.
OTERO-WARREN, NINA
PARTIDO DEL PUEBLO UNIDO
PACHECO, ROMUALDO
PATRÓN, JUAN B.
PEÑA, ALBERT A., JR.
PEÑA, FEDERICO
PEOPLE'S CONSTITUTIONAL PARTY
PICO, PIO
POLITICAL PARTICIPATION
PROPOSITION 187
PROPOSITION 209
PROPOSITION 227
RAZA UNIDA PARTY, LA
REYNOSO, CRUZ
RICHARDSON, BILL
ROYBAL, EDWARD R.
ROYBAL-ALLARD, LUCILLE
SECRETARIAT FOR THE SPANISH SPEAKING
SOLÍS, HILDA
TORRES, ART
VIGIL, DONACIANO
VOTING

RELIGION

BOYLE, EUGENE J.
CHÁVEZ, ANGÉLICO
CHURCHES
ELIZONDO, VIRGILIO P.
FLORES, PATRICK
GALLEGOS, JOSÉ MANUEL
GARRIGA, MARIANO S.
GUADALUPE, VIRGIN OF
HERMANDAD
LAMY, JEAN BAPTISTE
LAS HERMANAS
LUCEY, ROBERT E.
MARTÍNEZ, ANTONIO JOSÉ
METZGER, SIDNEY M.

SPORTS

TERMINOLOGY

AGABACHADO
ANGLO
AZTLÁN
BARRIO
BICULTURALISM
CALIFORNIO
CALÓ
CAMPESINO
CARNALISMO
CAUSA, LA
CHICANO
COCONUT
CODE SWITCHING
COMMUTER
COYOTE
GABACHO
GREASER
GRINGO
LATIN AMERICAN
MACHISMO
MALINCHE, LA
MANIFEST DESTINY
MAQUILADORA
MESTIZAJE, MESTIZO
MEXICAN AMERICAN
MUTUALISTAS
NATIVISM
NUEVOMEXICANO
OPEN BORDER
PACHUCO
PATRÓN POLITICS
POCHO
POLLERO/POLLO
RANGERS
RAZA, LA
SOUTHWEST
SPANISH AMERICAN
SPANISH SURNAME
TEJANO
TÍO TACO
TORTILLA CURTAIN
UNDOCUMENTED
VENDIDO
VIGILANTISM
WETBACK
ZOOT-SUITER

Preface

This reference work, *The Mexican American Experience*, has been broadly designed as a guide for those seeking basic information about the Mexicano, mainly in the Southwest, but also beyond, from 1848 to the present. It covers all aspects of that experience: the arts, education, labor, leadership, government, business, organizations, popular culture, religion, literature, science, and technology. It is organized alphabetically and is preceded by a guide to broad topics. Since some entries could legitimately fall into more than one category in the guide, a comprehensive index has been provided to further facilitate the reader's search for information. The index also provides valuable cross-reference access to significant information provided in related entries. When an entry mentions a topic covered in another entry, it is highlighted in boldface if the cross-reference adds significant further information.

Including all persons, places, and events of more than local importance, the authors aim to present as complete coverage as possible of the Mexican American historical experience. In general the subjects, whether persons, events, or concepts, have played a significant role in that experience beyond the local or immediate region. The authors have endeavored to be accurate, up-to-date, and as inclusive as constraints of space and time permitted. The entries vary in size and scope, ranging from a brief, concise paragraph to more than a page. Some are obviously of more importance and greater interest than others; commonly this difference is reflected in the length of the entry. The authors are confident that entries will be found to be accurate, balanced, and thorough.

All entries are followed by FURTHER READINGS, selected, up-to-date bibliographies for the user who wishes to pursue a more detailed investigation of a specific topic. The FURTHER READINGS serve to expedite the search for pertinent information about a topic but do not constitute exhaustive bibliographies; nor do they comprise all the sources consulted. Foreign language works, newspaper articles, and dissertations have generally been included in the FURTHER READINGS only when more readily available sources of specific information were lacking.

Mexican American is the identifying term regularly used for persons of Mexican cultural background born in the United States and for Mexicans legally and more or less permanently residing there. *Chicano*, a word derived from *Mexicano* by elision of the first syllable, has also been employed interchangeably with Mexican American, especially since World War II, when the term came into widespread popular use. It is used without political or social implications. However, the reader who seeks further information should be aware that some authors in the FURTHER READINGS use the term with a connotation of political activism.

The terms *Californio, Tejano,* and *Nuevomexicano* serve to denominate persons of Mexican cultural descent in those three areas of the Southwest. In order to avoid overuse of the terms *Mexican American* and *Chicano*, the authors use the widely accepted broader terms *raza* and *Mexicano* from time to time in a cultural sense. The latter term is especially useful in referring to groups that include, or may include, both Mexican Americans and Mexicans living or working in the United States. *Mexicano* and its English equivalent have been widely employed and still are, especially along the border, to refer to persons of Mexican cultural background without regard for their actual nationality. The broadly interchangeable terms *Hispanic* and *Latino*, encountered often in government statistics, have generally been avoided. When used without modifiers they may legitimately apply to all persons of Iberian cultural background, not just to those living in the United States. However, *Hispano* and *Hispanic* have been used in referring to Nuevomexicanos, many of whom prefer to think of themselves in those terms. The term *Anglo* is regularly used to denominate Americans of non-Mexican, European ancestry.

For Mexican Americans the 1848 Treaty of Guadalupe Hidalgo was a radical historic turning point. Accustomed to Spanish and Mexican governmental and cultural ways, they found themselves thrust overnight into an alien social and legal system that promised them greater democracy and economic opportunity, but ultimately failed to deliver on those promises. The years immediately after the Treaty of Guadalupe Hidalgo mark the Mexican Americans' initial efforts in the process of regaining influence in their lost land. As the demand for their labor increased, they expanded from a small conquered minority (in 1848), slowly in the second half of the 1800s and at a rapidly mounting tempo throughout the following century. At the beginning of the 1900s their growth gathered speed and then soared during the last quarter of the twentieth century.

As the twentieth century began, their cultural "reconquest" of the borderlands was accelerated first by the heavy influx of sojourners fleeing the chaos of the 1910 Mexican Revolution, many of whom subsequently remained as permanent immigrants. Then the labor demands of World War I, of the prosperity of the 1920s, of the World War II years, and the postwar economic boom attracted hundreds of thousands more, with documents and without. The 2000 census indicated that there are about twenty-two million persons of Mexican cultural ancestry in the U.S. population. By the time of the year 2010 census they will clearly be the largest minority group in the United States.

Acknowledgments

I would like to thank Sandra L. López and Roxanna Escobedo for their research assistance, and to Craig Schroer for the technical help. Thanks especially to Milton Jamail, Gabriel, and Jorge Jamail-Gutiérrez for their understanding of my disappearance acts and for the hot meals.

Margo Gutiérrez

I would like to thank Kelly Greenwalt, Ann Beyer, Gloria Hofer, and Steve Gelber, all of whom rescued me repeatedly from the vagaries of a computer program I fear I shall never completely understand.

Matt S. Meier

A

ABELARDO, 1931– . Poet-activist, community organizer. Abelardo Barrientos Delgado, commonly known simply by his first name, was born in the Mexican border state of Chihuahua and came to the United States in 1943 when his mother settled in El Paso, Texas. He received his higher education there, including a B.S. from the University of Texas (UTEP) in 1962. During the 1970s he did graduate work at UTEP and at the University of Utah.

From 1955 to 1964 Abelardo's work in El Paso as director of Our Lady's Youth Center helped develop his skills as a social worker and community organizer. In the years 1969 to 1971 he was employed as director of the Colorado Migrant Council in Denver. Because of his work he became widely recognized as one of the leaders in the Chicano Movement, and was the founder of several social service organizations.

While continuing to pursue his principal concerns, community organizing and social service work, Abelardo also taught at the University of Texas, El Paso and the University of Utah during the 1970s. A decade later he served on the faculties of the University of Colorado and several Colorado colleges. Over the years he has lectured and given dramatic poetry readings at numerous colleges and universities throughout the United States.

A prolific writer for many years, Abelardo has written over 1,000 poems in a combination of Spanish and English; he has published nearly a dozen collections of his poetry through Barrio Publications, which he founded in 1970. Many of his poems have also appeared in literary anthologies. Among his best-known works are *Chicano: 25 Pieces of a Chicano Mind*, 1969, and *It's Cold: 52 Cold Thought-Poems of Abelardo*, 1974. The most widely acclaimed of his poems is "Stupid America," in which he expresses his frustration at (and condemns) the waste of Chicano talent. His short novel *Letters to Louise* won the Tonatiuh–Quinto Sol literary award in 1977. His latest major work is *La Llorona: Forty-three Lloronas of Abelardo*, 1987.

Among the recent honors received by Abelardo are the Martin Luther King Human Rights Award and the Colorado governor's Award for Excellence in Poetry, both in 1997. In the following year he was given a Citation for Achievement in Literature by the Texas legislature. He is widely considered one of the most influential poets of the Chicano literary renaissance.

FURTHER READINGS: Bruce-Novoa, Juan. *Chicano Authors: Inquiry by Interview*, Austin: University of Texas Press, 1980; Krstovic, Jelena, ed. *Hispanic Literature Criticism*, vol. 1. Detroit: Gale Research, 1994; Lomelí, Francisco A., and Carl R. Shirley, eds. *Chicano Writers: First Series*. Detroit: Gale Research, 1989.

ACOSTA, OSCAR ZETA, 1936–1974?. Author, lawyer, activist. Oscar Acosta was born in El Paso, Texas, of immigrant parents and later grew up and received his early education in California's Central Valley. After high school he served in the U.S. Air Force during the Korean conflict, and then suffered a mental breakdown that climaxed in an attempted suicide and led to nearly a decade of psychiatric treatment. In the meantime he earned a college degree in creative writing and went to work for a San Francisco newspaper while he completed a law degree. In 1966 he was hired by the East Oakland Legal Aid Socicty as a legal aid attorney, but soon turned to political activism.

Acosta became widely known in the late 1960s for his legal defense of a number of Chicano Movement activists including Sal Castro, the Biltmore 7, and the East Los Angeles 13. An outspoken activist, he also took a major part in the 1970 National Chicano Moratorium events. His two semi-autobiographical novels, *The Autobiography of a Brown Buffalo* (1972) and *The Revolt of the Cockroach People* (1973), established him as an important member of the Chicano literary renaissance. The 1974 Bantam Press edition of *The Revolt of the Cockroach People* made him one of the first Chicano writers to be published by a mainstream press and secured his position as one of the leading writers in the **movimiento**.

Unconstrained in his criticism of racism and discrimination, Acosta was described by people who knew him as often anarchic and frequently out of control. He abandoned the Catholicism of his early years to become a Baptist minister for a short time. Throughout his adult life he apparently suffered intensely from feelings of inferiority and lack of identity, which he numbed by womanizing, carousing, and gross overindulgence in alcohol and drugs. In his two books he described his search for self-identity and also voiced his sincere concerns about Chicano problems. In 1971 Acosta gave up his practice of law, and during the following year made an unsuccessful run for sheriff of Los Angeles County on a quixotic anarchist platform under **La Raza Unida Party** label. The next year he teamed up with gonzo journalist Hunter Thompson on an extended trip to Las Vegas, Nevada. Thompson appears in *The Autobiography of a Brown Buffalo* as the journalist Stonewall, and Acosta shows up, thinly disguised, in Thompson's *Fear and Loathing in Las Vegas* as Gonzo, an attorney.

In 1974 Acosta mysteriously disappeared. He is believed to have died or been killed in Mazatlán, Mexico, possibly as a result of his drug involvement.

FURTHER READING: Kawalczyk, Kimberly A. "Oscar Zeta Acosta: The Brown Buffalo and His Search for Identity." *Americas Review* 19:3–4 (1989) 199–209; Lomelí,

Francisco A., and Carl R. Shirley, eds. *Chicano Writers: First Series.* Detroit: Gale Research, 1989; Stavans, Ilan. *Bandido: Oscar Zeta Acosta and the Chicano Experience.* New York: Icon Editions,1995; Thompson, Hunter S. "Fear and Loathing in the Graveyard of the Weird: The Banshee Screams for Buffalo Meat." *Rolling Stone* (15 December 1977) 48–54, 57, 59; Thompson, Hunter S. *Fear and Loathing: On the Campaign Trail '72.* San Francisco: Straight Arrow Books, 1973.

ACCULTURATION. *See* ASSIMILATION.

ACUÑA, RODOLFO F., 1932– . Activist, historian, educator. Rodolfo Acuña has been an outstanding Mexican American in three categories: educator, activist, and historian. He was born in Los Angeles and received his early education there. His post–high school studies were interrupted by two years of military service during the Korean conflict; he received his undergraduate degree from Los Angeles State College in 1957. While working on his doctorate in history and teaching, in 1966 he developed and taught the first course in the Mexican American experience at Mount St. Mary's College in Los Angeles. A few years later he founded the first **Chicano studies department** at San Fernando Valley State College, today California State University at Northridge. These two firsts are only his most outstanding contributions in developing the field of Chicano studies. In addition, he is one of the leading chroniclers of **la raza**, publishing his first history of the Mexican American experience in 1972.

Acuña has written a dozen books on the Chicano experience, including a popular textbook, *Occupied America: A History of Chicanos* (3rd edition 1988). Among his best-known works are *Anything but Mexican: Chicanos in Contemporary Los Angeles* and *A Chronicle of Chicanos East of the Los Angeles River, 1945–1975.* In his recent *Sometimes There Is No Other Side: Chicanos and the Myth of Equality,* 1998, he explores **discrimination** in university hiring. His 1996 book *Anything but Mexican: Chicanos in Contemporary Los Angeles* received the prestigious Gustavus Myers Award, an annual prize for the best scholarship on intolerance in America.

All of his adult life, activist Rudy Acuña has been vigorously involved in a wide variety of concerns, ranging from union organizing and the Delano farm workers' strike to support for bilingual education and civil rights issues. He endorsed **La Raza Unida Party** in the 1970s and called attention to university discrimination and police brutality in the 1980s and 1990s. He was the plaintiff in a suit against the Los Angeles police department for spying on his university classes. In 1995 he was awarded $326,000 by the U.S. District Court in a discrimination suit he had filed against the University of California four years earlier. For his many services to the Chicano community, Acuña has been the recipient of numerous honors and awards, including the highly respected Liberty Hill award given for his four decades of community leadership.

FURTHER READING: Acuña, Rodolfo. *Anything but Mexican: Chicanos in Contemporary Los Angeles.* New York: Verso, 1996; Acuña, Rodolfo. *Sometimes There Is No Other Side: Chicanos and the Myth of Equality.* Notre Dame: University of Notre Dame Press, 1998; *Acuña v. The Regents of the University of California et al.* Superior Court for Santa Barbara County, Case No. SB196297. U.S. District Court, Central District of California, Case No. CV93-1548HLH; Martínez, Julio A. *Chicano Scholars and Writers: A Bio-Bibliographical Dictionary,* Metuchen, N.J.: Scarecrow Press, 1979; *Who's Who among Hispanic Americans, 1994–1995.* Detroit: Gale Research, 1994.

AFFIRMATIVE ACTION. The concept of affirmative action came out of the Johnson administration's programs for his Great Society. With its base in the Civil Rights Act of 1964, it encompasses a variety of laws, regulations, practices, and programs having as their goal the redressing of past **discrimination** and incquities suffered by ethnic minorities and women in **education**, employment, and **housing**. The term is commonly used to describe the use of race, gender, or ethnic identity as a substantial factor in selection, admission, hiring, and promotion. Most of its supporters see affirmative action as an adjustment for past inequities; opponents argue that it serves to perpetuate the very stereotypes it finds offensive.

Preferential treatment given to members of minority groups quickly led to charges of reverse discrimination that first culminated in the successful 1974 **Bakke** lawsuit in California. During the 1980s President Ronald Reagan vigorously led a growing movement to abolish affirmative action practices in government agencies. By the middle of the 1990s affirmative action programs had been grievously weakened by court decisions and actions of governmental bodies, as well as by a noticeable change in popular attitudes toward them. A further blow to affirmative action came in November 1996 when California voters approved **Proposition 209**, which prohibited the use of race- and gender-based preferences in employment, contracts, and school admissions. Other types of preferences were still permitted. The proposition was immediately challenged in the courts.

In 2003, the U. S. Supreme Court handed down decisions in two cases affecting affirmative action. In the case of *Grutter v. Bollinger*, the court upheld the University of Michigan affirmative action policy regarding admission to the law school. The decision in the law school case is clearly a victory for advocates of affirmative action. In the case of *Gratz v. Bollinger*, the court ruled that the University of Michigan undergraduate admissions policy was not narrowly tailored to achieve educational diversity. While the court ruled against the specific policy being applied by the University of Michigan, it left the door open for other affirmative action policies.

FURTHER READING: Lydia Chávez, *The Color Bind: California's Battle to End Affirmative Action.* Berkeley: University of California Press, 1998; Terry Eastland, *Ending Affirmative Action.* New York: Basic Books, 1996; F. Chris García, "Latinos and the Affirmative Action Debate: Wedge or Coalition Issue?" In *Pursuing Power: Latinos and the Political System,* edited by F. Chris García. Notre Dame: University of Notre Dame Press, 1997; Kathanne W. Greene, *Affirmative Action and Principles of Justice.*

Westport, Conn.; Greenwood Press, 1990; Leiter, Samuel, and William M. Leiter. *Affirmative Action in Antidiscrimination Law and Policy: An Overview and Synthesis.* Albany: State University of New York Press, 2002.

AGABACHADO. *Agabachado* comes from the word *gabacho,* originally a derogatory term for a Frenchman. It is a derisive epithet for a Mexican American who has become acculturated to Anglo society but is not viewed as having totally rejected Mexican culture. One who has completely rejected his Mexican culture may be disparagingly referred to as a *vendido,* a sellout.

AGRICULTURE, SOUTHWESTERN. Southwestern agriculture began in prehistoric times with the arrival of corn-bean-squash subsistence farming from the central Mexican highlands. When Spaniards settled in the area beginning in the 1600s, they added the cultivation of wheat, olives, grapes, fruits, and various vegetables. They also introduced domestic animals, with sheep-raising prevalent in the semi-arid parts of Nuevo México and cattle-raising coming to dominate the south Texas and California *rancho* economies.

The influx of settlers resulting from the California gold rush after the Treaty of **Guadalupe Hidalgo** led to an expansion in grain growing as well as increased demand for cattle. In New Mexico and Texas little change from the mix of subsistence agriculture and cattle-raising took place. In the post–Civil War era, citrus fruit and grape culture began to develop in California, while in Texas cotton moved westward. Toward the end of the century, dam building and expansion of irrigation opened up vast new areas to cultivation, especially to cotton in California and Arizona. By 1900 California was number one in commercial agriculture; in Texas the Winter Garden area began providing East Coast tables with vegetables and citrus. This southwestern agricultural expansion was in large measure based on the labor contribution of Mexicanos.

In the twentieth century the trends already noted in southwestern agriculture continued, augmented by the demands of World War I and World War II as well as by population increase. The most notable change was the expansion of irrigation and mechanization, particularly in cotton. Family farming was in large measure replaced by the "factories in the fields" of **Carey McWilliams**. California continued to lead in southwestern farm production, producing over two hundred commercial crops.

FURTHER READING: Dethloff, Henry C., and Irvin M. May, Jr., eds. *Southwestern Agriculture: Pre-Columbian to Modern.* College Station: Agricultural History Society, Texas A&M University Press, 1982; Hutchinson, Claude H. *California Agriculture.* Berkeley: University of California Press, 1946.

ALAMO, THE. Originally the Franciscan mission San Antonio Valero, in 1836 the Alamo became the site of a bloody Mexican victory over the beleaguered

The Alamo, San Antonio, Texas, 1909.
© Library of Congress.

Texas and Tejano volunteers who were resisting **Santa Anna**'s efforts to force them into submission to his government. The few defenders who were not killed in the battle were executed in accord with Santa Anna's declared policy of no quarter. The defeat and the defenders' execution led to the battle cry "Remember the Alamo," used to rally Texas troops during the subsequent fighting. Since then the Alamo has oftentimes been used as a shorthand for Texas chauvinistic patriotism and ethnocentric anti-Mexican attitudes. Between 1883 and 1905 the state of Texas purchased the Alamo buildings and turned them into a historical monument.

FURTHER READING: Brear, Holly Beachley. *Inherit the Alamo: Myth and Ritual at an American Shrine.* Austin: University of Texas Press, 1995; Flores, Richard R. *Remembering the Alamo: Memory, Modernity, and the Master Symbol.* Austin: University of Texas Press, 2002; Hardin, Stephen L. *Texian Iliad: A Military History of the Texas Revolution.* Austin: University of Texas Press, 1984; Miller, Thomas L. "Mexican Texans in the Texas Revolution." *Journal of Mexican American History* 3 (1973) 105–130.

ALARCÓN, FRANCISCO X., 1954– . Poet, teacher. Born in Wilmington, a small town in Los Angeles County, Francisco Alarcón spent his early life in both the United States and Mexico. In his late teens he settled in the Los Angeles area, where he worked in restaurants and migrant agriculture while pursuing his education. He attended East Los Angeles College and received his B.A. from California State University, Long Beach, in 1977. Two years later he earned his M.A. at Stanford University, where he began to develop a reputation as a poet. In 1981 he was awarded the Rubén Darío prize by the Casa Nicaragua of San Francisco for his poetry. After several jobs in the publishing industry, a 1982 Fulbright grant took him back to Mexico and on a long side trip to Cuba. The experience had a direct impact on his writing and brought him wider recognition as a poet.

The poetry Alarcón wrote upon his return to California won him several awards. Then his tranquil life was rudely shaken by being unjustifiably singled out, particularly in the press, as a suspect in a San Francisco murder. This distressing and discriminatory experience led to the first volume of his poetry to be published, *Tattoos*, 1985. In the same year he accepted a position teaching Chicano literature at the University of California, Santa

Cruz, and contributed some fifteen poems to a collaborative work, *Ya vas, carnal*, in which he described for the first time his feelings as a gay person vis-à-vis the Latino community. His next published work was a collection of poems further speaking to his sexual orientation, titled *Body in Flames/Cuerpo en llamas*, 1990. Two years later he came out with *Snake Poems: An Aztec Invocation*, based on a manuscript written in the 1600s by a Spanish priest.

By the mid-1990s Alarcón's poetry had already won a number of prizes and awards and he was on his way to being considered one of the new stimulating young Chicano poets. In the second half of the 1990s he began writing poetry for children; he published several bilingual books of magical poems for children that had child-provocative titles like *Laughing Tomatoes and Other Spring Poems*, *From the Belly Button of the Moon and Other Summer Poems*, and *Angels Ride Bikes and Other Fall Poems*, 1999. Altogether he has written ten volumes of poetry. Although he identifies himself primarily as a poet, he also has written essays and short stories. Currently he heads the Spanish for Native Speakers program at the University of California, Davis. In April 2002 he was one of three poets who made the final selection list from which the first formally chosen poet laureate of the state of California will be named by Governor Gray Davis.

FURTHER READING: Lomelí, Francisco A., and Carl R. Shirley, eds. *Chicano Writers: Second Series*. Detroit: Gale Research, 1992; "Francisco X. Alarcón Finalist: California Poet Laureate." *Los Angeles Times* (29 March 2002).

ALATORRE, RICHARD, 1943– . Legislator. Born in Los Angeles, Richard Alatorre grew up and received his entire education there, earning degrees from California State University and the University of Southern California (USC). During his college years he became seriously involved in incipient Chicano student activism. After earning a 1965 undergraduate degree in sociology, he broadened his concerns for the marginalized by pursuing a master's degree in public administration at USC. In 1967 he took part in the black civil rights movement as western regional director of the NAACP Legal Defense Fund. Two years later he helped create a **Chicano studies department** at California State University, Long Beach.

In 1972 Alatorre won a seat in the California Assembly, where he served with distinction until 1986, becoming a close associate of Speaker Willie Brown, and one of California's most powerful Latino legislators. His continuing interest in the Chicano condition led him to resign in 1985 in order to run for the powerful city council of **Los Angeles** with its huge Latino population. Strongly supported by the community and Hispanic business leaders, he won a surprising upset victory, becoming the first Mexican American to serve on the council since **Edward Roybal** in the early 1960s. Because of extensive adverse publicity about backroom deals, possible political corruption, and his personal life, he retired in mid-1999 after fourteen years of distinguished service on the council and twenty-eight years representing

Eastside, Los Angeles. Since then, with strong labor support, he has accepted appointment to the California Unemployment Insurance Appeals Board.

Alatorre has been honored with a number of awards for his work as a legislator and his contributions to the Chicano struggle for human dignity. In addition to being appointed to various boards and committees, he was named legislator of the year in 1980, and subsequently Rutgers University's Eagleton Institute of Politics named him an Outstanding State Legislator. In 1988 the YMCA honored him with its Human Dignity Award.

FURTHER READING: Calderón, Thomas M. "To L.A. Council(?) To Mayor(?) To . . . (?)." *Hispanic Business* 7:11 (November 1985) 16–18, 52; Gold, Matea, and Peter Y. Hong. "A Bittersweet Conclusion to Alatorre Era at City Hall." *Los Angeles Times* (30 June 1999) A1; *Hispanic Business* 8:2 (February 1986) 12; Olivo, Antonio. "'Roast' a Sentimental Occasion for Alatorre." *Los Angeles Times* (2 April 2000) Metro, B1; *Who's Who among Hispanic Americans, 1994–1995*. Detroit: Gale Research, 1994.

ALBUQUERQUE WALKOUT, 1966. In late March 1966, fifty Mexican American delegates attending a federal **Equal Employment Opportunity Commission** (EEOC) hearing in Albuquerque, New Mexico stood up and walked out. Protesting that the EEOC lacked Mexican American commissioners and was also insensitive to minority needs and grievances, the leaders of the walkout demanded that President Lyndon Johnson host a White House conference on Mexican American problems. They also filed suit with the Civil Rights Commission, charging the EEOC with employment **discrimination** based on the fact that out of 150 staff members, only three were Latinos.

Two months later President Johnson met with Chicano leaders, and they arranged for a conference to be held in El Paso. However, a number of prominent Chicano leaders, including **César Chávez, Corky Gonzales,** and **Bert Corona,** boycotted the meeting and met in El Paso's south barrio, where they organized their own rump conference to articulate *raza* problems and grievances.

Most historians have seen the Albuquerque walkout as an extremely important milestone in the Mexican American struggle for civil rights. By supplying *la raza* with its first national forum, the walkout and subsequent rump session marked the clear beginning of the Chicano Movement.

FURTHER READING: Pycior, Julie Leininger. *LBJ & Mexican Americans: The Paradox of Power.* Austin: University of Texas Press, 1997; "Walkout in Albuquerque: The Chicano Movement Becomes Nationwide." In *Aztlán: An Anthology of Mexican American Literature*, edited by Luis Valdez and Stan Steiner. New York: Knopf, 1972.

ALDRETE, CRIS(TÓBAL), 1924–1991. Social activist. Cris Aldrete was born and grew up in Del Rio, Texas. As a youth he worked in the family grocery and also picked cotton to help with the family finances. The first member in a family of eleven children to complete high school, at the end of World

War II he took advantage of the G.I. Bill to enter the University of Texas at Austin. There he and some friends established the Alba Club for Mexican American students to help reduce their isolation and to provide opportunities for them to discuss *raza* problems. A civil rights pioneer, while still in college he also took an active role in the fight to end school **segregation** in Texas. Upon completing his undergraduate studies, he went on to obtain a law degree from Houston's South Texas College of Law in 1951.

After law school Aldrete returned to his hometown, Del Rio, where he entered law practice and also became deeply involved in the **American G.I. Forum** (AGIF), helping to recruit members and organizing new chapters. In 1953 he was elected the AGIF state chair. Three years later he was one of the team of AGIF lawyers who argued before the Supreme Court to overturn Pete Hernández's murder conviction. Aldrete was also active in the Del Rio city government, being elected a city commissioner and then city attorney. In 1961 he won election as attorney for Val Verde County. Four years later he was appointed a regional director of the **Office of Economic Opportunity**'s community action programs.

During the following decade Aldrete served as legislative assistant to Texas senator Lloyd Bentsen; when Jimmy Carter took over the presidency in 1977, he was named cochairman of the Southwest Border Regional Commission, an economic development agency. In the late 1980s he was executive director of the Hispanic Caucus in the Texas Senate. His death from cancer in 1991 ended a long and honorable political career.

FURTHER READING: Pycior, Julie Leininger. *LBJ & Mexican Americans: The Paradox of Power.* Austin: University of Texas Press, 1997; San Miguel, Guadalupe, Jr. *"Let All of Them Take Heed": Mexican Americans and the Campaign for Educational Equality in Texas, 1910–1981.* Austin: University of Texas Press, 1987; Tyler, Ron, ed. *New Handbook of Texas*, vol 1. Austin: Texas State Historical Association, 1996.

ALIANZA FEDERAL DE PUEBLOS LIBRES. Headquartered in Albuquerque, the Alianza, the Federal Alliance of Free Towns, was originally founded as the Alianza Federal de Mercedes (Grants) by **Reies López Tijerina** in 1963. Its principal goal was regaining lands awarded by the Spanish and Mexican governments to early settlers and lost after the U.S. takeover of the Southwest in 1848. As a result, it had strong appeal for many descendants of Nuevomexicano land grantees. Tijerina's aggressive leadership soon added a large following of youthful Chicano activists all over the Southwest.

With a membership estimated at several thousand by the mid-1960s, the Alianza's early strategy alternated between court petitions and direct confrontation. In October 1966 some three hundred members of the Alianza took over the Echo Amphitheater campground in the **Kit Carson National Forest**. The *aliancistas* asserted their claims to the land as heirs to the pueblo grant of San Joaquín del Rio Chama. To assert their rights they "arrested" and "tried" two forest rangers for trespassing. Their aggressive actions aroused considerable public concern, which reached a crescendo when they raided the **Tierra Amarilla**, New Mexico, courthouse in 1967.

The Alianza began to decline when it was deprived of Tijerina's dynamic leadership as a result of his jail sentences in 1970 and subsequent parole with the condition that he not hold any Alianza office for five years. The absence of Tijerina's guiding hand, along with a general weakening in the Chicano Movement's militancy by the second half of the 1970s, changed the nature and the tactics of the Alianza. These conditions also caused considerable loss in membership and reduction in the organization's activities. As a protest movement, the Alianza slid into a sharp decline in the 1980s and soon was attracting only limited local support in northwestern New Mexico.

FURTHER READING: Gardner, Richard. *Grito! Reies Tijerina and the New Mexico Land Grant War of 1967.* Indianapolis: Bobbs-Merrill, 1970; Jenkinson, Michael. *Tijerina: Land Grant Conflict in New Mexico.* Albuquerque: Paisano Press, 1968; Knowlton, Clark S. "Reies L. Tijerina and the Alianza Federal de Mercedes: Seekers after Justice." *Wisconsin Sociologist* 22 (Fall 1985) 133–144; Knowlton, Clark S. "Violence in New Mexico: A Sociological Perspective." *California Law Review* 58 (October 1970) 1054–1084; Swadesh, Frances L. "The Alianza Movement of New Mexico." In *Minorities and Politics,* edited by Henry J. Tobias and Charles E. Woodhouse. Albuquerque: University of New Mexico Press, 1969; Valdez, Armando. "Insurrection in New Mexico—Land of Enchantment." *El Grito* 1:1 (Fall 1967) 15–24.

ALIANZA HISPANO-AMERICANA (AHA). The Alianza was founded in 1894 in **Arizona** by *El Fronterizo* editor **Carlos Velasco**, José Elías, **Mariano Samaniego**, Carlos Tully, and others to defend Mexicanos' rights and eliminate discrimination. One of the earliest regional Mexican American organizations, initially it was largely mutualist in character, providing death benefits for its members and encouraging acculturation and civic virtues. However, influenced by changing attitudes in the community, the Alianza began providing members with various social services as well as help in cases involving discriminatory practices. By its fiftieth birthday it had nearly three hundred lodges and a membership of about twenty thousand, scattered over the Southwest but mostly in Arizona.

After World War II the Alianza started to concern itself more centrally with educational inequities and civil rights. In the early 1950s, despite a declining membership, it helped bring about an end to legal school segregation in Arizona, and in 1955 it created a separate civil rights department. It was active in developing the Arizona **Viva Kennedy clubs** that helped bring about a Democratic victory in the 1960 presidential election.

However, in the late 1950s the Alianza began to develop bitter personal rivalries and other internal problems. Mismanagement and theft of funds finally led to the Alianza president's conviction for embezzlement, and to receivership for the Alianza. In spite of financial and managerial reorganization, the Alianza continued to lose members to newer, more popular organizations like the **American G.I. Forum**. Efforts to attract new members from the World War II generation and *movimiento* Chicanos were unsuccessful. By the end of the 1960s the Alianza was moribund.

FURTHER READING: Arrieta, Olivia. "The Alianza Hispano-Americana in Arizona and New Mexico: The Development and Maintenance of a Multifunctional Ethnic Organization." *Renato Rosaldo Lecture Series*, vol. 7 (1989–1990) 55–82; Briegel, Kaye L. "Alianza Hispano-Americana, 1894–1965: A Mexican-American Fraternal Insurance Society." Ph.D. diss. Los Angeles: University of Southern California, 1974; Gonzales, Sylvia Alicia. *Hispanic American Voluntary Organizations*. Westport, Conn.: Greenwood Press, 1985.

ALINSKY, SAUL. *See* INDUSTRIAL AREAS FOUNDATION.

ALURISTA (URISTA, ALBERTO B.), 1947– . Poet, teacher. Alberto Urista was born in Mexico City and came to the United States as a youth. One of the first Chicano poets to write bilingually in English-Spanish, he uses poetry to arouse concern about Mexican American problems. Commonly known as Alurista, in the early 1970s he became the preeminent and most prolific poet of the Chicano Movement. In addition, he was extremely active in establishing various community and student organizations. He was one of the founders of the **Movimiento Estudiantil Chicano de Aztlán** and helped develop the **Plan Espiritual de Aztlán** in 1969. He was also cofounder of the Chicano Studies Department and the Chicano Studies Center at San Diego State University in California.

A charismatic academician with a doctorate in Spanish literature, Alurista has lectured and given poetry recitals at many colleges and universities. Remarkably well-read in religion, history, and philosophy, he has published numerous articles on Chicano history, culture, and literature, as well as nearly a dozen collections of his poetry. His two earliest publications, *Floricanto en Aztlán*, 1971, and *Nationchild Plumaroja, 1969–1972*, 1972, made his reputation as a major Chicano author, and are still considered his best works. He remains the undisputed seminal Chicano poet, even though some criticize his romanticizing the Indian past. His goal as a poet, he has said, is to use his skill as a writer to communicate, to reflect the Chicano experience. As a leading Chicano intellectual and as founder and coeditor of the literary magazine *Maize*, he has both explored and furthered the cause of Chicano rights.

FURTHER READING: Alurista. *Z Eros / Alurista*. Tempe, Ariz.: Bilingual Press/ Editorial Bilingüe, 1995; Alurista. *Et tu . . . raza?*. Tempe, Ariz.: Bilingual Press/Editorial Bilingüe, 1996; Bruce-Novoa, Juan. *Chicano Authors: Inquiry by Interview*. Austin: University of Texas Press, 1980; Lomelí, Francisco A., and Carl R. Shirley, eds. *Chicano Writers: First Series*. Detroit: Gale Research, 1989.

ALVARADO, JUAN BAUTISTA, 1800–1882. Governor. Aided by his family's position and an excellent education for the time and place, Juan Bautista Alvarado made himself an outstanding leader in northern **California**. During the Mexican federalist-centralist strife of the 1830s he took a strong anti-centralist action. In 1836 he ousted the officials from Mexico City and declared himself provisional governor of the free and sovereign state of California until Mexico restored the federal constitution of 1824. After six years he relinquished his authority to the new governor sent from Mexico.

When U.S. forces invaded California in 1846, Alvarado did not participate in the resistance and withdrew from public life. During the following year he sold his Mariposa land grant, which he had never visited, to a proxy for **John Charles Frémont** for $3,000 and retired to a large *rancho* owned by his wife in present-day Contra Costa County.

FURTHER READING: Bancroft, Herbert Howe. *History of California*, vols. 5–6. San Francisco: History Company, 1888–1889; Miller, Robert Ryal. *Juan Alvarado: Governor of California*. Norman: University of Oklahoma Press, 1998; Pitt, Leonard M. *The Decline of the Californios: A Social History of the Spanish-speaking Californians, 1846–1890*. Berkeley: University of California Press, 1966.

ÁLVAREZ, EVERETT, JR., 1937– . Aviator, engineer, attorney. Everett Álvarez was born of Mexican immigrant parents in Salinas, California, and received his early education there. Having completed his degree in electrical engineering at Santa Clara University in 1960, he became a naval pilot in the Vietnam conflict and was shot down in 1964. After spending eight and a half years as a prisoner—the longest captivity of the war—he was released in 1973 and returned to the United States.

Back in the United States, Álvarez continued in the navy at a desk job and attended the Naval Post-Graduate School, where he earned an M.S. degree. Upon his retirement from the navy seven years after his release, he completed a doctorate in jurisprudence at George Washington University. In 1981 he was appointed deputy director of the Peace Corps, and a year later was named deputy director in the Veterans Administration. Currently he owns a computer consulting firm in Virginia. Álvarez has received numerous medals and awards, military and civilian, and has a park and two housing developments named in his honor. In 2001 he was awarded an honorary doctorate by the University of North Texas.

FURTHER READING: Alvarez, Everett, Jr., and Anthony S. Pitch. *Chained Eagle*. New York: D. I. Fine, 1989; Alvarez, Everett, Jr., with Samuel A. Schreiner. *Code of Conduct*. New York: D. I. Fine, 1991; García, Ignacio. "America Says, 'Welcome Home.'" *Nuestro* (November 1982) 15–19; Hubbell, John. *P.O.W.* New York: Reader's Digest Press, 1976; Martínez, Al. *Rising Voices: Profiles in Leadership*. Glendale, Calif.: Nestle USA, 1993.

ÁLVAREZ, FRANCISCO S., 1928–1980. Chemical researcher. Born in the Mexican state of Veracruz, Francisco Álvarez grew up and received his early education in Jalapa. After completing undergraduate studies in chemistry at the Universidad Nacional Autónoma de México in 1953, he took a job as a researcher for Syntex (Mexico) while studying for his doctorate. He then did postdoctoral work at Harvard, returning to Syntex in 1957 as a development research scientist. Seven years later he moved to Syntex in Palo Alto, California as senior research chemist. In 1968 he was appointed head of the development research department, a position he held until his death.

Dr. Álvarez's most notable contribution in the field of chemistry was his work on the production of Norethindron, a principal ingredient in many birth control pills. He also contributed to the basic methodology of chemical synthesis, authored some fifteen scientific research papers, and was coinventor of about eighty patented drugs.

FURTHER READING: *American National Biography*, vol. 1. New York: Oxford University Press, 1999.

ÁLVAREZ, MANUEL, 1794–1856. Trader, merchant. A Spaniard who settled in Santa Fe as a trader, merchant, and later U.S. consul, Manuel Álvarez assisted General Stephen Kearny in the peaceful conquest of Nuevo México by American forces in 1846. After the Treaty of **Guadalupe Hidalgo**, he strongly advocated the admission of **New Mexico** as a state. When the Compromise of 1850 admitted New Mexico as a territory he became an official in the territorial government, and served until his death.

FURTHER READING: Chávez, Thomas E., ed. *Conflict and Acculturation: Manuel Alvarez's 1842 Memorial.* Santa Fe: Museum of New Mexico Press, 1988; Chávez, Thomas E. *Manuel Alvarez, 1794–1856: A Southwestern Biography.* Niwot, Colorado: University Press of Colorado, 1990.

AMADOR, LUIS VALENTINE, 1920– . Physician, teacher. Luis Amador was born in Las Cruces, New Mexico, and grew up and was educated there. After earning his B.S. from New Mexico State University, he entered Northwestern University and received his M.D. in 1944. He completed his residency in neurology and then served two years in the army Medical Corps.

Outstanding in neurosurgery, Amador became a Rockefeller research associate in 1950 and four years later was named a Guggenheim fellow. During the 1950s and 1960s he lectured on neurology and neurosurgery at various prestigious universities, societies, and congresses. From 1966 to 1978 he taught neurological surgery at the the University of Chicago; then he moved to Northwestern University. He is the author of numerous articles in his field of specialization.

FURTHER READING: Unterburger, Amy L. *Who's Who among Hispanic Americans, 1991–1992,* Detroit: Gale Research, 1992; *Who's Who in America, 1984–1985.* Chicago: Marquis Who's Who, 1984.

AMERICAN COORDINATING COUNCIL OF POLITICAL EDUCATION. ACCPE was an early effort in Mexican Americans' struggle for their political rights. Founded in Phoenix, Arizona, at the beginning of the 1960s, it was an offshoot of the **Political Association of Spanish-Speaking Organizations.** Its goals were mainstream and inclusive. It spread rapidly throughout

Arizona and ultimately became active in a majority of the state's fourteen counties. As a nonpartisan political organization it conducted citizenship programs, organized registration drives, and supported Chicano candidates for public office.

ACCPE elected Chicano candidates to town councils and school boards, but it was never able to move from its political success at the city level to victory in county or state contests, perhaps because of their more politically partisan nature.

FURTHER READING: Castro, Tony. *Chicano Power: The Emergence of Mexican America.* New York: Saturday Review Press, 1967; Gómez-Quiñones, Juan. *Chicano Politics: Reality and Promise, 1940–1990.* Albuquerque: University of New Mexico Press, 1990.

AMERICAN COUNCIL OF SPANISH-SPEAKING PEOPLE. The Council was established in 1951 at an El Paso convention of Mexican American civil rights groups in an effort to create a national umbrella organization. With **George I. Sánchez** as its key initiator and first executive director, it was able to obtain from the Robert C. Marshall Trust Fund a number of grants to carry on its struggle against discrimination and school segregation. During the first half of the 1950s these grants, and Mexican American contributions, enabled the Council to provide leadership as well as legal assistance in discrimination and desegregation lawsuits. In 1952 the Council joined the **Alianza Hispano-Americana** in segregation suits against discriminating Arizona school districts. It also played an important role in *Hernández v. Texas* and *Hernández v. Driscoll Consolidated Independent School District.*

In 1958 the Council lost the support of the Marshall Trust, its major source of funds, because the trustees felt its efforts were too localized. Unable to obtain sufficient further funding for its activities, the Council languished and finally expired in 1959.

The Council was the first effort to create a national civil rights organization; it provided leadership and funds to challenge discrimination and segregation in dozens of legal cases in the first half of the 1950s. Nearly a decade ahead of the broader American civil rights movement, it made an important contribution by providing precedents and a model for subsequent civil rights organizations.

FURTHER READING: Romo, Ricardo. "George I. Sánchez and the Civil Rights Movement: 1940–1960." *La Raza Law Journal* 1:3 (Fall 1986) 342–362; Tyler, Ron, ed. *The New Handbook of Texas*, vol. 1. Austin: Texas State Historical Association, 1996.

AMERICAN G.I. FORUM (AGIF). The American G.I. Forum was founded in **Texas** in the aftermath of World War II, largely through the efforts of Dr. **Héctor Pérez García.** As a result of the 1949 **Félix Longoria** case in Texas, some forty existing groups, which had been loosely organized the year before, met to provide themselves with a permanent formal structure. They adopted the name American G.I. Forum and elected Dr. García the first president. Under his leadership the AGIF grew steadily during the 1950s to become one of the largest and most influential Mexican American **organizations** with chapters in the Midwest as well as the Southwest.

Although originally veteran-oriented, the AGIF quickly developed a broad spectrum of interests, with special emphasis on civil and social rights for *la raza.* It took a significant part in all aspects of the fight against **segregation**, particularly segregation in Texas schools. It conducted annual drives to persuade more Mexican Americans to pay their poll taxes in order to vote. In the pursuit of its goals it has been active at all levels of government in an officially nonpartisan stance. Decidedly middle-class in leadership, it has encouraged members to participate actively in the American political process. In the 1960 elections several Forum leaders helped found the popular **Viva Kennedy clubs**, and nearly every AGIF chapter in the Southwest organized a club to support John F. Kennedy's presidential bid. Because of its moderate stance, the AGIF lost members during the decade of the Chicano Movement, but successfully regained and expanded its membership in the 1980s and 1990s by providing valuable services and unmistakable immediate benefits.

Stressing political action and recourse to the courts to advance the cause of *la raza,* the AGIF monitors state and federal legislative bills of particular interest to Chicanos. It has played a major role in various civil rights cases involving Mexican Americans and remains a valued pressure group for *raza* concerns.

FURTHER READING: Allsup, Carl. *The American G.I. Forum: Origins and Evolution.* Austin: Center for Mexican American Studies, University of Texas, 1982; García, Ignacio M. *Viva Kennedy: Mexican Americans in Search of Camelot.* College Station: Texas A&M Press, 2000; Pycior, Julie Leininger. *LBJ & Mexican Americans: The Paradox of Power,* Austin: University of Texas Press, 1997; Ramos, Henry A. J. *The American G. I. Forum: In Pursuit of the Dream, 1948–1983.* Houston: Arte Público Press, 1998. *www.agif.org*

ANAYA, RUDOLFO A., 1937– . Novelist. Rudolfo Anaya was born in the Llano Estacado area of New Mexico, but the family moved to the Pecos River town of Santa Rosa while he was still a baby. He grew up and received his early education there and in Albuquerque, to which the family moved in 1952. After obtaining his A.B. in literature from the University of New Mexico in 1963, he taught in Albuquerque public schools for seven years and then moved to the English department of the University of New Mexico, where he began teaching creative writing a few years later. He directed the creative writing program until his retirement.

Seriously interested in writing during his undergraduate days, while teaching in the public schools he began working on what eventually became *Bless Me, Ultima. Ultima* was extremely well received and won the Premio Quinto

Rudolfo Anaya (center) is congratulated by President and Mrs. Bush at the National Endowment for the Arts National Medal of Arts Awards ceremony, Washington, D.C., 2002. © AP/Wide World Photos.

Sol in 1971. It has been translated into Spanish, Italian, French, Russian, and Japanese. *Ultima* was soon followed by two other novels, *Heart of Aztlán*, 1976, and *Tortuga*, 1979; in addition, Anaya also coedited several works dealing with Chicanos in the Southwest. In 1980 he published *Cuentos: Tales from the Hispanic Southwest*, two years later *The Silence of the Llano*, and then a personal reminiscence, *A Chicano in China*, in 1986.

During the late 1980s Anaya began to expand his writing interests, publishing a beautifully illustrated children's story, *The Farolitos of Christmas*, in 1987. In the following decade he took another new tack, publishing four mystery thrillers featuring a Chicano detective. In addition, he also has written short stories published in various journals and magazines, as well as two plays.

As one of the foremost Chicano writers, professor emeritus Rudolfo Anaya has been the recipient of many national and international awards and honors. In addition to an honorary doctorate from the University of Albuquerque in 1981, he was given a three-year W. K. Kellogg Foundation fellowship the following year. He has also received the New Mexico Governor's Award for Excellence and the President's National Salute to American Poets and Writers. He has read his works at the White House as well as at numerous colleges and universities. Anaya continues to be active at book readings, lectures, and conferences.

FURTHER READING: Anaya, Rudolfo. *Conversations with Rudolfo Anaya.* Jackson: University Press of Mississippi, 1998; Bruce-Novoa, Juan. *Chicano Authors: Inquiry by Interview.* Austin: University of Texas Press, 1980; Fernández Olmos, Margarite. *Rudolfo A. Anaya: A Critical Companion.* Westport, Conn.: Greenwood Press, 1999.

ANAYA, TONEY L., 1941– . Lawyer, politician. Toney Anaya was born in the tiny town of Moriarity, New Mexico, of virtually unschooled parents who encouraged their children to get good educations. After high school he enrolled in New Mexico Highlands University on a scholarship, but then went to Washington, D.C., to work for Senator **Dennis Chávez**. He completed his B.A. in economics and political science in 1963 and got his law degree at American University four years later. In 1970 he returned to New Mexico, where he established himself in a private law practice and spent two years as administrative assistant to Governor Bruce King.

In 1974 Anaya ran for the state attorney general office and won; at the end of his four-year term he ran for the U.S. Senate, but lost to Pete Domenici in a close race. While continuing his law practice, he ran for governor in 1982 and won the election by a landslide. As governor, Democrat Anaya pursued an aggressive liberal course, proposing educational innovations, prison reform, and high-tech economic development. His combative leadership as governor provoked extensive negative reaction among New Mexico's conservative voters. Despite a legislature dominated by Republicans and conservative Democrats, he was able to obtain some strong affirmative action legislation.

Unable to succeed himself, at the beginning of 1987 Anaya took over the presidency of the **Mexican American Legal Defense and Educational Fund**. In 1999 he was one of a group of Hispanic investors who bought some 400,000 telephone lines from GTE Corporation in order to form a new company. He also is registered as a lobbyist in Washington, D.C., for the Mexican government. At various times in the 1980s and 1990s he was suggested as possible candidate for the vice presidency.

FURTHER READING: "Group Buying GTE Assets." *New York Times* (9 September 1999) C10; Lamar, Jacob V. "Unfriendly Fire; Flak for New Mexico's Anaya." *Time* 127 (24 March 1986) 38; "Looking Out for No. 1." *Time* (31 October 1983) 47; Mendosa, Rick. "The Business of Influence." *Hispanic Business* (September 1993) 34–36; Vigil, Maurilio. "The Election of Toney Anaya. . . ." *Journal of Ethnic Studies.* 12:2 (Summer 1984) 81–94.

ANGEL, FRANK, JR. 1914– . Educator. Frank Angel was born, grew up, and received his early education in Las Vegas, New Mexico. When he completed high school in 1932 he began teaching elementary grades in the state's rural areas, and rose to elementary principal. His teaching career was interrupted by service in World War II as a bomber pilot in the Pacific. Upon being mustered out, he returned to education, earning his B.S. in 1949, his M.S. two years later, and his doctorate in 1955. From 1955 to 1971 he taught at the University of New Mexico in educational administration and was active in educational associations. In 1972 he became the first Latino president of a four-year liberal arts institution, New Mexico Highlands University. During his tenure as president, from 1972 to 1976, he instituted policies to meet the academic needs of Chicano, Indian, and black students.

FURTHER READING: "First Hispano College President in the U. S.: New Mexico Highlands University." *La Luz* 3:3 (June 1974) 44–45; Martínez, Julio A., ed. *Chicano Scholars and Writers: A Bio-Bibliographical Directory*. Metuchen, N.J.: Scarecrow Press, 1979.

ANGLO. Short for Anglo-Saxon, the word may be simply descriptive or mildly pejorative. The term may be used to describe any non-Mexicano white American.

ANGUIANO, LUPE, 1929– . Civil rights leader, social worker, feminist, nun. Guadalupe Anguiano was born in Colorado of Mexican immigrant parents who moved to southern California when she was eight years old. After graduating from Ventura Junior College, she spent 1949 to 1964 as a teaching nun in the missionary sisters of Our Lady of Victory. Her classroom experience caused her to become deeply aware of the numerous problems in the Mexican American community, particularly discrimination against migrant workers' children. Later experience as a social worker and youth program organizer in the community convinced her that as a lay person she could do more to improve the lives of barrio dwellers. She therefore left the order to become more intimately involved in Chicano concerns.

Anguiano immediately immersed herself in community work, becoming first a counselor in a California youth program and then coordinator of a federal poverty program in East Los Angeles. In 1966 she was appointed by President Lyndon Johnson to create a Mexican American unit within the Department of Health, Education, and Welfare (HEW). As a result of her own experience growing up, she strongly advocated **bilingual education** and helped write the Bilingual Education Act passed by Congress in 1968.

Mildly disappointed by HEW limitations, Anguiano left Washington in 1967 to join the **United Farm Workers** (UFW) as an organizer. Soon she was tapped by **César Chávez** to head the grape boycott in Michigan. After a year with the UFW and a brief stint in the Legal Defense and Education department of the National Association for the Advancement of Colored People, she returned to HEW as a Civil Rights Specialist. She helped implement provisions of the Civil Rights Act of 1964, chiefly by monitoring affirmative action programs. She also became deeply concerned with the status of women, and was involved in the hearings on the Equal Rights Amendment.

Anguiano's reputation as a welfare reformer was established in 1973 when she led a group of 100 San Antonio welfare mothers in a "Let's Get Off Welfare Campaign." Subsequently she was appointed by the National Conference of Catholic Bishops as regional director in the Southwest with headquarters in San Antonio. Continuing to be concerned about women on welfare rolls, in 1977 she cofounded a feminist organization named National Women's Program Development, which she left two years later to create, with private funding, National Women's Employment and Education, Inc., which she headed from 1979 to 1991. During the 1980s she was also busily involved in a consulting firm she had organized. In the early 1990s she accepted appointment to the Division of Affirmative Recruitment in the U.S. Department of Personnel Management, where she was able to continue pursuing her concerns for women and minorities. A dedicated leader in the feminist and civil rights movements, she carries on, serving the needs of the poor and voiceless. Currently she heads a consulting firm in the San Fernando Valley. She has been the recipient of numerous awards and honors.

FURTHER READING: Anguiano, Lupe. "Employment and Welfare Issues As They Affect Low Income Women." *Comunidad* 1:6 (March 1976) 1–2; Newlon, Clarke. *Famous Mexican Americans.* New York: Dodd, Mead & Co., 1972; Spano, John. "Private Group to Help Welfare Mothers Work." *Los Angeles Times*, Metro (22 November 1988) 3; Telgen, Diane, and Jim Kamp, eds. *Notable Hispanic American Women.* Detroit: Gale Research, 1993; *Who's Who among Hispanic Americans, 1994–1995.* Detroit: Gale Research, 1994.

ANZALDÚA, GLORIA E., 1942– . Writer, poet, feminist. Gloria Evangelina Anzaldúa was born in 1942 to sharecropper and migrant worker parents in the Rio Grande valley of south Texas. When she was eleven, the family settled near Hargill in Hidalgo County. As a child she decided she was going to go to college because she wanted to write or be an artist. Since there were no art classes in her high school, she began teaching herself; later she took art classes in college. While in high school and college she continued to work in the family fields to help support the family after her father died in 1956.

In 1969 Anzaldúa graduated from Pan American University in Edinburg with a B.A. in English, education, and art. She then obtained her M.A. in English and education at the University of Texas in Austin and began teaching. She has taught at all levels, from preschool programs through high school and special education to university classes.

During the early 1970s Anzaldúa taught children of migrant families for the state of Indiana, and she began writing short stories there. From 1974 to 1977 she sought to pursue her student interests in the comparative literature department at the University of Texas at Austin, without success. Later she moved to California where she taught at San Francisco State University and worked as a tech writer for the University of California Medical Center. In the 1980s she taught at the University of California, Santa Cruz, and other colleges while she continued her writing.

This Bridge Called My Back: Writings by Radical Women of Color, 1981, which Anzaldúa coedited with Cherrie Moraga, received the Before Columbus

Foundation American Book award that year. A collection of her poems and essays titled *Borderlands/La Frontera: The New Mestiza*, published in 1987, examines society's treatment of people who are different; it was picked by the *Library Journal* as one of the Best Books of 1987. Her next book, *Making Face, Making Soul/ Haciendo caras: Creative and Critical Perspectives by Feminists of Color*, won the 1990 Lambda Lesbian Small Book Press award. During the 1990s she wrote three children's books, including a semiautobiographical novel, *La Prietita*. At the century's end she collaborated with AnaLouise Keating in publishing a collection of interviews she had given between 1982 and 1999, with the title *Interviews=Entrevistas*, 2000.

Anzaldúa continues to participate in workshops and panels, teaches, gives lectures, and does public readings of her poetry. She serves on several editorial boards, and since 1984 has been a contributing editor to the feminist journal *Sinister Wisdom*. Viewing her writing as a form of activism and a tool for change, she evinces a strong feminist and lesbian turn of mind in her poems and essays. Some critics have accused her of being overly emotional in her essays, but most find her poetry compelling. Anzaldúa has received many awards for her writing.

FURTHER READING: Anzaldúa, Gloria E. *Interviews=Entrevistas*. Edited by AnaLouise Keating. New York: Routledge, 2000; Lomelí, Francisco A., and Carl R. Shirley, eds. *Chicano Writers: Second Series*. Detroit: Gale Research Inc., 1992; Ramos, Juanita. "Gloria E. Anzaldúa." In *Contemporary Lesbian Writers of the United States: A Bio-bibliographical Sourcebook*, edited by Sandra Pollack and Denise Knight. Westport, Conn.: Greenwood Press, 1993; Steele, Cassie Premo. *We Heal from Memory: Sexton, Lord, Anzaldúa, and the Poetry of Witness*. New York: Pelgrave, 2000.

APODACA, JERRY, 1934– . Politician, businessman. Jerry Apodaca was born in Las Cruces, New Mexico, where his family had lived for over 100 years. At the University of New Mexico he excelled in sports and received his B.S. in education in 1957. After teaching for three years he turned to business, and then to politics. In 1966 he won election to the state senate. After two terms there he ran for the governor's office in an aggressive campaign and was elected. In January 1975 he became the first Hispano governor since **Octaviano Larrazolo** in 1920.

As governor, Apodaca showed interest in a wide variety of areas: education, state government reorganization, and energy issues. As a result the state's education budget was increased substantially, 117 state agencies were made responsible to 12 departments, and he was named chairman of the western governors' regional energy policy commission. Upon leaving the governorship, he returned to various business interests but combined them with politics by assuming the chair of the National Issues Council, an organization for advancing business interests in legislation and federal programs. He was on the short list for appointment as ambassador to Mexico in 1979, and two years later he was unsuccessful in a bid for the U.S. Senate. During the 1980s he served as president of the University of New Mexico's board of regents, and early in the following decade was president of the Hispanic Association for Corporate Responsibility. In the 1998 Democratic primary he failed to win his bid to run for a second term as governor. He heads the Washington-based firm of Apodaca Sosa and Associates, which lobbies for the Mexican government.

Apodaca has been the recipient of various awards, including two honorary doctorates, an Award for Distinguished Service to Higher Education, and appointment as chairman of the President's Council on Physical Fitness and Sports.

FURTHER READING: García, José Z. "Jerry Apodaca: Running Unscared." *Nuestro* (November 1978) 15–22; Mendosa, Rick. "The Business of Influence." *Hispanic Business* (September 1993) 34–36; Vigil, Maurilio. "Jerry Apodaca and the 1974 Gubernatorial Election in New Mexico: An Analysis." *Aztlán* 9:1 (1978) 133–149; *Who's Who among Hispanic Americans, 1994–1995*. Detroit: Gale Research, 1994.

ARAGÓN, JOHN A., 1930–1997. Educator, educational administrator. John Aragón was born and grew up in Albuquerque, New Mexico. He graduated from New Mexico Highlands University in 1952 and began teaching in high schools in Española and Los Alamos. From 1956 to 1959 he served as director of professional services for the New Mexico Education Association while completing the requirements for an M.A. in education. During the next six years he completed his Ed.D. while working as executive secretary to the New Mexico School Boards Association.

In 1965 Aragón accepted a teaching position at the University of New Mexico, and four years later became director of the university's Minority Groups Cultural Awareness Center. After being considered several times in the early 1970s for top administration positions, in 1975 he was appointed president of New Mexico Highlands University, where he served nine years.

Dr. Aragón has acted as a consultant to many private and government agencies. He has been the recipient of numerous awards from professional and civic groups. In 1973 he was given the George I. Sánchez Award by the National Education Association for his innovative work in bilingual education.

FURTHER READING: Martínez, Tomás O. "Dr. John Aragón: Leading New Mexico Educator." *La Luz* 3:2 (May 1974) 26-27; *Who's Who in America, 1984–1985*. Chicago: Marquis Who's Who, 1984.

ARCHULETA, DIEGO, 1814–1884. Political and military leader. Diego Archuleta was born in the Rio Arriba area of Nuevo México in the uncertain days of Mexico's war for independence. He was educated in Taos at Father Martínez's school, and then spent eight years studying for the priesthood at the seminary in Durango, Mexico. He returned to Nuevo México in 1840, joined the militia, and soon became the area's representative to the national government in Mexico City. Returning, he was advanced to colonel in the militia, second only to the governor. He took a leading role in the two abortive **Taos rebellion**s in 1846 and 1847, a role that caused him to flee to Chihuahua until passions had cooled.

Upon his return to **New Mexico**, Archuleta swore allegiance to the new American government and served as representative in the territorial assembly during the 1850s. In 1857 he was appointed a U.S. Indian agent. When the Civil War erupted, he returned to active duty in the territorial militia as a lieutenant colonel and reached the rank of brigadier general. In the 1860s and 1870s he won seven elections to the territorial Legislative Council, and twice served as its president. A leading Nuevomexicano in political and military matters, he died while serving in the legislature and was honored in death as befitted an able and dedicated citizen.

FURTHER READING: Kanellos, Nicolás. *The Hispanic American Almanac: A Reference Work on Hispanics in the United States.* Detroit: Gale Research, 1993; Twitchell, Ralph E. *The History of the Military Occupation of the Territory of New Mexico from 1846 to 1851.* Chicago: Rio Grande Press, 1963; Vigil, Maurilio E. *Los Patrones: Profiles of Hispanic Political Leaders in New Mexico History.* Washington, D.C.: University Press of America, 1980.

ARIZONA. Home of Pima, Papago (To hono O'odham), Hopi, Navajo, Apache, and other Indian groups, Arizona was explored by Europeans beginning at the end of the 1530s, first by Cabeza de Vaca and Fray Marcos de Niza and later by Francisco Vásquez de Coronado. Disappointment at the result of the Coronado expedition caused the area to be subsequently ignored by Spain except for limited missionary activity. In 1700 the noted Jesuit missionary-explorer Eusebio Kino established mission San Xavier del Bac and followed that with other missions in the area, but missionary work in Arizona was never very successful.

On the extreme northern frontier, Arizona remained sparsely settled during the Spanish and Mexican periods despite the discovery of silver deposits in the 1730s and some mining activity during periods of relatively peaceful Indian relations. The founding of a presidio at Tubac in 1752, after a serious Pima uprising against the missions, marked the real beginning of civilian settlement. Sheep and cattle ranching became important activities despite frequent Apache raids that inhibited expansion. By the time of Mexican independence in 1821, Arizona had about one thousand inhabitants, virtually all located around **Tucson** and southward.

After the United States acquired the area through the Treaty of **Guadalupe Hidalgo** in 1848 and the **Gadsden Purchase Treaty** five years later, Arizona remained as isolated from the rest of the United States as it had been from central Mexico. Until 1863 it was administered from **Santa Fe,** and most of the inhabitants continued to be more Mexican than American. Living in the Santa Cruz valley near the border, they remained closely linked to the adjoining Mexican state of Sonora through close familial, economic, and cultural ties. Because of Apache raiding and the border banditry of drifters and outlaws in this last U.S. frontier, there was considerable movement back and forth across the border by the inhabitants. However, the defeat of raiding Apaches after the U.S. Civil War and continuing unrest in Mexico made U.S. residence more appealing.

During the first decades of American control there was interaction in Arizona, including intermarriage, between Mexicano elites and the few Anglo males who arrived from the East. Spanish remained the language of everyday intercourse until the advent of the Southern Pacific Railroad in the 1870s. Mining, ranching, and subsistence farming, helped by Eastern capital and Anglo in-migration, expanded rapidly during the 1870s. The railroad brought both solid citizens and rascals who prolonged frontier conditions until the end of the century. Good relations faded as the frontier began to recede and as Arizona became increasingly linked to the East Coast and the national economy. By 1900 a majority of Anglos viewed Mexicanos primarily as unskilled labor. Middle and lower class Mexicanos increasingly became objects of discrimination, and Anglos more and more experienced preferential treatment in government and society.

Although rights to lands granted by Spain and Mexico were guaranteed by the Treaty of Guadalupe Hidalgo and the 1853 Gadsden Purchase Treaty, in many instances the guarantees failed to protect Mexicano ownership. When the **Court of Private Land Claims** concluded its task in 1904 it had confirmed title to 116,540 acres, about 14 percent of the land claimed in Arizona under Spanish and Mexican grants. In the sparsely settled northeastern part of the territory Anglos, who came to own nearly all the land, completely dominated local government offices and politics. Only in the Tucson-Santa Cruz River valley area did Mexican Americans retain some local political influence. Nevertheless, fear of Mexican American political control remained a recurrent theme throughout the territorial period and was an important factor in delaying statehood.

At the end of the 1800s, dual pay scales were the norm in Arizona's rapidly expanding **mining industry** areas, and acts of violence against Mexicanos became commonplace. Copper mining, ranching, and mercantile activity continued to dominate the area's economy, in which Mexicanos were assigned subordinate roles. As discrimination spread, segregation in schools, churches, and other public and semi-public areas increased. Mexican Americans began turning to mutualist and other organizations for protection and comfort. To defend themselves, in 1894 they created one of the earliest Mexican American civil rights groups, the **Alianza Hispano-Americana**.

The period from the beginning of the new century to the 1930s was one of further adjustment for the Mexican American elite as they continued to lose political influence. In 1901 the Arizona Rangers were created with the special objective of monitoring the Mexicano labor force. Early in the century the statehood movement and copper mining continued to dominate

Arizona's political and economic scene. Irrigated agriculture expanded rapidly, especially in the Salt River valley. In 1912 the **Liga Protectora Latina** was organized in Phoenix to secure Mexicano rights, particularly those of copper mine workers. It also concerned itself with educational issues in a state with very limited schools; in 1891 there were no high schools in the territory. Revolutionary unrest in Mexico and Arizona's demand for workers, especially in the expanding cotton fields, fostered a steady stream of immigrants.

The World War I demand for copper (and cotton) led to a new surge of Mexican immigration that faltered briefly at the war's end and then resumed. In the following decade the "**repatriation**" of the 1930s sent thousands of miners, farm workers, and their families (some of whom were American citizens) across the border. However, in the **Tucson** area, where the elite still retained some political power, urban Mexican Americans were less summarily treated. By 1940 Mexicanos made up about 20 percent of the state's population.

Except for copper mining and the defense industry, World War II had limited impact on Arizona. In the postwar period Arizona Mexicanos faced fewer legal barriers and less open bigotry, but the continuing heavy influx of agricultural labor from Mexico engendered considerable nativist sentiment among Anglos. Chicano leaders continued to work to end all segregation, and by the mid-1950s most Arizona schools had been desegregated. In the workplace, exclusion from unions and stereotyping on the part of management continued to be the chief causes of discrimination in employment and promotion. Although the working conditions of Chicanos had improved by 1960, equality in the workplace, especially in agriculture and mining, continued to be a major concern. Chicanas began playing an increasingly significant role in the urban workforce.

In 1962 Arizona Chicanos formed the **American Coordinating Council of Political Education** (ACCPE) to provide a support base to elect Mexican American candidates. Efforts of ACCPE had only limited success. In the late 1960s the Chicano Movement came to Arizona, following the California example. University and high school students carried the message of the **movimiento** to the community, but found that their elders tended to be more conservative than their California counterparts. Some less traditional movimiento ideas took a while to receive acceptance; however, youthful leaders did create a renewed demand for activism. **La Raza Unida Party** was relatively subdued in Arizona, and Mexican Americans gave only limited support to its candidates in the early 1970s. However, they did elect Chicanos to positions at the city and county level. By the mid-1970s, Mexican Americans made up about 19 percent of Arizona's population; they helped elect eleven state representatives and made **Raúl Castro** the state's first and only Mexican American governor. Despite advances, they lag behind California and Texas Chicanos in advancing economic, social, and political agendas. At the beginning of the twenty-first century, Phoenix, home of half of Arizona's Latino population, had no Latinos on the city council, and only a handful served in the state legislature.

FURTHER READING: *The Chicano Experience in Arizona, Part One: Mining, Agriculture, Ranching.* Tempe: University Libraries, Arizona State University, 1991; Crow, John E. *Mexican Americans in Contemporary Arizona: A Social and Demographic View.* San Francisco: R&E Research Associates, 1975; Dimas, Pete R. *Progress and a Mexican American Community's Struggle for Existence: Phoenix's Golden Gate Barrio.* New York: Peter Lang, 1999; Officer, James E. *Arizona's Hispanic Perspective.* Phoenix: Arizona Academy, 1981; Officer, James E. *Hispanic Arizona, 1536–1856.* Tucson: University of Arizona Press, 1987; Sheridan, Thomas E. *Los Tucsonenses: The Mexican Community in Tucson, 1854–1941.* Tucson: University of Arizona Press, 1986.

ARMIJO, MANUEL, 1792–1853. Governor, businessman. Manuel Armijo was born near Albuquerque on the hacienda of his wealthy parents. When the Santa Fe trade opened at the beginning of the 1820s, he became an active leader in the southern end of the trade. He served three times as territorial governor, first from 1827 to 1829 and then again in the late 1830s and 1840s. As governor, he awarded many large, and sometimes illegal, land grants to favored friends and business associates. Otherwise, he seems to have given Nuevo México reasonably good rule.

When American forces under Stephen W. Kearny invaded Nuevo México in 1846, Governor Armijo prepared to resist at first and then apparently changed his mind and fled southward to Chihuahua. At the end of the **U.S.- Mexican War** he returned to Lemitar on the Rio Grande south of Albuquerque and resumed his mercantile and cattle-raising activities. In 1850 he ran unsuccessfully for election to local office; he died three years later. Among the bequests in his will was $1,000 to establish a public school. Contemporary Anglos in New Mexico generally painted a very negative image of him.

FURTHER READING: Lecompte, Janet. "Manuel Armijo and the Americans." *Journal of the West* 19:3 (1980) 51–63; Perrigo, Lynn I. *Hispanos: Historic Leader in New Mexico.* Santa Fe: Sunstone Press, 1985; Weber, David J. *The Mexican Frontier, 1821–1846: The American Southwest under Mexico.* Albuquerque: University of New Mexico Press, 1982.

ARREGUÍN, ALFREDO MENDOZA, 1935– . Painter, sculptor, teacher. Alfredo Arreguín was born and grew up in Morelia, the capital of Michoacán. At age eight, he was enrolled in the local Bellas Artes academy, which aroused an early interest in art. Five years later he joined his father in Mexico City to continue his education at the Universidad Nacional Autónoma de México. One of his contacts with *norteamericano* tourists brought him to Seattle, where he enrolled in the University of Washington.

Arreguín was drafted into the U.S. Army in the late 1950s. After his discharge from the service he returned to Seattle, where he resumed his

Alfredo Mendoza Arreguín. © Susan R. Lytle.

university studies. He received his B.A. in 1967 and his Master of Fine Arts two years later. Meanwhile, he had begun to develop a distinctive, elaborately patterned, deeply layered painting style that featured broad vistas with calligraphically detailed flora and fauna of tropical Mexico. By the second half of the 1970s these kaleidoscopic paintings with vibrantly colored monkeys, felines, and birds began to win prizes. In 1979 he won the prestigious Palm of the People award at the International Festival of Painting at Cagnes-sur-Mer, France. Since then, Arreguín's painting style has continued to evolve over the years.

During the 1980s and 1990s Arreguín had over three dozen solo exhibits, and his paintings were also included in nearly fifty group exhibitions, in the United States, Chile, Japan, the former Soviet Union, and elsewhere abroad. On the occasion of the 450th anniversary of its founding, the Universidad de San Nicolás de Hidalgo in Morelia honored him in 1989 with a retrospective and the publication of a book on his life's work. In 2002 *Alfredo Arreguín: Patterns of Dreams and Nature / Diseños sueños, y naturaliza* by Lauro Flores, the third volume in the Jacob Lawrence Series on American Artists, was published by the University of Washington Press.

Arreguín has been the recipient of nineteen national awards and other honors. In 1994 the National Museum of American Art purchased his large triptych *Sueño* as one of its most important acquisitions of the year. Two years later the National Academy of Sciences in Washington, D.C. presented a solo exhibition of his works. In 1997 the government of Mexico gave him the highly prized OHTLI award for his extensive altruistic activities in the Mexican American community. His paintings grace more than three dozen corporate and public collections and adorn the covers of a dozen books of poetry, fiction, history, and even biology.

FURTHER READING: Chaplik, Dorothy. "Alfredo Arreguín," *Latin American Art* (Winter 1991) 40–41; Flores, Lauro. *Alfredo Arreguín: Patterns of Dreams and Nature / Diseños sueños, y naturaliza.* Seattle: University of Washington Press, 2002; Gallagher, Tess. "Viva la Vida" (Exhibition catalogue). Tacoma, Wash.: Tacoma Art Museum, 1992; Griswold de Castillo, Richard, Teresa McKenna, and Yvonne Yarbro-Bejarano, eds. *Chicano Art: Resistance and Affirmation, 1965–1985.* Los Angeles: Wight Art Gallery, 1991.

ARTS AND ARTISTS. Mexican American art may be divided into two broad categories: public and private art. Born of social and political circumstances, both generally derive from and reinforce the Mexican American experience and culture. Until the middle of the twentieth century, nearly all Mexican American art was private art.

Since early in the 1700s, *santeros* in Nuevo México had been carving and painting wooden religious figures called *santos*; most carved and painted in anonymity. They also carved statues called *bultos* and painted *retablos*, wooden panels covered with plaster. These folk art products were viewed with some disdain by the European clergy brought in by Bishop Jean Baptiste Lamy. During the 1930s depression, traditional folk arts were revived by the New Mexico Department of Vocational Training, which began programs designed to create cottage industries. One of the first *santeros* of this period to gain recognition outside of New Mexico was **Patrocinio Barela**, who exhibited his *santos* at the New York's World Fair in 1939. In the 1940s and 1950s, Texan **Consuelo (Chelo) González Amezcua** developed her unique filigree style of drawing. A decade later, **Luis Jiménez** made his satiric "pop art" fiberglass and epoxy sculptures a badge of the Chicano art renaissance. In 1994 his artistic stature was recognized by his receiving an endowed chair in the art department of the University of Houston.

The roots of the contemporary Chicano artistic renaissance go back to the folk arts developed in the American Southwest; however, the immediate cause of their revival in the 1960s was the Chicano Movement. The renaissance was seen as a visual expression of the **movimiento** ideology of brotherhood, cultural affirmation, and political assertion, while at the same time often addressing topics of family, home, and daily life. Many Chicano artists viewed the mural especially as a nonverbal language to be used to further their goal of teaching the community ethnic solidarity and cultural nationalism through public art. It conveyed its message through the use of images and symbols derived from Mexico's Indian past, its 1910 revolution, and its major muralists. It glorified and romanticized the past of native groups like the Aztecs and Maya. It also usually showed strong sentiments of idealism, and was often quite idiosyncratic.

The Chicano public art movement dates from the latter years of the 1960s. Much of the subject matter of this art renaissance was derived from the movimiento and the civil rights struggle in the 1960s and 1970s. Chicano artists, as part of the movimiento, looked for ways to protest societal inequities, to promote ethnic identity, and to express their own self-identification. A strong community orientation in public art led to an emphasis on murals and poster art, much of which depicted some aspect of the struggle for human rights. The **United Farm Workers** grape and lettuce boycotts, the Vietnam War protest, and the death of **Rubén Salazar** provided many artists with themes for murals and posters. The farm worker magazine *El Malcriado* popularized the caricatures of contemporary Andy

Zermeño, as well as the skeletal *calaveras* of long-dead Mexican printmaker José Guadalupe Posada. Posada's art also graced the pages of other Chicano journals.

In addition to Posada, the great Mexican muralists David Alfaro Siqueiros, Diego Rivera, and José Clemente Orozco especially influenced Chicano public art. Chicano artists borrowed or adapted themes, styles, and techniques from the mythology of their Aztec and Maya past, thereby creating new symbols for labor struggles and the civil rights movement. Pre-Columbian symbols and icons, 1910 Mexican revolutionaries Emiliano Zapata and Francisco Villa, Miguel Hidalgo, and the Virgin of Guadalupe tended to dominate posters and murals, most of which were painted in the style of social realism. Muralists, often self-taught artists and often with the help of untrained barrio youths, covered blank walls, mostly in large urban centers. Well-known poster artists like Rupert García, Amado Peña, and Malaquías Montoya reflected the ideals and goals of chicanismo in their works.

While early Chicano renaissance painters, and muralists especially, borrowed heavily from Mexico's historic roots, not all Chicano artists consciously sought to identify with these influences. Some Chicano painters like **Alfredo Arreguín, Porfirio Salinas, Carmen Lomas Garza,** Salvador Corona, and Margarita Herrera, while showing some influence of the Mexican muralists in techniques, sought new subject matter. Arreguín's paintings reflect Mexican geography more often than its Indian past or current politics, while Porfirio Salinas specialized in Texas landscapes dotted with bluebonnet flowers. Carmen Lomas Garza's paintings chronicle daily life among Mexicanos in Texas during the 1950s and 1960s. Today a growing number of Chicano artists pursue individual artistic inspiration for their subject matter. Their art is a mixture of personal expression and social commentary.

In the early years of the Chicano art renaissance, both public and nonpublic artists found it difficult to exhibit their work through the normal art channels. As a result, in the late 1960s and on into the 1970s numerous regional Chicano art groups sprang up: the Mexican American Liberation Art Front in Oakland, California, the Movimiento Artístico Chicano in Chicago, La Cofradía de Artes y Artesanos in New Mexico, Pintores de la Nueva Raza in Texas, and Las Mujeres Muralistas in San Francisco. Alternative art centers and galleries like San Antonio's Guadalupe Cultural Arts Center, El Grito de Aztlán in Denver, Mechicano Art Center in Los Angeles, Casa Aztlán in Chicago, and Galería de la Raza in San Francisco also provided loci for art lectures and student conferences. By the mid-1970s U.S. art museums began to recognize the importance of Chicano art, mounting exhibitions that included paintings by Arreguín, Gilbert Luján, Carlos Almaraz, and others. In 1990 a traveling exhibit, *Chicano Art: Resistance and Affirmation, 1965–1985,* began a U.S. tour that lasted for three years.

Performance art also began to draw the attention of Chicanos in the early 1970s. In southern California, artists Patssi Valdez, Willie Herrón, and Gronk were important in founding the performance art group ASCO in 1973. This avant-garde group experimented with various artistic forms, from alternative murals and street theater to graffiti and film presentations. Another special aspect of the Chicano art movement, sometimes referred to as **pachuco** art, is illustrated by the Royal Chicano Air Force barrio art program in Sacramento. Graffiti artists often used spray paint in combination with felt-tip markers to "tag" buildings, overpasses, and subways.

Despite long-held raza stereotypes in Chicano art circles dominated by males, **Chicanas** began taking an active part in the artistic upsurge of the 1960s. Focusing on feminist concerns, they adopted the Virgin of Guadalupe and Diego Rivera's wife, the painter Frida Kahlo, as feminist models and important sources of inspiration. Equally important, they organized their own groups to promote their art and advance feminist concerns. Among the prominent Chicana artists are southern California muralist Judith Baca; muralist and *retablo* artist Patricia Rodríguez; specialist in La Guadalupana Yolanda López; cultural chronicler Santa Barraza; family portraitist Carmen Lomas Garza; and portraitists Ester Hernández and Patssi Valdez.

Although the renaissance of Chicano art arose out of the movimiento, it has not only outlived it; it has continued to develop and expand. By the 1990s many Chicano artists joined a growing trend toward artistic multiculturalism. They recognized the societal changes that were taking place in the Mexican American community, particularly the expansion of the middle class. While continuing older art forms, they now experimented with video, film, sculpture, assemblage, and mixed media. As they entered mainstream art, their works appealed to a broader segment of American society. Increasingly they were accepted and welcomed, as the great success of the 1990–1993 touring exhibition, "Chicano Art: Resistance and Affirmation," would indicate.

FURTHER READING: Barrio, Raymond. *Mexico's Art and Chicano Art*. Sunnyvale, Calif.: Ventura Press, 1975; Cancel, Luis, et al., eds. *The Latin American: Art and Artists in the United States*. New York: Harry M. Abrams, Inc., 1988; Cockcroft, Eva Sperling, and Holly Barnet-Sánchez, eds. *Signs from the Heart: California Chicano Murals*. Albuquerque: University of New Mexico Press, 1993; Frank, Larry. *New Kingdom of the Saints: Religious Art of New Mexico, 1780–1907*. Santa Fe: Red Crane Books, 1992; Goldman, Shifra M., and Tomás Ybarra-Frausto, eds. *Arte Chicano: A Comprehensive Annotated Bibliography of Chicano Art, 1965–1981*. Berkeley: Chicano Studies Library Publications, University of California, 1985; Griswold del Castillo, Richard, Teresa McKenna, and Yvonne Yarbro-Bejarano, eds. *Chicano Art: Resistance and Affirmation, 1965–1985*. Los Angeles: Wight Art Gallery, University of California, 1991; Keller, Gary D., et al. *Contemporary Chicano Art: Artists, Work, Culture, and Education*. 2 vol. Tempe, Ariz.: Bilingual Press/Editorial Bilingüe, 2002; Maciel, David R., Isidro D. Ortiz, María Herrera-Sobek, eds. *Chicano Renaissance: Contemporary Cultural Trends*. Tucson: University of Arizona Press, 2000; Marín, Cheech. *Chicano Visions: American*

Painters on the Verge. Boston: Bullfinch Press, 2002; Quirarte, Jacinto, ed. *Chicano Art History: A Book of Selected Writings.* San Antonio: University of Texas, 1984; Quirarte, Jacinto. *Mexican American Artists.* Austin: University of Texas Press, 1973; Steele, Thomas J. *Santos and Saints: The Religious Folk Art of Hispanic New Mexico,* rev. ed. Santa Fe: Ancient City Press, 1994; Tatum, Charles M. *Chicano Popular Culture: Que hable el pueblo.* Tucson: University of Arizona Press, 2001.

ASOCIACIÓN DE JORNALEROS. The Asociación de Jornaleros was established in Laredo, Texas, in 1933 as a result of the New Deal's National Industrial Recovery Act. An independent union of workers in agriculture, mining, and construction, it obtained a charter from the American Federation of Labor in 1936 and began a statewide drive to organize workers. In the following year it became a part of the **United Cannery, Agricultural, Packing, and Allied Workers of America**, but then disintegrated, largely because of that organization's radical leadership.

FURTHER READING: Jamieson, Stuart M. *Labor Unionism in American Agriculture.* Washington, D.C.: U.S. Government Printing Office, 1945.

ASOCIACIÓN NACIONAL MÉXICO-AMERICANA (ANMA). In the wake of a 1949 clash between police and Mexicano miners in Arizona, ANMA was founded at Phoenix to protect the workers' rights. It was a militant organization with reform orientation, fighting against racist discrimination and stressing unity based on class and ethnicity. Strongly influenced by contemporary leftist ideology, it followed a popular front strategy during its short life.

Under the leadership of Mine, Mill, and Smelter Workers organizer-president Alfredo Montoya, ANMA called attention to intimidation and excessive use of force by police in dealing with Mexicano workers. During the infamous 1954–1955 "**Operation Wetback**" it strongly condemned Attorney General Herbert Brownell's sweeping raids and indiscriminate expulsion of Mexicans from the United States without judicial hearings.

In the repressive climate of the McCarthy era ANMA was listed by the attorney general as a subversive organization. Its activities and influence were undermined by intense FBI surveillance and other harassment from federal agencies. As a result, it languished and by the late 1950s ceased to function.

FURTHER READING: Acuña, Rodolfo. *Occupied America: A History of Chicanos,* 3rd ed. New York: Harper & Row, 1988; García, Mario T. *Mexican Americans: Leadership, Ideology, and Identity, 1930–1960.* New Haven: Yale University Press, 1989; Urrutia, Liliana. "An Offspring of Discontent: The Asociación Nacional México-Americana, 1949–1954." *Aztlán* 15:1 (Spring 1984) 177–184.

ASSIMILATION. A process, also referred to as acculturation, in which a person of a minor ethnic group adopts the cultural patterns of the majority society. The adaptation is usually gradual, and may vary in degree from surface acceptance to complete immersion. Typically the higher the socioeconomic level, the greater the degree of assimilation. Among Mexican

Americans the degree of assimilation may also be affected by their isolation, educational levels, proficiency in English, and type of employment, as well as skin color. Also, levels of Mexican assimilation have been obscured by the continuing heavy **immigration**. A 2002 poll indicated that Latino immigrants are assimilating into U.S. society at a normal rate, with English becoming the primary language of over 90 percent of the second generation.

FURTHER READING: Murgia, Edward. *Assimilation, Colonialism, and the Mexican American People.* Austin: University of Texas Press, 1975; Spicer, Edward H., and Raymond H. Thompson, eds. *Plural Society in the Southwest.* New York: Interbook, 1972.

ASSOCIATED FARMERS OF CALIFORNIA, INC. The Associated Farmers is a countermovement organization of California growers and groups with related interests. It grew out of the 1933 San Joaquin Valley cotton strike, and was formally established in the following year under the leadership of the California Chamber of Commerce and the Farm Bureau to vigorously counter the movement for unionization of agricultural labor. Supported financially by the railroads, Pacific Gas and Electric Company, Holly Sugar Corporation, and other companies, the Associated Farmers declared agribusiness's strong opposition to unions, the closed shop, hiring halls, and picketing. To advance its ideas it hired lobbyists, undertook so-called educational programs, accused union leaders of communist connections, and made use of tear gas and axe handles. After the 1939–1940 **LaFollette** Civil Liberties Committee investigation of the denial of workers' rights in agriculture and its damning report, the Associated Farmers declined in importance.

FURTHER READING: Pichardo, Nelson A. "The Power Elite and Elite-Driven Countermovements: The Associated Farmers of California During the 1930s." *Sociological Forum* 10:1 (March 1995) 21–49.

ATENCIO, ALONZO CRISTÓBAL, 1929– . Educator, biochemist. Alonzo Atencio was born and grew up in southern Colorado. After high school he enlisted in the U.S. Navy and served as a medical corpsman in the Korean conflict. In 1958 he received his B.S. in chemistry at the University of Colorado, Boulder, his M.S. at Denver six years later, and his Ph.D. in medicine in 1967. After a postdoctoral fellowship at Northwestern University, he accepted a dual position as professor in biochemistry and assistant dean for student affairs at the University of New Mexico School of Medicine. As a dean, he has been particularly concerned with the academic needs of Chicano students, especially in the sciences. The respected author of articles in various scientific journals, he remains active in professional societies and has served on national boards concerned with health issues.

FURTHER READING: *American Men and Women of Science,* 20th ed. New Providence, N.J.: R. R. Bowker, 1998; *Who's Who among Hispanic Americans, 1994–1995.* Detroit: Gale Research, 1994.

AUSTIN, STEPHEN FULLER, 1793–1836. Texas leader. Stephen Austin took over the Texas *empresario* colonizing project of his father Moses upon the latter's death in 1821. In the following year he brought in the first of about eight thousand Anglo colonists he was to introduce according to the terms of agreements made with Spain, then with independent Mexico, and finally with the state of Coahuila-Texas. Austin was a force for moderation, especially after Mexico virtually ended **Anglo** immigration in 1830, and he sought support from **Tejano**s for greater local rule in order to avoid more stringent centrist control. After Texans declared conditional independence as Mexican federalists in 1835, he was sent to Washington, D.C., to seek help. Upon his return six months later, he found Texas had already won complete *de facto* independence. He ran for president of the new republic but was defeated by **Sam Houston**, who appointed him to head the Department of State. Suffering from ill health, he died a few months later.

FURTHER READING: Barker, Eugene C. *The Life of Stephen F. Austin, 1793–1836.* Nashville, Tenn.: Cokesbury Press, 1925; Cantrell, Gregg. *Stephen F. Austin, Empresario of Texas.* New Haven: Yale University Press, 1999; Tyler, Ron, ed. *The New Handbook of Texas*, vol. 1. Austin: Texas State Historical Association, 1996.

AUSTIN MARCH, 1966, 1977. On the Fourth of July 1966, Texas agricultural workers, on strike for higher wages at La Casita Farms in Starr County, began a march from the Mexican border to Austin. In two months several hundred strikers, led by **César Chávez** lieutenant Eugene Nelson, among others, walked nearly three hundred miles from Rio Grande City to the state capital in order to present Governor John B. Connally with a list of demands, particularly the inclusion of farm workers in a proposed $1.25 per hour Texas minimum wage law. When the marchers arrived in Austin on Labor Day, Connally refused to meet with them, and agricultural workers were not included in the minimum wage legislation passed the following year by the Texas legislature.

Intimidation by the **Texas Rangers,** strikebreakers from Mexico, and inadequate planning contributed to the failure of the strike and the march it engendered. However, the march was not a total failure. It did call public attention to Texas farm workers' problems, and may have been a factor in later minor improvements in agricultural wages.

A second march to Austin took place in mid-1977. Labor leader **Antonio Orendain** led a group of farm workers to the state capital to request Governor Dolph Briscoe's support for legislation to establish collective bargaining rights for agricultural workers. In spite of thousands of signatures on the petition, Briscoe refused to support their demands, and the collective bargaining bill died in committee.

FURTHER READING: García, Ignacio M. "The Many Battles of Antonio Orendain." *Nuestro* (November 1979) 25–29; Procter, Ben H. "The Modern Texas Rangers: A Law Enforcement Dilemma in the Rio Grande Valley." In *The Mexican Americans: An Awakening Minority*, edited by Manuel P. Servín. Beverly Hills, Calif.:

Glencoe Press, 1970; Rhinehart, Marilyn D., and Thomas H. Kreneck. "The Minimum Wage March of 1966: A Case Study in Mexican American Politics, Labor, and Identity." *The Houston Review* 9:1 (1989) 27–44.

AYRES REPORT, 1942. At the time of the **Sleepy Lagoon** incident in 1942, Edward Duran Ayres, chief of the sheriff's Foreign Relations Bureau, made a report to the Los Angeles grand jury. In it he stated that males of Mexican descent had certain genetic characteristics, derived from their Indian ancestry, which predisposed them to violence, cruelty, and bloodlust. The report recommended the jailing of all Chicano gang members. Supported by sheriff Eugene Biscailuz, this pseudoscientific statement negatively influenced law enforcement attitudes toward Mexicanos in the greater **Los Angeles** area for years.

FURTHER READING: Acuña, Rodolfo. *Occupied America: A History of Chicanos,* 3rd ed. New York: Harper & Row, 1988; Ayres, Edward Duran. "Edward Duran Ayres Report." In *Readings on La Raza: The Twentieth Century,* edited by Matt S. Meier and Feliciano Rivera. New York: Hill and Wang, 1974.

AZTLÁN. Aztlán was the mythical Mexica (Aztec) place of origin from which, according to Mexican Americans' traditions, they migrated southward to ultimately dominate the central Mexican highlands. During the 1960s and 1970s many **movimiento** Chicanos in their search for identity applied the name Aztlán to the U.S. Southwest. The metaphor was in harmony with a stress on cultural nationalism and indigenous roots as well as the adoption of Mexican symbols.

The Aztlán concept was first articulated clearly by **Corky Gonzales** in his epic poem *Yo soy Joaquín.* In March 1969 it was enshrined by him in the **Plan Espiritual de Aztlán** at the first National Chicano Youth Liberation Conference in Denver, and became a new "fantasy heritage," replacing the earlier fantasy heritage of a Spanish Arcadia. Interrelated with *movimiento* ideas about self-determination and ethnic nationalism, for a few activists Aztlán became the physical homeland to be reclaimed. For others it was simply a metaphysical geographic area of Mexican cultural concentration.

FURTHER READING: Anaya, Rudolfo A., and Francisco A. Lomelí, eds. *Aztlán: Essays on the Chicano Homeland.* Albuquerque: Academia / El Norte Publications, 1989; Muñoz, Carlos Jr. *Youth, Identity, Power: The Chicano Movement.* New York: Verso, 1989; "El Plan Espiritual de Aztlán." *El Grito del Norte* 2:9 (6 July 1969) 5.

B

BACA, ELFEGO, 1865–1945. Folk hero, lawyer, private detective. Elfego Baca was born into the extensive Nuevomexicano Baca family just weeks before the end of the Civil War. Because his parents moved to Topeka, Kansas, he grew up and received his early education there, becoming completely bilingual. After his mother died in 1880 the family returned to New Mexico and his father became the marshal in the old Hispano town of Belen.

In 1884 the teenage Elfego had his famous confrontation with drunken, rampaging Texas cowhands. A self-appointed deputy, he undertook the arrest and disarming of one of the cowpokes, which escalated into a two-day standoff in which he killed four of his attackers. His subsequent jury trial in Albuquerque resulted in acquittal, and his reputation as a folk hero was made.

Baca's career took off. An ambitious youth, he studied law, passed the bar examination, and eventually was certified to practice before the U.S. Supreme Court. After he reached twenty-one, he ran for public office in nearly every election year and usually won, serving as county clerk, sheriff, mayor, district attorney, superintendent of schools, and deputy U.S. marshal. During the **Mexican revolution** his official representation of the Huerta government in the United States got him indicted for criminal conspiracy. He was exonerated, with no damage to his political career.

During the 1920s Elfego was intermittently the elected sheriff of Socorro County and was mentioned as a possible gubernatorial candidate. His longtime friendship with and support of **Bronson Cutting**, the U.S. senator from New Mexico, helped keep him in the political limelight until the latter's death in 1935, as did his ability to deliver the Nuevomexicano vote. In the early 1940s Baca's health began to fail, and he died as he had lived, running for public office. He was survived by five children and Francisquita, his feisty wife of sixty years.

FURTHER READING: Ball, Larry D. *Elfego Baca in Life and Legend.* El Paso: Texas Western Press, 1992; Bryan, Howard. *Incredible Elfego Baca: Good Man, Bad Man of the Old West.* Santa Fe: Clear Light Publishers, 1993; Crichton, Kyle S. *Law and Order, Limited: The Rousing Life of Elfego Baca of New Mexico.* Santa Fe: New Mexican

Publishing Co., 1928. Arno reprint, 1974; Keleher, William A. *Memoirs: 1892–1969: A New Mexico Item.* Santa Fe: Rydal Press, 1969.

BACA, POLLY B., 1941– . Political leader and activist. Polly Baca has been a woman of firsts: first woman to chair the Colorado House Democratic Caucus, first woman to be elected to the state senate, first minority woman to serve in a **leadership** position in any state senate. Baca was born and raised in a small town near Greeley, Colorado. Greatly influenced by her mother's independent spirit, in high school she was active in the Adlai Stevenson Young Democrats club, and in 1960 was the dynamic Viva Kennedy campus coordinator at Colorado State University in Fort Collins.

Baca graduated from college two years later with a degree in political science and with practical experience gained from working in several congressional campaigns. After college she worked as an editor on two union publications in Washington, D.C. and then became a public information officer in the Interagency Committee on Mexican-Americans during the Lyndon Johnson administration. In 1968 she took an active role in Robert Kennedy's bid for the Democratic presidential nomination. After his assassination she became research director for the Southwest Council of La Raza, a position she left two years later to accept a job as assistant to the chair of the Democratic National Committee.

In 1974 Polly Baca ran for a seat in the Colorado House of Representatives and won. Four years later she became the first woman elected to the state senate. She was reelected in 1982, but she was defeated in her bid for the U.S. Senate four years later. During her twelve years in the Colorado legislature, Baca sponsored and actively pushed over 250 bills, many of them reflecting her concern for the rights of the minority poor. Baca's success in politics was the result of her leadership skills; extensive involvement in the community; service on numerous committees, boards, and commissions; and close ties to Democratic party leaders.

Retired from elective politics, Baca served as special assistant to President Bill Clinton and was appointed director of the U.S. Office of Consumer Affairs. Currently she oversees Region 8 of the General Services Administration and heads a consulting firm, SierraBaca Systems.

In 1988 Baca was one of the first inductees into the National Hispanic Hall of Fame, and in the following year she was selected by the U.S. Information Agency to lecture in the Far East on race and ethnicity in American life. In 2000 she was inducted into the Colorado Women's Hall of Fame. For her community activism and advancement of minority rights she has been the recipient of numerous awards and laurels, including an honorary LL.D. from Warburg College in 1989.

FURTHER READING: Gloria Bonilla-Santiago. *Breaking Ground and Barriers: Hispanic Women Developing Effective Leadership.* San Diego, Calif.: Marin Publications, 1992; Lucy Chávez. "Colorado's Polly Baca-Barragán," *Nuestro* (April 1980) 18–19; Hardy, Gayle J. *American Women Civil Rights Activists.* Jefferson, N.C.: McFarland &

Co., 1993; Holzmeister, Michael. "Women's Hall of Fame Inductee Walks Her Talk." *La Voz*, Denver (22 March 2000) 4, 20; Mandel, Ruth B. *In the Running: The New Woman Candidate*. New Haven: Tichnor & Fields, 1981; *Who's Who among Hispanic Americans, 1994–1995*. Detroit: Gale Research, 1994.

BÁEZ, JOAN CHANDOS, 1941– . Singer, social activist, songwriter. Joan Báez was born on Staten Island, New York, but grew up in a variety of places in the United States and abroad where her Mexico-born physicist father taught or worked. When her father accepted an appointment at the Massachusetts Institute of Technology in 1958, she enrolled in Boston University but soon dropped out. Meanwhile, she had already begun a career singing folk songs in Harvard Square coffeehouses.

From the beginning of her musical career in the 1960s, Báez became deeply involved in U.S. civil rights protest movements. Motivated by a Quaker background and youthful self-confidence, in 1962 she led a concert tour of southern colleges, demanding integrated audiences. She later participated in southern civil rights marches, took a prominent role in the Vietnam protest movement, participated in the free speech movement on the campus of the University of California in Berkeley in 1964, and supported **César Chávez** and the **United Farm Workers** in their struggle. All of this was in addition to, or a part of, her singing career.

During the mid-1960s Báez performed in numerous concerts, some with Bob Dylan, with whom she also toured. In 1967 she undertook her first solo concert tour abroad, to Japan. Later that year she and her mother were among protesters arrested for blocking the Oakland, California, armed services induction center. Given a ten-day jail sentence, she later repeated her protest and received ninety days. After serving her time, she and fellow antiwar activist David Harris toured colleges and universities promoting draft resistance. They were married in March 1968, and a few months later Harris received a three-year sentence for draft resistance. Báez continued to tour the United States preaching her belief in resistance and nonviolence. In 1965 she founded the Institute for the Study of Nonviolence.

By the 1970s Joan Báez had become a nationwide symbol of earnest nonviolent protest, and soon she extended her concerns for rights worldwide. In 1979 she founded Humanitas International, a worldwide human rights organization over which she presided. An active supporter of Amnesty International, she met with Russian dissidents in the Soviet Union and also toured Latin America to investigate human rights abuses there. During the 1980s she met with famed international rights leaders such as Polish Solidarity chief Lech Walesa and the Dalai Lama. In 1993 Báez performed in refugee camps in war-torn Yugoslavia and did benefits in Sarajevo. During the second half of the 1990s she continued to be seriously involved in contemporary issues, albeit less vocally. All of her adult life she has been a dedicated activist, working for human rights and world peace.

At the end of the 1980s Báez decided to try to regain an audience lost through her years of political activism and changes in musical tastes. She regretfully closed Humanitas International. With the help of her new manager, Mark Specter, she seriously redirected her attention to her musical career, again touring clubs and doing concerts. In 1992 she issued her thirty-third album, "Play Me Backwards," and six years later "Gone From Danger," her most recent. Over the years she has had seven gold albums and many Grammy nominations. In July 1999 she celebrated the fortieth anniversary of her teenage debut at the Newport Folk Festival, and in the first year of the twenty-first century she began an extensive U.S. tour, declaring her intention to focus on her music. In October 2001 she did something quite different, a three-week stint in San Francisco dinner theater as the singing Countess Zinzanni in Teatro Zinzanni's *Le Palais Nostalgique.*

Joan Báez onstage with her guitar, 1967.
© Library of Congress.

FURTHER READING: Báez, Joan. *And a Voice to Sing With.* New York: Summit Books, 1987; Báez, Joan, and David Harris. *Coming Out.* New York: Pocket Books, 1971; *Current Biography, 1963.* New York, N.Y.: H. W. Wilson Co., 1963; Hadju, David. *Positively 4th Street: The Lives and Times of Joan Baez, Bob Dylan, Mimi Baez Farina, and Richard Farina.* New York: Farrar, Straus and Giroux, 2001; Telgen, Diane, and Jim Kamp. *Latinas! Women of Achievement.* Detroit: Visible Ink Press, 1996; Woliver, Robbie. "Joan Baez Fights Myth of Being Joan Baez." *New York Times* (15 October 2000) 14NJ: 13.

BAKKE SUIT, 1974–1978. When his application for admission to the medical school at University of California at Davis was rejected, Allan Bakke, a 34-year-old Anglo, filed suit against the University of California in 1974. His suit argued that he was the victim of reverse discrimination inasmuch as academically less qualified minority students had been admitted because of the university's **affirmative action** policy. California state courts accepted Bakke's widely debated contention that his Fourteenth Amendment rights had been violated. Upon appeal, the U.S. Supreme Court in June 1978 upheld the lower courts' ruling in a five-to-four decision. Bakke was admitted to the Davis medical school, and later graduated and went into private practice. The Bakke decision marked the beginning of a movement away from affirmative action policies.

FURTHER READING: Haro, Carlos M., ed. *The Bakke Decision: The Question of Chicano Access to Higher Education.* Los Angeles: Chicano Studies Center, University of California, 1976; *Regents of the University of California v. Bakke,* Supreme Court of the United States, 438 U.S. 265; Schwartz, Bernard. *Behind Bakke: Affirmative Action and the Supreme Court.* New York: New York University Press, 1988; Welch, Susan. *Affirmative Action and Minority Enrollments in Medical and Law Schools.* Ann Arbor: University of Michigan Press, 1998; Ball, Howard. *The Bakke Case: Race, Education, and Affirmative Action.* Lawrence: University Press of Kansas, 2000.

BANDITRY, SOCIAL. Lawlessness, ranging from highway robbery to murder, was endemic in much of the U.S. Southwest from frontier days until after World War I. Numerically there were probably more Anglo than Mexicano bandits, since the Southwest became the last refuge of murderers, rascals, and misfits during this period. Banditry among Mexicanos in this region was often social banditry, an extreme response to Anglo racist actions and land-grabbing. Often it led to a divided reaction in the community.

In California, as a result of the gold rush and frontier conditions, banditry was endemic from 1849 until the 1880s. There was an upsurge of social bandits and highwaymen in the 1850s arising from the gold rush, Anglo racism, and Californios' loss of lands, and then a lull until the late 1860s, when numerous small bands were active in cattle and horse rustling. The best-known Californio bandits were **Tiburcio Vásquez** and the largely legendary **Joaquín Murieta**, but there were others like Juan Flores, Juan Soto, and Solomón Pico who led small groups of followers in forays against gringos.

In New Mexico, Arizona, and Texas the causes of banditry were related to the Mexican border as well as their being the very last western frontiers. Often this so-called banditry arising from border problems had a decided political aspect, as in the cases of **Juan N. Cortina** and **Catarino Garza** in Texas. In addition, the border, unpoliced until the 1890s, provided a rugged refuge for outlaws of all sorts: escaped convicts, highwaymen, smugglers, felons, thugs, and simple ruffians. Although there continued to be occasional flare-ups, by the early 1890s closer policing by both the United States and Mexico had wiped out most of the bandit hideouts along the Texas border.

Unlike California and Texas, New Mexico and Arizona suffered little from social banditry. Most of the banditry there seems to have been practiced by Anglos, and their specialty was cattle rustling. After the Civil War the area had its share of uprooted and unsettled war veterans and midwestern toughs and rowdies. The Lincoln County war (1876–1878) brought in hired gunmen and employed local outlaws, but such real banditry as existed was largely limited to the border region. In the 1890s the **Gorras Blancas** (White Caps) brought to New Mexico some disorder that might be considered a form of social banditry. A decade later the Mexican revolution spewed up bandits and small gangs all along the border, but after that the era of the unpoliced frontier had passed.

FURTHER READING: Camarillo, Alberto, and Pedro Castillo, eds. *Furia y muerte: Los bandidos chicanos.* Los Angeles: Chicano Studies Center, University of California, 1973; Cortés, Carlos. "El bandolerismo social chicano." In *Aztlán: historia del pueblo chicano, 1848–1910,* David Maciel and Patricia Bueno, eds. Mexico City: SepSetentas, 1975; Rosenbaum, Robert J. *Mexicano Resistance in the Southwest: "The Sacred Right of Self-Preservation."* Austin: University of Texas Press, 1981.

BAÑUELOS, ROMANA ACOSTA, 1925– . Businesswoman, government official. Romana Acosta was born in the mining town of Miami, Arizona, to undocumented Mexican parents. During the 1930s depression she went to Mexico when the family returned, and grew up and received her early education on a small Sonora ranch. As a child she helped both her father in the field and her mother in the latter's entrepreneurial activities. After a teenage marriage, two children, and a divorce, she returned to the United States at age nineteen, settling in Los Angeles. To support herself and her two sons she worked in a clothing factory and a laundry.

By 1949 Romana had managed to save four hundred dollars, with which she started manufacturing and merchandising tortillas. She called her company Ramona's Mexican Food Products, after Helen Hunt Jackson's fictional heroine. By the middle 1960s her hard work and long hours paid off in booming sales and profits. In 1964 Romana diversified by becoming a prime mover and founding director of the Pan American National Bank in East Los Angeles. Later, as chairwoman of the board, she gave the bank strong leadership and received much credit for its success; she was twice reelected to chair the board by unanimous vote.

In 1971 President Richard Nixon selected Romana to become Treasurer of the United States. After a rancorous Senate hearing, her appointment was confirmed and she served until 1974, when she resigned. Although she retained some interest in politics, most of her time since has been devoted to family, civic interests, and business. In the early 1990s Romana became president of the Pan American Bank and continued as president of Ramona foods. She has been the recipient of numerous honors and awards for her business leadership and her civic activities, including an honorary doctorate in business administration.

FURTHER READING: Chacón, José. *Hispanic Notables in the United States of North America.* Albuquerque: Saguaro Publications, 1978; Martínez, Al. *Rising Voices: Profiles of Hispano American Lives.* New York: New American Library, 1974; Tardiff, Joseph C., and L. Mpho Mabunda, eds. *Dictionary of Hispanic Biography.* Detroit: Gale Research, 1996; Telgen, Diane, and Jim Kamp, eds. *Notable Hispanic American Women.* Detroit: Gale Research, 1993.

BARAJAS, GLORIA, 1952– . Activist, feminist. While still a student in a Texas high school, Gloria Barajas began to develop her political skills in its Latin American Club and in the local Catholic Youth Organization. She became deeply aware of the unmet needs in the Chicano community as the result of early jobs teaching and working for a local public housing authority. She also took an active part in local and national political campaigns.

In Washington, D.C. she was a member of the D.C. Commission on Latino Community Development. While vice president of a Washington consulting firm, Congressional Education Associates, Barajas helped establish a local chapter of the Mexican American Women's National Association (**MANA**). As its first vice president for programming, she developed and organized MANA's leadership training workshop. Elected national president of MANA in 1986, she brought to the organization her extensive experience and skills as a community and political activist. She worked to promote Chicana involvement in the electoral process and sought more governmental positions for Chicanas. After leaving the MANA presidency Barajas became coordinator of the Women's Leadership Training Program in the civil rights department of the National Education Association.

FURTHER READING: Elvira Valenzuela Crocker. *MANA: One Dream, Many Voices; A History of the Mexican American Women's National Association.* Washington, D.C.: MANA, 1991.

BARELA, CASIMIRO, 1847–1920. State senator, businessman. Casimiro Barela was born during the U.S.-Mexican war in Embudo, a small town north of Santa Fe. An eager student there and later in Mora, he came to the attention of **Jean Baptiste Salpointe**, the new Mora parish priest and future bishop and archbishop. With his parents' consent, Salpointe took Casimiro into his home to educate him. After four years with Salpointe he returned to his family and persuaded his parents to move to southern Colorado, which he had visited with Salpointe.

In 1869 Barela began what was to become a long and honorable political career by winning election as justice of the peace. From justice of the peace he moved to county assessor, and then to the territorial legislature. In 1875 he was selected as one of the delegates to the Colorado constitutional convention, in which he played a leading role as defender of Mexican American rights. In 1876 he was elected to the first state senate and regularly won reelection to that body. In 1916 at age 69 he was finally defeated, but kept his "title" of Perpetual Senator.

After his political defeat Barela devoted his time to his many business interests. He was just as active in business as he was in politics. He oversaw a huge network of businesses: raising thoroughbred horses, ranching, merchandising, railroading, printing, and banking—in Colorado, New Mexico, and old Mexico. Before the end of the century he was widely considered to be one of the richest men in Colorado. He died in December 1920 of pneumonia contracted while on a diplomatic mission to Mexico.

FURTHER READING: Burrola, Ray. "Casimiro Barela: A Case Study of Chicano Political History in Colorado." In *Perspectivas en Chicano Studies: Papers Presented at the Third Annual Meeting of the National Association of Chicano Social Science*, edited by Reyaldo F. Macías. Los Angeles: The Association, 1977; Fernández, José. *Cuarenta años de legislador: biografía del senador Casimiro Barela.* Reprint. New York: Arno Press, 1976; Meléndez, A. Gabriel. "Recovering Neomexicano Biographical Narrative: Cuarenta años de legislador, the Biography of Casimiro Barela." In *Recovering the U.S. Hispanic Literary Heritage*, vol. 3. Edited by María Herrera-Sobek and Virginia Sánchez Korrol. Houston: Arte Público Press, 2000.

BARELA, PATROCINIO, 1902–1964. Artist, **santero**. Patrocinio Barela was born in Bisbee, Arizona of an itinerant worker father and a *curandera* mother (see **curanderismo**). After his mother's death, he grew up in farm and labor camps where his father worked. Although he attended school from time to time, he remained illiterate but taught himself to draw and carve. Forsaken by his father, he traveled around the Southwest earning a below-subsistence living as an itinerant worker. In Denver he was turned over to an African American family to be raised; he was well treated and taught to speak English.

After years of migrant work, in 1930 Barela settled in Cañon, New Mexico, and married. While doing odd jobs to support himself and his family, he began to take his ability to carve more seriously and began making religious figures. During President Franklin D. Roosevelt's first term he found employment in a Works Progress Administration project where his carving skills were noticed. As a result he was invited to work for the Federal Art Project (FAP) as a wood carver. He carved doors and massive colonial-style furniture as well as *santos.* In 1936 eight of his pieces were included in an FAP exhibit at the Museum of Modern Art in New York City. His figures soon brought him wide acclaim, and three years later a collection of his carvings was displayed at the New York World Fair.

The FAP was ended in 1942 during World War II, but Barela continued to carve *santos* and *bultos* at home at night and when unable to find work in agriculture. In the postwar decades he continued to act as his own salesman despite his growing artistic fame. Throughout his entire life Barela struggled with an alcohol problem. He died as the result of a fire that erupted during the night in the workshop where he slept. His carvings are represented today in a number of outstanding museums and many private collections.

FURTHER READING: Crews, Mildred. "Saint-Maker from Taos." *Américas* 21:3 (March 1969) 33–37; Gonzales, Edward, and David L. Witt. *Spirit Ascendant: The Art and Life of Patrocino Barela.* Santa Fe: Red Crane Books, 1996.

BARRERA, ROY R., 1927–. Criminal lawyer, politician. Roy Barrera was born, grew up, and received most of his education in San Antonio, Texas. After a stint in the armed services he was able to earn a law degree from St. Mary's University in 1951 with the aid of the G.I. Bill. During the 1950s he occupied several positions in the local court system, and in 1957 went into private law practice. In the late 1960s he was named one of the state's top ten criminal lawyers, and Governor John Connally appointed him the Texas Secretary of State. Barrera has been active in local politics and has served on numerous civic boards and committees.

FURTHER READING: Salazar, Verónica. *Dedication Rewarded: Prominent Mexican Americans.* San Antonio: Mexican American Cultural Center, 1970.

BARRIO. *Barrio* is the Spanish word for district. In the United States it refers to a part of a town or city, usually in less desirable neighborhoods with substandard **housing,** inhabited mostly by Mexican Americans. Many barrios are characterized by a high incidence of poverty and disease, poor city services, little economic and political influence, and isolation. Barrios had diverse origins. Some resulted from early Mexican and Spanish settlements surrounding a plaza that were bypassed by later Anglo business and transportation centers. Other sources of barrios were suburban labor camps and farm worker communities.

BARRIO, RAYMOND, 1921–1996. Writer, painter, teacher. Raymond Barrio was born of Spanish immigrant parents in New Jersey and grew up there, but had since lived in California. After three years in the army during World War II he went to college; he earned a B.A. at the University of California, Berkeley, and a B.F.A. at the Art Center College of Los Angeles. After marriage and a family, his early successful career as a painter was replaced by teaching as a more regular source of income. While teaching he also began to write, and in 1968 published two books on modern art.

The following year Barrio self-published *The Plum Plum Pickers* after it was rejected by all the publishers he sent it to. Today it is widely considered one of the most important works in the early Chicano literary renaissance, and has been the most anthologized Chicano novel. Basically a study of the exploitation of migrant workers, *The Plum Plum Pickers* describes the difficult marginal lives of migrant agricultural workers. Barrio was one of the first writers to use the novel to expose Chicano social problems. He went on to publish on art and other topics in addition to writing short stories and a weekly newspaper column.

FURTHER READING: García, Nasario. "Nasario García Interviews Raymond Barrio." Revista Chicano-Riqueña 13:1 (Spring 1985) 75–90; Lomelí, Francisco A., and Carl R. Shirley, eds. *Chicano Writers: First Series.* Detroit: Gale Research Inc., 1989; *Who's Who in America, 1984–1985.* Chicago: Marquis Who's Who, 1984.

BEAR FLAG REVOLT, 1946. The Bear Flag revolt was an uprising against Mexican officials by Anglos in California immediately preceding the outbreak of the **U.S.-Mexican War.** Taking the northern California commandant, General **Mariano Vallejo,** prisoner, the Americans declared California an independent republic and raised their flag with its grizzly bear insignia. Captain **John Charles Frémont,** who was illegally in California with his command, incorporated the Bear Flag revolutionaries into his force and took over the presidio at San Francisco. Meanwhile, the United States having declared war on Mexico, Commodore John D. Sloat captured Monterey and raised the U.S. flag. The Bear Flag revolt and republic lasted only four weeks.

FURTHER READING: Hart, James D. *A Companion to California.* New York: Oxford University Press, 1978; Pitt, Leonard M. *The Decline of the Californios: A Social History of the Spanish-speaking Californians, 1846–1890.* Berkeley: University of California Press, 1966; Roberts, David. *A Newer World: Kit Carson, John C. Fremont, and the Claiming of the American West.* New York: Simon & Schuster, 2000; Warner, Barbara R. *The Men of the California Bear Flag Revolt and Their Heritage.* Spokane, Wash.: Clark, 1996.

BEAUBIEN, CARLOS, 1800–1864. Merchant, landowner. Charles H. Trotier, Sieur de Beaubien was born in Canada but as a young man traveled to New Mexico in the fur trade. Settling in Taos, he married a Nuevomexicana of a prominent family and became a Mexican citizen. In 1841, with partner Guadalupe Miranda, he was awarded a large land grant by Governor **Manuel Armijo** that later became notorious as the **Maxwell Land Grant**.

Beaubien supported the U.S. takeover of the Southwest, and was rewarded with a judgeship by acting governor Colonel Stephen Kearny. He presided at the trial of the Nuevomexicano leaders in the **Taos rebellion**. As a pre-eminent New Mexico landowner, he served in the unsuccessful statehood convention at Santa Fe in 1848. For the rest of his life he pursued the dream of an immense landed estate, but was unable to develop his grant, which he sold to his two sons-in-law.

FURTHER READING: Lamar, Howard R. *The Far Southwest, 1846–1912.* New York: W. W. Norton., 1977; Murphy, Lawrence R. "The Beaubien and Miranda Land Grant, 1841–1846." *New Mexico Historical Review* 42:1 (1967) 27–47; Twitchell, Ralph E. *The History of the Military Occupation of the Territory of New Mexico . . .* , reprint. New York: Arno Press, 1976.

BENAVIDES, SANTOS, 1823–1891. Politician, merchant, soldier. Santos Benavides was born in Laredo, Texas; he received an excellent education for the times and also acquired a basic knowledge of ranching and merchandising. During the late 1830s he participated in border separatist movements and after the U.S. takeover became active in local politics. During the **Civil War** he initially obtained the rank of major in the Confederate forces, was promoted to colonel, and was in line for promotion to general at the war's end. After the war he quickly accepted the northern victory and became extremely active in politics. He was elected mayor of Laredo, was named chief justice of Webb County, and won three terms to the state legislature, where he played a prominent role. Meanwhile he raised cotton and organized a Laredo mercantile business, which he operated for the rest of his life.

FURTHER READING: Larralde, Carlos. *Mexican American: Movements and Leaders.* Los Alamitos, Calif.: Hwong Publishing Co., 1976; Riley, John D. "Santos Benavides: His Influence on the Lower Rio Grande, 1823–1891." Ph.D. diss. Texas Christian University, 1976; Thompson, Jerry D. *Vaqueros in Blue and Gray.* Austin: Presidial Press, 1977.

BERNAL, JOE J., 1927– . Activist, political leader. One of nine children in a middle-class family, Joe Bernal was born and received his early education in San Antonio, Texas. Upon his graduation from Sidney Lanier High School, where he was a class officer for three years, he volunteered for military duty in World War II. Discharged from the armed services in 1946, he then used the G.I. Bill to obtain an undergraduate degree in sociology at Trinity University. In 1954 he earned an M.Ed., and twenty-four years later he received his doctorate. Meanwhile, thirteen years of teaching in Texas public schools and daily contact with young Chicanos and their problems gradually convinced him of the importance of legislation in solving the many *raza* problems.

In 1964 Bernal, one of the "new" Texas Democrats, won a seat in the Texas House of Representatives and two years later ran for the Texas senate. Elected in a close race, he quickly became known in the senate as an aggressive and effective reformer. He understandably had a special concern for education and was the author of the first Texas **bilingual education** law. In 1969 he received the National Education Association's Human Rights Award for his outstanding contributions to the field of human relations.

Bernal participated actively in San Antonio community affairs as well as in politics. He served on the **Mexican American Legal Defense and Educational Fund** board of directors, was active in the **American G.I. Forum**, and strongly supported the Texas political group Mexican American Democrats. Known as a coauthor with **Julian Samora** and **Albert Peña** of *Gunpowder Justice: A Reassessment of the Texas Rangers*, 1979, he also wrote on bilingual education.

FURTHER READING: Bernal, Joe, Julian Samora, and Albert Peña. *Gunpowder Justice: A Reassessment of the Texas Rangers*. Notre Dame, Ind.: University of Notre Dame Press, 1979; Chacón, José A. *Hispanic Notables in the United States of North America*. Albuquerque: Saguaro Publishing, 1978; Joe J. Bernal Papers, 1942–1981. Benson Latin American Collection, General Libraries, University of Texas at Austin.

BERREYESA FAMILY. The Berreyesas were members of an early Californio family with extensive land holdings in the San Francisco Bay area, including the valuable New Almaden mercury mines. After the U.S. takeover and the Treaty of **Guadalupe Hidalgo**, they were plagued by squatters on their lands, hounded by vigilantes, and denied justice by the courts. Ultimately they lost all their holdings. During the 1850s eight family members were lynched, were murdered, or met other untimely ends at the hands of Anglos; others had to flee to southern California or Mexico to get out of danger.

FURTHER READING: Pitt, Leonard M. *The Decline of the Californios: A Social History of the Spanish-Speaking Californians, 1846–1890*. Berkeley: University of California Press, 1966; Salonites, Eftimeos. *Berreyesa: The Rape of the Mexican Land Grant, Rancho Cañada de Capay*. Capay, Calif.: Mission Bell Marketing, 1994.

BICULTURALISM. Biculturalism is the state of being equally comfortable and able to function effectively in two distinct cultures. Truly bicultural persons are able to switch codes of personal and societal values and behavior as easily as the bilingual person switches languages.

Early Anglo in-migrants to the Southwest adopted aspects of Mexicano culture, while Mexican American elites accepted some Anglo practices, leading to widespread, if limited, biculturalism. By 1900 the heavy influx of Anglo in-migrants and the integration of the Southwest into the national economy and society led to a decline in this bicultural pattern.

FURTHER READING: Darder, Antonia, ed. *Culture and Difference: Critical Perspectives on the Bicultural Experience in the United States.* Westport, Conn.: Bergin & Garvey, 1995.

BILINGUAL EDUCATION. From its inception, the concept of bilingual education has meant different things to different people. Basically it refers to teaching students in two languages in a program designed to enable those with limited English language skills to develop sufficient proficiency to benefit fully from education in that language.

Used informally in the United States for many years, bilingual education became a major objective of the Chicano Movement in the late 1960s. The **movimiento** pushed demands for bilingual education as a civil right. That concept was officially recognized by the Bilingual Education Act of 1968. In 1974 the U.S. Supreme Court in the case *Lau v. Nichols* institutionalized bilingual education by ruling that failure to provide instruction in their native languages violated the civil rights of students.

However, bilingual programs aroused controversy from the beginning. There were, and are, widely differing views of what composes bilingual education. A basic issue was how bilingual education should be done—if it should be done at all. There is still no agreement as to the effectiveness of various programs. Without question, the lack of Anglo community support, well-trained teachers, and effective teaching materials has limited their success. The opposition of Republican presidents Richard M. Nixon and Ronald Reagan in the 1970s and 1980s undermined congressional mandates and court decisions. In 1992 California voters approved **Proposition 227**, ordering an end to bilingual education in that state. The proposition was immediately challenged in the courts.

Many Chicano activists have strongly supported bilingual education as an important prop to the retention of Mexican culture. Although support in the community has been more equivocal, most Mexican Americans and nearly all Chicano political and social organizations favor continuing the programs, which they view as improving educational opportunity. This support is accompanied by a virtually unanimous belief in the necessity of learning English. It seems abundantly clear that support for bilingual education does not mean opposition to English as the national language.

Protesters wave placards during a protest against bilingual education on the steps of the Colorado State Capitol, Denver Colo., June 19, 2001. © AP/Wide World Photos.

FURTHER READING: Arias, M. Beatriz, and Ursula Casanova, eds. *Bilingual Education: Politics, Practice, and Research.* Chicago: National Society for the Study of Education, 1993; Crawford, James. *Bilingual Education: History, Politics, Theory, and Practice,* 3rd ed. Los Angeles: Bilingual Educational Services, 1995; Donato, Rubén. *The Other Struggle for Equal Schools: Mexican Americans During the Civil Rights Era.* Albany: State University of New York Press, 1997; Feinberg, Rosa Castro. *Bilingual Education: A Reference Handbook.* Santa Barbara, Calif.: ABC-CLIO, 2002; García, Ofelia, ed. *Bilingual Education.* Philadelphia: J. Benjamins, 1991; Manuel, Herschel T. *Spanish-Speaking Children of the Southwest.* Austin: University of Texas Press, 1965; San Miguel, Guadalupe, Jr. "Conflict and Controversy in the Evolution of Bilingual Education in the United States—An Interpretation." In *The Mexican American Experience: An Interdisciplinary Anthology,* edited by Rodolfo O. de la Garza et al. Austin: University of Texas Press, 1985; Trujillo, Armando L. *Chicano Empowerment and Bilingual Education.* New York: Garland Publishing, 1998; Turner, Paul R. *Bilingualism in the Southwest,* 2nd ed. Tucson: University of Arizona Press, 1982.

BILINGUAL LEGISLATION. A federal **bilingual education** bill was introduced in the House of Representatives in mid-1967 and passed, with modifications, in the following January as an amendment to the Elementary and Secondary Education Act. The Bilingual Education Act of 1968 officially recognized the concept of bilingual education as a civil right; the act was later strengthened and refined by amendments in 1974 and 1978. In the benchmark case of ***Lau v. Nichols***, 1974, the U.S. Supreme Court by a unanimous vote held that failure to provide students instruction in their native languages violated the Civil Rights Act of 1964. As a result, bilingual education became institutionalized.

However, in 1969 Republican president Richard M. Nixon, reacting sharply to President Lyndon Johnson's Great Society goals, initiated a sharp attack on bilingual legislation, and during the 1980s the Ronald Reagan administration stepped up Republican opposition to the bilingual concept. By reducing or terminating federal funding for various bilingual programs, Reagan did much to undermine congressional mandates and decisions of the courts. In 1992 California voters ordered an end to bilingual education in that state by approving **Proposition 227**. Although challenged in the courts, the vote set off a national trend.

FURTHER READING: Bangura, Abdul Karim, and Martin C. Muo. *United States Congress & Bilingual Education.* New York: Peter Lang, 2001; Schmidt, Ronald J. "Language Education Policy and the Latino Quest for Empowerment: Exploring the Linkages." In *Latinos and Political Coalitions: Political Empowerment for the 1990s,* edited by Roberto E. Villarreal and Norma G. Hernández. Westport, Conn.: Greenwood Press, 1991; Trueba, Enrique T. *Raising Silent Voices: Educating the Linguistic Minorities for the 21st Century.* New York: Newbury House, 1989.

BILINGUALISM. Bilingualism is the ability to speak two languages like a native speaker. After the 1848 Treaty of **Guadalupe Hidalgo**, conditions in the Southwest contributed to a considerable degree of economic and social interaction between Anglos and Mexicanos, including intermarriage. In much of the area English, already in limited use, soon became the language of commerce while Spanish remained the language of daily life for Mexicanos and many Anglos who had frequent contact with them. Today New Mexico is the only state in which Spanish is an official language.

FURTHER READING: Baker, Colin, and Sylvia Prys Jones, eds. *Encyclopedia of Bilingualism and Bilingual Education.* Philadelphia: Multilingual Matters, 1998; Fishman, Joshua A. *Language Loyalty in the United States.* New York: Humanities Press, 1966; Goodenough, Ward H. *Culture, Language and Society.* Reading, Mass.: Addison-Wesley, 1971; Sánchez, Rosaura. "Chicano Bilingualism." In *New Directions in Chicano Scholarship,* edited by Ricardo Romo and Raymund Paredes, Santa Barbara, Calif.: University of California, Center for Chicano Studies, 1984; Turner, Paul R. *Bilingualism in the Southwest,* 2nd ed. Tucson: University of Arizona Press, 1982.

BISBEE "DEPORTATIONS," 1917. In the midst of the **World War I** copper boom, **Industrial Workers of the World** leaders at Bisbee, **Arizona** led some three thousand miners in a strike for higher wages in late June 1917. Two weeks later the protesters, many of whom were Mexicanos, were rounded up by a force of over two thousand men deputized by the sheriff and were held in the local ballpark. Charged with disturbing the peace, vagrancy, and treason, the strikers were given a last chance to return to work. More than one thousand holdouts who rejected the offer were loaded into boxcars and taken across the state border to Hermanas, New Mexico. Here they were abandoned in the desert, where they were later rescued by federal troops. Although the deportation was widely criticized and both state and federal charges of kidnapping were later filed, no one was convicted. Few of the deportees returned to Bisbee.

FURTHER READING: Bailey, Lynn Robinson. *Bisbee, Queen of the Copper Camps.* Tucson: Westernlore Press, 1983; Byrkit, James W. *Forging the Copper Collar: Arizona's Labor Management War, 1901–1921.* Tucson: University of Arizona Press, 1982; Taft, Philip. "The Bisbee Deportation." *Labor History* 13:1 (1972) 3–40.

BLACK BERETS. The Black Berets organization was an urban-oriented paramilitary youth group that arose in New Mexico and California during the Chicano **movimiento**. First established in Albuquerque, the Berets were based loosely on the contemporary Black Panther movement among African Americans. Acting as aggressive shock troops in the Chicano movement, they denounced police harassment and especially the indiscriminate and excessive use of force. They were dogmatically nationalistic, with goals of eventual self-determination as well as liberation through education.

The Black Berets' strident rhetoric appealed mostly to high school and college students. Although the organization was involved in various worthy community service projects, it attracted only a limited following, which it later lost to the more popular **Brown Berets**.

FURTHER READING: García, F. Chris. "Black Beret Organization." In *La Causa Política: A Chicano Politics Reader*, edited by F. Chris García. Notre Dame, Ind.: University of Notre Dame Press, 1974.

BLOODY CHRISTMAS, 1951. On Christmas Eve 1951, seven Chicano youths were arrested by the Los Angeles police and taken to the Lincoln Heights station, where they were charged with battery and interfering with the officers. While detained at the station they were brutally beaten by police during a Christmas Eve drinking party. The **Community Service Organization** pushed for the punishment of the officers, and the following year a Los Angeles grand jury indicted eight of the policemen involved. Resulting court trials led to conviction and prison terms for five of the officers; the remainder were reprimanded and disciplined.

FURTHER READING: Morales, Antonio. "A Study of Mexican American Perceptions of Law Enforcement Policies and Practices in East Los Angeles." Ph.D. diss., University of Southern California, 1972.

BOGARDUS, EMORY S., 1882–1973. Seminal sociologist. Emory Bogardus was a pioneer in the study of ethnic leadership, race relations, and immigration. Born and educated in the Midwest, beginning in 1911 he researched, wrote, and taught during a long and highly productive academic career based at the University of Southern California (USC). In 1915 he organized and became the first chairperson of the sociology department at USC. During World War I he was president of the Los Angeles Social Service Commission, and in the 1920s was research director for the Pacific Coast Race Relations Survey. Active in professional and civic groups, from 1929 to 1931 he was the founding president of the Pacific Sociological Society. His investigative studies in race relations and the problems of juveniles in Los Angeles became the point of departure for subsequent research by scholars and created a basis for public perception of the issues involved. During his lifetime he published hundreds of articles and twenty-four books dealing with race and immigration. He did an invaluable study of the **Zoot Suit**

Riots during the World War II years. Among his more important books are *Immigration and Race Attitudes*, 1928, and *The Mexican in the United States*, 1934.

FURTHER READING: Bogardus, Emory S. *The Mexican in the United States*, reprint of 1934 edition. New York: Arno Press, 1970; Chabrán, Richard, and Rafael Chabrán, eds. *The Latino Encyclopedia*, vol.1. New York: Marshall Cavendish, 1996; Garraty, John A., and Mark C. Carnes, eds. *American National Biography*, vol. 3. New York: Oxford University Press, 1999.

BONILLA, TONY, 1936– . Activist, politician. Born in Calvert, Texas, halfway between Dallas and the coast, Tony Bonilla attended a local junior college and received his B.A. in education from Baylor University in 1958. After obtaining his L.L.B. from the University of Houston two years later, Bonilla entered law practice and went into state politics immediately. In 1964 he won election to the Texas House of Representatives, where he served until 1967.

An outspoken Corpus Christi attorney, Bonilla led the fight for Tejano civil rights. He became deeply involved in the Texas political group Mexican American Democrats (MAD), of which he later was elected state chairman. Entrepreneurially oriented, he was also active in the Corpus Christi Chamber of Commerce and was chosen chairman of its board of directors in 1973. Deeply concerned about Mexican American problems, Bonilla had earlier helped establish the **Political Association of Spanish-Speaking Organizations** and played a vital role in the **League of United Latin American Citizens** (LULAC). As an extremely energetic member of the latter organization since receiving his law degree, he was elected state director at the beginning of the 1970s and a decade later became national president. During his two-year presidential term he worked assiduously to bring blacks and Chicanos together, meeting with Jesse Jackson, Coretta Scott King, and leaders of the Southern Christian Leadership Conference.

After stepping down as president of LULAC, in 1983 Bonilla was selected to chair the National Hispanic Leadership Conference, a Latino think tank that he still heads. In 1983 he ran for mayor of Corpus Christi and three years later he received the Cecil Burney Humanitarian Award from the Nueces County bar association. He is a trial lawyer for the Corpus Christi firm of Bonilla and Berlanga. He continues to be an active businessman, involved in real estate as well as the law.

FURTHER READING: Bonilla, Tony. "We Gave It Our Best Shot," *Latino* 54:4 (May–June 1983) 6; Cárdenas, Leo. "The Bonilla Years Come to an End," *Latino* 54:4 (May–June 1983) 8–9, 29; Kane, George. "The Entrepreneurial Professional," *Hispanic Business* (September 1983) 36–37, 80; Salazar, Veronica. *Dedication Rewarded: Prominent Mexican Americans*. San Antonio: Mexican American Cultural Center, 1976; Tardiff, Joseph C., and L. Mpho Mabunda, eds. *Dictionary of Hispanic Biography*. Detroit: Gale Research, 1996; *Who's Who among Hispanic Americans, 1994–1995*. Detroit: Gale Research, 1994.

BORDER CONFLICT. Unrest and conflict along the border between the United States and Mexico date from the Treaty of **Guadalupe Hidalgo** in 1848. Among the many causes of border problems until the 1900s were cattle rustling, smuggling, Indian depredations, banditry, filibustering, and political unrest in northern Mexico. Neither Mexico nor the United States was able to establish a reasonably firm control of the region until the last decades of the nineteenth century. Because of the wild, sparsely inhabited nature of nearly the entire twelve hundred mile frontier, adventurers, revolutionaries, and badmen were able to operate there with little concern for law.

Robbing people and looting villages on both sides of the border were constant irritants. Also, incursions into Mexico by slave owners trying to recapture runaways and by the **Texas Rangers** and the U.S. army to pursue bandit gangs aroused local antagonisms and Mexican government concerns. High points of the perennial conflict were the Carbajal incidents; the filibustering of Raousset de Boulbon, William Walker, and Henry Crabb; the **Cart War** of 1857; the border raids of **Juan Cortina**; and the **Salt War** of 1877.

The greater pacification of southwestern Indians in the United States during the 1870s and the coming to the presidency of Mexico of Porfirio Díaz marked the beginning of greater control and somewhat more settled conditions on the border. However, as a last frontier in both countries it continued to be plagued by some lawlessness and small-scale **banditry.** In the 1890s opponents of President Díaz began to disturb the region by using it as a convenient launching pad for their efforts to overthrow the old dictator. Because of the considerable sympathy and support they enjoyed from Mexicanos in the United States and the isolation of the area, the American government had great difficulty in controlling their actions. When the 1910 **Mexican revolution** actually broke out, conditions along the border became even more volatile. Tensions on both sides climaxed in "Pancho" Villa's raid on Columbus, New Mexico and the year-long search for Villa in northern Mexico by U.S. troops under General John Pershing.

Conflict in the remainder of the twentieth century was different. Mostly between governments rather than border peoples, it revolved around smuggling, border water resources, narcotics, and **undocumented** immigration from Mexico. Smuggling was an endemic problem that intensified during the Prohibition era in the United States. In the last quarter of the century the interdiction of narcotics smuggling became a high-priority activity of the U.S. government. As dams were built on the **Rio Grande** and some of its tributaries in both countries and Colorado River waters were diverted by the United States, the need for mutually agreed-to solutions was recognized. Although tensions became high at times, compromise solutions have been worked out. Undocumented immigration was, and continues to be, a more intractable problem, exacerbated by Mexico's population explosion, by downturns in the U.S. economy from time to time, and by not-infrequent unilateral border actions by the **Border Patrol**.

FURTHER READING: Andreas, Peter. *Border Games: Policing the U.S.-Mexico Divide.* Ithaca, N.Y.: Cornell University Press, 2000; Bowden, Charles. *Down by the River: Drugs, Money, Murder, and Family.* New York: Simon & Schuster, 2002; Dunn, Timothy J. *The Militarization of the U.S.-Mexico Border, 1978–1992: Low Intensity Conflict Doctrine Comes Home.* Austin: University of Texas, Center for Mexican American Studies, 1996; Fernández, Raúl A. *The Mexican-American Border Region: Issues and Trends.* Notre Dame: University of Notre Dame Press, 1989; Jackson, Robert H. *New Views of Borderlands History.* Albuquerque: University of New Mexico Press, 1998; Martínez, Oscar J. *Troublesome Border.* Tucson: University of Arizona Press, 1988; Martínez, Oscar J., ed. *U.S.-Mexico Borderlands: History and Contemporary Perspectives.* Wilmington, Del.: Scholarly Resources, 1996.

BORDER CULTURE. The United States–Mexico border culture is made up of a wide variety of elements: geographical, economic, political, and social. The region, especially along the **Rio Grande**, which unites as much as it separates, forms a distinct entity that is set apart from the mainstream of both countries. Elsewhere a generally arid land, sparsely inhabited, has inhibited any regional unity. The border's distinctiveness derives from long-term cross-borrowing as well as the incorporation of native American cultural elements. Until **World War II** the borderlands were socially and economically marginal to both the United States and Mexico. Cultural borrowing has grown out of the daily occasions for social interaction provided by a close economic interdependence. As a result, the intensity of this culture tends to vary with distance from the border.

The U.S.-Mexico borderlands culture is in constant transition. It is rooted in the many complex ways that the nature of the border influences the lives of the people who live there, their values, and their behavior. It is being Hispanicized casually by Mexican immigrants who arrive already partly Americanized by international commerce and exported U.S. mass culture. Continuing **immigration** from all regions of Mexico nourishes and reinforces the Mexican impact on border culture.

While not homogenous, border culture has been identified and defined by a disjunction or apartness. Until recently many border concerns have received relatively little attention from the heartland, from distant and generally indifferent Washington, D.C., and México, D.F., or so many border-landers feel. For most of its existence the border has seen smuggling as a way of life, in recent decades automobiles into Mexico and drugs into the United States. It has been a sometimes troubled region, its daily life often shaped by forces beyond its control: the **Mexican revolution** in the 1910s, U.S. Prohibition in the 1920s, and the North America Free Trade Agreement and drugs today. In the 1920s the rise of tourism gave a boost to the area and especially to the development of border twin cities, as Americans flocked into the Southwest and Mexicans moved to the border towns. El Paso's population reached over 600,000 in 1998 and Ciudad Juárez had over one million three years earlier. Border twins like El Paso/Ciudad Juárez and Laredo/Nuevo Laredo continue to provide a propitious environment for interaction in customs, language, values, economic interdependence, and family ties. Each city has taken on something of the character of its twin across the border.

This border interaction is conducive to creativity at all levels of society. It has produced a vibrant society thriving on cultural adaptation and experimentation. The border culture is expressed popularly in language, norteño **music**, local **corrido**s, and the popularity of Mexican foods. Holding on to its Mexican cultural roots, the Texas border region developed Tex-Mex: a "new" language, new cuisine, new music. In music the border culture centers on the *conjunto*, based on the accordion and leading to development of a vigorous regional musical style early in the twentieth century. The conjunto, a musical symbol of working class culture, remains the musical heart of border culture.

Mexican Americans in the border region tend to be bilingual and bicultural and to maintain links to Mexico. About three quarters of the borderlanders speak English well, but **caló** also persists and flourishes in border barrios. Both English and Spanish languages continue to undergo changes along the border.

FURTHER READING: Anzaldua, Gloria. *Borderlands = La Frontera*, 2nd ed. San Francisco: Aunt Lute Books, 1999; Croswaite, Luis Humberto, John William Byrd, and Bobby Byrd, eds. *Puro Border: Dispatches, Snapshots, & Graffiti from La Frontera*. El Paso, Tex.: Cinco Puntos Press, 2003; Fox, Claire F. *The Fence and the River: Culture and Politics of the U.S.-Mexico Border*. Minneapolis: University of Minnesota Press, 1999; Martínez, Oscar J. *Border People: Life and Society in the U.S.-Mexico Borderlands*. Tucson: University of Arizona Press, 1994; Richardson, Chad. *Batos, Bolillos, Pochos, & Pelados: Class & Culture on the South Texas Border*. Austin: University of Texas Press, 1999; Salvador, José David. *Border Matters: Remapping American Cultural Studies*. Berkeley: University of California Press, 1997; Sánchez-Bane, Mary, and Martha Oehmke Loustanau. *Life, Death and In-between on the U.S.-Mexico Border: Así es la vida*. Westport, Conn.: Bergin & Garvey/Greenwood, 1999; Vélez-Ibáñez, Carlos G. *Border Visions: Mexican Cultures of the Southwest United States*. Tucson: University of Arizona Press, 1996; Weisman, Alan. *La Frontera: The U.S. Border with Mexico*. San Diego: Harcourt, Brace, Jovanovich, 1986.

BORDER PATROL. The U.S. Border Patrol was created by Congress in 1924 primarily to supervise the southwestern border between the United States and Mexico. An agency under the Immigration and Naturalization Service, its primary function was, and is, to prevent undocumented (Mexican) immigrants from entering the United States.

BOX BILL, 1926. The Box Bill was an attempt in 1926 by Texas Democratic congressman John Box to apply the quota provisions of the 1924 Immigration Act to the Western Hemisphere. The bill was aimed at restricting **immigration** by Mexican nationals, who were entering the United States, without documents but legally, in large numbers during the preceding years. Southwestern business interests and the State Department, moving toward a Good Neighbor policy, were opposed to the bill. Despite strong support from U.S. union labor, the Box Bill died in committee.

FURTHER READING: Acuña, Rodolfo. *Occupied America: A History of Chicanos*, 3rd ed. New York: Harper & Row, 1988.

BOYCOTT, GRAPE. In the spring of 1968, **César Chávez** initiated a national boycott against all California table grapes when it was discovered that struck vineyards were using other growers' labels in order to circumvent the Delano strike. From the United States the boycott quickly spread to Canada, and then to Europe as well. Widely supported by students, labor unions, and religious and political leaders, the boycott proved an effective strategy and was important to the ultimate success of the **Delano grape strike.** Subsequently it was intermittently declared in effect until it was finally rescinded in 2000.

FURTHER READING: Ferris, Susan, and Ricardo Sandoval. *The Fight in the Fields: César Chávez and the Farmworkers Movement.* New York: Harcourt Brace, 1997; Levy, Jacques E. *César Chávez: Autobiography of La Causa.* New York: W. W. Norton, 1974.

BOYLE, EUGENE J. 1922– . Social activist. An Irish American teamster's son who was long interested in social justice, the Reverend Eugene Boyle became deeply involved in the Delano farm worker movement from its beginning. He participated in the 1966 **Sacramento march**, and during the next decade was jailed with Chávez at Fresno, California in 1973. He negotiated one of the **United Farm Workers'** (UFW's) first contracts, served as a mediator, coordinated boycotts, and protested. He worked as an organizer for César Chávez's UFW, becoming widely known as "César's Priest."

In 1974 Boyle ran for the California state assembly and came close to winning. During the 1970s and 1980s he continued his social action work and also served on the boards of various social justice organizations. After a long and distinguished career in social action, in 1996 he retired from his pastorate but not from the struggle for social justice. In 1998 Boyle was honored with the Harry A. Fagan Roundtable Award, and in 2001 the Santa Clara Human Relations Commission gave him the Director's Award for his longtime support of social justice and civil rights.

FURTHER READING: "Roundtable's 1998 Award to Father Eugene J. Boyle," *The Valley Catholic*, Santa Clara, Calif. 16:5 (17 March 1998) 1, 4; "Tribute to Father

A United Farm Workers' poster; "Boycott Lettuce and Grapes," 1978. © Library of Congress.

Boyle," *The Valley Catholic*, Santa Clara, Calif. 16:6 (14 April 1998) 2, 5.

BRACERO PROGRAM. The bracero program resulted from an executive agreement jointly developed by the United States and Mexico in 1942 to provide workers needed in U.S. agriculture during **World War II.** It was an important Mexican contribution to the Allied war effort, providing more than 200,000 workers for southwestern **railroads** and farms, most of them in California. Texas was excluded from the program by Mexico because of complaints about the treatment of Mexicano workers there.

Although the statutory basis of the bracero program ended in 1948, the importation of Mexican workers not only continued, but increased markedly after the war. Under various arrangements, thousands of workers continued to be brought in, partly to counter a widespread concern about the rapid rise in the number of **undocumented**s crossing the border.

In 1951 Public Law 78, delineating a new bracero program, was formalized as a treaty between the two countries. During the 1950s opposition to the increasingly heavy influx of Mexican labor mounted in both the United States and Mexico. Nevertheless, supporters of bracero importation managed to prevail until the mid-1960s. Influenced in part by the civil rights movement, in May 1963 the congress voted down a bill to extend Public Law 78 for two more years, but then approved a measure to provide one final year. In December 1964 Public Law 78 expired amid dire predictions of southwestern agricultural disaster.

FURTHER READING: Calavita, Kitty. *Inside the State: The Bracero Program and the I.N.S.* New York: Routledge, 1992; Craig, Richard B. *The Bracero Program: Interest Groups and Foreign Policy.* Austin: University of Texas Press, 1971; Driscoll, Barbara A. *The Tracks North: The Railroad Bracero Program of World War II.* Austin: Center for Mexican American Studies, University of Texas, 1999; Galarza, Ernesto. *Merchants of Labor: The Mexican Bracero Story.* San Jose, Calif.: Rosicrucian Press, 1965; Gamboa, Erasmo. *Mexican Labor and World War II: Braceros in the Pacific Northwest, 1942–1947.* Austin: University of Texas Press, 1990; Rasmussen, Wayne D. *A History of the Farm Labor Supply Program, 1943–1947.* Washington, D.C.: Department of Agriculture Monograph No. 13, 1951.

BRAVO, FRANCISCO, 1910–1990. Civic leader, physician. Francisco Bravo was born of immigrant parents in southern California, where he grew up and was educated. After high school he studied pharmacy at the University of Southern California, and then studied sociology and medicine while working as a pharmacist. After earning his M.D. from Stanford University and completing postgraduate work in surgery he returned to Los Angeles, where he entered private practice, which was interrupted for three years by service in World War II. At the war's end he resumed his medical practice but also became involved in various business ventures. In the mid-1960s he was a founder and president of The Pan American Bank in Los Angeles. He also participated widely and actively in political, philanthropic, and community affairs.

FURTHER READING: Martínez, Al. *Rising Voices: Profiles of Hispano-American Lives.* New York: New American Library, 1974; Palacios, Arturo, ed. *Mexican American Directory.* Washington, D.C.: Executive Systems Corp., 1969; Unterburger, Amy L., ed. *Who's Who among Hispanic Americans, 1991–1992.* Detroit: Gale Research, 1991.

BROWN BERETS, 1967–1972. The Brown Berets was a confrontational, apolitical organization of youthful Mexican Americans, originally called Young Chicanos for Community Action. Founded in East Los Angeles by college student David Sánchez in late 1967, it was one of the first highly militant Chicano groups, with close ties to both the community and high school students. It recruited from the barrio streets and from high school and college campuses, and played a decisive role in organizing the student "blowouts" in 1968.

In addition to protesting educational inequities, the Berets demanded an end to brutality and excessive use of force by police. They rapidly evolved into a paramilitary alert patrol patterned somewhat similarly to the Black Panthers. Distinguished by uniforms of brown berets, army fatigues, and military boots and by radical rhetoric, they alarmed most Anglos and some middle-class Mexican Americans. The Berets held that their strength lay in their "purity." They believed that any Mexican American who had become middle class or had achieved material success was somehow corrupt, even a *vendido*. Despite a concern for education, the youthful members generally distrusted educated and intellectual Chicanos as well as Anglos, thereby isolating themselves. The Berets had a strong appeal for high school and college students, quickly spreading throughout the Southwest and reaching a maximum membership of about four to five thousand in eighty-plus chapters, most in California and Texas.

In 1969 the Brown Berets, leading the protest against the high number of Chicano casualties in the Vietnam war, took an important part in organizing the **National Chicano Moratorium**. Three years later their occupation of Catalina Island as "Aztlán Libre" probably reduced their support in the community. The leadership's inability to define clearly the group's purpose and goals, plus internal power struggles, police harassment, and infiltration by agents provocateur led to a severe organizational crisis. As a result Sánchez declared the Brown Berets disbanded in late 1972.

In October 1992 Sánchez, now a professor at East Los Angeles College, revived the Brown Berets, prompted by the high number of Chicano homicides in Los Angeles County. The new Berets' crusade against violence is especially aimed at members of barrio gangs. Sánchez sees the immediate task as overcoming the idea of the gang as family and substituting the Brown Berets.

FURTHER READING: Carlson, Mike. "Joining a New Battle; *La Causa* for Brown Berets Switches to the Home Front." *Los Angeles Times* (4 November 1993) J1: 2; Fields, Rona M., and Charles J. Fox, "The Brown Berets," *The Black Politician* 3:1 (July 1971) 53–63; Christine Marín, "Go Home, Chicanos: A Study of the Brown Berets in California and Arizona." In *An Awakened Minority: The Mexican American*, edited by Manuel P. Servín. Beverly Hills, Calif.: Glencoe Press, 1974; David Sánchez. *Expedition Through Aztlán*. La Puente, Calif.: Perspectiva Publications, 1978; Torgerson, Dial. "'Brown Power' Unity Seen Behind School Disorders." In *Chicano Politics: Readings*, edited by F. Chris García. New York: MSS Information Corp, 1973.

BROWN POWER. The concept of Brown Power was one of the Chicano adaptations from the black civil rights movement, which had proclaimed "Black Power." Brown Power basically referred to the potential that lay in united action to achieve goals. Within the Mexican American community it had a spectrum of meanings, ranging from a simple buzzword to a hope of achieving ethnic separation and even cultural independence.

During the last years of the 1960s and the early 1970s the term was used by Chicano activists as a kind of shorthand for all **movimiento** goals. Many youthful participants in the Movement viewed the right to self-determination and the creation of a separate *raza* entity in the Southwest as the principal objective of Brown Power. By the end of the 1970s many of the moderate goals of the Brown Power movement were achieved as a result of Chicano activism and its sensitizing of Anglo society.

FURTHER READING: Acuña, Rodolfo. *Occupied America: A History of Chicanos*, 3rd ed. New York: Harper & Row, 1988; Rosales, F. Arturo. *Chicano!: The History of the Mexican American Civil Rights Movement*. 2nd ed. Houston: Arte Público Press, 1997.

***BROWN v. BOARD OF EDUCATION OF TOPEKA, KANSAS*, 1954, 1955.** In 1954 the U.S. Supreme Court, following a precedent set earlier by the lower federal courts in the Méndez case (1945, 1947), ruled by unanimous vote that **segregation** of minority students in the public schools was a violation of their Fourteenth Amendment rights. The court further asserted that the separate but equal concept that grew out of its 1896 *Plessy v. Ferguson* decision inevitably resulted in unequal treatment of minorities. In public education, it said, separate but equal facilities based on race were inherently unequal.

In the following year the court weakened this decision by ordering that public schools be desegregated with due speed. As a result, the Brown decision had only a limited immediate effect, but it later became an important precedent to cite in the struggle to advance the educational rights of Chicanos.

FURTHER READING: Burns, Haywood. "From Brown to Bakke and Back: Race, Law and Social Change in America," *Daedalus* 110:2 (Spring 1981) 219–231; Martin, Waldo E. Jr., ed. *Brown v. Board of Education: A Brief History with Documents.* Boston: Bedford/St. Martin's, 1998; Patterson, James T. *Brown v. Board of Education: A Civil Rights Milestone and its Troubled Legacy.* New York: Oxford University Press, 2000; Sarat, Austin, ed. *Race, Law, and Culture: Reflections on Brown v. Board of Education.* New York: Oxford University Press, 1997; Wilkinson, J. Harvie III. *From Brown to Bakke: The Supreme Court and School Integration, 1954–1978.* New York: Oxford University Press, 1979.

BURCIAGA, JOSÉ ANTONIO, 1940–1996. Muralist, journalist, essayist, poet. José Antonio Burciaga was born near El Paso, Texas, grew up there, and received his early education in its schools. After four years of service in the U.S. Air Force during the Korean conflict, he completed a degree in fine arts at the University of Texas at El Paso. After going to work in Washington, D.C. as a graphic artist for the Central Intelligence Agency, he began to participate in the Chicano **movimiento**, and met and married Cecilia Preciado in 1972. When she was hired by Stanford University two years later, the couple moved to California.

In California Burciaga began a career as a freelance journalist. In the mid-1970s he founded a publishing company, Diseños Literarios, which published his first collection of poems, *Restless Serpents,* in 1976. Nine years later Burciaga became a Stanford resident fellow as a poet, writer, and artist. Through both his writing and his mural paintings he called attention to the problems facing **la raza** in American society. His best-known mural is his somewhat controversial "Last Chicano Supper," in which the revolutionary Che Guevara replaces Jesus Christ. Like his murals, his often humorously ironic essays and poetry focused on political and social issues, particularly discrimination and racism. Through satire, usually humorous but sometimes with a biting edge, he illuminated the Chicano experience while demanding social justice and cultural freedom.

Burciaga's poems, short stories, and essays have been widely published. In addition to *Restless Serpents,* his best-known works are *Drink Cultura Refrescante,* 1979; *Weedee Peepo: A Collection of Essays,* 1988; *Undocumented Love,* 1992; and *Spilling the Beans,* 1995. He was a founding member of the San Francisco Chicano comedy group Culture Clash. Burciaga was the recipient of numerous literary and artistic awards. He died of cancer at age fifty-six.

FURTHER READING: Chabrán, Richard, and Rafael Chabrán, eds. *Latino Encyclopedia,* vol. 1. New York: Marshall Cavendish, 1996; Lomelí, Francisco A., and Carl

R. Shirley, eds. *Chicano Writers: Second Series.* Detroit: Gale Research, 1992; García, Nasario. "Interview with José Antonio Burciaga," *Hispania* 68:4 (December 1985) 821–825; "Latino artist, activist succumbs to cancer." *San Jose Mercury News* (8 October 1996) 1B; *Who's Who among Hispanic Americans, 1994–1995.* Detroit: Gale Research, 1994.

CABALLEROS DE LABOR. The Caballeros de Labor was a southwestern organization based on the national union, the Knights of Labor, founded in 1869 by Uriah Stephens and greatly expanded by Terence V. Powderly beginning in the following decade. In the late 1880s Juan José Herrera, a New Mexican organizer of Las **Gorras Blancas**, and others were successful in recruiting Nuevomexicanos in about twenty groups for the Knights. Many of the Hispanos in the Knights appear to have been active also in Las Gorras. While the Knights stressed the eight-hour day, the principal Nuevomexicano concern was resistance to Anglo land-grabbing. The Caballeros helped organize the **Partido del Pueblo Unido** at the beginning of the 1890s and, with the Gorras Blancas, had limited temporary success in holding back the tide of Anglo takeover of pueblo lands. Never chartered by the national Knights, they became defunct by the end of the century.

FURTHER READING: Meyer, Doris. *Speaking for Themselves: Neomexicano Cultural Identity and the Spanish-Language Press, 1880–1920.* Albuquerque: University of New Mexico Press, 1996; Rosenbaum, Robert J. *Mexicano Resistance in the Southwest: "The Sacred Right of Self-Preservation."* Austin: University of Texas Press, 1981.

CABEZA DE BACA, EZEQUIEL, 1864–1917. Politician, journalist. Political leader and newspaper editor and owner, Ezequiel Cabeza de Baca was the first Mexican American to be elected governor of New Mexico. His prominent family status and press affiliations placed him at the center of politics in northeastern New Mexico for two decades. As a politician and as a newspaperman he made use of his excellent education to speak out with a powerful voice for Nuevomexicano rights, especially in the areas of land grants and education.

In 1890 Cabeza de Baca was one of the founders of the **Partido del Pueblo Unido**, a populist movement that attracted many Nuevomexicanos who were angered by the corruption in the Republican and Democratic parties and by Anglo land takeover. Two decades later he opposed the proposed state constitution for New Mexico as being insufficiently protective of *raza* rights. When New Mexico became the forty-seventh state in 1912, Cabeza de Baca was elected its first lieutenant governor, a position he used to support educational reforms. In the following election he was the unanimous Democratic choice as candidate for the governorship, and won. He died a few weeks after his inauguration, after a long bout with pernicious anemia.

FURTHER READING: Meléndez, A. Gabriel. *So All Is Not Lost: The Poetics of Print in Nuevomexicano Communities, 1834–1958.* Albuquerque: University of New Mexico Press, 1997; Perrigo, Lynn I. *Hispanos: Historic Leaders in New Mexico.* Santa Fe: Sunstone Press, 1985; Vigil, Maurilio E. *Los Patrones: Profiles of Hispanic Political Leaders in New Mexico History.* Washington, D.C.: University Press of America, 1980.

CABINET COMMITTEE ON OPPORTUNITIES FOR SPANISH-SPEAKING PEOPLE, 1969–1974. The CCOSSP was a government agency established during the Lyndon Johnson administration to replace the earlier Inter-Agency Committee on Mexican American Affairs. It expanded the scope of the latter to include all U.S. Latinos and continued to pursue goals of aiding and motivating them through government programs and federal appointments. Its first chairman, Martín Castillo, a former deputy director of the Civil Rights Commission, achieved the major accomplishments of the agency's five-year life.

During the less supportive administration of President Richard Nixon, who succeeded Johnson, the CCOSSP became greatly politicized. Castillo's successor in 1971, **Henry M. Ramírez**, proved to be a politically oriented and somewhat lackluster leader but did secure appointment of a number of Mexican Americans to federal positions in the Republican bid for the *raza* vote. When the agency's five-year term expired, it was not renewed.

FURTHER READING: "Cabinet Committee on the Spanish Speaking: Its Information and Its History," *La Luz* 1:1 (1972) 18–19; Castro, Tony. "The 'Chicano Recognition' Strategy of a National Party." In *La Causa Política: A Chicano Politics Reader,* edited by F. Chris García. Notre Dame: University of Notre Dame Press, 1974; Isla, José de la. "The Politics of Reelection: Se habla español," *Aztlán* 7:3 (Fall 1976) 427–451; Pycior, Julie Leininger. *LBJ & Mexican Americans: The Paradox of Power.* Austin: University of Texas Press, 1997.

CADENA, CARLOS, 1915–2001. Lawyer, judge. Carlos Cadena was born into a large middle-class Mexican American family in San Antonio, Texas. His stature as an outstanding student both in high school and at the University of Texas, Austin, and its law school led to employment as assistant San Antonio city attorney in 1941. After service in the Army Air Corps in the South Pacific during World War II, he returned to his position as assistant city attorney. Several years in private law practice and teaching at St. Mary's University Law School followed. In 1954 Cadena became the San Antonio city attorney, and eleven years later he was appointed judge of the Texas Fourth Court of Civil Appeals by Governor John Connally.

To advance the cause of Mexican American equality and dignity Cadena devoted a lifetime to using the law to end discrimination and bigotry. As a lawyer, he helped obtain court decisions mandating an end to restrictive property covenants, school **segregation**, and the exclusion of Mexican Americans from jury panels. He was deeply involved in several prominent Mexican American civil rights cases, the most important of which was *Hernández v. Texas*. In this case, in which he wrote the Supreme Court brief, he and **Gus García** won a major civil rights victory in 1954. The recipient of various honors, Cadena was appointed Chief Justice of the Texas Fourth Court of Civil Appeals in 1977. He retired from the bench in 1990, but continued to serve as a senior appellate justice. He died a decade later of cancer.

FURTHER READING: "Carlos Cadena; Won Key Supreme Court Ruling." *Los Angeles Times* (19 January 2001) Metro, B6; García, Mario T. *Mexican Americans: Leadership, Ideology, and Identity, 1930–1960.* New Haven: Yale University Press, 1989; Salazar, Veronica. *Dedication Rewarded: Prominent Mexican Americans*, vol. 2. San Antonio: Mexican American Cultural Center, 1981.

CALIFORNIA. Although visited by Spanish explorers in the 1500s and 1600s, California did not begin to be colonized until the Franciscan missionary Junípero Serra established the mission San Diego de Alcalá in 1769. The chain of twenty-one missions that Serra and his successors established between 1769 and 1823 became the economic backbone of Alta California. Efforts of the Spanish and Mexican governments to attract civilian settlers to this far northern frontier had only limited success. By the 1840s three pueblos and four presidios were home to most of its eight thousand Mexican citizens. Secularization of the missions, begun in 1834, led to the end of the mission system and distribution of mission lands, mostly in large grants or by sale to members of the leading Californio families. After secularization these Californio *rancheros* completely dominated the area economically and politically until its takeover by the United States.

Mexico's tenuous control of Alta California ended in 1848 when the United States acquired the area by the Treaty of Guadalupe Hidalgo. Shortly thereafter Mexican Americans in California began to face serious problems. When gold was discovered in 1848, many of them who went to the mining areas soon became targets of racial violence. A rapid and overwhelming influx of Anglo miners and settlers in the next year reduced the Californios to a small and almost powerless minority. Despite treaty guarantees of property rights and ultimate citizenship, they soon found their lands in jeopardy and themselves considered as foreigners. The state's **Foreign Miners License Tax Law** of 1850 and the federal **Land Act of 1851** greatly increased violations of their rights, especially by Anglo squatter activity. The social **banditry** of Tiburcio Vásquez, Juan Flores, and the semi-legendary Joaquín Murieta was an indication of the deteriorating position of most Californios. While some elites had become assimilated into the majority society by the end of the century, most were largely disfranchised and relegated to low economic status. Because of the great population increase resulting from the gold rush, this decline of the Californios was rapid in the north. In southern California they were able to hold on to economic and political power longer; however, the decline of their pastoral economy toward the end of the century and the advent of a new national economic order ended their lingering influence.

At 1900 California had about twenty thousand Mexicanos in a population of a million and a half. As the state's economy mushroomed early in the twentieth century, it became the destination of a flood-tide of workers from the Southwest and refugees fleeing the Mexican revolution of 1910. Rapid economic development during the 1920s, especially in agriculture (Carey McWilliams's "factories in the fields"), accelerated the influx of unskilled and semiskilled laborers. By 1930 California's Mexicano population had risen to more than 360,000 and had buried the old Californio culture.

The increase in the state's Spanish-speaking population led to widespread and more overt anti-Mexican attitudes, especially when the economy began to falter toward the end of the 1920s. The **Great Depression** that followed the 1929 stock market crash brought the Mexican immigration torrent of the 1920s to a trickle and sent roughly a million Mexicanos southward across the border. This "**repatriation**," the result of minority scapegoating because of severe nationwide unemployment, was the occasion of numerous civil rights violations.

As the United States began to prepare for **World War II** at the end of the 1930s, California agriculture and industry again drew upon Mexico's large unskilled labor reservoir. The demand for labor was particularly insistent in agriculture, which was losing workers to war industries and the armed services. In July 1942 an executive agreement between the United States and Mexico created a regulated immigration plan to provide workers, commonly referred to as braceros. More than half of the 200,000 World War II braceros worked in California agriculture.

During the World War II years California's Mexicano population grew rapidly as migrants from the other southwestern states and Mexico took jobs in agriculture and rapidly expanding west coast industries. This increasingly urbanized population was concentrated in the southern half of the state. By the end of the war Los Angeles was second only to Mexico City in its Mexicano population, and anti-Mexican feeling was on the rise. The **Sleepy Lagoon** case in Los Angeles and the 1943 **Zoot Suit Riots** reflected ethnic tensions and also helped spur Chicano organizational development. At the war's end a large first and second generation Mexican American population in California began to demand its rightful place in American society. The creation of the aggressive **Mexican American Political Association** at the end of the 1950s initiated a new civil rights activism. During the next decade, the unionization of farm workers in the Central Valley under the leadership of **César Chávez, Dolores Huerta,** and others renewed the push for human rights and marked the beginning of a new stage in agricultural unionism. Establishment of the California Rural Legal Assistance in 1966 and the **Cali-**

fornia Agricultural Labor Relations Act a decade later confirmed this increased tempo of activity.

During the 1960s Mexican Americans became an "awakening minority," in the words of historian Manuel P. Servín. Los Angeles councilman **Edward Roybal** was elected to the U.S. Congress. Numerous student and community organizations arose to protest the low status of Chicanos in education, employment, and government. California played a leading role in the Chicano Movement, which marked a decisive step in the demand for full acceptance. The **movimiento** succeeded in getting many California colleges and universities to institute programs in Mexican American studies—history, literature, and sociology. Although its tempo had slowed by the end of the 1970s, the advances and spirit it had engendered continued to animate Mexican Americans in California.

Symbolic of the advances made, in 1980 President Jimmy Carter appointed as U.S. ambassador to Mexico historian **Julian Nava** of California, the first Mexican American to be appointed to such an important diplomatic post. In 1996 Cruz Bustamante's selection as the first Chicano speaker of the California Assembly was further evidence and recognition of Mexican American political power, as was his election three years later to the office of lieutenant governor. He was the first Mexican American to hold that position in a century and a quarter.

Not all was milk and honey. In a clearly anti-Mexican frenzy, a successful ballot initiative amended the state constitution in 1986 to make English California's official language. Moreover, less than a decade later Republican governor Pete Wilson used a race-baiting anti-immigrant strategy to win reelection by more than a million votes despite strong opposition and a heavy turnout by Asians and Latinos. Between 1990 and the end of the century California had an increase of 1.1 million registered voters, most of them Latinos. Despite greater electoral participation by Chicano voters, **Proposition 227**, which aimed at ending bilingual education, easily passed in 1998. By 2000 California counted 10,460,000 U.S. Latinos in the state, as they vied with black Americans as the number one ethnic minority in the country.

FURTHER READING: Acuña, Rodolfo F. *Anything but Mexican: Chicanos in Contemporary Los Angeles.* New York: Verso, 1996; Almanza, Arturo S. *Mexican-Americans and Civil Rights.* Los Angeles: County Commission on Human Relations, 1964; California. Mexican Fact-Finding Committee. *Mexicans in California.* Reprint. San Francisco: R & E Research Associates, 1970; Camarillo, Albert. *Chicanos in California: A History of Mexican Americans in California.* San Francisco: Boyd & Fraser, 1984; García, Matt. *A World of Its Own: Race, Labor, and Citrus in the Making of Greater Los Angeles, 1900–1970.* Chapel Hill: University of North Carolina Press, 2001; Guerin-Gonzales, Camille. *Mexican Workers and American Dreams: Immigration, Repatriation, and California Farm Labor, 1900–1939.* New Brunswick, N.J.: Rutgers University Press, 1994; Haas, Lisbeth. *Conquests and Historical Identities in California, 1769–1936.* Berkeley: University of California Press, 1995; Menchaca, Martha. *The Mexican Outsiders: A Community History of Marginalization and Discrimination in California.* Austin:

University of Texas Press, 1995; Monroy, Douglas. *Rebirth: Mexican Los Angeles from the Great Migration to the Great Depression.* Berkeley: University of California Press, 1999; Pitt, Leonard M. *The Decline of the Californios: A Social History of the Spanish-speaking Californians, 1846–1890.* Berkeley: University of California Press, 1966; Pitti, Stephen J. *The Devil in Silicon Valley: Northern California, Race, and Mexican Americans.* Princeton, N.J.: Princeton University Press, 2003; Romo, Ricardo. *East Los Angeles: History of a Barrio.* Austin: University of Texas Press, 1983; U.S. Commission on Civil Rights. *Political Participation of Mexican Americans in California.* Washington, D.C.: U.S. Government Printing Office, 1971; Wollenberg, Charles. *Ethnic Conflict in California History.* Los Angeles: Timmon-Brown, 1970.

CALIFORNIA AGRICULTURAL LABOR RELATIONS ACT, 1975. In 1975 newly elected California governor Jerry Brown called the legislature into special session to enact farm labor legislation he had proposed in his campaign. In May the legislature overwhelmingly passed the Agricultural Labor Relations Act. The new law aimed at giving California farm workers the same rights guaranteed to industrial workers by the 1935 National Labor Relations Act. It provided for secret elections to determine which union, if any, field workers wanted to represent them. Successful at first, the law was subsequently weakened by the failure of the legislature to provide funds for elections.

FURTHER READING: Mitchell, Robert Joseph. "Peace in the Fields: A Study of the Passage and Subsequent History of the California Agricultural Labor Relations Act of 1975." Ph.D. diss. University of California, Riverside, 1980; *The Sabotage and Subversion of the Agricultural Labor Relations Act: A United Farm Workers of America, AFL-CIO White Paper.* La Paz, Keene, Calif.: United Farm Workers of America, AFL-CIO, 1975(?).

CALIFORNIA ANTI-VAGRANCY ACT, 1855. In 1855 the California legislature passed a law restricting the freedom of Mexicanos in the state. It was widely known as the "greaser law" because it singled out persons "commonly known as Greasers" for special surveillance. In the following year the legislature removed the denigrating epithet.

FURTHER READING: Heizer, Robert F., and Alan F. Almquist. *The Other Californians: Prejudice and Discrimination Under Spain, Mexico, and the United States to 1920.* Berkeley: University of California Press, 1971.

CALIFORNIA RURAL LEGAL ASSISTANCE (CRLA). The CRLA was established in 1966 with a grant from the **Office of Economic Opportunity** to provide free legal services to poverty-level clients in order to protect their civil rights. Mexican Americans formed a majority of the persons it served. The nonprofit organization's activities aroused vocal opposition from many conservative Californians and especially from Republican governor Ronald Reagan, who tried to cripple it.

The CRLA task force was concerned with defending citizen rights in housing, education, and employment. The agency emphasized class-action suits that would benefit a maximum number of people. Its headquarters in San Francisco oversaw the activities of 160 employees who were handling over thirteen thousand cases annually in the 1980s.

FURTHER READING: Bennett, Richard, and Cruz Reynoso. "California Rural Legal Assistance: The Survival of a Poverty Law Practice." *Chicano Law Review* 1 (1972) 1–79; Street, Richard Steven. *Organizing for Our Lives: New Voices from Rural Communities.* Portland, Oregon: New Sage Press & California Rural Legal Assistance, 1992; Trillin, Calvin. "U.S. Letter: McFarland." *New Yorker* 43 (4 November 1967) 173–181.

CALIFORNIO. A Mexican-descent inhabitant of the state of California. More narrowly and commonly, the term is used to refer to Mexicans living in California when it became part of the United States, and their descendants. Even more narrowly, it is sometimes used to refer to the Mexican elites at the time of the United States takeover.

FURTHER READING: Pitt, Leonard. *The Decline of the Californios: A Social History of the Spanish-speaking Californians, 1846–1890.* Berkeley: University of California Press, 1966.

CALÓ. Caló is a dialect of Spanish commonly associated with barrio youths, especially along the Mexico-U.S. border. During the early days of the **movimiento** its use became a badge of commitment among some activists who proposed teaching it in lieu of Spanish.

FURTHER READING: Ornstein-Galicia, Jacob. "Chicano Caló: Description and Review of a Border Variety." *Hispanic Journal of Behavioral Sciences* 9:4 (1987) 359–373; Reyes, Rogelio. "The Social and Linguistic Foundations of Chicano Caló: Trends for Future Research." In *Research Issues and Problems in United States Spanish: Latin American and Southwestern Varieties,* edited by Jacob L. Ornstein-Galicia, George K. Green, and Dennis J. Bixler-Márquez. Brownsville, Texas: Pan American University, 1988.

CAMARILLO, LYDIA, 1958– . Community organizer. Lydia Camarillo was born in El Paso and received her early education there. After studying law at Hastings College in San Francisco, she worked for various antipoverty programs. From 1989 to 1994 she served as national director of the **Mexican American Legal Defense and Educational Fund**'s leadership development program. For the next five years she worked for the **Southwest Voter Registration Education Project**. As the SVREP executive director, she helped create and operate some two hundred voter registration campaigns that registered nearly 1.5 million new Latino voters. Her long career in community advocacy and organizing provided credentials for her next job. In the fall of 1999 she was offered and accepted the responsibility of chief executive officer of the 2000 Democratic convention in Los Angeles, a task she carried out admirably. She was the first Latina chief executive of any political party. In 2003 Lydia Camarillo was named vice-president of the SVREP.

FURTHER READING: García, James E. "Lydia Camarillo's Unconventional Convention." *Politico Magazine* (May 2000) 13–14; "Texas Native Crowns Long Journey as First Latina to head DNC." *The Houston Chronicle* (25 May 2000) A22.

CAMPA, ARTHUR LEÓN, 1905–1978. Folklorist, linguist. Arthur Campa was born in Mexico's west coast port of Guaymas, the son of Mexican American Methodist missionaries. His father, Daniel Campa, who served as a federal officer during Mexico's great revolution, was killed in an encounter with Pancho Villa's forces in 1914. Soon afterwards the family moved back to the United States, where Campa continued his education in El Paso, Texas, and Albuquerque, New Mexico. After high school he specialized in modern languages at the University of New Mexico, and graduated in 1928 with an emphasis on Spanish. Upon earning his master's degree two years later at Columbia University he began teaching Spanish and French at the university.

While teaching, Campa began doctoral studies at Columbia and completed the requirements in 1940. In World War II, at age thirty-eight, he enlisted in the armed services and served as a combat intelligence officer in the U.S. Army Air Force in North Africa and Europe. Returning to civilian life, he accepted the department chair at the Methodist-related University of Denver, where he remained until his retirement in 1972.

Before World War II Campa had been active in and briefly president of the leftist **Congreso de los Pueblos de Habla Española**; after the war he supported the efforts of the more centrist American G.I. Forum and the League of United Latin American Citizens. However, in the postwar years Campa remained less active politically than many of his academic peers and took a moderate position during the Chicano Movement of the 1960s.

Although Dr. Campa's primary training was as a linguist, his interests lay in **folklore** and he did most of his research and writing in that area, particularly in the folklore of the Hispanic Southwest. With a populist attitude toward scholarly activity, he viewed his role as combining folklore and history to provide a better understanding of the Nuevomexicano experience. He wrote voluminously about southwestern popular lore in theater, music, poetry, legends, religion, and, of course, language. His seven books and seventy-plus articles and bulletins earned him a well-deserved reputation as the outstanding authority on the folklore of the Southwest. The best-known of his works are *Treasure of the Sangre de Cristos: Tales and Traditions of the Spanish Southwest*, 1963, and the posthumously published *Hispanic Culture in the Southwest*, 1979.

FURTHER READING: García, Mario T. *Mexican Americans: Leadership, Ideology, & Identity, 1930–1960.* New Haven: Yale University Press, 1989; Ryan, Bryan, ed. *Hispanic Writers: A Selection of Sketches from Contemporary Authors.* Detroit: Gale Research, 1991; Philip Sonnichsen, "Arthur León Campa." *La Luz* 7:12 (December 1978) 20, 26.

CAMPESINO. A rural person. In the United States it is commonly used to refer to farm workers, regardless of their backgrounds.

CANALES, J. T. (JOSÉ TOMÁS), 1877–1976. Jurist, politician. J. T. Canales of Brownsville was a prominent south Texas lawyer. A close friend of activist **Alonso Perales**, he aggressively defended the civil rights of Mexicanos even though he was also part of the local Anglo political machine. During the border unrest resulting from the 1910 Mexican revolution he criticized the **Texas Rangers**' brutal treatment of Mexicanos and became widely known for filing formal charges against them in January 1918. An investigation of his charges eventually led to a reduction in the Ranger force to five companies.

In the 1920s J. T. was active in the development of the Latin American Citizens League (LACL), and in 1929 he was one of the founders of its successor, the **League of United Latin American Citizens** (LULAC). He played a leading role in developing the first LULAC constitution and held a number of important offices in the organization, including the presidency in 1932–1933. At the end of the 1930s he led the revision of LULAC's constitution to adapt to its expansion into a national organization.

A progressive but at times somewhat maverick politician, J. T. was active in south Texas politics throughout the first half of the twentieth century. During its second decade he served several terms in the Texas legislature, where he showed great interest in education and irrigation rights. He also supported broad reforms like Prohibition and the vote for women. Throughout his life he was influential in Mexican American political life in Texas. As an octogenarian, he supported Lyndon Johnson's political career.

Canales wrote prolifically: articles, pamphlets, and books; he is best known for the two-volume historical work *Bits of Texas History in the Melting Pot*.

FURTHER READING: Anders, Evan. *Boss Rule in South Texas.* Austin: University of Texas Press, 1982; Canales, José T. *Bits of Texas History in the Melting Pot.* 2 vols. Brownsville, Texas: 1950–1957; Canales, José T. *Juan N. Cortina Presents His Motion for a New Trial.* San Antonio: Artes Gráficas, 1951; Lynch, Michael J., III. "The Role of J. T. Canales in the Development of Tejano Identity and Mexican American Integration in Twentieth Century South Texas." *Journal of South Texas* 13:2 (2000) 220–239; Pycior, Julie Leininger. *LBJ & Mexican Americans: The Paradox of Power.* Austin: University of Texas Press, 1997; Tyler, Ron, ed. *The New Handbook of Texas,* vol. 1. Austin: Texas State Historical Association, 1996.

CANDELARIA, NASH, 1928– . Novelist, marketing expert. Although he was born in Los Angeles, California, Nash Candelaria's roots and cultural memories go back to the seventeenth-century New Mexico of his father's family. Armed with a B.S. in chemistry, he took a job with a Los Angeles pharmaceutical firm and also began taking evening courses in writing. During the Korean conflict he enlisted in the air force and after his service found a position as a technical writer, followed by work in marketing and communications, and he wound up becoming advertising manager for Varian Associates.

Meanwhile, he wrote half a dozen novels. In 1977 he self-published his somewhat autobiographical *Memories of the Alhambra*, which received wide acclaim. In 1982 he added *Not by the Sword*, then *Inheritance of Strangers* in 1985, and *Leonor Park* in 1992. *Not by the Sword* received the Before Columbus Foundation's American Book award, but Candelaria is probably best known for *Memories of the Alhambra*. He is also the author of two well received collections of short stories: *The Day the Cisco Kid Shot John Wayne*, 1988, and *Uncivil Rights*, 1998. Candelaria is considered by many to be one of the top ten novelists of the Chicano literary renaissance.

FURTHER READING: Bruce-Novoa, Juan. "Nash Candelaria: An Interview." *De Colores* 5:1 & 2 (1980) 115–129; Martínez, Julio A., and Francisco A. Lomelí. *Chicano Literature: A Reference Guide*. Westport, Conn.: Greenwood Press, 1985; Tardiff, Joseph C., and L. Mpho Mabunda, eds. *Dictionary of Hispanic Biography*. Detroit: Gale Research, 1996.

CANNERY AND AGRICULTURAL WORKERS INDUSTRIAL UNION. The CAWIU was an affiliate of the communist Trade Union Unity League (TUUL) active in agriculture, the **mining industry,** and textile manufacture. A leading California agricultural labor union of the 1930s, this radical union led over thirty-eight thousand California farm workers in strikes from late 1932 to early 1934, with some success. By mid-1934 a slight improvement in agricultural wages caused a decline in its support. The CAWIU's involvement in the high-profile 1934 San Francisco General Strike led to the arrest and jailing of many of its leaders under state criminal syndicalism legislation, and to the union's resulting decline. In the following year it ceased to exist when the **Communist Party** terminated the TUUL as part of its "popular front" policy. The CAWIU was an important step in California agricultural unionism in terms of successful strikes and especially as a training ground for future labor organizers.

FURTHER READING: Cletus, Daniel E. "Radicals on the Farm in California." *Agricultural History* 49:4 (1975) 629–645; Jamieson, Stuart. *Labor Unionism in American Agriculture*. Washington. D.C.: U.S. Government Printing Office, 1945; reprint, New York: Arno Press, 1976.

CARBAJAL, JOSÉ MARÍA JESÚS, ?–1874. Border political figure. Carbajal was born in San Antonio, Texas, and worked and studied for a while in the East. He returned to Texas as the official surveyor for empresario Martín de León, whose daughter he later married. When Texas revolted against Mexican centralism in 1836 he fought in the rebel cause. After Texas independence he continued to fight against both Mexico and the United States in favor of an independent buffer state. During the early 1850s he led border clashes sometimes referred to as the Merchants War or Carbajal disturbances. Later he crossed over the Rio Grande to fight against the French troops supporting the Mexican emperor Maximilian. He became governor of Tamaulipas during the regime of President Benito Juárez. After the U.S. Civil

War he returned to Texas for a few years and then recrossed the border to die in Soto La Marina. His ambivalent citizenship status was illustrative of the times.

FURTHER READING: Rippy, J. Fred. "Border Troubles along the Rio Grande, 1848–1860." *Southwestern Historical Quarterly* 23 (October 1919); Tyler, Ron, ed. *New Handbook of Texas*, vol. 1. Austin: Texas State Historical Association, 1996.

CÁRDENAS, ROBERTO L., 1920– . Army officer. Roberto Cárdenas was born in the Yucatán peninsula but grew up in San Diego, California. A few months before Pearl Harbor he won his pilot's wings and served in the European Theater of Operations, where he was wounded in a bombing flight over Germany. Sent back to the United States, he became a test pilot on the new jet planes. From 1949 onward he attended various air force service schools, earned a B.S. in engineering, and served in various administrative positions. After promotion to brigadier general, in 1969 he was sent to Spain as vice-commander of the Sixteenth Air Force, and was then assigned to the Joint Strategic Target Planning Staff. Among his many decorations are the Air Medal, Legion of Merit, and Distinguished Flying Cross.

FURTHER READING: Chacón, José A. "Brigadier General Roberto L. Cárdenas." *La Luz* 1:9 (January 1973) 61.

CARNALISMO. From *carnal*, related by blood, *carnalismo* was a term much used during the **movimiento** to describe an ethnic kinship based on common experiences undergone by Chicanos. For some Chicano activists it had an almost spiritual unifying force.

CARR, VIKKI (FLORENCIA BICENTA DE CASILLAS MARTÍNEZ CARDONA), 1940– . Singer, philanthropist. Florencia Cardona was born in El Paso, Texas, but grew up in southern California, to which the family had moved. Music was an important part of her family life and she began singing even before she entered school. While still in Rosemead High School she sang on weekends with various local bands.

After graduation, Florencia Bicenta began singing with Pepe Callahan's Mexican-Irish band, and soon adopted Vikki Carr as her professional name and expanded her repertoire of songs. After much effort she obtained a long-term contract with Liberty Records in 1961. Her early recordings, while not smash hits in the United States, had considerable success abroad. Between record sessions she engaged in moderately successful concert tours. In the second half of the 1960s her exposure on television as vocalist for Ray Anthony's band confirmed her position as one of the leading female vocalists. There followed sold-out tours of Europe, Japan, and later South America, and in 1967 she was invited by Queen Elizabeth II to give a royal command performance. Meanwhile Carr's albums with Liberty, Columbia, and CBS/Sony proved immensely popular, especially the ones in Spanish.

She recorded some fifty best-selling singles, and a dozen and a half of her albums have reached gold status. She has earned two Grammys.

At the end of the 1960s Carr began a new career as a philanthropist. In addition to her own scholarship program founded in 1971, she has raised thousands of dollars for other educational and medical groups, including the March of Dimes and the American Cancer Society. A politically active Republican, she has sung at the White House for Presidents Nixon, Ford, Reagan, and the elder Bush. In 1992 she recorded "Brinda a la Vida, al Bolero, y a Ti" for Sony, and two years later did "Recuerdo a Javier Solís." She continues a heavy schedule of nightclub and concert appearances, in addition to radio, stage, and television work.

Vikki Carr has been the recipient of honors and awards far too numerous to mention. Woman of the World, the title conferred on her by the International Orphans Fund, is the one of which she is proudest.

FURTHER READING: Tardiff, Joseph C., and L. Mpho Mabunda, eds. *Dictionary of Hispanic Biography*. Detroit: Gale Research, 1996; Telgen, Diane, and Jim Kamp, eds. *Notable Hispanic American Women*. Detroit: Gale Research, 1993.

CARRILLO, LEO(POLDO), 1881–1961. Actor. Leo Carrillo was the scion of a prominent old Californio family, and was born in an old Los Angeles plaza adobe house. After college, he took an engineering job with the Southern Pacific Railroad. His art studies in San Francisco then landed him a job as a cartoonist at the *San Francisco Examiner*, and that, in turn, led to work as an amateur in vaudeville doing dialect stories. During World War I he moved from vaudeville to the legitimate theater and in the 1920s played romantic roles in a number of Broadway stage productions.

At the end of the 1920s Carrillo returned to California, where he began to play romantic leads in the new talking pictures. During the two decades between 1930 and 1950 he appeared in more than 100 films. Widely known as "Mr. California" because of his great pride in the state's Hispanic history, he was appointed "Goodwill Ambassador to the World" by one California governor, and in the 1940s Governor Earl Warren named him a Beaches and Parks commissioner, a position he applied himself to seriously for a decade and a half.

FURTHER READING: Carrillo, Leo. *The California I Love*. Englewood Cliffs, N.J.: Prentice-Hall, 1961; Keller, Gary D. *A Biographical Handbook of Hispanics and United States Film*. Tempe, Ariz.: Bilingual Press/Editorial Bilingüe, 1997; Reyes, Luis, and Peter Rubie. *Hispanics in Hollywood: A Celebration of 100 Years in Film and Television*. Hollywood: Lone Eagle, 2000.

CARSON, KIT (CHRISTOPHER), 1809–1868. Scout, soldier, rancher. Kentucky-born Kit Carson joined a trading expedition to Santa Fe and Taos, Nuevo México while still a teenager. During the 1830s he traveled over much of the Southwest in search of beaver, and in 1842 he became a guide for **John Charles Frémont**'s expeditions.

Married to Josefa Jaramillo of Taos, Carson became a rancher in the area and took an active role in the local Anglo community. He also had considerable influence among pro-American Nuevomexicanos. He fought in the Civil War as commander of the New Mexico volunteers, and was breveted brigadier general for his action at Valverde in 1862. After the Civil War he moved to Colorado, where he died a few years later.

FURTHER READING: Carson, Christopher. *Kit Carson's Own Story As Dictated to Colonel and Mrs. D. C. Peters about 1856–57.* Santa Fe: Museum of New Mexico, 1926; Gordon-McCutchan, R. C., ed. *Kit Carson: Indian Fighter or Indian Killer?* Niwot: University Press of Colorado, 1996.

CART WAR, 1857. A U.S.-Mexican border incident arising out of assaults beginning in 1855 by Anglo teamsters attempting to take over the lucrative trade between the coast and San Antonio. Unsuccessful in competing economically, Anglo freighters launched a series of systematic violent attacks, destroying Mexicanos' oxcarts, stealing freight, and wounding and killing some carters. Local officials made little serious effort to stop the violence. After protest by the Mexican minister in Washington, D.C. in October 1857, a company of Texas Rangers was sent into the troubled area and by the end of 1857 the attacks had ceased.

FURTHER READING: "Cart War." *The Handbook of Texas Online. http://www.tsha.utexas.edu/handbook/online/index.html*; McWilliams, Carey. *North from Mexico: The Spanish-Speaking People of the United States,* rev. ed. Westport, Conn.: Praeger, 1990.

CASTAÑEDA, CARLOS E., 1896–1958. Historian, author, professor. Carlos Castañeda was born in the small Mexican border town of Ciudad Camargo, Tamaulipas. To escape the approaching 1910 Mexican revolution, the middle-class Castañeda moved first to Matamoros and then across the Rio Grande to Brownsville, Texas, where he completed his grade and high school education. His outstanding academic performance in high school won him a scholarship to the University of Texas as an engineering student. When the United States entered World War I in 1917 he dropped out to enlist in the U.S. Army. After he was discharged from the service he returned to the university but then had to drop out again, for financial reasons.

For a year Castañeda worked in the Tampico oil fields as an engineer, but wrote regularly to Texas history professor Eugene Barker, who had become his mentor and friend. In his correspondence he declared his intention to switch from engineering to history. Assisted by a scholarship, he was able to return to the university and complete his undergraduate history studies in 1921. With his B.A. he obtained a teaching job in Texas public schools while he also worked on his M.A. in history, constantly encouraged by Barker. With the completion of his M.A. he was able to obtain a position teaching Spanish at the College of William and Mary in Virginia. However, Castañeda

Carlos E. Castañeda speaking at the San Jacinto Monument, 1943. Courtesy of the Benson Latin American Collection, University of Texas at Austin.

longed to return to Texas, and during his four years in Virginia he continued to pester Barker about job opportunities there.

In 1927 Castañeda was offered a position as head of the new Latin American Collection at the University of Texas in Austin. He quickly accepted and immediately enrolled in the university's doctoral program in history. His doctoral thesis was an annotated translation of the "lost" *History of Texas* by Fray Juan Agustín Morfi, which he published in two volumes in 1935. Castañeda's work on Morfi attracted the attention of the Knights of Columbus, which commissioned him to write a history of the Catholic Church in Texas. The result was a monumental seven-volume work titled *Our Catholic Heritage in Texas, 1519–1936* and going far beyond its title in its coverage. It became the core of his life's research and publishing.

In 1939 Castañeda joined the Texas history department part-time, while retaining his library position half-time. In the same year he was elected president of the American Catholic Historical Association. A man of prodigious energies, he also was active in local, state, regional, national, and international historical societies and their meetings. He served as editor of several leading historical journals.

During World War II Castañeda took a leave of absence from the university to work for the **Fair Employment Practices Committee** as a fact-finding assistant to the chairman. At the war's end he returned to the history department at Austin, where he remained the rest of his life. Throughout his life Castañeda wrote voluminously, publishing some eighty-five articles and twelve books on the history and culture of the Southwest and Mexico. For his extensive and intensive historical work he was the recipient of numerous honors, including membership in various Latin American historical associations. He was awarded the Order of Isabel La Católica by the government of Spain and was knighted by the papacy.

FURTHER READING: Almaraz, Félix D., Jr. *Knight Without Armor: Carlos Eduardo Castañeda, 1896–1958.* College Station: Texas A & M University Press, 1999; García, Mario T. *Mexican Americans: Leadership, Ideology, and Identity, 1930–1960.* New Haven,

Conn.: Yale University Press, 1989; Mecham, J. Lloyd. "Carlos Castañeda, 1896–1958." *Hispanic American Historical Review* 38:3 (August 1958) 383–388.

CASTILLO, LEONEL J., 1939– . Government official. Leonel Castillo was born and educated in Texas. After receiving his B.A. from St. Mary's University in San Antonio he earned a Masters in Social Work from the University of Pittsburgh. During the early 1960s he served in the Peace Corps as a supervisor in the Philippines; in the early 1970s he became the Houston city comptroller and state Democratic Party treasurer. In 1977 he was appointed head of the Immigration and Naturalization Service by President Jimmy Carter; he was the first Mexican American to hold that position. Bitterly criticized by both Chicano activists and conservative Anglos, he stressed improving services to immigrants and tried to downplay the enforcement aspect of the agency without lasting success. With the inauguration of Ronald Reagan as president in 1981 he lost his job. From 1984 to 1989 he was president of the Hispanic International University; currently he is an aide in education matters to the mayor of Houston.

FURTHER READING: Martínez, Oscar J. *Border People: Life and Society in the U.S.-Mexico Borderlands.* Tucson: University of Arizona Press, 1994; *Who's Who among Hispanic Americans, 1994–1995.* Detroit: Gale Research, 1994.

CASTRO, RAÚL, 1916– . Governor, diplomat, lawyer. Raúl Castro was born in the Sonora mining town of Cananea, but grew up in Arizona to which his parents had moved to improve themselves economically. When his father died, he went to work at age twelve. In the mid-1930s he enrolled in Northern Arizona University at Flagstaff, where he also had a successful regional boxing career. He graduated in 1939 and became a U.S. citizen that same year. A decade later he obtained his law degree from the University of Arizona and then opened a private practice in Tucson and entered politics. Between 1951 and 1964 he served as Pima County attorney, superior court judge, and in other elective and appointive positions.

Castro was appointed by President Lyndon Johnson as U.S. ambassador to El Salvador in 1964, and became ambassador to Bolivia five years later, a position he held until 1971. He won election to the governorship in 1974, becoming the first Mexican American governor of Arizona. Three years later he resigned to accept from President Jimmy Carter the ambassadorship to Argentina, a position he held until Ronald Reagan's entry of the White House in 1981. He then returned to Arizona, practicing law in Phoenix; currently he practices international law in Nogales. He has been the recipient of numerous honors and awards.

FURTHER READING: "La Luz Interview: Governor of Arizona." *La Luz* 4:5 (October 1975) 11; Mawn, Geoffrey P. "Raúl Héctor Castro: Poverty to Prominence." In *The Mexican Americans: An Awakening Minority*, edited by Manuel P. Servín. Beverly Hills, Calif.: Glencoe Press, 1970; Pimentel, O. Ricardo. "Ex-Governor Shows Way for Mexican Americans." *The Arizona Republic* (8 July 2000) Opinions, B7; *Who's Who among Hispanic Americans, 1994–1995*. Detroit: Gale Research, 1994.

CASTRO, SAL(VADOR), 1933– . Activist, teacher. Sal Castro was born in southern California of undocumented immigrant parents. As an infant he returned with them to Mexico in their repatriation during the 1930s, and later came back to the United States. He served in the Korean conflict. Upon his return he entered college, where he participated in Democratic politics and later became active in the **Mexican American Political Association**. After college he obtained a position teaching in a Los Angeles high school.

From his teaching experience, Castro came to the conclusion that Mexican Americans students were being poorly educated and needed to take steps to obtain their educational rights. The **student walkout** as a coercive tool was his first step to solving the problem. In March 1968 Castro became a media headline when some five thousand students walked out of the classrooms of five Los Angeles high schools. He took an active part in picketing, sit-ins, demonstrations, and demands and quickly became the symbol as well as the leader of the "blowout," as the episode became known. In June, along with twelve other activists, he was indicted by a Los Angeles grand jury for felonious conspiracy and was convicted. Two years later on appeal the charges were found unconstitutional and were dropped, but Castro was barred from teaching for five years and continued to be harassed. In 1973 he returned to teaching at Belmont High School.

FURTHER READING: Muñoz, Carlos, Jr. *Youth, Identity, Power: The Chicano Movement*. New York: Verso, 1990; Chabrán, Richard, and Rafael Chabrán, eds. *The Latino Encyclopedia*, vol 1. New York: Marshall Cavendish, 1996.

CATÓLICOS POR LA RAZA. Católicos por la Raza was a militant group of Chicanos, founded in 1969 by Ricardo Cruz, a law student at Loyola University in Los Angeles. The group accused the Catholic Church of ignoring the many problems of *la raza* and demanded that it take a greater interest in social justice. On Christmas Eve the members demonstrated at wealthy St. Basil's church. When they tried to enter the church, they were expelled and about twenty, including Cruz, were arrested and tried for disturbing the peace.

FURTHER READING: Acuña, Rodolfo. *Occupied America: A History of Chicanos*, 3rd ed. New York: Harper & Row, 1988; Valdez, Luis, and Stan Steiner, eds. *Aztlán: An Anthology of Mexican American Literature*. New York: Vintage Books, 1972.

CATRON, THOMAS B., 1840–1921. Lawyer, politician, landowner. Thomas Catron moved to Santa Fe after fighting for the Confederacy during the Civil War. Admitted to the New Mexico bar, he began practicing law and in 1872 received appointment as U.S. attorney. He soon became a leading figure in territorial Republican politics. He was one of the principals in the ill-reputed **Santa Fe Ring** and was active in railroading, mining, banking, and land speculation. In the mid-1890s he held title to two million acres of land and had an interest in an additional four million acres, most of which he had acquired as attorney for Hispano grantees. He was active in the statehood movement and was elected New Mexico's first U.S. senator. A decade later his political dominance among Nuevomexicanos was broken by **Bronson Cutting.**

FURTHER READING: Simmons, Marc. *New Mexico: An Interpretive History.* Albuquerque: University of New Mexico Press, 1988; Westphall, Victor. "Thomas Benton Catron: A Historical Defense." *New Mexico Historical Review* 63:1 (1988) 43–57.

CAUSA, LA. Literally "the Cause," the term was used by many to describe the broad objectives of the **Delano grape strike** as well as of the Chicano Movement.

FURTHER READING: Levy, Jacques E. *César Chávez: Autobiography of La Causa.* New York: W. W. Norton, 1974.

CAVAZOS, LAURO, JR., 1927– . Educator, administrator. Lauro Cavazos was the son of a foreman on the King Ranch in southern Texas. Although his parents had limited schooling, they believed strongly in the benefits of education and actively pushed their children. When Lauro graduated from Kingsville High School in 1945 he enlisted in the army and served in the infantry during the last days of World War II. Upon his release from the service he enrolled in college, at his father's insistence, and received his B.A. in zoology three years later. Subsequently he earned an M.A. in cytology and his Ph.D. in physiology from Iowa State University in 1954.

Cavazos began his teaching career at the Medical College of Virginia, where he rose from instructor to associate professor in the next ten years. During this time he published numerous articles on cell replication and two guides on dissection in human anatomy. In 1964 he accepted the chair of the Department of Anatomy at Tufts University and in the next decade advanced to associate dean and in 1974 to full dean. In 1980 he was offered the presidency of his alma mater, Texas Technological University. He accepted. Overall Cavazos was an excellent president of Texas Tech for nearly a decade. He worked energetically to enroll more Mexican American and black students and to reduce their dropout rate. Because of his tendency to act arbitrarily, without consulting the faculty, in 1984 the faculty declared its lack of confidence in his leadership. Nevertheless, he managed to weather the crisis.

In 1988 Cavazos announced he was leaving the presidency to return to teaching. A few months later during the presidential election campaign, although a Democrat, he was nominated by President Ronald Reagan for the post of secretary of education and was unanimously confirmed by the Senate. He thus became the first American Latino to be appointed to a cabinet position. The elder George Bush continued his appointment. As secretary of education, Cavazos had goals at wide variance with those of the Bush administration and, as the result of overwhelming White House pressure, he resigned after less than two years amid sharp criticism of his leadership. He continues to be active in education, as an adjunct professor in community health at Tufts and as an education and business consultant.

FURTHER READING: *Current Biography Yearbook, 1989.* New York: H. W. Wilson Co., 1989; Tardiff, Joseph C., and L. Mpho Mabunda, eds. *Dictionary of Hispanic Biography.* Detroit: Gale Research, 1996; *Who's Who among Hispanic Americans, 1994–1995.* Detroit: Gale Research, 1994; *Who's Who in American Politics, 1993–1994*, vol. 2. New Providence, N.J.: R. R. Bowker, 1993.

CENSUS, 2000. The 2000 census showed that there were about 35.3 million Americans, up from 22.4 million in 1990, who identified themselves as Latinos, some 3 million more than the Census Bureau had predicted. Americans of Mexican descent, who make up about 58 percent of U.S. Latinos, increased from 13.5 million in 1990 to 20.6 million in 2000; a majority of them still reside in Texas and California. The census count indicates that U.S. Latinos are roughly equal in numbers to African Americans, a benchmark previously forecast for the 2010 census.

The unexpectedly large Latino increase since the 1990 census is mainly the result of substantially higher levels of immigration since 1990, higher fertility and birth rates, and undercounts in previous censuses. The 2000 count was characterized by a massive government campaign to encourage minority residents to be counted. The census figures are important because they affect federal funding and congressional district boundaries, as well as policy and other decisions.

Although the census offered sixty-three racial categories, many Latinos felt that none fitted them. Some 42 percent of America's Latinos checked the box labeled "some other race." For most, culture is their defining identifier; race, as defined largely by skin color, plays only a secondary role.

FURTHER READING: Grieco, Elizabeth M., and Rachel C. Cassidy. *Overview of Race and Hispanic Origin, 2000.* Washington, D.C.: U.S. Census Bureau, 2001. Martínez, Anne. "New Choices on 2000 Census Fail to Offer Right Racial Fit for Latinos." *San Jose Mercury News* (25 May 2001) 28A.

CENSUS DATA. Census data on Mexican Americans has somewhat limited value in making comparisons over time because of the varying identifiers used in the census counts. Until the 1930 census the identifier was birth in Mexico or one Mexico-born parent. The 1930 Census Bureau counted as Mexican American all those of Mexican descent who were not white, Negro, Indian, or Asian. In 1940 it identified as Mexican American those whose first language was Spanish. The 1950 and 1960 census counts used Spanish surnames as the identifier—which lumped together all U.S. Latinos. In 1970 the Spanish surname identifier continued to be used, with a special sampling to provide greater detail. The 1980 and 1990 censuses further refined the process; however, Mexican American leaders continued to assert that there was a considerable undercount, perhaps as much as 10 percent.

CENTRO CAMPESINO CULTURAL, INC. A center originally established in 1967 by **Luis Valdez** and others at Del Rey, California, for the presentation and advancement of the Mexican cultural heritage through theater, music, and films. Two years later the center was moved to the more populous town of Fresno, California, and ultimately to forty acres purchased in the old mission town of San Juan Bautista, California. While the organization centers on the **Teatro Campesino**, it also includes a publishing house (Cucaracha Publications); Pixan Films, which produces films and tapes; and Menyah Music, which manufactures records and albums.

FURTHER READING: Morton, Carlos. "La Serpiente Sheds Its Own: Changes in Aztlan." *La Luz* 4:8–9 (November–December 1975) 26–28; Saavedra, Pilar. "El Teatro Campesino: From the Picket Line to the Recording Studio." *Agenda* 7:3 (May–June 1977) 14–15.

CENTRO DE ACCIÓN SOCIAL AUTÓNOMA. CASA was founded in late 1968 to promote international solidarity as well as Chicano political awareness. Its membership consisted mostly of workers plus some students and professionals. It developed close ties in the Mexican American community and made available militant leaders for organizing workers and developing a vigorous activism. CASA became deeply involved with the problems of **undocumented** immigrants and other Mexicano working-class concerns.

From its inception, CASA's leftist leaders insisted on ideological purity and strong party discipline. Unresolved differences between factions periodically caused internal strife that sometimes erupted in divisive accusations and bitter denunciations. In 1972 these organizational conflicts led to a split that restructuring in the following years failed to heal. CASA ceased to exist as an organization, but some local chapter leaders remained active in the community.

During its short life CASA had some successes, but in the long run it had greater importance in developing aggressive leaders for successor organizations.

FURTHER READING: Mario T. García, *Memories of Chicano History: The Life and Narrative of Bert Corona.* Berkeley: University of California Press, 1994; Juan Gómez-Quiñones, *Chicano Politics: Reality and Promise, 1940–1990.* Albuquerque: University of New Mexico Press, 1990.

CERVANTES, LORNA DEE, 1954– . Poet. Lorna Dee Cervantes was born in San Francisco, California, but grew up in San Jose, to which her mother moved after the breakup of her marriage. At age eight she began writing poetry and had assembled a small "book" of poems before she graduated from high school. In the late 1960s she became active in the Chicano **movimiento** and in other liberal causes. In 1975 a number of her poems appeared in the *Revista Chicano-Riqueña*. By the latter 1970s Cervantes had gained a national reputation as a poet and as editor-publisher of a literary review, *Mango*. In 1978 she was awarded a National Endowment of the Arts grant. Three years later a collection of her poetry was published by the University of Pittsburgh Press under the title *Emplumada*. In 1991 she published *From the Cables of Genocide: Poems on Love and Hunger* with Arte Público Press. Her poems have also been published in various Mexican and English journals. Critics have characterized her poetry as carefully worked and polished; she is a leading Chicana poet.

FURTHER READING: Binder, Wolfgang, ed. *Partial Autobiographies: Interviews with Twenty Chicano Poets*. Erlangen, Germany: Palm & Enke, 1985; Monda, Bernadette. "Interview with Lorna Dee Cervantes." *Third Woman* 2:1 (1984) 103–107; Tardiff, Joseph C., and L. Mpho Mabunda, eds. *Dictionary of Hispanic Biography*. Detroit: Gale Research, 1996.

CHACÓN, BOBBY, 1952– . Boxer. Robert Chacón was born in the San Fernando valley of southern California. A Latino gang member with a reputation as a tough street fighter in the Los Angeles suburb of Pacoima, he dropped out of high school and began to box as an amateur. At twenty he turned professional and in his first year won fifteen consecutive fights, fourteen by knockouts. In 1976 he won the world featherweight championship by defeating Alfredo Marcano. However, success led to easy living, relaxed training, and a weight gain; a year later he lost the title by a knockout in a fight that lasted only two rounds. Although he won his next four fights, he quit the ring partly to please his wife. In 1978 "Schoolboy Bobby," as he was nicknamed because he went to college while he was a pro boxer, returned to boxing as a junior lightweight and racked up a nine-win, two-loss record. In 1982 he regained the world title, but then was denied it by the Boxing Commission because of a non-approved match. Today the ex-champion lives in obscurity.

FURTHER READING: Fournier, Carlos. "In the Ring." *Hispanic* (March 1989) 23–26; Konner, K. Patrick. "Bobby Chacón: Fighting Is All He Has Ever Known." *San Francisco Chronicle: This World* (January 1985); Medina, Harold. "Schoolboy's Return." *Nuestro* (February 1978) 14.

CHACÓN, EUSEBIO, 1870–1948. Interpreter, attorney, poet, historian, novelist. Although he lived most of his life in Colorado, Eusebio Chacón was born in Peñasco, New Mexico, and as an adult identified with Nuevomexicano literature. He was a leading figure in efforts to protect and encourage its development. While he was still an infant, the family moved from New Mexico to Colorado to homestead near Trinidad. An outstanding student, he attended primary school in Trinidad, and later earned his B.A. degree at the Jesuit *colegio* in Las Vegas, New Mexico, and then Notre Dame University in Indiana. After he completed his law degree at Notre Dame in 1889 he took a job teaching English in a school in Durango,

Mexico. Toward the end of 1891 a health problem caused him to return to Trinidad.

In Trinidad Chacón began a law practice, but was then appointed interpreter in the **Court of Private Land Claims** at Santa Fe, where he worked from 1892 to 1899. While working for the court he continued to write and publish poetry and other literary works. Over a period of years he also collected and compiled important documents of New Mexican history. In 1894 he was reported at work on a history of New Mexico. When the court completed its work in 1904 he returned to Trinidad, where he remained the rest of his life.

At the beginning of the 1890s Chacón began publishing his works. He was the author of two short novels (1892) and published a corpus of poetry in various New Mexican Spanish language newspapers. By 1894 he was widely known for his literary output. A staunch believer in literature to be read for pleasure, he called on his fellow Nuevomexicanos to follow his lead in creating a significant corpus of creative literature. In part, he saw such a literary output as a way of preventing the derogation of Nuevomexicano culture.

FURTHER READING: Martínez, Julio A., and Francisco A. Lomelí, eds. *Chicano Literature: A Reference Guide.* Westport, Conn. Greenwood Press, 1985; Meléndez, A. Gabriel. *So All Is Not Lost: The Poetics of Print in Nuevomexicano Communities, 1834–1958.* Albuquerque: University of New Mexico Press, 1997.

CHACÓN, FELIPE MAXIMILIANO, 1873–1949. Poet, writer, newspaper editor. Born in Santa Fe, New Mexico, Felipe M. Chacón was the son of Urbano Chacón, an early Nuevomexicano newspaper publisher. After receiving a college education he became active in various business ventures, particularly in Spanish language newspapers. During the second decade of the twentieth century he edited Spanish newspapers in Las Vegas, Mora, and various other New Mexican towns. Completely bilingual, he contributed essays and poetry in both English and Spanish. In 1924, while editor and general manager of *La Bandera Americana* in Albuquerque, he published *Obras de Felipe Maximiliano Chacón, "El Cantor Nuevomexicano": Poesía y Prosa*, which contained a large number of his writings spanning forty years and including fifty-six poems. His poetry, which he began writing as a teenager, was written in the florid style popular at the end of the nineteenth century.

FURTHER READING: Gonzales-Berry, Erlinda. "Vicente Bernal and Felipe M. Chacón: Bridging Two Cultures." In *Paso por aquí: Critical Essays on the New Mexican Literary Tradition, 1542–1988*, edited by Erlinda Gonzales-Berry. Albuquerque: University of New Mexico Press, 1989; Meyer, Doris. *Speaking for Themselves: Neomexicano Cultural Identity and the Spanish-language Press, 1880–1920.* Albuquerque: University of New Mexico Press, 1996.

CHAVES, JOSÉ FRANCISCO, 1833–1904. Rancher, politician, soldier, lawyer. José Francisco Chaves was born near Albuquerque into an extensive and politically and economically important Nuevomexicano family. His father occupied several high positions in the Mexican territorial government. José was educated in Nuevo México, Chihuahua, St. Louis (Missouri), and later in New York. As a youthful teenager he acted as an interpreter with the invading army of Stephen Kearny. Before he was twenty his father died, and he took over management of the family ranch. A decade later he served as a major and colonel in the territorial militia during the Civil War and fought in the battle of Valverde.

After the war, Chaves studied law and became active in politics. Between 1865 and 1871 he won three terms as delegate to the U.S. Congress and in 1875 was elected to the New Mexico territorial Legislative Council, where he played an important role the rest of his life. He served eight times as president of the territorial legislature and also held positions as superintendent of schools, district attorney, and delegate to the unsuccessful 1889 constitutional convention. Strongly opposed to the notorious **Santa Fe Ring**, he gave energetic leadership to Nuevomexicano opposition to its leaders and their activities. In November 1904 he was shot by an unknown attacker in a murder that was widely believed to be politically motivated. He was widely respected by his contemporaries, friend and foe.

FURTHER READING: Keleher, William A. *Memoirs: 1892–1969: A New Mexico Item.* Santa Fe: Rydal Press, 1969; Lamar, Howard R., ed. *New Encyclopedia of the American West.* New Haven, Conn.: Yale University Press, 1998; Perrigo, Lynn I. *Hispanos: Historic Leaders in New Mexico.* Santa Fe: Sunstone Press, 1985; Vigil, Maurilio E. *Los Patrones: Profiles of Hispanic Political Leaders in New Mexico History.* Washington, D.C.: University Press of America, 1980.

CHAVES, MANUEL ANTONIO, 1818–1889. Rancher, soldier, merchant. Manuel Chaves, born near Albuquerque, belonged to a family whose ancestors had been important in Nuevo México since the 1600s. In late 1839 young Chaves was forced to flee to Missouri because of a serious quarrel with his uncle, Governor **Manuel Armijo**. In Independence, Missouri, he gained practical experience as a frontier trader. Upon his return two years later he helped repulse the 1841 Texas invasion, and five years later prepared to repel the invading U.S. forces. Meanwhile he had settled down to ranching and trading, had married, and lived in Albuquerque.

When the Americans under General Stephen Kearny took over Nuevo México, Chaves became involved in the first **Taos rebellion**, and was arrested, charged with treason, and ultimately acquitted. He then helped put down the second Taos uprising and resumed his ranching and trading activities. During the 1850s he enhanced his reputation as a scout and military leader during several expeditions against marauding Utes and Apaches. In 1861 he was appointed commandant of Fort Fauntleroy on the edge of the Navajo lands.

During the **Civil War** Chaves became famous for leading a group of volunteers through Glorieta Pass to flank Confederate forces under General Henry A. Sibley and destroying their supply train. As a result the Confederates were forced to withdraw and finally to abandon all hope of occupying New Mexico. After the war Chaves again returned to his ranching and mercantile activities.

A decade later Chaves took his family to the far frontier in western New Mexico where, in his sixties, he undertook the daunting task of creating a new home. Despite old wounds that had not healed properly and that gave him considerable pain, he worked without respite, building up his rancho. Widely known as El Leoncito, the Little Lion, because of his bravery, he also remained a commander in the territorial militia.

FURTHER READING: Gonzales, Manuel G. *The Hispanic Elite of the Southwest.* El Paso: Texas Western Press, 1989; Simmons, Marc. *The Little Lion of the Southwest.* Chicago: The Swallow Press, 1973.

CHÁVEZ, ANGÉLICO, 1910–1996. Historian, priest, poet. Fray Angélico Chávez, named Manuel Ezequiel by his parents, was born in Mora County, New Mexico. At age fourteen he entered a Franciscan seminary and studied in their educational institutions in Ohio, Illinois, and Indiana. In 1937 he was ordained a Franciscan priest at Santa Fe, taking the name Angélico. He then began his priestly life among the Pueblo Indians and his fellow Nuevomexicanos, serving as pastor in several pueblos and towns. During **World War II** he volunteered as a Spanish-speaking chaplain and served in the South Pacific until the end of the war. He returned to his previous clerical activities, interrupted once more for chaplain service in the army during the Korean conflict.

All this time Chávez was writing. He started in high school, and continued in the seminary, on the Pueblo reservation, and in the army. Over the years his writings ranged from poetry and essays to historical fiction and history, all dealing with New Mexico's past. All of his works are concerned with the distinctive features of Nuevomexicano singularity. In poor health at the beginning of the 1970s, he left the Franciscan Order and priesthood and was appointed archivist of the Santa Fe archdiocese, where he continued his historical research and writing. Among the twenty-some books he published between 1939 and 1985, he is especially known for *Our Lady of the Conquest*, 1948; *When the Santos Talked*, 1957; *Origins of New Mexico Families in the Spanish Colonial Period*, 1954; *Coronado's Friars: The Franciscans in the Coronado Expedition*, 1968; *My Penitente Land*, 1974; and *The Domínguez-Escalante Journal* (translator), 1976. Perhaps his most important piece of New Mexican history is *But Time and Chance: The Story of Padre Martínez of Taos, 1793–1867*, published in 1981. He was widely respected as one of New Mexico's outstanding writers.

FURTHER READING: Briggs, Walter. "Biographical Sketch of Fray Angélico Chávez." *New Mexico Magazine* 51:1–2 (January–February 1973); Lomelí, Francisco and Carl R. Shirley, eds. *Chicano Writers: First Series.* Gale Research, 1989; McCracken, Ellen, ed. *Fray Angélico Chávez: Poet, Priest, and Artist.* Albuquerque: University of New Mexico Press, 2000.

César Chávez, leader of the United Farm Workers union, addresses followers in 1972. © National Archives.

CHÁVEZ, CÉSAR ESTRADA, 1927–1993. Social activist, union organizer. Although often facilely labeled a labor or farm worker leader, César Chávez was in reality much more than that. A great admirer of Mohandas Gandhi and Martin Luther King, he was able to convert the Mexican American farm workers' struggle into a civil rights movement to a considerable degree. His charismatic leadership in this struggle derived from his personal moral probity, his deep concern for the rights of others, and his strong commitment to nonviolence. This leadership in the struggle for human dignity made him a national metaphor for social justice.

Chávez was born near Yuma, Arizona, on a small farm homesteaded by his paternal grandfather. The Great Depression of the 1930s transformed the Chávezes into a typical Mexican American migrant farm worker family of that era. Eventually they joined thousands of other Americans in the trek to California, where they continued to work in migratory agriculture. Young César attended some thirty schools before he dropped out of the seventh grade, barely literate.

At seventeen Chávez enlisted in the U.S. Navy and served two years in the Pacific during the latter days of World War II. After the war he came back home to San Jose, California, returned to migrant agricultural work, and joined an early union. Half a decade later, during the summer of 1952, he became acquainted with **Fred Ross, Sr.**, a Saul Alinsky disciple who was organizing for the **Community Service Organization** (CSO) in southern California. Although skeptical of the CSO at first, he soon joined as an unpaid volunteer, working in voter registration. By 1958 he had become a director in the organization. Four years later when his repeated proposal to organize farm workers was again voted down, he resigned from the CSO to devote his time and energies to working for farm labor rights, a cause he believed in deeply.

With the help of his wife Helen, Fred Ross, **Dolores Huerta**, and a few other devoted followers, Chávez began his crusade in California's great central valley, creating the National Farm Workers Association, which later became the **United Farm Workers** (UFW). By 1965 some 1,700 families were enrolled in the the organization. In that year Chávez took the union into the **Delano grape strike.** By presenting the workers' plight in the context of the civil rights movement, he quickly converted the strike (La Huelga) from a labor dispute to a civil rights crusade—**La Causa** (The Cause). In April 1966 he led a march to the state capital, Sacramento, to demand from the governor justice for farm workers. Throughout the five difficult years of the strike he strongly stressed its moral basis, going on fasts, enduring jail, and constantly reinforcing its character as a nonviolent movement. In 1970 he and the grape growers signed a three-year UFW contract. Subsequent organizing efforts in California's lettuce and strawberry fields were less satisfying. His long struggle for the rights of harvest agricultural labor had limited immediate success, but made Americans vividly aware of the often inhumane conditions of the work.

Toward the end of the 1970s Chávez's leadership suffered a severe blow when a serious internal UFW disagreement over tactics and his leadership of the UFW led to the departure of some of his most able lieutenants. By the end of the decade the UFW had shrunk to one-fifth of its peak size. Nevertheless, even when a conservative trend began in the 1980s, Chávez remained a world-recognized Mexican American leader in the fight for human dignity and agricultural workers' rights. For Chicanos he was the closest thing to a national leader like Martin Luther King.

During the latter 1970s there was some talk of Chávez being a possible nominee for a Nobel Prize. Two decades later he received the Orden del Aguila Azteca from the president of Mexico, the highest honor the Mexican government can confer on a foreigner. A year after his unexpected death in 1993, César Chávez was posthumously awarded the Presidential Medal of Freedom by President Bill Clinton for his leadership in the cause of labor and in the Chicano rights movement. In August 2000 the California legislature created a new state holiday, César Chávez Day.

FURTHER READING: Day, Mark. *Forty Acres: César Chávez and the Farm Workers.* New York: Praeger, 1971; Ferriss, Susan, and Ricardo Sandoval. *The Fight in the Fields: César Chávez and the Farmworkers Movement.* New York: Harcourt Brace, 1997; Goodwin, David. *César Chávez: Hope for the People.* New York: Fawcett Columbine, 1991; Griswold del Castillo, Richard, and Richard García. *César Chávez: A Triumph of Spirit.* Norman: University of Oklahoma Press, 1995; Hammerback, John C., and Richard J. Jensen, *The Rhetorical Career of César Chávez.* College Station: Texas A & M University Press, 1998; Levy, Jacques E. *César Chávez: Autobiography of La Causa.* New York: W. W. Norton, 1974; *Remembering César: The Legacy of César Chávez.* Compiled by Ann McGregor. Clovis, Calif.: Quill Driver Books, 2000; Ross, Fred, Sr. *Conquering Goliath: César Chávez at the Beginning.* Keene, Calif.: United Farm Workers, 1989; Vizzard, James L. "The Extraordinary César Chávez." *Progressive* 30 (July 1966) 16–20.

CHÁVEZ, DENISE, 1948– . Playwright, novelist, poet, teacher, actress. Denise Chávez was born in Las Cruces, New Mexico, to a schoolteacher mother and an attorney father. As a young girl she was exposed to oral traditions of storytelling from the Mexican women who worked in the Chávez residence and helped raise her and her two sisters.

While a student at Madonna High School in Mesilla, New Mexico, Denise developed a strongly motivating interest in her theater class. As a result she obtained a drama scholarship at New Mexico State University in Las Cruces, where she completed her B.A. in 1971. She then enrolled in a master's program at Trinity University and received her master of fine arts degree in drama three years later. For the next decade she worked in the Dallas Theater Center while continuing her studies in drama and writing. During this time she was also writing plays, poetry, and short stories. In 1984 she completed a second M.A., in creative writing, at the University of New Mexico.

In 1986 a collection of her interrelated short stories was published as a novel with the title *The Last of the Menu Girls*; it won the Puerto del Sol Fiction Award and the Steele Jones Fiction Award. Nearly a decade later her *Face of an Angel* received the American Book Award in 1994. In 2001 she published her most recent novel, *Loving Pedro Infante*. A contributor of poetry and essays to various periodicals, she has written a score of plays that, like her short stories and poems, reflect the dignity and strengths of common, everyday people.

Chávez has been a writer and artist in residence at a number of institutions in New Mexico and does extensive workshops, lecturing, and readings for widely varied audiences. She has also taught English and drama at various colleges and universities, most in the Southwest. Until her retirement she taught creative writing at New Mexico State University in Las Cruces. She was the founder of the Border Book Festival in Las Cruces, where she lives.

Chávez has been favored with numerous honors and awards for her plays and fiction. Among them are grants from New Mexico Arts Division in 1979, 1981, and 1988; the Rockefeller Foundation in 1984; and the Cultural Arts Council of Houston in 1990. In 1995 she received the Governor's Award in Literature.

FURTHER READING: *Contemporary Authors,* vol. 131. Detroit: Gale Research, 1991; Esturoy, Annie O. "Interview with Denise Chávez." In *This Is about Vision: Interviews with Southwestern Writers,* edited by William Balassi, John Crawford, and Annie Esturoy. Albuquerque: University of New Mexico Press, 1990; Houston, Robert. "Face of an Angel; Book Review." *New York Times Book Review* (September 1994) 20.

CHÁVEZ, DENNIS (DIONISIO), 1888–1962. Hispano leader, senator. Dennis Chávez came from a family with New Mexican roots that went back to the late 1600s. From a family of eight children, he was born near Albuquerque, to which the family later moved when he was seven and where he attended grade school and grew up. To help with family finances he dropped out of the eighth grade, but continued his education by voracious reading of history and biography in the Albuquerque library. As a result of an intense attraction to Thomas Jefferson, he developed an early interest in politics and the law. Working as an interpreter for an Anglo candidate brought him to a clerkship in Washington, D.C., in 1918.

While working at various jobs related to politics, Chávez married and studied law through night classes. After earning his degree at the age of thirty-two, the ambitious young lawyer set up a successful practice in Albuquerque in 1920 and quickly entered the New Mexico political arena. Ten years later he won election to the U.S. House of Representatives and in 1934 he was almost successful in challenging New Mexico's outstanding liberal senator, **Bronson Cutting**. Upon the latter's death in the next year, he was appointed to the U.S. Senate by the governor. He was easily elected to the seat in the following year, the first Mexican American in the Senate, and was regularly reelected until his death.

In the U.S. Senate Dennis Chávez viewed his role primarily as that of advancing New Mexican interests in Washington. An energetic follower of Franklin D. Roosevelt, he was a strong supporter of legislation favoring national defense and military preparedness. His service in the committees on Indian Affairs, Education and Labor, Irrigation and Reclamation, Appropriations, Post Office and Post Roads, and Territories and Insular Affairs reflected his interests. He took his work seriously and consistently fought for the rights of his Nuevomexicano constituents. Senator Chávez's most important contribution, especially to his state's Hispanos, was his advocacy of and support for education and civil rights legislation. During World War II he introduced and strongly supported an Equal Rights Amendment to the U.S. Constitution. In the postwar years Chávez did some of his most statesmanlike work. He worked quietly and effectively to improve the lot of Native Americans. He was the dynamic leader over the years in writing and pushing a bill to establish a permanent federal **Fair Employment Practices Committee** (FEPC). In 1946 the bill lost by an eight vote margin.

In the early 1950s Chávez was one of a handful of senators who dared denounce the infamous Senator Joseph McCarthy for riding roughshod over constitutional and civil rights. He was always an individualist and at times a paradoxical politician. In committee discussions he often took independent stands that sometimes irritated his constituents as well as his fellow Democrats. In 1953 he introduced legislation to provide equal opportunity in employment; on the other hand, in 1960 he voted to send a civil rights bill back to committee, thereby effectively killing it.

A heavy smoker, in 1962 Chávez died of complications arising from throat cancer. After his death he was selected by the New Mexico Historical Society for the honor of representing the state in the Statuary Hall of the Capitol in Washington, D.C.

FURTHER READING: *Current Biography, 1946.* New York: H. W. Wilson, 1947; Luján, Roy. "Dennis Chávez and the Roosevelt Era, 1933–1945." Ph.D. diss. University of New Mexico, 1987; Perrigo, Lynn I. *Hispanos: Historic Leaders in New Mexico.* Santa Fe: Sunstone Press, 1985; Popejoy, Tom. "Dennis Chávez." In *Hall of Fame*

Essays. Albuquerque: Historical Society of New Mexico, 1963; Tardiff, Joseph C., and L. Mpho Mabunda, eds. *Dictionary of Hispanic Biography*. Detroit: Gale Research, 1996.

CHÁVEZ, LINDA, 1947– . Political commentator, writer. Linda Chávez was born in Albuquerque and grew up there and in Denver, Colorado, to which the family moved when she was ten. In high school she became active in both the National Association for the Advancement of Colored People and the Congress of Racial Equality as a result of the discrimination she was experiencing. However, as an English major at the University of Colorado in Boulder during the late 1960s, she was unswayed by the Chicano Movement and took no part in its campus activities.

Subsequently, as a doctoral student at the University of California, Los Angeles Linda Chávez was persuaded to teach a class in Chicano literature. Reluctant to accept the validity of Chicano literature as a college subject, she found herself frequently harassed by militant campus Chicanos. In 1972 she left the university and joined her husband, Christopher Gersten, in Washington, D.C., working first as a political staffer. A year and a half later she went to work as a lobbyist for the National Education Association and in 1975 accepted the position of assistant director of legislation for the more conservative American Federation of Teachers (AFT).

In 1977 Chávez was appointed director of research for the AFT, thereby becoming editor of its influential quarterly, *American Educator*, for the next six years. As editor she wrote a series of hard-hitting articles on the need to teach traditional values in the public schools. Her outspoken conservative views attracted favorable attention from the Republican administration of Ronald Reagan, and in August 1983 she was appointed staff director of the U.S. **Civil Rights Commission**. As director of the commission, the first woman to hold that position, she greatly helped President Reagan weaken the commission's work. She vehemently rejected busing policies and affirmative action and opposed the quota system.

In 1985 Chávez was appointed director of the White House Office of Public Liaison, making her the highest-ranking woman in the Reagan administration. Encouraged by the president, less than a year later she resigned and ran for the U.S. Senate from Maryland. Despite Reagan's support in an aggressive, mudslinging campaign against her liberal Democratic opponent, she failed to win the election.

In 1987 Linda Chávez assumed the presidency of **U.S. English,** a national right-wing anti-immigrant organization. Although in general agreement with U.S. English's objectives, she resigned a year later in protest an anti-Latino and anti-Catholic memo by its founder John Tanton. She then received appointment as a senior fellow with the Manhattan Institute for Policy Research, a conservative Washington-based think tank. In 1991 she published *Out of the Barrio: Toward a New Politics of Hispanic Assimilation*, which expounded her strongly conservative views on ethnic political involvement, affirmative action, and multiculturalism. Four years later she founded the Center for Equal Opportunity, which, among other objectives, provides support for efforts to defeat legal challenges to California's Proposition 209 and Proposition 227, both designed to do away with liberal advances.

An articulate, forceful speaker, Linda Chávez has spent the past several years as a print, radio, and television commentator. In 2001 she was selected by President-elect George W. Bush to be his Secretary of Labor, but then was embarrassed by evidence of hiring an undocumented worker. A crescendo of opposition immediately developed and she was forced to withdraw her nomination. In 2002 she published a second book, *An Unlikely Conservative.*

FURTHER READING: Barrett, Paul M. "Linda Chávez and the Exploitation of Ethnic Identity." *Washington Monthly* 17 (June 1985) 25–29; Chávez, Linda. *Out of the Barrio: Toward a New Politics of Hispanic Assimilation.* New York: Basic Books, 1991; Chávez, Linda. *An Unlikely Conservative: The Transformation of an Ex-liberal, or, How I Became the Most Hated Hispanic in America.* New York: Basic Books, 2002; Hernández, Macarena. "Conservative and Hispanic, Linda Chavez Carves Out Leadership Niche." *New York Times* (19 August 1998) A26; Saavedra-Vela, Pilar. "Linda Chávez: Commentary by a Political Professional." *Agenda* 7:5 (September/October 1977) 42–43; Telgen, Diane, and Jim Kamp, eds. *Notable Hispanic American Women.* Detroit: Gale Research, 1993.

CHICAGO. When Mexican Americans and Mexicans began moving out of the Southwest in numbers during the early twentieth century, Chicago became one of the important midwestern centers to which they were attracted by available employment at better wages than existed in agriculture. Chicago was an important railroad center and was also able to provide jobs in meatpacking plants and the steel industry. The 1919 steel strike brought in more Mexicanos, some as unwitting strikebreakers, and the 1920s saw thousands of them moving into hotel, restaurant, and other service work. By 1930 Chicago had a Mexican-descent population of about twenty thousand.

The **Great Depression** and repatriation movement of the 1930s caused a decline in Chicago's Mexicano population, but **World War II** demands for industrial workers in war production factories and agriculturally related industries reversed that trend. Chicago saw a considerable Mexicano population increase that continued and rapidly intensified in the postwar years.

By 1970 the Chicago metropolitan area boasted a Mexicano population of approximately 110,000, distributed in various barrios of the city. There was also a large Cuban and Puerto Rican population of about the same size. In 1990 the census indicated a Mexicano population of 607,000 as they moved out of the Southwest in ever-increasing numbers. Today Chicago has the largest Chicano population outside of the Southwest.

FURTHER READING: Hinojosa, Francisco. *Mexican Chicago.* Mexico, D.F.: Conacultura, 1999; Jones, Anita. *Conditions Surrounding Mexicans in Chicago.* San Francisco: R & E Research Associates, 1971; Kerr, Louise Año Nuevo. "The Chicano

Experience in Chicago, 1920–1970." Ph.D. diss. University of Illinois at Chicago Circle, 1976.

CHICANAS. Only in recent years have Chicanas, Mexican American women, begun to fully take their rightful place in American society. Until the 1960s gender-based **discrimination** and low societal expectations tended to keep them on the lowest rungs of the social, educational, economic, and political ladders. As a group within the Mexican American community, Chicanas have historically been at a considerable cultural disadvantage, usually deferring to parents or husbands, even though many contributed importantly to supporting their families through employment outside the home.

Already by the mid-1920s Chicanas made up more than one-third of the Mexicano labor force, employed mostly as maids, laundresses, clerks, and cannery, packinghouse, and garment workers as well as harvest laborers. During **World War II** many were able to enter the industrial labor market and earn higher wages in factories, shipyards, and other war-related industries. As husbands and fathers went into the armed services, in many cases Chicanas took on the heavy responsibilities of heads of families and community leaders. In the postwar period, more of them played active roles in business, law, and education as well as in community organizations, labor unions, and social agencies. They made up much of the organizational backbone for the new Chicano civil rights groups that developed from the 1950s onward.

After the war Chicanas as a group became intensely aware of their subordinate status, even within the community, despite their increasingly active and extensive participation throughout the Southwest in economic, social, and political spheres. They soon raised their voices in demands for gender equality, although most kept aloof from the Anglo-dominated feminist movement. Beginning in the 1970s, middle-class Chicanas were vigorously creating a variety of **organizations** whose broad goals were to advance the cause of their equal treatment in society as well as in law. One indication of the degree of their success is the fact that by 1990, Chicanas outnumbered Chicanos in mid-level managerial and executive positions. By the century's end Latinas owned hundreds of businesses and also made up nearly twenty-five percent of all *raza* elected officials. Their struggle for equality is, of course, a never-ending one, and Chicanas continue to work for complete parity with males.

FURTHER READING: Alarcón, Norma, et al. *Chicana Critical Issues.* Berkeley, Calif.: Third Woman Press, 1993; Anda, Roberto M. de. *Chicanas and Chicanos in Contemporary Society.* Boston: Allyn & Bacon, 1996; Córdova, Teresa, et al., eds. *Chicana Voices: Intersection of Class, Race, and Gender.* Austin: Center for Mexican American Studies, University of Texas, 1986; Cotera, Martha P. *Diosa y hembra: The History and Heritage of Chicanas in the U. S.* Austin: Information Systems Development, 1976; García, Alma M. *Chicana Feminist Thought: The Basic Historical Writings.* New York: Routledge, 1997; García, Juan R., ed. *Perspectives in Mexican*

American Studies: Mexican American Women Changing Images. Tucson: Mexican American Studies and Research Center, University of Arizona, 1995; Maciel, David R., and Isidro D. Ortiz. *Chicanas/Chicanos at the Crossroads.* Tucson: University of Arizona Press, 1996; Melville, Margarita, ed. *Mexicanas at Work in the United States.* Houston: Mexican American Studies Program, University of Houston, 1988; Melville, Margarita B., ed. *Twice a Minority: Mexican American Women.* St Louis: Mosby, 1980. Mora, Magdalena, and Adelaida R. Del Castillo. *Mexican Women in the United States: Struggles, Past and Present.* Los Angeles: Chicano Studies Research Center, University of California, 1980; *Las mujeres: Mexican American/Chicana Women.* Windsor, Calif.: National Women's History Project, 1991; Ruiz, Vicki L. *From Out of the Shadows: Mexican Women in Twentieth-Century America.* New York: Oxford University Press, 1998.

CHICANO. Apparently the word Chicano derives from the word *mexicano* with the first syllable elided, making it *xicano.* The term was popularized by **movimiento** activists who adopted the formerly somewhat pejorative term as a badge of pride in their ethnic culture. In the 1960s and 1970s it often had connotations of a militant ethnicity that rejected assimilation and favored confrontation tactics. At times a controversial term, it was disapproved of and repudiated by many older, more conservative Mexican Americans. Today the word is widely used simply as a convenient alternative to Mexican American.

In the late 1960s leaders in the Chicano Movement made use of the term in developing a concept of Chicanismo, a unifying bond between those members of *la raza* who accepted and advocated the ethnic self-awareness and comradeship ideals of the movimiento.

FURTHER READING: García, Ignacio M. *Chicanismo: The Forging of a Militant Ethos among Mexican Americans.* Tucson: University of Arizona Press, 1997.

CHICANO STUDIES DEPARTMENTS. Also called Chicano Studies centers and sometimes Ethnic Studies departments or programs, most of these agencies arose out of the unrest among Mexican American students in the 1960s. They were both the result of the civil rights ferment among Mexican Americans and an important factor in the further demand for those rights. They usually developed and taught courses in Chicano history, sociology, psychology, and folklore. Nevertheless, in most universities they had to struggle mightily to obtain academic legitimacy. The struggle for acceptance of university courses as legitimate still goes on.

Because of the historic roots of these departments, they developed some goals in addition to those of traditional university departments. They usually became involved in the Chicano community and its problems, and tended to be more activist politically. The research and publishing that they fostered greatly increased awareness among all Americans of past and current denial of social justice, especially to Mexican Americans. These departments encouraged both students and faculty in developing deeper concerns for bringing about change for *la raza.*

FURTHER READING: Acuña, Rodolfo F. *Sometimes There Is No Other Side: Chicanos and the Myth of Equality*. Notre Dame: University of Notre Dame Press, 1998; Bixler-Márquez, Dennis J., et al. *Chicano Studies: Survey and Analysis*, rev. ed. Dubuque, Iowa: Kendall/Hunt, 1999; Córdova, Teresa, ed. *Chicano Studies: Critical Connection Between Research and Community*. Albuquerque: National Association for Chicano Studies, 1992; *El Plan de Santa Barbara*. Santa Barbara, Calif.: La Causa Publications, 1969; National Association for Chicano Studies. *History, Culture and Society: Chicano Studies in the 1980s*. Ypsilanti, Mich.: Bilingual Press/Editorial Bilingüe, 1983; Nuñez, Rene, and Raoul Contreras. "Principles and Foundations of Chicano Studies: Chicano Organization on University Campuses in California." In *Chicano Discourse: Selected Conference Proceedings of the National Association for Chicano Studies*, edited by Tatcho Mindiola, Jr., and Emilio Zamora. Houston: Mexican American Studies Program, University of Houston, 1992.

CHURCHES. The Catholic and Protestant churches have played a significant religious and social role in the Mexican American community. After the Treaty of **Guadalupe Hidalgo** in 1848, both church groups, for somewhat differing reasons, worked to incorporate Mexicanos into American society. Until the early decades of the twentieth century Catholic and Protestant clergy looked at Mexicanos primarily from a missionary perspective. In their work, all southwestern church leaders faced cultural differences, conditions of limited manpower, lack of organizational structure, and weak financial support. The vast distances and small, often isolated settlements in much of the Southwest tended to make the missionaries' task additionally difficult.

After the Treaty of Guadalupe Hidalgo, Mexican Americans, in part because of their rural demographic distribution, soon became marginalized and were largely unrepresented in the Catholic church's hierarchy. French priests, brought in by Bishop **Jean Baptiste Lamy,** quickly replaced Mexican clergy in the New Mexico territory. In California the sheer numbers of Anglo parishioners resulting from the gold rush led to considerable neglect of Californios. The U.S. Catholic Church, totally unprepared in the second half of the nineteenth century for cultural differences, failed its Mexicano flock. Until the late 1800s Protestant missionary efforts among Mexicanos were extremely limited.

The beginning of the social gospel movement among some Protestant groups in the late 1800s signaled a growing realization by church leaders of their poverty-ridden Mexicano followers' need for social justice. The 1891 encyclical of Pope Leo XIII, *Rerum Novarum,* spoke out for the rights of workers, but only a scant handful of Catholic leaders saw social justice as a part of their pastoral stewardship. While generally taking care of Mexicanos' spiritual requirements, most showed almost no concern for the urgent unmet temporal needs of their parishioners.

At the beginning of the twentieth century, the relationship between the churches and Mexican Americans continued to be largely limited to religious matters. The Catholic Church, to which most Mexicanos belonged, lagged behind Protestant denominations in publicly advocating an active social Christianity with its emphasis on the needs of the poor. A 1920 survey in Los Angeles showed that Catholic and Protestant churches alike had established few social services centers, and the great "repatriation" movement, 1929–1936, brought only limited objections from churchmen. However, in Texas a few Catholic bishops like **Robert Lucey** and Francis Furey did begin to concern themselves about the economic exploitation of their parishioners. On the Protestant side the interdenominational **Migrant Ministry,** founded in the 1920s with support from the National Council of Churches, began to do some excellent social work. Nevertheless, until the 1960s the churches provided little assistance directly aimed at obtaining social justice for marginalized Mexicanos.

After World War II greater strides were made as social action began to attract the attention of younger Catholic Church leaders. In 1945, under Lucey's leadership, the Bishops Committee for the Spanish Speaking was organized and began developing various programs. In farming areas the National Catholic Rural Life Conference began to support the aspirations of agricultural workers and to train leaders. The Catholic Youth Organization was founded to give young urban Chicanos an ideology of social service in addition to training in leadership and organizational skills. However, at the century's end relatively few Latinos were choosing the religious life. There was only one Latino priest for each ten thousand Latino parishioners and a great majority of parishes were headed by non-Latinos.

Various Protestant denominations also played a significant part in Chicanos' post–World War II struggle for social justice. In 1964 the Presbyterian Church sponsored a conference in Phoenix titled "The Role of the Church in the Civil Rights of the Spanish Speaking." Episcopalian, Presbyterian, and Methodist leaders provided considerable leadership in the quest for social justice, while fundamentalist ministers, often operating out of storefronts, placed less emphasis on social problems. Some storefront ministers were Mexican Americans who also occupied additional leadership roles within the community.

The **Delano grape strike** in the second half of the 1960s witnessed a widespread outpouring of church support, Protestant and Catholic. The Migrant Ministry and the ad hoc Catholic Bishops Committee on Farm Labor played important roles in the successful conclusion of the strike. The Mexican American civil rights movement of the 1960s and 1970s further awakened the churches to widespread social problems and a high level of alienation. Chicano activists occupied Catholic Church property, held demonstrations, and demanded that Church resources be more equably distributed. In 1968 Chicano priests in Texas created their own organization, **Padres Asociados Para Derechos Religiosos, Educativos y Sociales**. An expanded vision of social justice was adopted by most younger Catholic and Protestant clergy, who then took an important part in organizing, promoting, and supporting local organizations like the **United Neighborhoods Organization** (UNO) and **Communities Organized for Public Service** (COPS). In a 1984 pastoral statement "Catholic Social Teaching and the United States Economy," U.S. bishops pledged the church's commitment to social and economic justice. Today Protestant and Catholic churches continue the fight to put an end to discriminatory practices and to improve social conditions by supporting community leaders and organizations like COPS and UNO.

FURTHER READING: "Bishops Support César Chávez." *America* 122:21 (30 May 1970) 574; *Church Views of the Mexican American.* Reprint. New York: Arno Press, 1974; Dolan, Jay P., and Gilberto M. Hinojosa. *Mexican Americans and the Catholic Church, 1900–1965.* Notre Dame: University of Notre Dame Press, 1994; Hurtado, Juan. *An Attitudinal Study of Social Distances between the Mexican American and the Church.* San Antonio: Mexican American Cultural Center, 1975; Maldonado, David Jr., ed. *Protestantes/Protestants: Hispanic Christianity within Mainline Traditions.* Nashville: Abingdon Press, 1999; Mosqueda, Lawrence J. *Chicanos, Catholicism, and Political Ideology.* Lanham, Md.: University Press of America, 1986; "Protestants and Mexicans." In *The Mexican American People: The Nation's Second Largest Minority,* edited by Leo Grebler, Joan W. Moore, and Ralph C. Guzmán New York: Free Press, 1970; Sandoval, Moisés. *Fronteras: A History of the Latin American Church in the USA since 1513.* San Antonio: Mexican American Cultural Center, 1983; Sandoval, Moisés, ed. *The Mexican American Experience in the Church: Reflections on Identity and Mission: Mexican American Cultural Center Tenth Anniversary Forum.* New York: Sadlier, 1983; Steele, Thomas J., Paul Rhetts, and Barbe Await, eds. *Seeds of Struggle, Harvest of Faith: A History of the Catholic Church in New Mexico.* Albuquerque: LPD Press, 1999; Stevens Arroyo, Antonio M., ed. *Prophets Denied Honor: An Anthology on the Hispano Church in the United States.* Maryknoll, N.Y.: Orbis Books, 1980; Walker, Randi Jones. *Protestantism in the Sangre de Cristos, 1850–1920.* University of New Mexico Press, 1991.

CINCO DE MAYO. The Fifth of May is the number two civic holiday in Mexico after Independence Day. It commemorates the Mexican triumph over invading French forces at the fortified city of Puebla in 1862. Mexican forces under Texas-born General Ignacio Zaragoza and Brigadier Porfirio Díaz soundly defeated the French soldiers, then reputed to be the best in Europe. Like St. Patrick's Day, Cinco De Mayo has been celebrated in the United States since the late 1800s as an assertion of ethnic cultural pride.

FURTHER READING: "Cinco de Mayo: A Renewal for Mexican Americans." *Nuestro* (June/July 1984) 52–55; La France, David G. "A Battle for Nationhood." *Vista* (May 1990) 8–10.

CISNEROS, HENRY GABRIEL, 1947– . Henry Cisneros was born in San Antonio, Texas into a comfortable middle-class Mexican American family, the eldest child of George and Elvira Cisneros. He attended parochial schools and was in the Reserve Officer Training Corps (ROTC) at Central Catholic High, from which he graduated at sixteen. In the fall of 1964 Cisneros enrolled in Texas A & M University at College Station, where he earned his A.B. degree in city planning. Taking advantage of resources available to him, he then got an M.A. in urban and regional planning. His advanced degree was followed by a White House fellowship and a Ford Foundation grant that took him to Harvard and a second M.A., in public administration. In 1974 he earned a doctorate in public administration at George Washington University.

Strongly influenced by both his father, who rose from migrant farm worker to a colonel in the U.S. Army Reserves, and his journalist maternal grandfather, Cisneros plunged into local politics upon his return to San Antonio from Washington, D.C. While teaching at the University of Texas, he was elected to the city council in 1975, the youngest councilman in the city's history. Six years later his energy and dedication made him San Antonio's first Mexican American mayor since the 1840s; he was easily reelected to three subsequent terms. Viewing politics as a way "to change things," as mayor he worked with dedication and discipline to bring San Antonio's Anglo and Mexicano communities closer together.

Cisneros's meteoric political rise made him a contender for the Democratic vice presidential nomination in 1984. Nine years later he was appointed by President Bill Clinton as Secretary of Housing and Urban Development (HUD), into which he breathed new life. Moderate to conservative in many respects, in public office Henry Cisneros showed deep liberal concerns about social issues. To enable HUD to better serve the minority poor, he ordered the reversal of federal policies that he characterized as abetting racial **segregation** in housing. He labeled racism as a malignancy at the heart of big city problems and worked diligently to eradicate it.

Because of problems in his personal life, particularly an extramarital affair, at the end of Clinton's first term Cisneros resigned from HUD. The target of a ten-million-dollar, four-year investigation of his minimizing the amount he paid his ex-mistress, he left Washington and politics. The investigation led to eighteen federal charges of lying, conspiracy, and obstruction of justice and ended in late 1999 with his pleading guilty to a single misdemeanor, a $10,000 fine, and an apology by Cisneros. His honorable handling of the whole affair won him a good deal of popular respect. Meanwhile, in January 1997 he became president and chief executive officer of Miami-based Univisión Communications, which dominates U.S. Spanish-language television. In mid-2000 he resigned from Univisión to join with Kaufman and Broad Home Corporation to create a new company, America City Vista, to build homes in the inner city. As chairman and chief executive officer of ACV he hopes to rejuvenate San Antonio's south side by building as many as six hundred mid-priced homes. He also is chairman of Cisneros Asset Management Company, a bond market investment firm. He declares that he has no future plans to run for political office.

FURTHER READING: Chavira, Richard, and Charlie Ericksen. "An American Political Phenomenon Called Cisneros." *La Luz* 19:6 (August–September 1981)

26–27; *Current Biography Yearbook 1987*. New York: H. W. Wilson Co., 1987; Diehl, Kemper, and Jan Jarboe. *Cisneros: Portrait of a New American*. San Antonio: Corona, 1985; Lehman, Nicholas. "First Hispanic." *Esquire* 102:6 (December 1984) 480–486; Radelat, Ana. "Henry Cisneros Sets A New Course." *Hispanic* (September 2000) 18, 28.

CISNEROS, SANDRA, 1954– . Writer, poet. Sandra Cisneros was born in Chicago, Illinois, the only daughter of a middle- class Mexican American couple. Her parents stressed the importance of education, and early in life Sandra became a regular library patron and an avid reader. While still in grade school she began to write poetry, a habit she continued in high school. Encouraged by one of her teachers, she eventually became the editor of the school literary magazine.

After high school Cisneros entered Chicago's Loyola University as an English major. Upon receipt of her B.A. she enrolled in the University of Iowa's prestigious Writers Workshop. During her two years in Iowa City she sharpened her writing skills and published some poems in Latino journals. She then returned to Chicago, where she read her poetry in libraries and schools while earning her living as a part-time teacher.

A 1982 National Endowment for the Arts fellowship enabled Cisneros to travel to Europe and helped secure her an artist-in-residence position at the Foundation Michael Karolyi in France. Next came a job in San Antonio as an arts administrator, followed by a Dobie Paisano fellowship at the Texas Institute of Letters in Austin. After her Dobie Paisano residency expired, Cisneros accepted a visiting professorship at Chico State University in northern California. At this point a National Education Association fellowship in fiction writing revived her flagging spirits and led to her second important work, *Woman Hollering Creek and Other Stories*.

Sandra Cisneros's first loosely constructed novel, *The House on Mango Street*, was published by Arte Público Press in 1984 and has been reprinted several times since by mainstream publishers. Three years later her first book of poems, *My Wicked, Wicked Ways*, was issued by the Third Woman Press. When her next fictional work, *Woman Hollering Creek*, was published by Random House in 1991 she became the first Chicana printed by a major publisher. The book won several prestigious awards, including the PEN Center West award for best fiction of 1991. A collection of her poems titled *Loose Woman* was published by Knopf in 1994 and was praised highly for attacking the stereotype of the fatalistic, passive Latina. In the following year a Spanish translation of *The House on Mango Street* was put out by Random House, as was a children's book, *Hairs/Pelitos*. In the same year Cisneros was one of twenty-four Americans awarded a MacArthur Foundation "genius grant." Her most recent and long-awaited novel, *Caramelo*, was published in 2002 to high praise for its complex multi-generational folk saga organization.

FURTHER READING: Cisneros, Sandra. "Do You Know Me? I wrote *The House on Mango Street*." *Americas Review* 15:1 (Spring 1987) 77–79; Cisneros, Sandra. Sandra

Cisneros in Conversation with Dorothy Allison. Videocassette. Santa Fe: Lannan Foundation, 1999; Kevane, Bridget, and Juanita Heredia. *Latina Self-Portraits: Interviews with Contemporary Women Writers.* Albuquerque: University of New Mexico Press, 2000; Magill, Frank N. *Masterpieces of Latino Literature.* New York: HarperCollins, 1994; *New York Times Book Review* (26 May 1991) 6; Sagel, Jim. "PW Interviews Sandra Cisneros." *Publishers Weekly* 238:15 (29 March 1991) 74–75.

CISNEROS v. CORPUS CHRISTI INDEPENDENT SCHOOL DISTRICT, 1970.

Cisneros v. the CCISD was an important early step in advancing the struggle of Mexican Americans against **segregation** in the schools. Following the arguments of the U.S. Supreme Court in the 1956 **Hernández v. the State of Texas** case, the federal district court held that Mexican Americans were white, but an identifiable ethnic minority, comparable to Italian Americans. This recognition of Mexican Americans as a distinguishable ethnic minority helped deter school districts from avoiding court-ordered desegregation by integrating Chicanos with black students while continuing all-Anglo schools.

FURTHER READING: Salinas, Guadalupe. "Mexican-Americans and the Desegregation of Schools in the Southwest." In *Voices: Readings from El Grito, 1967–1973*, 2nd ed. Edited by Octavio I. Romano-V. Berkeley, Calif.: Quinto Sol Publications, 1973; San Miguel, Guadalupe. "*Let All of Them Take Heed": Mexican Americans and the Campaign for Educational Equality in Texas, 1910–1981.* Austin: University of Texas Press, 1987.

CITIZENSHIP. Until the **World War II** era the Mexicano attitude toward United States citizenship was characterized by a lack of interest on the part of many. This apathy resulted from various causes: the scarcity of institutions promoting naturalization in the Southwest, where most Mexicanos lived; the widespread exclusion, by law and custom, of Mexican American citizens from the political process; the Anglo attitude in the Southwest that a person of Mexican descent was a Mexican no matter what; the widely held belief of many Mexicanos that they would eventually return to Mexico; and the general unresponsiveness of government to Mexican American concerns. Low levels of economic, educational, and social status (generally associated with low naturalization rates), limited proficiency in English, migrant-work lifestyles, a long history of border crossing for seasonal employment dating back to the late 1800s, and not uncommonly lack of official documentation—all influenced the low levels of naturalization. Indifference to citizenship was often encouraged among immigrants as well as sojourners by the local Mexican consul who, understandably, tried to maintain their identification with Mexico.

Relatively low levels of naturalization reduced the potential political power of Mexican-descent persons. Until World War II, fully one-third of Mexicanos were not citizens and were therefore ineligible to vote. In the postwar period levels of naturalization have shown a marked increase. An unprecedented

255,000 Mexicans became American citizens in 1996—a historical record for any group in a single year.

FURTHER READING: Flores, William V., and Rina Benmayor, eds. *Latino Cultural Citizenship: Claiming Identity, Space, and Rights.* Boston: Beacon Press, 1997; Grebler, Leo. "The Naturalization of Mexican Immigrants in the U.S." *International Migration Review* 1 (Fall 1966) 17-32; Grebler, Leo., Joan W. Moore, and Ralph C. Guzmán, eds. *The Mexican American People: The Nation's Second Largest Minority.* New York: The Free Press, 1970; McNamara, Patrick. *Mexican Americans in Los Angeles County: A Study in Acculturation.* San Francisco: R & E Research Associates, 1975; Sheridan, Clare. "A Genealogy of Citizenship: Mexican Americans, Race and National Identity." Ph.D. diss. Austin: University of Texas, 1999.

CIVIL RIGHTS COMMISSION. First established by President Harry Truman, the commission is a nonpartisan, independent federal board of six commissioners appointed by the President and confirmed by the Senate. The commission acts as a clearinghouse for civil rights information and complaints through seven regional offices. It has broad powers to collect information on abuses of civil rights, to investigate grievances, and to evaluate federal legislation, policies, and enforcement. Although lacking enforcement powers, it has been able to influence considerably the attitude of federal agencies toward civil rights. It was incorporated into the Civil Rights Act of 1957 by Congress. Its greatest success was the Voting Rights Act of 1965. Its 1970 report, *Mexican Americans and the Administration of Justice in the Southwest*, highlighted numerous problems including serious underrepresentation on juries and in employment, widespread police and other official misconduct, and inadequacy of local remedies for these problems. The commission later reported that Chicano children were unfairly treated in schools and penalized for language and cultural differences. It noted that, despite some recent improvements, the administration of justice to Mexican Americans left much to be desired.

FURTHER READING: Castro, Tony. *Chicano Power: The Emergence of Mexican America.* New York: Saturday Review Press, 1974; *Racial and Ethnic Tensions in American Communities: A Report of the United States Commission on Civil Rights.* Washington, D.C.: The Commission, 1993; U.S. Commission on Civil Rights. *The Mexican American.* Washington, D.C.: U.S. Government Printing Office, 1968; U.S. Commission on Civil Rights. *Mexican Americans and the Administration of Justice in the Southwest.* Washington, D.C.: U.S. Government Printing Office, 1970; *United States Commission on Civil Rights.* Washington, D.C.: The Commission, 1995.

CIVIL RIGHTS LEGISLATION, HISTORY OF. Historically, the earliest protection of the rights of citizens was embodied in the first ten amendments to the U.S. Constitution, ratified in 1791. Article IX of the 1848 Treaty of **Guadalupe Hidalgo** promised eventual full **citizenship** and in the meantime guaranteed the rights of the new Mexican American nationals to be "protected in the free enjoyment of their liberty and property and secured in the free exercise of their religion." The Fourteenth Amendment to the Constitution, which was ratified twenty years later in 1868, included the important phrase "equal protection of the laws." Nearly a century later, in the 1950s and 1960s, the courts vigorously used the Fourteenth Amendment guarantees to support a broad attack on discrimination and denial of civil rights.

The Civil Rights Act of 1957 was the first legislation of consequence since the 1800s in the move toward more active federal government support of civil rights. The law mandated the creation of a Civil Rights Commission to investigate and report on compliance with the Fourteenth Amendment provision prohibiting the denial or abridgement of citizens' rights. It specifically forbade interference with the process of voting and made available federal protection at the polls. Within the Justice Department it established a Civil Rights Division that could obtain court injunctions against interference with citizens' right to vote. Although aimed at black Americans, it also helped Chicanos by establishing a more favorable climate during elections.

Seven years later the comprehensive 1964 Civil Rights Act greatly extended the scope of the federal government's guarantees of citizens' rights. Proposed by President John F. Kennedy, it was passed after his assassination and only after a lengthy filibuster by opponents in the Senate. It created a federal **Equal Employment Opportunity Commission** and outlawed **discrimination** because of race or sex by employers, unions, public schools, and voting registrars. It also provided for equality of treatment in theaters, hotels, restaurants, and other places of public accommodation and gave the U.S. Attorney General powers to hasten school desegregation, in which there was much foot-dragging at the time. Despite very determined opposition, the constitutionality of the law's far-reaching scope was confirmed by the U.S. Supreme Court.

The Voting Rights Act of 1965, also known as the Civil Rights Act of 1965, made possible direct federal intervention to enable citizens to register and vote. The law specifically rejected English-speaking and literacy as requirements for voting. Like the 1957 Civil Rights Act, it was written primarily to protect the voting rights of black Americans. However, it also served to pave the way for voter registration and get-out-the-vote drives among Chicanos.

In 1970 the Voting Rights Act was extended by Congress for five years with an added provision to prevent the erection of new barriers to participation in politics. In 1975 the act was again renewed with important additions for Mexican Americans. New provisions included a requirement for bilingual ballots in certain language-dominated areas, and allowed individuals to file suit for denial of voting rights. Seven years later the act was extended to the year 2007 and included an absolute prohibition of various discriminatory practices. The 1975 and 1982 changes in the law aimed specifically at language minority groups like Mexican Americans. The benefits of these voting rights acts for Chicanos can be seen in the much larger numbers voting and the growing numbers elected to public office.

Meanwhile, Congress also passed the 1968 Civil Rights Act prohibiting **housing** discrimination based on race or ethnicity. Concerned with rioting, this act made various activities in fomenting unrest federal offenses—a reflection of the turbulent times. Like the 1957 and 1964 legislation, it was in large part a response to the black civil rights movement. However, it also helped prepare the way for the Mexican American civil rights struggle in the last quarter of the twentieth century.

In general, over the years the protective shield of civil rights has been advanced by federal and state constitutions, federal and state legislation, and by decisions of the courts, especially the U.S. Supreme Court. In the post–World War II era, court decisions took the lead in reducing discrimination and promoting the rights of Mexican Americans.

FURTHER READING: Bardolph, Richard, ed. *The Civil Rights Record.* New York: Thomas Y. Crow Co., 1970; García, John A. "The Voting Rights Act and Hispanic Political Representation in the Southwest." In *Land Grants, Housing, and Political Power,* edited by Antoinette Sedillo López. New York: Garland Publishing, 1995; Graham, Hugh Davis. *The Civil Rights Era, 1960–1972.* New York: Oxford University Press, 1990; Grofman, Bernard, ed. *Legacies of the 1964 Civil Rights Act.* Charlottesville: University Press of Virginia, 2000; Loevy, Robert D., ed. *The Civil Rights Act of 1964: The Passage of the Law That Ended Racial Segregation.* Albany: State University of New York Press, 1997; "New Accent on Civil Rights: The Mexican American." *Civil Rights Digest.* 2: 1 (Winter 1969) 16–23; *Revolution in Civil Rights, 1945–1968,* 4th ed. Washington, D.C.: Congressional Quarterly, 1968; Rosales, F. Arturo, ed. *Testimonio: A Documentary History of the Mexican American Struggle for Civil Rights.* Houston: Arte Público Press, 2000.

CIVIL RIGHTS VIOLATIONS. From the 1850s to the present there have been numerous instances of notorious abuse of Mexican Americans' civil rights. Among the more outrageous were the U.S. **Land Act of 1851**, which despoiled many Californios of their lands, and the 1855 California anti-vagrancy law, which singled out persons "commonly known as Greasers." In Texas the **Cart War** of 1857 saw Mexicano teamsters assaulted for months (and some even murdered) by Anglo competitors before federal troops ended the attacks. Throughout the years from the Treaty of Guadalupe Hidalgo to the end of the 1910 Mexican revolution, the fanatical pursuit and often killing of presumed Mexican bandits by the **Texas Rangers** terrorized Mexicanos and kept the border area in turmoil. More recently the Los Angeles **"Sleepy Lagoon"** case, the **Zoot Suit Riots** in 1943, and the **Bloody Christmas** case of 1951, in which seven Los Angeles youths were brutally beaten in jail by police officers, exemplified wider violations of civil rights. In post–World War II there was the refusal of restaurant service to Medal of Honor winners José Mendoza López and Sergeant **Macario García** in Texas, as well as the 1948 **Félix Longoria** case, which showed that even in death Mexican Americans might be denied equality.

In addition to these outrageous incidents there was school **segregation** and much harrying and hounding, including punishment in many schools for speaking Spanish, even on the playground. Long-term over-policing of barrios elicited frequent complaints. With little understanding of Mexican culture, the overwhelmingly Anglo police force generally held stereotypes of Mexicanos that encouraged abuse. In the post–World War II era Chicanos made continuing abuses in schools, the workplace, and society the targets of their civil rights movement. Perceiving only limited improvement from the 1960s civil rights movement and ensuing legislation, they used their growing political power to call attention to their concerns in politics and education.

FURTHER READING: Almanza, Arturo S. *Mexican-Americans and Civil Rights.* Los Angeles: County Commission on Human Relations, 1964; Burma, John H. "The Civil Rights Situation of Mexican Americans and Spanish Americans." In *Race Relations: Problems and Theory,* edited by J. Masouka and P. Valien. Chapel Hill: University of North Carolina Press, 1961; "Civil Rights." *La Luz* 8:6 (February–March 1980) 10–14, 41, 43; McWilliams, Carey. *North from Mexico: The Spanish-Speaking People of the United States,* rev. ed. Westport, Conn.: Praeger, 1990; Mirandé, Alfredo. *Gringo Justice.* Notre Dame: University of Notre Dame Press, 1987; Rosales, Francisco A. *Chicano! The History of the Mexican American Civil Rights Movement,* 2nd rev. ed. Houston: Arte Público Press, 1997; U.S. Commission on Civil Rights. *Mexican Americans and the Administration of Justice in the Southwest.* Washington, D.C.: U.S. Government Printing Office, 1970.

CIVIL WAR, 1861–1865. Although the focus of the struggle between the North and the South lay elsewhere, the fighting did have some impact on Mexican Americans. A large majority of them had only a limited notion of the quarrel and remained indifferently unionist. However, some elites, particularly in New Mexico, equated slavery with their own practice of peonage and empathized with Confederate views.

New Mexico formed five infantry and one cavalry units in which many Nuevomexicanos served. When Confederate forces invaded from Texas, they helped repel the invasion in the battle of Glorieta Pass in 1862 and continued harassing the southern troops as they were forced to withdraw to safety in Texas. In Texas some **Tejano**s were drafted into the Confederate forces, while others supported the North at least in part simply because most Anglo Texans favored the Confederacy. California's involvement in the Civil War was extremely limited, and nearly all Californios remained at least passively loyal to the Union. Salvador Vallejo commanded a battalion of Californio cavalry that patrolled the southern border.

FURTHER READING: Crocchiola, Stanley F. L. *The Civil War in New Mexico.* Denver: World Press, 1960; Thompson, Jerry D. *Mexican Texans in the Union Army.* El Paso: Texas Western Press, 1986; Thompson, Jerry D. *Vaqueros in Blue & Gray.* Austin: Presidial Press, 1976.

COCONUT. A mildly pejorative term for a Mexican American who gives up his Mexican culture and tries to assimilate more or less completely into Anglo society. The reference is to the coconut being brown on the outside and white within.

CODE SWITCHING. Code switching is the alternation or mixing of two languages by bilingual speakers. The speakers may intermix words, phrases, or whole clauses from two languages while maintaining normal continuity of thought. Code switching is not entirely a random process; frequently the switch is caused by a word or phrase that is more expressive (or lacking) in one language.

FURTHER READING: Bayley, Robert, and José Zapata. *Prefiero español porque I'm More Used to It: Code-Switching and Language Norms in South Texas.* San Antonio: Hispanic Research Center, University of Texas, 1993; Lance, Donald M. "Spanish-English Code Switching." In *El lenguage de los Chicanos,* edited by E. Hernández-Chávez, A. Cohen, and A. Beltramo. Virginia: Center for Applied Linguistics, 1975; Lipski, John M. *Linguistic Aspects of Spanish-English Language Switching.* Tempe: Center for Latin American Studies, Arizona State University, 1985.

COLEGIO CÉSAR CHÁVEZ. Colegio César Chávez was a liberal arts institution earlier known as Mount Angel College. It was part of the effort during the Chicano movement to create *raza* institutions of higher learning. Many Mexican Americans saw a need for an academic base for Chicano intellectual development such as black Americans had possessed ever since their emancipation. Established in Mount Angel, Oregon, the college was a four-year institution granting both associate and bachelor of arts degrees during its decade of existence.

FURTHER READING: Maldonado, Carlos S. *Colegio César Chávez, 1973–1983: A Chicano Struggle for Educational Self-Determination.* New York: Garland, 2000.

COLMENARES, MARGARITA H., 1957– . Engineer. Born to Mexican immigrant parents in Sacramento, California, Margarita Colmenares was the eldest of five children. Despite financial stringency, her parents, who believed strongly in the value of education, sent her to the local parochial school and then to the all-girl Bishop Manogue High School. Influenced by the Chicano Movement, in high school she founded the Asociación Juvenil Mexicano Americana to push for Chicano students' academic needs. Nevertheless, she found herself being counseled away from college preparatory courses. Upon graduation she entered Sacramento State University as a business major, but soon found that she had a serious interest in engineering. Lacking the background coursework needed for engineering, she enrolled in junior college courses. As a result she was able to get a part-time job in engineering and also to win several scholarships that took her to Stanford University.

At Stanford, Colmenares divided her time between her studies, research assistant duties, tutoring, and the dance. She codirected the Stanford Ballet Folklórico one year. As a junior she entered the Chevron co-op education program and when she graduated in 1981 took a job with the Chevron Corporation, for which she worked in a wide variety of engineering capacities. While working in the Bay Area she founded a local chapter of the Society of Hispanic Professional Engineers (SHPE), and served as its president for two years.

Colmenares continued to move up the Chevron success ladder. At the end of the 1980s she was named to head a multimillion-dollar cleanup of Chevron's El Segundo plant in southern California. She also moved up in engineering professional organizations. While working in Texas she was elected regional vice-president of SHPE, then became national chairwoman for leadership development, and in 1989 was elected its first woman national president. She took a year's leave from her Chevron job to devote all her energies to her presidency. In 1991 she was selected as a White House fellow, serving, at her request, as a special assistant in the Department of Education.

Because of her deep interest in technological education, particularly of young Mexican Americans, Margarita Colmenares has been the recipient of a number of prestigious awards.

FURTHER READING: *Hispanic Business.* (October 1992) 78; "Margarita H. Colmenares." *Replica* 21 (July 1990) 23; "Profiles in Leadership." *Hispanic Engineer* (Fall 1989) 22–25; Telgen, Diane, and Jim Kamp, eds. *Notable Hispanic American Women.* Detroit: Gale Research, 1993; *Who's Who among Hispanic Americans, 1994–1995.* Detroit: Gale Research, 1994.

COLONIA. A small unincorporated settlement or subdivision usually on the edge of a town and inhabited largely by one ethnic group, mostly recent Latino immigrants. Colonias typically lack paved streets, piped water, and a sewerage system. Housing is often a collection of ramshackle buildings made from salvaged materials. More broadly, the term may be applied to any enclave of a Latino group; in larger cities the term *barrio* is more often used in this sense.

FURTHER READING: Rochín, Refugio, and Monica D. Castillo. *Immigration and Colonia Formation in Rural California.* Berkeley: University of California, Chicano/Latino Policy Project, 1995; Ward, Peter M. *Colonias and Public Policy in Texas and Mexico: Urbanization by Stealth.* Austin: University of Texas Press, 1999.

COLONIALISM, INTERNAL. A construct, widely advanced by activists in the early years of the Chicano Movement, that held that Mexican Americans are the victims of a colonialist economic structure that exists within the United States and that keeps them in inferior positions. By the mid-1970s the theory had been largely abandoned by Chicano academicians.

FURTHER READING: Barrera, Mario. *Race and Class in the Southwest: A Theory of Racial Inequality.* Notre Dame: University of Notre Dame Press, 1979.

COLORADO. Colorado, the sparsely settled far northern frontier of the New Mexico–Arizona region, had fewer than a thousand settlers at the end of the Mexican period in 1848, mostly subsistence farmers, ranchers, and a few traders. Mining development in the latter 1800s brought in Anglo American settlers and large numbers of miners from Europe, rapidly changing the area's demographics. A mere handful of elite Mexican Americans, or **Hispano**s, as they preferred to call themselves, continued participating in territorial and state politics. In the 1875 state constitutional convention **Casimiro Barela**, "The Perpetual Senator," was the only Hispano delegate. He was able to obtain some protection for Spanish-speaking Coloradans in the state's 1876 constitution. In the southern part of the state a Mexican American majority made possible limited control of local political offices.

Development of the sugar beet industry at the turn of the century led to an influx of Mexicanos from adjacent New Mexico and Texas to work in the beet fields. Soon Colorado growers were recruiting workers from northern Mexico, helped by the 1910 Mexican revolution, which uprooted thousands of rural Mexicans. During the 1920s American Federation of Labor organizer C. N. **Idar** was active in trying to unionize Colorado beet workers. The depression of the following decade sent many workers back to Mexico, but had limited economic effects on Colorado Hispanos. The 1930s saw a serious decline both in the sugar beet industry and in coal mining, as oil increasingly replaced coal as a source of heating. Employment of Mexicanos in both activities never recovered. Today Colorado's sugar beet industry, a mere shadow of its former self, is almost completely mechanized.

A second heavy influx of Anglos in the post–World War II era greatly reduced the number of towns and counties in which Chicanos still wielded political power. In order to retain influence in local and state politics, Colorado Mexican Americans began to organize. The 1960s saw the development of community associations and student organizations. With the advent of **Corky Gonzales**'s aggressive **Crusade for Justice** in the late 1960s they began to take a significant political role. Gonzales organized Chicano youths, supported high school walkouts, voiced complaints about police attitudes, demanded educational reforms, and led a strongly nationalist movement. In 1970, at the height of Gonzales's Colorado **La Raza Unida Party**, Crusade for Justice leaders ran Albert Garrule for governor on an LRUP ticket. He garnered less than 2 percent of the vote. However, in the early 1980s **Federico Peña** was elected mayor of Denver and served ably until 1991.

In 1960, 9 percent (157,173) of Colorado's population was Spanish-surnamed; 76 percent of them lived in urban areas. The 2000 census listed 14.9 percent as Latinos.

FURTHER READING: C. de Baca, Vincent, ed. *La Gente: Hispano History and Life in Colorado*. Denver: Colorado Historical Society, 1998; Campa, Arthur L. *Hispanic Culture in the Southwest*. Norman: University of Oklahoma Press, 1979; Deutsch, Sarah. *No Separate Refuge: Culture, Class, and Gender on an Anglo-Hispanic Frontier in the American Southwest, 1880–1940*. New York: Oxford University Press, 1987; Pappas, George, and María Guajardo, eds. *Latinos in Colorado, U.S.: A Profile of Culture, Changes, and Challenges*. Denver: Latin American Research and Service Agency, 1997.

COMISIÓN FEMENIL MEXICANA NACIONAL, INC. An early Chicana organization coming out of the **movimiento**, the commission was established in 1970 in Los Angeles as the Comisión Femenil de Los Angeles. Under founding president **Gloria Molina** it established chapters elsewhere in the Southwest. It operated two bilingual child-development centers and established a Chicana Action Service Center. Primarily concerned with advancing the role and contributions of Chicanas to the community, it helped develop many of today's community leaders. In recent years it has been involved in the struggles of migrant farm workers and the economic empowerment of inner-city **Chicanas**. With the objective of promoting the cause of Chicana leadership, it provides information and training for positions in management and administration. Headquartered in Los Angeles, its membership is largely limited to California.

FURTHER READING: Flores, Francisca. "Comisión Femenil Mexicana." *Regeneración* 2:4 (1975) 24–25; Gonzales, Sylvia A. *Hispanic American Voluntary Organizations*. Westport, Conn.: Greenwood Press, 1985.

COMISIÓN HONORÍFICA MEXICANA. Initially an organization established by Mexican consuls in the Southwest to help Mexican citizens with a variety of problems. Established first in Texas at the end of World War I and immediately afterwards in California, the commissions were made up of local volunteers who provided Mexican nationals with emergency assistance until they could obtain help from the nearest Mexican consul, who might be one hundred or more miles away. Although the commissions' early objectives centered on retaining loyalty of Mexicans to the fatherland, in the aftermath of World War II they were broadened to include concerns of the Chicano community, especially educational opportunity and civil liberties as well as economic and social betterment.

FURTHER READING: Balderrama, Francisco E. *In Defense of La Raza: The Los Angeles Mexican Consulate and the Mexican Community, 1929–1936*. Tucson: University of Arizona Press, 1982; Tyler, Ron, ed. *The New Handbook of Texas*, vol. 2. Austin: Texas State Historical Association, 1996.

COMMUNIST PARTY. During the 1920s, and especially in the 1930s, the Communist Party targeted Mexican Americans, using its position in labor unionism to appeal to them. Although Mexican Americans benefitted from the training and skills learned in communist-dominated unions, the basic doctrines of communism had little or no appeal for most of them.

COMMUNITIES ORGANIZED FOR PUBLIC SERVICE. COPS is a nonpartisan community service group based on Catholic parishes and greatly influenced by the community organizing ideas of Saul Alinsky. It was founded in 1974, principally by **Ernie Cortés,** who trained at the Industrial Areas Foundation (IAF) in Chicago. He was supported by San Antonio's bishop, Francis Furey, some Catholic laymen, and several young priests. Similar to the **Community Service Organization**, COPS likewise favored Alinsky's persuasive confrontation tactics.

COPS is self-sufficient, like other IAF-inspired groups, and is completely nonpartisan. Its policy has been to support its friends in local government and to withhold its support from their opponents, regardless of party affiliation. It has helped augment the political clout of the San Antonio Mexican American community by politicizing it as well as by voter registration and get-out-the-vote campaigns. The growth of COPS in the 1980s enabled it to achieve some statewide as well as local reforms objectives.

Ultimately the success of COPS has been the result of its energetic and capable leadership, including many Chicanas; of wide support from a large civil service population in San Antonio; and of the endorsement and help of local Catholic clergymen strongly supported by bishops Francis Furey and **Patrick Flores.**

FURTHER READING: Cortés, Ernesto Jr. "Changing the Locus of Political Decision-Making." *Christianity and Crisis* 47:1 (2 Feb. 1987) 18–22; Rips, Geoffrey. "Texas Mavericks Take on Big Boys." *Progressive* (June 1984) 20–22; Rogers, Mary Beth. *Cold Anger: A Story of Faith and Power Politics.* Denton, Texas: University of North Texas Press, 1990; Sekul, Joseph D. "Communities Organized for Public Service: Citizen Power and Public Policy in San Antonio." In *Latinos and the Political System*, edited by F. Chris García. Notre Dame: University of Notre Dame Press, 1988; Skerry, Peter. *Mexican Americans: The Ambivalent Minority.* New York: Free Press, 1993.

COMMUNITY SERVICE ORGANIZATION. The CSO is a broad-based nonpartisan, nonpolitical organization. Although membership is without citizenship or language qualifications, it seeks to make Mexicanos aware of civic rights and responsibilities and encourages political participation. Aiming at integration, it promotes learning English, **citizenship**, voter registration, and get-out-the-vote programs.

The first Community Service Organization was established in the Los Angeles area during the fall of 1947 under the leadership of **Fred Ross, Sr.**, a Saul Alinsky disciple. Initially its principal objective was to support the candidacy of **Edward Roybal** for a seat on the city council. After Roybal was successfully elected, it turned to the broader community issues of citizenship and civil rights. Led by World War II veterans, it soon spread elsewhere within California and outside, especially in Arizona.

However, during the latter 1960s it underwent a decline in membership because of competition from new, more aggressive Chicano organizations and the more confrontational mood of the decade. During the early 1970s it expanded its mutual benefit programs. When the Chicano Movement subsided in the latter 1970s, the CSO regained some of its lost membership and began again to enjoy a wider community support. The CSO has been particularly notable as the training ground for **César Chávez, Dolores Huerta**, Fred Ross, Sr., **Antonio Orendain**, and other leaders.

FURTHER READING: Brigham, Jack. "CSO; Working for the People." *Caminos* 2:3 (May 1981) 32–33; García, F. Chris. *La Causa Política.* Notre Dame: University of Notre Dame Press, 1974; Gonzales, Sylvia A. *Hispanic American Voluntary Organizations.* Westport, Conn.: Greenwood Press, 1985; Ross, Fred W. (Sr.) *Community Organization in Mexican-American Communities.* Los Angeles: American Council on Race Relations, 1947.

COMMUTER. The term *commuter* is used to describe a Mexican national who lives in Mexico and crosses the border on a regular basis, usually daily or weekly, to work in the United States. They are employed in service positions, agriculture, and to a lesser extent in construction and industry. A majority of commuters hold green cards that make them resident aliens and enable them to take jobs in the United States. Over one million more Mexicans possess border-crossing cards, which do not allow them to work legally in the United States. According to some authorities, commuters tend to have a depressing effect on border area working conditions and wages. Efforts to reduce their numbers have had limited success.

FURTHER READING: Herzog, Lawrence A. "Border Commuter Workers and Transfrontier Metropolitan Structure along the United States-Mexico Border." *Journal of Borderlands Studies* 5:2 (Fall 1990) 1–20; Jones, Lamar B. "Alien Commuters in United States Labor Markets." *International Migration Review* 4:3 (Summer 1970) 65–86.

COMPEÁN, MARIO C., 1940– . Activist, political leader. Mario Compeán was born and grew up in San Antonio, Texas. After working in migrant agriculture he entered San Antonio's St. Mary's University, where he became closely associated with **José Angel Gutiérrez**. In 1967 he, Gutiérrez, and other students founded the **Mexican American Youth Organization** (MAYO). He soon became deeply involved in electoral politics as well as student activism. In April 1969 he ran for mayor of San Antonio on the Committee for Barrio Betterment ticket. Although he did not win, the votes he received nearly forced a runoff election between the two leading candidates.

Having served as vice-chairman of MAYO, in 1969 Compeán replaced Gutiérrez as state chairman and then in 1970 became one of the founders and leaders of **La Raza Unida Party** (LRUP) in Texas. Two years later at the party's first convention he was named state chairman of LRUP. In 1978 he ran for governor of Texas but suffered a devastating defeat, garnering less than 2 percent of the votes. The lack of enthusiasm among Mexican Americans for his candidacy was blamed on his failure to develop a grassroots community base.

During the 1980s Compeán headed the Chicano studies program at the University of Wisconsin in Madison, and in the next decade was a policy researcher for the Minnesota Spanish-Speaking Affairs Council while working on a doctorate in education.

FURTHER READING: García, Ignacio M. *United We Win: The Rise and Fall of La Raza Unida Party*. Tucson: University of Arizona, Mexican American Studies and Research Center, 1989; "LRUP Leaders Today." *Hispanic* (April 1989) 46; Navarro, Armando. *Mexican American Youth Organization: Avant-Garde of the Chicano Movement in Texas*. Austin: University of Texas Press, 1995.

CON SAFOS. An intellectual Chicano periodical established in 1968. It published essays, short stories, and poetry that tended to reflect life in the barrio. Until it ceased publication in 1971, it served as an important forum for Chicano literary endeavors. The journal took its name from a **pachuco** expression meaning roughly "the same to you."

CONFEDERACIÓN DE UNIONES DE CAMPESINOS Y OBREROS MEXICANOS (CUCOM). The Confederation of Mexican Farm Laborers' and Workers' Unions grew out of the 1933 **El Monte Berry Strike** in Los Angeles County. Some of the strike leaders, trained in the **Confederación de Uniones Obreras Mexicanas** (CUOM), formed the CUCOM as the strike progressed and expanded. After the strike the CUCOM was established as a permanent union and quickly assumed a leading role in the agricultural strikes of the 1930s. During 1936 and 1937 the CUCOM also participated in several unsuccessful efforts to create a statewide federation of farm worker unions. By the outbreak of World War II the CUCOM had been greatly weakened by jurisdictional disputes, aggressive grower opposition, and the use of state criminal syndicalism legislation.

FURTHER READING: Gómez-Quiñones, Juan. "'. . . down the valleys wild:' Epilogue, Prologue, Medias-res Still; the Strikes of the Thirties." *Aztlán* 1:1 (Spring 1970) 119–123; Jamieson, Stuart. *Labor Unionism in American Agriculture*. Washington, D.C.: U.S. Government Printing Office, 1945.

CONFEDERACIÓN DE UNIONES OBRERAS MEXICANAS (CUOM). One of the first Mexicano labor organizations, the Confederation of Mexican Workers Unions was established in the Los Angeles area in the 1920s by Chicanos and immigrants from Mexico. Modeled on the Confederación Regional Obrera Mexicana in Mexico, it peaked in 1928 with about three thousand workers in some twenty-two unions, and then dwindled with the onslaught of the depression. The CUOM was important as a training ground for future labor leaders and for clearly describing in its constitution the objectives of *raza* workers.

FURTHER READING: Gómez-Quiñones, Juan. "'. . . down the valleys wild:' Epilogue, Prologue, Medias-res Still; the Strikes of the Thirties." *Aztlán* 1:1 (Spring 1970) 119–123; Jamieson, Stuart. *Labor Unionism in American Agriculture*. Washington, D.C.: U.S. Government Printing Office, 1945; Montoya, Alfredo C. "A Brief Look at Labor Union History in the West and Southwest." *Journal of Hispanic Policy* (1989–1990) 117–126.

CONGRESO DE LOS PUEBLOS DE HABLA ESPAÑOLA. The left-leaning Congreso was founded in 1938 by **Luisa Moreno, Josefina Fierro de Bright, Bert Corona,** and other community and union leaders as an umbrella organization. One of the early Mexican American organizations with specific civil rights goals, it held its first convention in Los Angeles, which attracted Latinos from all over the United States. The Congreso and many of its leaders became intensely involved in union organizing as well as in protesting racial and ethnic discrimination.

The Congreso, concerned with achieving greater equality through education, denounced the **segregation** of Chicano students in Los Angeles schools and worked to improve the substandard facilities and education they were subjected to. It provided Mexicanos with counseling services for immigration and naturalization questions and protested a number of southern California cases of excessive use of force by the police. It also concerned itself with employment **discrimination** in defense industries at the end of the 1930s.

The Congreso's militancy and often radical stance focused government attention on its activities, and some leaders were investigated and harassed by the Federal Bureau of Investigation. Its left-leaning leadership and forthright positions on concerns like union organizing, discrimination, police brutality, and vigilantism caused it often to be labeled a communist organization in the press despite a lack of documentary evidence for the charge. After the United States entered **World War II**, Congreso leaders continued to demand and work for civil and human rights reforms despite early wartime pressures to "all pull together."

As a result of a leadership split and other developments during World War II, the Congreso virtually ceased to function as an organization by the end of 1942, although individual leaders continued their activism. Hopes for a revival of the Congreso after the war were dashed by McCarthyism and the deportation of Moreno and Fierro in the early 1950s. Although short-lived, the Congreso inspired many community activists and had a valuable role in developing community leadership.

FURTHER READING: Acuña, Rodolfo. *Occupied America: A History of Chicanos*, 3rd ed. New York: Harper & Row, 1988; Albert Camarillo, *Chicanos in California*. San Francisco: Boyd and Fraser, 1984; García, F. Chris. *La Causa Política*. Notre Dame:

University of Notre Dame Press, 1974; García, Mario T. *Memories of Chicano History: The Life and Narrative of Bert Corona.* Berkeley: The University of California Press, 1994; Mario T. García. *Mexican Americans: Leadership, Ideology, and Identity, 1930–1960.* New Haven: Yale University Press, 1989.

CONGRESS OF MEXICAN AMERICAN UNITY. The CMAU was formally established in 1968 to create an umbrella organization for Chicano groups in the Los Angeles area. It represented over two hundred associations and served to consolidate a variety of community concerns. Among its early successes was the election of historian **Julian Nava** to the Los Angeles Board of Education; in 1970 it played an important part in the **National Chicano Moratorium** march in East Los Angeles. During its early years it provided an important forum for discussion of civil rights concerns of southern California Chicanos. It declined as the movimiento waned in the latter 1970s. It later dissolved largely as a result of the often radical positions taken by its youthful leaders and their unwillingness or inability to compromise in the face of a nationwide conservative trend.

FURTHER READING: "C.M.A.U. (Congress of Mexican-American Unity)." Los Angeles: *La Causa* 1:5 (28 February 1970) 5; Steiner, Stan. "Militance among the Mexican Americans: Chicano Power." *New Republic* 162:25 (20 June 1970) 16–18.

CONGRESSIONAL HISPANIC CAUCUS. The Caucus was formally established in December 1976 by Latino members of the U.S. House of Representatives, led by Mexican American **Edward Roybal** of California. Its principal object is to establish a Hispanic agenda and to influence national policies that affect U.S. Latinos. It routinely monitors legislative action in Congress, but is also concerned with policies and practices in the executive branch and the judiciary. In addition, the Caucus aims to strengthen and expand the role of Latinos at all levels of government.

Most of the Caucus's activity takes place within the House of Representatives, where it acts as a forum for Latino members of Congress and speaks out against all legislation it considers detrimental to U.S. Latinos. During the past quarter century it has concerned itself with issues of **bilingual education, housing** discrimination, immigration policy, **affirmative action**, health care, and police brutality. Despite its limited membership, the Caucus has considerable impact, particularly within congressional committees.

During the Jimmy Carter administration, 1977–1981, the Caucus met regularly with the president to discuss concerns, especially education and minority representation in government. In the 1990s it was regularly consulted by the Clinton administration in matters of its concern. As a result of funding cuts by the new Republican Congress in 1995, the Caucus reorganized as a Congressional Member Organization in order to continue its work. Under the chairmanship of congressman Silvestre Reyes of El Paso it continues to serve as a forum for Latino issues in the new millennium. It publishes a bimonthly newsletter, *Avance*.

FURTHER READING: Menard, Valerie Avila. "Hispanic Journal: Caucus Alive and Well Despite Changes." *Hispanic* (30 April 1996) 16; Yzaguirre, Raúl. "The Hispanic Congressional Caucus: A New Sign of Unity." *Agenda* 7;3 (May–June 1977) 2. www.chci.org

CORONA, BERT N., 1918–2001. Activist, community leader, union organizer, professor. Bert Corona was born of immigrant parents in El Paso and received his early education there. In 1936 he moved to Los Angeles, where he attended the University of Southern California and the University of California while working as a stevedore to support himself. Between 1936 and 1942 he was also active organizing for the Congress of Industrial Organizations.

Bert Corona devoted his life to working for social, economic, educational, and political betterment of *la raza*. Often described as a kind of urban César Chávez, he had an important part over the years in the creation and development of many community **organizations**, including the Asociación Nacional México-Americana, the Community Service Organization, the Congreso de Los Pueblos de Habla Española, and the Hermandad Mexicana Nacional.

In 1959 Corona was one of the principal founders of the **Mexican American Political Association** (MAPA). As an officer in California MAPA he took an important role in campaigns to achieve greater civil rights for minorities. He was deeply involved in liberal California Democratic politics, and helped Edward Roybal win his first election to the U.S. House of Representatives in 1962. He was also active in the 1960 **Viva Kennedy clubs** and the Viva "Pat" Brown movement two years later, and was cochairman of the national Viva Johnson campaign in 1964. In 1967 he was appointed to the U.S. **Civil Rights Commission** by President Lyndon Johnson.

As a lifelong battler against ethnic discrimination, Corona had some influence on the Chicano Movement but distanced himself from those people in the movimiento who advocated a strong nationalism. During the Movement and beyond he repeatedly spoke out forthrightly for the rights of immigrants, particularly of **undocumented** sojourners. In 1981 he opposed the Simpson-Mazzoli immigration bill, some parts of which he found unacceptable. As director of La Hermandad Mexicana Nacional until his death, he led the fight in defense of undocumented workers' rights.

Over the years Corona's unswerving support for civil and human rights and his outspoken opposition to discrimination highlight his importance as a significant Chicano leader. Often labeled a radical and sometimes accused of being a communist, Bert Corona was in reality a fairly moderate social reformer who deserves great credit for his many contributions to the struggle for Chicano and labor rights. He died in Los Angeles on January 15, 2001 as a result of complications of gallbladder and kidney ailments.

FURTHER READING: Corona, Bert N. *Bert Corona Speaks on La Raza Unida Party and the "Illegal Alien" Scare.* New York: Pathfinder Press, 1972; Hammerback, John

C. "An Interview with Bert Corona." *Western Journal of Speech Communication* 44:3 (Summer 1980) 214–220; Garcia, Mario T. *Memories of Chicano History: The Life and Narrative of Bert Corona.* Berkeley: University of California, 1994; Ortega, C. F. "The Legacy of Bert Corona." *Progressive* 65:8 (2001) 26–27; Ramos, George. "Bert Corona; Labor Activist Backed Rights for Undocumented Workers." *Los Angeles Times* (17 January 2001) Metro B, 10.

CORONEL, ANTONIO FRANCO, 1817–1894. Civic leader, educator, landowner. Antonio Coronel was born in Mexico City and moved to the northwestern frontier town of Los Angeles when he was seventeen. During the Mexican period he served as schoolteacher, street commissioner, irrigation commissioner, territorial deputy, justice of the peace, and inspector of the secularized mission properties. He actively opposed the American invasion of California in 1846, but after the Treaty of **Guadalupe Hidalgo** accepted and embraced his new nationality.

Under the American government Coronel continued his career of service to the community. Among many local governmental positions, he served on the Los Angeles city council and the irrigation board; he was a teacher, superintendent of schools, county assessor, and mayor of Los Angeles. In spite of some Anglo opposition, as mayor he spearheaded a movement to create a public school and opened the first school in 1855. He was a founder of the Historical Society of Southern California.

Coronel was one of the few **Californio**s who made a modest fortune as a miner in the early months of the 1848–1849 gold rush. Unlike many of his compatriots, he adapted well to the new economic environment and had a comfortable income from his real estate, grape growing, and money lending. In the post–Civil War years he continued to take an active part in local Democratic politics. As a kind of Californio elder statesman he was often sought out by Anglo political leaders and in 1867 was elected state treasurer. Nearly a decade later he moved from treasurer to the state senate, where he voiced a Californio viewpoint as the sole Californio senator. In addition to his civic activities and state political involvement, during this time he was also busy managing his various properties. For several years in the mid-1870s he was active in directing the weekly *La Crónica*, of which he was a part owner. His death in 1894 ended a remarkably distinguished career of public service.

FURTHER READING: Barrows, H. D. "Antonio F. Coronel." *Historical Society of Southern California Quarterly* 5:1 (1900); Coronel, Antonio Franco. "De cosas de California de Antonio Franco Coronel." In *Nineteenth Century Californio Testimonials*, edited by Rosaura Sánchez, Beatrice Pita, and Bárbara Reyes. La Jolla: University of California, San Diego, Ethnic Studies, 1994; Newmark, Marco. "Antonio Franco Coronel." *Historical Society of Southern California Quarterly* 36:2 (June 1954).

CORRIDO. The corrido is a folk ballad, the theme of which is usually an important historic event or person. Generally in Spanish, it recites in simple language the details of the person's life or of the historic occurrence. The 1910 **Mexican revolution** and its leaders have been particularly popular topics for corridos, but contemporary themes are also used. The lives of both John F. Kennedy and **César Chávez** have been celebrated in corridos. The corrido can provide valuable source materials for the historian, especially in understanding the popular assessment of the person or event it describes, as in the Corrido of Gregorio Cortez.

FURTHER READING: Arteaga, Alfred. "The Chicano Mexican Corrido." *Journal of Ethnic Studies* 13 (Summer 1985) 75–105; Herrera-Sobek, María. *The Mexican Corrido: A Feminist Analysis.* Bloomington: Indiana University Press, 1990. McDowell, John Holmes. "The Mexican Corrido." *Journal of American Folklore* 85 (1972) 205–220.

CORTÉS, CARLOS E., 1934– . Historian, teacher. Carlos Cortés was born in Oakland, California, grew up in Kansas City, and returned to California to get his B.A. at Berkeley in 1956. After receiving an M.A. in journalism at Columbia University a year later, he spent two years in the army, and then worked as editor for the Phoenix weekly Sunpapers. Deciding that his real interest was Latin America, he obtained his doctorate in Latin American history at the University of New Mexico in 1969. Meanwhile he began teaching at the University of California, Riverside, where he still teaches.

A scholar of great industry, Cortés has authored, coauthored, edited, and coedited numerous books and articles in a variety of fields: ethnic history, education, media, and popular culture, especially film studies. His *Gaucho Politics in Brazil* won the Hubert Herring award for 1974. He has served on numerous governmental and private boards and acted as consultant to over two hundred agencies and businesses. He has been the recipient of a number of fellowships, awards, and honors.

FURTHER READING: Cortés, Carlos E. *The Making and Remaking of a Multiculturalist.* New York: Teachers College Press, 2002; Gaona, Thomas. "Hispanics' Impact on America: An Interview with Professor Carlos Cortés." *Hispanic Times* 6:2 (March–April 1985) 60–62; Martínez, Julio A. *Chicano Scholars and Writers: A Bio-Bibliographical Dictionary.* Metuchen, N.J.: Scarecrow Press, 1979.

CORTÉS, ERNIE (ERNESTO, JR.), 1943– . Activist, organizer. Ernie Cortés is best known as one of the principal founders of **Communities Organized for Public Service** (COPS) in San Antonio. As a college student in the early 1960s he became active in the black civil rights movement and then was caught up by César Chávez's charismatic leadership in the struggle for farm workers' rights. During the second half of the 1960s, while still a graduate student in economics at the University of Texas, he began organizing support for the struggle of Texas farm workers to gain recognition of their union.

Through his work in the United Farm Workers, Cortés became aware of Saul Alinsky's organizing ideas, and spent nearly three years with Alinsky's

Industrial Areas Foundation (IAF) of Chicago, where he worked with midwestern Chicanos. He became a firm believer in Saul Alinsky's ideas for teaching minority communities how to work for their rights. In 1974 he returned to San Antonio and began putting IAF organizing ideas into practice. Supported by local Catholic Church officials, he created COPS by organizing Mexican Americans in local, parish-oriented groups. COPS achieved considerable local success. Cortés then moved on to East Los Angeles, where in 1975, he created a similar organization that he called the **United Neighborhoods Organization** (UNO). UNO proved less effective, although Cortés had a few successes.

In 1987 Cortés was appointed supervisor of all IAF-affiliated organizations in Texas. As southwestern regional director for the Industrial Areas Foundation, he oversees two dozen associated organizations, most of which he founded. In the mid-1980s over half of the IAF-inspired groups in the United States resulted from his founding efforts. At the century's end he was still working on a renewed effort to organize communities in southern California.

Cortês sees his work primarily as an educational job. He has been the recipient of numerous honors. In 1990 he was a MacArthur Foundation fellow ("a genius grantee"), and in January 1998 he received a $250,000 Heinz Award for leadership in public policy. That same year he was the Martin Luther King visiting professor at the Massachusetts Institute of Technology.

FURTHER READING: Cortés, Ernesto Jr. "Changing the Locus of Political Decision Making." *Christianity and Crisis* 47:1 (2 February 1987) 18–22; Northcott, Kaye. "To Agitate the Dispossessed." *Southern Exposure* 13:4 (July–August 1985) 16–23; Rogers, Mary Beth. *Cold Anger: A Story of Faith and Power Politics.* Denton: University of North Texas Press, 1990.

CORTEZ, GREGORIO LIRA, 1875–1916. Folk hero. Gregorio Cortez was born in the north Mexican state of Tamaulipas, but crossed over the Rio Grande at age twelve when his family settled northeast of Austin, Texas. As an unmarried young man he followed the itinerant life of ranch hand and farm worker for more than a decade; after his marriage he settled down on a rented farm southeast of San Antonio.

In June 1901 Karnes County sheriff W. T. Morris, in a typical ethnic profiling move, undertook to arrest Gregorio and his brother Romaldo for horse-stealing. Morris spoke little Spanish and Gregorio spoke little English. An incompetent job of interpreting caused a major misunderstanding. Gregorio protested his innocence, and an altercation ensued in which Morris wounded Romaldo but missed Gregorio. Gregorio fired back, wounding and killing the sheriff in the exchange of fire. Knowing what he might expect in the way of justice from a vigilante posse, he fled northward, where he hoped to lose his pursuers. Meanwhile his family, including the children, were held in jail.

As the result of encountering a large posse, Gregorio decided to reverse directions and head for the Mexican border. Now mounted, for more than four hundred miles he managed to elude the various posses that were chasing him. Almost in sight of the Rio Grande, he was betrayed by an acquaintance and captured by the **Texas Rangers**. After joining his family in jail he underwent a series of trials that lasted four years. His defense was financed by many Mexicanos, who undoubtedly saw him as a proxy in their struggle for justice. Eventually he was acquitted of two murder charges but convicted of a third and given a life sentence.

Cortez was a model prisoner and aroused a great deal of support from Anglos and Mexicanos who over the years supported appeals for his release. After serving eight years in Huntsville Penitentiary he received a conditional pardon, although the parole board had recommended a full pardon. Upon his release from prison in 1913 he traveled throughout Texas thanking his many supporters, and then crossed the Rio Grande to fight against the 1910 revolutionaries. Wounded in a battle, he recrossed into Texas to recuperate. As a result of his long trial he became the object of much female attention. While celebrating his fourth wedding in 1916, he apparently suffered a fatal heart attack or stroke.

FURTHER READING: Castillo, Pedro, and Albert Camarillo, eds. *Furia y muerte: Los bandidos chicanos.* Los Angeles: Chicano Studies Center, University of California, 1973; Paredes, Américo. *"With His Pistol in Hand!" A Border Ballad and Its Hero.* Austin: University of Texas Press, 1958, 1971; Tyler, Ron, ed. *The New Handbook of Texas,* vol. 2. Austin: Texas State Historical Association, 1996; Webb, Walter P. *The Texas Rangers.* Austin: University of Texas Press, 1965.

CORTINA, JUAN NEPOMUCENO, 1824–1894. Bandit-revolutionary, rancher, Mexican governor. "Cheno" Cortina was born in Camargo on the south side of the **Rio Grande** into a family that owned land on both sides of the river. As a young man he fought against the United States in the U.S.-Mexican War. After becoming a U.S. national in 1848 by the Treaty of **Guadalupe Hidalgo**, Cortina gradually became aware of the declining position of **Tejanos**. As their land grant rights were attacked and they lost their lands, he saw their political and civil rights also being endangered and disregarded. To protect them he suggested the creation of a buffer republic between Mexico and the United States, to be controlled by Tejanos. His move to direct action in order to secure protection for Tejanos aroused the concern of officials on both sides of the border.

As the result of an incident in 1859 Cheno became the de facto leader of a growing opposition to the routine ignoring of Mexicano rights in the border region. In September he led a raid on Brownsville, issued a declaration of grievances, and proclaimed a buffer Republic of the Rio Grande. The episode marked the beginning of Cortina's activities as a border revolutionary-reformer-bandit. From a family rancho in Cameron County, Texas he issued a statement outlining his goals and affirming his determination to defend the rights of all Tejanos. His outspoken and aggressive leadership for Mexicano rights attracted a large following even after he moved across the

A portrait of Juan Nepomuceno Cortina, taken from a sketch made in 1864. © Library of Congress.

Rio Grande to Matamoros, Tamaulipas. His active efforts to better the condition of Mexicanos were misperceived by some Texans as an attempt at reconquest by Mexico.

After the Civil War, in which his sympathies lay with the North, he helped the Mexican Liberal Party leader, Benito Juárez, expel the occupying French forces from Mexico. He rose to the rank of general in the Liberal army and was named acting governor of Tamaulipas by President Juárez. His subsequent petition to be allowed to return to his Texas ranch holdings was rejected by the Texas state legislature.

In 1875, several years after Juárez's death, Cortina was charged with cattle rustling and jailed without trial by Mexican authorities, who feared his leadership in the continuing border separatist movement. He was ultimately paroled but not allowed to leave Mexico City. When he died in 1894, his earlier career as a defender of Tejano rights was long forgotten and his last wish, to be buried in Texas, was denied. In many ways his life mirrored the turbulent conditions of the Southwest border in the second half of the 1800s.

FURTHER READING: Canales, José T., ed. *Juan N. Cortina Presents His Motion for a New Trial.* San Antonio: Artes Gráficas, 1951; Cortina, Juan N. "The Death of Martyrs." In *Aztlán: An Anthology of Mexican American Literature,* edited by Luis Valdez and Stan Steiner. New York: Alfred A. Knopf, 1972; Goldfinch, Charles W. *Juan Cortina, 1824–1892: A Reappraisal.* Brownsville, Texas: Bishop's Print Shop, 1950; Heintzelman, Samuel P. *Fifty Miles and a Fight: Major Samuel Peter Heintzelman's Journal of Texas and the Cortina War,* edited by Jerry Thompson. Austin: Texas State Historical Association, 1998; Larralde, Carlos, and José Rodolfo Jacobo. *Juan N. Cortina and the Struggle for Justice in Texas.* Dubuque, Iowa: Kendall/Hunt, 2000; Thompson, Jerry D. *Juan Cortina and the Texas-Mexico Frontier, 1859–1877.* El Paso: Texas Western Press, 1994.

COTERA, MARTHA P., 1938– . Activist, educator. Born in Mexico, Martha Cotera immigrated to Texas, where she received her education at today's University of Texas at El Paso; she then attended Antioch College in Ohio. After college she worked as a university librarian, first at El Paso and then at Austin. In 1964 she was named director of documents in the Texas State

Library. Moved to action by the discrimination she encountered in Austin, she became deeply involved in the Chicano Movement. In 1969 Cotera and her husband helped organize the high school protest walkouts in Crystal City, Texas. After Crystal City she became a hardworking activist in **La Raza Unida Party** (LRUP), moved into a leadership position, and in 1972 ran unsuccessfully for the State Board of Education as the LRUP candidate.

Cotera has been quite active as an educator. In 1970 she was one of the founders of Jacinto Treviño College (which later became Juárez-Lincoln University) in Austin and taught there for five years. Three years later she helped establish the Texas Women's Political Caucus and in 1974 founded the Chicana Research and Learning Center in Austin. Then she organized a publishing company named Information Systems Development. In 1980 she was a cofounder of Mexican American Business and Professional Women, another effort to politicize Chicanas, also in Austin. For the past several decades she has organized training sessions and conducted workshops to inform Mexican Americans of their rights and to call Chicanas' attention to existing gender inequities. Currently she continues to be active in voter registration drives and political campaigns and has taught courses in Mexican American history at Austin Community College.

Martha Cotera is the author of numerous works, most having to do with education and women's rights. She has received a number of prestigious awards.

FURTHER READING: Cotera, Martha P. *Diosa y hembra: The History and Heritage of Chicanas in the U.S.* Austin: Information Systems Development, 1976; Cotera, Martha P. *Las Mujeres: Mexican American / Chicana Women.* Windsor, Calif.: National Women's History Project, 1991; Telgen, Diane and Jim Kamp, eds. *Notable Hispanic American Women.* Detroit: Gale Research, 1993.

COTTON STRIKE, SAN JOAQUIN, 1933. The San Joaquin cotton strike of 1933 was the largest and best organized farm workers' strike of the early 1930s. Led by **Cannery and Agricultural Workers Industrial Union** organizers, cotton pickers walked out of the fields at Cocoran, California, at the beginning of the harvest in early October, demanding higher wages than the offered sixty cents per hundred pounds. The walkout quickly spread over most of the San Joaquin valley and soon encompassed between twelve and eighteen thousand pickers. The strikers, mostly Mexicanos, faced the daunting task of picketing several thousand fields in an area covering over a hundred miles. The growers' refusal to accept mediation and their resort to vigilantism led to the killing of two strikers and wounding of others at Pixley when the union hall there was riddled by rifle fire.

In the increasingly tense situation, California governor James Rolf called out the National Guard and at the same time appointed a fact-finding commission. The commission condemned the growers' use of violence against the strikers and recommended a compromise wage increase. Both sides reluctantly accepted the compromise. By the end of October most strikers had returned to work, but bad feelings between the workers and growers lingered.

FURTHER READING: Chacón, Ramón D. "Labor Unrest and Industrialized Agriculture in California: The Case of the 1933 San Joaquin Valley Cotton Strike." *Social Science Quarterly* 65:2 (June 1984) 336–353; Weber, Devra. *Dark Sweat, White Gold: California Farm Workers, Cotton, and the New Deal.* Berkeley: University of California Press, 1994.

COUNCIL OF MEXICAN AMERICAN AFFAIRS. The CMAA was an early effort to create a Mexican Americans umbrella organization for community groups. It was established in Los Angeles in 1953 with over forty member organizations, and developed conferences on various community concerns including education and employment opportunities. However, efforts to coordinate the activities of the various groups dwindled because of insufficient finances. Also, the middle-class orientation of the CMAA's leadership made it difficult to attract sufficient community support from working-class Chicanos.

In 1963 the CMAA was reorganized. The new leaders had ideas for helping the community that were even less acceptable to most community organization members. The leaders saw themselves as an elitist political and social pressure group working for all Mexican Americans, a concept that ran counter to widely held grassroots community attitudes.

FURTHER READING: Gómez-Quiñones, Juan. *Chicano Politics: Reality and Promise, 1940–1990.* Albuquerque: University of New Mexico Press, 1990; Tirado, Miguel David. "Mexican American Community Political Organization." In *La Causa Política,* edited by F. Chris García. Notre Dame, Ind.: University of Notre Dame Press, 1974.

COURT OF PRIVATE LAND CLAIMS, 1891–1904. Established by the fifty-second U.S. Congress in early 1891, the Court of Private Land Claims was created to address the problem of determining the validity of Spanish and Mexican land grant titles in New Mexico, Colorado, and Arizona. Because of the urgent need to end ambiguity in land ownership, Congress established a court of five judges to adjudicate the validity of about three hundred claims to some thirty-five million acres. The court's verdicts were appealable only directly to the U.S. Supreme Court.

Loss of documents and lack of other records caused many claimants to be unable to establish their rights in about two-thirds of the claims filed. There was also a problem of greatly inflated claims. The court ruled that claims to more than thirty-two million acres were invalid.

FURTHER READING: Bradfute, Richard W. *The Court of Private Land Claims: The Adjudication of Spanish and Mexican Land Titles, 1891–1904.* Albuquerque: University of New Mexico Press, 1975; Briggs, Charles L., and John R. Van Ness, eds. *Land, Water, and Culture: New Perspectives on Hispanic Land Grants.* Albuquerque: University of New Mexico Press, 1987; Ebright, Malcolm. *Land Grants and Lawsuits in Northern New Mexico.* Albuquerque: University of New Mexico Press, 1994.

COURTS. The Mexican American experience with U.S. courts and the American system of justice began with the 1848 Treaty of **Guadalupe Hidalgo**. Despite treaty guarantees of their civil and property rights, they soon found themselves generally deprived of both. Many lost part or all of their lands and because of their ethnicity they found themselves excluded from juries and even denied the right to give testimony in court.

Mexican Americans quickly discovered that the courts belonged to the Anglos. They saw the **Land Act of 1851** and the 1891 **Court of Private Land Claims** as Anglo devices to use the courts to take their lands. Also, courts and juries often applied rules of justice more stringently to Mexicanos, usually victimizing them in the process. Because the courts gave them little hope for receiving justice, they were made little use of in the nineteenth century by most Mexican Americans except Nuevomexicanos.

In the twentieth century the rise of the Mexican American generation and of their organizations with civil rights goals led to more widespread use of the courts. Chicano leaders realized that the courts could be used as an alternative or addition to confrontation tactics in order to obtain and defend raza rights. The establishment of the **California Rural Legal Assistance** in 1966 and the **Mexican American Legal Defense and Educational Fund** two years later resulted from this viewpoint. Court victories in various cases of segregation, especially in the schools, confirmed the helpfulness of the legal approach to achieving civil rights. Although more conservative in their rulings in recent years, the courts continue to be useful in helping Chicanos achieve full citizen rights.

FURTHER READING: Cortner, Richard. *The Supreme Court and Civil Liberties Policy.* Palo Alto, Calif.: Mayfield Publishing Co., 1975; *The Mexican-American and the Law.* New York, Arno Press, 1974; *The Mexican American Experience: An Interdisciplinary Anthology*, edited by Rodolfo O. de la Garza et al. Austin: University of Texas Press, 1985; Mirandé, Alfredo. *Gringo Justice.* Notre Dame: University of Notre Dame Press, 1987; Morales, Armando. "Justice and the Mexican American." *El Grito* 1:4 (Summer 1968) 42–48.

COYOTE. *Coyote* is the term used to designate a professional smuggler who specializes in bringing **undocumented** Mexicans across the border into the United States. It also sometimes refers to a **labor contractor** who sells strikebreakers.

CRUSADE FOR JUSTICE. In 1966 **Corky Gonzales** founded the Crusade for Justice in Denver, Colorado, basically as a civil rights organization. It grew out of Los Voluntarios, an organization created by Gonzales to scrutinize police activities and demonstrate against law enforcement brutality in the apprehension and detention of Chicanos. Los Voluntarios led directly to the development of the Crusade for Justice.

Appealing strongly to young Chicanos, the Crusade soon attracted a large following, particularly in the greater Denver area. In 1968 the Crusade acquired a former church property that became El Centro de la Cruzada para la Justicia and was used to provide social services and cultural programs. In the following year, after passionate student demonstrations in Denver for better and more meaningful education, the Crusade sponsored the national Chicano Youth Liberation Conference. The Denver conference produced the **Plan Espiritual de Aztlán**, an important exposition of cultural nationalism that aimed at uniting the various Chicano youth groups that had arisen in the Southwest from California to Texas.

The Crusade for Justice played a major role in the Chicano Movement for a decade. After the mid-1970s its activities declined considerably, even in Colorado, where it still retained some importance.

FURTHER READING: Larralde, Carlos. *Mexican American: Movements and Leaders.* Los Alamitos, Calif.: Hwong, 1976; Vigil, Ernesto B. *The Crusade for Justice: Chicano Militancy and the Government War on Dissent.* Madison: University of Wisconsin Press, 1999.

CRYSTAL CITY, TEXAS. Crystal City first made newspaper headlines in 1963 when Mexican Americans elected their slate of councilmen, thereby abruptly ending decades of complete Anglo political and economic control. However, widespread intimidation from the city's powerful Anglo minority checked Chicano efforts to do away with local discrimination and to advance civil rights. The elected Mexican Americans immediately found themselves without jobs, and two years later Anglos were able to regain political control of the town.

A second overturn of the city's rulers in 1969 grew out of ethnic discrimination in the town's high school and led to broad educational changes and to organization of **La Raza Unida Party** (LRUP) by José Angel Gutiérrez, a native of Crystal. Chicanos now gained control of the school system and city government and introduced innovative programs in both. These efforts were denigrated as communist-inspired by Texas governor Dolph Briscoe, and an exodus of businesses and finance resulted. After a decade, Mexican American political control ended because of well financed Anglo political and economic opposition, fratricidal Chicano rivalries, and the severe decline of LRUP.

Early on, Crystal City became an icon of the Chicano **movimiento** in Texas principally because of its organization and able leadership; the revolt ultimately failed because of factionalism and lack of economic power, as well as adamant Anglo opposition.

FURTHER READING: Gutiérrez, José Angel. *The Making of a Chicano Militant: Lessons from Cristal.* Madison: University of Wisconsin Press, 1998. Hirsch, Herbert, and Armando Gutiérrez. *Learning to Be Militant: Ethnic Identity and the Development of Political Militance in the Chicano Community.* San Francisco: R & E Research Associates, 1977; Navarro, Armando. *The Cristal Experiment: A Chicano Struggle for Community Control.* Madison: University of Wisconsin Press, 1998; Shockley, John S. *Chicano Revolt in a Texas Town.* Notre Dame, Ind.: University of Notre Dame Press, 1974.

CUAUHTÉMOC, 1502–1525. Cuauhtémoc was the last ruler of the Aztec people. In 1521 he succeeded Cuitláhuac, who had taken over after the death of Moctezuma a year earlier. He led the Aztecs in the final defense of their capital Tenochtitlán and was captured by the Spaniards. His resistance to torture by the Spaniards, who tried to force him to reveal the location of Aztec treasure, and his later execution by Hernán Cortés made him a Mexican folk hero. Many youthful Chicanos in the **movimiento** adopted Cuauhtémoc, along with **Emiliano Zapata**, as a symbol of their resistance to oppression.

CUENTO. A folktale, an important aspect of Mexican popular culture. The *cuento* often illustrates standards of social conduct or imparts bits of folk wisdom. It may contain elements of the preternatural.

CULTURE CLASH. Although currently two of its three members are Salvadorean Americans, the comedy team Culture Clash considers itself a Chicano group. When the group made its 1984 debut in San Francisco at a Cinco de Mayo variety night, there were six performing members. Originally calling themselves Comedy Fiesta, in 1990 the performers, now down to three, quit their day jobs and took their broad humor to Los Angeles, seeking a larger audience in its extensive Latino population. "The Mission," which they put on there, was an outstanding success and brought them to the attention of Cheech Marín and ultimately to Fox TV and a sitcom that died aborning. A second TV show, called "Culture Clash," over which they had greater artistic control, was more successful but was canceled after thirty episodes because of insufficient syndication.

Culture Clash has been characterized as commedia dell'arte, part Marx brothers, part Cantinflas, and part Chaplin—a heady and irreverent mix of comedy and political ideology. Specializing in comedic ethnic sketches, it mocks stereotypes to expose shallow thinking and ridiculousness. In its 1992 Miami, Florida, debut Culture Clash moved from the Chicano to the Latino, and beyond, in its topics. One of the results was a commission to do a piece about the city. They came up with "Radio Mambo," which won an Obie award. The striking success in Miami led to "Culture Clash in Bordertown," presented at the San Diego Repertory Theater in 1998, and then to a take on New York City, "Nuyorican Stories" in the following year. In 2002 the group had further expanded its horizons to "Culture Clash in AmeriCCa," described as a response to the jingoism following the September 11 terrorist attack.

Culture Clash has performed in comedy nightclubs, colleges, universities, and many prestigious venues including the Lincoln Center, the Kennedy Center, and the Mark Taper Forum in Los Angeles. The group members have also appeared in films both as individuals and as Culture Clash. Their first book, a collection of their sketches titled *Culture Clash: Life, Death, and*

Revolutionary Comedy, is in its second printing. In 1998 they published a second collection of their skits titled *Radio Mambo.*

FURTHER READING: "Crossing Over?" *Frontera,* 7 (1998) 18–19, 37; Monaghan, Constance. "Mambo Combo." *American Theater* 15:3 (March 1998) 10–13; Rousuck, J. Wynn. "Starting a Revolution with Humor." *The Baltimore Sun* (12 December 1999) F8.

CURANDERISMO. A folk healing system that uses herbs, diet, massage, and religious rituals to treat physical, emotional, and psychological illnesses. *Curanderismo* usually considers the patient to be a passive victim of outside forces, sometimes ones of malicious preternatural origins. With the increasing acknowledgment of the value of alternative medicine, *curanderismo,* as practiced in the community, has modified its techniques to expand the use of psychological and psychiatric tools.

FURTHER READING: Garza, Mary Jane. "Healing Spirits: The Growing Acceptance of Alternative Medicine Enhances the Popularity of Curanderismo." *Hispanic* (June 1998) 30, 32, 34, 36, 38; Trotter, Robert T., and Juan Antonio Chavira. *Curanderismo: Mexican American Folk Healing,* 2nd ed. Athens: University of Georgia Press, 1997.

CURSILLO DE CRISTIANDAD MOVEMENT. The Cursillo movement, originally a Spanish Catholic religious concept, came to the Southwest via Mexico after World War II. It stresses individual self-reform and personal responsibility and emphasizes involvement in the community. As a result of these ideas it has also developed social action activities and provided leadership training, especially for isolated rural Mexican Americans. In parts of the Southwest it has played a valuable role in alleviating some community problems.

FURTHER READING: Marcoux, Marcene. *Cursillo: Anatomy of a Movement, the Experience of Spiritual Renewal.* New York: Lambeth Press, 1982; Rodríguez, Edmundo. "The Hispanic Community and Church Movements: Schools of Leadership." In *Hispanic Catholic Culture in the U.S.: Issues and Concerns,* edited by Jay P. Dolan and Allan Figueroa Deck. Notre Dame, Ind.: University of Notre Dame Press, 1994.

CUTTING, BRONSON, 1888–1935. Senator, journalist. Bronson Cutting was born in New York, was educated at Groton and Harvard, and moved to New Mexico because of his health. There he became active in journalism and politics and gradually acquired a reputation as a champion of the Nuevomexicanos. After service in World War I he returned to Santa Fe, journalism, and Republican politics. In 1927 the governor appointed him to fill a vacancy in the U.S. Senate, where he served until his death in a 1935 airplane crash. A liberal Republican of great charisma and an admirer of Hispanic culture, in Congress he spoke out vigorously for the poor and for progressive government. By his opposition to ethnic discrimination and racism he helped Nuevomexicanos retain political power in New Mexico.

FURTHER READING: Gonzales, Phillip B. "El Jefe: Bronson Cutting and the Politics of Hispanic Interests in New Mexico, 1920–1935." *Aztlán* 25:2 (2000) 67–108; Lowitt, Richard. *Bronson M. Cutting: Progressive Politician.* Albuquerque: University of New Mexico Press, 1992.

D

DE LA GARZA, KIKA (ELIGIO), 1927– . Legislator, lawyer. Born and educated in Hidalgo County, Texas, Kika de la Garza decided early on he wanted to become a lawyer. He volunteered in the navy during the latter days of World War II and served for two years as an artillery officer in the army during the Korean conflict. After a law degree in 1952 from St. Mary's University in San Antonio, he started his legal practice and a career in Texas Democratic politics, winning a seat in the state's lower house, in which he served without particular distinction from 1953 to 1965. In 1964 he won election to the U.S. House of Representatives where, as a conservative southern Democrat representing an impoverished rural district, his main concern was legislation agriculture. He was also interested in making available greater educational opportunities for all children. Winning consecutive terms, often unopposed, until his retirement in 1996, he was the first Mexican American to chair a standing House committee, the Agriculture Committee.

Although a longtime member of the **League of United Latin American Citizens** and an active participant in the 1976 founding of the **Congressional Hispanic Caucus,** de la Garza upset many of his Mexican American constituents by his notable lack of enthusiasm for civil rights issues. He often spoke out critically against the militant leadership in the Chicano Movement. Despite a rather lackluster career except for his chairmanship of the House Agriculture Committee, in 1978 he was honored by Mexico with the Aguila Azteca award. In 1996 he retired after thirty-two years in the House, and headed home for McAllen, Texas to practice law.

FURTHER READING: Ehrenhalt, Alan, ed. *Politics in America.* Washington, D.C.: Congressional Quarterly, 1983; Ralph Nader Congress Project. *Eligio de la Garza, Democratic Representative from Texas.* Washington, D.C.: Grossman Publishers, 1972; "Representative de la Garza of Texas to Quit." *New York Times* (19 December 1995) B11; "Hispanic Journal: De La Garza Reflects on Long Career." *Hispanic* (December 1996) 16.

DE LA HOYA, OSCAR, 1973– . Oscar de la Hoya was born in East Los Angeles and grew up there in a family with a boxing history and tradition. Both his father and grandfather had fought in the ring. However, as a youngster he preferred baseball in the park and skateboarding near home. Pushed by his father and older brother to learn to defend himself, he started going to the Eastside Boxing Gym, and began training and fighting. He quickly discovered that he had a powerful left hand that augured well for a career in the ring. One of the top amateur boxers in the late 1980s and early 1990s, he won 223 of his 228 fights, 163 of them by knockouts. In 1990 he won a gold medal in the Goodwill Games.

At nineteen de la Hoya won a gold medal in the Summer Olympics at Barcelona. He then turned professional and soon became a four-time world champion boxer. He won his first thirty-one fights, capturing the junior lightweight title in 1994, the lightweight title later in the year, the super lightweight title in 1996, and the welterweight title in 1997. However, eight fights later he lost his welterweight title in 1999 to Félix Trinidad in a twelve-round decision bout. After two further ring defeats he decided to take time off and reexamine his professional life. Inspired by his mother, who was a professional singer, he essayed a singing career. His album *Oscar*, released in 2000, was a resounding success and a single from it was nominated for a Grammy. However, after a layoff of less than a year he returned to boxing and soon won the super welterweight title by defeating the reigning champion, Spaniard Javier Castillejo. In December he announced his entrance into the boxing promotion business by the formation of Golden Boy Promotions, of which he is the owner-president. Over the years de la Hoya has earned over $125 million in the ring, plus millions more in merchandise endorsements.

De la Hoya has not forgotten his roots. He has donated millions to support programs in the East Los Angeles Mexican American community through the Oscar de la Hoya Foundation. He also contributes liberally to other causes.

FURTHER READING: Price, S. L. "He Says He's a Gladiator . . ." *Sports Illustrated* (19 June 2000) 80+; "Oscar de la Hoya." *Playboy* (June 2002) 125, 150–151; Springer, Steve. "Promoters Looking for Gold." *Los Angeles Times* (24 November 2001) D5.

DE LEÓN, NEPHTALÍ, 1945– . Activist, poet, playwright. Nephtalí de León was born in Laredo and grew up and was educated in Lubbock, Texas. At the beginning of the Chicano **movimiento** he was a psychology student at Texas Tech University. After a period in the U.S. Army and travel in the United States and Mexico he returned to Lubbock, where he founded a bilingual weekly called *La Voz de los Llanos* that he edited until 1973.

De Léon's first published work was a volume of militant essays titled *Chicanos: Our Background and Our Pride*, 1972. In the following year his two children's books, *I Color My Garden* and *I Will Catch the Sun*, were published. Both were adopted by the State Board of Education in California and by other states. During the 1970s he published a number of varied poetic works: his book-length *Chicano Poet*, 1972, included the long poem "Coca Cola

Dream," published separately in 1973; *Hey, Mr. President Man*, 1975, was a bitter denunciation of President Gerald Ford and the U.S. government.

In 1979 De Léon moved to San Antonio, where he continued writing his poetry and plays. The death of his ten-year-old daughter in 1985 from leukemia desolated him and deeply affected his literary output. He has turned more to painting, poetry readings, and lecturing. The recipient of several prestigious awards, he has had his poems published in various magazines and literary anthologies.

FURTHER READING: Lomelí, Francisco A., and Carl R. Shirley, eds. *Chicano Writers: First Series*. Detroit: Gale Research, 1989; Garza, Sabino C. "Nephtalí de León." *La Luz* 6:12 (December 1977) 15–19; Martínez, Julio A. *Chicano Scholars and Writers: A Bio-Bibliographical Dictionary*. Metuchen, N.J.: Scarecrow Press, 1979.

DE LEÓN DE VEGA, SONIA MARIE, 1960s?– . Musician, conductor. The daughter of a Tejano show business couple, Sonia Marie de León was born in San Antonio, Texas, and grew up in Los Angeles in a family musical atmosphere created by her guitarist father. She studied music at California State University in Los Angeles and then earned a graduate degree in conducting in 1984. Two years later she was well enough known as a conductor to receive an invitation to conduct before Pope John Paul II, the first woman to conduct at the Vatican. From 1986 to 1992 she was guest conductor for various opera companies and orchestras in the United States, Europe, and Latin America.

In 1993 De León de Vega established the Santa Cecilia Orchestra in Los Angeles with two goals: to bring classical music to the city's large Latino population and to train young musicians. As the orchestra's director, every year she produces and directs "Opera under the Stars," in part to give high visibility to talented young operatic vocalists about to launch their careers. She also organized an outreach program called Discovering Music in order to introduce classical music, and especially its Spanish roots, to inner-city Latino children.

With the support of various businesses and public agencies, De León de Vega has developed concerts and children's musical workshops for the city of Los Angeles. Committed to bringing opera to the Latino community, she has offered concerts through Santa Cecilia's "Neighborhood Concert Series." Her performances have been televised in Europe and Latin America as well as in the United States. In October 2000 she was given Outstanding Latina Woman of the Year awards by Univisión TV, Target stores, and Mervyns.

FURTHER READING: "Executive Director/Conductor Santa Cecelia Orchestra." *Hispanic Business* (October 2001) 56; Terry-Azíos, Diana A. "A Classical Act." *Hispanic* (May 2001) 78–79; Trino, Pedro. "Sonia Marie de León de Vega Conducts the Santa Cecilia Orchestra." *Latin Style* 40 (August/September 2001) 12.

DELANO GRAPE STRIKE, 1965–1970. For half a decade, from 1965 to 1970, the Delano grape strike dominated the California agricultural scene.

In 1965, on 16 September, Mexican independence day, **César Chávez** led his newly organized union, the National Farm Workers Association, into what was to be a five-year struggle with grape growers for the right of workers to organize and to have the union recognized as their bargaining agent. The strikers also demanded a wage increase. Following a strict policy of nonviolence, the Delano strikers squared off against giant companies like Schenley Industries and the **Di Giorgio Corporation**. Despite various provocations, including grower and police harassment and the importation of green card workers, the strike endured. Through Chávez's dedicated leadership the strike was converted into a moral crusade that sought and obtained support from numerous labor, civil rights, and religious groups. Chávez's involving state and national politicians, labor leaders, and churchmen gave the movement wide newspaper publicity, as did the nationwide **boycott** of table grapes after 1967.

The intrusion into the strike of the Teamsters Union, favored by most of the grape growers, caused Chávez to take his small union into the AFL-CIO as the **United Farm Workers** Organizing Committee. By the end of 1967 most wine-grape growers had agreed to accept field elections to determine union representation. However, table-grape growers held out until mid-1970 when the last of the growers, led by John Giumarra, Sr., signed three-year contracts with the union. When the contracts expired, most were not renewed. Although in some ways the strike was only a temporary success, it had a nationwide impact by bringing the miserable conditions of harvest farm workers sharply to the consciousness of the American public.

FURTHER READING: Dunne, John Gregory. *Delano.* New York: Farrar, Straus & Giroux, 1971; Mark Day. *Forty Acres: César Chávez and the Farm Workers.* New York: Praeger, 1971; Ferris, Susan, and Ricardo Sandoval. *The Fight in the Fields: César Chávez and the Farmworkers Movement.* New York: Harcourt Brace, 1997; Griswold del Castillo, Richard, and Richard A. García. *César Chávez: A Triumph of Spirit.* Norman: University of Oklahoma Press, 1995; Levy, Jacques E. *César Chávez: Autobiography of La Causa.* New York: W. W. Norton, 1975.

DELGADO ET AL. v. BASTROP INDEPENDENT SCHOOL DISTRICT ET AL.,

1948. This class action suit was filed by the **League of United Latin American Citizens** (LULAC) on behalf of Minerva Delgado and other parents. Alleging violations of their children's civil rights, the plaintiffs argued that the arbitrary **segregation** of Mexicano students in separate schools was discriminatory and violated the Fourteenth Amendment to the U.S. Constitution. They pointed out that the Texas state attorney general had already declared the practice illegal.

Agreeing that the school district's practices violated the Fourteenth Amendment and were arbitrary and discriminatory, Judge Ben H. Rice, Jr. held for the plaintiffs after they dropped a request for damages. Although Judge Rice's June 1948 decision did allow for the possible separation in the first grade only, of non-English-speaking children, he stipulated that their classrooms could not be on a separate campus. His decree was followed in the same month by an antisegregation policy statement from the state superintendent of public instruction and a later confirmation of this policy by the Texas State Board of Education. Nevertheless, school districts used various evasive schemes to postpone desegregation. Mexican American advocacy groups continued the fight for compliance for the next decade.

FURTHER READING: Allsup, Carl. "Education Is Our Freedom: The American G.I. Forum and the Mexican American School Segregation in Texas, 1948–1957." *Aztlán* 8 (1977) 27–50; Sánchez, George I. *Concerning Segregation of Spanish-Speaking Children in the Public Schools.* Austin: University of Texas, 1951; San Miguel, Guadalupe Jr. *"Let All of Them Take Heed": Mexican Americans and the Campaign for Educational Equality in Texas, 1910–1981.* Austin: University of Texas Press, 1987.

DI GIORGIO CORPORATION. One of the largest fruit growers in the United States, the Di Giorgio Corporation also had interests in a number of associated businesses. It became deeply involved in two strikes by its mostly Mexicano workers. From 1947 to 1950 it successfully resisted a strike by the **National Farm Labor Union** at its Arvin, California, farms. A strike by César Chávez's National Farm Workers Association (NFWA) and the Filipino Agricultural Workers Organizing Committee (AWOC) against Di Giorgio in the mid-1960s led to Di Giorgio bringing in the competing Teamsters union, which in turn caused Chávez to convert the NFWA and the AWOC into the **United Farm Workers** Organizing Committee (UFWOC) of the AFL-CIO. In 1967 the UFWOC won the union elections that were held and Di Giorgio signed a contract with the union.

FURTHER READING: Ferriss, Susan, and Ricardo Sandoval. *The Fight in the Fields: César Chávez and the Farmworkers Movement.* New York: Harcourt Brace, 1997.

DIEZ Y SEIS DE SEPTIEMBRE. The date of the Grito de Dolores by which, according to tradition, Father Miguel Hidalgo y Costilla set off the Mexican movement for independence from Spain in 1810. It has been celebrated by Mexican Americans since the late 1800s and is generally considered second in importance to **Cinco de Mayo**.

DISCRIMINATION. Discrimination against Mexican Americans has been a cancer in southwestern society since the mid-1800s. Based on skin color, ethnic culture, and the low economic status assigned to Mexicanos by American society, discrimination has resulted in the denial of rights in **education**, employment, **housing**, and politics. Segregated schools for Mexican American children continued until long after **World War II.**

Mexican American veterans returning from World War II found that their fight against Axis tyranny had not won them equality of treatment in their own country. The **Longoria** case in Texas in 1948 was only the most notorious of many denials of their rights as Americans—in this instance, even beyond this life. Many Texas town cemeteries still maintained a segregated section for persons of Mexican ancestry.

Chicano family migration to the cities in the postwar years disrupted existing societal patterns and aggravated segregationist attitudes by increasing Anglo angst. As a result, Chicanos began creating **organizations** to protect themselves and fight for their rights. Their organizing efforts were hindered by the large number of postwar Mexican immigrants and sojourners who generally had limited involvement in the struggle. Restrictive housing covenants and low incomes helped keep Mexican Americans in the **barrio**. Today many still find it difficult to obtain the better, higher-paying jobs; decision-making managerial positions often remain beyond their reach. The economic progress they have made has been blurred by the continuing heavy influx of immigrants with low levels of job skills and education.

The increased size of the Mexican American middle class and the accompanying growth of the Latino consumer market have served to moderate Anglo attitudes. Today Anglo discrimination against Mexican Americans tends to be covert rather than overt, de facto rather than de jure. Much of it is historical and institutional and therefore difficult to eradicate. Discrimination by other Latinos is usually based on economic class or country of origin. In the past several decades the long fight to end discrimination has made considerable progress, but there are lingering effects of historical discrimination. Complete elimination is yet to be achieved.

FURTHER READING: Acuña, Rodolfo. *Occupied America: A History of Chicanos.* 3rd ed. New York: Harper & Row, 1988; McWilliams, Carey. *North From Mexico: The Spanish-Speaking People of the United States*, rev. ed. Westport, Conn.: Praeger Publishers, 1990; Rodríguez, Roberto. *Justice: A Question of Race.* Tempe, Arizona: Bilingual Press, 1997; Rosales, F. Arturo, ed. *Testimonio: A Documentary History of the Mexican American Struggle for Civil Rights.* Houston: Arte Público Press, 2000.

DOMINGO, PLÁCIDO, 1941– . Operatic tenor, conductor, administrator. Although born in Madrid, Spain, Plácido Domingo spent his formative years and was educated in Mexico. He studied music under various well-known faculty members at the National Conservatory in Mexico City. In 1961 he made his operatic debut in Monterrey, Nuevo León, and later that year appeared with the Dallas Civic Opera. Since 1965 Domingo's operatic career has been based in the United States. From his early success at the New York City Opera he moved to the Metropolitan Opera, where he sang his four hundredth performance in 1996.

In the mid-1980s Domingo began a career in conducting at the Metropolitan and Los Angeles Music Center and followed that with another new role as administrator. In 1994 he assumed the post of artistic director of the Washington, D.C., opera and six years later was named artistic director of the Los Angeles opera. A workaholic of boundless energy, in the mid-1990s he also embarked on a series of triumphant world tours with fellow

Plácido Domingo waves to the crowd in Wembley Stadium during an encore of the Three Tenors concert, 1996. © AP/Wide World Photos.

tenors Luciano Pavarotti and José Carreras. He was the founder, in 1993, of Operalia, an international vocal competition.

FURTHER READING: Domingo, Plácido. *My First Forty Years.* New York: Alfred Knopf, 1983; Gunther, Louise T. "Conquistador." *Opera News* 60:13 (16 March 1996) 8–11, 47; Schauber, Cornelius. *Plácido Domingo.* Boston: Northeastern University Press, 1997; Snowman, Daniel. *The World of Plácido Domingo.* New York: McGraw-Hill, 1985; Sunier, John. "Plácido Domingo, Grandissimo." *American Record Guide* 56:2 (March–April 1993) 204.

EAST LOS ANGELES COMMUNITY UNION, THE. TELACU came out of the Lyndon Johnson administration's "Great Society" program. Originally conceived in 1968 and backed with a $60,000 Ford Foundation grant, it was organized to create community economic development in order to provide jobs and create financial support for social programs. Concerned with housing and other economic goals, its crowning achievement is TELACU Industrial Park, begun in the 1970s, and today the location of companies employing over two thousand people. It has a for-profit subsidiary, TELACU Industries, that provides funds for a wide variety of activities including student tutoring, counseling, and other educational support. It has assets of over $350 million.

In 1982 TELACU officials were charged with the misuse or embezzlement of $47 million in federal funds. Ultimately the widely publicized charges led only to TELACU being ordered to repay a $1 million agricultural grant the federal court judge considered misused.

FURTHER READING: Chávez, John R. *Eastside Landmark: A History of the East Los Angeles Community Union, 1968–1993.* Stanford, Calif.: Stanford University Press, 1998; Guernica, Antonio J. "TELACU: Community Change Through Economic Power." *Agenda* 7:6 (November–December 1977) 14–16; "TELACU: America's Leading Model in Massive Community Economic Development." *La Luz* 9:3 (March 1981) 7–9; "TELACU's Strategy: Community Capitalism." *Hispanic Business* (June 2000) 36. www.telacu.com

ECONOMIC OPPORTUNITY ACT, 1964. The Economic Opportunity Act of 1964, a part of President Lyndon Johnson's War on Poverty program, created a Job Corps, an agency named Volunteers in Service to America (VISTA), and a community action program. These three programs aimed at a sort of Peace Corps approach to urban problems.

FURTHER READING: Brecher, Charles. *The Impact of Federal Antipoverty Policies.* New York: Praeger, 1973; Jackson, Alice M., et al. "Constituency and the War on Poverty." *Journal of Public Affairs and Issues* 1 (Fall 1998) 41–65.

EDUCATION. Mexican Americans almost unanimously believe that education holds promise of a way out of poverty and is therefore among their most

A Mexican school, ca. 1935. Courtesy of the Benson Latin American Collection, University of Texas at Austin.

important rights as citizens. Early in the 1900s they began the fight against the "separate Mexican school" policy generally in effect throughout the Southwest. Despite their long struggle to end **discrimination** in school systems, de facto **segregation** began to be terminated only after **World War II**. Even then, language difficulties and ethnically biased testing procedures caused some Chicano students to continue to be placed in classes for the mentally retarded. Low levels of education and skills have retarded the improvement of their economic condition.

During the 1960s and 1970s the Chicano Movement stepped up the struggle to reshape the American educational system in order to provide a better and more meaningful school experience for Chicano children. Some progress has been achieved. The Civil Rights Act of 1964 ultimately initiated widespread desegregation in school districts, and the 1974 decision by the U.S. Supreme Court in *Lau v. Nichols* marked a giant step in the **bilingual education** movement throughout the United States. Programs like Upward Bound have helped to reduce the educational problems of Mexican Americans, as has the sensitizing of teachers to stereotyping conduct.

Since World War II Mexican American educational issues have increasingly become a leading concern of civic **organizations** like the **American G.I. Forum**, the **Mexican American Legal Defense and Educational Fund**, and the **League of United Latin American Citizens**. Working through these and other groups, Chicanos have sought and obtained redress of many grievances concerning the education of their children.

Between 1984 and 1995 Latino college enrollment doubled, but the original base was extremely low. By 1995 the percentage of high school graduates had crept up from about 50 percent to 58.6 percent, and the percentage of adult Latino immigrants with high school diplomas has doubled in the past quarter-century. Despite the gains made, a 1997 study indicated that today fewer California Chicano high school graduates are eligible to enter college than a few years ago. Less than 12 percent of California Latino high school graduates are able to qualify to enroll in the state universities and under 4 percent qualify for admission to the University of California system.

The predicament of migrant workers' children continues to be particularly bleak. Typically they are two grades or more behind their age groups and have little hope of ever catching up. They are hampered by a variety of impediments: language, single-parent families, poor health, lack of mentors, poverty, and all that poverty implicates. The excessive dropout rate among Latino students remains a crying shame in a society that sees education as a basic civil right as well as the best route to upward mobility. Nevertheless, there has been a strong movement to deny free public education to the children of **undocumented** workers.

At a symposium in Los Angeles in December 1997 **Antonia Hernández,** president of the Mexican American Legal Defense and Educational Fund, was quoted as saying "To me, the most important civil right for Latinos, bar none, is education." In the June 1998 election Californians voted overwhelmingly for **Proposition 227**, which aimed at terminating bilingual education programs.

FURTHER READING: Carter, Thomas P., and Roberto Segura. *Mexican Americans in the Public Schools: A History of Neglect.* Princeton, N.J.: College Entrance Examination Board, 1979; *Education and the Mexican American.* Reprint. New York: Arno Press, 1974; García, Juan R., ed. *Community, Identity and Education.* Vol. 3, Perspectives in Mexican American Studies. Tucson: University of Arizona, Mexican American Studies & Research Center, 1992; Getz, Lynne Marie. *Schools of Their Own: The Education of Hispanos in New Mexico, 1850–1940.* Albuquerque: University of New Mexico Press, 1992; Moreno, José F., ed. *The Elusive Quest for Equality: 150 Years of Chicano / Chicana Education.* Cambridge, Mass.: Harvard Educational Review, 1999; Romo, Harriet D., and Toni Falbro. *Latino High School Graduation: Defying the Odds.* Austin: University of Texas Press, 1995; Valencia, Richard R., ed. *Chicano School Failure and Success: Past, Present, and Future.* London: Routledge/Falmer Press, 2002; Valenzuela, Angela. *Subtractive Schooling: U.S.-Mexican Youth and the Politics of Caring.* Albany: State University of New York Press, 1999.

EL CLAMOR PÚBLICO. *El Clamor Público,* Los Angeles's first Spanish-language newspaper, was published from 1855 to 1859 by Francisco Ramírez. It voiced complaints of mistreatment and discrimination against Latinos in southern California. Ramírez's editorials reflected Californio disappointment with the Anglo version of equal justice for all. At one point he urged Californios to cross the border into Sonora in a **repatriation** movement.

FURTHER READING: Acuña, Rodolfo. *Occupied America: A History of Chicanos.* 3rd ed. New York: Harper & Row, 1988; Rodríguez, América. *Making Latino News: Race, Language, Class.* Thousand Oaks, Calif.: Sage, 1999.

EL GRITO: A JOURNAL OF CONTEMPORARY MEXICAN AMERICAN THOUGHT. *El Grito* was one of the earliest and most important journals of the Chicano literary renaissance in the 1960s. Founded in 1967 by **Octavio Romano** and Nick Vaca, until its end in 1974 it provided an outlet for young Chicano writers who encountered difficulties in getting acceptance of their work in mainstream publications. It fostered the renaissance, awarding prizes for outstanding works by Chicano writers like **Rudolfo Anaya**, **Rolando Hinojosa-Smith**, and **Tomás Rivera**.

FURTHER READING: Ybarra-Frausto, Tomás. "The Chicano Movement and the Emergence of a Chicano Poetic Consciousness." In *New Directions in Chicano Research*, edited by Ricardo Romo and Raymund Paredes. Santa Barbara: Center for Chicano Studies, University of California, 1984.

EL GRITO DEL NORTE. *El Grito* was a newspaper established in Española, New Mexico, by Chicano activists of the **Alianza Federal de Pueblos Libres.** In 1968 **Betita (Elizabeth) Martínez** joined **Reies López Tijerina**'s Alianza and undertook to develop a journalistic voice in the fight for lost pueblo lands. To this end she helped create and then edited a bilingual newspaper, *El Grito del Norte.* Under her editorship *El Grito* became an important voice for the rural Hispanic poor of northwestern New Mexico.

FURTHER READING: *Las Mujeres: Mexican American/Chicana Women.* Windsor, Calif.: National Women's History Project, 1991; Ybarra-Frausto, Tomás. "The Chicano Movement and the Emergence of a Chicano Poetic Consciousness." In *New Directions in Chicano Research*, edited by Ricardo Romo and Raymund Paredes. Santa Barbara: Center for Chicano Studies, University of California, 1984.

EL MEXICANO PREPARADO, LISTO, EDUCADO Y ORGANIZADO. EMPLEO, the acronym for this organization, is Spanish for *employment.* The organization was begun by Chicano inmates of San Quentin prison in 1966 to prepare prisoners for successful employment and reentry into society upon release. Its objective was to foster discipline, self-esteem, and pride in ethnic identity.

FURTHER READING: Espinosa, Rudy. "Mi casa es su casa." *El Grito* 3:2 (Winter 1970) 19–27.

EL MONTE BERRY STRIKE, 1933. The strike was called in May 1933 because wages in the strawberry fields at El Monte, on the outskirts of Los Angeles, dipped below ten cents an hour. During the weeks-long strike, leaders used the training gained in the earlier **Confederación de Uniones Obreras Mexicanas** as the basis for their **Confederación de Uniones de Campesinos y Obreros Mexicanos**, which ultimately won a wage increase to $1.50 for a nine-hour day.

FURTHER READING: Hoffman, Abraham. "The El Monte Berry Pickers Strike, 1933: International Involvement in a Local Labor Dispute." *Journal of the West* 12:1 (1973) 71–84; López, Ronald W. "The El Monte Berry Strike of 1933." *Aztlán* 1:1 (Spring 1970) 101–104.

EL PASO, TEXAS. El Paso primarily owes its origins, as its name indicates, to a suitable ford across the **Rio Grande.** The original settlement, on the south bank of the river, was recognized as a key location by early Spanish explorers of Mexico's northern frontier, who began referring to it as *el paso del norte* in the late sixteenth century. By the mid-1800s it was a flourishing trade and irrigated agricultural center with some four to five thousand inhabitants, a few of whom were spilling over to the north bank of the river.

At the time of the Treaty of **Guadalupe Hidalgo**, which ended the **U.S.-Mexican War** in 1848, the north shore, which became today's El Paso, had a population of about three hundred. In the following year the California gold rush gave the north bank settlement a new population growth spurt. In the second half of the 1800s ranching, agriculture, and commerce continued to flourish. Anglos, with eastern capital and mercantile connections, soon came to dominate the trade with Mexico that passed through the town. The advent of transcontinental **railroads** at the beginning of the 1880s marked a further step in El Paso's growth as an important transportation crossroads having both east-west and north-south traffic patterns. Its location on the border and the railroad network also contributed to its becoming a major southwestern labor reservoir.

The railroads brought many more Anglos, temporarily ending the Mexicano majority and causing a further decline in their economic and social position. By the end of the century new infusions of capital from the U.S. east coast had made it the center for processing, smelting, and refining ores from the surrounding mineral-rich areas, activities heavily dependent on Mexicano labor. As El Paso became further integrated into the national economy, it became increasingly important for agriculture and light industry as well as **mining** and trade.

At the beginning of the twentieth century El Paso had become the leading urban center on the U.S.-Mexican border with a population of nearly forty thousand. By 1925 the population had doubled, and Mexicanos again became the majority ethnic group. The 1910 **Mexican revolution**, which persisted for over a decade, caused much of this significant increase in El Paso's population, as Mexican emigrés crossed the river to avoid revolutionary chaos and violence. Many of the refugees belonged to the middle and upper classes and brought capital and skills as well as changes to the Mexican American community with their leadership. The Mexican-descent population found itself regaining some of its previously lost political power and social influence.

Historically, El Paso, like the entire Southwest, has encouraged the immigration of Mexicans to provide cheap labor and has sent them back in difficult economic times. At the onset of the post–World War I recession in the early 1920s and again during the 1930s **Great Depression**, thousands of Mexican workers found it expedient to leave El Paso. The outbreak of **World War II** in 1939 again created a demand for their labor, and back they came in even greater numbers. After World War II a new generation of native-born Mexican American El Pasoans began to push more energetically for their civil rights. As a result, they have been elected and appointed to numerous positions in city government, including the office of mayor. While progress has been made, Chicanos continue to strive for greater political and economic representation and for participation proportionate to their numbers in the city's population.

Throughout the 1900s Mexicanos have remained in a majority in El Paso, usually hovering about the two-thirds mark. In the 1950s, largely as the result of a downtrend in the border economy, there was an exodus from El Paso to interior cities of the Southwest, the Midwest, and **California**. However, the emigrants were quickly replaced by Mexican **immigration** from across the river and by easterners. In 1960 El Paso had a population of 276,000 and twenty years later had 425,000. In the 1990s El Paso's population increased at double the annual national rate of 1.3 percent; at the century's end it approached 680,000, of whom over 530,000 were Hispanics.

El Paso's population remains one of the poorest and most undereducated in the United States; 20 percent of its citizens have only an eighth-grade education. Some 43 percent are under 25 years of age. With a populace that is 78 percent Latino today (of whom about two-thirds are Mexicano), up from 70 percent in 1990, it remains a bilingual and bicultural frontier.

FURTHER READING: *El Paso, A Centennial Portrait*. El Paso: El Paso County Historical Society, 1973; García, Mario T. *Desert Immigrants: The Mexicans of El Paso, 1880–1920*. New Haven: Yale University Press, 1981; Martínez, Oscar J. *The Chicanos of El Paso*. El Paso: University of Texas Press, 1980; Sonnichsen, Charles L. *Pass of the North: Four Centuries on the Rio Grande*. El Paso: Texas Western Press, 1968, 1980; Timmons, W. H. *El Paso: A Borderlands History*. El Paso: Texas Western Press, 1990; Vila, Pablo. *Crossing Borders, Reinforcing Borders: Social Categories, Metaphors, and Narrative Identities on the U.S.-Mexico Frontier*. Austin: University of Texas Press, 2000.

EL PASO INCIDENT, 1948. In a struggle over wages for the cotton harvest, American immigration officials opened the border at **El Paso** to Mexican workers in mid-October 1948. In spite of Mexican officials' efforts to deter them, in five days some six to seven thousand **undocumented**s entered the United States, where they were loaded onto growers' trucks and taken to the cotton fields. The Mexican government, various Mexican American organizations, and U.S. labor unions protested this unilateral action as a violation of a February 1948 U.S.- Mexican agreement on workers.

The U.S. government issued a statement of regret, but the cotton was picked at the wage rate set by the growers.

FURTHER READING: Martínez, Oscar J. *Border Boom Town: Ciudad Juárez Since 1848.* Austin: University of Texas Press, 1978.

ELIZONDO, VIRGILIO P., 1935– . Priest, activist, writer. Nearly a grade school dropout because of language difficulties, Virgilio Elizondo, son of Mexican immigrant parents, was turned around by a caring teacher. He went on to complete high school and college and to become a Catholic priest. As a result of the 1960s liberation theology movement he became convinced that social justice should be an integral part of the Gospel message. Strongly supported by Archbishop **Robert Lucey,** in 1972 he established the **Mexican American Cultural Center** in San Antonio as a community-centered agency to sensitize, train, and develop social activist nuns, clergy, and laypersons to work with Mexican Americans. He remained director and guiding spirit of the center until 1983 when he was named rector of San Antonio's cathedral.

Elizondo is the author of numerous articles and nine books, primarily concerned with Chicanos and the Church; he has often spoken out in defense of Mexicano folk Catholicism. During the 1970s he was active in **Padres Asociados para Derechos Religiosos, Educativos, y Sociales**, the *raza* priests' association. More recently he has concentrated on the study of *mestizaje* and the Virgin of **Guadalupe**, a central theme in Mexican Catholicism.

FURTHER READING: Martínez, Julio A. *Chicano Scholars and Writers: A Bio-Bibliographic Directory.* Metuchen, N.J.: Scarecrow Press, 1979; Maeroff, Gene I., ed. *Sources of Inspiration: 15 Modern Religious Leaders.* Kansas City: Sheed & Ward, 1992; Matovina, Timothy, ed. *Beyond Borders: Writings of Virgilio Elizondo and Friends.* Maryknoll, N.Y.: Orbis, 2000; Zapa, Patricia. "His Roots Are in San Antonio, But His World Is the Globe." *Migration World Magazine* 24:5 (1996) 43–44.

EMIGRANT AGENCY LAW, 1929. The Emigrant Agency law was one of a series of **Texas** laws passed by the state legislature in the 1920s at the behest of Texas growers to curtail the outflow of Mexicano labor. Texas farmers were angered by out-of-state growers, mostly sugar beet companies, luring away local workers with higher wages. The law required labor recruiters in Texas to pay a license fee and a large occupational tax, and to post a sizable bond. The legislation seems to have had little impact on restraining the movement of Mexicano workers to more remunerative work outside of Texas and the Southwest.

FURTHER READING: Coalson, George O. *The Development of the Migratory Farm Labor System in Texas, 1900–1954.* San Francisco: R & E Research Associates, 1977; Reisler, Mark. *By the Sweat of Their Brow: Mexican Immigrant Labor in the United States, 1900–1940.* Westport, Conn.: Greenwood Press, 1976.

ENGANCHADOR. The Mexicano term for a **labor contractor,** also known as an *enganchista* or *contratista.* The *enganchador,* usually a Mexicano, provided workers for U.S. agriculture and other industries. He was often an independent operator, but might work for growers' associations, the **railroads,** or other employers of unskilled labor. He might provide workers for a flat head fee and in agriculture might also supervise their harvest work. The *enganchador* often had a reputation for sharp dealing and cheating workers. Today labor contracting is regulated by law and licensing.

ENGLISH ONLY MOVEMENT. The English Only movement arose in the late 1970s to protect American society from what its advocates viewed as a threat from heavy immigration, principally Mexican. Through California senator S. I. Hayakawa, a well-known specialist in linguistics, the group was able to get legislation introduced into the U.S. Congress to make English the official language of the United States. The movement found little support in the U.S. Congress, but at state and local levels it was more successful as the result of a rising tide of xenophobia. By the 1990s half the states, and even some municipalities, had passed resolutions or legislation designating English as their sole official language.

Early in January 1999 the U.S. Supreme Court refused to review an Arizona English Only law, which the state Supreme Court had struck down by unanimous vote. After an emotional debate that same month, the Utah legislature for the fourth time turned down English Only legislation. While English Only laws have had very little noticeable effect, the possibility exists that such nativist legislation could mandate the use of English in a number of citizen-government interactions such as court cases and driver-testing, as well as in printed information and forms.

In the early 1980s a well-financed Washington-based lobbying organization named **U.S. English** was founded with Hayakawa as its honorary chairman. English Only and U.S. English people have ties to anti-immigration groups, advocate a written English-proficiency test for **citizenship,** and oppose **bilingual education** programs. The real heart of their shrill "defense" of English seems to be opposition to Mexican immigration and to the use of Spanish. To counter English Only, Mexican American activists formed the English-Plus Information Clearinghouse, which supports mastery of English along with retention of Spanish.

FURTHER READING: Adams, Karen L., and David T. Brink, eds. *Perspectives on Official English: The Campaign for English as the Official Language of the USA.* New York: Mouton de Gruyler, 1990; Baron, Dennis. *The English-Only Question: An Official Language for Americans?.* New Haven: Yale University Press, 1990; Lang, Paul. *The English Language Debate: One Nation, One Language?.* Springfield, N.J.: Enslow Publishers, 1995; Piatt, Bill. *Only English? Law and Language Policy in the United States.* Albuquerque: University of New Mexico Press, 1990; Tatalovich, Raymond. *Nativism Reborn? The Official English Language Movement and the American States.* Lexington: University Press of Kentucky, 1995.

EQUAL EDUCATIONAL OPPORTUNITY ACT, 1974. Public Law 93-380, named the Equal Educational Opportunity Act, was passed by the U.S. Congress in 1974. It created an Office of Bilingual Education within the U.S. Office of Education and provided financial assistance for bilingual programs.

It amended the Elementary and Secondary Education Act of 1965 and expanded existing **bilingual education** programs.

FURTHER READING: Avila, Joaquín G. "Equal Education Opportunities for Language Minority Children" (Symposium: Educational Equality Thirty Years After *Brown v. Board of Education*). *University of Colorado Law Review* 55:4 (Summer 1984) 559–569; Haft, Jonathan D. "Assuring Equal Education Opportunity for Language Minority Children: Bilingual Education and the Equal Educational Opportunity Act of 1974." *Columbia Journal of Law and Social Problems* 18:2 (1983) 209–293; "Public Law 93-380: Educational Amendments of 1974." *Congressional Information Service Annual,* Part 1. Washington, D.C.: Congressional Information Service, 1975.

EQUAL EMPLOYMENT OPPORTUNITY COMMISSION. The EEOC was created by the Civil Rights Act of 1964 as an independent agency within the executive branch of the government. Its purpose was to end **discrimination** in the workplace. While not completely successful in reaching this goal, it has served to reduce discrimination in business.

FURTHER READING: Gonzales, Claire. *The Empty Promise: The EEOC and Hispanics.* Washington, D.C.: National Council of La Raza, 1993; Pycior, Julie Leininger. *LBJ & Mexican Americans: The Paradox of Power.* Austin: University of Texas Press, 1997.

ESCOBAR, ELEUTERIO, JR., 1894–1970. Educational activist, organizer. Familiar at firsthand with the dire conditions of Mexicanos in south **Texas** at the beginning of the twentieth century, Eleuterio Escobar early came to the conclusion that education was a key to improving life for *la raza*. After service in World War I he returned to San Antonio, where he soon became an important officer in the **Knights of America** and later in the **League of United Latin American Citizens** (LULAC). Early in the 1930s he, **Alonso Perales,** and others began organizing Mexican Americans for greater participation in Texas electoral politics. The short-lived Association of Independent Voters, of which he was a founder and first president, set the stage for further Mexican American political activity.

Distressed by the gross inferiority of educational facilities for Mexican American children in San Antonio, Escobar, heading a LULAC committee, vainly tried to move the school board to make improvements. Eased out of his committee chairmanship, he was quickly offered the presidency of a new umbrella organization, the Liga Pro-Defensa Escolar, which at its peak spoke for some seventy community groups. Under Escobar's leadership, in the late 1930s the Liga succeeded in obtaining the upgrading and enlarging of westside (Mexican American) educational facilities. With the advent of World War II the Liga's school campaign languished.

In 1947 Escobar was elected president of a revitalized Liga that demanded an end to the still dangerously substandard westside school facilities. As a result of his leadership a majority of the Liga's incisive recommendations were adopted and carried out. Although Escobar was unable to achieve fully his goals for educational equality, he did force the school board to take action and at the same time demonstrated to the community what could be achieved by organized militancy. In 1958 Escobar was honored for his leadership by having his name given to a new high school.

FURTHER READING: Eleuterio Escobar Papers, 1906–1971. Benson Latin American Collection, General Libraries, University of Texas at Austin; García, Mario T. *Mexican Americans: Leadership, Ideology, and Identity, 1930–1960*. New Haven: Yale University Press, 1989.

ESCOVEDO, PETE(R), 1935– . Musician. Pete Escovedo was inevitably drawn into Latino **music** by his father, who sang with local Mexican bands in the Sacramento, California delta region. Pete began to play the drums with various musical groups in the Bay Area and in the late 1960s began to receive recognition nationally as a drummer in Carlos Santana's band. In 1970 Pete and his brother Coke organized a small band they named AZTECA. A subsequent contract with Columbia Records resulted in two albums of the group's music. In 1972 and 1973 the band, expanded to twenty-four members, toured the United States with Stevie Wonder. Its size made it increasingly difficult to support, and finally it broke up.

After the mid-1970s Escovedo played Bay Area club gigs with his daughter Sheila and made two successful albums for Fantasy Records. In 1977 he rejoined Santana's band to do tours and records. He continues to perform in the Bay Area, often with his daughter. In addition to being a percussionist of note, he also is a highly regarded local painter.

FURTHER READING: Holston, Mark. "All in the Family." *Hispanic* (June 2003) 60-63; Romero, Pedro S. "Pete Escovedo: A Study in Versatility," *Nuestro* (December 1982) 63–64; *Who's Who among Hispanic Americans, 1994–1995*. Detroit: Gale Research, 1994.

ESPARZA, CARLOS, 1828–1885. Rancher, poet, activist. Carlos Esparza was a border rancher like **Juan N. Cortina**, whom he supported in the struggle to maintain Tejano rights after the Treaty of **Guadalupe Hidalgo**. A believer in a separate Territory of the **Rio Grande,** he acted as a spy for Cortina and helped provide him with funds and military supplies. He was also a poet and literary figure.

Hopeful of the promise of a democratic society, after the Civil War Esparza made an unsuccessful effort to defend the lands and rights of Mexicanos in the Texas political arena. His defeat there made him a cynic about politics; in the last decade of his life political despair replaced his earlier idealism. He ultimately came to believe that education was the only way to improve the lot of *la raza*, while recognizing that it was available to few border Mexicanos.

FURTHER READING: Larralde, Carlos. *Carlos Esparza: A Chicano Chronicle*. San Francisco, Calif.: R & E Research Associates, 1977; Larralde, Carlos. "Josiah Turner, Juan Cortina and Carlos Esparza." *Mexican War Journal* 5:1 (Fall 1995) 5–14.

ESPARZA, MOCTEZUMA, 1949–. Film producer. Born in 1949, Moctezuma Esparza grew up in the Boyle Heights neighborhood of Los Angeles. Although at first classified as a slow learner, he went on to achieve status as an honor student and student organization leader in high school. At sixteen, attendance at a Mexican American Youth Leadership Conference in Los Angeles marked the beginning of his youthful activism. He protested for the civil rights of Chicano students and against the war in Vietnam. In college he was one of the founders of the **United Mexican American Students**, a cofounder of the **Brown Berets,** and one of the organizers of the Young Citizens for Community Action. He was also one of the dozen Chicanos indicted by the grand jury for criminal conspiracy in 1968 for his role in the high school **student walkouts**. The indictment was dropped three years later.

After high school Esparza enrolled in the University of California at Los Angeles where, following a longtime bent, he began to study for a career in films. He completed his B.A. in 1971 and earned his Master's in Fine Arts two years later; his thesis film, *Cinco Vidas*, won him an Emmy. Over the next two decades he produced or coproduced ten successful films; his first independent film, *Agueda Martínez: Our People, Our Country*, was nominated in 1978 for an Oscar in the documentary category. Six years later he formed a partnership with Richard Katz. In 2000, *Introducing Dorothy Dandridge*, a television movie he coproduced with Katz, received an Emmy nomination. Although no longer the only Chicano producer in Hollywood, Esparza was the first and is still the best-known.

FURTHER READING: Laezman, Rick. "Moctezuma Esparza." *Latino Leaders* (June–July 2001) 30–36.

ESPINOSA, AURELIO M., 1880–1958. Linguist, folklorist. Aurelio Espinosa was born and grew up in southern Colorado. Encouraged in his studies by his parents, he earned his B.A. and M.A. in Spanish from the University of Colorado and in 1909 completed his Ph.D. in philology at the University of Chicago. Meanwhile he taught Spanish at Chicago and the University of New Mexico; with his doctorate he accepted a position at Stanford University, where he taught for the rest of his life. He chaired the modern language department there from 1932 to 1953.

Espinosa was active in various professional societies and served as editor of several journals, including the *Journal of American Folklore* from 1914 to 1946. An academician of tremendous energy, he authored nearly two hundred scholarly articles, a dozen learned monographs, and thirty-some textbooks. For his great contributions to the Spanish language and **folklore** he received from Spain the Order of Isabel La Católica in 1922 and the Grand Cross of Alfonso El Sabio in 1950. In addition to these and other honors, he was admitted to a number of prestigious societies, including the Royal Spanish Academy.

FURTHER READING: Espinosa, J. Manuel. "Espinosa's New Mexican Background and Professional Career." In Espinosa, Aurelio M., *The Folklore of Spain in the American Southwest.* Norman: University of Oklahoma Press, 1985; McSpadden, George. "Aurelio M. Espinosa (1880–1958)." *Hispania* 42:1 (March 1959) 20–21.

FAIR EMPLOYMENT PRACTICES COMMITTEE, 1941. The FEPC was created in 1941 by a presidential order of Franklin D. Roosevelt to uncover and eliminate employment **discrimination** in companies having government contracts. University of Texas historian Dr. **Carlos Castañeda** was appointed regional director in the Southwest to monitor the concerns of Mexican Americans, particularly in the **mining industry**. The agency had some success in eliminating discrimination in employment and promotion, but was allowed to expire when Congress rejected President Harry Truman's recommendation that it be given permanent status. In 1964 Congress established the **Equal Employment Opportunity Commission** with essentially the same powers and goals as the FEPC.

FURTHER READING: Almaraz, Félix D., Jr. *Knight without Armor: Carlos Eduardo Castañeda, 1896–1958.* College Station: Texas A & M University Press, 1999; Daniel, Clete. *Chicano Workers and the Politics of Fairness: The FEPC in the Southwest, 1941–1945.* Austin: University of Texas Press, 1991.

FANTASY HERITAGE. Fantasy heritage describes the overly romantic and greatly sentimentalized picture of the American Southwest during the time of Spanish and Mexican control. To a considerable extent it was the result of a literary movement initiated by Helen Hunt Jackson's *Ramona*, a romantic novel published in 1884. *Ramona* told a story of the loss of **Californios'** lands to Anglo in-migrants and of the latter's mistreatment of California Indians and Mexicanos. It painted a picture of an earlier cultural Eden inhabited by beautiful señoritas and handsome dons who were Spanish rather than Mexican.

This sentimental fiction was nurtured by other Anglo writers like Charles F. Loomis and John Steven Groarty. It has led to the establishing of associations to recall and preserve the Hispanic heritage of the Southwest with fiesta parades, while ignoring the degree to which it was a Mexican rather than Spanish culture. Jackson's novel was important in helping create what **Carey McWilliams** later dubbed the "fantasy heritage" of the Hispanic Southwest in his book *North from Mexico*.

FURTHER READING: Jackson, Helen Hunt. *Ramona: A Story*. Madison, Wisc.: Turtleback Books, 1988, 1884; McWilliams, Carey. *North from Mexico: The Spanish-Speaking People of the United States.*, rev. ed. New York: Praeger, 1990; Monroy, Douglas. *Thrown Among Strangers: The Making of Mexican Culture in Frontier California.* Berkeley: University of California Press, 1990; Rodríguez, Joseph A. "Becoming Latinos: Mexican Americans, Chicanos, and the Spanish Myth in the Urban Southwest." *Western Historical Quarterly* 29:2 (1998) 165–185.

FARAH STRIKE, 1972–1974. In May 1972 over four thousand employees of the Farah Manufacturing Company, El Paso's second-largest employer, went on strike against unfair labor practices and for recognition of their union. Strike-breakers were brought in from Ciudad Juárez across the Rio Grande as well as locally. In June the strikers called for a national boycott of Farah clothes, thus converting a local dispute into a nationwide campaign. Supported by unions and local Catholic church leaders, particularly Bishop Sidney Metzger, the strikers held out until January 1974 when the National Labor Relations Board ordered Farah to allow union organizing. As a result Farah signed a contract favorable to the workers. However, for a variety of economic reasons, in subsequent contracts the union was unable to retain all its initial gains. The five plants employing nearly ten thousand workers dwindled to one factory and fewer than six hundred workers by 1992. All of the assembly work was transferred to overseas factories. The strike resulted in the politicizing of some of the female strikers, who continued their activism long after the strike ended.

FURTHER READING: Coyle, Laurie, Gail Hershatter, and Emily Honig. "Women at Farah: An Unfinished Story." In *Mexican Women in the United States: Struggles Past and Present*, edited by Magdalena Mora and Adelaida R. Del Castillo. Los Angeles: University of California, Chicano Studies Research Center, 1980; Honig, Emily. "Women at Farah Revisited: Political Mobilization and Its Aftermath among Chicana Workers in El Paso, Texas, 1972–1992." *Feminist Studies* 22:2 (1996) 425–452.

FARM LABOR ORGANIZING COMMITTEE. FLOC was created by **Baldemar Velásquez,** with the help of his father and a small circle of fellow farm workers. Developed in the late 1960s, it was envisioned as an agency to combat **discrimination**, poor working conditions, and the wretched standard of living endured by farm workers in the Midwest.

With deep convictions about social justice, FLOC has become a leading force in midwestern farm labor affairs over the years. The organization's leaders have consistently maintained a close association with harvest field workers and a high level of commitment to their welfare. One of FLOC's characteristics has been its reliance on outside groups—civic organizations, churches, and unions—to help it achieve its objectives. In turn, FLOC has publicly supported civil rights and labor groups like César Chávez's **United Farm Workers** union, with which it cooperated closely.

FURTHER READING: Barger, W. K. and Ernesto M. Reza. *The Farm Labor Movement in the Midwest.* Austin: University of Texas Press, 1994; Rosenbaum, René Pérez. "Unionization of Tomato Field Workers in Northwest Ohio, 1967–1969." *Labor History* 35:3 (1994) 329–344. www.floc.com

FEDERATION FOR AMERICAN IMMIGRATION REFORM. FAIR is a Washington, D.C.–based anti-immigrant organization that seems particularly concerned about immigration from Mexico. It states as its aim "to restore reasonable and moderate levels of immigration," and argues that today's entrants are permanent immigrants, unlike their nineteenth- century predecessors, who, it alleges, were merely sojourners. It was founded in the late 1970s by John Stanton, a Michigan ophthalmologist and lawyer, and today claims over fifty thousand dues-paying members. In 1980 FAIR filed suit in the courts to require the Census Bureau to make a separate count of **undocumented** aliens. The suit was rejected. In 1989 it still had a suit pending against the Bureau.

Many of Stanton's critics accuse him of **racism** and white supremacy ideas, pointing out FAIR's early connection with the Pioneer Fund, a racial purity organization, and Stanton's more recent anti-Latino and anti-Catholic statements. In the 2000 election FAIR spent $700,000 allegedly to defeat a proposed bill to increase the number of visas for foreigners with high-tech skills.

FURTHER READING: Barfield, Chet. "Immigration Perils U.S., Group Fears; Critics Charge Lobbyists Breed Fear, Racism." *The San Diego Union-Tribune* (3 March 1989) A-1; Blake, Andrew. "Sides Are Drawn in Fight over 'Official' Language." *The Boston Globe* (25 February 1990) Metro/Region, 26; Marks, Peter. "Special Interest Groups Widening Political Attack Ads." *The New York Times* (14 May 2000) Section 1:22.

FENDER, FREDDY, 1937– . Musician, guitarist. Born Baldemar Huerta in San Benito, Texas, he is much better known as Freddy Fender, a name he took in the late 1950s to become more acceptable to Anglo audiences. He worked as a migrant field hand in the 1950s and served in the Marines while still a teenager. After a tour in the Marines, he entered the music field in 1956. Since then he has had three musical careers: a singer of pop music in the late 1950s, a country/pop star in the 1970s, and a member of the Texas Tornadoes in the 1990s. In the first stage his high tenor helped establish him as a regional Hispanic pop star, known as El Bebop Kid.

Busted for pot in Baton Rouge in 1960, Fender served almost two and a half years in the Louisana state penitentiary before being paroled. His parole kept him in Louisiana and prevented him from playing in clubs where alcohol was sold. When his parole ended, he returned to music, working on Bourbon Street in New Orleans. In 1969 he returned to Texas, where he began the second phase of his musical career, playing music on weekends while he worked as a welder and mechanic during the week. Soon he was playing in the clubs.

Fender's singing rock and roll themes in Spanish was a first, and made him a country/pop star in a short time. In 1975 his bilingual rendition of "Before the Next Teardrop Falls," a plaintive country ballad, was selected by the Country Music Association as its Single of the Year and won him two other awards including "Artist of the Year." In the mid-1970s he had nine country hits in the Top 10, with four reaching number one. However, success and prosperity had their costs; for the next few years alcohol and cocaine, plus a three-pack-a-day cigarette habit and constant battle with diabetes, put a brake on his musical career. In the mid-1980s he finally kicked the drug habit and even gave up smoking, but found recording contracts eluding him because of the mistrust his past had engendered in the music business.

In the early 1990s, nearly a decade later, Fender joined the Texas Tornadoes, a move he saw as a way out of his impasse. It put him back on the pop music map while enabling him to avoid agents, managers, and record company executives. Prickly and bullheaded, he has always had trouble with the business side of music, which he considers filled with leeches and sharks. He has no manager; he and his wife handle the details of his contracts. Overall, his musical career has probably been held back by the lack of a manager to deal with the business side of music.

Texas's gift to popular music won Grammys in 1990 and 1999 for "Best Mexican/American Performance" and in February 1999, at age sixty-one, he had his name inscribed in the Hollywood Walk of Fame. His "Wasted Days and Wasted Nights," which he wrote in the late 1950s, remains his signature song.

FURTHER READING: Infantes, Victoria. "Estrella para Freddy Fender: Pionero de la música tejana inscribe su nombre en el Paseo de la Fama." *La Opinion* (5 February 1999) 2B; Morthland, John. "Wasted Days." *Texas Monthly* 23:10 (October 1995) 64.

FIERRO DE BRIGHT, JOSEFINA, 1920–1998. Political activist, labor organizer. Josefina Fierro came from a politically active Mexican family. During the 1910 Mexican revolutionary period her mother, a staunch supporter of the Mexican prerevolutionary socialist leader **Ricardo Flores Magón**, settled in a Los Angeles, California exile, and Josefina grew up there. While still a teenager, she married Hollywood screenwriter and Communist Party (CP) member John Bright and quickly became a part of Hollywood's 1930s leftist community.

As an eighteen-year-old student at the University of California in Los Angeles, Josefina helped **Luisa Moreno** found the reformist **Congreso de Los Pueblos de Habla Española**. She became secretary of the Congreso and remained its staunch supporter until its demise in the mid-1940s. During

World War II she was one of the leaders in organizing the **Sleepy Lagoon** Defense Committee. Although a leftist, she was probably never a CP member; not self-consciously feminist, she fought for equal rights for women.

As part of a serious political effort by the **Asociación Nacional México-Americana**, Fierro ran for Congress in 1951 but lost. During the McCarthyite red scare at mid-century she was accused of being a subversive and, as a result, voluntarily left the United States for Mexico in the 1950s.

FURTHER READING: García, Mario T. *Memories of Chicano History: The Life and Narrative of Bert Corona.* Berkeley: University of California Press, 1994; García, Mario T. *Mexican Americans: Leadership, Ideology, and Identity, 1930–1960.* New Haven: Yale University Press, 1989.

FLORES, PATRICK, 1929– . Archbishop, activist. The son of illiterate Texas sharecroppers, Patrick Fernández Flores had a sporadic education until he decided to become a priest. At age twenty he finally graduated from high school and seven years later was ordained. As a parish priest he became strongly influenced by the charismatic **Cursillo** movement among Mexican Americans in the Southwest, and soon became widely known in Texas as the *mariachi* pastor. Flores became deeply concerned about the needs of his impoverished Chicano parishioners for jobs, housing, and education. He strongly backed **César Chávez** and his **United Farm Workers**, supported the Chicano Movement, and helped found and gave continuing support to **Communities Organized for Public Service** in San Antonio.

Patrick Flores. © Matt Meier.

On Cinco de Mayo 1970, Patrick Flores became the first Mexican American and second U.S. Latino to be named a bishop in the Roman Catholic Church. As bishop of El Paso (1977) and then archbishop of San Antonio (1979), he continued to be deeply active in the temporal as well as the religious welfare of his flock. As bishop and archbishop he spoke out for *raza* rights and against the abuse of Mexicanos by local and federal agencies as well as by private businesses.

Flores was chairman of the Texas Advisory Committee to the U.S. Commission on Civil Rights and a founder and national chairman of **Padres Asociados para Derechos Religiosos, Educativos y Sociales**, the Mexican American priests' rights group. He has been especially concerned with better educational opportunities for Mexican American youths. Many of his reformist ideas and programs derive from his acquaintance with Saul Alinsky's Industrial Areas Foundation, of which he was a director. In late June 2000 he was held hostage for nine hours by an immigrant who feared deportation.

FURTHER READING: *American Catholic Who's Who, 1980–1981*, vol. 23. Washington, D.C.: N.C. News Service, 1980; Bacon, John, Guillermo X. García, and John Larrabee. "Archbishop Taken Hostage for 9 hours." *USA TODAY* (29 June 2000) News, 3A; Cook, Joy. "Bishop Patrick Flores: The Barrio Bishop." *La Luz* 1:4 (August 1972) 19–21; McMurtrey, Martin. *Mariachi Bishop: The Life Story of Patrick Flores.* San Antonio: Corona Publishing, 1985.

FLORES, TOM, 1937– . Football player, coach. Tom Flores was born in Fresno, California, the son of a refugee from Mexico's great revolution of 1910. He grew up the Great Central Valley and as a youth worked in migratory agriculture. At both Fresno City College and College (now University) of the Pacific he had an enviable record in football and was selected for several All-American teams. After coaching at Fresno High School for two years, he joined the Oakland Raiders in 1960 and in the next seven years made an outstanding reputation as quarterback. He then spent two seasons with the New York Buffalo Bulls, after which he finished out his career in football as a player with the Kansas City Chiefs.

In 1972 Flores was hired by the Raiders' coach, John Madden, as receivers coach. His seven years as assistant coach were eminently successful; the Raiders reached the play-offs six times and won one Super Bowl. When Madden retired in 1979, Flores was named head coach and led the Raiders to another Super Bowl victory. In 1982 he was named Coach of the Year and then led the team to yet another Super Bowl win. From 1989 to 1994 he worked for the Seattle Seahawks, first as general manager and then as head coach. In 1994 he and his staff were all fired.

FURTHER READING: Olmos, Frank del. "The Ice Man." *Nuestro* (October 1979) 18–19; Díaz, Katherine A. "And This Year's Winners Are . . ." *Caminos* 4: 1–2 (January–February 1983) 39–54; Smith, Craig. "Seahawks Fire Flores and his Entire Staff." *Seattle Times.* (29 December 1994).

FLORES MAGON, RICARDO, 1873–1922. Political leader. Ricardo Flores Magón, along with his brothers Enrique and Jesús, were early leaders in the liberal movement to oust lifetime president Porfirio Díaz of Mexico. Exiled from Mexico in 1904, Ricardo began publishing his anti-Díaz journal, *Regeneración,* in San Antonio, where he sought support from border Mexicanos in his early efforts to overthrow Díaz. However, the increasingly radical anarchism he preached there and later in Los Angeles reduced his popular appeal. His denunciations of nearly all the leaders of the 1910 revolution increasingly isolated him from the Mexican political struggle. Arrested in 1918 for violating U.S. neutrality laws and on other charges, he was sentenced to twenty years in prison, where he died four years later, apparently of a heart attack. In the 1960s he became one of the icons of the Chicano Movement.

FURTHER READING: Albro, Ward S. *Always a Rebel: Ricardo Flores Magón and the Mexican Revolution.* Fort Worth: Texas Christian University Press, 1992; Cockcroft, James D. *Intellectual Precursors of the Mexican Revolution, 1900–1913.* Austin: University of Texas Press, 1968; MacLachlan, Colin M. *Anarchism and the Mexican Revolution: The Political Trials of Ricardo Flores Magón in the United States.* Berkeley: University of California Press, 1991.

FOLKLORE. The popular beliefs, customs, proverbs, oral tales, legends, songs, superstitions, traditional arts, and medicine of a people, most of which express cultural attitudes, values, and aspirations. At the beginning of the twentieth century **Aurelio Espinosa** became the first scholar to study Mexican American folklore as a rigorous discipline. He emphasized its roots in Spain. His students and successors, like Professor **Arthur Campa,** greatly expanded the investigation of folklore in the Southwest, generally stressing its Mexican roots. Campa specialized in the folklore of the New Mexican region, particularly collecting folk songs during the 1930s. Two decades later **Américo Paredes** further advanced the study of Mexican American folklore beginning with the publication of his corrido study, *With His Pistol in His Hand,* in 1958. Paredes placed his emphasis on the fact that southwestern folklore had many indigenous roots. He also pointed out the value of folklore as a tool in recovering more fully the history of a people whose traditions were primarily oral. Today folklore continues to be seen as a valuable tool to understand the culture and history of Mexican Americans.

FURTHER READING: Castro, Rafaela G. *Dictionary of Chicano Folklore.* Santa Barbara, Calif.: ABC-CLIO, 2000; Espinosa, Aurelio M. *The Folklore of Spain in the American Southwest.* Norman: University of Oklahoma Press, 1985; Heisley, Michael. *An Annotated Bibliography of Chicano Folklore from the Southwestern United States.* Los Angeles: University of California, 1977; Leal, Luis. "Américo Paredes and Modern Mexican American Scholarship." *Ethnic Affairs* 1 (Fall 1987) 1–11; Paredes, Américo. *Folklore and Culture on the Texas-Mexican Border.* Austin: Center for Mexican American Studies, University of Texas at Austin, 1993; Sonnichsen, Philip H. "Arthur León Campa." *La Luz* 7:12 (December 1978) 20, 26.

FOREIGN MINERS LICENSE TAX LAW, 1850. The Foreign Miners License Law was passed by the California legislature in 1850; it imposed a twenty-dollar monthly fee on all noncitizen miners. Aimed principally at the Spanish-speaking, it included as foreigners the former Mexicans recently made U.S. nationals by the Treaty of **Guadalupe Hidalgo**. The legislation was clearly a violation of their rights as guaranteed by the Treaty of Guadalupe Hidalgo and the U.S. Constitution. Having largely achieved its objective of ousting the Spanish-speaking from the mines, it was replaced in the following year with a more limited law directed primarily at Chinese miners.

FURTHER READING: Hart, James D. *A Companion to California.* New York: Oxford University Press, 1978; Johnson, Susan Lee. *Roaring Camp: The Social World of the California Gold Rush.* New York: W. W. Norton, 2000; Patterson, Richard H. "Anti-American Nativism in California, 1848–1953: A Study of Cultural Conflict." *Southern California Quarterly* 62:4 (1980) 309–327.

FRÉMONT, JOHN CHARLES, 1813–1890. Soldier, politician. In the 1830s John Charles Frémont, a second lieutenant in the Topographical Corps of the U.S. army, married Jessie, the ambitious daughter of powerful Senator Thomas Hart Benton of Missouri. With his father-in-law's help, Frémont was appointed to lead expeditions to the Far West in the early 1840s; the widely publicized report of his second expedition brought him national recognition. On a third expedition, from 1845 to 1846, he led sixty armed men into California, defied the Mexican governor's order to leave, and later participated in the **Bear Flag revolt**. Named military governor of **California** after the American takeover, he refused to obey General Stephen Kearny, was court-martialed, and then received a presidential pardon.

Frémont resigned from the army and returned to California, where he had bought **Juan B. Alvarado**'s Mariposa grant. The discovery of a rich vein of gold on the grant in 1849 made Frémont a wealthy man. In the following year he became the new state's first senator, and in the 1856 election

An 1856 lithograph of John C. Frémont. © Library of Congress.

ran as the new Republican Party's first presidential candidate but failed to win. After the Civil War he lost Mariposa, unsuccessfully dabbled in western railroad promotion, and from 1878 to 1883 served as governor of the New Mexico Territory.

FURTHER READING: Frémont, John C. *Memoirs of My Life.* New York: Bedford, Clarke, 1887; Rolle, Andrew. *John Charles Frémont: Character as Destiny.* Norman: University of Oklahoma Press, 1991.

G

GABACHO. A Chicano term for an Anglo American, somewhat more pejorative than *gringo*. Also sometimes spelled *gavacho, con B/V chica.*

GADSDEN PURCHASE TREATY, 1853–1954. Railroad entrepreneur James Gadsden, the U.S. minister to Mexico, was instructed by President Franklin Pierce's Secretary of State to buy for a future transcontinental railway route as much of northern Mexico as its president, **Antonio López de Santa Anna,** would sell. Pressured by the threat of U.S. troops sent to the border "to preserve order," and politically weak, Santa Anna agreed to sell a twenty-nine-million-acre triangle of mineral-rich land in southern **Arizona** and **New Mexico** for ten million dollars. Despite some opposition, the treaty was ratified by the U.S. Congress in June 1854.

As a result of the Gadsden Purchase, some hundreds of Mexicans who had moved across the 1848 **Guadalupe Hidalgo Treaty** border in order to remain under Mexico were thrust back into the United States. The terms of the Gadsden Treaty were somewhat less protective of land claims and other property rights than was the Treaty of Guadalupe Hidalgo.

FURTHER READING: Davis, William C. "The Gadsden Purchase." *American History Illustrated* 4:2 (1969) 41–48; Garber, Paul N. *The Gadsden Treaty.* Philadelphia: University of Pennsylvania Press, 1923; Rippy, J. Fred. "The Boundary of New Mexico and the Gadsden Treaty." *Hispanic American Historical Review* 4 (November 1921) 715–742.

GALARZA, ERNESTO, 1905–1984. Labor organizer, author, teacher. Ernesto Galarza was born in the tiny mountain village of Jalcocotán in Mexico's west coast state of Nayarit. The family fled Mexico's Great Revolution of 1910 by crossing into the United States, finally settling in central California, where Galarza grew up. Excelling in school, he graduated from Occidental College and then completed an M.A. in history and political science at Stanford University. Ultimately he earned his doctorate from Columbia University in New York. After doing research work for the Foreign Policy Association and the Pan American Union (PAU) in Washington, D.C., he was promoted at the beginning of the 1940s to the directorship of the

PAU's new Division of Labor and Social Information. This appointment resulted in a lifelong focus on the rights of Latino workers, particularly in agriculture.

When his policy recommendations to the PAU were ignored, Galarza resigned to undertake the organizing of California agricultural workers. As first vice president of the **National Farm Labor Union** from 1947 to 1963, he spent the next dozen years working to unionize farm laborers, most of them Mexicanos. He then left the agricultural labor scene and during the next decade took on a variety of jobs related to urban workers. During this time he served on the board of the **Mexican American Legal Defense and Educational Fund** and also became involved in the developing Chicano Movement.

Widely recognized as a leading Mexican American intellectual, Galarza added education to his special interests, writing books about labor problems and teaching at Harvard, Notre Dame, and several California state universities. At the beginning of the 1970s he was involved in developing Spanish language teaching materials and **bilingual education** programs. In this connection he wrote a number of mini-books for children. In spite of his poor health during the last decade of his life, he continued to be a frequent and active participant in conferences and workshops devoted to workers and their rights.

Because of a lifetime devoted to fighting for the rights of workers, in 1979 Ernesto Galarza became the first Mexican American to be suggested for a Nobel prize.

FURTHER READING: Chabran, Richard. "Activism and Intellectual Struggle in the Life of Ernesto Galarza (1905–1984)." *Hispanic Journal of Behavioral Sciences* 7:2 (June 1985) 135–152; Galarza, Ernesto. *Barrio Boy.* Notre Dame: University of Notre Dame Press, 1971; Galarza, Ernesto. *Spiders in the House and Workers in the Field.* Notre Dame: University of Notre Dame Press, 1970; Guilbault, Rose del Castillo. "Scholar, Labor Leader, Poet, Hero." *San Francisco Chronicle: This World* (23 September 1990) 3–4; London, Joan, and Henry Anderson. "Man of Fire: Ernesto Galarza." In *Chicano: The Evolution of a People,* edited by Renato Rosaldo, Robert Calvert, and Gustav Seligmann. Minneapolis: Winston Press, 1973.

GALINDO, RUDY (VALENTÍN JOSEPH), 1970– . Skating champion. Rudy Galindo was born into a lower-middle-class family in an East San Jose, California, trailer park. As a result of accompanying his sister Laura to her ice-skating lessons, he became interested in the sport and soon became adept. By his thirteenth birthday he had become the national junior solo skating champion. Rudy partnered with Kristi Yamaguchi from 1986 to 1991, during which time the pair won various championships. In 1991 Kristi's decision to go solo plunged Rudy into a trough of dejection and self-doubt, augmented by the feeling that he was being discriminated against because he was openly gay. He was also depressed by the death of his father and elder brother. As a result, he did poorly on the ice, placing eighth in the 1995 U.S. championships.

In 1996, after a self-imposed eight months' absence from the skating scene, Galindo returned to the competition. In an outstanding display of virtuosity, he bested sixteen competitors to win the U.S. men's title and to become the first Latino U.S. ice-skating champion. Later that year he took third place in the World Figure Skating Championships at Edmonton, Canada.

Six months after Edmonton, Galindo turned professional and began touring. In the spring of 2000 he announced that he tested HIV positive. He continues touring with the group Champions on Ice.

FURTHER READING: Galindo, Rudy, with Eric Marcus. *Icebreaker: The Autobiography of Rudy Galindo.* New York: Pocket Books, 1997; Harvey, Randy. "Galindo Is Not Simply Skating Through Life." *Los Angeles Times* (14 May 2000) Sports, D1; Longman, Jere. "After Years of Struggle, the Veteran Galindo Lands an Upset for the Ages." *New York Times* (21 January 1996) S2(L); Martínez, Katynka Zazueta. "A Natural Talent." *El Andar* 6:9 (March 1996) 22–25.

GALLEGOS, HERMAN E., 1930– . Community organizer, entrepreneur. Herman Gallegos was born in the Colorado mining town of Aguilar and received his higher education in two California state colleges, from 1948 to 1952, and the University of California at Berkeley, from 1955 to 1958. After graduating from San Jose State College in 1952, he took employment with Santa Clara County while working with Saul Alinsky to organize a local **Community Service Organization** (CSO). From 1958 to 1960 he was national president of the CSO.

In the mid-1960s Gallegos became a consultant to the Ford Foundation and, with **Ernesto Galarza** and **Julian Samora**, helped it become involved in providing financial support for the Chicano civil rights movement. In 1968 with a Ford grant he helped establish the Southwest Council of La Raza (now the National Council) and became its first executive director. In the early 1970s he accepted a teaching appointment at San Jose State University, and subsequently began to turn his attention more to the private sector while continuing his social concerns for Mexican Americans.

Firmly committed to issues of justice and equity, Gallegos was a member of the California Fair Employment Practices Commission and later served on the boards of various philanthropic grant organizations, including the Rockefeller and Rosenberg foundations. He has been a trustee of the University of San Francisco and of the University of California at San Francisco. In the early 1970s he was one of the first Mexican Americans elected to serve on the board of directors of a private corporation. In addition, he was a founder and CEO of several business firms. In 1990 he established the first Latino-owned brokerage house in California, Gallegos Institutional Investors. He is also a private consultant but continues to be concerned with social issues, especially housing. While holding that government has a responsibility to protect citizen rights, he also strongly believes that the private sector can help *la raza* achieve its economic goals.

Gallegos has received various honors for his active participation and leadership in numerous service organizations. He sees his activity in the creation and development of the Community Service Organization during the 1950s as his important contribution to *la raza*. His activism there helped make available a training ground for future Chicano leaders. Among his published writings is "U.S. Foundations and Minority Group Interests," 1975, a seminal study profiling philanthropic support for minority causes.

FURTHER READING: Gallegos, Herman E. "Equity and Diversity: Hispanics in the Nonprofit World." Berkeley: University of California, The Bancroft Library, Regional Oral History Office, 1989; Gallegos, Herman E. "Hispanics Need a Strategy for the 90s." *Hispanic Business* (February 1985) 10; Gallegos, Herman E., and Michael O'Neil, eds. *Hispanics and the Nonprofit Sector.* New York: The Foundation Center, 1991; Watson, Lloyd. "A Brokerage for the Socially Conscious." *The San Francisco Chronicle* (28 December 1990) Business, C3.

GALLEGOS, JOSÉ MANUEL, 1815–1875. Priest, political leader, José Gallegos was born in Abiquiu, Nuevo México, attended Fr. Martínez's school in Taos, and graduated from the Durango (Mexico) seminary in 1840. In addition to his priestly activities in Nuevo México, he became seriously involved in politics and was elected to the provincial assembly in 1843. After the American takeover he served in the first territorial Council in 1851. Excommunicated by Bishop **Jean Baptiste Lamy** for concubinage, he plunged more intensely into politics. In 1853 he was elected territorial delegate to the U.S. Congress, but lost two years later to **Miguel Otero, Sr.**, in a hotly disputed election. In 1860 he won a seat in the territorial House of Representatives and was elected speaker.

During the **Civil War** Gallegos, an unyielding unionist, was imprisoned by Confederate forces from Texas; at the war's end he became treasurer of the New Mexico Territory. In 1867 he returned to the lower house of the territorial legislature and three years later was elected delegate to the U.S. Congress but, as before, failed to win reelection.

FURTHER READING: Chávez, Angélico. *But Time and Chance: The Story of Padre Martínez of Taos, 1793–1867.* Santa Fe: Sunstone Press, 1981; Horgan, Paul. *Lamy of Santa Fe.* New York: Farrar, Straus and Giroux, 1975; Vigil, Maurilio E. *Los Patrones: Profiles of Hispanic Political Leaders in New Mexico History,* Washington, D.C.: University Press of America, 1980.

GALLUP INCIDENT, 1935. In the early 1930s the leftist National Miners Union (NMU) began organizing the mostly Mexicano coal miners near Gallup, New Mexico. When a local landowner tried to force the miners to buy, at highly inflated prices, the houses they were renting, the union planned and directed the miners' resistance. As miners were evicted from their homes, feelings ran high. When a sheriff was shot and killed in a scuffle during the evictions, over one hundred Mexicano workers, many of them NMU officials, were arrested and jailed. Ten were later indicted for murder, and three were convicted. About one hundred mine workers who were Mexican nationals were deported, and the NMU local was destroyed.

FURTHER READING: Rubinstein, Harry R. "The Great Gallup Coal Strike of 1933." *Southwest Economy & Society* 3:2 (Winter 1977/78) 33–53.

GAMIO, MANUEL, 1883–1960. Anthropologist. Manuel Gamio, a leading Mexican anthropologist during the second quarter of the twentieth century, centered his studies on Mexican **immigration** to the United States. His research resulted in two seminal works: *Mexican Immigration to the United States*, 1930, 1971 and *The Mexican Immigrant: His Life's Story*, 1931, 1969. Gamio also made recommendations that were applied in the **bracero** program during World War II.

FURTHER READING: León Portilla, Miguel. "Manuel Gamio, 1883–1960 [obituary]." *American Anthropologist* 64:2 (1962) 356–366; Nahmad Sittón, Salomón, and Thomas Weaver. "Manuel Gamio, el primer antropólogo aplicado y su relación con la antropología norteamericana." *América Indígena* 50:4 (1990) 291–321.

GARCÍA, GUS(TAVO) C., 1915–1964. Civil rights activist, lawyer. After an outstanding record at the University of Texas law school, in 1938 Gus García became San Antonio assistant city attorney, then Bexar County assistant attorney, and later a legal advisor to the **League of United Latin American Citizens** (LULAC). During World War II he served in the Judge Advocate Corps.

Upon his return to San Antonio from the army, García immediately began an active career in politics, working with the **American G.I. Forum,** LULAC, and other Mexican American civic groups, especially in the area of school segregation. In the 1948 case of ***Delgado et al. v. Bastrop Independent School District et al.***, he led the team of attorneys who succeeded in bringing an end to the legal **segregation** of Mexican American schoolchildren in Texas. He was also directly involved in both ***Hernández v. the State of Texas*** and the **Félix Longoria** case.

Gus García's single most important contribution to *la raza*'s struggle for equality before the law was his work as chief counsel in the landmark case of *Hernández v. State of Texas*. Before the U.S. Supreme Court he argued successfully that the exclusion of Mexican Americans from the jury violated Pete Hernández's Fourteenth Amendment rights. His eloquence persuaded the court to a rare unanimous decision in 1956.

García was frequently reviled by the Anglo press and legal establishment in Texas because of his civil rights work for Mexicanos. At the same time his work was underappreciated in the Chicano community. Bitterly disappointed and disillusioned, he later destroyed his career and ultimately his life through overindulgence in alcohol.

FURTHER READING: Chacón, José A. *Hispanic Notables in the United States of North America*. Albuquerque: Saguaro Publishing Co., 1978; García, Arnold, Jr. "A Tough

Competitor Speaks from the Grave." *Austin American-Statesman* (21 September 1997); García, Mario T. *Mexican Americans: Leadership, Ideology, and Identity, 1930–1960.* New Haven: Yale University Press, 1989; Reyna, Abel A. Jr. "Gus García." *La Luz* 4:2 (May 1975) 38; Tyler, Ron, ed. *The New Handbook of Texas*, vol. 3. Austin: Texas State Historical Association, 1996.

GARCÍA, HÉCTOR PÉREZ, 1914–1996. Physician, community organizer, activist, ambassador. Mexican-born Héctor García, like many others of his generation, crossed the Rio Grande into the United States when his family fled the 1910 **Mexican revolution**. The Garcías settled in Mercedes, Texas, where Héctor grew up, attending the local public schools. After completing his A.B. at the University of Texas at Austin in 1935, he entered the University of Texas School of Medicine as a result of parental influence and older sibling example. After completing his M.D. degree four years later, he then did his internship at Creighton University in Nebraska because of discriminatory attitudes in Texas.

In **World War II** García volunteered, serving in the infantry, the engineers, and lastly in the Medical Corps as a combat surgeon. Upon his release from the army he returned to Corpus Christi to practice family medicine. When he contracted with the Veterans Administration (VA) to provide medical care for veterans, he soon became aware that Mexican American veterans were being subjected to **discrimination** by the VA, often being denied basic rights.

In 1948 Dr. García took a leading part in the protest against the refusal of the Three Rivers, Texas, mortuary to handle the reburial of World War II casualty **Félix Longoria**. To do something more enduring about the denial of rights to Mexican American veterans, he then organized a meeting of Mexican American veterans, from which the **American G.I. Forum** (AGIF) developed. In the following decade he traveled extensively in Texas, working to develop voter registration drives and urging the importance of education. Despite threats and physical harassment at times, he continued his deeply held commitment to the goals of the **League of United Latin American Citizens** and the AGIF.

Dr. García's concerns for *la raza* inevitably drew him into the political arena. He became active in Democratic politics and in the 1960 presidential election was named national coordinator of the **Viva Kennedy clubs**. In the postelection period he led efforts to create a nationwide Mexican American civil rights organization from which the **Political Association of Spanish-Speaking Organizations** resulted. He was elected its first president.

García played a major role in the Pete Hernández and other civil rights cases as well as in the Longoria case. Because of his profound commitment to the civil rights struggle and his devotion to community affairs as well as to the Democratic Party, in 1968 he was appointed to the U.S. **Civil Rights Commission** by President Lyndon Johnson. In the following year he was given a civil rights award by the National Association for the Advancement of Colored People. In addition to an intense involvement in numerous civil rights activities, Dr. García continued his medical practice well into his seventies.

During his lifetime Héctor García was honored by numerous groups for his outstanding leadership. In 1967 he was appointed by President Lyndon Johnson as a delegate to the United Nations with the rank of ambassador. Seventeen years later he became one of the first U.S. Latinos given the Presidential Medal of Freedom, awarded to him by Ronald Reagan. In 1989 he was honored by a Texas senate resolution recognizing his life's work for civil and human rights. He was also the recipient of numerous appointments, awards, and high honors resulting from his lifetime of service. After suffering from cancer for more than a decade, he died in July 1996.

FURTHER READING: Allsup, Carl. *The American G. I. Forum: Origins and Evolution.* Austin: University of Texas, Center for Mexican American Studies, 1982; García, Ignacio M. *Hector P. García: In Relentless Pursuit of Justice.* Houston: Arte Público Press, 2002; García, Ignacio M. *Viva Kennedy: Mexican Americans in Search of Camelot.* College Station: Texas A & M University Press, 2000; Green, George N. "The Felix Longoria Affair." *Journal of Ethnic Studies* 19:3 (1991) 23–49; "Hector Pérez García Dies: Led Hispanic Rights Group." *New York Times* (29 July 1996) A17; "President Honors G.I. Forum Founder." *Nuestro* (May 1984) 27–31; Ramos, Henry A. J. *The American G.I. Forum: In Pursuit of the Dream, 1948–1983.* Houston: Arte Público Press, 1998.

GARCÍA (MACARIO) INCIDENT. In 1945 Sergeant Macario García, a **World War II** veteran and Congressional Medal of Honor recipient, was refused service in a restaurant in the small town of Richmond, Texas, near Houston. When he protested the refusal to serve him, he was arrested on a charge of assault. The Houston council of the **League of United Latin American Citizens** supported him with a defense committee.

FURTHER READING: Morín, Raúl R. *Among the Valiant: Mexican Americans in World War II and Korea.* Los Angeles: Bordon, 1963; Perales, Alonso. *Are We Good Neighbors?* Reprint. New York: Arno Press, 1974.

GARRIGA, MARIANO S., 1886–1965. U.S. Latino bishop. Mariano Garriga was born in Port Isabel, Texas, of Spanish immigrant parents. Ordained to the priesthood in 1911, he was appointed coadjutor bishop in the Corpus Christi diocese in 1936, becoming the first U.S. Latino bishop since Mexican Francisco García Diego y Moreno nearly a century earlier. He was actively involved in Texas history and strongly supported **Carlos E. Castañeda** in his writing the seven-volume *Our Catholic Heritage in Texas, 1519–1936.*

FURTHER READING: Almaraz, Félix D., Jr. *Knight without Armor: Carlos Eduardo Castañeda, 1896–1958.* College Station: Texas A & M University Press, 1999.

GARZA, CARMEN LOMAS, 1948– . Painter. Carmen Lomas Garza was born in Kingsville, Texas, about thirty miles southwest of Corpus Christi. Several generations of her family on the maternal side were connected with the King Ranch. She attended an elementary school in which all the students were Mexican American; nevertheless, she was affected by community concerns about discrimination and racism. Carmen's first contact with Anglo students was in junior high. Her parents were deeply involved in the **American G.I. Forum**. Later in college, in her early twenties, she actively participated in the Chicano Movement.

Carmen grew up in a household in which her mother, a self-taught artist, did pen and ink drawings, watercolors, and oil painting. Having taught herself the basic elements of drawing, at age thirteen Carmen decided she wanted to become an artist. Her parents were very supportive of her goal. As a junior in high school she began taking art classes, and in her senior year the art teacher helped her get a tuition scholarship at Texas A&I University, today Texas A&M at Kingsville. After getting her B.S. degree there, she obtained a master's in education through the Juárez-Lincoln Center in San Antonio. Later she earned a Master of Arts from San Francisco State University with concentration on painting and lithography.

While attending graduate school at Washington State University, Carmen came to San Francisco in 1976 and became involved in the local Chicano art scene, going to work for the Galería de la Raza. Dropping out of WSU, she set up her studio and has remained in San Francisco ever since. Although she lives there, her paintings celebrate a wide range of activities from everyday Chicano life in Kingsville during the 1950s and early 1960s; they call to mind happy scenes from her childhood for both her and viewers.

Between 1979 and 1986 Carmen Garza received four artist-in-residence grants from the California Arts Council, followed by two fellowships from the National Endowment for the Arts. In 1996 she received from the National Endowment for the Arts a special International artist-in-residence grant to spend two months in Mexico.

Garza has shown her paintings in several group traveling exhibitions and has had one-person shows in a number of U.S. museums, including the Whitney Museum of American Art in New York. Her paintings may be found in over a dozen public collections. In 2000 she completed a commission for the San Francisco International Airport, a 16- by 24-foot metal cutout of Mexican dancers. She is also the author of children's books combining pictures and short stories arising from her art work: *Family Pictures/Cuadros de familia*, 1990; *In My Family/En mi familia*, 1996; and *Magic Windows/ Ventanas mágicas*, 1999.

FURTHER READING: Alba, Victoria. "Artists with a Mission." *San Francisco Examiner* (20 May 1990) Image Magazine, 22–31; "Arte: Carmen Lomas Garza." *Magazin* 1:9 (September 1973) 57–61; Cárdenas de Dwyer, Carlota, ed. *Chicano Voices.* Boston: Houghton Mifflin Co., 1975; Karlstrom, Paul J. *Oral History Interview with Carmen Lomas Garza, 10 April 1997.* Smithsonian Archives of American Art, 1997; Moreno, José Adán. "Carmen Lomas Garza: Traditional & Untraditional." *Caminos* 5:10 (November 1984) 44–45, 53; Simmons, Jeff. "Artist, Activist, Educator: Carmen

Lomas Garza in Profile." *Hispanic Outlook* (11 August 2000) 13–16; Ybarra-Frausto, Tomás. *Carmen Lomas Garza, Lo Real Maravilloso: The Marvelous/The Real.* San Francisco: Mexican Museum, 1987.

GARZA, CATARINO ERASMO, 1859–1895. Revolutionary, journalist. As a young liberal, Catarino Garza became interested in journalism partly in order to counter the negative stereotyping of Mexicanos by the Anglo press in **Texas**. During the 1880s he edited ephemeral Spanish-language newspapers in Brownsville, Eagle Pass, Corpus Christi, and San Antonio, using them to spread his enthusiasm for *mutualista* societies, his liberal political ideas, and his trenchant criticism of and attacks upon the ill-treatment and **lynching** of Mexicanos in Texas. His caustic editorials often bitterly criticized the not-infrequent ruthless actions of the **Texas Rangers** and made him the target of that organization's anger, leading to his arrest. They also served to make him a leading figure among border Mexicanos, especially among those exiles who were plotting the overthrow of Mexican president Porfirio Díaz.

More revolutionary than reformer, toward the end of the 1880s Garza began using his leadership position on the border to organize a guerrilla movement to unseat Díaz. In 1890 he led a force across the border in an unsuccessful foray against the Mexican garrison at San Ignacio, Tamaulipas. A second border crossing was thwarted by American troops, and in 1891 a third try with about two hundred followers ended in his crushing defeat.

Continual harassment by the U.S. Army and a long manhunt by the Texas Rangers soon turned Garza into a folk hero for many along the border. He persisted in his guerrilla activities until 1893, when he left the United States with a handful of associates. A sincere revolutionary, he joined the ongoing Cuban fight for independence from Spain. In 1895 he was killed while fighting in the Panamanian struggle for separation and independence from Colombia.

FURTHER READING: Cuthbertson, Gilbert M. "Catarino E. Garza and the Garza War." *Texana* 13:4 (1975) 335–348; Garza, Catarino E. "La lógica de los hechos, o sean observaciones sobre las circunstancias de los mexicanos en Texas desde el año 1877 hasta 1889," tomo I. Corpus Christi, ca. 1890. Ms. in Benson Latin American Collection, General Libraries, University of Texas at Austin; Young, Elliott G. "Remembering Catarino Garza's 1891 Revolution: An Aborted Border Insurrection." *Mexican Studies/Estudios Mexicanos* 12:2 (1996) 231–272.

GARZA, REYNALDO G., 1915– . Federal judge, politician. Growing up in Brownsville, Texas, Reynaldo Garza personally experienced little discrimination, but he early became aware of the existence of racism and the inferior position of Latinos. Influenced by liberal immigrant parents, as a university student at Austin he worked to make Anglo leaders more sensitive to segregation and aware of other *raza* educational concerns. After earning his law degree in 1939, he returned to Brownsville to put his legal education to use in the service of Mexican Americans. In the following year he joined the **League of United Latin American Citizens** and within twelve months was elected the Brownsville chapter president.

After four years service in **World War II**, Garza returned to Brownsville, resumed his civic activities, and re-entered local politics. A decade later he was appointed to the **Texas Good Neighbor Commission**, and in 1961 he was named a judge in the U.S. District Court by President John F. Kennedy, becoming the second Mexican American on a federal bench, the first after Harold Medina. Subsequently he was appointed chief judge of a federal judicial district. As a judge he supported the rights of students suspended for distributing antiwar leaflets during the war in Vietnam.

During the 1970s Garza presided over numerous cases arising out of the Civil Rights Act of 1964. Although his position on the rights of labor was fairly conservative, in the 1972 *Medrano et al. v. Allee et al.* suit he ruled for the union and against the **Texas Rangers**. After turning down a possible cabinet position, in 1979 he was named by President Jimmy Carter to the Fifth Circuit Court of Appeals in New Orleans, where he continues to rule against school segregation and political discrimination against minority voters. Now on "senior status," he is in effect on phased retirement.

FURTHER READING: DeLeón, Jessica. "Federal Judge Sets Benchmark for Success in South Texas." *The Houston Chronicle* (29 December 1996) State, 4; Fisch, Louise Ann. *All Rise: Reynaldo G. Garza, the First Mexican American Federal Judge.* College Station, Texas A&M University Press, 1996.

GERRYMANDERING. The setting of electoral district boundaries so as to benefit a political group. When the decennial census mandates reapportionment, the party in power tries to create voting districts that will maintain or improve its electoral chances. Gerrymandering's primary purpose is to divide the voting strength of minority groups and opposition parties. The **Voting Rights Act** of 1970 attempts to prevent gerrymandering.

FURTHER READING: Griffith, Elmer C. *Rise and Development of the Gerrymander,* Reprint. New York: Arno Press, 1974; Lubin, David. *The Paradox of Representation: Racial Gerrymandering and Minority Interests in Congress.* Princeton, N.J.: Princeton University Press, 1997.

GILBERT, FABIOLA CABEZA DE BACA, 1898–1993. Teacher, folklorist, author. Fabiola Cabeza de Baca was born in northeastern **New Mexico** of parents from distinguished old Nuevomexicano ranching families. After completing her formal education under the Sisters of Loretto in Las Vegas, she began a teaching career and also entered New Mexico Normal School, from which she graduated in 1921. She taught in various rural public schools for the next several years, during which time she became aware of the great need for home economics education among the rural poor. As a result she went back to college and earned a B.S. degree in home economics in 1929.

Upon graduation, Fabiola went to work for the New Mexico State Extension Service, where she was to spend the next thirty years helping rural

Nuevomexicanos. While respecting their traditional ways, she introduced newer techniques of preparing and preserving food, including use of the pressure cooker. Her promotion of family gardens was credited with mitigating the dire effects of the severe drought years, 1933 to 1935. Through her intense involvement with New Mexico's isolated villages she came to deeply respect and admire Hispano and Indian cultures. Meanwhile she also collected their cooking recipes, herbal remedies, and folkloric tales.

Fabiola used her new knowledge to write bulletins and pamphlets for the extension service and articles for popular magazines. In 1934 she published *Los alimentos y su preparación*, which was subsequently revised and expanded several times. Five years later her *Historic Cookery* was an immediate success, going through several printings and editions. In 1949 she published *The Good Life*, a folkloric account of the Nuevomexicano annual cycle of work and fiestas, for which some critics accused her of romanticizing the Hispano experience. Her next and most successful book, *We Fed Them Cactus*, 1954, a potpourri of memoir, **folklore**, and history, made her widely known outside the Southwest.

After her retirement from the extension service in 1959, Fabiola continued lecturing and writing on southwestern culture, folklore, and foods. During the 1960s she also worked for the Peace Corps, training volunteers and acting as a consultant. She spent her final years in an Albuquerque convalescent home.

FURTHER READING: Jensen, Joan M. "Crossing Ethnic Barriers in the Southwest: Women's Agricultural Extension Education, 1914–1940." *Agricultural History* 60:2 (Spring 1986) 169–181; Jensen, Joan M., and Darlis Miller. *New Mexico Women: Intercultural Perspectives*. Albuquerque: University of New Mexico Press, 1985; Lomelí, Francisco A., and Carl R. Shirley, eds. *Chicano Writers: Second Series*. Detroit: Gale Research, 1992; Ponce, Merrihelen. *Lives and Works of Five Hispanic New Mexican Woman Writers, 1878–1991*. Working Paper No. 119. Albuquerque: Southwest Hispanic Research Institute, University of New Mexico, 1992; Rebolledo, Tey Diana, ed. *Nuestras mujeres*. Albuquerque: El Norte, 1992.

GLORIETA PASS, BATTLE OF, 1862. In late March, 1862 Confederate forces from Texas, after having captured **Santa Fe**, New Mexico, were soundly defeated at Glorieta Pass, southeast of the capital. As a result of their rout they were forced to withdraw completely from the New Mexico Territory, effectively bringing to an end **Civil War** fighting in the territory.

FURTHER READING: Scott, Robert. *Glory, Glory, Glorieta: The Gettysburg of the West*. Boulder, Colo.: Johnson Books, 1992; Simmons, Marc. *New Mexico: An Interpretive History*. Albuquerque: University of New Mexico Press, 1988. Westphall, David. "The Battle of Glorieta Pass: Its Importance in the Civil War." In *New Mexico Historical Review* 44:2 (1969) 137–154.

GÓMEZ-QUIÑONES, JUAN, 1940– . Historian, activist, poet. Mexico-born Juan Gómez-Quiñones has been a social activist since his student days at the

University of California, Los Angeles (UCLA) in the early 1960s. Cofounder of the **United Mexican American Students** organization, he also helped create and develop a number of other Chicano educational groups and community organizations. A historian with special interests in Chicano political movements, labor history, and the Mexican revolution, he has taught at his alma mater, UCLA, since 1969, a year before he received his Ph.D. there. In 1970 he founded the preeminent Chicano journal *Aztlán: International Journal of Chicano Studies Research* at UCLA's Chicano Studies Research Center and was its first editor. From 1974 to 1987 he acted as director of the center. He has served on the boards of the California State Universities and Colleges, the Los Angeles Urban Coalition, the **Mexican American Legal Defense and Educational Fund**, and the Latino Museum of History, Art & Culture.

Among his many publications, Gómez-Quiñones is the author of major works on Chicano and Mexican history: *Sembradores: Ricardo Flores Magón y el Partido Liberal Mexicano*, 1973, *Mexican Students por La Raza*, 1978, *Porfirio Díaz, los intelectuales y la Revolución*, 1981, *Chicano Politics: Reality and Promise, 1940–1990*, 1990, and *Mexican American Labor, 1790–1990*, 1994. He also coauthored several books and published numerous journal articles dealing primarily with labor organizing and the student movement, in which he played an active role.

Gómez-Quiñones is also a poet of some distinction. His poetry has been published in various prestigious Chicano literary journals and several anthologies. His poems, often personal and sometimes even lyrical, seem to reflect the evolution of his political thought.

FURTHER READING: Gómez-Quiñones, Juan. *Mexican Students por La Raza: The Chicano Student Movement in Southern California, 1967–1977*. Santa Barbara, Calif.: Editorial La Causa, 1978; Lomelí, Francisco A., and Carl R. Shirley, eds. *Chicano Writers: Second Series*. Detroit: Gale Research, 1992.

GONZALES, CORKY (RODOLFO), 1928–. Activist, community organizer, political leader. Rodolfo Gonzales was born, grew up, and attended school in Denver, Colorado. Even before graduating from high school he began to envision the boxing arena as a way out of barrio poverty. While still in his teens he won the national and international Golden Gloves amateur championships. As a professional after 1947, he won sixty-five of his seventy-five bouts. In 1955 he quit the ring and went into business for himself. He soon moved from a retired prize-winning young boxer and successful businessman to an active participant in **Colorado** Democratic politics. In 1960 he was state coordinator for the successful "Viva Kennedy" election campaign.

Corky's involvement in politics and various local social service agencies focused his attention on the many problems of Colorado Mexican Americans. Active earlier in the **American G.I. Forum**, in the second half of the 1960s he created La Cruzada para la Justicia (The **Crusade for Justice**), an organization with goals of improving economic and political opportunities for Mexican Americans. The Crusade took over an old church and school complex and in 1970 converted it into the Escuela Tlatelolco Centro de Estudios—a cultural center, school, nursery, gymnasium, and theater. During the decade 1968 to 1977 the Crusade became a preeminent training arena for youthful urban activists from all over the Southwest.

In 1968 Gonzales led several hundred Mexican Americans in the **Poor People's March** to Washington, D.C. As the leading advocate of Chicano cultural nationalism, he issued his **Plan del Barrio** there, listing Chicano objectives and demands. In the following year he organized a follow-up conference at Denver to discuss concerns of youthful Mexican Americans. Under his sponsorship some fifteen hundred young delegates to this national Chicano Youth Liberation Conference drew up the **Plan Espiritual de Aztlán**, which stressed goals of ethnic nationalism and self-determination. The conference also called for the creation of a Chicano political party. After the conference, Gonzales continued to articulate concerns about the problems of young Chicanos, sharply criticizing their education, strongly supporting **student walkouts**, vociferously defending the rights of those arrested in demonstrations, and persistently protesting police brutality.

In 1970 Corky Gonzales formed the (Colorado) **La Raza Unida Party** (LRUP) to raise Mexican American political consciousness and to advance his political ideas. In the meantime he had begun to move from Chicano **nationalism** to concepts of class struggle and internationalism. Two years later at the first national LRUP convention in El Paso, convened to develop greater political unity among Chicanos, he lost a bitter battle for leadership to the more politically pragmatic **José Angel Gutiérrez** of Texas.

In the second half of the 1970s Gonzales's confrontational leadership declined further as the American people turned more conservative and the Chicano Movement ebbed. Also, his ideas of Chicano nationalism and an independent homeland in the Southwest became mired down by partial victories. He remained the charismatic head of a considerably diminished Crusade, now largely limited to Colorado. A heart attack in 1987 and a severe automobile injury later that year left him with a difficult and long, drawn-out recovery. In the mid-1990s a visibly aging Corky Gonzales still spoke out for Chicano concerns, although perhaps somewhat less passionately than earlier. Although forced into semiretirement by his ill health, he still goes to the Escuela Tlatelolco, where he encourages Chicano youths to keep the faith.

For many urban Mexican Americans Corky Gonzales was the most important Chicano leader of the 1960s. In addition to his varied endeavors as a civic leader, political reformer, and Chicano nationalist, he was known to all for his 1967 epic poem, *I Am Joaquín*, which provided inspiration for thousands of youthful Chicano activists.

FURTHER READING: Gonzales, Rodolfo. *Message to Aztlán: Selected Writings of Rodolfo "Corky" Gonzales.* Antonio Esquibel, comp. Houston: Arte Público Press, 2001;

Hammerback, John C., Richard J. Jensen, and José Angel Gutiérrez. *A War of Words: Chicano Protest in the 1960s and 1970s.* Westport, Conn.: Greenwood Press, 1985; Larralde, Carlos. *Mexican American: Movements and Leaders.* Los Alamitos, Calif.: Hwong, 1976; Marín, Christine. *A Spokesman for the Mexican American Movement: Rodolfo "Corky" Gonzales and the Fight for Chicano Liberation, 1966–1972.* San Francisco, Calif.: R & E Research Associates, 1977; Vigil, Ernesto B. *The Crusade for Justice: Chicano Militancy and the Government's War on Dissent.* Madison: University of Wisconsin Press, 1999.

GONZALES, M. C. (MANUEL C.), 1900–1986. Activist, judge, community leader. Manuel C. Gonzales, known throughout his adult life simply as M.C., got an early taste for the law as a teenager by clerking for a district judge in southeast Texas, by working as a chief clerk in the state capital, and later as a secretary in an Austin law firm. After the American entrance into **World War I** in 1916, he received an appointment as interpreter for the U.S. military attachés in Madrid and later in Paris, although he was not yet twenty. After the war he studied law, passed the bar, and went to work for the district attorney of Bexar County, Texas.

While still a teenager, M.C. took a dynamic part in creating **La Liga Protectora Mexicana** and in the 1920s helped organize other local associations. In 1929 he was secretary of the convention that created the **League of United Latin American Citizens** (LULAC), and two years later he was elected president of the organization. He remained an active participant in LULAC for the rest of his life. Widely acknowledged in Texas as one of *la raza*'s principal leaders, Gonzales took a vital role in all community affairs. During the 1930s he worked indefatigably for the San Antonio Mexicano community, filed class action petitions against school segregation, and organized protests against unpopular school board decisions. In his many published writings M.C. stressed the obligations of citizenship as well as its rights. In his newspaper, *El Luchador,* his constant theme was that Mexican Americans should unite as citizens to fight for their rights. He strongly supported the "Better Government" group in its campaign against machine politics in San Antonio. When he died in 1986 he left a legacy of vigorous leadership that was acknowledged throughout the Southwest.

FURTHER READING: Garcia, Richard A. *Rise of the Mexican American Middle Class: San Antonio Texas, 1929–1941.* College Station: Texas A&M University Press, 1991; Salazar, Veronica. *Dedication Rewarded: Prominent Mexican Americans.* San Antonio: Mexican American Cultural Center, 1976; Tyler, Ron, ed. *The New Handbook of Texas,* vol. 3. Austin: Texas State Historical Association, 1996.

GONZALES, PANCHO (RICHARD ALONZO), 1928–1995. Tennis great. Richard Alonzo Gonzales was born in Los Angeles, California of immigrant parents, both of whom worked to support the family. As a youth Gonzales was very active in sports, winning certificates in basketball and football as a freshman in junior high school. The gift of a tennis racquet from his mother, who feared football injuries, opened up a new sport vista for the teenager.

Gonzales developed his tennis game by observing other players. Without taking a single lesson, within three years he became a top-ranking teen tennis player in southern California. On his seventeenth birthday he enlisted in the navy and served eighteen months in the Pacific during World War II. Upon his discharge he returned to tennis, and in May 1947 he entered the Southern California championship tournament, in which he reached the finals. In the following year he won the U.S. singles title at Forest Hills, becoming the second-youngest champion in tennis history. In 1949 he won the U.S. Indoor Championship, turned pro, and joined a tennis tour.

Although Gonzales's record as a professional was not completely consistent, from 1953 to 1962 he dominated

Pancho Gonzales during his marathon match against Charles Pasarell of Puerto Rico at Center Court, Wimbledon, 1969. © AP/Wide World Photos.

professional tennis, winning a number of world championships and earning himself a reputation as one of the finest tennis players in the world. He won the U.S. Open eight times. Twice during this time he retired, but his retirements never lasted long. In 1968 he was inducted into the International Tennis Hall of Fame and in the next year he played the longest match in Wimbledon history—112 games—and won. In 1971, at age forty-three and still ranking among the top ten in world tennis, he won the World Series of Tennis.

During his various retirements Gonzales taught and coached young players and occasionally sallied forth to play exhibition games, much to the joy of his many admirers. His brilliant power game attracted huge crowds to a sport previously little attended. Driven by the lure of competition and the thrill of winning as well as his desire for recognition and respect from his peers, he continued to play, consistently defeating his opponents. He was finally defeated by cancer of the stomach in July 1995.

FURTHER READING: *Current Biography, 1949.* New York: H. W. Wilson, 1949; Doviak, Joan, and Arturo Palacios. *Catorce personas lindas.* Washington, D.C.: Educational Systems Corp., 1970; Frayne Trent. *Famous Tennis Players.* New York: Dodd, Mead, 1977; Gonzales, Pancho. *Man with a Racket: The Autobiography of Pancho Gonzales.* New York: Barnes, 1959; Obituary. *New York Times.* (5 July 1995) A15.

GONZALES, SYLVIA ALICIA, 1943– . Feminist, writer, teacher. After university studies that culminated in a doctorate in education at the University of Massachusetts, Sylvia Gonzales began her professional career in 1968 as an analyst for the **U.S. Civil Rights Commission**. She later left Washington, D.C. and in 1974 accepted a position teaching in Mexican American studies at California State University in San Jose. She took an active role in the **Mexican American Women's National Association** (MANA) and in 1977 was a delegate at the International Women's Year Conference held in Houston, Texas.

Primarily known for her writings, Gonzales had concerns tending to be as much feminist as *raza.* In 1971 she edited *Women in Action* for the U.S. Civil Service Commission. Over the years she has been a contributor to half a dozen books. Her best-known work is *Hispanic American Voluntary Organizations,* 1985. In addition to writing broadly about feminist issues, she has devoted herself especially to the political empowerment of Chicanas. Decrying the divisiveness and factionalism among Latinas, she sees the need for changes both within the community and in the larger society. These, she believes, can be achieved only by group consciousness and close cooperation.

FURTHER READING: Fisher, Dexter, ed. *The Third Woman: Minority Women Writers of the United States.* Boston: Houghton Mifflin, 1977; Gonzales, Sylvia. "The Latino Feminist: Where We've Been, Where We're Going," *Nuestro* (August/September 1981) 45–47; Telgen, Diane, and Jim Kamp, eds. *Notable Hispanic American Women.* Detroit: Gale Research, 1993.

GONZALES ET AL. v. SHEELY ET AL., 1951. At the beginning of the 1950s Porfirio Gonzales and other petitioners filed suit against **Arizona** public school authorities for segregating their children. They argued that the school officials were discriminating and denying their children rights guaranteed by the U.S. Constitution. In March 1951 the U.S. District Court ruled in their favor, holding that placing Mexican American children in separate school buildings with inferior facilities violated their constitutional rights and was therefore illegal.

FURTHER READING: *Gonzales et al. v. Sheely et al.* Civ. No. 1473. 96 F. Supp. 1004. United States District Court D Arizona, March 26, 1951; San Miguel, Guadalupe. "The Origins, Development, and Consequences of the Educational Segregation of Mexicans in the Southwest." In *Chicano Studies: A Multidisciplinary Approach,* edited by Eugene E. García, Francisco Lomclí, and Isidro D. Ortiz. New York: Teachers College Press, 1984.

GONZÁLEZ, HENRY BARBOSA, 1916–2000. Political leader. Like many Mexican Americans of his age group, Henry González was born in the United States of parents who had recently fled the **Mexican revolution** of 1910. He was born in, grew up in, and was educated in San Antonio, Texas. Convinced by his parents of the vital importance of education, he began engineering studies but was forced to abandon them because of the Great Depression of the early 1930s. Later in that decade he was able to graduate from St. Mary's University in San Antonio with a bachelor of law degree. During World War II he worked in the armed forces intelligence service, and from the immediate postwar years until the end of the 1940s he was a juvenile probation officer.

After first failing in a bid for a seat in the Texas legislature, in 1953 González was elected to the San Antonio city council, where he soon became involved in

Henry Barbosa González. Courtesy of Matt Meier.

civil rights issues, particularly **segregation**. Now firmly committed to a political career, he won election to the state senate three years later. The first Mexican American to serve in that body since the mid-1800s, he quickly became known as an outspoken foe of racist legislation and a champion of minority rights. In the late 1950s González attracted national attention by leading the longest filibuster in Texas senate history, thirty-five hours, in order to defeat a group of racist bills.

In 1961 Henry González won a seat in the U.S. House of Representatives, becoming the first **Tejano** in history elected to a national office. For the next three decades he was regularly reelected to the House, where he continued to demonstrate his concern for the rights of the disadvantaged. He sponsored and supported numerous bills to protect the rights of minorities and expand their economic and political opportunities, bills that included abolition of the poll tax, basic adult education, educational benefits for Vietnam veterans, manpower training, and a conservation corps for youths. He served actively in numerous congressional committees in which his sometimes irascible and pugnacious manner irritated some colleagues. Fiercely independent and at times disruptively obstinate, he staunchly supported what he believed to be right. During the Chicano Movement González opposed the strident anti-gringo rhetoric of the **Mexican American Youth Organization** in Texas and its progeny, **La Raza Unida Party**. In 1976 he was one of the founders of the **Congressional Hispanic Caucus.**

At the end of 1998 the eighty-two-year-old González retired from the U.S. House of Representatives for reasons of health. During his more than thirty-five years of service in Washington and five years in the Texas legislature, Henry B. González consistently supported and furthered legislation making secure the rights of the poor and powerless. The well-being of his constituents was always his primary concern.

FURTHER READING: Conroy, Ed. "Give 'em Hell, Henry." *Mother Jones* 16:4 (July–August 1991) 12; Marquis, Christopher. "Henry Gonzalez, 84; Served 37 Years in the House." *The New York Times* (29 November 2000) A 33; "Profile of a Public Man." *Nuestro* (March 1983) 13–19, 50; Rodríguez, Eugene. *Henry B. González: A Political Profile.* New York: Arno Press, 1976; Sloane, Todd A. *González of Texas: A Congressman for the People.* Evanston, Ill.: John Gordon Burke, 1996; Vigil, Maurilio E. *Hispanics in Congress: A Historical and Political Survey.* Lanham, N.Y.: University Press of America, 1996.

GONZÁLEZ, PEDRO J., 1895–1995. Musician, activist. Pedro González became one of the first Spanish-language radio announcers in the Los Angeles area. After fighting in the Mexican revolutionary army of Pancho Villa, crossing into the United States in 1923, and working as a dockhand in Los Angeles, he became the leader of a musical group named Los Madrugadores. During his widely popular early morning musical program he spoke out boldly against **discrimination** and human rights violations, especially the mass deportation of Mexicanos in the 1930s depression.

González's outspokenness led to harassment and finally to his conviction in 1934 on a trumped-up rape charge. His teenage accuser later admitted she had lied, and after serving six years of a fifty-year sentence he was released from San Quentin and then deported as an undesirable alien. Across the border in Tijuana, González renewed his musical career on radio and again spoke out forcefully against injustice and denial of rights.

In 1971, after three decades in exile, González was allowed to return to the United States, and became a citizen in 1984. In his declining years he continued his long fight for Mexican American rights to equality of treatment. By the time of his death at age ninety-nine he had received numerous honors for his battle for social justice. A 1983 TV documentary, *Ballad of an Unsung Hero* and a subsequent film, *Break of Dawn* recounted his life's story.

FURTHER READING: Parlee, Lorena M. "Ballad of an Unsung Hero." *Nuestro* (December 1984) 22–24; "Pedro J. González, 99, Folk Hero and Advocate for Social Justice." *The New York Times* (24 March 1995) B7.

GONZÁLEZ AMEZCUA, CHELO (CONSUELO), 1903–1975. Artist, poet. Consuelo González was born in the Mexican border town of Piedras Negras, twin city to Eagle Pass, Texas. Because of the violence and upheaval of the **Mexican revolution** the González family crossed the river, settling in Del Rio in 1913. During her six years in the Del Rio schools, Consuelo showed an aptitude for drawing and artwork, using whatever materials came to hand. After leaving school she worked in a Del Rio store and continued to draw and write poetry. In the mid-1930s she sought an art scholarship from Mexican president Lázaro Cárdenas but then was unable to accept it because of her father's death.

Chelo and her sister Zaré took care of their widowed mother and worked to support the family. Over the years she continued to write poems, compose songs, and make pen and ink drawings using a wide variety of subjects. Without formal art training, she developed her own idiosyncratic style and often incorporated suitable poems into her "filigree" drawings. At first she used ballpoint pens and paper or cardboard; toward the end of her life she added felt-tip pens and crayons.

Chelo's pen and ink drawings and her poetry became well-known around Del Rio, and in 1968 the Marion Koogler McNay Art Institute in San Antonio mounted a solo exhibition of her work. In the following years she had exhibitions in New York, San Antonio, and Dallas as well as various venues in Mexico, and her poetry won prizes. She died in June 1975. Posthumously her drawings have had several gallery exhibitions, and in 1991 the Del Rio Council for the Arts organized a traveling exhibition of her works.

FURTHER READING: Quirarte, Jacinto. "Image and Text (Poetry) in the Work of Consuelo (Chelo) González Amezcua, a Texas Artist (1903–1975)." *Research Center for the Arts Review* 5:1 (January 1982) 1–3; Quirarte, Jacinto. *Mexican American Artists.* Austin: University of Texas Press, 1973; Quirarte, Jacinto, and Rolando Hinojosa-Smith. *Mystical Elements/Lyrical Imagery: Consuelo González Amezcua, 1903–1975.* Del Rio, Texas: Del Rio Council for the Arts, 1991; Telgen, Diane, and Jim Kamp, eds. *Notable Hispanic American Women.* Detroit: Gale Research, 1993.

GORRAS BLANCAS, 1889–1995. Las Gorras Blancas (White Caps) was one of the first secret organizations created to defend Nuevomexicano rights. Organized in the late 1880s by Juan José Herrera and others in response to encroachment on pueblo grant lands, especially by **railroads** and **Anglo** cattlemen, it hoped to halt and roll back the private takeover of what had been public lands. The fencing-in of common lands previously available to all for grazing aroused great concern among Nuevomexicano herdsmen, especially in San Miguel County, and led to the destruction of miles of fencing and thousands of railroad ties.

The aggressive actions of the white-hooded Gorras Blancas had extensive popular support, and they soon claimed fifteen hundred members, most in northeastern **New Mexico**; however, the organization antagonized many elite Nuevomexicanos and most Anglos. The indictment of alleged members of the group in November 1889 led to an avalanche of support for the jailed suspects.

In 1890 the Gorras entered the political arena in support of the newly organized **Partido del Pueblo Unido**. While the Gorras had temporarily stemmed the tide of land-grabbing, internal dissent and the turn to political action ended its effectiveness. By the mid-1890s it had lost popular support, and its political extension, the People's Party, had faded away.

FURTHER READING: Martínez, Félix. "Las Gorras Blancas." In *Foreigners in Their Native Land: Historical Roots of the Mexican American*, edited by David J. Weber. Albuquerque: University of New Mexico Press, 1973; Rosenbaum, Robert J. *Mexican Resistance in the Southwest: "The Sacred Right of Self-Preservation."* Austin: University of Texas Press, 1981; Schlesinger, Andrew B. "Las Gorras Blancas, 1889–1891." *Journal of Mexican American History* 1 (Spring 1971) 87–143.

GREASER. *Greaser*, a pejorative **Anglo** term for a Mexican, was widely used in the nineteenth century. In a broader application it has been used to refer to Mexican Americans and to Latinos generally. The origin of the term is widely disputed.

GREAT DEPRESSION. The serious U.S. economic decline usually dated from the stock market crash of 1929 to the outbreak of **World War II** ten years later. Like other Americans, Mexican Americans and Mexican immigrants found jobs hard to get as the Depression sent midwestern Anglos into the low-paying migrant agricultural circuits of the Southwest. After 1933, New Deal programs helped alleviate some of the most serious problems, providing work and food. Singled out as scapegoats for the Depression, nearly half a million Mexican nationals left the country during the decade, some voluntarily, many more coerced. The **repatriation** occasioned long-term feelings of resentment in the Mexican American community. In the long run it also contributed to the urbanization of Mexican Americans.

FURTHER READING: Balderrama, Francisco E., and Raymond Rodríguez. *Decade of Betrayal: Mexican Repatriation in the 1930s.* Albuquerque: University of New Mexico Press, 1995; Hoffman, Abraham. *Unwanted Mexican Americans in the Great Depression.* Tucson: University of Arizona Press, 1974.

GREENCARDER. An alien possessing a Form I-151, a permanent document establishing his or her immigrant status in the United States. Many Mexican greencarders live in the border regions of Mexico and regularly commute to work in the U.S. border areas.

FURTHER READING: Ross, Stanley R., and Sidney Weintraub. *Temporary Alien Workers in the U. S.* Boulder, Colo.: Westview Press, 1982.

GRINGO. *Gringo* is a moderately pejorative Latino term for an Anglo. Often it suggests a cultural attitude of ethnocentric paternalism rather than a racial designation. It has its origin in the Spanish word *griego*, Greek, used to indicate foreignness.

GUADALUPE, VIRGIN OF. The Virgin of Guadalupe has served as a unifying symbol for Mexicanos since the sixteenth century. In 1531, according to a sixteenth-century oral tradition, the Virgin Mary appeared on the Hill of Tepeyac to a lowly Indian. A devotion to the dark-skinned Virgin quickly spread, not only among the Indian converts to Catholicism but also among mestizos and even criollos. By the mid-1600s she was depicted in association with the Mexican eagle and nopal cactus. In 1737 La Guadalupe was declared "Patroness of the Mexican Nation," and in the 1810 Mexican revolution for independence her image was immediately adopted as a standard for the forces of both Miguel Hidalgo and José María Morelos.

In the nineteenth and twentieth centuries, as federalists and centralists fought bitterly to rule the nation, Guadalupe continued to be the only thing that all Mexicans could agree on. Even the most anticlerical elements excepted her from their fulminations against the Church, while her colors shaded from blue, rose, and white to the colors of the Mexican flag, green, red, and white.

A lithograph of Our Lady of Guadalupe by Currier and Ives, 1848. © Library of Congress.

The Mexicans who began settling the Southwest at the end of the sixteenth century brought with them the devotion to Guadalupe. In the Southwest as in Mexico, she served as a unifying symbol of Mexican ethnic identity as well as a religious icon. During the **Delano grape strike** César Chávez used her image to rally support for la **causa**. She has also been adopted by some Chicana feminists as a unifying symbol. She remains at the heart of Mexican ethnicity.

FURTHER READING: Elizondo, Virgilio P. *Guadalupe, Mother of the New Creation.* Maryknoll, N.Y.: Orbis Books, 1999; Meier, Matt S. "María Insurgente." *Historia Mexicana* 23:3 (January–March 1974) 466–482; Poole, Stafford. *Our Lady of Guadalupe: The Origins and Sources of a Mexican National Symbol, 1531–1797.* Tucson: University of Arizona Press, 1996; Rodríguez, Jeanette. *Our Lady of Guadalupe: Faith and Empowerment among Mexican-American Women.* Austin: University of Texas Press, 1994.

GUADALUPE HIDALGO, TREATY OF, 1848. On February 2, 1848 the Guadalupe Hidalgo Treaty ended the war between the United States and Mexico. By the terms of the treaty Mexico ceded the territories of **California** and **New Mexico** to the United States and accepted the **Rio Grande** as the boundary for **Texas** in exchange for fifteen million dollars. The treaty stipulated that the approximately eighty thousand Mexicans living in the area acquired by the U.S. had the choice of remaining Mexican citizens or of becoming nationals, and eventually citizens, of the United States. Those who opted to become U.S. nationals were to enjoy "all the rights of citizens of the United States according to the principles of the Constitution." Whichever choice they made, their property rights and religious liberty were guaranteed. About 97 percent became U.S. nationals by choice or default. The property rights guaranteed by the treaty, particularly in the matter of land ownership, were later often ignored or violated by "reinterpretation" of the treaty's intent.

FURTHER READING: Bloom, John Porter, ed. *The Treaty of Guadalupe Hidalgo, 1848: Papers of the Sesquicentennial Symposium, 1848–1998.* Las Cruces, N.M.: Yucca Tree Press, 1999; Conmy, Peter T. *A Centennial Evaluation of the Treaty of Guadalupe Hidalgo, 1848–1948.* Oakland, Calif.: Oakland Public Library, 1948; Griswold Del Castillo, Richard. *The Treaty of Guadalupe Hidalgo: A Legacy of Conflict.* Norman: University of Oklahoma Press, 1990; Miller, Hunter, ed. *Treaties and Other International Acts of the United States of America,* vol. 5. Washington, D.C.: U.S. Government Printing Office, 1937.

GUERRERO, LALO (EDUARDO), 1917– . Singer, composer. Eduardo Guerrero was born and grew up in Tucson, Arizona. A driving interest in music at a very early age resulted in his learning to play the piano and guitar as a child. He dropped out of high school to help support the family by playing in local bars for tips. With three other musicians he formed a group named Los Carlistas; in 1937 the popular quartet went to Los Angeles, where they played in clubs, made some recordings, and appeared in a Gene Autry film. Returning to Tucson as heroes, they were sent to New York by the Chamber of Commerce to appear on the radio in Major Bowes Amateur Hour. Los Carlistas dissolved and Lalo returned to Los Angeles and Tucson.

After Pearl Harbor, Lalo went to work in the defense industry in San Diego, where he also entertained at military installations and played in hospitals. At the end of World War II he moved permanently to Los Angeles, where he continued his musical career. From 1956 to 1968 he operated a club there and then opened one in Tucson. Five years later he entered into a long-term contract with a Mirage, California, restaurant and moved to nearby Palm Springs. In 1975 he was among those selected to play at the Festival of American Folklife in Washington, D.C. In recent years he has been writing lyrics for his son Mark's music.

Lalo has made some twenty albums and has written over two hundred songs. Among his most popular songs, which range from ballads to parodies, are "Cancíon Mexicana," "Nunca Jamás," "Los Chucos Suaves," "Las Ardillitas," "Tacos for Two," and "Pancho Claus."

FURTHER READING: Burr, Ramiro. *Billboard Guide to Tejano and Regional Mexican Music*. New York: Billboard Books, 1999; Guerrero, Lalo, with Sherilyn Meece Mentes. *Lalo: My Life and Music*. Tucson: University of Arizona Press, 2002; Loza, Steven. *Barrio Rhythm: Mexican American Music in Los Angeles*. Urbana: University of Illinois Press, 1993; Sheridan, Thomas E. "From Luisa Espinel to Lalo Guerrero." *Journal of Arizona History* 25:3 (Fall 1984) 285–300; Sonnichsen, Philip. "Lalo Guerrero, Pioneer in Mexican-American Music." La Luz 6:5 (May 1977) 11–14; Tatum, Charles M. *Chicano Popular Culture: Que hable el pueblo*. Tucson: University of Arizona Press, 2001.

GUTIÉRREZ, JOSÉ ANGEL, 1944– . Politico, activist, judge. José Angel Gutiérrez, son of a physician who had fled the **Mexican Revolution**, was born and grew up in **Crystal City, Texas**. Highly motivated and studious, he did well academically. After his early education he earned his B.S. in political science in 1966 and obtained a master's degree at St. Mary's University in San Antonio two years later. In 1976 he completed the requirements for a doctorate in political science at the University of Texas in Austin. In the late 1980s he earned a doctorate in jurisprudence at the University of Houston.

While at St. Mary's University, Gutiérrez was one of five Chicanos who formed the **Mexican American Youth Organization**, and he was elected its first president. After completing his master's degree in political science and working as a research investigator for the **Mexican American Legal Defense and Educational Fund** he returned to Crystal City to put into practice his ideas for organizing Mexican Americans in politics. A 1969 high school student walkout over racist discrimination provided an opportunity that Gutiérrez used to organize a political power base, **La Raza Unida Party** (LRUP).

With the help of the LRUP organization Gutiérrez and two other raza candidates were elected to the school board, and in 1970 two Chicanos won seats on the city council. Crystal City Mexican Americans achieved some immediate political power and were able to institute bilingual and bicultural programs in the schools. Gutiérrez favored a continuing focus on local issues, but the success in Crystal City created pressure to take La Raza Unida national. At the 1972 El Paso LRUP convention he lost the battle to keep LRUP local, but won a divisive leadership victory over his Colorado rival, **Corky Gonzales.** In the 1972 elections the party did poorly, but two years later Gutiérrez won a Zavala County judgeship. Of the principal Mexican American political leaders at the beginning of the 1970s, José Angel Gutiérrez unquestionably showed the most promise. However, he soon found himself involved in a power struggle with the Anglo court establishment, and after a long feud with the Texas judicial commission resigned his judgeship in 1981.

After stints teaching at two Oregon colleges, in 1986 José Angel Gutiérrez returned to Texas, where he resumed his civil rights interests as the director of the Greater Dallas Legal and Community Development Foundation. Having obtained his doctorate in jurisprudence, he became an administrative law judge for the city of Dallas in 1990. Three years later he entered the race for a vacated U.S. Senate seat on the Democratic ticket. Despite an energetic campaign, he continued to be perceived by many, both Mexican Americans and Anglos, as an extremist rather than a political pragmatist. In a contest with two dozen candidates he failed to win. He still operates a legal aid center as part of his continuing fight for Mexican American equality and rights.

FURTHER READING: García, Ignacio. *United We Win: The Rise and Fall of La Raza Unida Party.* Tucson: Mexican American Studies and Research Center, University of Arizona, 1989; Gutiérrez, José Angel. *The Making of a Chicano Militant: Lessons from Cristal.* Madison: University of Wisconsin Press, 1998; Gutiérrez, José Angel. *La Raza and Revolution.* San Francisco: R & E Research Associates, 1972; Hammerback, John C., Richard J. Jensen, and José Angel Gutiérrez. *A War of Words: Chicano Protest in the 1960s and 1970s.* Westport, Conn.: Greenwood Press, 1985; Navarro, Armando. *Mexican American Youth Organization: Avant-Garde of the Chicano Movement in Texas.* Austin: University of Texas Press, 1995; Navarro, Armando. *La Raza Unida Party: A Chicano Challenge to the U.S. Two-Party Dictatorship.* Philadelphia: Temple University Press, 2000; Shockley, John S. *Chicano Revolt in a Texas Town.* Notre Dame, Ind.: University of Notre Dame Press, 1974.

GUZMÁN, RALPH C., 1924–1985. Activist, professor. Ralph Guzmán played an important part in the Chicano rights struggle during the early years of the Chicano Movement. With an academic background in political science, in 1955 he was named director of the **Alianza Hispano-Americana**'s newly established civil rights department, where he soon became known for his skill in developing community support organizations. He was one of the founders of the **Community Service Organization** in the **Los Angeles** area.

Even before he obtained his doctorate Guzmán began a long and successful academic career. As a director in the Mexican American Study Project at the University of California, Los Angeles, he helped develop *The Mexican American People: The Nation's Second Largest Minority*, 1970, an outstanding resource book. Meanwhile, in the Department of Politics and Community Studies at the University of California, Santa Cruz, he had already begun educating an entire generation of students in the many aspects of racism, discrimination, and denial of rights in the United States. In addition to his teaching he served in the State Department and was a widely employed and respected consultant. He was also a prolific author who published extensively on various facets of racism and civil rights.

FURTHER READING: Acuña, Rodolfo. *Occupied America: A History of Chicanos*, 3rd ed. New York: Harper & Row, 1988; Guzmán, Ralph C. *The Political Socialization of the Mexican American People.* New York: Arno Press, 1976; Gutiérrez, Félix. "Ralph Guzmán Remembered." *La Red/The Net* 91 (October 1985) 1–2; "Ralph C. Guzmán." *PS* 19:1 (Winter 1986) 125–127.

HARRIS BILL, 1930. The Harris Bill was a response to the high levels of **immigration** from Mexico during the 1920s. As originally introduced by Senator William Harris, it would have added all Western Hemisphere countries except Canada to the quota system of the 1924 Immigration Act. Objections of southwestern employer interests resulted in efforts to defeat the bill by adding numerous amendments. Finally amended to apply the quota system only to Mexico, the bill passed the Senate but then died in the House.

The reduction of immigration to a trickle because of the 1930s depression and the **repatriation** of a quarter million Mexicans greatly lessened concerns about a quota for Mexican immigration.

FURTHER READING: Bogardus, Emory. "The Mexican Immigrant and the Quota." *Sociology and Social Research* 12:4 (March–April 1928) 371–378; Divine, Robert A. *American Immigration Policy, 1924–1952.* New Haven: Yale University Press, 1957; Taylor, Paul S. "More Bars against Mexicans." *Survey* 64 (April 1930) 26–27.

HEAD START. Project Head Start was part of President Lyndon B. Johnson's 1964 "War on Poverty" program. In part, Head Start had its origins in a preschool English language program called The Little School of the 400, started in 1957 by the **League of United Latin American Citizens.** Head Start programs were developed to meet perceived community needs by providing compensatory educational training to children of poor families. By actively involving parents in the educational process, it was hoped that more children might achieve their full potential.

In 1966 Head Start was transferred from the **Office of Economic Opportunity** to the Department of Health, Education and Welfare. Most observers have seen Head Start as an excellent effort at encouraging greater self-realization in underprivileged families by providing a much-needed initial boost on the ladder of upward mobility.

FURTHER READING: Currie, Janet, and Thomas Duncan. *Does Head Start Help Hispanic Children?* Cambridge, Mass.: National Bureau of Economic Research, 1996;

Ziegler, Edward. *Head Start: The Inside Story of America's Most Successful Educational Project.* New York: Basic Books, 1992.

HERMANDAD. A lay religious group, also sometimes called a *cofradía* (a brotherhood), originally created to organize observation of feast days, processions, and other church celebrations. Some *hermandades* also took on aspects of **mutualistas** and provided social benefits like insurance for their members. The **Penitentes** of New Mexico provide an outstanding example of the *hermandad.*

FURTHER READING: Pulido, Alberto L. *The Sacred World of the Penitentes.* Washington, D.C.: Smithsonian Institution Press, 2000; Vigil, Maurilio E. *The Hispanics of New Mexico: Essays on History and Culture.* Bristol, Ind.: Wyndham Hall Press, 1984; Weigle, Marta. *Brothers of Light, Brothers of Blood: The Penitentes of the Southwest.* Albuquerque: University of New Mexico Press, 1976.

HERNÁNDEZ, ALFRED J., 1917– . Activist, judge, lawyer. Judge Alfred J. Hernández was one of the leaders of the rump caucus that followed the walkout of fifty Mexican American delegates to the March 1966 **Equal Employment Opportunity Commission** meeting in Albuquerque, New Mexico. At the time president of the **League of United Latin American Citizens** (LULAC), Hernández pointed out the lack of Mexican American representation on the commission and the government's indifference to *la raza* as the chief reasons for the rump caucus.

At the annual LULAC convention three months later, he advocated a more militant policy for the organization. In July he helped organize the four-hundred-mile march to Austin and in the following April took an important part in a "**Brown Power**" conference in Sacramento, California. Later that year he testified before the U.S. **Civil Rights Commission** on abuses of migrant workers' rights.

In the 1970s Judge Hernández left the bench and returned to private law practice. In mid-1999 he was awarded the League of United Latin American Citizens' Lifetime Achievement Award, for his work establishing the **Head Start** Program and other contributions to *la raza.*

FURTHER READING: Chacón, José A. *Hispanic Notables in the United States of North America.* Albuquerque: Saguaro Press, 1978; *The Houston Chronicle* (7 May 1999) A43.

HERNÁNDEZ, ANTONIA, 1948– . Attorney, activist. Antonia Hernández was the daughter of immigrant parents who believed strongly in public service. As a college student she was active in several Chicano organizations and served on an admissions committee of the University of California Los Angeles law school. She also worked as a clerk in the **California Rural Legal Assistance** program. After obtaining her law doctorate in 1974, she took a position as an attorney in the East Los Angeles Center for Law and Justice and a year later became directing attorney for the Legal Aid Foundation.

In 1978 she accepted a staff position on the U.S. Senate Judiciary Committee in Washington, D.C., where she specialized in the area of **immigration** for the next three years.

Hernández lost her staff job when the Republican party won the U.S. Senate majority in 1981. She then took a position as an attorney in the Washington office of the **Mexican American Legal Defense and Educational Fund** (MALDEF), where she had an important part in the 1982 defeat of the Simpson-Mazzoli bill. Later she was employment litigation director in MALDEF's Los Angeles office, fostering **affirmative action** and wider federal employment opportunities for Latinos. In 1985 she became the president of MALDEF. As that agency's president and general counsel she highlighted a litany of civil rights concerns, especially voting rights, at-large elections, redistricting, equal educational opportunities, discrimination in employment, and immigrant rights.

Hernández led MALDEF in strong opposition to employer sanctions provisions in the **Immigration Reform and Control Act** of 1986. She believed that sanctions would lead to increased discrimination against U.S. Latinos, and persuaded the 1990 Leadership Conference on Civil Rights to support their repeal. Because of her extensive community involvement she was appointed to the Rebuild Los Angeles commission by Mayor Tom Bradley after the 1992 rioting there. In the beginning of 2001 she was appointed to the California Community Colleges Board of Governors by Governor Gray Davis. She continues to give MALDEF the benefits of her vigorous leadership.

FURTHER READING: Groller, Ingrid. "Law in the Family." *Parents' Magazine* (March 1985) 96; Gross, Lisa L. "Antonia Hernández: MALDEF's Legal Eagle." *Hispanic* (December 1990) 16–18; Hernández, Antonia. "Affirmative Action Services' Close Brush with Bush." *Hispanic Business* (February 1992) 10; Shaw, Katherine. "Antonia Hernández." *Vista* (October 1985) 16; Telgen, Diane, and Jim Kamp, eds. *Latinas! Women of Achievement.* Detroit: Visible Ink Press, 1996.

HERNÁNDEZ, MARÍA LATIGO, 1896–1986. Community activist, organizer. Born in Mexico at the end of the nineteenth century into a professional family, María Latigo grew up in a small town near Monterrey. After teaching elementary school in Monterrey, at age nineteen she married a Tejano and three years later they settled in San Antonio. As a young woman she began organizing Mexicano workers to fight for their rights, and she soon became a collaborator of civil rights activist **Alonso Perales** in San Antonio. With him and her husband, Pedro Hernández she helped organize several early civil rights groups in the 1920s, including the Order of **Knights of America** and the **League of United Latin American Citizens** (LULAC) in 1929. She viewed political activism as a citizen's duty toward the community.

An early feminist, in 1932 María became the first female radio announcer in San Antonio, a position she used to promote LULAC objectives. Two years later she helped found the Liga Pro-Defensa Escolar to articulate the educational needs of Mexican American children in Texas. During the 1938 San Antonio **pecan shellers' strike** she spoke out publicly for workers' rights despite strong opposition to the strike from city and church leaders.

Hernández remained an untiring fighter on the cutting edge of the Chicano rights struggle. During and after World War II she continued to organize protests in support of educational reforms and civil rights, to lead marches, and to make speeches. To promote cultural awareness she spoke only in Spanish. In her early seventies she took an active part in the Chicano Movement and was an active figure in the Texas **La Raza Unida Party**.

María Latigo Hernández. Courtesy of the Benson Latin American Collection, University of Texas at Austin.

In her late seventies María Hernández remained an active community leader. She participated in nearly all the important *raza* human rights struggles in Texas during the twentieth century. She died of pneumonia in January 1986.

FURTHER READING: Cotera, Martha. *Profile of the Mexican American Woman.* Austin: National Educational Laboratory, 1976; Hammerback, John, Richard J. Jensen, and José Angel Gutiérrez. *A War of Words: Chicano Protest in the 1960s and 1970s.* Westport, Conn.: Greenwood Press, 1985; *Las Mujeres: Mexican American/ Chicana Women.* Windsor, Calif.: National Women's History Project, 1991.

HERNÁNDEZ v. DRISCOLL CONSOLIDATED INDEPENDENT SCHOOL DISTRICT, 1957. In 1955 the **American G.I. Forum** (AGIF) and the **League of United Latin American Citizens** filed suit in the federal district court accusing the Driscoll school district of ethnic **discrimination**. The AGIF was represented by attorney **Gus García,** who argued that the placement of Mexican American children in separate classes was a violation of their Fourteenth Amendment rights. School officials of the southwest Texas town argued that the **segregation** was based on language deficiencies, although they admitted that no formal language tests were given the students. They were unable to explain why one Mexican American child who spoke no Spanish, only English, was included in the segregated class.

The court ruled, in January 1957, that the district's "separate grouping" of Mexican American children was unreasonable, arbitrary, and discriminatory. It ordered an end to the practice and issued an injunction against grouping based on ethnic ancestry. Despite the court's ruling, local officials found subterfuges and delaying tactics that enabled them to continue de facto segregation in the schools.

FURTHER READING: Allsup, Carl. "Education Is Our Freedom: The American G.I. Forum and Mexican American School Segregation in Texas, 1948–1957." *Aztlán* 8 (Spring-Summer-Fall 1977) 27-50; San Miguel, Guadalupe. "*Let All of Them Take Heed*": *Mexican Americans and the Campaign for Educational Equality in Texas, 1910–1981.* Austin: University of Texas Press, 1987.

HERNÁNDEZ v. THE STATE OF TEXAS, 1956. In a unanimous decision the U.S. Supreme Court under chief justice Earl Warren set aside the murder conviction of farm worker Pete Hernández of Texas, declaring that he had not received a fair trial because no Mexican Americans served on the jury. In this landmark civil rights case the court held that the exclusion of Mexican Americans from Texas juries violated the equal protection clause of the Fourteenth Amendment. A momentous aspect of the court's decision was its recognition, for the first time, that Mexican Americans formed a distinguishable ethnic group within the "white" classification and suffered from discriminatory practices as a result. The case was argued before the Supreme Court for the **American G.I. Forum** and the **League of United Latin American Citizens** by five attorneys headed by **Gus García** and **Carlos Cadena**. Hernández received a second trial in which he was again convicted of murder.

FURTHER READING: Baca, Balthazar A. "Hernández v. Texas." *Hispanic* (July 1989) 26; García, Mario T. *Mexican Americans: Leadership, Ideology, and Identity, 1930–1960.* New Haven: Yale University Press, 1989; Pycior, Julie Leininger. *LBJ & Mexican Americans: The Paradox of Power.* Austin: University of Texas Press, 1997.

HERRERA, EFRÉN, 1951– . Football player. Efrén Herrera was born near Guadalajara, Jalisco, where he lived until he was fourteen years old. Then the family immigrated to La Puente in southern California. He excelled in high school football, a skill that brought him a scholarship at the University of California, Los Angeles (UCLA). His prowess as a field goal kicker led to the establishing of new records at UCLA. When he graduated in 1974 he had offers to play both football and soccer.

Herrera accepted the Detroit Lions' offer but then was picked up by the Dallas Cowboys, where his outstanding ability as a kicker earned him a place on the All-Rookie team and later on the All-Pro team. At his request, in 1977 he was traded to the Seattle Seahawks, where he spent the next four years, ending his professional career a year later with the Buffalo Bills. In the mid-1980s he did TV commercials for Miller's beer and United Way; he also did sports commentary in Spanish for the Fox chain. Since his retirement from football he has spent time giving talks in high schools against drugs and gangs. He also has established a scholarship program for Latino students who want to go to the university.

FURTHER READING: Domínguez, Fernando. "Getting His Kicks." *Nuestro* (November 1972) 20-21; Rabago-Mussi, Angela. "Herrera se esfuerza por ser buen ejemplo para los jovenes." *The Arizona Republic/The Phoenix Gazette.* (24 January 1996) Special Section, 6.

HIDALGO KUNHARDT, EDWARD, 1912–1995. Secretary of the Navy, lawyer. Eduardo Hidalgo was born in Mexico City, came to the United States as a child, and became a citizen as a young man. He earned a B.A. magna cum laude from College of the Holy Cross in 1933 and a J.D. from Columbia three years later. In 1959 he obtained a civil law degree from the Universidad Nacional Autónoma de México. After a year as a law clerk, in 1937 he went into private practice. His law career was interrupted by **World War II**, in which he served in naval air combat intelligence for two years.

In 1946 Hidalgo resumed his international corporate law career in Mexico City and two years later established his own Mexican law partnership in which he worked for two decades. Because of his earlier experience as assistant to Secretary of the Navy James Forrestal, in 1965 he was appointed special assistant to Secretary Paul Nitze. From 1966 to 1972 he was the European representative of the Washington law firm of Cahill, Gordon & Reindel. Upon his return to the United States he served as special assistant and then general counsel to the U.S. Information Agency. In 1977 he was appointed assistant secretary of the navy, and was named secretary by President Jimmy Carter two years later.

While at the navy, Hidalgo made a settlement with General Dynamics Corporation in a controversial contract issue involving multimillion-dollar overruns; less than a year after he left the navy in 1981, he took a consultant job with General Dynamics for which he was paid $66,000. He defended his action before a 1985 congressional committee as not improper since his position had nothing to do with the navy. For his services Hidalgo has been the recipient of various honors, including the order of the Aguila Azteca from Mexico.

FURTHER READING: "Edward Hidalgo; Former Secretary of the Navy." *Los Angeles Times* (23 January 1995) A22; "Hidalgo, Valdez Nominated to High Positions." IMAGE *Newsletter* (Fall 1974); Mendosa, Rick. "The Business of Influence." *Hispanic*

Business (September 1993) 34–36; *Who's Who in America, 1984–1985.* Chicago: Marquis, 1984.

HIGH SCHOOL WALKOUTS, 1968. See STUDENT WALKOUTS.

HINOJOSA-SMITH, ROLANDO, 1929– . Writer, teacher, poet. Rolando Hinojosa-Smith was born in Mercedes, Texas, into a middle-class family that was both bilingual and bicultural. The youngest of five children, he grew up in a Mexicano barrio and at first attended a barrio school. By the time he reached public high school he had become an insatiable reader, and had also begun writing as well as playing football and acting in school plays.

Having completed high school, Rolando enlisted in the army for three years, after which he entered the University of Texas, but then returned to active service during the Korean conflict. When the Korean fighting ended, he was transferred to the states, where he was put to work as an army newspaper editor. Out of the army, he completed his undergraduate degree in Spanish language and literature and began teaching in high school. After several years he started graduate studies, earned his M.A. at Highlands University, and in the late 1960s completed his Ph.D. at the University of Illinois, Urbana. After a decade of teaching and administration positions in three universities he returned to his alma mater, the University of Texas at Austin, as the Ellen Clayton Garwood Centennial Professor.

In spite of time-consuming duties Hinojosa began writing, based on his early recollections and experiences in the lower Rio Grande valley. In 1973 his first work, *Estampas del valle y otras obras,* won the Quinto Sol award as an outstanding Chicano novel. His next work, *Klail City y sus alrededores,* was received even more warmly, winning the prestigious international Premio Casa de las Américas in 1976. Among his many subsequent books, *Mi querido Rafa* won the 1981 Best Book in the Humanities award. In 1993 Rolando published *The Useless Servants,* the purported Korean war diary of Rafe Buenrostro, which paints a harshly realistic picture of that conflict in which he participated. His most recent work is *Ask a Policeman,* 1998. He is best known for his many novels composing the Klail City Death Trip Series, but is also the author of a satirical work based on Ambrose Bierce's *Cynic's Work Book.* He titled it *El Grito* or *Devil's Dictionary.* He has been the recipient of honors and awards too numerous to list.

FURTHER READING: Bruce-Novoa, Juan. *Chicano Authors: Inquiry by Interview.* Austin: University of Texas Press, 1980; Bruce-Novoa, Juan. "Chicano Wins Major Prize." *Hispania* 53:3 (September 1976) 521; Lee, Joyce Glover. *Rolando Hinojosa and the American Dream.* Denton: University of North Texas Press, 1997; Martínez, Julio A., and Francisco A. Lomelí. *Chicano Literature: A Reference Guide.* Westport, Conn,: Greenwood Press, 1985; Saldívar, José D. *The Rolando Hinojosa Reader: Essays Historical and Cultural.* Houston: Arte Público Press, 1985; Zilles, Klaus. *Rolando Hinojosa: A Reader's Guide.* Albuquerque: University of New Mexico Press, 2001.

HISPANIC CAUCUS. *See* CONGRESSIONAL HISPANIC CAUCUS.

HISPANO SUBCULTURE. In **New Mexico** there exists a distinctive subculture, usually referred to as *Hispanic* or *Hispano*, that has resulted from a prolonged settlement pattern dating as far back as the end of the sixteenth century and from the area's subsequent isolation. This subculture has a number of distinguishing characteristics. Among them are Hispano folklore—proverbs, ballads, riddles, and myths—many of which have Spanish rather than strictly Mexican origins. There are also folk arts, particularly carvings such as *santos* (painted wooden religious images), *bultos* (statues), and *retablos* (altar panels); distinctive family and given names; and the persistence of religious practices like that of the **Penitente** Brotherhood. While New Mexico Hispanos pay homage to the Virgin of **Guadalupe** like other Mexican Americans, they also give nearly equal veneration to the Virgin under the title "La Conquistadora," a reference to her role in the settlement of Nuevo México. Although increasingly urbanized in the second half of the twentieth century, many Hispanos remain dependent on traditional agriculture and livestock-raising. Finally, Hispano cuisine differs from that of other Mexican Americans in that it is noted for the extensive use of red chili peppers.

This Hispano culture has retained its distinctive characteristics partly because it developed in a distant outpost of New Spain, then Mexico, and later the United States. After the Treaty of **Guadalupe Hidalgo**, Hispano New Mexico attracted little immigration from Mexico and also continued to remain relatively isolated from Anglo settlement. When peon-class immigrants began to flood into the Southwest at the beginning of the twentieth century, Hispanos saw themselves as losing social position by being identified with the newcomers. They distanced themselves from the "new" immigration by stressing their Spanish roots and rejecting or at least greatly downplaying Mexican aspects of their culture.

FURTHER READING: Gonzales-Berry, Erlinda, and David A. Maciel, eds. *The Contested Homeland: A Chicano History of New Mexico*. Albuquerque: University of New Mexico Press, 2000; Montgomery, Charles. *The Spanish Redemption: Heritage, Power, and Loss on New Mexico's Upper Rio Grande*. Berkeley: University of California Press, 2002; *The New Mexican Hispano*, reprint. New York: Arno Press, 1974; Nostrand, Richard L. *The Hispano* Homeland. Norman: University of Oklahoma Press, 1992; Sánchez, George I. *Forgotten People: A Study of the New Mexicans*. Albuquerque: University of New Mexico Press, 1996 (1940); Simmons, Marc. *New Mexico: An Interpretive History*. Albuquerque: University of New Mexico Press, 1988; Vigil, Maurilio E. *The Hispanics of New Mexico: Essays on History and Culture*. Bristol, Ind.: Wyndham Hall Press, 1984; Weigle, Marta. *Brothers of Light, Brothers of Blood: The Penitentes of the Southwest*. Albuquerque: University of New Mexico Press, 1976.

***HOPWOOD v. STATE OF TEXAS*, 1992–1996.** In 1992 Anglos Cheryl Hopwood and others filed suit against the state of Texas, alleging discrimination in the University of Texas law school's admissions policy, which gave preference to Mexican and African Americans. Four years later the 5th U.S. Circuit Court of Appeals ruled that the policy led to reverse discrimination by denying the equal protection guarantee of the Fourteenth Amendment to the plaintiffs and barred the use of racial factors of any kind in admissions. The Hopwood decision resulted in the dismantling of racially based recruitment policies, admission programs, scholarships, and financial aid packages and led to a decrease in minority enrollment at Texas universities and colleges. The U.S. Supreme Court ruling in the 2003 case of *Grutter v. Bollinger* regarding the admissions policy of the the University of Michigan law school, swept away the restrictions of the Hopwood decision.

FURTHER READING: Adam, Michelle. "Hopwood/Proposition 209 and Minority Enrollment in Texas and California." *Hispanic Outlook in Higher Education* (18 November 2002) 39–40; Denniston, Lyle. "Race-Based Admissions Await Another Test Case." *The Boston Globe* (26 June 2001) National/Foreign, A8; Eastland, Terry. "Perspective on Affirmative Action; . . ." *Los Angeles Times* (22 March 1996) Metro 9B; Gwynne, S. C. "Undoing Diversity: A Bombshell Court Ruling Curtails Affirmative Action." *Time* (1 April 1996) 54.

HOUSING. Historically, most towns of the Southwest have had well-defined **barrios** to which Mexicanos were restricted until recently by economic status and real-estate covenants. Rural housing has generally been inadequate as well as inferior, while housing in the barrio has typically been both substandard and overcrowded. In the large urban centers of Texas and California only dilapidated tenements and the least desirable housing have been widely available to *la raza.* Housing **segregation** has also frequently been reflected in school segregation. Substandard barrio housing is often accompanied by poor quality in urban services. For many Mexicanos in these cities, housing segregation has increased rather than decreased.

Housing conditions have generally been somewhat better for Mexican

An adobe house with chili peppers drying, Concho, Arizona, 1940. © Library of Congress.

Americans in Arizona, Colorado, and New Mexico. These states have higher levels of Chicano home ownership than do California and Texas. The differing levels of home ownership in the Southwest seem to be partly related to percentages of recent immigrants in the Mexicano population of the different states. Income is also an obvious factor. Since World War II, higher levels of family income have enabled many Mexican Americans to procure better rental housing and to achieve home ownership.

Decent housing available to all without discrimination has long been an important Mexican American goal. In August 2001 the Department of Housing and Urban Development announced that minority home ownership had reached a record 48.8 percent. In the past half century, housing available to Mexicanos has improved but has not kept up with the improvement in housing and home ownership among Anglos. Despite protests by Mexican Americans, disruption of communities by urban renewal or new freeways has continued. Ethnic prejudice against la raza in housing continues to be a salient element in urban segregation.

FURTHER READING: Cubillos, Herminia L. "Fair Housing and Latinos." In *Land Grants, Housing, and Political Power*, edited by Antoinette Sedillo López. New York: Garland, 1995; Dolbeare, Cushing N. *The Hispanic Housing Crisis.* Washington, D.C.: National Council of La Raza, 1988; "Housing Conditions" and "Residential Segregation." In *The Mexican American People*, edited by Leo Grebler, et al. New York: Free Press, 1970; Santiago, Anna M. "Trends in Black and Latino Segregation in the Post-Fair Housing Era: Implications for Housing Policy." *La Raza Law Journal* 9:2 (Fall 1996) 131–153.

HOUSTON, SAM(UEL), 1793–1863. Politician, soldier. Originally from Virginia, Sam Houston grew up in Tennessee. At sixteen he ran away from home and lived with the Cherokee Indians for three years. He joined the U.S. Army when the War of 1812 broke out and was wounded in action. Five years later he was named sub–Indian agent to the Cherokees and assisted in their removal across the Mississippi. He then read law for six months and opened a law office. As a frontier lawyer he became active in politics, was elected to the U.S. Congress in 1823, and four years later became governor of Tennessee. A marital crisis caused him to resign suddenly. He fled to the Cherokees for three years and later moved to **Texas**, where he settled at Nacogdoches. When the Texas revolt against Mexican centralism broke out in 1835 he was elected commander of the Texas forces. His defeat of the Mexican army and capture of President **Santa Anna** at San Jacinto ended the latter's attempts to retake Texas.

Houston then was voted the first president of the Texas republic and was later elected for a second term. When Texas was admitted to the United States he was elected to the U.S. Senate and served from 1846 to 1859. In the latter year he won election to the governorship of Texas, but his anti-secession stance when the **Civil War** erupted caused him to be removed from

Photographic portrait of Samuel Houston, c. 1860.
© Library of Congress.

office in 1861. He died two years later of pneumonia.

FURTHER READING: Campbell, Randolph B. *Sam Houston and the American Southwest.* New York: HarperCollins, 1993; Houston, Sam. *The Autobiography of Sam Houston.* Edited by Donald Day and Harry H. Ullom. Norman: University of Oklahoma Press, 1954; Williams, John Hoyt. *Sam Houston: A Biography of the Father of Texas.* New York: Simon and Schuster, 1993.

HOYOS, ANGELA DE, c. 1940– . Poet. Angela de Hoyos was born in Coahuila but grew up in San Antonio, Texas, to which her parents had moved. Strongly influenced by her mother's recital of poetry, as a child she composed poems that were published in her high school newspaper. While she was still in her early twenties her poetry began to receive wide recognition. Under the influence of the Chicano **movimiento**, in the late 1960s she turned to socioeconomic themes in her work.

Hoyos's prolific poetic output appeared widely in literary journals, but only in 1975 did she have a book of her poems published, *Arise, Chicano! and Other Poems.* In the same year her *Poems/Poemas* was published in Buenos Aires and in the following year *Selecciones* was printed in Mexico City. Widely considered one of the leading Chicana poets, she has been published on five continents and won awards on four.

FURTHER READING: Aguilar-Henson, Marcella. *The Multi-faceted Poetic World of Angela de Hoyos.* Austin: Relampago Books, 1982; Binder, Wolfgang, ed. *Partial Autobiographies: Interviews with Twenty Chicano Poets.* Erlangen, Germany: Palm & Enke, 1985; Martínez, Julio A., and Francisco A. Lomelí. *Chicano Literature: A Reference Guide.* Westport, Conn.: Greenwood Press, 1985; Ramos, Luis A. *Angela de Hoyos: A Critical Look.* Albuquerque: Pajaritos Publications, 1979.

HUELGA. The term *huelga*, the Spanish word for strike, is commonly used in reference to the **Delano** *grape strike* led by César Chávez in the second half of the 1960s. Its symbol, the huelga black eagle, became the banner of the United Farm Workers union.

HUERTA, DOLORES FERNÁNDEZ, 1930– . Labor organizer, activist. Dolores Fernández was born in northeastern New Mexico but the family moved to Stockton, California, while she was still a young child. Here she grew up and received her early education. After high school and a failed early marriage, she returned to school with strong support from her mother in order to pursue a career in teaching. Her post–World War II experiences in the classroom and the community led her to social activism, registering and organizing voters for the **Community Service Organization** (CSO) in the Stockton area. During this time she met and married fellow community activist Ventura Huerta. After a stint in Sacramento as a CSO lobbyist, she later moved to Los Angeles as director of the CSO there.

Strongly politicized by Chicano activism, Huerta became somewhat disillusioned with the CSO after a few years and in 1962 joined **César Chávez** in organizing farm workers in California's Central Valley. Her early role in the Chávez union was to recruit new members in the Stockton area, and later in the decade she took an important leadership role in the **Delano grape strike**. Developing into a dynamic speaker and fund-raiser, in time she also became a cagey union strategist and a highly adept contract negotiator. She made herself Chávez's most valuable, if sometimes contentious, associate. Her critics within the **United Farm Workers** (UFW) saw her as often unable or unwilling to follow agreed-upon organizational plans.

During the late 1970s Huerta headed a UFW political arm, the Citizenship Participation Day department, in an unsuccessful effort to obtain enforcement of the California Labor Relations Act of 1975. In the following decade she carried a heavy program of speaking tours, fund-raising engagements, and boycott management. She has been arrested a score of times. During the 1988 political campaign she was seriously injured with a ruptured spleen and broken ribs as a result of excessive use of force by police during a peaceful San Francisco demonstration against Republican presidential candidate George Bush. She was later awarded $825,000 in damages for the assault. Ill, on and off, since her beating in San Francisco, in 2000 she underwent successful surgery for internal bleeding. In the 1990s Dolores Huerta gradually resumed her work in the UFW, concerning herself primarily with immigration reform, pesticide abuse, and general farm labor health conditions.

In sum, the combative Huerta was second only to César Chávez in shaping the United Farm Workers. Like Chávez, she saw the union's struggle as part of a larger fight for greater equality and human rights, and she used her skills to advance toward these objectives. As a result she became an important symbol in the Mexican American workers' struggle for their rights, particularly since Chávez's death in 1993. She has been the recipient of numerous awards and honors including induction into the National Women's Hall of Fame and the 1999 Eleanor Roosevelt Award for Human Rights.

FURTHER READING: Bonilla-Santiago, Gloria. *Breaking Ground and Barriers: Hispanic Women Developing Effective Leadership.* San Diego, Calif.: Marin Publications,

1992; Coburn, Judith. "Dolores Huerta: La Pasionaria of the Farmworkers." *Ms.* (November 1976) 11–16; Garcia, Richard A. "Dolores Huerta: Woman Organizer, and Symbol." *California History* 72:1 (Spring 1993) 56–71; James Rainey, "The Eternal Soldadera," *Los Angeles Times Magazine* (15 August 1999) 13–15, 35–36; Margaret Rose, "Traditional and Nontraditional Patterns of Female Activism in the United Farm Workers of America, 1962 to 1980." *Frontiers* 11:1 (1990) 26–32.

I AM JOAQUÍN. The title of the epic poem published by **Corky Gonzales** in 1967. *I Am Joaquín*, which vividly expressed the Chicano's torturous search for identity and self-understanding, was unquestionably the outstanding inspirational work of the **movimiento** and held special appeal for Chicano youths. It has been reprinted, anthologized, recited, performed, quoted, cited, and analyzed over the years. It also became the basis of a film made by **Luis Valdez.**

FURTHER READING: Gonzales, Rodolpho. *I am Joaquín—Yo Soy Joaquín: An Epic Poem.* New York: Bantam Books, 1972 (1967).

IDAR FAMILY. Activists. Three generations of the Idar family: grandfather Nicasio (1855–1914); his three children Jovita (1885–1946), Eduardo (1887–1947), and Clemente (1893–1934); and grandson Ed, Jr. (1020–) all played important roles in the Tejano struggle for Mexican American rights. Perhaps the family's most important contribution was the calling of the **Primer Congreso Mexicanista** at Laredo in 1911. Nicasio, publisher of *La Crónica,* an important Spanish language weekly in Laredo, and a strong believer in the benefits of organization, used his paper to lead the fight for Mexicano rights. Daughter Jovita, a journalist on her father's paper, took an outstanding role in organizing and developing the Primer Congreso Mexicanista, through which she established a women's organization, La Liga Femenil Mexicanista. Son Eduardo also participated in the Congreso of 1911; at the end of the following decade he played an important role in the creation of the **League of United Latin American Citizens** (LULAC), particularly taking a significant part in writing its constitution. Younger brother Clemente was an American Federation of Labor union organizer and participated in founding the **Order Sons of America** in the early 1920s. Later he became deeply involved in LULAC as well. Ed, Jr., throughout his life has been active as an officer in the **American G.I. Forum**, the **Political Association of Spanish-Speaking Organizations**, and the **Mexican American Legal Defense and Educational Fund**. He served in World War II, earned a journalism degree, then completed his law studies in 1956, and served as Texas assistant attorney general from 1970 until his retirement in 1983. Ed Idar dedicated the greater part of his adult life to improving the lot of Mexican Americans by fighting for equal rights and greater opportunities through better education and increased political participation.

FURTHER READING: Berson, Robin Kadison. *Marching to a Different Drummer: Unrecognized Heroes of American History.* Westport, Conn.: Greenwood Press, 1994; Limón, José E. "El Primer Congreso Mexicanista de 1911: A Precursor to Contemporary Chicanismo." *Aztlán* 5:1 & 2 (Spring and Fall 1974) 85–117; Martínez, Liliana. "A Thirst for Helping Others." *Narratives: Stories of the U.S. Latinos and Latinas and World War II.* 2:1 (Fall 2000 and Spring 2001) Latinos and Latinas and World War II Oral History Project, School of Journalism, University of Texas at Austin; Tyler, Ron, ed. *The New Handbook of Texas*, vol. 3. Austin: Texas State Historical Association, 1996; Zamora, Emilio. *The World of the Mexican Worker in Texas.* College Station: Texas A&M University Press, 1993.

IMMIGRATION. Immigration has been a dominant theme in the Mexican American experience. While immigration northward from the Mexican heartland has been a continuous process for centuries, for convenience it may be divided into four broad periods, each greater in volume than its predecessor. The first period begins at the end of the sixteenth century with the Oñate settling expedition and ends in the second half of the nineteenth century. Most immigrants of this stage settled in the Nuevo México area. Immigration to Texas began early in the 1700s and the colonizing of California developed half a century later. At the end of this first period, when the area became a part of the United States through the 1848 Treaty of **Guadalupe Hidalgo**, it had a population of about eighty thousand.

The second wave of Mexican immigration, from the 1880s to 1910, was a response to three push-pull factors: the incorporation of the Southwest into the U.S. national economy, the reduced availability and ultimate exclusion of Asian workers, and worsening social and political conditions in Mexico. Most of the immigrants came from the north border states of Mexico and crossed into Texas. By 1910 they had tripled the number of Mexico-born persons in the United States to a total of approximately 250,000.

The third surge of immigration from Mexico was triggered by the 1910 **Mexican revolution**. The violence and chaotic conditions in northern and central Mexico caused a massive movement from rural areas to the relative safety of urban environments and the even safer alternative of crossing into the United States. In addition to this push, there was also the pull of U.S. agricultural and industrial labor needs during World War I and the 1920s economic boom. **Mining**, cotton farming, the sugar beet industry, and railroads led in the demand for cheap labor. Approximately half of the Mexicans in this immigration came from the border states and the other half from the north central interior. They left at least another 250,000 in the United States, most in the Southwest but also increasing numbers in the Northwest and industrial Midwest. This third group, largely from the middle and lower

Mexican immigrant Maria Teresa Camino waves an American flag, along with hundreds of others who have just been sworn in as new American citizens, Los Angeles Sports Arena, March 2003. © AP/Wide World Photos.

economic classes, has given Mexican American culture most of its current configuration and content.

World War II set the fourth Mexican immigrant wave into motion. As a result of wartime labor needs, the United States and Mexico agreed on a temporary contract worker program to be regulated by the two governments. This **bracero** program and its successors ran from 1942 until 1964, during which time they brought in nearly five million Mexicans (with many repeaters) to work, primarily in U.S. agriculture and on the railroads. During this period an equal or possibly greater number of **undocumented** Mexican sojourners entered the country, and the termination of the bracero program accelerated the number of undocumented entries. In the early 1990s an economic downturn led to another of the periodic spasms of anti-immigrant agitation and legislation like California's **Proposition 187**. Polls have indicated widespread concern, even among Mexican Americans, about levels of immigration, particularly by undocumenteds. Studies show that informal

A U.S. Border Patrol agent marches a group of undocumented immigrants across a stretch of the Yuha Desert after they were spotted hiding in the brush, August 1997. © AP/Wide World Photos.

networking over the years has established patterns of regional origins and U.S. destinations that persist today.

From its beginnings, immigration from Mexico has been made up of both settlers and sojourners; a majority considered themselves sojourners but ultimately became settlers. The 2000 census counted approximately 20.6 million persons of Mexican descent in the United States. Of these, about 10 percent trace their ancestry to the eighty thousand who were living in the Southwest when the Treaty of Guadalupe Hidalgo made them U.S. nationals. The remaining eighteen million are more recent immigrants and their descendants. The unbroken stream of settlers and sojourners from Mexico for a century and a half has provided constant cultural reinforcement that helps to explain the deep persistence of Mexican culture in the United States.

FURTHER READING: Andreas, Peter. *Border Games: Policing the U.S.-Mexico Divide.* Ithaca: Cornell University Press, 2000; Cornelius, Wayne A. *Mexican Migration to the United States: Causes, Consequences, and the U.S. Response.* Cambridge: Massachusetts Institute of Technology Press, 1978; Gamio, Manuel. *Mexican Immigration to the United States.* Chicago: University of Chicago Press, 1930, reprint, New York: Arno Press, 1970; Gutierrez, David G., ed. *Between Two Worlds: Mexican Immigrants in the United States.* Wilmington, Del.: Scholarly Resources, 1996; Juárez-Orozco, Marcelo M., ed. *Crossings: Mexican Immigration in Interdisciplinary Perspectives.* Cambridge: Harvard University, David Rockefeller Center for Latin American Studies, 1998; Martínez, Oscar J. *Mexican-Origin People in the United States: A Topical History.* Tucson: University of Arizona Press, 2001; *Mexican Immigration to the United States*. New York: Arno Press, 1976.

IMMIGRATION LEGISLATION. Immigration to the United States was unregulated until the demand for cheap immigrant labor increased greatly toward the end of the nineteenth century. The Chinese Exclusion Act of 1882 was a first step, followed that same year by a general immigration law that applied only to entrants by sea. Aimed at inexpensive labor from southern and eastern Europe, it was followed three years later by legislation prohibiting immigration of workers under contract. Two decades later in 1906 a federal bureau of immigration was established to enforce these restrictions. Immigration by land from Mexico and Canada remained unregulated.

During World War I the need for workers caused the Department of Labor to explicitly sanction the importation of Mexican agricultural workers. Fear of a flood of European refugee labor at the end of the war led to passage of the Emergency Immigration Act of 1921, which established a quota system and an annual immigration maximum of 357,000. Western Hemisphere nations were exempted from the quota. Three years later Congress reduced the total to 150,000, revised the quota system to favor northern European immigrants, and completely excluded Asians.

The **McCarran-Walter Immigration and Nationality Act** of 1952, which had a declared purpose of screening communists and other subversives, ended the exclusion of Asians and empowered the government to deport naturalized citizens as well as aliens. In 1965 heavy immigration, legal and **undocumented**, from Mexico was the main factor in new immigration legislation that put Western Hemisphere nations under the quota system. Continued efforts during the next two decades to reduce undocumented immigration led to the **Immigration Reform and Control Act** of 1986 (IRCA). The IRCA aimed at greater border control and at curtailing employer abuses; it also included penalties for employers of illegal aliens and a complex amnesty program.

FURTHER READING: Andreas, Peter. *Border Games: Policing the U.S.-Mexico Divide.* Ithaca: Cornell University Press, 2000; Bean, Frank D., Barry Edmondston, and Jeffry S. Passel, eds. *Undocumented Migration to the United States: IRCA and the Experience of the 1980s.* Washington, D.C.: Urban Institute Press, 1990; Cornelius, Wayne A. *Building the Cactus Curtain: Mexican Migration and U.S. Responses, from Wilson to Carter.* Berkeley: University of California Press, 1980; Cornelius, Wayne A. *Mexican Migration to the United States: Causes, Consequences, and the U.S. Response.* Cambridge: Massachusetts Institute of Technology Press, 1978; U.S. National Commission for Manpower Policy. *Manpower and Immigration Policies in the United States.* Washington, D.C.: U.S. Government Printing Office, 1978.

IMMIGRATION REFORM AND CONTROL ACT, 1986. After years of efforts to reform and tighten the U.S. i**mmigration** policy by penalties and stricter enforcement, Congress passed the Immigration Reform and Control

Act (IRCA) in 1986. The IRCA had three principal goals: to curtail **undocumented** immigration by stricter control of the border, to lessen job availability by imposing sanctions on employers of undocumenteds, and to provide an amnesty program for undocumenteds already in the United States. The legislation also included efforts to reduce abuse of workers by employers. Mexican American reaction to the law was mixed.

The IRCA legislation's greatest success was in reducing the undocumented alien population in the United States through its amnesty program. By the end of the decade over three million undocumenteds, including more than two million Mexicans of whom more than one million were seasonal agricultural workers, had applied for amnesty. It is less evident that the law appreciably reduced the number of employers willing to hire undocumented aliens. Lastly, the expanded **Border Patrol** and tighter border controls have not deterred those who continue to regard the United States as a land of opportunity. The situation is exacerbated by the fact that there is a huge visa waiting list for Mexicans, over one million in the 1990s.

FURTHER READING: Bean, Frank D., Barry Edmondston, and Jeffry S. Passel, eds. *Undocumented Migration to the United States: IRCA and the Experience of the 1980s.* Washington, D.C.: Urban Institute Press, 1990; Meier, Matt S., and Feliciano Ribera. *Mexican Americans / American Mexicans: From Conquistadors to Chicanos.* New York: Hill and Wang, 1993; Muñoz, Cecilia. *Unfinished Business: The Immigration and Control Act of 1986.* Washington, D.C.: National Council of La Raza, 1990.

IN RE RICARDO RODRÍGUEZ, 1897. *In re Ricardo Rodríguez* was a benchmark case in the Mexican American struggle for civil rights. Rodríguez, a resident of San Antonio, Texas, for ten years, filed in the federal courts for final approval of his application for citizenship. His request moved the issue of U.S. **citizenship** for Mexicans into the judicial system and unleashed a movement to disenfranchise all Mexicanos in **Texas**. A highly vocal Anglo opposition argued that Mexicans were not eligible by law since they were neither black nor white. The case naturally aroused strong and widespread interest among Texas Mexicanos.

In May 1897, federal district judge Thomas Maxey held that Rodríguez had the right to become a citizen and to vote. In his ruling he cited the Fourteenth Amendment and the Treaty of **Guadalupe Hidalgo**, and further pointed out that race and skin color were not legal determinants in citizenship. While his decision discouraged and reined in attempts by Texans to deny Mexicanos their full civil rights, it by no means ended them.

FURTHER READING: De León, Arnoldo. *In Re Ricardo Rodríguez: An Attempt at Chicano Disenfranchisement in San Antonio, 1896–1897.* San Antonio: Caravel Press, 1979; Padilla, Fernando. "Early Chicano Legal Recognition: 1846–1897." *Journal of Popular Culture* 13:3 (Spring 1980) 564–574.

INCORPORATED MEXICAN AMERICAN GOVERNMENT EMPLOYEES. National IMAGE, Inc., as it is also referred to, was formally organized in 1972 by a group of Mexican American federal government employees. Initially its basic purpose was to counter discrimination against the Spanish-speaking, particularly in government hiring. IMAGE soon expanded its membership to include all Latino employees at all levels of government.

IMAGE's goal is to increase hiring opportunities for U.S. Latinos at federal, state, and local government levels as well as to promote the careers of U.S. Latinos already employed. It is also concerned with achieving equality of treatment for Latinos in all aspects of public service. National IMAGE goes beyond merely fighting existing discrimination in hiring by actively recruiting and training Latinos for federal jobs. It holds an annual women's training conference, and local chapters regularly conduct job fairs and sponsor workshops on affirmative action, voting rights, voter registration, and citizenship. Its Washington, D.C., office maintains a Latino talent bank, and its more than 120 chapters in forty states publicize information about available positions and encourage qualified candidates to apply for them.

To avoid confusion with the group Involvement of Mexican Americans in Gainful Endeavors (IMAGE), a Texas-based youth-oriented association, Incorporated Mexican American Government Employees is frequently referred to as National IMAGE.

FURTHER READING: "Civil Rights: National Image Inc.: The Concern for Equality." *La Luz* (February–March 1980) 12; Córdova, José. "IMAGE Is No Mirage; It's Here to Stay." *La Luz* (September 1972) 36–37; Gonzales, Sylvia A. *Hispanic American Voluntary Organizations.* Westport, Conn.: Greenwood Press, 1985; Treviso, Rubén. "National IMAGE." *Caminos* (September 1982) 37–38. www.nationalimageinc.org

INDUSTRIAL AREAS FOUNDATION. The IAF is an aggressive community advocacy organization that teaches people relatively simple techniques for organizing effectively to develop and use their political power. It was begun in 1940 by Chicagoan Saul Alinsky with support from Marshall Field III and Chicago's Catholic bishop, Bernard Sheil. The IAF was based on Alinsky's academic training in criminology and his experience in urban sociology. Its purpose was to train social activists in techniques and tactics for empowering the powerless poor and for enabling them to defend their rights.

In the post–World War II period the IAF helped Chicano barrios to organize in their struggle for rights. Its organizational structure was adapted by many Mexican American community groups, particularly forming the basis for the **Community Service Organization** and **United Neighborhoods Organization**. The success of IAF techniques attracted numerous social organizers like **Ernie Cortés** and **Fred Ross, Sr.**, who used Alinsky's ideas and carried on IAF work in the Southwest after his death in 1972.

FURTHER READING: Alinsky, Saul. *Reveille for Radicals.* 2nd ed. New York: Vintage Press, 1969; Finks, P. David. *The Radical Vision of Saul Alinsky.* New York: Paulist Press, 1984; Horwitt, Sanford D. *Let Them Call Me Rebel: Saul Alinsky, His*

Life and Legacy. New York: Random House, 1989; Márquez, Benjamin. "The Industrial Areas Foundation and the Mexican-American Community in Texas: The Politics of Issue Mobilization." In *Pursuing Power: Latinos and the Political System,* edited by F. Chris García. Notre Dame: University of Notre Dame Press, 1997; Márquez, Benjamin. "Standing for the Whole: The Southwest Industrial Areas Foundation on Identity and Mexican American Politics." *Social Service Review* 74:3 (2000) 453–473.

INDUSTRIAL WORKERS OF THE WORLD. The IWW was established in Chicago in 1905 to organize and support a class struggle against capitalism. A militant radical union, it had its greatest success in the West, where it recruited membership in lumbering, mining, and agriculture among unskilled casual workers, many of whom were Mexicanos. Among its most dramatic involvements were the 1913 Durst Ranch strike at Wheatland, California, and the 1914 Ludlow miners strike in **Colorado.** At its peak, the IWW claimed a membership of more than ten thousand. Its importance for Mexicanos was in making them aware of the benefits of unionization and providing them with experience in developing organizing skills.

FURTHER READING: Dubofsky, Melvyn. *We Shall Be All: A History of the Industrial Workers of the World.* 2nd ed. Urbana: University of Illinois Press, 1988; Jamieson, Stuart M. *Labor Unionism in American Agriculture.* Washington, D.C.: Government Printing Office, 1945.

INTER-AGENCY COMMITTEE ON MEXICAN AMERICAN AFFAIRS. The agency was created by President Lyndon Johnson in 1967 to alert Mexican Americans to federal programs intended for them and to make sure that they were receiving the services offered. Two years later it was converted into the **Cabinet Committee on Opportunities for Spanish-Speaking People**, which was allowed by the Republicans to die at the end of its five-year term.

FURTHER READING: Ortego, Philip D. "The Minority at the Border Cabinet Meeting in El Paso." *Nation* 207:2 (11 December 1967) 624–627; Pycior, Julie Leininger. *LBJ & Mexican Americans: The Paradox of Power.* Austin: University of Texas Press, 1997.

INTERNATIONAL BROTHERHOOD OF TEAMSTERS. The Teamsters union was organized in 1903 and grew to become the nation's largest union toward the end of the century, despite repeated charges of internal corruption. The member unions have been divided on the question of local versus national policy control; member unions have not always agreed with decisions made at the national level. This conflict sometimes has led local leaders to refuse to accept national agreements, as in the **Delano grape strike** and the Salinas **lettuce strike**, in which locals refused to abide by jurisdictional boundaries agreed to by the national leadership after bitter struggles against the United Farm Workers.

FURTHER READING: Brill, Steven. *The Teamsters.* New York: Simon and Schuster, 1978; Zeller, F. C. Duke. *Devil's Pact: Inside the World of the Teamster's Union.* Secaucus, N.J.: Carol, 1996.

J

JARAMILLO, MARÍ-LUCI, 1928– . Ambassador, teacher, educational administrator. Marí-Luci Jaramillo was born in Las Vegas, New Mexico, where she grew up and received her early schooling. Encouraged by parents who believed strongly in education, after high school graduation she entered New Mexico Highlands University, but then dropped out to marry. After three children and several part-time jobs, she resumed her university studies and completed her B.A. magna cum laude in 1955. While teaching elementary school she began graduate studies and received her master's degree four years later.

Marí-Luci next entered a doctoral program at the University of New Mexico (UNM), where she also began teaching English and then other subjects to foreign students. Because of her work with students from Latin America, in 1969 she was appointed assistant director in the university's Minority Group Cultural Awareness Center. By this time, in addition to her teaching and administrative duties she was also doing consulting work for various state and federal programs. As a consultant she traveled extensively in Central and South America, working with local teachers, setting up workshops, and making recommendations for improvements in teacher-training programs.

In 1970 Marí-Luci received her doctorate in education and was immediately hired in the UNM education department. She quickly rose to associate and full professor, and then was appointed to the department chair. During this time she was a frequent speaker at regional and national conferences and workshops because of her expertise, especially in bilingual education. In 1977 she was appointed by President Jimmy Carter as ambassador to Honduras, becoming the first Latina to represent the United States to another country. Three years later she returned to the United States to become deputy assistant secretary for Inter-American Affairs in the State Department. After Republican Ronald Reagan became president in 1981 she resigned, in part because of disagreement over his educational policies.

Jaramillo returned to New Mexico to become special assistant to the president of UNM, from which position she soon moved to dean of the college of education and then to vice president for student affairs. In 1987 she accepted a position as northern California director of the Educational Testing Service. Five years later she was promoted to vice-president for its field services in the United States. In addition to her ambassadorship, Marí-Luci Jaramillo has been the recipient of honors and awards far too numerous to list in their entirety.

FURTHER READING: Jaramillo, Mari-Luci. *Madame Ambassador: The Shoemaker's Daughter.* Tempe, Ariz.: Bilingual Press, 2002; Rebolledo, Tey Diana, ed. *Nuestras mujeres.* Albuquerque: El Norte, 1992; Telgen, Diane, and Jim Kamp, eds. *Notable Hispanic American Women.* Detroit: Gale Research, 1993; Vásquez, Olga. "Marí-Luci Jaramillo." In *Women Educators in the United States, 1820–1993: A Bio-Bibliographical Sourcebook,* edited by Maxine Schwartz Seller. Westport, Conn.: Greenwood Press, 1994.

JARAMILLO, PEDRITO, c. 1850–1907. Faith healer, *curandero.* Pedrito Jaramillo was born in the mid-1800s near Guadalajara, Jalisco, where he learned *curandero* skills as a young man. In the early 1880s he moved into southeastern Texas, where he continued to practice folk medicine without charge, becoming widely esteemed among local Mexicanos. As his reputation increased and spread, people began coming from considerable distances to his home in Los Olmos, near present-day Falfurrias. Sometimes several hundred people, Mexicanos and Anglos, would be waiting for him when he returned from his rounds of local ranches. After more than two decades of caring, unselfish service, Don Pedrito died and was buried near Falfurrias; nearly a century later his grave continues to be a shrine to which the children of his patients came to pay their respects.

FURTHER READING: Dodson, Ruth. *Don Pedrito Jaramillo: Curandero.* Corpus Christi, Tex.: Henrietta Newbury, 1994 (1934); Hudson, Willliam M., ed. *The Healer of Los Olmos and Other Mexican Lore.* Dallas: Southern Methodist University Press, 1966 (1951); Romano, Octavio. "Don Pedrito Jaramillo: The Emergence of a Mexican-American Folk Saint." Ph.D. diss. University of California, Berkeley, 1964.

JIMÉNEZ, FRANCISCO, 1943– . Writer, teacher, academic administrator. Born in San Pedro Tlaquepaque, now a suburb of Guadalajara, Francisco Jiménez crossed the border into California with his family without documentation when he was four. As a young child Francisco worked in migrant agriculture with the rest of the family. Because of his limited understanding of English and irregular school attendance he was labeled mentally retarded, but he persevered, began learning English, and continued his education.

When Francisco was fourteen, he was taken out of his Santa Maria Junior High School classroom by Immigration and Naturalization Service officers. The entire Jiménez family was deported to Mexico, but soon were able to return with proper papers. Francisco resumed his studies and worked part-time as a school janitor to help support the family. An outstanding student, he graduated from high school in 1962 with three university scholarship

Francisco Jiménez. © Francisco Jiménez.

offers. While attending Santa Clara University he became a U.S. citizen and continued his outstanding scholastic record, graduating with honors and a Woodrow Wilson fellowship. He then undertook graduate studies at Columbia University in New York, receiving his Ph.D. in Spanish and Latin American literature in 1972.

Having taught Spanish at Columbia while working on his doctorate, Jiménez now began teaching it and its literature at Santa Clara University. His ability, dedication, and hard work enabled him to rise from assistant to full professor by 1981, in which year he was also named to the University Board of Trustees. Five years later he was honored with the Sanfilippo Chair. From 1981 to 1990 he served as director of the division of Arts and Humanities. From there he moved to associate vice-president for academic affairs, a position he held until 1994, when he stepped down to chair the department of modern languages and to devote more time to his writing.

In 1973 Jiménez was a cofounder of the *Bilingual Review* and later joined the editorial board of the Bilingual Review Press. As a writer he is best known for his literary criticism and his semiautobiographical vignettes of migrant worker life as seen by a child. His highly regarded short stories have been published and reprinted in English, Spanish, and Chinese in numerous textbooks and literary anthologies. In addition to his short stories, he is the author or editor of a number of books, including *Los episodios nacionales de Victoriano Salado Álvarez*, 1974; *The Identification and Analysis of Chicano Literature*, 1979; and *Poverty and Social Justice: Critical Perspectives*, 1987. His *The Circuit: Stories from the Life of a Migrant Child*, 1997, won several awards and has been published in both Chinese and Japanese as well as in Spanish. *La Mariposa*, published in 1998, was a Smithsonian Notable Book; and his bilingual children's book *Christmas Gift/El regalo de Navidad*, 2000 was selected as an American Library Association Notable Book. His most recent work, *Breaking Through*, published in 2001, garnered rave notices. It has received seven notable book awards. Early in 2002 it received the Pura Belpré Authors Honor Book Award, followed by the even more prestigious Americas Award in June. Later in the year it was issued in Spanish under the title *Senderos fronterizos*. In November 2002 Jiménez received further national recognition, being named one of four "2002 U.S. Professors of the Year."

FURTHER READING: Carger, Chris Liska. "Talking with Francisco Jiménez." *Book Links* (December 2001/January 2002) 14–19; Cassidy, Jack, et al., eds., *Follow the Wind.* New York: Scribner's, 1987; Farrell, Harry. "How Francisco Jiménez Became the Pick of the Crop." *California Today* (19 October 1980); Martínez, Julio A., ed. *Chicano Scholars and Writers: A Bio-Bibliographical Directory.* Metuchen, N.J.: Scarecrow Press, 1979; Penahich, Loretta. "Former Illegal Migrant Worker Gains University Honors." *Migration World Magazine* 23:4 (September–October 1995) 43.

JIMÉNEZ, LUIS A., 1940– . Painter, sculptor. Luis Jiménez was born and grew up in El Paso, Texas, where he learned his father's trade of sign painting. After graduating from the University of Texas in 1964 with a degree in art and architecture he traveled to Mexico on a scholarship, studying at the Universidad Nacional Autónoma de México. He also studied in New York with the well-known sculptor Seymour Lipton. Interested in machines as a symbol of United States culture, he devised "machine man," an epoxy and fiberglass sculpture blending the human body and the machine. His 1983 *Southwest Pieta*, commissioned by the National Endowment for the Arts, became the center of a heated controversy in Albuquerque. His most popular work is perhaps *Border Crossing*, which depicts a bone-weary immigrant couple crossing the border with their baby. His works have been shown in a number of group exhibits and he has also had one-man shows. Each spring he teaches art at the University of Houston.

FURTHER READING: Dingman, Tracy. "Dialogue: Luis Jiménez's Sculptures Draw Debate." *Hispanic* (2002) 56–58; Ennis, Michael. "Luis Jiménez." *Texas Monthly* (Sept. 1998) 112–113; *Man on Fire: Luis Jiménez.* Albuquerque: Albuquerque Museum, 1994; Quirarte, Jacinto. *Mexican American Artists.* Austin: University of Texas Press, 1973; Sandback, Amy Baker. "Signs: A Conversation with Luis Jiménez." *Art Forum International* 23 (Sept. 1984) 84–87.

JUÁREZ-LINCOLN UNIVERSITY. Established in Fort Worth in 1971 by Andre Guerrero, Leonard J. Mestas, and others, Juárez-Lincoln University was a split-off from the earlier Jacinto Treviño College in Mercedes, Texas. Emphasizing bilingual and bicultural education, it sought to create an academic program more suited to Chicano students than traditional college programs were, and also committed to social change. Referring to itself as the *universidad sin paredes* and the *universidad en la comunidad*, it provided programs based on community work and study in addition to classroom instruction. It also administered an information agency, the National Migrant Information Clearinghouse. Through affiliation with Antioch College in Ohio it initially made available a master's degree in education. In 1975 it established a separate campus in Austin and in the following year offered a Bachelor of Arts program. In 1979 it closed down because of problems—legal, financial, and administrative.

FURTHER READING: Juárez-Lincoln University Records, 1969–1978. Benson Latin American Collection, General Libraries, University of Texas, Austin.

KIBBE, PAULINE R., 1909– . Pauline Kibbe was born in Pueblo, Colorado, but later moved to San Antonio, Texas. After travel in Mexico in 1939, she worked for a San Antonio bilingual secretarial and purchasing organization and became active in inter-American affairs. In 1942 and 1943 she wrote and produced a series of weekly programs on Latin America, chaired the citywide Central Planning Committee for Inter-American Understanding, and wrote a weekly newspaper column. In 1943 she was appointed the first executive secretary of the **Texas Good Neighbor Commission**, created in September.

As executive secretary, Kibbe traveled in Texas and Mexico promoting inter-American understanding through speeches, workshops, and conferences. In 1946 she wrote *Latin American in Texas*, outlining problems in discrimination, segregation, and exploitation. This indignant indictment of the treatment of Mexicanos was followed in the next year by a paper documenting the extreme exploitation of undocumenteds, which led to her resignation from the Commission under pressure from growers and the governor. Subsequently she worked for the political arm of the Congress of Industrial Organizations and wrote about Hispanic America.

FURTHER READING: Kibbe, Pauline R. *Latin American in Texas*. Albuquerque: University of New Mexico Press, 1946; Kingrea, Nellie Ward. *History of the First Ten Years of the Texas Good Neighbor Commission*. Fort Worth: Texas Christian University Press, 1954. Tyler, Ron, ed. *New Handbook of Texas*, vol. 3. Austin: Texas State Historical Association, 1996.

KIT CARSON NATIONAL FOREST. Reies López Tijerina and his followers in the Alianza Federal de Mercedes occupied the Echo Amphitheatre in the Kit Carson National Forest in October 1966. Tijerina then declared it a "republic" based on the fact that part of the area had once belonged to San Joaquín del Rio Chama as a pueblo land grant. The squatters "arrested" and tried two Forest Service officers who tried to evict them. The activist stance of the *aliancistas* in the Kit Carson confrontation attracted many youthful urban Chicano militants to the group. Three years later a second confrontation between *aliancistas* and forest rangers resulted in Tijerina's arrest, trial, conviction, and imprisonment.

FURTHER READING: Knowlton, Clark S. "Tijerina, Hero of the Militants." In *An Awakened Minority: The Mexican-Americans*, 2nd ed. Edited by Manuel P. Servín. Beverly Hills: Glencoe Press, 1974; Valdez, Armando. "Insurrection in New Mexico–Land of Enchantment." *El Grito* 1:1 (Fall 1967) 15–24.

KNIGHTS OF AMERICA. The Knights was a group of San Antonio Mexican Americans that splintered from the **Order Sons of America** in the mid-1920s. At the end of the decade it joined other organizations to form the League of United Latin American Citizens.

FURTHER READING: Márquez, Benjamín. *LULAC: The Evolution of a Mexican American Political Organization.* Austin: University of Texas Press, 1993.

LABOR, AGRICULTURAL. Over the years agricultural labor in the U.S. Southwest has had various sources. In the eighteenth and first half of the nineteenth century, southwestern agriculture was largely subsistence; family members, local native Americans, and recent immigrants from central Mexico provided the workers needed. However, by the last quarter of the 1800s an extensive market economy based on seasonal crops had emerged, especially in **California**, leading to a demand for large numbers of workers at harvest time. Unskilled Chinese workers, recently left jobless by the completion of the Central Pacific Railroad, at first filled that need and dominated the agricultural workforce in California until the end of the 1880s. Their place was then taken largely by Japanese and Filipino immigrants, who in turn were displaced by Mexicans fleeing the revolutionary ferment in Mexico.

During the last quarter of the nineteenth century the amount of land under cultivation in the West nearly tripled, increasing the need for workers. In **Texas**, citrus and vegetable production in the Winter Garden area and the lower Rio Grande valley and the rapid expansion of cotton acreage created a need for large numbers of harvest workers. At first blacks from the Old South filled most of that demand, especially in the greatly expanded cotton fields of central Texas. However, already by the 1890s migrant Mexicans were crossing the border to pick cotton in Texas and Arkansas. In California the shift to citrus, fruit, grapes, raisins, and truck gardening in the last quarter of the nineteenth century required increasing numbers of agricultural workers, as the state rapidly advanced on its way to becoming the nation's major farming area.

New Mexico and **Arizona** lagged behind Texas and California in agricultural expansion, but completion of the Roosevelt and Elephant Butte dams in the first quarter of the twentieth century made irrigation available for the expansion of cotton acreage. Mexicanos provided most of the additional seasonal labor needed. Mexicans fleeing their country's long, chaotic 1910 revolution crossed the border in large numbers and were welcomed by growers seeking cheap labor. Mexican sojourners were soon wintering over in agricultural worker *colonias* established by growers.

In the new century Mexicano agricultural workers were essential to the expansion of western commercial crops like sugar beets and cotton. World War I greatly increased the demand for cotton, and thousands of acres in the Southwest were converted from other crops to cotton; in this change migrant Mexicanos increasingly replaced tenant farmers and sharecroppers. By the last year of the war Arizona and **Colorado** growers had begun to recruit workers in Mexico to top beets and pick cotton. In the postwar decade of the 1920s, southwestern agriculture shared in the general economic boom, and thousands of Mexicans, now the chief source of western agricultural labor, were recruited by growers as the Southwest became a reservoir of migrant labor for the entire West. El Paso and San Antonio, Texas, became centers in which recruiters for midwestern agriculture sought harvest workers. In the early 1920s recruiters for the railroads, meatpacking plants, stockyards, and steel mills of the Midwest began seeking workers, sometimes as strikers, in the borderlands. By the end of the decade Denver, Colorado, and Kansas City, Missouri had become secondary reservoirs of immigrant workers. In California Los Angeles became a center from which workers were recruited for the entire west coast from San Diego to Alaska. Every year migrant worker families followed the harvests from Texas to Colorado and from California to Oregon and Washington.

When farm prices collapsed during the **Great Depression** of the 1930s, much work in commercial agriculture disappeared and the migration from Mexico was reversed. About a quarter of a million Mexicans, with their wives and children, were repatriated or persuaded to return to their home villages. The coming of World War II at the end of the 1930s again reversed this movement of Mexican workers. The **bracero** program, initiated with Mexico in 1942 and finally terminated in 1964, supplied several million agricultural workers to the Southwest and undoubtedly prevented serious food shortages during the war years.

Increased mechanization in commercial agriculture since World War II has somewhat lessened the demand for harvest labor. So have the farm labor unionization efforts of leaders like **César Chávez**, **Antonio Orendain**, and **Baldemar Velásquez**. Deeply concerned with the abysmal conditions of farm labor, during the 1960s and 1970s Chávez spearheaded a movement that spotlighted the plight of harvest workers.

In recent decades many Mexican Americans and Mexican sojourners have turned from agriculture to better-paying, less backbreaking, and more stable industrial and service employment. Less than 15 percent of Chicano workers remain in agriculture; the actual total number of Mexicano agricultural workers is difficult to determine because of the widespread use of undocumented and commuter workers.

FURTHER READING: Barger, W. K., and Ernesto M. Reza. *The Farm Labor Movement in the Midwest*. Austin: University of Texas Press, 1994; Coalson, George O. *The Development of the Farm Labor System in Texas, 1900–1954*. San Francisco: R & E Research Associates, 1977; Galarza, Ernesto. *Farm Workers and Agri-business in California, 1947–1960*. Notre Dame: University of Notre Dame Press, 1977; Gamboa, Erasmo. *Mexican Labor and World War II: Braceros in the Pacific Northwest, 1942–1947*. Austin: University of Texas Press, 1990; García, Matt. *A World of Its Own: Race, Labor, and Citrus in the Making of Greater Los Angeles, 1900-1970*. Chapel Hill: University of North Carolina Press, 2001; Martínez, Rubén. *Crossing Over: A Mexican Family on the Migrant Trail*. New York: Metropolitan Books, 2001; Mitchell, Don. *The Lie of the Land: Migrant Workers and the California Landscape*. Minneapolis: University of Minnesota Press, 1996; Rothenberg, Daniel. *With These Hands: The Hidden World of Migrant Farmworkers Today*. New York: Harcourt Brace, 1998; Valdés, Dennis N. *Al Norte: Agricultural Workers in the Great Lakes Region, 1917–1970*. Austin: University of Texas Press, 1991.

LABOR CONTRACTOR. A person who acts as an intermediary between employers and laborers, providing workers as needed by the employer. The labor contractor was especially important in agriculture, but he also had a role in railroads and some other industries. Typically he provided workers for a flat fee per worker. The contractor, who was usually a Mexicano, was known historically as a *contratista, enganchista*, and *enganchador* and often had a reputation for sharp dealing and cheating the workers. As a result of complaints, labor contracting came under the scrutiny of legislators and in 1964 the U.S. Congress passed the Farm Labor Contractor Registration Act. Today farm labor contracting is closely regulated by law.

FURTHER READING: Rothenberg, Daniel. *With These Hands: The Hidden World of Migrant Farmworkers Today*. New York: Harcourt Brace, 1998.

LABOR ORGANIZATION. As the borderlands became more integrated with the national economy after the Treaty of **Guadalupe Hidalgo**, they increasingly became a part of the evolving U.S. industrial complex. Texas and California were the loci of early mechanization and industrialization in the Southwest in the late 1800s. Labor unionism, which was just beginning to develop in the United States after the Civil War, was hindered among Mexicanos by the proximity of cheap labor from Mexico and by restrictive racism practiced by early Anglo unions. Among Mexicanos initial efforts at unionizing tended to develop out of **mutualista** organizations and earlier artisan guilds.

The first extensive effort to develop unions in the borderlands was undertaken by the Knights of Labor in the 1880s, but Mexicano locals soon turned from organizing workers to politics and concerns about Anglo land-grabbing. In the first decade of the twentieth century there was a spate of organizing in both California and Texas among street railway workers and harvest laborers. Texas smelter workers also organized and struck for higher wages. In New Mexico and Arizona the Western Federation of Miners, founded in 1896, recruited copper mine workers into Spanish-speaking unions and led them in subsequent strikes bitterly contested by mine owners. Those southwestern labor organizations that managed to survive the struggle remained weak; most generally excluded Mexicanos.

During the first decades of the twentieth century, attempts at union organizing among Mexicanos were sporadic, localized, and generally short-lived. In Texas the American Federation of Labor (AFL) and later the Congress of Industrial Organizations did limited recruiting among agricultural and cannery workers, without lasting success. The **Industrial Workers of the World** led efforts in Colorado to organize Mexicano coal miners, and AFL organizer Clemente **Idar** spent some time working with sugar beet workers. In California the influx of World War I workers from Mexico greatly increased the state's Spanish-speaking population and buttressed unionizing concepts. Several Spanish-language agricultural unions were founded in the late 1920s.

The decade of the 1930s saw depressed farm prices, wage cuts, and worker unrest. Mexican American agricultural worker leaders, many apprenticed in the communist-led Cannery and Agricultural Workers Industrial Union and its parent, the Trade Union Unity League, spearheaded the numerous strikes in California agriculture. Except for the **Confederación de Uniones Obreras Mexicanas**, most of the Mexicano unions they founded were unable to survive the incidents that created them. Growers' resistance to the unionization of farm workers was typically hostile and unrelenting; they formed their own union, the **Associated Farmers of California**, to suppress union organizing.

World War II greatly increased the demand for foodstuffs and led to the supervised importation of workers from Mexico in the **bracero** program, which nullified unionizing efforts in southwestern agriculture. At the war's end **Ernesto Galarza** of the **National Farm Labor Union,** AFL began organizing agricultural laborers in California's Central Valley. The NFLU had considerable success in recruiting workers but little success in getting employers to recognize labor's right to organize. Its prolonged 1947–1950 strike against the leading grower, Di Giorgio Farms, ultimately failed. Despite reorganization as the National Agricultural Workers Union in 1952, its membership went into a long decline and seven years later it was replaced by the AFL-CIO Agricultural Workers Organizing Committee (AWOC).

In the 1960s **César Chávez,** having left the **Community Service Organization**, began using his skills to organize agricultural workers in the Central Valley. His National Farm Workers Association joined the AWOC in 1965 to pursue the **Delano grape strike**, and the two later merged to form the United Farm Workers Organizing Committee (UFWOC). In 1972 the UFWOC became a full-fledged AFL-CIO union, the **United Farm Workers**.

In Texas, labor organizing among Mexicanos was even more difficult than in California. Efforts early in the twentieth century to unionize led to harsh reprisals from local police and the **Texas Rangers.** Inspired by Chávez's example in California, Eugene Nelson and **Antonio Orendain** began recruiting farm workers in Texas in the late 1960s, but with indifferent success. Texas sweatshop industries like pecan-shelling and garment-making strongly resisted union activities. The International Ladies Garment Workers Union began organizing on the border just before World War II, with limited success. The Amalgamated Clothing Workers of America organized the **Farah** employees, who struck in 1972 demanding recognition of their union and better working conditions. The strike, which lasted over two years, was successful.

FURTHER READING: Ferriss, Susan, and Ricardo Sandoval. *The Fight in the Fields: César Chávez and the Farmworkers Movement.* New York: Harcourt Brace, 1997; García, Mario T. *Mexican Americans: Leadership, Ideology, and Identity, 1930–1960.* New Haven: Yale University Press, 1989; Gómez-Quiñones, Juan. *Mexican American Labor, 1790–1900.* Albuquerque: University of New Mexico Press, 1994; González, Gilbert G. *Mexican Consuls and Labor Organizing: Imperial Politics in the American Southwest.* Austin: University of Texas Press, 1999; Jamieson, Stuart M. *Labor Unionism in American Agriculture.* Washington, D.C.: Government Printing Office, 1945; Mellinger, Philip J. *Race and Labor in Western Copper: The Fight for Equality, 1896–1918.* Tucson: University of Arizona Press, 1995; Ruiz, Vicki L. *Cannery Women, Cannery Lives: Mexican Women and the California Food Processing Industry, 1930–1950.* Albuquerque: University of New Mexico Press, 1987; Zamora, Emilio. *The World of the Mexican Worker in Texas.* College Station: Texas A&M University Press, 1993.

LAFOLLETTE COMMITTEE, 1936–1940. In 1936 Senator Bob LaFollette headed the Civil Liberties Committee, a U.S. Senate subcommittee created to investigate the denial of workers' right to organize. After hearing testimony on the problem in manufacturing and mining, the committee, in part prodded by publication of John Steinbeck's *Grapes of Wrath*, held hearings in California agriculture during 1939 and 1940. The committee's report was issued in 1942. It reported that violence and infringement of civil liberties by farm owners and their agents were common, and recommended remedial legislation. However, no legislative action resulted, largely because of the United States's somber involvement in World War II by that time.

FURTHER READING: Auerbach, Jerold S. "The La Follette Committee: Labor and Civil Liberties in the New Deal." *Journal of American History* 51:3 (1964) 435–459.

LAMY, JEAN BAPTISTE, 1814–1888. Archbishop. In 1850 the Reverend Jean Baptiste Lamy was appointed to head the Catholic Church in the southwestern territory acquired from Mexico by the **Guadalupe Hidalgo Treaty**. As bishop of the vast diocese of Santa Fe, he found most of the nine Mexican clergymen there not to his Jansenist tastes and quickly brought in missionary priests from Europe, particularly his native France. His lack of toleration for Mexican folk Catholicism, puritanical Jansenism, and long conflict with the **Penitentes** created some problems in his thirty-five years of leadership. By the time he retired in 1885 he had succeeded in an ambitious school and church construction program and had Americanized the Church in the Southwest.

FURTHER READING: Horgan, Paul. *Lamy of Santa Fe.* New York: Farrar, Straus & Giroux, 1975; Lamy, Jean Baptiste. *Archbishop Lamy: In His Own Words.* Translated and edited by Thomas J. Steele. Albuquerque: LPD Press, 2000.

LAND ACT OF 1851. The 1851 Land Act enacted by the U.S. Congress created a three-man commission to determine the validity of land grant claims in California. It was to weed out invalid titles ostensibly in order to clarify Californios' rights to lands granted by Spain or Mexico. The commission met from January 1852 to March 1856. Its basic attitude was that Californio claims were fraudulent until proved otherwise, and that its function was to declare a maximum amount of land available to (Anglo) settlers. The decisions of the commission led to decades of costly litigation for Californios.

Of the 813 claims heard by the commission, 273 were originally declared invalid; 132 of the invalidated claims were appealed to the courts, which declared 98 of them valid. Of the 521 claims originally confirmed by the commission, 417 were appealed by the U.S. government; only 5 were reversed by the courts. So ultimately 614 titles, or 75 percent, were validated. This gross attack on the property rights guaranteed by the Treaty of **Guadalupe Hidalgo** was an important factor in the loss of economic position by Californios and their subsequent political disenfranchisement.

FURTHER READING: Baker, Charles C. "Mexican Land Grants in California." *Annual Publications of the Historical Society of Southern California.* Los Angeles: California Historical Society, 1914; Gates, Paul. "The California Land Act of 1851." *California Historical Society Quarterly* 50 (December 1971) 395–430; Pitt, Leonard. *The Decline of the Californios.* Berkeley: University of California Press, 1966; *Spanish and Mexican Land Grants and the Law.* Edited by Malcom Ebright. Manhattan, Kans.: Sunflower University Press, 1989.

LAND GRANTS. From the first settlement of Mexico's northern frontier at the end of the sixteenth century until 1846, Spain and Mexico used land grants in order to attract settlers to this vast region. Three types of grants were made over the years: individual, *empresario*, and communal or pueblo. Individual grants were the most common, being awarded throughout the entire northern frontier. Pueblo (town) grants were more common in present-day New Mexico and Colorado, while *empresario* grants were most common in Texas. The terms under which grants were made varied. Some gave the grantee full ownership upon completion of the established requirements; some remained use-only grants, principally for grazing.

Validation of the Spanish-Mexican land grants under U.S. law was complicated by vague boundaries and scarcity or lack of records, as well as by cultural and historical differences. Most grants had their boundaries defined by natural features: rivers, hills, and trees; but some were "floating" grants in which a total amount of land was specified but location and boundaries were not set. Only rarely was the same area given in error to two grantees, but boundaries sometimes overlapped due to poor geographic knowledge.

(Alta) California was the location of over 800 grants, made between 1779 and 1846. Almost 30 percent of these were made to non-Hispanics. The New Mexico territory had a total of nearly 200 grants, and Texas had about 300. In Texas the Republic (1836–1845) officially declared its recognition of valid Spanish and Mexican grants, and by the terms of the 1845 treaty of annexation to the United States, Texas retained control over its public lands. Texas, therefore, rather than the federal government determined the validity of land grants in that state. In the late 1800s the Texas legislature set up a commission that confirmed about 250 land grants. In 1923 the remaining claims became part of a U.S.-Mexican agreement, which led to a 1941 treaty to discharge claims of the two countries against each other. To date Mexico has not settled with the hundreds of heir-claimants.

In California, squatter pressure, which arose as a result of the 1849–1850 gold rush, led to the passage by the U.S. Congress of the Land Act of 1851. A three-man Board of Land Commissioners was to determine the validity of grants. As administered, the legislation put the onus on grantees to prove legal ownership. Although ultimately 614 titles, or 75 percent of the claims, were validated, the grantees who won confirmation found themselves losing as much as a third of their grants to pay lawyers' fees, court costs, taxes, and travel expenses. By 1870 Californio elite families, which composed no more than 3 percent of the Mexicano population, held only about 25 percent of land parcels valued at ten thousand dollars or more.

Initially Nuevomexicano landowners fared somewhat better. New Mexico was spared the problems and pressures that the gold rush brought to California. In 1854 the U.S. Congress created the position of Surveyor General for the New Mexico Territory (New Mexico, Colorado, and Arizona). The validity of each grant had first to be approved by the Surveyor General and then confirmed by the U.S. Congress. Between 1854 and 1886, 205 claims were filed; 141 were approved, but only 46 confirmed by Congress.

The New Mexico land problem was complicated by the large number of pueblo grants, vague boundary lines (in seventeenth- and eighteenth-century grants especially), and aggressive efforts by claimants to expand their boundaries. For example, the famous **Maxwell land grant** (originally the Beaubien-Miranda grant) was increased from 97,000 to 1,714,764 acres. Claims were made to more land than existed in the Territory, and Anglo lawyers like **Thomas Catron** acquired immense tracts of land as their fees for successfully defending these extravagant claims.

Because of problems arising as railroads, ranchers, and settlers moved into the Territory, in 1891 Congress created the **Court of Private Land Claims** for New Mexico, Colorado, and Arizona. The court completed its work in 1904. It heard 301 petitions for a total of more than thirty-five million acres, rejected nearly three-fourths of them, and confirmed title to about two million acres. Altogether about five million acres of private grants and two million acres of pueblo grants were confirmed in New Mexico. Ultimately Anglos came to control about 80 percent of the grant lands.

As their lands were taken over, Mexican Americans fought back. Nuevomexicanos especially never completely accepted the loss of their grants. The activities of the **Gorras Blancas** at the end of the 1880s are one example of this resistance. During the 1960s the grievances of grantee heirs were reanimated by **Reies López Tijerina** and his Alianza Federal de Mercedes (Federal Alliance of [land] Grants). The failure of the United States government to abide by the spirit of Article IX of the Treaty of Guadalupe Hidalgo remains an issue in the Southwest.

FURTHER READING: Baker, Charles C. "Mexican Land Grants in California." *Annual Publications of the Historical Society of Southern California.* Los Angeles: California Historical Society, 1914; Briggs, Charles L., and John R. Van Ness, eds. *Land, Water, and Culture: New Perspectives on Hispanic Land Grants.* Albuquerque: University of New Mexico Press, 1987; De la Garza, Rodolfo O., and Karl M. Schmitt. *Texas Land Grants and Chicano-Mexican Relations.* Austin: University of Texas, Institute of Latin American Studies, 1986; Ebright, Malcolm. *Land Grants and Law Suits in Northern New Mexico.* Albuquerque: University of New Mexico Press, 1994; Knowlton, Clark S., ed. "Spanish and Mexican Land Grants in the Southwest: A Symposium." *Social Science Journal* 3:3 (1976). Rubio, Abel G. *Stolen Heritage: A Mexican American's Rediscovery of His Family's Lost Land Grant.* Austin: Eakin Press, 1986.

LARRAZOLO, OCTAVIANO A., 1859–1930. Governor, senator, lawyer. Octaviano Larrazolo was born near the north Mexican city of Chihuahua and came to the United States when he was eleven. A protégé of Bishop **Jean Baptiste Salpointe**, a family friend, he completed his formal education at St. Michael's College in Santa Fe after Salpointe became archbishop there in 1875. Meanwhile he began teaching school in El Paso County, Texas, where he began to take a serious interest in local Democratic politics, studied law, and was admitted to the bar in 1888.

In 1894 Larrazolo moved back to New Mexico, set up a law practice in Las Vegas, and became active in politics. Between 1900 and 1908 his three attempts to win election as a delegate to the U.S. Congress were unsuccessful. After three decades as a Democratic politico, Larrazolo became convinced that his failure to win elections was the result of ethnic discrimination within the party. In 1911 he switched his allegiance to the Republican Party. He worked strenuously to assure that Nuevomexicano rights were included in the New Mexico constitution when statehood was achieved in 1912. As a Republican, Larrazolo continued to fight so single-mindedly for ethnic equality in New Mexico politics that opponents sometimes accused him of dragging the race issue into every election. He strongly supported Nuevomexicano candidates for public office and in 1918 he himself won the governorship. As chief executive he showed himself a dedicated administrator, especially concerned with the many problems of Nuevomexicanos. He energetically pursued efforts to improve their lives and vigorously supported bilingual education as a path to improving their economic condition. At the end of his term the Republicans did not renominate him, and he returned to his law practice.

In 1928 Larrazolo became the first Latino elected to the U.S. Senate, where he employed his outstanding oratorical skills in his continuing campaign to obtain economic equality and greater political access for Nuevomexicanos. After serving in a single congressional session, he died early in 1930 after a lingering illness.

FURTHER READING: Chacón, José A. "Octaviano Larrazolo: New Mexico's Greatest Governor." *La Luz* 1:7 (November 1972) 37–39; Córdova, Alfred C. and Charles B. Judah. *Octaviano Larrazolo: A Political Portrait.* Albuquerque: University of New Mexico, Dept. of Government, 1952; Meyer, Nicholas E. *The Biographical Dictionary of Hispanic Americans.* New York: Facts on File, 1997; Perrigo, Lynn I. *Hispanos: Historic Leader in New Mexico.* Santa Fe: Sunstone Press, 1985; Walter, Paul A. "Octaviano Ambrosio Larrazolo." *New Mexico Historical Review* 7:2 (April 1932) 99–104.

LAS HERMANAS. Las Hermanas was organized in Houston at the beginning of the 1970s by U.S. Latino nuns headed by Sister Gregoria Ortega who were concerned about the Catholic Church's failure to fully understand the religious and social needs of Mexicanos. Influenced by the new liberation theology, its objectives were to make U.S. Catholicism, and particularly the hierarchy, more aware of cultural differences and to advance the cause of social change in the society at large. It lobbied for the appointment of Latino bishops and also encouraged **Chicanas** to participate in a more active ministry.

FURTHER READING: Díaz-Stevens, Ana María. "Latinas and the Church." In *Hispanic Catholic Culture in the U.S*, edited by Jay P. Nolan and Alan Figueroa Deck. Notre Dame, Ind.: University of Notre Dame Press, 1994; Gonzales, Sylvia A. *Hispanic American Voluntary Organizations.* Westport, Conn.: Greenwood Press, 1985; Iglesias, María. "Hermanas." In *Prophets Denied Honor: An Anthology on the Hispanic Church of the United States,* edited by Antonio M. Stevens-Arroyo. Maryknoll, N.Y.: Orbis Books, 1980.

LATIN AMERICAN. *Latin American* is a broad term referring to a person in or from Middle and South America and the Spanish-speaking countries of the Caribbean. Historically the term has been used, especially in Texas, to avoid the word "Mexican," which was often used derogatorily, disparagingly, or at least condescendingly by Anglo racists as an ethnic epithet. To refer to a person in the United States of Spanish cultural background, a more appropriate term might be U.S. Latino.

LATIN AMERICAN RESEARCH AND SERVICE AGENCY. LARASA, the brainchild of Bert Gallegos, Bernie Valdez, Lena Archuleta, and others, was founded in 1964 in Denver, Colorado. It had its roots in World War II, President Lyndon Johnson's War on Poverty, the civil rights movement, and the urbanization of Mexican Americans. Its principal purpose was to put pressure on elected officials to end their neglect of U.S. Latino concerns and to raise the consciousness of Anglos and Mexican Americans. It hoped to bring about community involvement in political decision making. An important issue was the gross discrimination that Latinos were still experiencing in **Colorado**'s main industries: mining, meatpacking, and sugar beets. It was also concerned with police harassment and brutality, housing discrimination, and the general marginality of *la raza*.

Today LARASA acts as the voice of the Mexican American community in supporting innovative approaches to solving issues of social justice. It combines coalition-building with the development of grassroots organizations to promote active participation by parents in their children's education. It has been important in developing Chicano leadership in Colorado. It publishes a monthly bulletin titled *LARASA Reports*.

FURTHER READING: "LARASA's Enduring Mandate to Carry on the 'Big Fight.'" *LARASA Reports* (August/September 1999). www.larasa.org

LAU v. NICHOLS, **1970–1974.** *Lau v. Nichols* was a class action lawsuit filed in California against the San Francisco School District alleging discrimination against one Kinney Lau because the school failed to deal with his limited comprehension of English. The lower courts ruled against Lau, but in 1974 the U.S. Supreme Court under chief justice Warren Burger unanimously ruled that Lau must be taught in his first language. The court held that the district's failure to meet his linguistic needs violated his civil rights, guaranteed by the Fourteenth Amendment to the Constitution and the Civil Rights Act of 1964.

Lau v. Nichols was a landmark legal case; for the first time the court stated unambiguously that non-English-speaking students had the right to be taught in their own language. The Lau decision led to expansion of bilingual and bicultural education programs. In 1980 the California Secretary of Education issued formal regulations to implement the court's ruling. *Lau* also created widespread controversy, and during Ronald Reagan's two presidential administrations, 1981–1989, enforcement of the *Lau* remedies was considerably weakened. In the 1990s neoconservatives continued to attack *Lau*.

FURTHER READING: De Avila, Edward A., and Sharon E. Duncan. *A Few Thoughts about Language Assessment: The Lau Decision Reconsidered.* Los Angeles: National Dissemination and Assessment Center, California State University, Los Angeles, 1978; Donato, Rubén. *The Other Struggle for Equal Schools: Mexican Americans During the Civil Rights Era.* Albany: State University of New York Press, 1997; Moran, Rachel F. "Language and the Law in the Classroom: Bilingual Education and the Official English Initiative." In *Perspectives on Official English: The Campaign for English as the Official Language of the USA*, edited by Karen L. Adams and Daniel T. Brink. Berlin; New York: Mouton de Gruyter, 1990; Weyr, Thomas. *Hispanic U.S.A.: Breaking the Melting Pot.* New York: Harper & Row, 1988.

LEADERSHIP. Leadership in the Mexican American community has had a long but uneven history. After the Treaty of **Guadalupe Hidalgo** in 1848

and the U.S. takeover of the Southwest, leadership became divided between elites and social bandits. Social **banditry** created heroic folk leaders like **Juan Cortina** in Texas and **Tiburcio Vásquez** in California who provided a kind of informal leadership. Although they generally lost some of their earlier political and social influence, landed elites of the Southwest were able to retain a more formal leadership based on their education and achievements. In the second half of the 1800s Nuevomexicano leaders developed political networking in order to retain power under the new conditions. Leadership efforts among the middle and lower classes were largely limited to the organizing of **mutualista** groups for minimal economic and social security.

In the twentieth century, greater educational attainment by some Mexican Americans began to provide a new base for leadership. After World War I, the initial steps in creating organizations with broad political, economic, and social goals were taken by first- and second-generation Mexican Americans with better formal educations. However, only after the upheavals of the **Great Depression** in the 1930s and **World War II** did leaders begin to organize more methodically for specific goals. These changes tended to emphasize a new, less individualistic leader—an intermediary between the community and Anglo American society. The leader's effectiveness was often circumscribed by the imperative of broad acceptance by both groups. The new leadership frequently used ethnic symbols, some historical like Cinco de Mayo, some cultural like the Virgin of Guadalupe, to appeal to its followers.

The new leaders were often entangled in the contradiction between radical rhetoric and more limited reformist goals. The conflict in this ambiguous position may clearly be seen in some leaders of the Chicano Movement during the 1960s and 1970s. Additionally, the success of these leaders was, in part, limited by the fact that none was successful in developing a national organization. On the other hand, leaders of nationwide groups like the **National Council of La Raza** and the **National Association of Latino Elected and Appointed Officials** seemed to lack the charisma required for dynamic leadership.

A notable weakness of many early senior leaders was their failure to recognize and encourage young politicians who seemed to be on their way to becoming a political force. This reluctance to share the leadership role and personalism have historically been seen as hindering the development of Mexican American organizations. *Raza* leaders, often highly individualistic and competitive, have sometimes found cooperation difficult, even when the common good clearly dictated it. When they were able to agree on goals, there was often little consensus on the most expedient way to go about achieving them. The bitter struggle in the early 1970s between **Corky Gonzales** and **José Angel Gutiérrez** to control the Raza Unida Party provides an outstanding example of this divisive and ultimately destructive competition.

Quarreling among leaders also undoubtedly contributed to mistrust of leadership and to political cynicism. A fairly widespread reluctance, until the

1950s, to identify more closely with the Democratic and Republican parties probably served to hinder the development of *raza* leadership. So has the exclusion until quite recently of potential Chicano political leaders from higher-level party positions by both Republicans and Democrats. Lastly, exclusion from and isolation within government employment have clearly limited development of Chicano political leadership.

Mexican American leaders have made considerable advances in the past three decades. However, at the beginning of the twenty-first century, with Gonzales, Gutiérrez, and *Reies López Tijerina* inactive on a national level and *César Chávez* dead, there exists a considerable individual and organizational leadership vacuum at the top.

FURTHER READING: García, Mario T. *Mexican Americans: Leadership, Ideology, and Identity, 1930–1960.* New Haven: Yale University Press, 1989; "Ethnic Organization and Leadership." In *The Mexican American People*, edited by Leo Grebler, Joan W. Moore, and Ralph C. Guzmán. New York: Free Press, 1970; Martínez, John R. "Leadership and Politics." In *La Raza: Forgotten Americans*, edited by Julian Samora. Notre Dame: University of Notre Dame Press, 1966; Ortiz, Isidro D. "Latino Organizational Leadership Strategies in the Era of Reaganomics." In *Latinos and Political Coalitions*, edited by Roberto E. Villarreal and Norma G. Hernández. Westport, Conn.: Greenwood Press, 1991; Sosa, Luis R. *An Analysis of Chicano Organizations and Their Leadership.* Ph.D. diss. University of California, 1981; Vigil, Maurilio. *Hispanics in American Politics: The Search for Political Power.* Lanham, Md.: University of America, 1987.

LEAGUE OF LATIN AMERICAN CITIZENS. The League was an ephemeral 1920s Texas organization that arose out of the desire of younger members of the **Order Sons of America** to create a wider membership base. When their overtures to expand the Sons were rebuffed, the leaders, led by Clemente **Idar**, met in Harlingen in 1927 to form the group. Two years later at Corpus Christi the Sons, the LACL, and the **Knights of America** united to form the new League of United Latin American Citizens.

FURTHER READING: Tyler, Ron, ed. *The New Handbook of Texas*, vol. 4. Austin: Texas State Historical Association, 1996.

LEAGUE OF UNITED LATIN AMERICAN CITIZENS. LULAC was formed as the result of a 1929 Corpus Christi meeting of three existing groups: the League of Latin American Citizens, **Knights of America**, and **Order Sons of America**. Because of the shift away from Mexico as a source of identity among second-generation Mexican Americans, the new organization was based on American rather than Mexican models. English was its official language. Its social and economic goals, to be achieved via education and hard work, stressed the rights and duties of Mexican Americans as U.S. citizens. Its middle-class male leadership strongly denounced discrimination and segregation and extended full membership to women in 1933, but only in gender-segregated councils. In the same decade it filed its first lawsuit against segregation in public schools.

League of United Latin American Citizens convention in Corpus Christi, Texas, May 1929. Courtesy of the Benson Latin American Collection, University of Texas at Austin.

Although LULAC showed a sincere concern for less fortunate members of *la raza*, it was slow in developing and implementing community action programs on their behalf. During World War II LULAC president **George I. Sánchez** used his position in the Office of Coordinator of Inter-American Affairs to advance the organization's demand for full civil rights. In the postwar era LULAC leaders called for more direct and active involvement in civil rights issues. Continuing concerns about segregation and racism in the schools led the group to take an active role in two lawsuits: the 1946 Méndez case in California and the 1948 Delgado case in Texas. Its intervention helped lead to success in both cases.

Under the presidency of **Mario Obledo,** after 1968 LULAC became even more militant in pushing for citizen rights. However, with the development of the Chicano Movement it became less vital to the community and therefore less effective politically. By the beginning of the 1980s the **movimiento** had declined, and LULAC experienced a resurgence. Its area of influence outside the Southwest grew to include Idaho, Georgia, and the Carolinas. However, in the early 1980s it suffered a financial crisis, followed toward the end of the decade by a series of internal scandals and **leadership** squabbles. As a result, it seemed unable to resolutely push community concerns.

Although it still boasts a large membership, over 50 percent women, LULAC is seen by its critics as no longer the preeminent leader in the

Chicano struggle for political, social, and civil rights. This loss of position seems due to a combination of successes, failures, and internal weaknesses. LULAC has had some difficulty adjusting to extensive changes within the Mexican American community since the 1980s. In 1994 it elected its first female national president. It continues to pursue social, political, and economic goals on various fronts.

FURTHER READING : Garza, Edward D. *LULAC: League of United Latin American Citizens.* San Francisco: R & E Research Associates, 1972; "History of LULAC." *La Luz* 6:5 (May 1977) 15–19; Márquez, Benjamín. *LULAC: The Evolution of a Mexican American Political Organization.* Austin: University of Texas Press, 1993; Orozco, Cynthia E. "Alice Dickerson Montemayor's Feminist Challenge to LULAC in the 1930s." *IDRA Newsletter* (March 1996) 11–14; Orozco, Cynthia E. "The Origins of the League of United Latin American Citizens (LULAC) and the Mexican American Civil Rights Movement in Texas. . . ." Ph.D. diss., University of California, Los Angeles, 1992. www.lulac.org

LEMON GROVE INCIDENT, 1931. A group of Mexican immigrant parents in the community of Lemon Grove near San Diego, California, rejected the **segregation** of their children in the Lemon Grove school. The children had previously not been segregated. The parents organized a committee, instituted a boycott, and hired Anglo lawyers to file a legal suit, *Alvarez v. Lemon Grove,* against the school district.

The court ruled in favor of the parents in spite of the school administrators' argument that the special school was established to help *raza* students learn English. The judge pointed out that establishing a separate school for all Mexicano children without regard for their individual proficiency in English violated California statute law. The Lemon Grove case set a benchmark as the first wholly successful effort against the segregation of Mexicano schoolchildren.

FURTHER READING: Alvarez, Robert R. "The Lemon Grove Incident: The Nation's First Successful Desegregation Court Case." *Journal of San Diego History* 32:2 (1986) 116–135; Donato, Rubén. *The Other Struggle for Equal Schools: Mexican Americans during the Civil Rights Era.* Albany: State University of New York Press, 1997; Reynolds, Annie. *The Education of Spanish-Speaking Children in Five Southwestern States.* Bulletin No. 11, Washington, D.C.: Department of the Interior, 1933. Reprinted in *Education and the Mexican-American.* New York: Arno Press, 1974.

LETTUCE STRIKE, SALINAS. After the successful conclusion of the **Delano grape strike** in 1970, the **United Farm Workers** Organizing Committee (UFWOC) stepped up its efforts to unionize lettuce workers in the Salinas valley, California. Here the UFWOC ran into competition from the Teamsters union, with which nearly all the lettuce growers now signed five-year contracts. In early August about seven thousand lettuce workers went on strike. An agreement between UFWOC and the Teamsters' national organization to delimit their individual areas of organizing was ignored by the Teamsters' locals. In the following month César Chávez inaugurated a boycott of "nonunion" lettuce.

In mid-March 1971 a new accord was reached by the UFWOC and the Teamsters national headquarters and was again rejected by the Teamsters' locals. Meanwhile the dispute was taken to the courts in 1971 and to the political arena in the 1972 elections. Efforts of the Bishops Committee on Farm Labor to mediate the dispute were unsuccessful, and the Teamsters initiated an all-out organizing drive, while the United Farm Workers (the former UFWOC) stepped up the boycott. For the rest of the decade the struggle between the Teamster locals and the UFW went on. It proved to be much more difficult to enforce a boycott on lettuce than on grapes, and to many the struggle seemed to be more a jurisdictional dispute over who would unionize the workers than a fight for field worker rights.

FURTHER READING: Ferris, Susan, and Ricardo Sandoval. *The Fight in the Fields: César Chávez and the Farmworkers Movement.* New York: Harcourt Brace, 1997; Meister, Dick, and Anne Loftis. *A Long Time Coming: The Struggle to Unionize America's Farm Workers.* New York: Macmillan, 1977.

LIGA OBRERA DE HABLA ESPAÑOLA. The Liga was a union founded in the mid-1930s by Jesús Pallares among his fellow Mexicano coal miners in New Mexico. The Liga's organizing efforts around Gallup and Madrid succeeded in signing up some eight thousand workers. Although an attempt by the mine owners to get a criminal syndicalism law passed to deter union organizing failed, they continued to refuse to recognize the union, and it soon disintegrated. Pallares was arrested and was deported in June 1935 as an undesirable alien.

FURTHER READING: Acuña, Rodolfo. *Occupied America: A History of Chicanos*, 3rd ed. New York: Harper & Row, 1988; Dinwoodie, D. H. "Deportation: The Immigration Service and the Chicano Labor Movement in the 1930s." *New Mexico Historical Review* 52:3 (July 1977) 193–206.

LIGA PROTECTORA LATINA. The Liga was a **mutualista** society officially established in Arizona in 1916. In the following year it became involved in uniting Mexicano workers in Arizona's copper mines in opposition to the revolutionary workers' organization, the **Industrial Workers of the World** (IWW). In the 1917 **Bisbee** strike it worked to unite Mexicanos against the IWW efforts to disrupt copper production in World War I. With the suppression of the IWW by the government and the arrest and trial of its leaders in 1918, Liga membership peaked and began to decline. Internal dissention and the depression that began at the end of the 1920s finished it off.

FURTHER READING: McBride, James D. "The Liga Protectora Latina: A Mexican American Benevolent Society in Arizona." *Journal of the West* 14:4 (1975) 82–90; Peterson, Herbert B. "Twentieth Century Search for Cibola: Post-World War I Mexican Labor Exploitation in Arizona." In *The Mexican Americans: An Awakening Minority*, 2nd ed. Edited by Manuel P. Servín. Beverly Hills, Calif.: Glencoe Press, 1974.

LIGA PROTECTORA MEXICANA. The Liga Protectora Mexicana was an ephemeral grassroots organization established in Kansas City shortly after

World War I. In the postwar economic downturn it addressed concerns about the likely **repatriation** of Mexicans who had been recruited earlier for the United States war effort. During its short existence the league supplied food and clothing to the needy, worked to protect the rights of immigrant workers, and also found jobs for the unemployed. The short postwar depression that fueled the threat of expulsion from the United States ended in 1921, and renewed demands for Mexican labor eliminated the league's raison d'être. It soon faded away.

FURTHER READING: Tirado, Miguel David. "Mexican American Political Organization: 'The Key to Chicano Political Power.'" In *La Causa Política: A Chicano Politics Reader*, edited by F. Chris García. Notre Dame: University of Notre Dame Press, 1974.

LIGHT UP THE BORDER. A campaign initiated in 1989 by Muriel Watson, longtime activist and widow of a Border Patrol pilot, to dramatize illegal immigration from Mexico. In 1989 and 1990 she organized several nighttime rallies in which hundreds of area residents shined their automobile headlights on sections of the border where undocumenteds congregated in preparation for crossing. Prospective border crossers patiently waited for the rallies to end and then began their trek north. Blaming **undocumented**s for a wide variety of U.S. problems, even traffic congestion, Watson denied being anti-Mexican or racist and argued that her movement had achieved some positive results. Critics and counterprotesters saw the movement as an expression of nativism and an encouragement to vigilantism.

FURTHER READING: Martínez, Oscar J. *Border People: Life and Society in the U.S.-Mexico Borderlands*. Tucson: University of Arizona Press, 1994; McDonnell, Patrick. "1,000 Flip Switches to 'Light Border.'" *Los Angeles Times* (17 March 1990) Metro, B1; McDonnell, Patrick. "Tactic of Lighting up the Border Raises Tensions." *Los Angeles Times* (26 May 1990) Metro, A1.

LIMÓN, JOSÉ ARCADIO, 1908–1972. Dancer, choreographer, teacher. José Arcadio Limón was born of artistically inclined middle-class parents in Culiacán, Sinaloa, an important city on Mexico's west coast. In 1915 the Limón family fled Mexico's revolutionary chaos across the border, first into Arizona and later to Los Angeles, California. There José received his high school education and then enrolled in the University of California.

In 1928 Limón moved to New York City to pursue his interest in painting at the New York School of Design, but soon found his baroque style was at odds with the current modernist vogue. He dropped out of art school and drifted aimlessly until friends took him to a modern dance recital. Here he found what he wanted to do with the rest of his life; the next day he enrolled in dance classes. Although his height and his angular body militated against success in dance, his intense dedication won out in the end.

During the 1930s Limón danced in a number of Broadway shows, performed concert duets, and began choreographing. In 1937 his promise as a choreographer was recognized by a fellowship at the Bennington School of Dance in Vermont. While there, he decided to specialize in concert dance and began using Mexican and Spanish dance forms in his choreography. In 1939 his *Danzas mexicanas* premiered; it was well received by the critics, especially during its subsequent West Coast tour.

World War II interrupted Limón's career, but after two years in the U.S. Army he returned to concert dance, organizing his own small company, José Limón and Dancers. In January 1947 the Limón company made its Broadway debut in *Lament for Ignacio Sánchez Mejías*, to critical acclaim. Although Limón was at his artistic peak during the 1950s, to support his wife and himself he found it necessary to teach at a number of colleges and universities, as well as the Juilliard School. For several months each year he performed and taught in Mexico at the Academia Nacional de la Danza; four times during the 1950s and 1960s he was selected by the Department of State to tour abroad in its cultural exchange program. For a quarter of a century he was widely acknowledged as the outstanding American choreographer and male dancer.

After 1960 Limón devoted his time almost entirely to choreography and teaching. The author of over sixty outstanding works, he was the recipient of many honors and awards and was a repeat guest at White House functions during the Kennedy and Johnson administrations. He died in 1972, but the Limón troupe still carries on.

FURTHER READING: *José Limón: The Artist Re-viewed*. Amsterdam: Harwood Academic, 2000; Limón, José. *José Limón: An Unfinished Memoir*. Edited by Lynn Garafola. Hanover, N.H.: University Press of New England, 1999; Obituary. *New York Times* (3 December 1972) 1, 85; Pollack, Barbara. *Dance Is a Movement: A Portrait of José Limón in Words and Pictures*. Pennington, N.J.: Princeton Book Co., 1993.

LITERATURE, CHICANO. The writings of Mexicans living in the United States and of their descendants. In the century and a half since the Treaty of **Guadalupe Hidalgo**, Mexican American authors, using various literary forms, have written on a wide variety of topics in English, Spanish, and combinations of the two languages. After the Treaty of Guadalupe Hidalgo a concern about retaining the use of Spanish as basic to cultural survival led to a lively literary movement. Newspapers like Las Vegas–based *La Voz del Pueblo* and *El Nuevo Mexicano* in Santa Fe provided support for Hispanic writers all over the Southwest. Until the Chicano literary renaissance in the late 1950s, most of their literary output was in the form of poetry, folktales, corridos, local history, and a handful of novellas, published in local or regional newspapers and journals. Since the mid-1900s it has become even more heterogeneous and more representative of the diversity within Chicano culture as writers pursue a variety of inspirations and concerns.

When Chicano literature began to come of age in the second half of the twentieth century, its themes, for the most part, derived directly from the experience of growing up Chicano in an Anglo society. *Pocho*, **José Antonio**

Villarreal's 1959 work, which is usually taken as the benchmark Chicano novel, is an excellent example of this inspiration. For many writers an important aspect of that experience has been segregation and an embittering racism. In the mid-1960s Chicano writers' perceptions of their relations to Anglo society were clarified and further refined by the opinions and attitudes of the black civil rights movement and by ideas of self-definition, self-realization, and human rights boiling out of the Chicano Movement's ferment. Chicano literature became an integral part of the **movimiento.**

Literature was seen by many Chicano writers as a natural way to articulate their feelings about discrimination, racism, and civil rights as well as to develop their search for identity and roots. In this search some sought an identity through an ethnic nationalism that stressed pride in Mexican culture. Topics of ethnic discrimination have loomed large in Mexican American writing, as authors channeled feelings of indignation and anger into literary outlets. Works like **Raymond Barrio**'s *The Plum Plum Pickers*, 1969, decried and criticized the ill-treatment and suffering of migrant Mexican workers. Five years later *Peregrinos de Aztlán* by Miguel Méndez called attention to human rights abuses at the U.S.-Mexican border and social injustice in the workplace. **Tomás Rivera**'s award-winning *. . . y no se lo tragó la tierra*, 1971, marked a new milestone in the Chicano novel, and five years later *Klail City y sus alrededores* by **Rolando Hinojosa-Smith,** published in Havana, began the development of an international reputation for Chicano literature.

In addition to the novel, the short story has been a favorite literary form of many Chicano writers. Publishing his work in various journals, **Francisco Jiménez** used a child's viewpoint to describe the typical experiences of migrant workers in the fields and the education system. His published collection, *Cajas de cartón*, 2000, has been compared to Tomás Rivera's writing, and in 2002 his *Breaking Through* received the prestigious Americas Award along with six other notable awards. **Sandra Cisneros,** the first Chicana to be published by a mainstream press, has provided a trenchant feminine perspective on the Chicano experience with her vignettes of strong-willed women fighting the denial of their rights by both Chicano males and Anglo society. Her second book, *Woman Hollering Creek*, 1991, won several awards and made her reputation secure. In 2002 it was followed by *Caramelo*, which received rave notices.

Poetry, always a popular literary genre in the Spanish language, has been widely employed by Chicanos in Spanish, English, and combinations of the two languages. **Corky Gonzales**'s *I Am Joaquín* towers in the genre. A powerful evocation of an Indian past, it strongly expresses the repressed Chicano anger at racism and discrimination. There were outstanding Chicanas in poetry, too; many took the discussion of denial of rights a step further. For example, **Bernice Zamora** crafted poems that illustrated the inferior position to which Chicanas were relegated in both Anglo and Mexican American society. The poetry of **Lorna Dee Cervantes,** on the other hand, is sometimes personal, sometimes political; it has been published in Mexico and England as well as by a mainstream U.S. press.

In drama the outstanding name is **Luis Valdez,** who almost single-handedly created the Chicano theater movement. His play *Zoot Suit* recalled the story of popular hysteria against young Chicanos and a gross miscarriage of justice in Los Angeles during World War II. **Estela Portillo-Trambley** of El Paso was one of many other dramatists; she published a number of plays as well as short stories and a novel, all of which carry her message of equality and liberation for women.

Lastly, Chicano journals like *El Grito, Caracol, Aztlán,* and others, many of them short-lived, provided Mexican American writers with forums from which they could expound on their societal concerns, make their readers aware of widespread repression, and condemn victimization, discrimination, and racism.

FURTHER READING: Aranda, Jose F. *When We Arrive: A New Literary History of Mexican America.* Tucson: University of Arizona Press, 2003; Candelaria, Cordelia. *Chicano Poetry: A Critical Introduction.* Westport, Conn.: Greenwood Press, 1985; Eysturoy, Annie O. *Daughters of Self-Creation: The Contemporary Chicana* Novel Albuquerque: University of New Mexico Press, 1996; Huerta, Jorge A. *Chicano Drama: Performance, Society, and* Myth. New York: Cambridge University Press, 2000; Jiménez, Francisco, ed. *The Identification and Analysis of Chicano Literature.* New York: Bilingual Press, 1979; Lomelí, Francisco A., ed. *Handbook of Hispanic Cultures in the United States: Literature and Art.* Houston: Arte Público Press, 1993; Lomclí, Francisco A., and Donaldo W. Urioste, eds. *Chicano Perspectives in Literature.* Albuquerque, N.M.: Pajarito, 1976; Madsen, Deborah L. *Understanding Contemporary Chicana Literature.* Columbia: University of South Carolina Press, 2000; Paredes, Raymond A. "The Evolution of Chicano Literature." *MELUS* 5 (Spring 1978) 71–110; Saldívar, Ramón. *Chicano Narrative: The Dialectics of Difference.* Madison: University of Wisconsin Press, 1990; Shirley, Carl R., and Paula W. Shirley. *Understanding Chicano Literature.* Columbia: University of South Carolina Press, 1988; Tatum, Charles M. *Mexican American Literature.* Orlando, Fla.: Harcourt Brace Jovanovich, 1990; Tatum, Charles M. *Chicano Popular Culture: Que hable el pueblo.* Tucson: University of Arizona Press, 2001.

LIVESTOCK INDUSTRY. When Spanish-Mexican pioneers entered the Southwest at the end of the sixteenth century they brought horses, cattle, sheep, and goats to an area devoid of domesticated grazing animals. By the end of the 1700s they had solidly established a pervasive pastoral economy, based on experience and traditions developed in central Mexico, in semi-arid areas from Texas to California. After the Treaty of Guadalupe Hidalgo, the daily routines and skills of Mexican American livestock culture were available to incoming Anglo cattlemen.

Toward the last third of the 1800s, Anglo cattlemen had acquired most of the large Spanish and Mexican land grants (with some exception in the Territory of New Mexico) on which they adopted and adapted techniques earlier pioneered by Mexican *vaqueros.* To herd their range cattle they hired cowboys, mounted on broncos or mustangs (*mesteño*) and using the traditional Mexican equipment, the names of which were sometimes anglicized: lariat (*la reata*), lasso (*lazo*), chaps (*chaparejos*), hackamore (*jáquima*), and quirt (*cuerda*). The urban demand for beef in the East and the world market as well created an ongoing need for cowboys and an opportunity for Mexicano *vaqueros* whose widespread employment continued to reinforce the distinctive character of western cattle-raising. When the **railroads** reached the West in the mid-1870s, the long drive became feasible and the cattle industry took off on the large ranches of the Southwest. High profits fostered the industry's expansion, and investment from the East and Europe poured in during the early 1880s, creating a spectacular, if short, prosperity.

The high profitability of the western livestock industry depended heavily on its ability to range cattle on government lands, unregulated and without payment. Cattlemen competed with sheep men, and settlers, for the best lands. The raising of sheep was common throughout the Southwest, but it was of particular importance to Nuevomexicanos, who had pastured their sheep for generations on extensive communal grant lands, much of which was declared public land after the Americans took over. Conflicts of Anglo cattlemen with sheep herders, usually Mexicanos, as well as with settlers, were common in the 1870s and 1880s and led to casual violence and various shooting frays such as the Tonto Basin War.

The droughts of the years 1885–1886 and 1886–1887 forced cattle ranchers to sell off their large herds at sacrifice prices, while the subzero winters of the same years killed off many animals on the overstocked range. In order to survive, the western cattle industry began to change from range-based to ranch-based. Some larger ranchers, like Richard King in Texas, developed virtual baronies employing numerous workers, mostly Mexicanos, in an almost feudal relationship. In some areas, even in parts of Texas, hardier sheep replaced less rugged cattle. As the Department of the Interior began to take over and police public lands more closely early in the twentieth century, livestock raisers increasingly found themselves in conflict with the federal government over grazing fees and overgrazing.

During the twentieth century the livestock industry became a highly organized big business, but the public image of the industry and the cowboy continues to be shaped considerably by its Mexican roots.

FURTHER READING: Clayton, Lawrence, Jim Hay, and Jerald Underwood. *Vaqueros, Cowboys, and Buckaroos*. Austin: University of Texas Press, 2001; Dale, Edward E. *The Range Cattle Industry*. Norman: University of Oklahoma Press, 1960; Dary, David. *Cowboy Culture: A Saga of Five Centuries*. New York: Alfred A. Knopf, 1981; Monday, Jane, and Betty Colley. *Voices of the Wild Horse Desert: The Vaquero Families of the King and Kennedy Ranches*. Austin: University of Texas Press, 1997; Rojas, Arnold. *California Vaquero*. Fresno, Calif.: Academy Library Guild, 1953; Slatta, Richard W. *Cowboys of the Americas*. New Haven: Yale University Press, 1990.

LONGORIA, FÉLIX, 1919–1945. During World War II, Félix Longoria was killed in the fighting on the Philippine island of Luzon and was buried there. In 1948 his widow tried to arrange for his reburial in the small town of Three Rivers, Texas, but the only funeral home denied use of its chapel because Longoria was Mexican American. The mortuary's refusal to accept Longoria led to an acrimonious and emotional debate, arousing nationwide attention and indignation over the denial of full equality to the dead veteran. The Texas legislature held hearings on the case and in a four-to-one vote asserted that no discrimination had occurred.

At the request of Longoria's activist sister-in-law, Sara Moreno, Dr. **Héctor García** tried to get a reversal of the mortuary's decision, without success. Ultimately he persuaded freshman U.S. senator Lyndon Johnson of Texas to intervene in the case. As a result, Longoria was buried in Arlington National Cemetery. The incident helped formalize the organization of the **American G.I. Forum** later that year by Dr. García and other activists. It also led to the establishment of the **Texas Good Neighbor Commission**.

FURTHER READING: Allsup, Carl. "A Soldier's Burial." *Revista Chicano-Riqueña* 4:4 (Fall 1976) 77–87; Carroll, Patrick J. *Felix Longoria's Wake: Bereavement, Racism, and the Rise of Mexican American Activism.* Austin: University of Texas Press, 2003; Dyer, Stanford P., and Merrell A. Knighten. "Discrimination after Death: Lyndon Johnson and Félix Longoria." *Southern Studies* 17 (1978) 411–426; Green, George Norris. "The Felix Longoria Affair." *Journal of Ethnic Studies* 19:3 (Fall 1991) 23–49; Pycior, Julie Leininger. *LBJ & Mexican Americans: The Paradox of Power.* Austin: University of Texas Press, 1997.

LÓPEZ, IGNACIO L., 1908–1973. Journalist, activist. Ignacio López was the crusading editor of the San Bernardino, California, weekly *El Espectador* for over a quarter century. From the 1930s until the 1960s he spoke out fearlessly, voicing concerns of Mexican Americans about discrimination, segregation, and violation of civil rights. An outstanding Mexican American leader in southern California during the 1940s and the 1950s, he strove to obtain the full acceptance and integration of Mexican Americans into a pluralistic American society. López publicized incidents of police brutality and obvious discrimination against Mexicanos. Vigilant but not confrontational, he advocated use of the boycott and other peaceful economic weapons as well as the courts to achieve greater respect for Mexicanos' rights in the use of public facilities: theaters, swimming pools, and cemeteries. As a fervent disciple of American democracy, he strongly stressed the need for Mexican Americans to take more forceful steps under the law to defend their rights.

López's activist leadership in the desegregation of public facilities was of great importance in establishing the Unity Leagues and Community Service Organization groups in the greater Los Angeles area after World War II. It was the chief ingredient in a number of victories for civil rights, including the case of *Méndez et al. v. Westminster School District et al.,* 1945–1947. Over a decade later he was one of the organizers of the **Mexican American Po-**

litical Association. During the 1950s his editorials helped elect two dozen Mexican Americans to city and county offices. Often considered by Anglos to be radical, during the 1960s he began to be seen for what he had always been, a determined moderate in Mexican Americans' struggle for their rights. He received appointment as Spanish-speaking Coordinator in the Department of Housing and Urban Development during the Nixon administration.

FURTHER READING: García, Mario T. *Mexican Americans: Leadership, Ideology, and Identity, 1930–1960.* New Haven: Yale University Press, 1989; López, Enrique M. "Community Resistance to Injustice and Inequality: Ontario, California, 1937–1947." *Aztlán* 17:2 (Fall 1986) 1–29.

LÓPEZ, LINO M., 1910–1978. Educator, activist. Lino López spent most of his life working to create greater opportunities for young Mexican Americans, particularly in education. After graduating from Loyola University in Chicago in the mid-1940s, he became involved in social welfare work. He served as director of the Catholic Youth Center in Pueblo, Colorado, for over half a decade and in 1953 moved to Denver, where he worked as an educational consultant and a member of the mayor's Commission on Human Relations.

In 1963 López moved to San Jose, California. In San Jose he established the Mexican American Community Service Agency to respond to ingrained injustices, and continued his educational work with young Chicanos. He helped organize clubs for Mexican American high school students and pioneered in persuading local schools to develop bilingual programs. At the expansion of the Chicano movimiento in the late 1960s he accepted a position at Redlands University in southern California, where he continued his life's work of teaching and advising Chicano students. A severe auto accident followed by an incapacitating stroke led to his return to Denver, where he died a tragic death. Lino López was one of the very early leaders in the struggle for Mexican American educational rights.

FURTHER READING: Valdés, Daniel. *Who's Who in Colorado.* Denver: Who's Who in Colorado, 1958.

LÓPEZ, NANCY, 1957– . Professional golfer. Although born in the Los Angeles, California, suburb of Torrence, Nancy López grew up in Roswell, New Mexico, to which the family moved. Both her parents were avid golfers and Nancy tagged along when they played on weekends. Imitating her father and other good golfers, she soon gave evidence of unusual skills. At age nine Nancy took first place in a Pee Wee tournament, and three years later she won the New Mexico Women's State Amateur tournament.

At Godard High School in Roswell, Nancy was number one on the otherwise all-male golf squad. An all-around athlete, she was also active in gymnastics, track, swimming, basketball, and touch football. After high school she initially accepted a University of Tulsa athletic scholarship and later was awarded a four-year golf scholarship at Colgate University. In her sophomore year she was named the school's Most Valuable Player and Female Athlete of the Year. At age nineteen she turned professional and left the university.

In February 1978 Nancy won the Bent Tree Classic at Sarasota, Florida, and then won five consecutive Ladies Professional Golf Association (LPGA) tournaments, earning her the titles LPGA Rookie of the Year, LPGA Player of the Year, and Associated Press Female Athlete of the Year. In 1979 she won eight tournaments, and placed within the top ten scorers in the twenty-two tournaments she entered. An outstanding favorite for her winning smile and sunny disposition, as well as her playing, with the increasing number of golf fans who came out to see her, she was a predominant factor in doubling LPGA tournament purses by 1984.

After a maternity leave to have her first child, she returned to the tournament circuit. By 1985 she again dominated women's golf. Two years later, with over thirty-five tournament wins, she became the youngest golfer to be installed in the LPGA Hall of Fame. Induction into the PGA World Golf Hall of Fame followed a few years later. In the latter 1980s Nancy López again took time out to give birth to twin daughters. Maternity and weight gain took their toll on her golf game, and at the beginning of the twenty-first century she was struggling to again become a contender in women's golf. Since turning pro she has won a total of forty-eight tourneys. A diabetic, she participates in charitable activities and promotes concern about strokes and heart disease.

FURTHER READING: Barnes, Jill. "The Winning Formula of Nancy Lopez. *Vista* 2:12 (1 August 1987) 6–9; "Committed Lopez Plays for a Cause." *USA Today* (14 May 1997) 2C; *Current Biography, 1978.* New York: H. W. Wilson, 1979; López, Nancy, with Peter Schwed. *The Education of a Woman Golfer.* New York: Simon and Schuster, Inc., 1979; Phillips, Betty Lou. *The Picture Story of Nancy López.* New York: J. Messner, 1980; Purkey, Mike. "At Home with Nancy López." *Golf Magazine* 32:5 (1 May 1990) 86; Stachura, Mike. "The Class of '78." *Golf World* 54; 22 (24 November 2000) 30–33.

LÓPEZ, TRINI(DAD), 1937– . Singer. Trinidad López was born in the "Little Mexico" barrio of Dallas, Texas, of undocumented parents from Guadalajara. Encouraged by his musical father, he early showed an aptitude and love for music. While in high school he formed a small band that within a short time became popular in much of the Southwest. Dropping out of school at the end of the 1950s, he took his combo to Los Angeles, where it soon was playing in prominent nightclubs. In 1963 he was signed up by Frank Sinatra's Reprise Records. His first album, "Trini Lopez Live at PJ's," went platinum, and a single from it, "If I Had a Hammer," became the number one song in twenty-three countries, selling more than four million copies. As a result, Trini spent the next several years making tours of the U.S., Europe, Australia, Japan, the Philippines, and South Africa.

By 1970 Trini had recorded fourteen albums, appeared on numerous TV shows, and made three movies, the best-known of which was *The Dirty Dozen.*

A quiet, reserved man, the international recording star invested his earnings in commercial real estate and music companies and has used his wealth to finance his philanthropies. During the 1970s and 1980s he also gave numerous benefit performances for educational and charitable institutions. At sixty-four he plays at the Mohegan Sun Casino (Conn.) every Sunday.

FURTHER READING: *Current Biography, 1968.* New York: H. W. Wilson, 1968; Reyes, Luis, and Peter Rubie. *Hispanics in Hollywood: A Celebration of 100 Years in Film and Television.* Hollywood: Lone Eagle, 2000; Newlon, Clarke. *Famous Mexican Americans.* New York: Dodd, Mead & Co., 1972; Roybal, Rose Marie. "Trini López." *La Luz* 4:8–9 (November–December 1985) 10.

Singer-guitarist Trini López with Jack Benny, November 1966. © AP/Wide World Photos.

LOS ANGELES. Although the area of Los Angeles was first sighted in the mid-1500s by Spanish explorers, its settlement from Mexico did not begin until the Portolá-Serra expedition reached it from Baja California in 1769. The pueblo was officially established in 1781; governor Felipe de Neve gave it the name Nuestra Señora de los Angeles de la Porciúncula. By 1800 the Mexican town, the largest settlement in Alta California, had about three hundred inhabitants. Independence from Spain two decades later had little impact initially, but soon local officials admitted the first Anglo merchants and adventurers, many of whom married into prominent Californio families, accepted Catholicism, and became Mexican citizens.

During the **U.S.-Mexican War** American naval forces initially seized Los Angeles with little difficulty, but the harsh occupation rule of Captain Archibald Gillespie led to an uprising that was finally put down in January 1847. After the war an exodus of gold-seekers to the northern mines left the town a struggling frontier settlement in which Californios kept a degree of control. The gold miners' need for food brought on an era of prosperity, particularly for the land-owning elites, based chiefly on cattle sales. After the cattle boom was ended by the long drought of the early 1860s, the town began to become more important for commercial farming and trading.

The advent of the transcontinental **railroads** in the next two decades completely changed Los Angeles. The arrival by rail of thousands of Anglo settlers from the Midwest and East marked a real estate boom and a rapid decline in lingering Angeleno influence. Mexicanos found themselves relegated to barrios in which urban services were lacking or inferior; many of them moved east from the plaza area, known as Sonoratown, to Boyle Heights. When the real estate prosperity collapsed at the end of the 1880s, it left a total population of 50,000. Ten years later, at the beginning of the next century, Los Angeles boasted a population exceeding 100,000, of whom Mexicanos formed about 15 percent.

Toward the end of the nineteenth century Mexican Americans in Los Angeles began to develop a deeper ethnic consciousness, often illustrated by use of a new term, *la raza*, and the creation of formal organizations. Except for a handful of acculturated upper-class Californios, they were excluded from most benefits of the city's economic growth. Most continued to be largely limited to employment in unskilled and semiskilled work in agriculture, meatpacking, harness-making, blacksmithing, garment making, trade, the railroads, and personal service. Only a handful were able to enter the professions as bookkeepers, lawyers, and nurses.

The **Mexican revolution** of 1910 set in motion the next stage of Los Angeles growth. Between 1900 and 1930 the city's population went from 100,000 to 2.2 million as refugees and job seekers from Mexico poured in and as a commercial real estate boom brought more midwestern Anglos. By 1920 the Mexicano population was nearly 30,000, and the next census showed over three times that many, most of them living in East L.A. Many were skilled and semiskilled workers in furniture-making, iron, oil, and construction; they also continued to predominate in meatpacking, the service sector, and agriculture. The expansion of citrus crops in eastern Los Angeles county provided employment for the immigrant influx of the 1920s. The expatriation of thousands during the Depression of the following decade created a bitterness and antagonism that was then reinforced by the **Sleepy Lagoon** affair in 1942 and the so-called **Zoot Suit Riots** of the following year.

During World War II, shipbuilding and the rapid industrial expansion in the Los Angeles area, especially in steel, rubber, and automobiles, provided more opportunities for Mexicanos in the workforce, while service in the armed forces moved a new, American-born generation farther into the U.S. mainstream. Using the G.I. Bill, returning L.A. Chicano veterans bought homes, started businesses, and went to college, from which they began to enter the professions in larger numbers. With greater self-confidence now, they also became actively involved in community affairs and politics. In 1949 they elected **Edward Roybal** to the L.A. city council, the first step in his long political career, and later helped elect **Julian Nava, Richard Alatorre**, **Art Torres**, and **Gloria Molina** to political offices. In 1991 Molina became the first woman and the first Mexican American in over a century to be elected to the county board of supervisors.

From mid-century onward, the problems of inferior barrio schools attended by their children became an increasingly important concern for Angelenos. As a result, the Chicano Movement and the 1968 **student walkouts** in Los Angeles elicited widespread community support. The L.A. area led in creating student organizations that pushed school administrations to take remedial action about various educational issues closely affecting Chicanos. The 1970 National Chicano Moratorium march in East Los Angeles to protest the large number of Chicano casualties in the Vietnam War illustrated the new spirit and climaxed long-held grievances against officialdom. The senseless death of reporter **Rubén Salazar** during the march served further to bring together all L.A. Mexican Americans.

In the 1980s Los Angeles county Latinos increased by 1.5 million, but fewer jobs were available to them as heavy industry and agriculture in the area declined. Between 1980 and 1995 some 2 million Mexicans, many of them **undocumented**, came to the United States and a majority of them, perhaps as many as 1.2 million, settled in the Los Angeles metropolitan area. The 1990 census indicated that L.A. county had 2,519,514 Mexicanos, approximately one-third of its total population. It had the largest concentration of Mexicanos outside Mexico City. Los Angeles school districts became predominantly Latino districts by the mid-1990s, with the majority of their students classified as having limited English proficiency. In the 2000 census L.A. (city) Hispanics numbered 1.7 million, accounting for 46 percent of the total city population and outnumbering Anglos.

Over 40 percent of Mexican immigrants who arrived in the Los Angeles area before 1980 owned their own homes by 1990. But the increasingly high cost of real estate has led to crowded **housing** and heightened stress for Mexicanos, who have an index of 1.7 persons per room. East Los Angeles, which is 60 percent Latino, has a housing density of over 20,000 persons per square mile, more than two and one half times the Los Angeles average.

According to the 1990 census, almost half of the Mexicanos living in Los Angeles had been born in Mexico. About 40 percent of the county population is noncitizen, but amnesty provisions of the 1986 **Immigration Reform and Control Act** (IRCA) and **Proposition 187**'s denial of medical and education benefits to undocumenteds in 1994 later led to a surge in **citizenship** applications. Although the enlarging Latino electorate increases the opportunities for Mexican American politicians, it has also increased racial and ethnic politicizing. In June 2001 former speaker of the state assembly **Antonio Villaraigosa**, the leader in initial balloting, lost his bid for the mayor's office in the runoff primarily because of ethnic bias, but Rocky Delgadillo won election to the office of Los Angeles city attorney.

FURTHER READING: Acuña, Rodolfo. *Anything But Mexican: Chicanos in Contemporary Los Angeles.* New York: Verso, 1996; Balderrama, Francisco E. *In Defense of La Raza: The Los Angeles Mexican Consulate and the Mexican Community, 1929–1936.* Tucson: University of Arizona Press, 1982; Chávez, Ernesto. *"Mi raza primero!" Nationalism, Identity, and Insurgency in the Chicano Movement in Los Angeles, 1966–1978.*

Berkeley: University of California Press, 2002; Clark, William A. *The California Cauldron: Immigration and the Fortunes of Local Communities*. New York: The Guilford Press, 1998; Fogelson, Robert. *The Fragmented Metropolis: Los Angeles, 1850–1930*. Cambridge, Mass.: Harvard University Press, 1967; García, Matt. *A World of Its Own: Race, Labor and Citrus in the Making of Greater Los Angeles, 1900–1970*. Chapel Hill: University of North Carolina Press, 2001; Griswold del Castillo, Richard. *The Los Angeles Barrio, 1850–1890: A Social History*. Berkeley: University of California Press, 1979; Leclerc, Gustavo, Raul Villa, and Michael J. Dear, eds. *Urban Latino Cultures: La vida latina en L. A.* Thousand Oaks, Calif.: Sage, 1999; Monroy, Douglas. *Rebirth: Mexican Los Angeles from the Great Migration to the Great Depression*. Berkeley: University of California Press, 1999; Romo, Ricardo. *East Los Angeles: History of a Barrio*. Austin: University Of Texas Press, 1983; Sánchez, George I. *Becoming Mexican American: Ethnicity, Culture, and Identity in Chicano Los Angeles, 1900–1945*. New York: Oxford University Press, 1993.

LOZANO, IGNACIO E., JR., 1927– . Ambassador, publisher. Ignacio Lozano, Jr. was born and received his early education in San Antonio, Texas. After graduation from Notre Dame University with a B.A. in journalism he went to work on his father's newspaper, *La Opinión*. When his father's health failed in 1953, he took over the management of *La Opinión*. As a prominent southwestern publisher, he became active in journalism organizations and in civic affairs. In 1964 he was appointed by President Lyndon Johnson as a consultant in the State Department, and also served on various commissions including the California advisory committee to the U.S. Civil Rights Commission. A dozen years later he was named ambassador to El Salvador by President Gerald Ford. In 1991 he sold one-half ownership in *La Opinión* but continued to be directly involved in the paper as publisher. President of Lozano Enterprises, Inc., he also serves on the boards of a number of other companies.

FURTHER READING: "Ignacio Lozano: Continuing a Tradition." *Caminos* 5:2 (February 1984) 37; "The *Hispanic Business* Rich List." *Hispanic Business* (March 1993) 48; "Ignacio E. Lozano Jr. Named U.S. Ambassador to El Salvador." *La Luz* 5:9 (September 1976) 20; *Who's Who in America, 1978–1979*. Chicago: Marquis, 1978.

LOZANO, IGNACIO E., SR., 1887–1953. Journalist. Ignacio Lozano, Sr., was born in the north Mexican state of Nuevo León and moved to San Antonio, Texas at age twenty-one. Five years later he began publishing *La Prensa*, a Spanish-language weekly that he converted into a daily. In 1926, following the trend of Mexican immigrants who now viewed California as El Norte, he began publishing *La Opinión* in Los Angeles. Aimed at immigrants rather than Mexican Americans, both papers were highly successful, with *La Opinión* reaching a circulation of twenty-five thousand by 1930. Lozano was active in the two papers until his severely deteriorating health forced him to step down early in 1953.

FURTHER READING: Di Stefano, Onofre. "'Venimos a luchar': A Brief History of *La Prensa*'s Founding." *Aztlán* 16:1–2 (1986) 95–118; "*The Blossoming of the Hispanic Press.*" *Nuestro* (October 1984) 22–27; Ríos-McMillan, Nora. "A Biography of a Man and His Newspaper." *The Américas Review* 17:3–4 (Fall–Winter 1989) 136–149.

LUCEY, ROBERT E., 1891–1977. Archbishop, civil rights advocate. Robert Lucey, a native of Los Angeles, was a longtime advocate and supporter of the Mexican American struggle for civil and social rights. As archbishop of San Antonio after 1941, he strongly defended the right of farm workers to form and join unions and he advocated federal labor legislation to protect migrant workers. In 1950 he was appointed by Harry Truman to the President's Commission on Migratory Labor. During the 1966 Texas melon pickers' march on Austin he spoke out vigorously in their support and urged them to persevere in their struggle.

During the nearly three decades of his bishopric, Lucey encouraged the priests of his diocese to become involved in civil rights concerns. In 1945 he was one of the leaders in founding the Bishops Committee for the Spanish Speaking, and remained its executive chairman for a quarter of a century, until his 1969 retirement.

Although Lucey was sometimes referred to by conservatives as the "pink bishop," he actually was fairly conservative in many instances. However, his liberal views on socioeconomic matters led him to champion the rights of poor Mexicanos and earned him a national reputation as a strong supporter of their struggle for social justice.

FURTHER READING: Bronder, Saul. *Social Justice and Church Authority: The Public Life of Robert E. Lucey.* Philadelphia: Temple University Press, 1982; Lucey, Robert E. "Migratory Workers." *Commonweal* 59 (15 January 1954) 370–373; Privett, Stephen A. *The U.S. Catholic Church and Its Hispanic Members: The Pastoral Vision of Archbishop Robert E. Lucey.* San Antonio: Trinity University Press, 1988.

LUDLOW MASSACRE, 1914. At the beginning of the twentieth century the Colorado Fuel and Iron Company pursued a policy of absolute feudal domination in the Trinidad coal mining district. It adamantly opposed the miners' efforts at unionization. In September 1913, after an intensive and successful unionization drive by the United Mine Workers, the union called a strike when the company refused to negotiate over the issue of wages and various civil rights abuses. The violence that erupted between company guards and the miners was suppressed by the **Colorado** National Guard after eleven people had been killed. Many of the strikers, including United Mine Workers organizer Mother Jones, were arrested and held incommunicado.

During the next six months, tensions between the miners, many of them Mexicanos, and the guardsmen and company guards continued, becoming increasingly bitter. On April 20, 1914, fighting broke out between the strikers and the guards. The militia brought in a mobile machine gun and burned down the tent city in which the miners had been living since their eviction from company housing. The melee resulted in the killing of sixty-six persons, of whom thirteen, women and children, were burned to death. This massacre resulted in open warfare with a vengeful rampage of burning and killing on the part of the enraged miners. A week later President Woodrow Wilson, having been asked to intervene by the Colorado governor, sent in federal troops who brought an end to the fighting. However, the strike dragged on until the end of the year. The Ludlow Massacre became a cause célèbre and in the long run served to advance the struggle for mine workers' rights. Finally, with the New Deal legislation of the 1930s the miners gained recognition of their union.

FURTHER READING: Eastman, Max. "Class War in Colorado." In *Echoes of Revolt: The Masses, 1911–1917*, edited by William L. O'Neill. Chicago: Ivan R. Dee, Inc., 1989; Gitelman, Howard M. *Legacy of the Ludlow Massacre: A Chapter in American Industrial Relations.* Philadelphia: University of Pennsylvania Press, 1988; Vallejo, M. Edmund. "Recollections of the Colorado Coal Strike, 1913–1914." In *La Gente: Hispano History and Life in Colorado*, edited by Vincent C. de Baca. Denver: Colorado Historical Society, 1998.

LUJÁN, MANUEL, JR., 1928– . Congressman. Manuel Luján, scion of a politically prominent old Nuevomexicano family, was born and raised in San Ildefonso. After college he worked in the family insurance business for a decade. Then, like his father before him, he entered politics. As a candidate for the state senate he lost, but in 1968 he was elected to the U.S. House of Representatives, where he ultimately served more terms than any other New Mexico Republican congressman.

A pro-business conservative, Luján was an ardent advocate of private initiative and of easing government controls. On environmental issues he was closely associated with the pro-development camp, and in the 1970s spoke out for opening more federal lands to logging, mining, and grazing. Impeccably credentialed by oil, timber, mining, and ranching interests, in 1989 he was made steward of the country's natural treasures by president George H. W. Bush, who named him Secretary of the Interior, with seventy thousand employees, a budget of eight billion dollars, and the oversight of one-quarter of the U.S. landmass. As Interior Secretary he called for a stepping back from environmentalism in favor of a greater "balance" with development. During his tenure, conservation-minded staffers were apt to find themselves transferred out of important positions to new, less significant assignments.

In 1999 Luján was one of a dozen Latino investors who bought some 400,000 telephone lines from the GTE Corporation in order to form a new company.

FURTHER READING: "Group Buying GTE Assets." *The New York Times* (9 Sept. 1999) C10; Gup, T. "The Stealth Secretary." *Time* 139:21 (25 May 1992) 57; Ralph

Nader Congress Project. *Manuel Luján Jr. Republican Representative from New Mexico.* Washington, D.C.: Grossman Publishers, 1972; Valdez, William J. "Crossing Swords With the Liberals." *Hispanic Review of Business* (May 1986) 6–13.

LUNA, SOLOMÓN, 1858–1912. Politician, rancher, businessman. Solomón Luna was born in Los Lunas, New Mexico, named after his prominent and well-to-do family. After private tutoring and a college education in Santa Fe and St. Louis, Missouri, he inherited a large sheep ranch in Valencia county. He married into the prominent Otero family and entered politics, serving as court clerk, then sheriff for two terms, and finally as county treasurer. His repeated reelection as treasurer made him the Republican boss of Valencia county for many years and gave him great political power. In 1897 he became a close advisor to governor **Miguel Otero, Jr**.

By the beginning of the twentieth century, Luna had become one of the wealthiest men in the New Mexico territory, active in banking and real estate as well as ranching. He was deeply interested in statehood and worked successfully to include in the state constitution guarantees for Hispanic culture and the Spanish language. Prominent in Republican politics, he nevertheless rejected suggestions that he run for governor of the new state. His sudden death from a stroke only months after New Mexico became the forty-seventh state ended a promising career.

FURTHER READING: Perrigo, Lynn I. *Hispanos: Historic Leaders in New Mexico.* Santa Fe, N.M.: Sunstone Press, 1985; Vigil, Maurilio E. *Los Patrones: Profiles of Hispanic Political Leaders in New Mexico History.* Washington, D.C.: University Press of America, 1980.

LYNCHING. The lynching of Mexicanos was widespread in the second half of the nineteenth century along the entire U.S.-Mexican border, but especially in Texas. In California lynching became fairly commonplace during the gold rush. Frequently it resulted from Mexicanos being accused of stealing gold or horses or of killing Anglos. The 1851 Downieville lynching of "Juanita" was a widely noted example of a Mexicana murdered for the death of an Anglo. Between 1850 and 1895 Mexicanos formed nearly 40 percent of California lynch mob victims at a time when they formed no more than 15 percent of the population.

In Texas, rape was the most common charge leading to lynching, which was the most extreme form of widespread violence there against *la raza* in the second half of the 1800s. Both the **Texas Rangers** and impromptu civilian vigilante committees and posses often took "justice" summarily into their own hands. Since all Mexicanos were considered foreigners and therefore without rights, protests against extralegal mob action were rarely successful in deterring vigilante violence. The Spanish-American War in 1898 and the Mexican revolution, 1910–1920, resulted in outbursts of persecution and the lynching of Mexicanos.

After the turn of the century, lynchings declined in number as Mexican Americans organized for their defense. However, from time to time economic recessions have created a climate in which night-riding, terrorism, and home-burning plagued Mexicanos. During the depression that lasted through most of the 1930s, for example, the Ku Klux Klan actively pursued such activities, including some lynching.

FURTHER READING: Acuña, Rodolfo. *Occupied America: A History of Chicanos*, 3rd ed. New York: Harper & Row, 1988; Riss, Jean F. "The Lynching of Francisco Torres." *Journal of Mexican American History* 2 (Spring 1972) 90–121; Rosales, Francisco A. *Chicano!: The History of the Mexican American Civil Rights Movement.* 2nd ed. Houston: Arte Público Press, 1997.

MACHISMO. From the Spanish word *macho*, male, machismo is a sociological term for the cult of maleness as expressed in aggressiveness and courageousness. In Mexican culture it is also associated with honor, responsibility, and dependability. Among some males it may at times connote arrogance, sexual rapacity, and compensation for a personal sense of insecurity.

FURTHER READING: González, Ray, ed. *Muy Macho: Latino Men Confront Their Manhood.* New York: Anchor Books, 1996; Mirandé, Alfredo. *Hombres y Machos: Masculinity and Latino Culture.* Boulder, Colo.: Westview Press, 1997.

MACHUCA, ESTHER NIETO, 1895–1980. Activist. Esther Machuca was a leader in the El Paso women's group Ladies League of United Latin American Citizens, known as the Ladies LULAC. One of the early organizers in the **League of United Latin American Citizens** (LULAC), she became unhappy at the lack of male support for the women's group, founded in 1933. As a result, in 1936 she dissolved the two-year-old auxiliary, but then helped reestablish it in the following year. Her important role in Texas LULAC was recognized by her selection as the official hostess of the 1938 national convention held in El Paso.

After the convention Machuca was appointed Ladies' Organizer General (1938–1939), a position she used effectively to increase the number of women's auxiliaries. She remained active in the El Paso Ladies LULAC into her early eighties. Although not a feminist in the modern mold, throughout her life she held that LULAC women should have complete equality with male members. By 1970 most women were active in integrated councils, and two decades later there were fewer than ten Ladies LULAC chapters in Texas.

FURTHER READING: García, Mario T. *Mexican Americans: Leadership, Ideology, and Identity, 1930–1960.* New Haven: Yale University Press, 1989; Tyler, Ron, ed. *The New Handbook of Texas,* vol. 4. Austin: Texas State Historical Association, 1996.

MALINCHE, LA. Malinche, also known as Doña Marina, who spoke both Nahuatl and Mayan, was given to Hernán Cortés in 1519 by the Tabascan Indians after his men defeated them. Because of her linguistic abilities and cultural savvy, Cortés soon made her his intermediary with the Aztecs as well as his mistress. She served him well as an advisor and interpreter of Aztec customs and politics, achieving great influence in the process. Although always viewed ambivalently, in Mexico she has commonly been seen as a symbol of betrayal because of her aid to the Spaniards. Among modern Chicanas she sometimes has been pictured as the symbolic mother of the mestizo "race."

FURTHER READING: Cypress, Sandra Messinger. *La Malinche in Mexican Literature: From History to Myth.* Austin: University of Texas Press, 1991; Díaz del Castillo, Bernal. *The Conquest of New Spain.* Baltimore: Penguin Books, 1963; Lanyon, Anna. *Malinche's Conquest.* St. Edwards, N.S.W.: Allen and Unwin, 1999. Sánchez, Rosaura, and Rosa Martínez Cruz, eds. *Essays on La Mujer.* Los Angeles: Chicano Studies Center, University of California, 1978.

MANA: A NATIONAL LATINA ORGANIZATION. MANA was founded in 1974 as Mexican American Women's National Association with Evangeline Elizondo of Texas as its first president. Its immediate goal was to advance Chicana status and obtain equality with men by developing self-esteem and **leadership** qualities among Chicanas. In 1984 it established a national academic program, the Raquel Márquez Frankel Scholarship Fund. It also operates a mentoring program called HERMANITAS.

MANA's development owes much to **Gloria Barajas,** president from 1985 to 1986. With extensive experience as a community and political activist, she focused the organization's goal on securing greater economic equality, especially more elective and administrative jobs in government for Chicanas. Her successor as president, Rita Jaramillo, emphasized stronger financing for MANA's expanded programs. Headquartered in Washington, D.C., MANA publishes a monthly newsletter and holds local and national conventions to alert Spanish-speaking women about current issues affecting them and to encourage the mentoring of teenage Latinas.

In 1998 the association's name was changed to MANA: A National Latina Organization to reflect the broadened scope of its membership. In June 2000 Alma Morales Riojas, a longtime Tejana activist, was named president; she has stressed the nurturing of Chicana leaders. With a membership of over four thousand in two-thirds of the states, MANA is one of the largest Chicana/Latina organizations. More than 80 percent of its members have university degrees.

FURTHER READING: Cadavíd, Fresia Rodríguez. "The Face of MANA." *Latina Style* 9:1 (2003) 12–13; Crocker, Elvira Valenzuela. *MANA: One Dream, Many Voices; A History of the Mexican American Women's National Association.* Washington, D.C.: MANA, 1991; Márquez, Benjamin. *Constructing Identities in Mexican American Political Organizations: Choosing Issues, Taking Sides.* Austin: University of Texas Press, 2003; Sarracent, Mari Carmen. "MANA: Women Informed and Active." *Hispanic Outlook in Higher Education* 11:10 (26 February 2001) 37–39. Segura, Denise A and Beatriz M. Pesquera. "Chicana Feminisms: Their Political Context and Contemporary Expressions." In *The Latino Studies Reader: Culture, Economy, and Society,* edited by

Antonia Darder and Rodolfo D. Torres. Malden, Mass.: Blackwell, 1998.
www.hermana.org

MANIFEST DESTINY. *Manifest destiny* was the name given to an aggressive
manifestation of U.S. nationalism in the nineteenth century. Its adherents
believed that it was the destiny, even the duty, of the United States to take
over and rule areas held by "inferior" peoples in order to bring them the
benefits of the democratic American political system and democracy in general. They held that it was the destiny of the country to expand to the Pacific Ocean and even beyond. The war with Mexico, 1846–1848, and the
acquisition of half of her territory were, in part, an early outstanding expression of this jingoist doctrine.

FURTHER READING: González, Juan. *Harvest of Empire: A History of Latinos in
America.* New York: Viking, 2000; Horsman, Reginald. *Race and Manifest Destiny: The
Origins of American Racial Anglo-Saxonism.* Cambridge: Harvard University Press, 1981;
Merk, Frederick. *Manifest Destiny and Mission in American History.* New York: Alfred
A. Knopf, 1966; Weinber, Albert. *Manifest Destiny.* Chicago: Quadrangle Books, 1967.

MANUEL, HERSCHEL THURMAN, 1887–1976. Educator, psychologist.
Herschel T. Manuel was born, grew up, and received his education in the
Midwest. After earning a doctorate from the University of Illinois, army service during World War I, and early university teaching, in 1925 he moved
to the University of Texas, where he remained the rest of his academic life.
A 1928 research grant to study the schooling of Spanish-speaking children
led to a lifelong interest in their problems, and to his seminal 1930 study,
The Education of Mexican and Spanish-speaking Children in Texas. He continued
his studies in the education of Mexicano children in Texas schools and argued strongly for their educational rights. He was one of the earliest scholars to point out the importance of their education to the future of Texas.

Manuel's pioneering studies in the problems of Spanish-speaking children
in an English-speaking educational environment soon earned him a reputation as a leading educational psychologist. He was especially noted for his
expertise in bilingual testing, and developed a series of tests that were published in 1950. A Hogg Foundation grant led to further research and the
1965 publication of his second work, *Spanish-Speaking Children of the Southwest: Their Education and the Public Welfare.*

FURTHER READING: Davis, Matthew D. "Herschel T. Manuel: 'The Doyen of
Mexican American Education.'" Ph.D. diss., University of Texas at Austin, 2000;
Tyler, Ron, ed. *New Handbook of Texas*, vol. 4. Austin: The State Historical Associa-
tion, 1996.

MAQUILADORA. *Maquiladora*, or *maquila*, is the name for a factory located in designated free zones in Mexico, especially in the border region,
to which materials or parts are brought under bond for labor-intensive
processing or assembly by Mexican workers and then returned to the

United States. Begun in the mid-1960s, maquiladoras were expected to ease employment problems created by the ending of the bracero program in 1964. They have expanded greatly since then. U.S. labor unions and some Mexican American groups have criticized the maquiladoras as making cheap labor available to U.S. companies and thereby taking jobs away from American workers.

FURTHER READING: Fatemi, Khosrow, ed. *The Maquiladora Industry: Economic Solution or Problem?* New York: Praeger, 1990; Kamel, Rachel, and Anya Hoffman, eds. *The Maquiladora Reader: Cross-Border Organizing Since NAFTA.* Philadelphia: Mexico-U.S. Border Program, American Friends Service Committee, 1999; Kopinak, Kathryn. *Desert Capitalism: Maquiladoras in North America's Western Industrial Corridor.* Tucson: University of Arizona Press, 1996. Salzinger, Leslie. *Genders in Production: Making Workers in Mexico's Global Factories.* Berkeley: University of California Press, 2003.

MARTÍNEZ, ANTONIO JOSÉ, 1793–1867. Priest, political activist. Antonio José Martínez was born in Abiquiu, Nuevo México, and spent most of his clerical life as pastor in Taos, where he started a school and minor seminary. A member of a large and politically powerful Nuevomexicano family, he was the territory's most prominent and controversial historical personage and unarguably its nineteenth-century genius.

A staunch republic-minded and patriotic citizen of Mexico, Father Martínez opposed the United States's encroachment and takeover of the Southwest; however, he developed substantial positive expectations for New Mexico and its people under U.S. rule. To meet the new conditions he added the study of English and civil law to the curriculum in his school at Taos. He also took advantage of those aspects of the U.S. government that he viewed as favorable to Nuevomexicanos. He himself became intensely active in politics, taking a vigorous role in the statehood convention that met after the 1848 Treaty of **Guadalupe Hidalgo**. In the convention discussions he expressed his concerns about the rights of Nuevomexicanos under United States rule.

Continuing his active role in politics, Martínez served three terms in the territorial Legislative Council during the 1850s, one term as its president. At the time of the Civil War he supported President Abraham Lincoln's policies on the slavery issue. He also spoke out for the plight of southwestern Indians. In 1865 he sent his critical views of U.S. policy to the congressional Doolittle Committee, asserting that under the United States the Indians had even fewer rights than under Mexico.

Father Martínez's conflict with his new French-born bishop, **Jean Baptiste Lamy**, began in part as an aspect of his defense of Nuevomexicano rights, including his own. After his conditional resignation in 1856 as pastor at Taos, it evolved into a bitter personal quarrel between two strong-willed men. Martínez ignored various public episcopal admonitions and was suspended and finally excommunicated in 1858 by Lamy. Using his home chapel, he continued to officiate as a priest until his death in July 1867, mourned by many.

FURTHER READING: Chávez, Fray Angélico. *But Time and Chance: The Story of Padre Martínez of Taos, 1793–1867*. Santa Fe, N.M.: Sunstone Press, 1981; Mares, E. A., ed. *Padre Martínez: New Perspectives from Taos*. Taos: Millicent Rogers Museum, 1988; Perrigo, Lynn I. *Hispanos: Historic Leaders in New Mexico*. Santa Fe, N.M.: Sunstone Press, 1985; Sánchez, Pedro. *Recollections of the Life of the Priest Don Antonio José Martínez*. Santa Fe, N.M.: Lightning Tree Press, 1978.

MARTÍNEZ, BETITA (ELIZABETH), 1925– . Activist, community organizer, journalist. Betita Sutherland Martínez was born and grew up in Washington, D.C. After graduating from Swarthmore College, she worked as a researcher and editor. Not unfamiliar with discrimination as a youngster, in 1963 she joined the black Student Non-Violent Coordinating Committee (SNCC) as a civil rights worker in the South. In the following year she became director of SNCC's New York office, with the job of fund-raising and calling media attention to civil rights abuses. In early 1966 she was sent by SNCC to California to give a speech in solidarity with the United Farm Workers, then on their march to Sacramento. As a result she became involved in the Chicano Movement.

In 1968 Martínez joined Reies López Tijerina's **Alianza Federal de Pueblos Libres** in Albuquerque, New Mexico, putting her experience in the black civil rights movement to use for the Alianza. Her first task was to develop a voice for the Alianza in its demands for the return of pueblo lands. To this end she helped create and then edited *El Grito del Norte*, a bilingual newspaper. Under her editorship *El Grito* became an important voice in the Chicano Movement throughout the entire Southwest.

Since the mid-1970s Martínez has worked with various community groups, and during the 1990s she was a visiting lecturer and college professor. Convinced of the wisdom of and necessity for cooperation between African Americans and Chicanos, she has stressed this point in her writing and lectures and has engaged in speaking tours with the goal of improving Latino-black relations. Her most recent project is the Institute for Multiracial Justice, a resource center for developing alliances among people of color. She is the author of five books and numerous journal articles on the Chicano experience and civil rights movement. The most recent of her books is titled *De Colores Means All of Us: Latina Views for a Multicolored Century*, published in 1998.

FURTHER READING: Betita Martínez. *De Colores Means All of Us: Latina Views for a Multicolored Century*. Cambridge, Mass.: South End Press, 1998; *Las Mujeres: Mexican American/Chicana Women*. Windsor, Calif.: National Women's History Project, 1991; Palmisano, Joseph M., ed. *Notable Hispanic American Women, Book II*. Detroit: Gale Research, 1998.

MARTÍNEZ, FÉLIX T., JR., 1857–1916. Businessman, publisher. Born in New Mexico just south of Taos, Félix Martínez grew up there and in southern Colorado. At age fourteen he began working as a retail clerk and at twenty-one opened his own store, then expanded, and at twenty-nine sold his mercantile interests in order to invest in real estate. Meanwhile he also had become deeply interested in New Mexico journalism and politics.

After an unsuccessful run for San Miguel county treasurer in 1884, he was elected tax assessor two years later and then won a seat in the territorial assembly. A political orator of note, at the beginning of the 1890s he was a leader in the Partido del Pueblo Unido movement and was elected to the territorial council in 1892. Two years earlier he bought a leading Las Vegas weekly, *La Voz del Pueblo*, to support his political career and in the later 1890s also published and edited the *Valley Optic* in Las Vegas while he served as court clerk. He used the *La Voz del Pueblo* with such vitriol to voice Nuevomexicano unhappiness at ethnic inequities that he antagonized some in the community as well as most Anglos. He soon became persona non grata in San Miguel County.

In 1898 Martínez moved to El Paso, Texas because of his real estate and other investment interests there and bought the *El Paso Daily News*, adding it to *La Voz del Pueblo*. After publishing the *Daily News* for a decade he bought a controlling interest in the Albuquerque *Tribune-Citizen*. During these years he was also involved in a variety of successful businesses, and served on the boards of banks, real estate companies, and community organizations. At the time of his death he was a member of the Dallas Federal Reserve Board and was widely respected as a pioneering business entrepreneur in New Mexico and Texas.

FURTHER READING: Meléndez, A. Gabriel. *So All Is Not Lost: The Poetics of Print in Nuevomexicano Communities, 1834–1958.* Albuquerque: University of New Mexico Press, 1997; Vigil, Maurilio E. *Los Patrones: Profiles of Hispanic Political Leaders in New Mexico History,* Washington, D.C.: University Press of America, 1980; White, Robert Rankin. "Félix Martínez: A Borderlands Success Story." *Palacio.* 87:4 (1981–82) 12–17.

MARTÍNEZ, VILMA SOCORRO, 1944– . Attorney, activist. While still a high school student in San Antonio, Vilma Martínez worked one summer for leading Texas civil rights lawyer **Alonso Perales**. As a result of his example she decided that she too would become a lawyer in order to be of service to *la raza*. She graduated from the University of Texas at Austin with a political science degree and in 1964 began her legal training at Columbia University, graduating three years later.

In 1967 Vilma Martínez took a position with the National Association for the Advancement of Colored People (NAACP). While working in the NAACP Legal Defense Fund department, she also helped create a new Chicano organization, the **Mexican American Legal Defense and Educational Fund** (MALDEF). In 1970 she joined the New York State Division of Human Rights, Equal Employment Opportunity Council, as a counselor.

A member of MALDEF since its inception, Martínez was named its director in 1973 and served until 1982. As director, she emphasized using the law and the courts to obtain for Mexican Americans equality before the law, the elimination of discriminatory practices, and greater access to education. Among her important successes was persuading the courts that Mexican Americans qualified for the protection of the Voting Rights Act of 1965. She also was successful in the case of *Plyler v. Doe,* assuring children of undocumenteds the right to free public school education. By the end of her presidency, she had greatly remolded and expanded MALDEF and put it on a secure financial basis.

In 1982 Martínez went into private practice, joining the Los Angeles law firm of Munger, Tolles, and Olson as a litigator in labor problems. She also continued her involvement in community service and civil rights. From 1980 to 1989 she served on the board of the **Southwest Voter Registration Education Project**, and at the beginning of the 1990s she returned to MALDEF's board of directors. She has been active on numerous important commissions, boards, and committees, including the University of California Board of Regents. As a result of outstanding work at all levels of the U.S. courts early in her career, she has been mentioned as a potential candidate for a Supreme Court appointment.

FURTHER READING: Johnson, Dean. "Chair of the Board. " *Nuestro* (September 1985) 34–36; O'Connor, Karen, and Lee Epstein. "A Legal Voice for the Chicano Community." In *The Mexican American Experience: An Interdisciplinary Anthology,* edited by Rodolfo O. de la Garza, et al. Austin: University of Texas Press, 1985; Diane Telgen and Jim Kamp, eds. *Notable Hispanic American Women.* Detroit: Gale Research, 1993.

MARTÍNEZ Y OROZCO, XAVIER T., 1869–1943. Painter, art teacher. Born in Guadalajara, Javier Martínez moved to San Francisco, California, when his foster father was appointed consul general there in 1882. He studied painting and sculpture, graduating from the Mark Hopkins Institute with honors in 1897 and then continuing art studies in Europe. His paintings received Honorable Mention in the 1900 Paris Universal Exposition.

In the following year Martínez returned to San Francisco, where he quickly became a leading figure in local art circles. His studio soon came to be a meeting place for the Bay Area's artists, literary figures, and politicos. The first extensive exhibition of his paintings, held in San Francisco in 1905, was a great success, but his studio and most of his paintings were destroyed in the 1906 San Francisco earthquake and fire. Undaunted, he moved across the Bay and resumed painting. In the 1915 Panama-Pacific Exposition at San Francisco his paintings received Honorable Mention. During the 1920s he exhibited in galleries in California and New York, where his dramatic southwestern and Mexican landscapes gained him national recognition and acclaim. In 1940 he was elected to the Hall of Fame at the New

York World's Fair. He taught at the California College of Arts and Crafts from 1908 until six months before his death.

A year-2000 exhibition of "California Paintings, 1910–1940" at Leband Art Gallery, Loyola Marymount University in Los Angeles included some of Martínez's work.

FURTHER READING: "Best Bets Friday 8/25." *Los Angeles Times* (24 August 2000) F3; Neubert, George W. *Xavier Martínez (1869–1943)*. Oakland, Calif.: The Oakland Museum, 1974; Quirarte, Jacinto. *Mexican American Artists*. Austin: University of Texas Press, 1973; "Xavier Martínez, Noted Californian, Dies." *Art Digest* 17 (15 February 1943) 18.

MAXWELL LAND GRANT. Famous in the land grant history of the Southwest, the Maxwell grant in northeastern New Mexico was originally called the Beaubien-Miranda grant after its two original owners. After Carlos Beaubien's death, his son-in-law Lucien B. Maxwell bought out all other claimants and in 1869 sold the 97,000 acres to a group of speculators for $1.35 million. The new owners organized the Maxwell Land Grant and Railroad Co., claimed 2,000,000 acres, and sold the grant to a group of English speculators. In 1871 the Department of the Interior ruled that the grant covered only 97,000 acres. The company's claim to more was contested by settlers and ranchers in the disputed area, but the company, using its political influence, was able to get patents to 1,714,765 acres in 1879. Finally, in the 1890s the patents were recognized as valid by the U.S. Supreme Court.

FURTHER READING: Keleher, William A. *The Maxwell Land Grant–A New Mexico Item*. Santa Fe: Rydal Press, 1942; Montoya, María E. *Translating Property; The Maxwell Land Grant and the Conflict Over Land in the American West, 1840–1900*. Berkeley: University of California Press, 2002; Murphy, Lawrence R. "The Beaubien and Miranda Land Grant, 1841–1846." *New Mexico Historical Review* 42:1 (1967) 27–47; Pearson, Jim Berry. *The Maxwell Land Grant*. Norman: University of Oklahoma Press, 1961.

McCARRAN-WALTER IMMIGRATION AND NATIONALITY ACT, 1952. The McCarran-Walter Act kept, but somewhat liberalized the 1924 immigration quota system established by Congress. It enabled undocumented aliens living in the United States since 1924 to legalize their status without leaving the country. However, it also provided for the exclusion of aliens deemed politically threatening and the deportation of undesirable naturalized U.S. citizens. President Harry Truman vetoed the bill as a potential threat to civil liberties, but his veto was overturned by Congress, which responded to the red scare of the 1950s. The law was subsequently used to deport Mexican immigrants active in labor organizing.

FURTHER READING: Edwards, Jerome E. *Pat McCarran, Political Boss of Nevada*. Reno: University of Nevada Press, 1982; Schrecker, Ellen. "Immigration and Internal Security: Political Deportations during the McCarthy Era." *Science and Society* 60

(Winter 1996) 393–426; Shanks, Cheryl. *Immigration and the Politics of American Sovereignty, 1890–1990.* Ann Arbor: University of Michigan Press, 2001.

McWILLIAMS, CAREY, 1905–1980. As a young lawyer with a special interest in U.S. labor issues, Carey McWilliams became aware of the many problems of minority peoples in the United States. Because of his decade-long concerns about discrimination and racism, in 1943 he was asked by editor Louis Adamic to write a history of Mexicans in the United States for J. B. Lippincott Co. Over the next five years McWilliams researched and wrote *North from Mexico: The Spanish-Speaking People of the United States.* Published in 1949, the book was destined to become the primer of Mexican American history two decades later as a result of the Chicano Movement. McWilliams viewed the book as a part of his lifelong learning and his critical efforts to make democracy work better in America. In all he wrote fourteen books, most dealing with California.

McWilliams was not merely a chronicler of the Mexicano experience; he was also an active participant in that history. During World War II his vigorous leadership in the **Sleepy Lagoon** Defense Committee helped secure the reversal of the conviction of seventeen Chicano youths in the sensational Los Angeles case. In the postwar McWilliams was hired by the progressive journal *The Nation* to work on a special issue dealing with civil liberties. After the issue he remained as a staff member and in 1955 was appointed editor, a position he held until he retired twenty years later. During his long and successful career as a journalist he was an indefatigable fighter for the rights of minorities, especially Mexican Americans.

FURTHER READING: California, Governor. *Citizens Committee Report on the Zoot Suit Riots.* Sacramento: Printing Office, 1943; Corman, Catherine A. "Teaching—and Learning From Carey McWilliams." *California History* 80:4 (Winter 2001) 205–243; McWilliams, Carey. *The Education of Carey McWilliams.* New York: Simon & Schuster, 1979; McWilliams, Carey. *North from Mexico: The Spanish-Speaking People of the United States.* New York: Praeger Publishers, 1990.

MEDINA, HAROLD R., 1888–1990. Jurist, teacher, author. Judge Harold Medina was the son of a Mexican father who had immigrated to the United States as a youth. He grew up in Brooklyn, where he attended Public School 44. He graduated from Columbia University law school in 1912 and three years later began a thirty-two-year career there as a teacher.

As the result of two trials early in the twentieth century, Medina became a nationally known figure in the United States. In the first trial he was the court-appointed defender of Anthony Cramer, charged with treason during World War I. Medina ultimately won acquittal for his client on appeal to the U.S. Supreme Court. In the second he was the federal judge, appointed in 1947 by President Harry Truman, in the nine-month, highly emotional 1949 Smith Act trial of eleven U.S. Communist party leaders for conspiracy. His control of the court and dignified conduct during the long trial, despite abuse and great provocation from defense attorneys, exemplified the finest spirit of American jurisprudence.

Into his early nineties Medina remained active as a teacher, author, lecturer, and champion of the First Amendment. At age ninety-two he retired as a senior judge of the U.S. Court of Appeals. His deep concern for issues of free speech and freedom of the press led him to write seven books on the First Amendment and other legal matters. He was the recipient of numerous awards and honors, and became a role model for many young Chicano lawyers during the movimiento years. After an extremely long and productive life, he left behind a proud legacy as one of the outstanding American jurists of the twentieth century.

FURTHER READING: "Harold Medina, U.S. Judge, Dies at 102." *New York Times* (16 March 1990) B7; Hawthorne, Daniel. *Judge Medina: A Biography.* New York: W. Funk, 1952; Moore, Leonard P. "Dedication to Judge Harold R. Medina on the Occasion of His Ninetieth Birthday." *Brooklyn Law Review* 44:4 (1978) xiii–xiv; Okun, Stacey. "Judge Medina's 100th Birthday: Time for Tributes." *New York Times* (16 February 1988) B3; *Who's Who in American Law,* 2nd ed. Chicago: Marquis Who's Who, 1979.

MEDRANO ET AL. v. ALLEE ET AL., 1972. Following the 1966–1967 farm workers' strike in Texas's Lower Rio Grande Valley, Francisco Medrano and other workers filed a class action suit against the **Texas Rangers** and ranger captain A. Y. Allee for use of excessive force and interfering with their efforts to organize. The suit charged that the rangers had deprived them of rights guaranteed under the First and Fourteenth Amendments. In 1972 the federal district court ruled in favor of the strikers and enjoined the rangers from intimidating strikers and from interfering with peaceful union activities. On appeal, the U.S. Supreme Court in 1974 upheld the lower court's decision.

FURTHER READING: Samora, Julian, Joe Bernal, and Albert Peña. *Gunpowder Justice: A Reassessment of the Texas Rangers.* Notre Dame: University of Notre Dame Press, 1979.

MÉNDEZ, CONSUELO HERRERA, 1904–1985. Activist, teacher. Consuelo Méndez was an Austin school teacher and an early Tejana political activist. From the 1940s to the 1960s she was a leader in the Texas Ladies **League of United Latin American Citizens**, particularly in the Austin chapter. She was also deeply involved in local politics and worked persistently to persuade Mexican Americans to participate in elections. She even ran for the Austin city council. For her political activism and a lifetime of work in education she was awarded various honors and had a school named after her.

FURTHER READING: Tyler, Ron, ed. *The New Handbook of Texas,* vol. 4. Austin: Texas State Historical Association. 1996.

MÉNDEZ ET AL. v. WESTMINSTER SCHOOL DISTRICT ET AL., 1946, 1947. In 1945 Mexican American parents in Orange County, California filed suit against Westminster and three other elementary school districts. They asserted that the districts had placed their children in separate classes solely on the basis of their ethnicity. The **League of United Latin American Citizens** attorneys, who argued the case, pointed out that this segregation violated constitutional guarantees embodied in the Fifth and Fourteenth Amendments to the Constitution.

In February 1946 federal judge Paul McCormick ruled that such segregation ignored both the U.S. Constitution and California statute law. He ruled that separate schools, even though they might have equal facilities, did not provide "equal protection of the laws" and ordered the school districts to end the separation. He added that segregation was also unhealthy for society because it fostered antagonisms and denied students the benefits of interaction with other cultures.

The school districts appealed McCormick's decision, arguing that the facilities were completely equal and that the federal court lacked jurisdiction. In 1947 the Ninth Circuit Court in San Francisco, California, upheld Judge McCormick's ruling that the school districts were in violation of California statute law and the Fourteenth Amendment. Although the decision in the Méndez case did not end *de facto* segregation, it set a precedent for the more important 1954 *Brown v. Board of Education* victory, in which the court held that separate facilities were inherently unequal.

FURTHER READING: *A Family Changes History: "Méndez vs. Westminster, Fiftieth Anniversary, 1947–1997."* Irvine: University of California, Division of Student Services, 1998; Arriola, Christopher. "Knocking on the Schoolhouse Door: *Méndez v. Westminster,* Equal Protection, Public Education, and Mexican Americans in the 1940s." *La Raza Law Journal* 8:2 (Fall 1995) 166–207; Sánchez, George I. *Concerning Segregation of Spanish-Speaking Children in the Public Schools.* Austin: University of Texas, 1951; Wollenberg, Charles. "*Méndez vs. Westminster:* Race, Nationality and Segregation in California Schools." *California Historical Quarterly* 53:4 (Winter 1974) 317–332.

MENDOZA, LYDIA, 1916– . Singer, musician, songwriter. Lydia Mendoza, the Lark of the Border, was born in Houston, Texas, of parents who had fled the turmoil of Mexico's 1910 revolution. After two moves back and forth across the border, Lydia's mother made a firm family decision to remain in the United States. Although both parents had some education, Lydia did not attend school because her father saw no reason to educate girls. However, she did receive a basic education from her mother, who also exposed her to the joys of music.

Before she reached her teen years, Lydia played the guitar and the mandolin and was learning to play the violin. When her father lost his railroad job, the Mendoza family began playing and singing on street corners and in restaurants and *cantinas,* surviving on tips. Her father, who had worked for Cuauhtémoc Brewery, named them the Cuarteto Carta Blanca after the

Mexican beer. In the late 1920s the Mendozas signed up to work in the midwestern sugar beet fields, but soon were back to playing music and singing in Pontiac, Michigan, and later Detroit.

In 1930, when the Great Depression settled on the United States, the Mendoza family returned to Texas, locating in San Antonio where they earned a precarious living by again playing and singing for tips. At the Plaza de Zacate, where musicians-for-hire gathered, Lydia's singing came to the attention of a local radio announcer. She quickly became a regular on radio and was soon known throughout the Southwest, which she regularly toured with the family musical group. Between 1934 and 1939 she cut about 100 platters for Blue Bird Record Company, but then World War II erupted, gasoline shortage ended the tours, and Lydia faded from the musical scene.

In 1947 the Mendoza band resumed touring the Southwest and Mexico, until Lydia's mother's death in 1952, after which Lydia performed solo. During the 1950s and 1960s she recorded extensively for a dozen or more record companies, playing the guitar and singing corridos, rancheras, boleros, tangos, polkas, and waltzes. She has recorded more than twelve hundred songs.

By the beginning of the 1970s Lydia Mendoza's extensive repertoire of Mexicano folk music began to be more widely appreciated, and she began a third musical career. She was invited to perform in the Smithsonian Festival of American Folklife in 1971, and five years later she was featured in *Chulas Fronteras*, an outstanding border music film. Early in 1977 she was a leading artist recording ethnic folk music for the Library of Congress at the American Folk Life Center. During the 1980s she was featured at numerous folk music festivals and made several tours of Latin America.

Awarded one of the first National Heritage fellowships in 1982, Lydia Mendoza was inducted into the Tejano Music Hall of Fame two years later and in 1985 she entered the Texas Women's Hall of Fame. Six years later she was installed in the Conjunto Hall of Fame. Especially famous for her rendition of "Mal Hombre," which she recorded at eighteen, she is known everywhere in Spanish-speaking America as a singer and instrumentalist. She is a musical institution.

FURTHER READING: Broyles-González, Yolanda. *Lydia Mendoza's Life in Music: Norteñ-Tejano Legacies.* New York: Oxford University Press, 2001; Gil, Carlos B. "Lydia Mendoza: Houstonian and First Lady of Mexican American Song." *Houston Review* 3:2 (Summer 1981) 250–260; Miller, Dale. "Lydia Mendoza: The Lark of the Border." *Guitar Player* 22:8 (August 1988) 38–41; Strachwitz, Chris, and James Nicolopulos. *Lydia Mendoza: A Family Autobiography.* Houston: Arte Público Press, 1993.

MESTER, JORGE, 1935– . Musician, conductor. Jorge Mester was born in Mexico City of Hungarian immigrant parents and received his very early musical education there. When he was eleven, his parents sent him to California to further his violin studies. As the result of an introduction to Leonard Bernstein he began studying conducting at the Juilliard School of Music and at age twenty-one became its youngest professor of conducting in 1956. After teaching there for a dozen years he accepted appointment as conductor of the Louisville (Kentucky) Orchestra, which he molded into one of America's leading city orchestras. While at Louisville he also served as guest conductor of various orchestras and festivals in the United States, South America, Europe, Australia, and the Far East. After twelve years in Kentucky he returned to teaching at Juilliard. In 1988 he became the artistic director of the National Orchestra Association's New Music Orchestral Project. He has continued to accept invitations to be guest conductor of outstanding orchestras all over the world.

FURTHER READING: Orozco, Mario. "Jorge Mester: Conductor." *Caminos* 4:11 (December 1984) 27–28; Oestereich, James R. "A Resurrected Ensemble Helps Nurture New Music." *New York Times* (2 March 1990) C25; Saavedra-Vela, Pilar. "The Musical World of Jorge Mester." *Agenda* 8:5 (September/October 1978) 28–31.

MESTIZAJE, MESTIZO. *Mestizaje* is a mixture, a blending of two or more racial and cultural types, for example, Indian and European, producing the mestizo. A majority of Mexican Americans exemplify the concept, giving evidence of varying combinations of European (mostly Spanish) and indigenous cultural and racial roots.

FURTHER READING: Lewis, Stephen E. "Mestizaje." In *Encyclopedia of Mexico: History, Society & Culture*, vol. 2. Edited by Michael A. Werner. Chicago: Fitzroy Dearborn, 1997.

METZGER, SIDNEY M., 1902–1986. Cleric, educator. Born in Fredricksburg, Texas, Sidney Metzger was educated there, in San Antonio, and in Rome, where he was ordained a priest in 1926. He then returned to Texas, where he taught at Saint John's Seminary and St. Mary's University Law School in San Antonio. In 1940 he was appointed auxiliary bishop of Santa Fe, New Mexico, and became coadjutor bishop of El Paso two years later. Over the years he strongly supported Mexican American efforts to form unions, and made friends of some El Paso labor leaders. Personally involved in numerous labor disputes in the El Paso area from 1944 onward, he actively supported the **Farah** workers in their 1972–1974 strike. His involvement with labor antagonized some Catholics, particularly Anglos, a few of whom became quite bitter. When he retired in 1978, he had been the recipient of numerous honors and awards for his educational leadership and his support for labor.

FURTHER READING: Carrillo, Emilia F. *Bishop Has Kept His Word*. New York: Carlton Press, 1966; *Who Was Who In America*, vol. 9. Chicago: Marquis, 1989.

MEXICAN AMERICAN. By a strict definition, Mexican Americans are persons of Mexican heritage who are citizens of the United States. Largely urban-dwellers, over three-fourths of them have been born in the United States. Some Mexicans who have lived in the U.S. for years without going through the official process of becoming citizens think of themselves and may be viewed as Mexican Americans.

MEXICAN AMERICAN CULTURAL CENTER. The Mexican American Cultural Center was established in San Antonio in 1972 by Reverend **Virgilio Elizondo.** Designed to sensitize and train laypersons and religious for social activism in the Chicano community, it continues to pursue that goal and to be concerned with developing Mexican American leaders. It also provides a community-centered agency for education and research. In the 1970s it made available a master's degree in education through Juárez-Lincoln University. The Center was directed by Elizondo until he stepped down in 1983. It has continued to be an important center for developing social activists.

FURTHER READING: Sandoval, Moisés, ed. *The Mexican American Experience in the Church: Reflections on Identity and Mission: Mexican American Cultural Center Tenth Anniversary Forum.* New York: Sadlier, 1983; Tyler, Ron, ed. *The New Handbook of Texas,* vol. 4. Austin: Texas State Historical Association, 1996; Zapa, Patricia. "His Roots Are in San Antonio, but His World Is the Globe." *Migration World Magazine* 24:5 (1996) 43–44.

MEXICAN AMERICAN DEMOCRATS. MAD was founded in 1975 as a Texas state organization by **Joe Bernal** and others in a move away from the third-party stance of **La Raza Unida**. It aimed at obtaining full Chicano representation at all levels of government through activity within the Democratic Party. With Matt García of San Antonio as its first permanent chairman, it peaked at the end of the 1970s with 6,000 members in forty-seven chapters. By 1991 it had declined to thirty-three chapters and 3,226 members, many of them Chicanas. MAD endorses candidates at local, county, and state levels and seeks to place qualified Mexican Americans in decision-making federal positions. It works with other organizations in voter registration and support of legislation.

FURTHER READING: Tyler, Ron, ed. *The New Handbook of Texas,* vol. 4. Austin: Texas State Historical Association, 1996.

MEXICAN AMERICAN JOINT COUNCIL. The Mexican American Joint Council was founded in 1967 in Austin, Texas, by representatives of various Chicano organizations under the leadership of **George I. Sánchez.** The council proposed to research the situation of Mexican Americans in education and employment and to work to improve their social and economic position. With Sánchez as chairman, it supported voter registration, get-out-the-vote drives, and efforts to form unions. One of its first motions was a resolution for disbanding the **Texas Rangers**. Sánchez also protested the segregation of Mexican American children in Texas schools and urged the inclusion of the Spanish language and Hispanic culture in the public school curriculum. After 1970 the council languished.

FURTHER READING: Tyler, Ron, ed. *The New Handbook of Texas*, vol. 4. Austin: Texas State Historical Association, 1996.

MEXICAN AMERICAN LEGAL DEFENSE AND EDUCATIONAL FUND.

Incorporated in Texas in 1967, MALDEF is dedicated to using the legal system to protect and advance the civil rights of American citizens of Mexican descent. **Vilma Martínez** of the NAACP Legal Defense Fund (LDF) helped prepare the MALDEF grant application, which succeeded in obtaining a $2.2 million five-year grant from the Ford Foundation. She then continued to act as liaison between MALDEF and the LDF.

MALDEF's initial goal was to bring about social and economic change by attacking racism and segregation in the courts. Its early activities were largely reactive in nature, focused on individual cases of civil rights denial. Later it sought constitutionally significant issues to take to the U.S. Supreme Court. Since its inception, it has filed suits in issues ranging from educational practices to police harassment and citizen rights under welfare legislation. It has won some important court cases in the area of equality of educational opportunity and has been successful in attacking barriers to Mexican American participation in politics and government.

MALDEF's first executive director, **Pete Tijerina,** established its headquarters in San Antonio, with a second office in Los Angeles because of that city's large Mexicano population. Partly because the Ford Foundation wanted a more national image for MALDEF, its headquarters were moved out of Texas in 1970 and Tijerina stepped down as director.

MALDEF's new headquarters were established in San Francisco, California, and former LULAC leader **Mario Obledo** took over the directorship. Under Obledo MALDEF widened its geographical scope by adding offices in Albuquerque, Denver, and Washington, D.C. Obledo's most important contribution to MALDEF, perhaps, was his decision to take more cases to the U.S. Supreme Court on constitutional issues. After one term he retired from office at the end of 1973 after MALDEF's first successful litigation before the U.S. Supreme Court in the case of *White v. Regester.* Vilma Martínez became the new director.

Under Vilma Martínez MALDEF made a number of changes, strengthened its staff by recruiting young Mexican American attorneys with civil rights experience, instituted an internship program to train young Chicano litigators, and initiated a new fund-raising plan. In 1974 a Chicana Civil Rights Project and other specialized projects were established. Most important, by carefully choosing its court cases MALDEF built up legal precedents in areas such as politics and education. In *Plyler v. Doe* (1982) the court accepted MALDEF's argument that Texas could not exclude the children of

undocumented aliens from its public schools. MALDEF also participated in political campaigns, having an important role in the election of **Gloria Molina** to the Los Angeles Board of Supervisors in the early 1990s. Under **Antonia Hernández,** who replaced Martínez as president in 1985, it has continued stressing civil and political rights, female equality, and concerns for equality of opportunity.

FURTHER READING: Johnson, Dean. "Chair of the Board." *Nuestro* (September 1985) 34–36; O'Connor, Karen, and Lee Epstein. "A Legal Voice for the Chicano Community: The Activities of the Mexican American Legal Defense and Educational Fund." In *The Mexican American Experience,* edited by Rodolfo O. de la Garza, et al. Austin: University of Texas Press, 1985; Oliveira, Annette. *MALDEF: Diez Años.* San Francisco: MALDEF, 1979; Ortega, Joe. "The Privately Funded Legal Aid Office: The MALDEF Experience." *Chicano Law Review* 1 (1972) 80–84; Salas, Abel. "In the Trenches with MALDEF." *Hispanic* (October 1997) 32; Vigil, Maurilio. "The Ethnic Organization as an Instrument of Political and Social Change: MALDEF, a Case Study." *Journal of Ethnic Studies* 18:1 (1990) 15–31. www.maldef.org

MEXICAN AMERICAN MOVEMENT. MAM grew out of the annual Older Boys Conference initiated by the YMCA for Los Angeles Chicano youths in 1934. It was established four years later with the object of promoting civic and social consciousness in the Mexican American community through education. It also provided a platform from which to voice unhappiness with the accessibility and quality of public higher education for Mexican Americans in California. MAM continued to be active into the early 1950s, but no longer remained strictly a Chicano youth organization.

FURTHER READING: García, Mario T. *Memories of Chicano History: The Life and Narrative of Bert Corona.* Berkeley: University of California Press, 1994; Gómez-Quiñones, Juan. *Roots of Chicano Politics, 1600–1940.* Albuquerque: University of New Mexico Press, 1994; Muñoz, Carlos Jr. *Youth, Identity, Power: The Chicano Movement.* New York: Verso, 1989.

MEXICAN AMERICAN POLITICAL ASSOCIATION. MAPA was founded in 1959 by a group of California political activists, including **Bert Corona**, **Herman Gallegos**, and **Eduardo Quevedo**, who met in Fresno to discuss ways to increase and make use of potential Chicano political power. It was one of the first Mexican American groups to formally declare its primary interest in politics. In the political arena it centered its goals on supporting Chicano issues and candidates. In addition to its purely political goals MAPA has involved itself in a wide variety of civil rights issues, from police brutality to discrimination in public places and segregation in schools. It was particularly important to rural Mexican Americans by providing outside support for efforts to defend their civil rights.

With broad community support from its beginning, MAPA helped secure the appointment of several Mexican American judges to California courts and was instrumental in the election of **Edward Roybal** to the U.S. Congress in 1962. Although officially nonpartisan, it has usually supported Democratic Party candidates. Its early success led to wide interest in the organization as a model for Chicanos elsewhere in the Southwest. In spite of efforts, especially in the late 1970s, to go national, MAPA has remained largely a California organization. At the beginning of the 1980s MAPA claimed a membership of about five thousand in sixty semiautonomous California chapters.

FURTHER READING: Benavides, Ben. "Toward 'the Decade of the Chicano-Mexicano.'" *Crossroads* 10 (May 1991) 14–16; Mario T. García. *Memories of Chicano History: The Life and Narrative of Bert Corona.* Berkeley: University of California Press, 1994; Navarro, Armando. "The Cucamonga Experiment: A Struggle for Community Control and Self-Determination." *Perspectives in Mexican American Studies* 7 (2000) 47–68; Santillán, Richard A. "Third Party Politics: Old Story, New Faces." *The Black Politician* 3:2 (October 1971) 10–18; "What is MAPA?" In *Minority Group Politics: A Reader,* compiled by Stephen J. Herzog. New York: Holt, Rinehart and Winston, 1971.

MEXICAN AMERICAN STUDENT ASSOCIATION. MASA was founded in 1967 by students at East Los Angeles College to improve the opportunities in higher education for Chicano youths. Initially its goal was largely limited to providing tutoring and scholarships. Its example was quickly followed by students at other Los Angeles institutions, and by the end of the year the Chicano student movement had spread throughout California. In mid-May, 1967 MASA participated in the establishment of the broadly based **United Mexican American Students**, of which it then became a part. In 1969 it became absorbed into the **Movimiento Estudiantil Chicano de Aztlán**.

FURTHER READING: Gómez-Quiñones, Juan. *Mexican Students por La Raza: The Chicano Student Movement in Southern California 1967–1977.* Santa Barbara, Calif.: Editorial La Causa, 1978.

MEXICAN AMERICAN STUDENT CONFEDERATION. The MASC was one of the early Chicano student organizations, founded in the northern California Bay Area in the late 1960s. It was more politically oriented than similar southern California youth groups and also tended to be more confrontational. In 1969 it was incorporated into the **Movimiento Estudiantil Chicano de Aztlán**.

FURTHER READING: Sanchez, Alfredo. "Chicano Student Movement at San Jose State." In *Parameters of Institutional Change: Chicano Experiences in Education.* Hayward, Calif.: Southwest Network, 1974.

MEXICAN AMERICAN UNITY COUNCIL. The MAUC was a Texas development corporation, established in 1968 as a resource for the **Mexican American Youth Organization** (MAYO). It was the brainchild chiefly of **José Angel Gutiérrez, Juan Patlán,** and **Willie Velásquez,** who had founded MAYO. Velásquez, who became its first president, established its basic goal of helping the Mexican American community of San Antonio tackle its economic problems.

Following Velásquez as president, Juan Patlán successfully pursued funding to finance a variety of social service and economic development projects in San Antonio. With the help of Ford Foundation money, the agency, in conjunction with other Chicano organizations, set up community programs in low-cost housing, job training, and health care. Despite strong criticism and opposition from U.S. Representative Henry B. González of Texas, MAUC was able to achieve a considerable degree of success, especially in providing community services and fostering local business development.

FURTHER READING: García, Ignacio M. *United We Win: The Rise and Fall of La Raza Unida Party.* Tucson: University of Arizona, Mexican American Studies and Research Center, 1989; Navarro, Armando. *Mexican American Youth Organization: Avant Garde of the Chicano Movement in Texas.* Austin: University of Texas Press, 1995.

MEXICAN AMERICAN YOUTH ORGANIZATION. One of the most important Chicano student groups of the 1960s, MAYO was founded at St. Mary's College in San Antonio in 1967 by Los Cinco: **José Angel Gutiérrez, Mario Compeán, Willie Velásquez,** and two other students. Originally it was financed by the Southwest Council of La Raza with Ford Foundation funds. It had strong grassroot ties and was loosely structured to give its local chapters latitude to experiment and improvise in attacking community problems. From the beginning it had a special concern for education and sought to force Texas schools to adapt their curricula to the particular needs of Chicano students. It also sought to create a greater awareness among Chicanos of their civil rights and to encourage them to participate actively in politics. MAYO provided education and training in political participation to a generation of Tejanos.

Stressing oppression and exploitation of Chicanos, MAYO leaders rejected existing middle-class Mexican American organizations as ineffectual. As its first president, Gutiérrez took an aggressive stance that included provocative rhetoric and frequent confrontation. MAYO's combination of an Alinskyite approach with a strong cultural nationalism had special attraction for high school and college students. During the late 1960s it played a leading role in various school walkouts in Texas and in the elections at Crystal City. MAYO angered and frightened Anglos and stirred some conservative Mexican Americans, like U.S. Congressman **Henry B. González,** into vocal opposition.

At the beginning of the 1970s MAYO was absorbed into **La Raza Unida Party,** which it had generated, and by 1972 only a handful of chapters continued to function. By the end of the 1970s even they had disappeared, and many MAYO leaders had achieved positions of some influence in Democratic politics, particularly through a new Tejano pressure group, **Mexican American Democrats**.

FURTHER READING: García, Ignacio M. *United We Win: The Rise and Fall of La Raza Unida Party.* Tucson: University of Arizona, Mexican American Studies and Research Center, 1989; Gutiérrez, José Angel. *The Making of a Chicano Militant: Lessons from Cristal.* Madison: University of Wisconsin Press, 1998; Muñoz, Carlos Jr. *Youth, Identity, Power: The Chicano Movement.* New York: Verso, 1989; Navarro, Armando. *The Mexican American Youth Organization: Avant-Garde of the Chicano Movement in Texas.* Austin: University of Texas Press, 1995.

MEXICAN CIVIC COMMITTEE. The committee was established in **Chicago** during the 1940s by Frank M. Paz. A community-based organization, its chief concern was the socioeconomic status of Mexican Americans in the Midwest.

FURTHER READING: Kerr, Louise Año Nuevo. "The Chicano Experience in Chicago, 1920–1970." Ph.D. diss. University of Illinois at Chicago Circle, 1976.

MEXICAN REVOLUTION, 1910. The 1910 Mexican revolution grew out of efforts to overthrow the long dictatorship of Mexican president Porfirio Díaz. It quickly turned into a staunchly nationalistic socioeconomic upheaval with a goal of agrarian as well as political reform. It lasted at least ten years, but some of its manifestations continued on into the 1920s. The chaotic conditions engendered in Mexico by the revolution had considerable impact on the Southwest. The border region became an area of asylum for Mexican political dissidents and those simply fleeing the violence and destruction of the conflagration. It also provided a base as well as a vital stockpile of arms and other supplies for contending revolutionary forces.

Mexicanos in the border area were strongly affected by the cataclysm. To an area that was still largely frontier, it brought even more turbulent conditions. Long-held racist feelings among Anglos and resentment at discrimination among Mexicanos were exacerbated by the quixotic **Plan de San Diego** in 1915. The plan generated rumors and fears that antagonized Anglos, deepened their prejudices, and increased their ill-treatment of Mexicanos. Support for Francisco Villa among Mexicanos and his raid on Columbus, New Mexico, likewise resulted in retaliatory actions.

In the long run the large-scale Mexican emigration to the United States, unleashed by the revolution and continuing into the 1920s, was to have an important and permanent impact on the Mexican American community. These border-crossers, many of whom evolved from sojourners to permanent immigrants, and their children have formed the heart of contemporary Mexican American culture and community.

FURTHER READING: Cumberland, Charles. "Border Raids in the Lower Rio Grande Valley—1915." *Southwestern Historical Quarterly* 57 (January 1954) 285–311; Hall, Linda B., and Don M. Coerver. *Revolution on the Border: The United States and Mexico, 1910–1920.* Albuquerque: University of New Mexico Press, 1988; Knight, Alan. *The Mexican Revolution.* 2 vol. New York: Cambridge University Press, 1986; Martínez, Oscar J., ed. *Fragments of the Mexican Revolution: Accounts from the Border.*

Albuquerque: University of New Mexico Press, 1983; Sandos, James A. *Rebellion in the Borderlands: Anarchism and the Plan of San Diego, 1904–1923*. Norman: University of Oklahoma Press, 1992.

MIDWEST CHICANOS. Mexicano migration to the Midwest was, and still is, predominantly a labor migration. Early in the 1900s Mexicano agricultural workers began to develop annual migratory patterns from Texas border areas to the midwestern United States. By the time of World War I they had begun to replace European immigrants in the expanded beet fields, and small groups had begun to overwinter in cities like Chicago, Detroit, Gary, Toledo, and St. Paul. As they settled in these urban centers, some remained in agriculturally related work while others found better-paying and more stable jobs on the railroads, and in the stockyards, meatpacking plants, steel mills, and auto assembly factories. Seeking cheap labor, employers began to actively recruit Mexicanos in Texas by the 1920s for work in the Midwest's expanding industrial economy, sometimes as unwitting strikebreakers. At the end of the decade Inland Steel had become the largest employer of Mexicanos in the country.

Like their cohorts in the Southwest, midwestern Mexicanos tended to cluster in barrios where **housing** was often deplorable. However, as merely one of many ethnic groups recently arrived in U.S. industrial centers, they found qualified acceptance; earlier patterns of ethnic isolation and cohesion began to weaken as they worked, associated, and lived with immigrants from various European countries. When the big depression began at the end of the 1920s, midwestern Mexicanos, having been "last hired," usually were "first fired." More or less voluntary early **repatriation** was followed by coerced expulsion in the 1930s, and most barrios were heavily depopulated. A decade later, because of labor demands during World War II and in the postwar era, greatly expanded numbers of Mexicanos from the southwestern border region were again able to obtain jobs in midwestern industry. From 1942 to 1964 **bracero** programs brought additional Mexican workers to the Midwest. In the Midwest Mexicanos were somewhat less singled out by discriminatory attitudes than they often were in the Southwest.

In the post–World War II years, urbanized midwestern Mexican American settlers, like those in the Southwest, began to develop **organizations** to assert and protect their rights. They lagged Chicanos in the Southwest, possibly because of smaller numbers, greater dispersal, and less intense discrimination. Generally they remained heavily dependent on the Southwest for organizational models, and adopted or adapted ideas and organizations developed there. During the early 1960s the **Viva Kennedy** movement and later the Delano grape strike strengthened their already aroused interest in serious political and economic involvement. In the late 1960s they established the **Farm Labor Organizing Committee** to protect the rights of agricultural workers.

Although earlier organizational efforts had some limited success, the establishment of the Midwest Council of La Raza in 1970 at Notre Dame University was a benchmark in midwestern regional self-identification and separateness. Midwestern leaders began to develop a distinct course, differing somewhat from southwestern trends. As further migratory waves from the Southwest continued during the 1970s, Chicanos in the Midwest initiated aggressive voter registration drives in their enlarged communities. The political clout of these new voters enabled them to convince some state legislatures to create agencies to deal with Mexican American concerns. In the 1990s the Iowa-Nebraska Immigrants' Rights Network was established with Ford Foundation support. At the same time Chicanos, moving up the hierarchical ladders within labor unions, were able to develop **leadership** skills and to further their political influence.

In recent years seasonal and temporary migration from the Texas border region continues to add to the Midwest's Mexican American population. Much of this migration is internal rather than international; however, the number of undocumented workers coming to the region directly from Mexico has increased and is sizable. In 1998 the Immigration and Naturalization Service instituted Operation Vanguard, a sweep designed to catch undocumented workers at the job.

Today **Chicago,** the traditional immigrant destination in the Midwest, has the largest Chicano population outside the Southwest. Most midwestern Mexicanos continue to be employed in service, industrial, artisan, clerical, and sales work; only about 15 percent are employed in managerial, professional, and administrative positions. In the past two decades they have spread out to smaller cities and towns in nearby Iowa and Nebraska where low-paying jobs in meatpacking are available. In some of these towns they make up nearly half of the population and cause predictable strains in education, housing, and health services. These changes have brought tensions and, in turn, have led to a number of organizations that concern themselves with immigrant rights, particularly in the workplace.

FURTHER READING: Barger, W. K., and Ernesto M. Reza. *The Farm Labor Movement in the Midwest.* Austin: University of Texas Press, 1994; Cárdenas, Gilbert. "Los Desarraigados: Chicanos in the Midwestern Region of the United States." *Aztlán* 7:2 (Summer 1976) 153–201; García, Juan R. *Mexicans in the Midwest, 1900–1932.* Tucson: University of Arizona Press, 1996; López, D. A. *The Latino Experience in Omaha: A Visual Essay.* Lewiston, N.Y.: E. Mellon Press, 2001; Santillán, Richard A. "Latino Political Development in the Southwest and the Midwest Regions: A Comparative Overview, 1915–1989." In *Latinos and Political Coalitions: Political Empowerment for the 1990s,* edited by Roberto E. Villarreal and Norma G. Hernández. Westport, Conn.: Greenwood Press, 1991; Valdés, Dennis N. *Al norte: Agricultural Workers in the Great Lakes Region, 1917–1970.* Austin: University of Texas Press, 1991; Valdés, Dionicio Nodín. *Barrios Norteños: St. Paul and Midwestern Communities in the Twentieth Century.* Austin: University of Texas Press, 2000; Vargas, Zaragoza. *Proletarians of the North: A*

History of Mexican Industrial Workers in Detroit and the Midwest, 1917–1933. Berkeley: University of California Press, 1993.

MIGRANT HEALTH ACT, 1962. The Migrant Health Act, Public Law 87-692, was passed by Congress during President John F. Kennedy's administration. It authorized the appropriation of federal funds for grants to support agencies providing health services to migratory workers. Behind the act was a congressional assumption that since many migratory workers travel interstate, their health problems could affect the national health and were therefore a federal concern.

FURTHER READING: Shenkin, Bud. *Health Care for Migrant Workers: Policies and Politics.* Cambridge, Mass.: Ballinger, 1974; U.S. Department of Health, Education, and Welfare. Public Health Service. *Interim Report on the Status of Program Activities under the Migrant Health Act (Public Law 87-692).* A Report to the Subcommittee on Migratory Labor of the Committee on Labor and Public Welfare, United States Senate. Washington, D.C.: GPO, 1964.

MIGRANT MINISTRY. The Migrant Ministry, an interdenominational Protestant group, was founded in 1920 through the National Council of Churches. Its main purpose was to promote social Christianity, particularly in the areas of housing, employment, and education. In spite of some opposition from more conservative Protestant sects and their clergy, in the 1960s the Migrant Ministry became directly involved in labor concerns, especially the right of workers to organize. It strongly supported **César Chávez** in the long Delano grape strike, and later also became involved in labor organizing in Texas.

FURTHER READING: Day, Mark. *Forty Acres: César Chávez and the Farm Workers.* New York: Praeger, 1971; Hoffman, Patricia L. *Ministry of the Dispossessed: Learning from the Farm Worker Movement.* Los Angeles: Wallace Press, 1987.

MIGRATORY LABOR. The migration of agricultural workers in the United States dates from the end of the nineteenth century. The development in the West of large-scale agriculture based on seasonal crops created a cyclical demand for large numbers of workers for limited time periods such as harvest. This demand was met in part by a rapidly growing influx of **undocumented** Mexican workers willing to work for substandard wages. They, in turn, forced many southwestern Mexican Americans into the migrant stream. The greater availability to workers of relatively cheap automobiles and trucks expanded the worker pool and made feasible the replacing of sharecroppers and tenant farmers with migrant workers.

Already in the 1880s Mexicans were crossing into Texas to work in the cotton fields, often displacing African Americans. By the end of World War I Tejanos were becoming increasingly aware of better pay and working conditions outside the state. Then the Depression of the 1930s forced many Mexicano families into the migrant stream. From wintering bases in Texas and southern California they trekked northward, picking strawberries in California, following fruit and nut harvests north into Oregon and Washington, topping sugar beets in Colorado and Idaho, and picking cotton in Arizona. Over the years many developed regular migratory patterns, working for the same farms year after year and returning to their winter quarters early in winter. This pattern of migration prevented most from developing strong community roots, from participating in the political arena, and from obtaining an adequate education for their children. They were thus condemned to a cycle of poverty from which escape was virtually impossible.

Carrot pullers working in the fields, Coachella Valley, California. Photograph by Dorothea Lange, 1937. © Library of Congress.

The various **bracero** arrangements with Mexico from World War II until 1964 meant fewer jobs in migratory agriculture available to Mexican Americans. Large-scale farming, "factories in the fields," and the subsequent unionization movement led to increased mechanization. Higher wages further reduced the use of migratory labor, and increasingly families tended to drop out of the migrant stream and remain in one place. By the end of the century, migratory farm work employed only a small minority of Mexican Americans, who had become overwhelmingly an urban people. Those who remained in migrant agricultural work continued to play an important role in producing the food we eat.

FURTHER READING: Dunbar, Anthony, and Linda Kravitz. *Hard Traveling: Migrant Farm Workers in America.* Cambridge, Mass.: Ballinger Publishing Co., 1976; Griffith, David, and Ed Kissam. *Working Poor: Farm Workers in the United States.* Philadelphia: Temple University Press, 1995; McWilliams, Carey. *Ill Fares the Land: Migrants and Migratory Labor in the United States.* Boston: Little, Brown & Co, 1942; Martin, Philip L. *Harvest of Confusion: Migrant Workers in U.S. Agriculture.* Boulder: Westview Press, 1988; Martínez, Rubén. *Crossing Over: A Mexican*

Migrant workers cutting broccoli, 1938. Courtesy of the Benson Latin American Collection, University of Texas at Austin.

Family on the Migrant Trail. New York: Metropolitan Books, 2001; Rothenberg, Daniel. *With These Hands: The Hidden World of Migrant Farmworkers Today.* New York: Harcourt Brace, 1998; Valle, Isabel. *Fields of Toil: A Migrant Family's Journey.* Pullman: Washington State University Press, 1994.

MINING INDUSTRY. The mining industry of the Southwest owes much to Mexican Americans: labor, mining techniques, and legislation developed earlier in Spain and Mexico. These skills and regulations were adapted and used in silver and copper mining on Mexico's northern frontier beginning in the 1600s. Until modified in the late eighteenth century, Spanish legal codes dating from the sixteenth century governed mining in the Southwest.

From the 1500s onward, much of the Spanish activity in Mexico was devoted to the search for and extraction of precious metals. In 1540 Francisco Vásquez de Coronado, lured by reports of the Seven Cities of Gold (Cíbola), explored much of the Southwest, but failed to find precious metals. Nevertheless, the later colonization of Mexico's northern frontier continued to be pushed in part by the hope of finding mineral wealth. Silver was discovered at Arizonac in 1736 and brought about a rush that lasted about five years. Later in the same century the rich copper deposits at Santa Rita in Nuevo México employed hundreds of miners and supplied the mint in Mexico City. Gold was not found in any quantity on the northern frontier until after the Treaty of **Guadalupe Hidalgo**.

The discovery of gold at Sutter's mill in 1848 led to a rush that included not only Californios but also about eight thousand Sonorans, who introduced their mining techniques and some of Mexico's mining code as well as terms like placer and bonanza. While gold mining was always of great interest, ultimately copper, in southern Arizona and New Mexico, provided more employment and brought greater wealth. Mexicanos predominated in southwestern copper mining and led in organizing unions in their efforts to improve working conditions and end wage discrimination. In the two World Wars Mexicano copper miners helped provide the United States with an essential sinew of war.

FURTHER READING: Colquhoun, James. *The Early History of the Clifton-Morenci District.* London: W. Clowes & Sons, 1935; Jackson, Joseph H. *Anybody's Gold.* New York: Appleton Century, 1941; Johnson, Susan Lee. *Roaring Camp: The Social World of the California Gold Rush.* New York: W. W. Norton, 2000; Mellinger, Philip J. *Race and Labor in Western Copper: The Fight for Equality, 1896–1918.* Tucson: University of Arizona Press, 1995; Parrish, Michael E. *Mexican Workers, Progressives and Copper: The Failure of Industrial Democracy in Arizona during the Wilson Years.* La Jolla, Calif.: Chicano Research Publications, 1979; Paul, Rodman W. *The Mining Frontiers of the Far West, 1848–1880.* New York: Holt, Rinehart and Winston, 1963.

MOLINA, GLORIA, 1948– . Political activist. The eldest of ten children, Gloria Molina was born in Los Angeles and grew up in Pico Rivera in southern California. After graduating from high school she entered East Los

Angeles City College, where she first became politically active. She was a volunteer in Robert Kennedy's 1968 bid for the presidential nomination and took part in the National Chicano Moratorium march two years later. Upon graduation from California State University, Los Angeles, in 1970, she went to work as a job counselor for The East Los Angeles Community Union.

Strongly influenced by the Chicano Movement, Gloria continued her involvement in community affairs after graduation. She was an active member of the Latin American Law Enforcement Association and in 1973 became the founding president of the Comisión Femenil de Los Angeles. As national president from 1974 to 1976, she created several programs to arouse Mexican Americans to greater awareness of their economic and political exploitation. Her special concerns for the poor and children led her to become cofounder of the Centro de Niños in Los Angeles. She also helped organize a number of local political groups.

Molina's development into an influential political leader was based on her extensive community activities and networking over the years. From a position as administrative assistant to California Democrat Art Torres, she soon moved to regional director in the Department of Health, Education and Welfare. In 1980 she became chief deputy to Willie Brown, then the powerful speaker of the California Assembly. Two years later, when Torres was elected to the state Senate, Molina ran aggressively for his Assembly seat and won despite a lack of enthusiasm on the part of the male-dominated Latino political establishment. She was the first Chicana to be elected to the California legislature.

After four years in the Assembly, Molina was elected to the Los Angeles city council in 1987. As the first Chicana to serve on the council she continued her energetic representation of her constituents. Supported by the **Mexican American Legal Defense and Educational Fund** and Congressman Edward Roybal, in 1991 she was elected to the powerful Los Angeles County board of supervisors, the first woman and only Mexican American in the twentieth century. On the board she has been an issue-oriented representative with a serious regard for community problems and Chicano empowerment. Elected chair of the board in her third term, she pushed community concerns about issues like drugs, street gangs, and affordable housing. Always independent, candid, and direct, she energetically pursues a variety of liberal causes regardless of the opposition that her outspokenness at times engenders.

Molina has been the recipient of various awards for her extensive community service.

FURTHER READING: Bonilla-Santiago, Gloria. *Breaking Ground and Barriers: Hispanic Women Developing Effective Leadership.* San Diego, Calif.: Marin Publications, 1992; Díaz, Katherine. "Hispanic of the Year: Gloria Molina." *Caminos* 4: 1–2 (January–February 1983) 39–54, 74; "Galaxy of Rising Stars." *Time* 138:20 (18 November 1991) 73; Laezman, Rick. "Gloria Molina." *Latino Leaders* (June–July 2001) 38–46;

Mills, Kay. "Gloria Molina." *Ms.* 13 (January 1985) 80–81, 114; *Notable Hispanic American Women.* Telgren, Diane and Jim Kamp, eds. Detroit: Gale Research,, 1993; Tobar, Héctor. "Gloria Molina and the Politics of Anger." *Los Angeles Times Magazine* (3 January 1993) 10–13, 32–34.

MONDRAGÓN, ROBERTO A., 1940– . Politician. Roberto Mondragón was born in La Loma, New Mexico, where he received his early education in a one-room school. He graduated from Albuquerque High School in 1958 as senior class president and then studied electronics. A technician job at station KABC led to his creating Albuquerque's first Spanish language radio talk show in the 1960s. Intensely active in local politics, in 1966 he won election to the legislature and was reelected two years later. In 1970 he became the youngest as well as the first full-time New Mexican lieutenant governor.

During the 1970s Mondragón was prominent in national Democratic politics. In 1980 he won a second term as lieutenant governor but two years later failed in his bid for the U.S. House of Representatives. Also an actor, he had a role in Robert Redford's 1988 film, *The Milagro Beanfield War.* As a political activist he has been especially concerned about education issues, civil rights, equality of opportunity, and election reforms. In 1994 he ran for governor of New Mexico on the Green Party ticket but lost; two years later his bid for the state Assembly was equally unsuccessful.

FURTHER READING: Brooke, James. "The 1998 Campaign: New Mexico." *New York Times* (31 October 1998) A11; Maldonado, Jim. "Lt. Governor of New Mexico." *La Luz* 1:8 (December 1972) 20; Martínez, Al. *Rising Voices: Profiles in Leadership.* Glendale, Calif.: Nestle USA, 1993.

MONTALBÁN, RICARDO, 1920– . Actor. Born in Mexico City of middle-class Spanish-immigrant parents, at age seventeen Ricardo Montalbán followed his older brother to Los Angeles, California, where he pursued an acting career. A small part in Tallulah Bankhead's Broadway play *Her Cardboard Lover* led to a film career in Mexico, and his success there brought him a long-term contract with Metro-Goldwyn-Mayer (MGM) after World War II. In 1953 he was dropped by MGM and his career slumped for the next decade.

Influenced by the atmosphere of the latter 1960s, Montalbán became increasingly concerned about the way Hollywood depicted *la raza* as well as its reluctance to hire Latino actors. Although not an activist, early in 1969 he, along with some other Latino actors and businessmen, founded Nosotros, an organization committed primarily to promoting job opportunities for Latinos in the film industry. He was elected Nosotros's first president. Nosotros later added the goal of improving civil rights for Latinos, and Montalbán made some commercials in Spanish for the **Southwest Voter Registration Education Project**, urging Latinos to take part in the political process by registering and voting.

Under Montalbán Nosotros achieved some minor improvements for Latinos, but he felt his leadership in the organization caused him to be the victim of a Hollywood backlash. His acting career languished. At the end of the 1970s television came to his rescue with long-term leads in "Fantasy Island" and "Dynasty," followed by substantial roles in other TV presentations during the 1980s and 1990s. He has had important roles in over eighty films. For his contributions to the economic improvement and social rights of Mexican Americans Ricardo Montalbán was given the Golden Aztec Award by the Mexican American Opportunity Foundation in 1988.

FURTHER READING: Duarte, Patricia. "Welcome to Ricardo's Reality." *Nosotros* 3:9 (October 1979) 25–26; Montalbán, Ricardo (with Bob Thomas). *Reflections: A Life in Two Worlds.* Garden City, N.Y.: Doubleday, 1980; "The Most Influential Latinos." *Hispanic* (Sept. 2000) 28; Reyes, Luis, and Peter Rubie. *Hispanics in Hollywood: A Celebration of 100 Years in Film and Television.* Hollywood: Lone Eagle, 2000; "Ricardo Montalbán." *La Luz* 1:9 (January 1973) 42–45.

MONTEMAYOR, ALICE DICKERSON, 1902–1989. Feminist, activist. Alicia Dickerson was born in Laredo, Texas, where she grew up in a bilingual home. After high school she attended Laredo Business College at night for a year, but gender and ethnic barriers hindered her getting a college education. In 1947, when she was forty-two, she enrolled in the recently opened Laredo Junior College.

When the **League of United Latin American Citizens** (LULAC) extended membership to women in 1933, Montemayor became a charter member of the Ladies LULAC. During the 1930s she aggressively fought attitudes of male superiority within the organization and promoted equality for women. In 1937 she was elected second national vice-president, the first woman to hold a LULAC position not specifically designated for women. In the late 1930s she also was associate editor of *LULAC News* and director general of Junior LULAC. In her position as vice-president she fostered more substantial roles for women within LULAC and worked to establish more women's councils. As a stalwart feminist, she felt that LULAC suffered from the chauvinism and egotism of its male leaders and their often petty internal bickering. After the 1930s she turned to other, non-civic activities and developed an interest in art, especially painting.

An outspoken critic of Chicana oppression long before Chicana feminism became a popular movement, in the 1980s Montemayor reminisced about the machismo that prevailed in LULAC, but continued to hope that men could change. Unfortunately she did not live to see the election of LULAC's first female president in 1994.

FURTHER READING: *Las Mujeres: Mexican American/Chicana Women.* Windsor, Calif.: National Women's History Project, 1991; Orozco, Cynthia E. "Alice Dickerson Montemayor's Feminist Challenge to LULAC in the 1930s." *IDRA Newsletter* (March 1996) 11–14; Tyler, Ron, ed. *The New Handbook of Texas,* vol. 4. Austin: Texas State Historical Association, 1996.

MÓNTEZ, PHILIP, 1931– . Teacher, activist. Phil Móntez has been active as a civil rights advocate as well as a teacher. A high school teacher and college professor, he was the founder-president of the Association of Mexican American Educators; he also served as director of the Foundation of Mexican American Studies. As a result of his involvement in the struggle for Chicano civil rights, he was appointed director of the western field office of the U.S. Civil Rights Commission by President Lyndon Johnson in 1967. Móntez is the author of various works on **biculturalism** and cultural differences.

FURTHER READING: Pycior, Julie Leininger. *LBJ & Mexican Americans: The Paradox of Power.* Austin: University of Texas Press, 1997.

MONTOYA, JOSÉ. 1932– . Poet, artist. José Montoya was born on a ranch in rural New Mexico south of Albuquerque. When he was five, the family moved to Albuquerque, where he began attending elementary school; in 1941 the family relocated to California and soon he was enrolled in school at Delano. During World War II his father decided to move to Oakland to obtain work in the defense industry and José was sent to New Mexico to finish his elementary schooling. In 1948 he was back in California and three years later completed high school.

During the Korean conflict Montoya served in the U.S. Navy and on being mustered out in the mid-1950s, married and moved to San Diego, where he began studying at City College. He received his Associate of Arts degree in 1956 and was given a scholarship at Oakland's California College of Arts and Crafts. In 1962 he graduated with a B.A. in art education and began teaching in high school. Eight years later Montoya moved to Sacramento, where he continued to paint and write, became one of the founders of Rebel Chicano Art Front (The Royal Chicano Air Force), entered a master's program, and taught at the state university. In 1971 he earned his Master of Fine Arts. He has continued to teach at Sacramento State, moving up the academic ladder to full professor by 1981. During this time he also developed a successful community program called Art in the Barrio.

A talented painter and graphic artist whose paintings have been exhibited in the United States and abroad, Montoya draws his subject matter from the barrio. In addition to painting, he also wrote poetry based on barrio themes for some time but only in 1969 did he begin to publish his poetic work. In that year nine of his poems appeared in the anthology *El Espejo*; among them was "La Jefita," which became one of his most widely known poems. Three years later his poem about a pachuco, "El Louie," also achieved immense popularity; like "La Jefita" it has been widely anthologized. His poetic ability was recognized in 1979 with a Writers Fellowship from the state university at Sacramento and two years later by a Writing Fellowship from the National Endowment for the Arts. Montoya's early poetry was influenced by Walt Whitman and William Carlos Williams. In the late

1960s, under the influence of the Chicano Movement and the beat poets, he began to write about social issues affecting Chicanos and started using more Spanish in his poems. He continues to write and perform with his musical group, Casindio.

FURTHER READING: Godina, Fox. *José Montoya's Pachuco Art: A Historical Update.* Los Angeles: Royal Chicano Air Force, 1977; "José Montoya: Pachuco Artist!" *Low Rider Magazine* 2:4 (1978) 11–13; Lomelí, Francisco A., and Carl R. Shirley, eds. *Chicano Writers: Second Series.* Detroit: Gale Research, 1992. Quirarte, Jacinto. *Mexican American Artists.* Austin: University of Texas Press, 1973; Riggs, Thomas, ed. *St. James Guide to Hispanic Artists: Profiles of Latino and Latin American Artists.* Detroit: St. James Press, 2002.

MONTOYA, JOSEPH M., 1915–1978. Senator. Joseph Montoya was born in the small village of Peña Blanca, New Mexico, the descendant of immigrants who had come there from central Mexico in the 1700s. Upon graduating from Bernalillo High School he entered the Jesuit Regis College in Denver in 1931, and three years later began studying law at Georgetown University in Washington, D.C. While at Georgetown he was elected to the New Mexico legislature. In 1938 he received his bachelor of laws degree and also was reelected to the legislature.

Montoya served a total of twelve years in the state's lower house and senate; between 1946 and 1956 he served four terms as lieutenant governor. In the following year he was elected to the U.S. House of Representatives and was reelected to three more terms. In 1964 he was chosen to complete the unexpired term of Senator **Dennis Chávez** when the latter died. Subsequently he was elected to two full U.S. Senate terms. In the Senate, as in the House, he supported bills to protect consumers and to help Indians, the poor, and the elderly. His voting record was highly esteemed by labor and farm interests, but in the late 1970s his fairly conservative stance caused his popularity to decline and he failed to win a third Senate term. In poor health, he died from complications of cancer surgery.

FURTHER READING: "The Dean." *Nuestro* (August 1978) 8–10; Vigil, Maurilio E. "Parallels in the Careers of Two Hispanic U.S. Senators." *Journal of Ethnic Studies* 13:4 (Winter 1986) 1–20; Vigil, Maurilio E. *Los Patrones: Profiles of Hispanic Political Leaders in New Mexico History,* Washington, D.C.: University Press of America, 1980.

MORENO, CARLOS R., 1948– . Jurist, lawyer. Carlos Moreno, the son of a produce wholesaler, was born and grew up in East Los Angeles. After grade and high school there he attended Yale University, obtaining his B.A. degree in 1970. From Yale he entered Stanford Law School and graduated with a J.D. degree in 1975.

In that same year Moreno went to work in the Los Angeles city attorney's office as deputy city attorney prosecuting consumer fraud and criminal cases. After four years in that position he entered private practice, serving as a civil litigator in the Los Angeles law firms of Mori & Ota, and Kelly, Drye &

Warren until 1986. He also became active in a number of professional law organizations and in 1982 was elected president of the Mexican American Bar Association.

Although he is a Democrat, Moreno received appointment to the Compton (California) Municipal Court from Republican governor George Deukmejian in 1986. Seven years later he was named by Republican governor Pete Wilson to Los Angeles Superior Court. In 1997 he was the recipient of the Court Judge of the Year award from Los Angeles County Bar Association and in the following year he was appointed to the federal U.S. District Court in Los Angeles by president Bill Clinton. On the federal bench he heard a broad range of complex criminal and civil cases.

In October 2001 Moreno accepted appointment by California governor Gray Davis to the state Supreme Court, the third Mexican American to serve there in its century and a half history. He gave up lifetime tenure on a prestigious federal bench to accept a state position that is subject to voter approval for renewal.

FURTHER READING: Barnett, Stephen R. "Dear Justice Moreno." *California Lawyer* 22 (January 2002) 16.

MORENO, LUISA, 1907–1990. Labor organizer, social activist. Luisa Moreno was born in Guatemala, grew up in Mexico, and received most of her education in the United States. As a result of personal experience working in a New York sweatshop she became one of the early twentieth century leaders in the Mexican American struggle for labor union recognition. In the 1930s she began organizing Latino garment workers for the American Federation of Labor (AFL) and in 1937 she switched from the AFL to the Congress of Industrial Organizations (CIO), organizing workers in agriculture. In the following year she replaced local leader **Emma Tenayuca** in the San Antonio **pecan shellers'** strike.

Moreno subsequently devoted her time and energies to the broader task of fighting racist discrimination in the Los Angeles area. To this end in 1938 she helped found one of the early Mexican American civil rights organizations, the **Congreso de Los Pueblos de Habla Española** (Congress of Spanish-Speaking People). The leftist Congreso, which was to have a national scope, was short-lived, dying out during World War II because of the inhibiting wartime climate and Federal Bureau of Investigation harassment.

During the war Moreno helped publicize the vicious attacks on **Zoot Suiters** in Los Angeles and was active in organizing the **Sleepy Lagoon** Defense Committee. Meanwhile, she continued her work as a labor union organizer in agriculture and related industries. As a vice president in the CIO and its affiliate, the radical **United Cannery, Agricultural, Packing and Allied Workers of America**, she headed a committee investigating discriminatory workplace practices. In 1947 she retired from union activities.

In the early 1950s Moreno's foreign birth and her former activity in the left-wing labor movement brought her to the attention of the House Un-American Activities Committee. She was deported as an undesirable alien, and never returned to the United States. At the end of the 1950s she participated briefly in the early days of Fidel Castro's overthrow of the dictator Fulgencio Batista in Cuba. She then returned to Mexico, where she lived quietly in retirement until her death a quarter century later.

FURTHER READING: Camarillo, Albert. *Chicanos in California.* San Francisco: Boyd and Fraser, 1984; García, Mario T. *Memories of Chicano History: The Life and Narrative of Bert Corona.* Berkeley: The University of California Press, 1994; Hardy, Gayle J., ed. *American Women Civil Rights Activists.* Jefferson, N.C.: McFarland, 1993; Larralde, Carlos M., and Richard Griswold del Castillo. "Louisa Moreno and the Beginnings of the Mexican American Civil Rights Movement in San Diego." *Journal of San Diego History* 41:4 (1995) 284–311.

MORÍN, RAÚL R., 1913–1967. Author, political activist. Returning to his Los Angeles sign-painting shop after World War II, Texas-born army veteran Raúl Morín soon took note of the continuing discrimination against Mexican Americans. As an officer in the local **American G.I. Forum** (AGIF), and later in the **Mexican American Political Association**, he became concerned about the frequent denial of their civil rights. As an antidote to this situation, he began to chronicle the service and valor of Mexican Americans in World War II and the Korean conflict. In the mid-1950s he completed his account but found publishers uninterested in his book, which he titled *Among the Valiant.* It was finally published in 1963 through the efforts of the AGIF.

Meanwhile Morín took an active role in community groups, veteran and civic organizations, and politics. He ran for a seat in the California senate but was unsuccessful. However, he continued his fight for Chicano rights through energetic participation in various local committees and boards. By the time of his death in 1967 he had become widely known in southern California for his consuming interest in the struggle for Mexican American rights.

FURTHER READING: Morín, Raúl R. *Among the Valiant: Mexican Americans in World War II and Korea.* Los Angeles: Bordon, 1963.

MORTON, CARLOS, 1947– . Poet, dramatist, editor. Carlos Morton was born in Chicago of a U.S. Army sergeant whose postings caused young Carlos to grow up in various army stations. Entering the University of Texas at El Paso as an English major, he wrote and published poetry, short stories, and plays while still a student. In 1975 he received his B.A. and four years later earned his M.F.A. at the University of California, San Diego. He completed his doctorate at the University of Texas at Austin in 1987.

Because of Morton's interest in theater, he did some early work with the San Francisco Mime Troupe and with **Luis Valdez**. He also worked as assistant editor of *Nuestro, La Luz,* and *Revista Chicano-Riqueña.* His first book of poetry, *White Heroin Winter,* was published in 1971 while he was a student at El Paso. As a graduate student in San Diego he published two plays: *El Cuento de Pancho Diablo,* 1976 and in the next year *Las Many Muertes de Richard Morales,* which he later revised as *The Many Deaths of Danny Rosales.* A prolific writer, he is the author of a baker's dozen plays, most appearing in print during the 1990s, and has published poetry, fiction, and essays in various periodicals. The message of his writing is generally nonviolence and racial harmony.

Morton has taught drama at Laredo Junior College, University of California at Berkeley, and the University of Texas at Austin. After teaching in the theater arts department of the University of California, Riverside, he moved to the University of California at Santa Barbara, where he recently was appointed director of the Center for Chicano Studies.

FURTHER READING: Daniel, Lee A. "Carlos Morton: Chicano Dramatist." In *Johnny Tenorio and other Plays,* Carlos Morton. Houston: Arte Público Press, 1992; Franco, Marco A. "His Work Is All Play." *Vista* 3:12 (August 1988) 32; Huerta, Jorge A. *Chicano Theater: Themes and Forms.* Ypsilanti, Mich.: Bilingual Press, 1982; Huerta, Jorge A. *Chicano Drama: Performance, Society, and Myth.* New York: Cambridge University Press, 2000; Lomelí, Francisco A., and Donaldo W. Urioste. *Chicano Perspectives in Literature.* Albuquerque, N.M.: Pajarito, 1976.

MOVIMIENTO, EL. The Movement was conceived by many Mexican Americans as a peaceful revolution to end the basic inequities in American society faced by Chicanos. Not precisely defined, it had a wide variety of political, economic, and social origins, goals, and perspectives. Set into motion by the expectations of Chicano veterans of World War II and the Korean conflict, it leaned heavily on the often humble and frustrating work of earlier seekers of social justice, whose contributions were unknown or undervalued by many in the *movimiento.* In its early years it followed the example of the black civil rights movement. For national **leadership** it sought Chicano role models comparable to Dr. Martin Luther King. In the late 1960s **César Chávez** came closest to that model, but his low-key, nonviolent stance had a limited attraction for the more confrontational youthful Chicano activists. Moreover, his primary concern for agricultural workers limited his appeal to barrio urbanites, who formed a large majority of Movement militants.

Most *movimiento* activity took place in the community and on high school and college campuses. Chicano students, whose needs were being ignored, took a leading role in the demand for greater voice in their education. Within the Movement Chicanas demanded an end to their inferior position and to a demeaning machismo. Nearly all stressed *chicanismo,* a vaguely defined and culturally oriented Mexicanness that was underscored by a view of themselves as a conquered people. They marched and demonstrated for equality of educational opportunity, which many saw as the key to gaining their rightful economic and political place in America. They manifested their

The march on Congress Ave. in Austin, Texas, during the Economy Furniture Co. strike, 1971. Courtesy of the Benson Latin American Collection, University of Texas at Austin.

unhappiness through high school walkouts, university sit-ins, face-to-face confrontation, and civil disobedience. Their leaders often boldly questioned many older Mexican American political leaders as well as the "system." They called for extensive reforms, particularly in education.

Appalled at high Chicano casualty rates in the Vietnam conflict, younger Mexican Americans became intensely politicized, working in voter registration and get-out-the-vote drives and running for political office. For a few years **La Raza Unida Party,** which they created, raised the hope for an influential third force in American politics. Paradoxically, in their search for dignity and a positive identity, many demanded equality as U.S. citizens and at the same time espoused some measure of political as well as cultural nationalism.

To a degree the *movimiento* succeeded in obtaining many of its demands. Although it did not achieve all its goals in the areas of political rights, education, land ownership, and the eradication of institutional racism, incremental gains were made. Its successes, as well as destructive internal power struggles, ultimately brought about the decline of the multifaceted Movement. Its inability to agree and unite on goals and strategies and to broaden its appeal to more sectors of the community also weakened it. As the country was swept by a tide of neoconservatism in the 1980s, many *movimiento* supporters turned to less confrontational activities like voter registration, election turnout, election of Chicanos to public office, and resort to the courts for solutions to their problems.

Among the achievements of its decade of intense activity, the Chicano Movement raised group consciousness and strengthened cultural pride and a sense of ethnic identity. It pointed out that Mexican Americans had made, and were making, significant contributions to American culture. Of even greater importance, it initiated and nurtured a deep concern for civil rights. That concern constitutes a lasting legacy of the movimiento.

FURTHER READING: García, Ignacio M. *Chicanismo! The Forging of a Militant Ethos among Mexican Americans.* Tucson: University of Arizona Press, 1997; García, Juan A. "The Chicano Movement: Its Legacy for Politics and Policy." In *Chicanas/Chicanos at the Crossroads: Social, Economic, and Political Change,* edited by David Maciel and Isidro D. Ortiz. Tucson: University of Arizona Press, 1996; Maciel, David R., Isidro D. Ortiz, and María Herrera-Sobek, eds. *Chicano Renaissance: Contempory Cultural Trends.* Tucson: University of Arizona Press, 2000; Marín, Marguerite V. *Social Protest in an Urban Barrio: A Study of the Chicano Movement, 1966–1974.* Lanham, Md.: University Press of America, 1991; Mirandé, Alfredo. *The Chicano Experience: An Alternative Perspective.* Notre Dame: University of Notre Dame Press, 1985; Navarro, Armando. *Mexican American Youth Organization: Avant-Garde of the Chicano Movement in Texas.* Austin: University of Texas Press, 1995; Rosales, F. Arturo. *Chicano! The History of the Mexican American Civil Rights Movement,* 2 nd ed. Houston: Arte Público Press, 1997; Rosen, Gerald. "The Development of the Chicano Movement in Los Angeles from 1967–1969." *Aztlán* 4:1 (Spring 1973) 155–183.

MOVIMIENTO ESTUDIANTIL CHICANO DE AZTLÁN (MEChA).

MEChA was an umbrella student organization established in 1969 by combining a number of existing Chicano campus groups during a meeting at the University of California's Santa Barbara campus. MEChA leaders developed and articulated the **Plan de Santa Bárbara**, outlining the organization's philosophy and educational goals. Leaders of the Chicano Coordinating Council on Higher Education, which hosted the three-day conference, hoped MEChA (fuse or match) would ignite educational and political change, both on campus and in the community.

This broad goal of MEChA leaders later led to internal bickering and divisions that widened as time went on. A patronizing attitude toward Chicanas further aggravated tensions within the organization. During the 1980s MEChA lessened its involvement in community politics and began concentrating more on campus issues, particularly affirmative action. Internal ideological splits continued to plague groups on various campuses. Although MEChA has declined since the late 1970s and has had limited success outside of California, it remains the principal Chicano student organization.

FURTHER READING: Gómez-Quiñones, Juan. *Mexican Students por La Raza: The Chicano Student Movement in Southern California 1967–1977.* Santa Barbara, Calif.: Editorial La Causa, 1978; Martínez, Douglas R. "El Movimiento Estudiantil: From the Sixties to the Seventies." *Agenda* 8:3 (May–June 1978) 19–21; Muñoz, Carlos,

Jr. *Youth, Identity, Power: The Chicano Movement.* New York: Verso, 1989; *El Plan de Santa Bárbara.* Santa Barbara, Calif.: La Causa, 1969; Valle, María Eva. "MEChA and the Transformation of Chicano Student Activism: Generational Change, Conflict, and Continuity." Ph.D. diss. University of California, San Diego, 1996.

MUÑIZ, RAMSEY, 1943– . Political activist, attorney. Ramsey Muñiz, an articulate young Chicano lawyer, was an early member of **La Raza Unida Party** (LRUP) in which his popularity rivaled that of **José Angel Gutiérrez**. He was born in Corpus Christi, where he attended Cunningham Junior High. A high school football hero, he went to Baylor University on an athletic scholarship. After completing his undergraduate degree and law school, in the late 1960s he took a position as administrative assistant in the Department of Health, Education and Welfare's Model Cities program in Waco, from which he resigned to run for the Texas governorship as the LRUP candidate in 1972.

During his election campaign Muñiz, charismatic and eloquent, appealed to a grassroots Chicano yearning for social justice. In a three-man race, his 214,000 votes, almost 7 percent of the total, nearly caused the first Republican gubernatorial victory in Texas since the 1870s. For many Mexican Americans his vote-getting ability indicated the potential of the electoral path to greater economic and social justice. However, when he ran again two years later he received only 94,000 votes. He returned to Corpus Christi and opened a law office.

In 1976 Muñiz was arrested twice within months on marijuana smuggling charges and pleaded guilty in a plea bargain that gave him a five-year prison term with ten additional years' probation. His conviction on drug charges ended a promising political career and helped bring an end to LRUP. He was released from prison in 1981 and was apprehended in June 1982 on a charge of possessing cocaine for sale. He returned to jail for two years, and then spent ten years working as a paralegal and avoiding trouble. Then in March 1994 he was arrested for driving a car with forty kilos of cocaine in the trunk. His conviction on a third federal narcotics charge sent him to Leavenworth, where he is currently serving a life sentence.

FURTHER READING: Chávez, Ray. "Marijuana, Mystery and Muñiz." *Nuestro* (February 1978) 56–57; García, F. Chris, and Rudolph O. de la Garza. *The Chicano Political Experience: Three Perspectives.* North Scituate, Mass.: Duxbury Press, 1977; García, Ignacio M. *United We Win: The Rise and Fall of La Raza Unida Party.* Tucson: University of Arizona, Mexican American Studies and Research Center, 1989; Moore, Evan. "The Muñiz Mystery: Downfall from Destiny." *The Houston Chronicle* (10 July 1994) A1; Terry-Azios, Diana A. "Where Are They Now? Ramsey Muñiz." *Texas Monthly* (November 2002) 58.

MURIETA, JOAQUÍN, fl.1850s. Folk hero. The bandit Joaquín Murieta was probably a legendary composite developed by romantic writers from a number of California outlaws referred to as Joaquín. According to the usual account, Murieta was forced into banditry during the gold rush period in order to avenge the rape and murder of his wife by Anglo miners.

Historically certain is the fact that early in 1853 the California legislature created a temporary ranger force to capture bandits known as the five Joaquíns. Nearing the expiration of their three month commission, the rangers encountered and shot up a small group of Mexicanos. They identified the body of one as Joaquín Murieta and preserved his head in a large jar of whiskey. A year later John Rollin Ridge, a pulp fiction writer, used this event as the basis for an essentially fictional account of *The Life and Adventures of Joaquín Murieta, the Celebrated California Bandit*. The immediate widespread success of his short novel led to numerous reprints, pirated editions, and elaborations.

Popular enthusiasm for the Murieta story in its many variations and its lack of any real documentation have continued down to the present. In its evolution the historical Murieta has been all but completely lost. He has been identified as a Sonoran, a Californio, even a Chilean. Whatever his origins, in the second half of the 1800s he became an evocative symbol to many Californios of their loss of economic and social position and the continuing erosion of their rights. The Murieta story has been the basis for movies, plays, epic poems, and even a biography. In the 1960s he joined Pancho Villa and Emiliano Zapata as one of the mythic heroes of the Chicano movimiento.

FURTHER READING: Latta, Frank. *Joaquín Murrieta and His Horse Gang*. Santa Cruz, Calif.: Bear State Books, 1980; Nadeau, Remi. *The Real Joaquín Murieta*. Corona del Mar, Calif.: Trans-Anglo Books, 1974; Paz, Ireneo. *Life and Adventures of the Celebrated Bandit Joaquín Murieta: His Exploits in the State of California*. Houston: Arte Público Press, 2001; Ridge, John Rollin. *The Life and Adventures of Joaquín Murieta, the Celebrated California Bandit*. New ed. Norman: University of Oklahoma Press, 1955; Secrest, William B. *The Return of Joaquín*. Fresno, Calif.: Saga-West , 1973; Varley, James F. *The Legend of Joaquín Murieta: California's Gold Rush Bandit*. Twin Falls, Idaho: Big Lost River Press, 1995.

MUSIC, CHICANO. Within the U.S.-Mexican border region an exuberant musical tradition has developed over the past century and a half. This music is a harmonious combination derived from European, pre-Columbian, Mexican folk, and African American roots. Additional musical elements and styles were added in the Southwest during the nineteenth and twentieth centuries. As the result of Polish and German immigration to both northern Mexico and Texas, Tejanos developed an instrumental style usually referred to as Tex-Mex, in which the accordion and the bass viol dominate. All over the Southwest mariachi music, brought to Mexico by the emperor Maximilian's entourage in the 1860s and introduced to the Southwest by the heavy *norteño* immigration of the 1920s, became widely accepted in the following decades and remains very popular today.

The most prevalent early musical form to emerge in the southwestern border region was the corrido, a sort of musical broadside that recited news of important events, especially the deeds of independence fighters, revolutionaries, and other popular heroes. The influx of refugees during the 1910 **Mexican revolution** added a nationalistic edge to many of the corridos in the Southwest, and they were also affected by the *indianismo* that influenced Mexican art and music at that time. In Texas, corridos adopted as topics such disparate events as the launching of space satellites, the assassination of John F. Kennedy, and the Vietnam War, but were also frequently based on the theme of border conflict. The corridos are especially rich in cultural significance, usually reflecting the feelings and history of the common people. During the Chicano Movement of the 1960s and 1970s some Mexican Americans used them to express an ethnic nationalism.

Carlos Santana (left) performs with Mana at the first annual Latin Grammy Awards in Los Angeles, September 13, 2000. © AP/Wide World Photos.

Among Mexican American vocalists, **Lydia Mendoza** of Texas began a long singing career at the end of the 1920s that was to have three phases and gain for her the affectionate title of "The Lark of the Border." In the 1930s she performed on the radio and recorded about 100 songs, mostly ballads; during the 1950s and 1960s she made hundreds of records; and in the 1970s and 1980s she became widely known as a leading Chicana ethnic folk music artist. Other internationally known Mexican American singers like **Joan Báez**, **Vikki Carr, Trini López,** Andy Russel, and **Linda Ronstadt**, who sing in both Spanish and English, have brought Mexicano music to the attention of Anglo listeners.

The most widely known male Mexican American musicians include southern California's **Lalo Guerrero**, who became famous for "Tacos for Two" and other parodies of popular American songs. Elsewhere Tejanos **Freddy Fender**, famous for his bilingual song "Before the Next Teardrop Falls," and Flaco (Santiago) Jiménez, widely known for his accordion improvisation, have attracted large followings. In northern California instrumentalists like **Pete Escovedo** and Carlos Santana have developed a large Anglo following.

Among bands, Los Lobos del Este of Los Angeles and Los Tigres del Norte of San Jose have successfully mixed rock and roll with boleros, blues, corridos, cumbias, rancheras, and Tex-Mex since the mid-1970s, to the delight of audiences. By the end of the century Los Tigres had pressed 130 discs and sold some 30 million albums. In the early 1990s singer Selena Quintanilla, known simply as **Selena** to her thousands of fans, dominated the Tejano vocal music scene and gave promise of an even more stunning future until her unfortunate death in 1995.

FURTHER READING: Burr, Ramiro. *Billboard Guide to Tejano and Regional Mexican Music.* New York: Billboard Books, 1999; Dicky, Dan. *The Kennedy Corridos: A Study of the Ballads of a Mexican American Hero.* Austin: University of Texas Press, 1978; Hornsby, Nick. "The Entertainers: Learning from Los Lobos." *The New Yorker* (23 & 30 April 2001) 182–186; Loeffler, Jack, with Katherine Loeffler and Enrique R. Lamadrid. *La música de los viejitos: Hispano Folk Music of the Rio Grande del Norte.* Albuquerque: University of New Mexico Press, 1999; Loza, Steven. *Barrio Rhythm: Mexican American Music in Los Angeles.* Urbana: University of Illinois Press, 1993; Paredes, Américo. *A Texas-Mexican Cancionero: Folksongs of the Lower Border.* Urbana: University of Illinois Press, 1976; Peña, Manuel. *Música tejana: The Cultural Economy of Artistic Transformation.* College Station: Texas A & M Press, 1999; Peña, Manuel. *The Texas-Mexican Conjunto: History of a Working Class Music.* Austin: University of Texas Press, 1985; Reyes, David, and Tom Waldman. *Land of a Thousand Dances: Chicano Rock 'n' Roll from Southern California.* Albuquerque: University of New Mexico Press, 1998; Roberts, John S. *The Latin Tinge, The Impact of Latin American Music on the United States.* New York: Oxford University Press, 1979; San Miguel, Guadalupe Jr. *Tejano Proud: Tex-Mex Music in the Twentieth Century.* College Station: Texas A & M Press, 2002; Tatum, Charles M. *Chicano Popular Culture: Que hable el pueblo.* Tucson: University of Arizona Press, 2001.

MUTUALISTAS. *Mutualistas* were Mexicano self-help groups that evolved during the second half of the 1800s. Their primary function was to provide funeral benefits and similar minimal insurance protection. Growing out of the local Mexicano cultural experience, they also became the basis for organizing popular festive occasions like Cinco de Mayo and Diez y Seis de Septiembre. In addition, they supplied a socializing focus and a forum for the discussion of community problems. Filling important community needs, they developed widely throughout the towns and villages of the Southwest.

At the time of World War I, mutualistas began to take on new tasks such as providing employment information and legal assistance. Some became important in the development of community and labor organizations. They began to decline during the 1930s and all but disappeared by mid-century.

FURTHER READING: Hernández, José Amaro. *Mutual Aid for Survival: The Case of the Mexican American.* Malabar, Florida: Robert A. Krieger, 1983; Rivera, José A. "Self-Help As Mutual Protection: The Development of Hispanic Fraternal Benefit Societies." *Journal of Applied Behavioral Science* 23:3 (1987) 387–396.

NATIONAL ASSOCIATION FOR CHICANA AND CHICANO STUDIES.
NACCS was started in 1972 by California Mexican Americans involved in education. First called the National Caucus of Chicano Social Scientists, it was named National Association of Chicano Social Scientists in 1973, became the National Association for Chicano Studies three years later, and finally settled on National Association for Chicana and Chicano Studies. From its inception, its goals have been to promote greater awareness of Mexicano contributions to American culture and to encourage educational achievement among Chicanas/Chicanos. To help in achieving these ends, it viewed providing mentors for both students and new faculty as an important part of its task. It has supported the creation and development of Chicano academic programs and studies centers. It also advocated and fostered greater Chicano involvement in the political process. Its largest membership is in California, but it has chapters in the Southwest and Midwest as well.

FURTHER READING: Gonzales, Sylvia A. *Hispanic American Voluntary Organizations.* Westport, Conn.: Greenwood Press, 1985; http://clnet.ucr.edu/research/NACCS/

NATIONAL ASSOCIATION OF LATINO ELECTED AND APPOINTED OFFICIALS. NALEO is the primary national organization of Latino political empowerment. It was largely the brainchild of California congressman **Edward Roybal.** An issue-oriented nonpartisan association, it was founded in 1976 to provide a clear Latino lobbying voice and pressure group in the nation's capital and to encourage Latino participation in government at all levels. Its founders envisioned it as a nationwide organization of Latino government officials who would network and combine their efforts in pursuit of important objectives like voter education and registration, civil rights, and economic betterment for *la raza.* Since its concern is primarily with issues, it monitors and analyzes proposed legislation and government policies, particularly as they affect U.S. Latinos. It reports its views on matters of concern and government policies via a quarterly newsletter.

NALEO is financed principally from individual and corporate sponsorship fees and membership dues. Fairly simple in organization, it has an elected board headed by a president, a national director, and a secretary-treasurer. Membership is open to all appointed and elected officials, and associate membership is available to anyone interested in helping to further the organization's goals. In 1981 it established an Educational Fund to finance workshops and seminars for young people in order to develop future leaders among Latino youths, and to encourage programs to integrate immigrants into American civic life. Today it continues its work of sponsoring institutes and leadership training seminars.

FURTHER READING: Eherenhalt, Alan, ed. *Politics in America*. Washington, D.C.: Congressional Quarterly, 1983; Gonzales, Sylvia A. *Hispanic American Voluntary Organizations*. Westport, Conn.: Greenwood Press, 1985; "NALEO: Challenging and Moving Ahead." *Caminos* 5:3 (March 1984) 36–37. www.naleo.org

NATIONAL CHICANO COUNCIL ON HIGHER EDUCATION. NCCHE was founded in 1975 at a Los Angeles meeting of Chicano academicians who saw a need for an organization to deal with the problems of Mexican Americans in colleges and universities. Funded by a Ford Foundation grant, it set two primary goals: to investigate and develop policies on Chicano educational issues and to foster academic advancement among Chicanos. It sponsored a postdoctoral program to increase the number of Mexican Americans teaching at the university level.

FURTHER READING: Gonzales, Sylvia A. *Hispanic American Voluntary Organizations*. Westport, Conn.: Greenwood Press, 1985; McCurdy, Jack. "Chicanos Mark Their Gains in Colleges, Call for More." *Chronicle of Higher Education* 25:10 (3 November 1982) 12.

NATIONAL CHICANO MORATORIUM, 1970. The national Chicano moratorium arose out of widely held and deeply felt Mexican American grievances, especially long-suffered rebuffs from U.S. government officials. The immediate occasion was the rising concern about the country's military involvement in Vietnam and the high percentage of Chicano casualties. In December 1969 an antidraft conference in Denver began plans for a demonstration in Los Angeles, and in the following March final arrangements for the march were completed by the second Chicano Youth Conference in Denver. The Los Angeles march was to climax earlier demonstrations throughout the Southwest.

In August 1970 the largest group of Chicano demonstrators ever assembled, more than twenty-five thousand, met in East Los Angeles to rally in protest against the Vietnam conflict. The war had politicized and polarized even conservative middle-class Mexican Americans, so the national moratorium march was supported by most community organizations.

To avoid possible problems the rally was closely monitored. However, trouble in a liquor store on the march route precipitated massive police interference, which was immediately extended to Laguna Park where early marchers were enjoying lunch while listening to music and speakers like

Corky Gonzales. Some five hundred helmeted police and sheriff deputies began a sweep of the park. Tear gas canisters were fired. Panic ensued. Rock and bottle throwing in the park quickly escalated into rioting, vandalizing, and looting on the Whittier Boulevard route, and led to the arrest of several hundred marchers and to three deaths. Among those killed was veteran journalist and TV station KMEX news director **Rubén Salazar.** The televised thirteen-day coroner's inquest into Salazar's death became an occasion for denouncing the marchers and condemning the moratorium march.

In the aftermath of the moratorium there were small outbreaks of confrontation and violence between demonstrators and police in the Southwest. These occurrences served to strengthen ethnic solidarity. They also served to attract Chicanos to the platform of the new *La Raza Unida Party*, particularly in California.

FURTHER READING: Acuña, Rodolfo. *Occupied America: A History of Chicanos.* 3rd ed. New York: Harper & Row, 1988; Escobar, Edward J. "The Dialects of Repression: The Los Angeles Police Department and the Chicano Movement, 1968–1971." *Journal of American History* 79:4 (March 1993) 1483–1514; Morales, Armando. "The 1970–71 East Los Angeles Police Riots." In *La Causa Política: A Chicano Politics Reader*, edited by F. Chris García. Notre Dame, Ind.: University of Notre Dame Press, 1974; Ruiz, Raúl. "Chicano Eyewitness Report." *La Raza* 1:3 (September, 1970) 46–52; Trujillo, Charley, ed. *Soldados: Chicanos in Viet Nam.* San Jose, Calif.: Chusma House Publications, 1991.

NATIONAL CONGRESS OF HISPANIC AMERICAN CITIZENS. The NCHAC was founded in 1971 by a group of Mexican American leaders including **Polly Baca** and **Raúl Yzaguirre.** With headquarters in Washington, D.C., the Congress aimed to provide a highly visible and vocal lobby for Mexican American concerns before all three branches of government, at both federal and state levels. The Congress, which included representatives from every major Hispanic organization, was soon restructured to reflect more closely the interests of the entire Latino community. Concerned with voting rights, educational problems, and housing needs, in its short life the Congress provided leadership through workshops on these issues and on the lobbying process. It had some successes in getting the U.S. Congress to pass laws that benefitted *la raza.* The Congress disintegrated by the end of the 1970s, largely as the result of internal leadership conflicts. Most of its agenda was taken over by the **Congressional Hispanic Caucus** and the **National Association of Latino Elected and Appointed Officials.**

FURTHER READING: Baca, Fernie. "Frank L. 'Hank' Lacayo–A Biography of an Outstanding Labor Leader." *La Luz* (April 1976) 16–19; Fierro, Manuel D. "An Open Letter to President Ford." *La Luz* (March 1976) 8–9; Gonzales, Sylvia A. *Hispanic American Voluntary Organizations.* Westport, Conn.: Greenwood Press, 1985.

NATIONAL COUNCIL OF LA RAZA. The National Council of La Raza was organized originally in 1968 as the Southwest Council of La Raza with a

$630,000 Ford Foundation grant. Envisioned by its founders as an umbrella organization with the broad goal of moving Mexican Americans into the American mainstream, it chose as its first executive director labor and community organizer Henry Santiestevan. The Council worked to strengthen Chicano organizations in the Southwest by providing a persistent voice for community concerns and objectives through leadership, subgrants, and other support for community empowerment. When it moved from San Antonio to Washington, D.C. in 1973 because of its expanded activities, the name was changed to reflect its wider scope.

A private, nonprofit group, the Council devoted most of its early energies to bridging the gulf between Chicanos and Anglo society. Working closely with the private sector, it has achieved a broad and secure financial base. It provided seed money to various groups including the **Mexican American Legal Defense and Educational Fund** and the **Southwest Voter Registration Education Project.** Among its successful early efforts was the creation of La Raza Investment Corporation, a small business investment company that made loans and provided managerial assistance to Mexican American entrepreneurs. Its Policy Analysis Center is the outstanding U.S. Latino think tank.

Under **Raúl Yzaguirre**'s able leadership since 1972, the Council has grown to become an institution of national influence. With more than 270 formally affiliated organizations plus a broad network of more loosely affiliated thousands, it is the largest Latino umbrella institution in the country, providing valuable research, information, and assistance to community groups. For more than three decades it has led the fight to improve education and housing for Latinos and to provide programs dealing with immigration, leadership, health, and community development. Its consistent support of voter registration has helped create a more effective Latino voice in government. The nation's largest Latino advocacy organization with branch offices in Arizona, Illinois, New Mexico, and Texas, it is widely accepted by Chicanos as speaking for the community.

FURTHER READING: Frase-Blunt, Martha. "Committed to Unity." *Hispanic* (July 1992) 11–14; Gonzales, Sylvia A. *Hispanic American Voluntary Organizations.* Westport, Conn.: Greenwood Press, 1985; Martínez, Douglas. "Yzaguirre at the Helm." *Américas* 32:6–7 (June–July 1980) 49; "Shaping a Greater America in the 21st Century: A Portrait of the National Council of La Raza." *Hispanic Journal* (NCLR Special Edition, July 2–5, 2001) 4–5; Sierra, Christine Marie. "The Political Transformation of a Minority Organization: The Council of La Raza, 1965–1980." Ph.D. diss., Stanford University, 1983; Weise-Peredo, Martha. "An American Institution Three Decades Strong." *Agenda* 13:4 (Spring 1998) 1–2. www.nclr.org

NATIONAL ECONOMIC DEVELOPMENT ASSOCIATION. The NEDA, established in 1970, was a nonprofit corporation formed by Mexican American businessmen. First headquartered in Los Angeles and then moving to Washington, D.C., it was funded through arrangements made with federal and state government agencies. With an annual budget of over five million dollars, it sought to develop Chicano-owned businesses. By 1980 it operated twenty-five offices in the Southwest, providing a complete range of services to potential Chicano entrepreneurs. It had a record of considerable initial success but ran into conflict with its funding agency, the Minority Business Development Agency.

FURTHER READING: "NEDA Turns 10." *Hispanic Business* (June 1980) 10–13, 19.

NATIONAL FARM LABOR UNION. The NFLU was an American Federation of Labor affiliate established in 1947 to replace the earlier Southern Tenant Farmers Union. Headed by **Ernesto Galarza** and Hank Hasiwar, it attempted to unionize agricultural workers in California's central valley beginning in 1947. During the next five years lengthy strikes against the **Di Giorgio Corporation**, melon growers in the Imperial Valley, and the Schenley Corporation all failed to gain recognition of the union as bargaining agent for the workers.

In 1952 the NFLU was reorganized as the National Agricultural Workers Union and a new spurt of organizing took place. Its membership reached a high point of about four thousand but declined to less than three hundred by the mid-1960s. In 1964 it finally closed down by merging with another AFL union, the Amalgamated Meat Cutters and Butcher Workmen of America.

FURTHER READING: Galarza, Ernesto. *Farm Workers and Agri-business in California, 1947–1960.* Notre Dame, Ind.: University of Notre Dame Press, 1977; Grubbs, Donald H. "Prelude to Chávez: The National Farm Labor Union in California." *Labor History* 16:4 (1975) 453–469.

NATIONAL HISPANIC LEADERSHIP CONFERENCE. The NHLC is a Latino think tank founded in Corpus Christi by **Tony Bonilla** and other Mexican Americans in 1976. Under the leadership of its president, Bonilla, it has as its goal both the economic and social improvement of *la raza*. Among its most important concerns are civil rights, education, employment, and the criminal justice system. It has established drug abuse prevention and support programs in Latino communities and has worked with other groups like the League of United Latin American Citizens to increase the economic opportunities available to Latinos. In the mid-1990s the NHCL helped negotiate agreements with the 7-Eleven convenience stores and the Miller Brewing Company to increase minority opportunities within those companies. At its quadrennial conferences it has stressed the manifest importance of education for both Chicanos and the nation.

FURTHER READING: "Hispanic Leadership Conference Report." *Hispanic Times* (August–Sept. 1988) 34; "Tony Bonilla." In *Dictionary of Hispanic Biography*, edited by Joseph C. Tardiff and L. Mpho Mabunda. Detroit: Gale Research, 1996.

NATIONAL ORGANIZATION OF MEXICAN AMERICAN SERVICES. NOMAS was one of the earlier institutions created to articulate Mexican

American concerns at the national level. Founded in 1964 by **Raúl Yzaguirre,** its goal was to make available to the community information about federal policies and to coordinate the efforts of local and regional Chicano groups. Although crippled by President Lyndon Johnson's ignoring its leadership during the 1966 **Equal Employment Opportunity Commission** meeting in Albuquerque, it lingered on for several more years. In its short life NOMAS prepared the way for the **National Council of La Raza** and initiated efforts among Mexican American congressmen to maintain communication with each other that led to the founding of the **National Association of Latino Elected and Appointed Officials** in 1975. It also made two important contributions to the Chicano Movement; it made young Chicanos aware of organizing techniques and it opened lines to sources of private funding like the Ford Foundation.

FURTHER READING: Gómez-Quiñones, Juan. *Chicano Politics: Reality and Promise, 1940–1990.* Albuquerque: University of New Mexico Press, 1990; Moore, Joan, and Harry Pachon. *Hispanics in the United States.* Englewood Cliffs, N.J.: Prentice-Hall, Inc., 1985.

NATIONALISM, CHICANO. Chicano nationalism, challenging assimilation as a goal for *la raza,* runs a gamut from full political independence to a banner for cultural escapism. During the Chicano Movement a few extreme militants talked about creating in the Southwest an independent nation-state that some referred to as **Aztlán. Reies López Tijerina** belonged to this school, using land grant claims as the basis for his position. **Corky Gonzales** was committed to a degree of economic and cultural separation, espousing a more moderate nationalism in which Chicanos would exercise greater economic and political control of their communities. Using the name Aztlán as a rallying cry, he argued that their common culture and history provided the basis for such a separateness. **José Angel Gutiérrez,** on the other hand, realized that any real political independence for Mexican Americans was a chimerical goal, and worked to obtain their political and economic rights within the system. Taking a sharply anti-Anglo stance in his rhetoric, he used their pent-up feelings of alienation from American society to organize them into his **La Raza Unida** party.

Some moderate and conservative Mexican Americans supported a degree of ethnic nationalism based on their concerns about corruptive effects of American society. Viewing their cultural values as superior to those of Anglos, they supported a cultural nationalism based on retention of Spanish and other ethnic appurtenances. In general, most Mexican Americans have wished to preserve some aspects of their inherited cultural identity, and the community has widely supported moderate stances on ethnic nationalism.

FURTHER READING: Acuña, Rodolfo. *Occupied America: A History of Chicanos.* 3rd ed. New York: Harper & Row, 1988; Anaya, Rudolfo A. *Aztlán: Essays on the Chicano Homeland.* Albuquerque: Academia/El Norte, 1989; Marín, Christine. *A Spokesman for the Mexican American Movement: Rodolfo "Corky" Gonzales and the Fight for Chicano*

Liberation, 1966–1972. San Francisco, Calif.: R & E Research Associates, 1977; Hammerback, John C., Richard J. Jensen, and José Angel Gutiérrez. *A War of Words: Chicano Protest in the 1960s and 1970s.* Westport, Conn.: Greenwood Press, 1985.

NATIVISM. Nativism is an attitude or practice of favoring native-born citizens over immigrants. Ethnocentrism and a belief in Anglo cultural superiority over other ethnic groups often forms an integral part of nativism. In the United States it often was expressed in the favoring of Anglo-descent persons over more recently arrived minority immigrants. This attitude has been oppressive of Mexican Americans and has often led to violence against them.

Early in the twentieth century nativism energized the movement to limit and restrict immigration to the United States. It also was one of the attitudes that justified the massive **repatriation** of Mexican sojourners in the 1930s and 1950s. Today it fuels groups like the **English Only movement** and the **Federation for American Immigration Reform.**

FURTHER READING: Higham, John. *Strangers in the Land; Patterns of American Nativism, 1860–1925.* New Brunswick, N.J.: Rutgers University Press, 1988; Perea, Juan F., ed. *Immigrants Out: The New Nativism and the Anti-Immigrant Impulse in the United States.* New York: New York University Press, 1997.

NAVA, GREGORY, 1949– . Director, screenwriter. Born in San Diego, California, Gregory Nava studied filmmaking at the University of California, Los Angeles. After graduating from the UCLA film school, in 1977 he cowrote with his wife and directed the movie *The Confessions of Amans;* five years later his second coauthored film, *The End of August,* came out.

A scene from *El Norte,* 1983, directed by Gregory Nava. © The Kobal Collection/Independent Productions/AM Playhouse.

The third film Nava directed, *El Norte*, became an immediate hit when it was released in 1984. The story of two young Guatemalan undocumented immigrants, it was nominated for an Academy Award in the following year. In 1988 Nava followed *El Norte* with a fourth film, *A Time of Destiny*; it received only a so-so reception from both audiences and critics when it was released. During the 1990s he had renewed success in his film work. His highly acclaimed *Mi Familia/My Family*, with Edward James Olmos, won high marks when it premiered in 1995. He both wrote and directed the film, which celebrates the ultimate victory of the Latino spirit. Two years later he produced *Selena*, a film he wrote and directed at the behest of the Texas singer's family. His most recent film, titled *Why Do Fools Fall in Love*, was released in 1998. Most recently he writes and directs a TV series titled *American Family*, which first aired on the Public Broadcasting System in January, 2002.

FURTHER READING: Reyes, Luis, and Peter Rubie. *Hispanics in Hollywood: A Celebration of 100 Years in Film and Television*. Hollywood: Lone Eagle, 2000; Rossi, Patrizia. "Tales: Gregory Nava Wants to Tell a Wonderful Story." *Latino Leaders* 3:2 (April/May 2002) 33–35; Ryan, Bryan, ed. *Hispanic Writers*. Detroit: Gale Research, 1991.

NAVA, JULIAN, 1927– . Historian, ambassador, civic leader. Born in East Los Angeles, California, Julian Nava was the American-born son of parents who had fled the turmoil of the 1910 **Mexican revolution**. He grew up in the Boyle Heights barrio, attended local schools, and in the summers followed the fruit harvests with his parents and siblings. In 1944 he volunteered for service in World War II and after a year was mustered out. His U.S. Air Force service helped make him aware of possibilities beyond the barrio.

In 1947 Nava enrolled in the East Los Angeles Community College, received his A.A. degree two years later, and went on to Pomona College. An excellent student, he graduated from Pomona with two scholarships that took him to Harvard University, where he earned his M.A. and Ph.D. He then taught for two years at the Universidad de Puerto Rico, after which he returned to California to teach Latin American history at California State University, Northridge. In the 1950s and early 1960s he took several leaves of absence to teach in Latin America and Spain.

Returning from abroad in 1965, Nava became caught up in Chicano students' rising concern about educational issues. Two years later he won election to the governing board of the Los Angeles Unified School district and was reelected in 1971 and 1975. During this time he also was active on numerous educational and community boards and councils including the National Hispanic Scholarship Foundation. In 1980 he was appointed by President Jimmy Carter as ambassador to Mexico. He acquitted himself well as ambassador, initiating a number of collaborative educational programs between the United States and Mexico. On his return from Mexico he resumed teaching. In 1993 he ran for mayor of Los Angeles but lost. Currently he teaches at California State University, Northridge.

In addition to his civic leadership, Nava is notable for his pioneering work in Chicano history. In 1969 he published *Mexican Americans: Past, Present, and Future,* one of the first ethnic-oriented high school texts, and followed that with two books of readings on the Mexican American experience. Among his many other publications are *Our Hispanic Heritage,* 1974 and *California: Five Centuries of Cultural Contrast,* 1976. He has been the recipient of various awards, the result of his extensive civic involvement and academic achievements.

FURTHER READING: Chacón, José A. *Hispanic Notables in the United States of North America.* Albuquerque: Saguaro Publishing Co., 1978; Martínez, Al. *Rising Voices: Profiles of Hispano-American Lives.* New York: New American Library, 1974; Nava, Julian. *Julian Nava: My Mexican American Journey.* Houston: Piñata Books/Arte Público Press, 2002; Nieto, Jess G. "Julian Nava, Our Voice in Mexico." Caminos 1:7 (November 1980) 11-14, 46.

NAVARRO, JOSÉ ANTONIO, 1795–1871. "Co-creator of Texas," merchant, political leader. José Antonio Navarro was born in San Antonio and grew up there and in Saltillo, Coahuila, where he obtained a basic education. When Tejano patriot forces were defeated during Mexico's revolution for independence from Spain, the Navarro family was forced to flee to Louisiana. After three years Navarro returned to San Antonio and at age twenty-one began a mercantile career.

In 1821 Mexico achieved independence and five years later Navarro was elected to the local legislature. At this time he became acquainted with the Anglo *empresario* **Stephen Austin,** with whom he forged a lifelong friendship. During the early 1830s he worked to develop better relations between Mexicans and the flood of Anglo immigrants. A staunch federalist, in 1835 he was a signer of the declaration of conditional Texas independence from the centralist government of Mexico, and helped write the Texas constitution.

Always a mediator, in 1841 he accompanied the ill-starred Santa Fe expedition as a commissioner, was captured, and as a former Mexican citizen was condemned to death for treason. His sentence was later commuted to life imprisonment. When the other expedition members were released by the Mexican government, he was transferred to Mexico's most wretched prison, San Juan Ulúa, where he remained until late 1844, when he managed to escape. Upon his return to Texas and his physical recovery he was elected to the convention called to write the constitution of Texas as a U.S. state.

After the annexation of Texas to the United States, Navarro was elected to the state upper house but declined to run for reelection in 1849 because of increasing discrimination against Mexicanos. He retired to pursue business interests and family obligations. Not even the divisive events leading up to the Civil War were able to draw him out of his retirement. In 1869 he was nominated for the Texas senate, but refused the nomination for health reasons. He died two years later of cancer.

FURTHER READING: Chabot, Frederick. *With the Makers of San Antonio.* San Antonio: Artes Gráficas, 1937; Dawson, Joseph M. *José Antonio Navarro: Co-Creator of Texas.* Waco: Baylor University Press, 1969; Miller, Thomas L. "José Antonio Navarro, 1795–1871." *Journal of Mexican American History* 2 (Spring 1972) 71–89; Navarro, José Antonio. *Defending Mexican Valor in Texas: José Antonio Navarro's Historical Writings, 1853–1857.* Austin: State House Press, 1995.

NEW MEXICO. The settlement of Nuevo México was undertaken at the end of the sixteenth century to forestall possible English control of the supposed Straits of Anián between the Atlantic and the Pacific oceans. Mexican and Spanish settlers under Juan de Oñate trekked up from central Mexico in 1598, and **Santa Fe** was established eleven years later. Throughout the colonial period, settlement of the area was encouraged by Spain because of a persisting fear of English, and later French, intrusion. The area's **mining** potential and the founding of missions among its sedentary Indians also helped attract settlers from central Mexico. As a result, Nuevo México was by far the most populous northern frontier area when the Treaty of **Guadalupe Hidalgo** made the southwest region part of the United States.

In 1848 New Mexico boasted some sixty thousand Mexican inhabitants, about 80 percent of the Mexican population acquired by the United States through the treaty. Unlike California, New Mexico was denied statehood in 1850 by the U.S. Congress to avoid potential political control of this newly acquired area by its large Hispanic American population, which outnumbered the Anglos by twenty-five to one. Instead it became a territory. During the six decades of its territorial era, most upper-level officials were Anglo appointees, but Nuevomexicanos managed to maintain a degree of local political power by electing many Hispanic legislators, judges, and other lesser officials. By 1900 they still had approximately a two-to-one majority in the population. The integration of New Mexico into the national economy, which began in the early 1880s with the arrival of the railroads, attracted considerable capital investment from the East.

The booming economy in mining and expanded commerce provided employment to many Hispanos, and attracted workers from Mexico as well. Numerous Anglo in-migrants also entered New Mexico from nearby states, particularly Texas, Oklahoma, and Kansas. Because of the increasing racial polarization that resulted from this expanded in-migration, Nuevomexicanos had begun to prefer thinking of themselves as **Hispano**s rather than Mexicanos. The latter term soon took on a deeply pejorative connotation, while the former became an indispensable mark of status. Nuevomexicano elites, who earlier had developed a precarious political and economic equilibrium with Anglo arrivals, saw their economic position eroding toward the end of the nineteenth century, as they lost lands, social status, and political influence.

New Mexico finally achieved statehood in 1912, with a constitution that Nuevomexicanos had helped craft. It went far beyond the Guadalupe Hidalgo Treaty by including assurances of raza cultural as well as civil rights. It preserved **bilingual education** and made New Mexico the only state in which Spanish is an official language. These constitutional guarantees and New Mexico's long, unbroken cultural traditions mitigated feelings of loss in ethnic identity among Nuevomexicanos.

As a result of steady Anglo in-migration, by 1930 the Spanish-speaking had lost their numerical majority despite moderate, but increasing immigration from Mexico. However, they were able to retain their strong foothold in local and state elective positions. At the end of the decade, World War II created defense jobs for Nuevomexicanos at Los Alamos, Alamogordo, and White Sands and greatly increased the population of Albuquerque. By 1960 nearly two-thirds of Hispanos lived in urban areas, and had begun to demonstrate a greater interest in their civil rights. However, problem-oriented organizations like the **League of United Latin American Citizens and the Mexican American Legal Defense and Educational Fund** aroused only limited enthusiasm in New Mexico, and the **La Raza Unida Party** had little success there. **Reies López Tijerina,** perhaps the state's most widely known citizen in the 1960s and 1970s, found little favor with Hispanic elites; U.S. senator **Joseph Montoya** of New Mexico publicly denounced him and his **Alianza Federal de Pueblos Libres**.

Nuevomexicanos continued to win elections as lieutenant governors, state legislators, mayors, and lesser government officials, but had only limited success at the governorship level. Most of the Hispanos who ran for governor in the 1900s failed to garner enough votes to win, but in 1974 **Jerry Apodaca** was successful in his bid, as was **Toney Anaya** eight years later. Throughout the entire twentieth century Nuevomexicanos were appointed or elected in considerable numbers to federal, state, and local courts, agencies, and commissions. At one time or another, they have held nearly every state elective office, have served at all levels in the state judiciary, and have won election to the U.S. Senate and House of Representatives. They have also taken increasingly influential and generally conservative leadership roles in the state's Democratic and Republican parties.

Although there is still room for improvement, during the past decades New Mexico has seen considerable increase in the total number of Hispanic elected officials. This change has come about as a result of more intense activism by Hispanic politicians, their greater acceptance within the Democratic and Republican parties, increasing political involvement on the part of Hispanic voters, and their bloc-voting. Today New Mexico continues to have a larger percentage of Hispanics in its population than any other state—more than 36 percent. Demographic changes have led to increased tensions because of intense and more widespread Nuevomexicano concerns about political influence and power.

While advancing in political participation and importance, over the years Nuevomexicanos have maintained and continued to develop a Latino culture unique in the Southwest. Because there was less economic opportunity in New Mexico than in California and Texas, there was never a heavy immigration from Mexico, even after 1900, to strongly exert its cultural influence on Hispanos. As a result, until the mid-twentieth century New Mexico's rural areas and numerous small villages retained much of their nineteenth-century ambience and culture despite some changes.

In the second half of the nineteenth century, Archbishop Lamy's French and Italian priests imported European religious art to replace the classic *retablos* and *bultos* of Nuevomexicano artisans in the churches of larger towns. The market for folk art also declined among the general population. After the 1880s, locally made art objects in many homes were replaced by the new commercially produced art brought from the East by the railroads. However, some religious folk art continued to be fostered by *cofradías* and some businesses, employing local artists.

A renewed interest in and greater appreciation of the local folk arts began to develop at the beginning of the 1920s with the arrival of Anglo artists, who established themselves in Taos and Santa Fe. In 1929 they founded the Spanish Colonial Arts Society to promote traditional Nuevomexicano arts, and six years later La Sociedad Folklórica was established in Santa Fe. In the late 1920s the New Mexico Department of Vocational Education began encouraging the revival of folk arts. By 1936 there were some forty community vocational schools, funded by the New Deal's Works Progress Administration (WPA). The Federal Art Project of the WPA provided employment to many Nuevomexicano artisans and artists who collected and created regional arts. The results of their visual arts projects are still evident in various public buildings.

The Chicano **movimiento** of the 1960s and 1970s added to the focus on Nuevomexicano folk art and encouraged the performing as well as visual arts. There was some expansion of the theater in New Mexico, much of it in connection with the universities and much of it ephemeral. In 1965 the National Endowment for the Arts was established to provide grants and fellowships to artists in various fields. The 1970s and 1980s saw an revived interest in *santos*, and the last two decades of the century witnessed the development of many fine carvers, both men and women. In 1989 the Museum of International Folk Art, established in Albuquerque thirty-six years earlier, opened its large Hispanic Heritage wing. Three years later some two hundred local artisans, scholars, and artists made presentations illustrating various aspects of Nuevomexicano culture at the Smithsonian Institution's annual Folk Life Festival in Washington, D.C.

FURTHER READING: Cummings, Richard M. *Grito! Reies Tijerina and the New Mexico Land Grant War of 1967.* Indianapolis: Bobbs-Merrill, 1970; Fincher, Ernest B. *Spanish-Americans As a Political Factor in New Mexico, 1912–1950.* Reprint. New York: Arno Press, 1974; Gandert, Miguel A. *Nuevo México profundo: Rituals of an Indo-Hispanic Homeland.* Santa Fe: Museum of New Mexico Press, 2000; García, F. Chris. "New Mexico: Urban Politics in a State of Varied Political Cultures." In *Politics in the Urban Southwest,* edited by Robert D. Wrinkle. Albuquerque: University of New Mexico, Division of Government Research, 1971; Gonzales-Berry, Erlinda, and David R. Maciel. *The Contested Homeland: A Chicano History of New Mexico.* Albuquerque: University of New Mexico Press, 2000; Lomelí, Francisco A., Victor A. Sorell, and Genaro M. Padilla, eds. *Nuevomexicano Cultural Legacy: Forms, Agencies, and Discourse.* Albuquerque: University of New Mexico Press, 2002; Montaño, Mary. *Tradiciones nuevomexicanas; Hispanic Arts and Culture of New Mexico.* Albuquerque: University of New Mexico Press, 2001; Montgomery, Charles. *The Spanish Redemption: Heritage, Power, and Loss on New Mexico's Upper Rio Grande.* Berkeley: University of California Press, 2002; *The New Mexican Hispano.* Reprint. New York: Arno Press, 1974; Nunn, Tey Mariana. *Sin nombre: Hispana and Hispano Artists of the New Deal Era.* Albuquerque: University of New Mexico Press, 2001; Ortiz, Roxanne Dunbar. *Roots of Resistance: Land Tenure in New Mexico, 1680–1980.* Chicano Studies Center, University of California at Los Angeles, 1980; Rosenbaum, Robert J. *Mexicano versus Americano: A Study of Hispanic-American Resistance to Anglo-American Control in New Mexico Territory.* Austin: University of Texas Press, 1972; Sánchez, George I. *Forgotten People: A Study of New Mexicans.* Albuquerque: University of New Mexico Press, 1996 (1940); Simmons, Marc. *New Mexico: An Interpretive History.* Albuquerque: University of New Mexico Press, 1988.

NOGALES, LUIS, 1943– . Businessman, lawyer. Luis Nogales was the son of migrant farm workers, and was born in the border town of Calexico. He grew up and received his early education there; in summer he worked in the fields with the family. After high school, a scholarship took him to San Diego State, where his scholastic record in political science won him admission to the Stanford University law school in 1966. At Stanford he became deeply involved in minority concerns and was appointed advisor to the president before he received his law degree in 1969. Three years later he left Stanford to accept a one-year appointment as a White House fellow.

From Washington, Nogales returned to southern California, where he served for five years as legal counsel for Los Angeles station KTLA; from there he advanced to executive vice president and board member of Golden West Broadcasters, only to be fired three years later in a policy disagreement. In 1981 he joined the consulting firm of Fleischman-Hilliard as vice president of its Hispanic division. Two years later he went to work for United Press International (UPI), where he held serially the positions of executive vice president, chairman of the executive committee, and then general manager. Although as manager he turned the UPI's finances around, he was fired in March 1985. The next day he was back in charge and those who fired him were out; in July he resigned. Two years later he was briefly president of Univisión, the Spanish language television network, and then became Chief executive officer of Embarcadero Media. Currently he is president of Nogales Partners, a Los Angeles media company.

From 1988 to 1998 Nogales served on the Stanford University Board of Trustees. He is also a board member of the Ford Foundation as well as various large companies, including the Southern California Edison Company. A tireless worker in both the community and the business world, he has served as national chairman of the **Mexican American Legal Defense and Educational Fund** and as advisor to United Way of America. In July 2000 he was elected to the board of the J. Paul Getty Trust.

FURTHER READING: Díaz, Tom. "Man on Top of a Roller Coaster." *Hispanic Review of Business* (October 1984); "Luis Nogales Moves to UPI." *Caminos* 4:7 (July–August 1983) 44; Tardiff, Joseph C., and L. Mpho Mabunda, eds. *Dictionary of Hispanic Biography*. Detroit: Gale Research, 1996.

NOVARRO, RAMÓN, 1899–1968. Actor. Novarro was born José Ramón Gil Samaniego into a professional family in the Mexican mining town of Durango. To escape the Mexican revolution and Pancho Villa's forces, in 1913 his dentist father took his wife and children to Los Angeles. Because his father was too ill to work, Ramón took jobs as a grocery clerk, theater usher, singer, and dancer. His dancing ability brought him to the attention of leading Hollywood director Rex Ingraham, who hired him in the early 1920s for *The Prisoner of Zenda*. The film was a big hit and was followed by starring roles for Novarro in several other successful films. However, his acting career failed to take off because Rudolf Valentino and John Gilbert had already preempted the niche of Hollywood's male Latino sex symbols. Nevertheless, in the second half of the 1920s he continued to be a box office draw of considerable magnitude. The classic epic *Ben Hur* in 1926 probably marked the high point of his film career. Then came the talkies and the decline of the lush romantic films of the early 1920s.

Novarro was able to survive the changes partly because of his ability as a singer. In 1932 he costarred with Greta Garbo in *Mata Hari*, then in 1933 with Helen Hayes in *The Son-Daughter*, and in 1934 he made what some critics felt was his best film, *The Cat and the Fiddle*. After the mid-1930s Novarro, miffed with Hollywood, made films in Mexico and Italy and appeared on stage and in concert. He also made guest appearances in TV shows while writing, painting, and managing his real estate holdings in California and Mexico. His last performance in films, a supporting role to Sophia Loren in *Heller in Pink Tights*, 1960, received good reviews. Eight years later he was bludgeoned to death in his home by a young man he had picked up.

FURTHER READING: Ellenberger, Allan R. *Ramón Novarro: A Biography of the Silent Film Idol, 1899–1968*. Jefferson, N.C.: McFarland, 1999; Shipman, David. *The Great Movie Stars: The Golden Years*. New York: Hill & Wang, 1979; Soares, Andre. *Beyond Paradise: The Life of Ramon Novarro*. New York: St. Martin's Press, 2002.

NUEVOMEXICANO. The term *Nuevomexicano* is used to refer to an inhabitant of Nuevo México during the colonial and Mexican eras. Today it often describes a New Mexican descended from one of the colonial Spanish-Mexican families. More broadly, it may be used to refer any New Mexican citizen of Mexican cultural background.

OBLEDO, MARIO GUERRA, 1932–. Lawyer, civil rights leader. Mario Obledo was born in San Antonio, Texas, the son of Mexican immigrant parents. As a youth he took on various jobs to help support the poverty-stricken family. Studying pharmacology, he worked his way through college, interrupted by four years of service in the navy during the Korean conflict. After receiving his B.S. degree he was employed as a pharmacist while he studied law at St. Mary's University in San Antonio.

In 1965 Obledo was appointed as an assistant attorney general for the state of Texas. Three years later he became president and general counsel of the **Mexican American Legal Defense and Educational Fund** (MALDEF), which he had helped establish. He also was active in the Southwest Voter Registration Education Project and the **League of United Latin American Citizens** (LULAC). During his tenure in MALDEF he supervised civil rights litigation, and toward the end of his presidency began the practice of taking cases to the U.S. Supreme Court on constitutional grounds, basing arguments heavily on Fourteenth Amendment guarantees.

While on the faculty of Harvard Law School, in 1975 Obledo was named Secretary of the Department of Health and Welfare for the state of California, to which MALDEF's headquarters had been moved. Seven years later he resigned to make what turned out to be an unsuccessful bid to become the Democratic party's candidate for governor. In 1983 he was elected national president of LULAC, in which he had long been active and had held important positions. After his two-year term in office, he stepped down to enter private law practice in Sacramento, although he retained his interest in Chicano concerns.

In 1998 the elder statesman was awarded the Presidential Medal of Freedom by President Bill Clinton and, despite his infirmities, also returned to activism. His provocative comments about Taco Bell's Chihuahua and a billboard near Blythe, California, and threats encouraging civil disobedience found the Mexican American community divided. Many felt this 1960s-type activism was no longer the path to follow at the end of the century. The former chairman of Jesse Jackson's Rainbow Coalition for four years, he is currently president of California Coalition of Hispanic Organizations, an umbrella organization for about fifty advocacy groups.

FURTHER READING: "A Close Look at Mario Obledo." *Latino* 54:5 (August–Sept. 1983) 10; Muñoz, Carlos Jr. *Youth, Identity, Power: The Chicano Movement.* New York: Verso, 1989; Reyes, David. "Seasoned Activist's Passions Burn Bright Again." *Los Angeles Times* (2 August 1998) A3; Whisler, Kirk. "Mario Obledo." *Caminos* 3:4 (April 1982) 18–20; *Who's Who among Hispanic Americans,* 1994–1995. Detroit: Gale Research, 1994.

OCHOA, ELLEN, 1958– . Engineer, astronaut. Ellen Ochoa was born in Los Angeles and grew up in La Mesa in a family atmosphere in which education was valued highly and individual intellectual pursuit was encouraged. In grade and high school she excelled in all her studies, but gravitated toward mathematics and the sciences. From high school she entered San Diego State University, where she tried various majors and settled on physics. After completing her B.S. in physics in 1980 she went to Stanford University, where she earned her M.S. degree in electrical engineering in the following year. Aided by a fellowship, she obtained her doctorate in electrical engineering in 1985, specializing in the use of photo-refractive crystals to filter images from space. She then accepted a position as a research engineer at Sandia National Laboratories, where she continued her work on space imaging. After three years with Sandia, Dr. Ochoa moved to Ames Research Center as part of a team studying optical recognition systems. Six months later she was appointed head of the Intelligent Systems Technology Branch, leading a team of thirty-five scientists and engineers.

Ever since her student days Ochoa had been interested in the U.S. astronaut program. In 1985 she was one of two thousand who applied for admission to the NASA astronaut school, two years later made it to the top ten finalists, and in 1990 was one of twenty-three chosen for astronaut training. In 1993 she was selected as a member of the five-person crew of the space shuttle *Discovery* on its sixteenth flight, the first Hispana in NASA history. Part of a long-term study of solar energy, her task during the nine days in space was demanding but also gratifying. In 1994 she spent ten days aboard the space shuttle *Atlantis* in her second space mission. Five years later she was flight engineer and mission

Astronaut Ellen Ochoa. © NASA.

specialist of the *Discovery*'s ten-day trip into space, her third flight. Altogether she has spent over seven hundred hours in space. She continues to be active in the NASA program in technical support positions.

Ochoa holds a number of patents in the field of optical imaging and is the author of numerous papers presented at conferences and published in professional journals. Her contributions to the U.S. space program have won her five medals and several other awards. Among them are the Outstanding Leadership Medal from NASA in 1995 and the Exceptional Service Medal two years later. Considered an outstanding role model for young Chicanas, she takes that position and honor seriously. Encouraging them in talks and conferences to complete their educations, she continues to make way for them in the new frontiers of science.

FURTHER READING: "Biographical Data." Houston: Lyndon B. Johnson Space Center, 1993; "Dr. Ellen Ochoa: Education . . . The Stepping Stone to the Stars." *Hispanic Times* (Spring 2002) 24–25; "Ellen Ochoa: Not Even the Sky's the Limit." *Hispanic Engineer* 6:3 (Fall 1990) 22–25; "New Astronaut's Higher Profile an Opportunity." *Houston Post* (23 July 1990) A9–A10; Telgen, Diane, and Jim Kamp, eds. *Notable Hispanic American Women.* Detroit: Gale Research, 1993.

OCHOA, ESTEBAN, 1831–1888. Entrepreneur, civic leader. Esteban Ochoa was born in the Mexican state of Chihuahua to a leading ranching and mining family. As the Santa Fe trade increased in importance, his father, Jesús, decided to move to Nuevo México, the southern axis of that trade. As a result, Esteban was sent to Missouri to learn English and the freighting business. Having become a prominent civic leader by the late 1850s, he chaired a committee working to create an **Arizona** Territory separate from New Mexico.

When southern Arizona was occupied by southern troops during the Civil War, Ochoa refused to take an oath of allegiance to the Confederate States of America and left **Tucson**, knowing his businesses would be confiscated. After northern troops reoccupied Tucson he returned, recovered most of his property, and soon joined an Anglo freighter to create Tully, Ochoa and Company. As a partner in a highly successful freighting business, Ochoa became the widely accepted spokesman for the Spanish-speaking population of southern Arizona.

Ochoa was twice elected to the territorial legislature in the 1860s and 1870s and was elected mayor of Tucson in 1875. As a legislator he took a leading role in creating Arizona's public school system and donated the land on which Tucson's first public school was built. During the 1880s the newly arrived **railroads** cut deeply into the freighting business, and his fortunes declined as he failed to adapt to the new national economy. He died of pneumonia at age fifty-seven, relatively poor but highly respected in the Southwest for his integrity and moral rectitude.

FURTHER READING: Gonzales, Manuel G. *The Hispanic Elite of the Southwest.* El Paso: Texas Western Press, 1989; Lockwood, Frank C. *Pioneer Portraits.* Tucson:

University of Arizona Press, 1968; Meier, Matt S. "Esteban Ochoa, Enterpriser." *Journal of the West* 25:1 (January 1986) 15–21; Officer, James E. *Hispanic Arizona, 1536–1856.* Tucson: University of Arizona Press, 1987; Sheridan, Thomas E. *Los Tucsonenses: The Mexican Community in Tucson, 1854–1941.* Tucson: University of Arizona Press, 1986.

OFFICE OF ECONOMIC OPPORTUNITY. The OEO was an agency in President Lyndon Johnson's War on Poverty program. It oversaw programs created as a result of the Economic Opportunity Act of 1964, such as the Job Corps and VISTA, Volunteers in Service to America. Using federal funds, it helped local community agencies mobilize resources to fight unemployment and poverty.

FURTHER READING: Anderson, James E. "Coordinating The War on Poverty." *Policy Studies Journal* 2:3 (1974) 174–179; Pycior, Julie Leininger. *LBJ & Mexican Americans: The Paradox of Power.* Austin: University of Texas Press, 1997.

OFFICE OF INTER-AMERICAN AFFAIRS. The Office was established in mid-1941 primarily to work toward reducing discrimination against Mexican Americans, as a part of President Franklin D. Roosevelt's Good Neighbor policy. During World War II it was directed by Nelson Rockefeller, with **Carey McWilliams** as head of the Spanish-Speaking Peoples Division. McWilliams created workshops and held conferences in the Southwest, but was never able to fully implement his ideas. At the end of the war President Harry Truman closed down the Office, transferring some of its functions to other government agencies.

FURTHER READING: Haines, Gerald K. "Under the Eagle's Wing: The Franklin Roosevelt Administration Forges an American Hemisphere." *Diplomatic History* 1:4 (1977) 373–388.

OLIVÁREZ, GRACIELA, 1928–1987. Social activist. At sixteen Graciela Olivárez dropped out of her Arizona high school, but continued her education in a Phoenix business school. After graduation she became the city's first female disc jockey, a position that soon led to her selection as the women's program director for Spanish language station KIFN. Her subsequent organizational work in the community led her to active involvement in the Chicano civil rights movement during the 1960s.

At a Southwest civil rights conference Graciela so impressed Theodore Hesburgh, the president of Notre Dame University, that he invited her to study law at that institution. In 1970, at age forty-two, she became the first woman to receive a law degree from Notre Dame. She returned to the Southwest, where she taught law at the University of New Mexico and held leadership positions in several government agencies while continuing her civil rights involvement. As a result of her strong advocacy of civil rights, in 1977 she was named director of the Community Services Administration by President Jimmy Carter. Three years later she resigned to become a senior consultant for a national service organization, United Way of America.

In 1982 Olivárez was named to a bipartisan federal board to oversee enforcement of legislation prohibiting discrimination based on race, ethnicity, age, sex, or religion. She also served on the boards of several nationwide organizations devoted to protecting and advancing civil rights, including Common Cause. For the last three years of her life she headed a consultant and public relations firm in Albuquerque. A lifetime spent helping the weak and unprotected resulted in her receiving numerous honorific awards.

FURTHER READING: Breiter, Toni. "Dr. Oliverez [sic] Awarded Honorary Law Degree." *Agenda* 8:4 (July–August 1978) 45; Hardy, Gayle J., ed. *American Women Civil Rights Activists.* Jefferson, N.C.: McFarland & Co., 1993; "An Interview with Graciela Olivárez." *Hispanic Business* (March 1980) 8–10, 12–13; Telgen, Diane, and Jim Kamp, eds. *Latinas! Women of Achievement.* Detroit: Visible Ink Press, 1996; Velez, Larry. "Washington's Top Advocate for the Poor." *Nuestro* (June–July 1979) 33; *Who's Who in America, 1980–1981.* Chicago: Marquis, 1980.

OLMOS, EDWARD JAMES, 1947– . Actor, writer, director, producer. Edward Olmos was born in Boyle Heights, East Los Angeles. After his parents divorced he lived with his mother in Montebello, California, where he attended high school. As a teenager he was deeply interested in baseball, but in high school his interest switched from baseball to music and in the mid-1960s he formed a band that he named Eddie and the Pacific Ocean. After graduating from East Los Angeles Junior College with an A.A. in sociology, he studied dance and drama at California State University, Los Angeles, moving gradually from music to acting.

To improve his acting skills Olmos participated in workshops and worked in local experimental theaters while he earned a livelihood as a furniture deliverer. Meanwhile he also pursued a film career, first with walk-on parts and then with minor roles in television sitcoms. In 1978 he was selected, out of some three hundred applicants, for the role of El Pachuco in Luis Valdez's play *Zoot Suit.* His portrayal won him several awards and nomination for a Tony, and the outstanding success of the play gave his acting career a rocket boost. As a result he obtained supporting movie roles, and in 1982 his portrayal of Gregorio Cortez in a television film gave him another breakthrough advance in his career. Two years later his role as Martin Castillo in the TV series *Miami Vice* won him an Emmy and a Golden Globe award. Altogether he has been nominated for three Emmys, an Oscar, and a Tony.

After *Miami Vice* Olmos played Jaime Escalante in the film *Stand and Deliver,* a performance that won him a Best Actor nomination in 1989. During the 1990s he demonstrated his acting abilities by appearing in widely varied roles in film and television movies that illuminated his societal concerns, the best of which was *My Family/Mi Familia.* YOY Productions, a company he and Robert Young formed, has given him the opportunity to produce and direct films that he believes in. He is outspoken on issues affecting the Latino community, condemning Eurocentrism in school curricula and rancorous organizations like **English Only**. In 1988 *Time* magazine featured him on its

Edward James Olmos (right) with Harrison Ford in *Blade Runner*, 1982. © The Kobal Collection/Ladd Company/Warner Brothers.

cover, and two years later a *Hispanic* magazine poll found him to be the Most Influential Latino. In 2000 he became the seventh person to be honored with a plaque on the Latino Walk of Fame.

In August 2001 Olmos was arrested and jailed for trespassing on U.S. Navy land in protest against the Navy's use of the Puerto Rican island of Vieques for war games.

FURTHER READING: Aufderheide, Pat. "An Actor Turns Activist." *Mother Jones* 8:9 (November 1983) 60; Breiter, Toni. "Eddie Olmos and the 'Ballad of Gregorio Cortez.'" *Nuestro* (May 1983) 14-19; *Current Biography, 1992.* New York: H. W. Wilson Co., 1992; Díaz, Katharine A. "Man of Influence." *Hispanic* (Sept. 2000) 22–23, 25, 27; Montane, Diana. "Edward James Olmos." *Vista* 1:1 (8 September 1985) 8–12; Mooney, Louise, ed. *Newsmakers: The People behind Today's Headlines.* Detroit: Gale Research, 1990; "Olmos Sentenced in Vieques Protest." *The San Diego Union-Tribune* (11 August 2001) A9; Reyes, Luis, and Peter Rubie. *Hispanics in Hollywood: A Celebration of 100 Years in Film and Television.* Hollywood: Lone Eagle, 2000.

OPEN BORDER. The concept of an immigration policy in which there is little restriction against foreigners who wish to work in the United States. It was essentially the policy, or absence thereof, of the United States until the mid-1920s when the U.S. Congress created the Border Patrol. Until then Mexicans freely crossed and recrossed the border, to visit and to work.

OPERATION WETBACK, 1954–1955. Operation Wetback resulted from demands for stricter enforcement of immigration legislation and for the expulsion from the United States of all **undocumented** aliens. The post–World War II decade saw a rapid increase in undocumented Mexican workers, the result of a ballooning demand for cheap labor by western agribusiness and light industry on the border with Mexico.

In the atmosphere of Senator Joseph McCarthy's red-baiting during the early 1950s, U.S. Attorney General Herbert Brownell ordered a massive roundup and deportation of undocumented aliens, allegedly in order to protect the United States from communist infiltration. Mobile forces were organized on a military basis under retired general Joseph Swing. To encourage voluntary **repatriation** the coming dragnet operation was announced in May 1954. The Special Mobile Force began its work in California, moved to Texas, and then went on to large urban centers in the states of Illinois, Missouri, and Washington. Over one million Mexicanos were rounded up and sent across the border. The commonplace use of excessive force and intimidation in the process routinely ignored the civil and human rights of Mexican Americans. American-born children saw one or both parents seized, undocumented husbands were separated from their American wives and families, and American citizens were expelled.

The Attorney General's office announced that the deportations had solved the problem of undocumented aliens; however, the results proved temporary. A decade later the number of illegal entrants again soared as the **bracero** program was terminated in 1964, while the demand for cheap labor continued in agriculture and industry, especially in the Southwest.

FURTHER READING: García, Juan Ramón. *Operation Wetback: The Mass Deportation of Undocumented Workers in 1954.* Westport, Conn.: Greenwood Press, 1980; Hayes, Edward F. et al. "Operation Wetback: Impact on the Border States." *Employment Security Review* 22:3 (March 1955) 16–21. ; Langham, Thomas C. "Federal Regulation of Border Labor: Operation Wetback and the Wetback Bills." *Journal of Borderlands Studies* 7:1 (Spring 1992) 81–91.

ORD, ANGUSTIAS DE LA GUERRA, 1815–1880. Historian. Born in San Diego, Angustias de la Guerra came to Santa Barbara, Alta California, while still an infant. There she received the typically meager education available to girls on Mexico's northern frontier in the early nineteenth century. Married at fifteen to an important Mexican government official, she spent a quarter of a century in Monterey, the capital and political center of Alta California. Three years after her husband's death in 1853, she married a U.S. army doctor, James L. Ord. In 1878 she recalled, for an assistant of historian Hubert Howe Bancroft, her memories of California's turbulent history from her childhood to the Treaty of Guadalupe Hidalgo. Her memoirs were published in 1956 under the title *Occurrences in Hispanic California.*

FURTHER READING: Ord, Angustias de la Guerra. *Occurrences in Hispanic California.* Washington, D.C.: Academy of American Franciscan History, 1956; Sánchez,

Rosaura. *Telling Identities: The California Testimonios.* Minneapolis: University of Minnesota Press, 1995; Scanlon, Jennifer, and Sharon Cosner. *American Women Historians, 1700s–1990s.* Westport, Conn.: Greenwood Press, 1996.

ORDER SONS OF AMERICA. Founded in San Antonio, Texas in 1921, the Order Sons of America (Orden Hijos de América) was one of the first politically oriented Mexican American organizations. It developed out of the greater consciousness among World War I veterans about the benefits and duties of their U.S. citizenship and an increased awareness of the potential gains from political action. After nearly a decade of organizing and recruitment among middle-class Mexican Americans, it became the heart of an expanded organization, the **League of United Latin American Citizens,** which it helped create in Corpus Christi in 1929.

FURTHER READING: Márquez, Benjamín. *LULAC: The Evolution of a Mexican American Political Organization.* Austin: University of Texas Press, 1993; Tyler, Ron, ed. *Handbook of Texas,* vol. 4 Austin: Texas State Historical Association, 1996.

ORENDAIN, ANTONIO, 1930– . Labor organizer. Antonio Orendain was born in the Mexican state of Jalisco and came to California in 1950. In the following year he became acquainted with **Fred Ross, Sr.** and **César Chávez,** who were developing the **Community Service Organization** (CSO) in southern California. For the next decade he worked for the CSO under Chávez, mostly in voter registration. In 1962 he left the CSO to help Chávez establish and organize what later became the **United Farm Workers** (UFW).

Orendain had a leadership role in the **Delano grape strike.** At the beginning of the strike he headed the grape boycott in the Chicago area and then returned to take part in the 1966 march to Sacramento. Later he was sent to Texas by Chávez to persuade Mexicanos not to accept employment as strikebreakers in the California vineyards. In Texas he began to aggressively organize farm workers in spite of Chávez's orders to the contrary, and was recalled to California.

Back in California, Orendain started a radio news program in Spanish for farm workers. After two years of success he was again sent to Texas in 1969. With the help of a small grant he created, produced, and hosted a weekly radio program called "La Voz del Campesino," similar to his California newscast. Chávez and Orendain, both men of strongly held convictions, finally split over the question of the timeliness of a farm workers' strike in Texas and Orendain's confrontational and publicity-oriented strike tactics.

Orendain left the UFW in 1975 to create his own local organization, the Texas Farm Workers Union (TFWU). Two years later he led a march of hundreds from the Rio Grande Valley to Austin (and from there to Washington, D.C.), where Governor Dolph Briscoe met them but rejected their demands for collective bargaining legislation. In spite of Orendain's dedicated leadership, the TFWU achieved little. Texas farm workers seemed to be wanting in motivation and were never able to develop sufficient liberal support. Orendain, while an excellent leader in many ways, lacked the charisma of a César Chávez.

In 1982 Orendain stepped down as director of the TFWU. During the 1980s he worked as a consultant and organizer for various unions. In 1990 he took a job as consultant for the Hidalgo County Juvenile Probation Department while continuing his concerns about discriminatory labor practices through a radio program called "Contrapunto." He still promotes the rights of labor but is not currently associated with any particular union.

FURTHER READING: García, Ignacio M. "The Many Battles of Antonio Orendain." *Nuestro* (November 1979) 25–29; Holly, Joe. "The Texas Farmworkers' Split." *The Texas Observer* 73:8 (17 April 1981) 4–8; Martínez, Oscar J. *Border People: Life and Society in the U.S.-Mexico Borderlands.* Tucson: University of Arizona Press, 1994; *Who's Who among Hispanic Americans, 1994–1995.* Detroit: Gale Research, 1994.

ORGANIZATIONS. During the past two centuries Mexican Americans have created numerous organizations with a multiplicity of political, economic, and social goals. Most of these groups were organized at the local level, based on shared cultural values: language, religion, ethnic symbols, and historical experience in the United States. Most were formed as a response to an immediate crisis and declined when the crisis passed.

In the second half of the nineteenth century, Mexicano organizations were nearly all *mutualistas*, self-help groups that provided basic insurance and had, at best, limited goals of economic or social betterment. In the late 1800s this pattern began to change, with a few groups like **Gorras Blancas** (White Caps) acting more aggressively in defense of economic rights, primarily rights to land. Until the 1900s severe discrimination and bigotry made most Mexican American reformist goals seem unachievable.

Continued denial of participation in the American mainstream caused Mexican American veterans returning from World War I to begin organizing civic clubs to make *la raza* more aware of its rights. In Texas, veterans created the first politically-oriented groups, like the **Order Sons of America** in 1921; eight years later the Sons led to founding the **League of United Latin American Citizens** (LULAC). Chicanas also participated in the struggle for ethnic and political equality. They established women's auxiliaries to male-dominated organizations and founded La Sociedad Protectora Mexicana, the Mexican American Civic Council, and El Comité Mexicano Contra El Racismo. Generally middle-class in their orientation, these groups tended to stress U.S. citizenship, the learning and use of English, and assimilation. Politically, most of them were low-key and nonpartisan.

After World War II a new Mexican American generation of politicized veterans led in the creation of organizations that advocated a more active participation in the political process. They refused to accept continuing discrimination, and many rejected the politics of accommodation. They began to organize political associations, most of which emphasized civil rights as well as social and economic improvement. The new leaders were usually more militant, and the struggle was thereby intensified.

The post–World War II era also saw a noticeable trend toward organizational participation by younger community leaders and students. There was an increase in self-help groups and also in business and professional associations with concerns about civil and social rights. Among these new organizations were the **Community Service Organization**, 1947; the **American G.I. Forum**, 1947; the Council of Mexican American Affairs, 1953; **Mexican American Political Association**, 1959; the **Political Association of Spanish Speaking Organizations**, 1960; the **Mexican American Legal Defense and Educational Fund**, 1968; **National Association of Latino Elected and Appointed Officials**, 1975; and numerous student groups that consolidated into the **Movimiento Estudiantil de Chicanos de Aztlán** in 1969.

In the immediate postwar decades some earlier organizations of middle-class orientation like LULAC and the Unity Leagues began to put less stress on earlier assimilationist goals and to devote greater attention and resources to civil rights problems. Local community groups like **United Neighborhoods Organization** and **Communities Organized for Public Service** received a positive jolt from the Chicano movimiento. Despite repeated efforts to create truly national umbrella groups, only the **National Council of La Raza** succeeded.

Between the mid-1960s and 1970s the organizational movement was centered in Texas and California, where intense large-scale political organizing took place. The resulting groups, which usually developed around charismatic regional leaders, typically were deficient in organizational structure. The development of organizations was at times hindered by the view of many youthful activists that structure was inherently elitist. By the mid-1970s ideological disagreements, personality conflicts, and FBI surveillance, infiltration, and use of agents provocateurs had greatly weakened many smaller militant groups.

The creation of **La Raza Unida Party** (LRUP) in 1970 seemed at the time to signal the beginning of more effective political action by Mexican Americans through organization. However, LRUP failed to fulfill its early promise. However, it did pressure both the Democratic and Republican parties to be more responsive to Mexican American concerns. Ultimately it also led to the organizing of **Mexican American Democrats** (MAD), which assumed an increasingly important role in the Texas Democratic party. Beginning in the late 1970s MAD leaders initiated energetic membership and get-out-the-vote drives.

In the 1980s and early 1990s a strong nationwide move to the right led to the resurgence of older, more moderate groups like LULAC and the American G.I. Forum. Increasingly the basic goal of political empowerment became a more paramount concern than earlier demands for self-determination and cultural nationalism. This trend toward working within the system was further advanced by the enlarged *raza* middle class, which increasingly favored electoral politics as the principal road to its economic and social goals.

FURTHER READING: Alvarez, Salvador. "Mexican-American Community Organizations." *El Grito* 4:3 (Spring 1971) 68–77; Briegel, Kaye. "The Development of Mexican American Organizations." In *The Mexican-Americans: An Awakening Minority*, edited by Manuel P. Servín. Beverly Hills, Calif.: Glencoe Press, 1970; Del Castillo, Adelaida R. "Mexican Women in Organization." In *Mexican Women in the United States: Struggles Past and Present*, edited by Magdalena Mora and Adelaida R. Del Castillo. Los Angeles: University of California, Chicano Studies Research Center, 1980; Gómez-Quiñones, Juan. *Roots of Chicano Politics, 1600–1940*. Albuquerque: University of New Mexico Press, 1994; Gonzales, Sylvia A. *Hispanic American Voluntary Organizations*. Westport, Conn.: Greenwood Press, 1985; Márquez, Benjamin. *Constructing Identities in Mexican American Political Organizations: Choosing Issues, Taking Sides*. Austin: University of Texas Press, 2003; Martínez, Douglas. "Overview: Hispanic Organizations, Meeting the Challenge of the 1980s." *La Luz* 8:6 (February–March 1980) 8–9, 43; Rodríguez, Roy C. *Mexican-American Civic Organizations: Political Participation and Political Attitudes*. San Francisco, Calif.: R&E Research Associates, 1978; Vigil, Maurilio E. *Hispanics in American Politics: The Search for Political Power*. Lanham, Md.: University Press of America, 1987.

ORTEGA, KATHERINE D., 1934– . U.S. Treasurer, banker, businesswoman. Born in Tularosa, New Mexico, Katherine Ortega grew up and received her early education there. She showed an aptitude for and interest in mathematics in school and studied accounting in high school. Upon graduation she worked in a bank for two years to finance her college education. Majoring in economics and business, she graduated with honors in 1957 and went to work for a Roswell oil company. With a sister she later opened an accounting firm in Alamogordo.

In the second half of the 1960s Ortega moved to Los Angeles, California. In 1972 she became a vice-president in the Pan American National Bank, and three years later was named director and president of the Santa Ana State Bank, becoming California's first female bank president. In 1979 she returned to New Mexico and completed her training to become a certified public accountant.

Coming from a staunch Republican family and as a result active in Republican politics since her college days, at the beginning of the 1980s Ortega was appointed to the President's Advisory Committee on Small and Minority Business by then-President Reagan. In 1983 she was named Treasurer of the United States by Ronald Reagan, and in the next year was selected to deliver the keynote address at the Republican national convention. She served six years as Treasurer and then left to return to the business world. After years of mostly self-employment she is now semiretired. She has been the recipient of various honors from business groups and has served on the boards of several corporations. She has also been the recipient of honorary university degrees.

FURTHER READING: Saikowski, Charlotte. "GOP Keynoter Radiates Self-Help Ideal." *Christian Science Monitor* (17 August 1984); Telgen, Diane, and Jim Kamp, eds. *Notable Hispanic American Women*. Detroit: Gale Research, 1993; Wittenauer, Cheryl. "Making Money in Washington." *Hispanic Business* (May 1984) 16, 36.

ORTEGO Y GASCA, FELIPE D., 1926– . Educator, publisher, poet. Felipe Ortego was born in the Chicago suburbs and grew up in Pittsburgh. He dropped out of high school to work at various jobs, and served in the Marines from 1944 to 1947. He used the G.I. Bill to continue his education but then partially interrupted it to serve nine years in the Air Force. Meanwhile, he continued his education, earning his B.A. from Texas Western College (now the University of Texas, El Paso—UTEP) in 1959. Resigning from the military as a captain, he received his M.A. in 1966 at UTEP and five years later completed his doctorate at the University of New Mexico. During this time he also taught in the English department at UTEP and was founding director of UTEP's Chicano Studies program. In 1972 he was named senior editor of the Hispanic magazine *La Luz*.

In the early 1970s Ortego accepted a position as assistant to the president of Denver's Metropolitan State College and then moved to California as a member of San Jose State University's newly established Mexican American Graduate Studies department. A decade later he was named chairman of the Hispanic Foundation, a Washington-based research organization, and then became editor in chief, and in 1991 the publisher, of the *National Hispanic Reporter*. Meanwhile he had also become associate publisher of the magazine *La Luz*. In the 1990s he taught at Texas Woman's University and Sul Ross State University. He now is semiretired and lives in Kingsville, Texas.

In addition to his other activities, Felipe Ortego has been a very productive scholar, with some 150 poems, short stories, essays, and reviews to his credit as well as several books. He has received a number of notable awards.

FURTHER READING: *Directory of American Scholars*, 6th ed. New York: R. R. Bowker, 1974; Martínez, Julio A. *Chicano Scholars and Writers: A Bio-Bibliographical Directory*. Metuchen, N.J.: Te Scarecrow Press, 1979; *Who's Who among Hispanic Americans, 1994–95*. Detroit: Gale Research, 1994.

ORTIZ, FRANK V., JR., 1926– . Ambassador. Francis Ortiz was born, grew up, and received his early education in Santa Fe, New Mexico. He served in the army Air Force during the last two years of World War II and earned his B.S. at Georgetown University in 1950. From Georgetown he entered the Foreign Service and continued his postgraduate education while serving in various U.S. embassies. In 1961 he was appointed special assistant to the U.S. ambassador to Mexico, and two years later returned to Washington to head the State Department's Spanish affairs section.

From 1967 to 1970 Ortiz was stationed in the U.S. embassy at Lima, Peru and then three years in Montevideo, Uruguay, after which he returned to Washington as the State Department country director for Argentina,

Uruguay, and Paraguay. In 1977 he was appointed U.S. ambassador to Barbados and Grenada and two years later was moved to Guatemala. In the following year he was dismissed by the Jimmy Carter administration after a bitter U.S. policy quarrel in which he supported Guatemala's repressive right-wing military government. At the time of his removal he was the highest-ranking Latino in the U.S. foreign service.

When conservative Republican Ronald Reagan became president, Ortiz returned to favor and was named ambassador to Peru, 1981–1983, and then to Argentina for three years. Retired from the foreign service, in 1986 he was appointed diplomat-in-residence at the University of New Mexico. He has received various honors and awards.

FURTHER READING: Peterson, Cass. "Back in the Saddle." *The Washington Post* (31 August 1981) A13; *Who's Who among Hispanic Americans, 1994–1995*. Detroit: Gale Research, 1994; *Who's Who in Government, 1975–1976*. Chicago: Marquis, 1975.

ORTIZ, RAMÓN, 1813–1896. Priest, patriot. Ramón Ortiz, the scion of an old Nuevomexicano family, was promised to the Church as the result of a vow his mother made. He studied at the seminary in Durango and was ordained in 1834. Three years later he was named pastor at Paso del Norte (Ciudad Juárez today), where he won Anglo friends by helping traders and particularly the survivors of the 1841 Santa Fe expedition from Texas.

When the U.S. invaded Mexico in 1846, Ortiz was active in resisting and was briefly imprisoned by the Americans. Upon his release he returned to Paso del Norte and successfully ran for the Mexican lower house, where he passionately opposed acceptance of the Treaty of **Guadalupe Hidalgo**. After transfer of the Southwest to the United States he was appointed by the Mexican government to oversee the removal of those who wanted to relocate in Mexican territory. In the post-treaty years he frequently acted as an intermediary and peacemaker between Anglos and Mexicans. He retired from his priestly duties in the 1880s because of ill-health, and died from cancer in 1896.

FURTHER READING: Puckett, Fidelia Miller. "Ramón Ortiz: Priest and Patriot." *New Mexico Historical Review* 25:4 (October 1950) 265–295; Taylor, Mary D. "Cura de la frontera, Ramón Ortiz." *U.S. Catholic Historian* 9:1–2 (1990) 67–85.

ORTIZ Y PINO DE KLEVEN, CONCHA, 1910– . Legislator, rancher. Concha Ortiz y Pino was born in the tiny town of Galisteo, about twenty miles south of Santa Fe. As a young girl she attended the widely famed Loreto Academy in Santa Fe. After graduation she began a folk arts vocational school on the extensive family ranch with financial backing from her father.

Belonging to a family that had been politically active since the 1600s, Concha was early tutored in politics by her legislator father. While still in her mid-twenties she ran for the New Mexico House of Representatives and was elected. In the legislature Concha introduced bills to make jury service possible for women and to establish bilingual education as provided for in the New Mexico constitution. She strongly believed that women should take a more active role in politics, and encouraged greater community political involvement. Serving in the lower house from 1936 to 1942, she was the first woman to be elected to the powerful position of majority whip. She left the legislature in 1942 and entered the University of New Mexico, where she earned a B.A. degree. At the university she met professor Victor Kleven, whom she married.

When her father died at the beginning of the 1950s, Concha was appointed by the court to manage the large family ranch. However, the death of her husband in 1956 caused her to lease the ranch and return to Albuquerque, where she became intensely active in a variety of civic affairs. Deeply committed to Hispanic and civic concerns, she served on numerous local, state, and national boards and commissions and was given national appointments by three presidents. She received many local and national honors in recognition of her lifetime of devoted service; in 1995 she was awarded the Order of the Holy Sepulchre by Pope John Paul II.

FURTHER READING: *Las Mujeres: Mexican American/Chicana Women.* Windsor, Calif.: National Women's History Project, 1991; Rebolledo, Tey Diana. *Nuestras mujeres: Hispanas of New Mexico, Their Images and Their Lives, 1582–1992.* Albuquerque: El Norte Publications, 1992; Palmisano, Joseph M., ed. *Notable Hispanic American Women, Book II.* Detroit: Gale Research, 1998.

OTERO, MIGUEL ANTONIO, JR., 1859–1944. Governor, businessman. Miguel Otero, Jr., was born and grew up, learning from both Mexican and Anglo cultures, on the booming southwestern U.S. frontier. Much of his early education came from the streets of railroad towns in which his father's freighting firm, Otero, Sellar & Company, prospered. Like his father, he attended St. Louis University, but he also studied at the U.S. Naval Academy and Notre Dame University. When his father died, the twenty-two-year-old youth was able to take a decisive role in the family businesses as the result of his previous experience as cashier, bookkeeper, and manager in various Otero companies.

Otero's business activities and his father's example almost inevitably led to his involvement in politics. Between 1883 and 1890 he advanced from city treasurer to probate court clerk, to county clerk, to district court clerk. As New Mexican delegate to the Republican National Convention in 1888 he made the acquaintance of William McKinley, who, when he became president ten years later, appointed him territorial governor. The thirty-seven-year-old Otero gave New Mexico vigorous leadership and was appointed to a second term, during which the statehood issue came to the fore. In 1901 he called a convention to discuss all aspects of the issue. His opposition to President Theodore Roosevelt's conservationist national forest policy cost him a possible third term as governor, and he switched his allegiance to the Democratic Party. After Democrat Woodrow Wilson won the presidency he received various political appointments. He died at age eighty-four toward the end of World War II.

FURTHER READING: Crocchiola, Stanley. *The Otero, New Mexico, Story.* Pantex, Texas: Pampa Print Shop, 1962; "Miguel Otero Dies; Leader in West, 84." *New York Times* (8 August 1944) 17; Montoya, María E. "The Dual World of Governor Miguel A. Otero: Myth and Reality in Turn-of-the-Century New Mexico." *New Mexico Historical Review* 67;1 (1992) 13–31; Otero, Miguel A., Jr. *My Life on the Frontier, 1864–1882.* New York: Press of the Pioneers, 1935; Otero, Miguel A., Jr. *My Life on the Frontier, 1882–1897.* Albuquerque: University of New Mexico Press, 1939; Otero, Miguel A., Jr. *My Nine Years As Governor of the Territory of New Mexico, 1897–1906.* Albuquerque: University of New Mexido Press, 1940; Otero, Miguel A., Jr. *Otero: An Autobiographical Trilogy*, Reprint of his three works above. New York: Arno Press, 1974.

OTERO, MIGUEL ANTONIO, SR., 1829–1882. Politician, businessman. Miguel A. Otero, Sr. was born near Albuquerque and educated in Nuevo México and the United States. In 1841 he enrolled in St. Louis University and eight years later began to study law. After being admitted to the bar in Missouri in 1852, he returned to the Territory of New Mexico, began a law practice in Albuquerque, and entered the political arena. He won election to the territorial legislature that same year and then served three terms as territorial delegate to the U.S. Congress from 1855 to 1861. Though not opposed to slavery and sympathetic to the Confederacy, he did not favor the secession of the southern states that led to the Civil War.

During the Civil War, Otero moved to the Midwest and busied himself with his freighting and mercantile activities, establishing Otero, Sellar & Co in the postwar period. During the 1870s he was an early advocate of railroads, a director of the Atchison, Topeka, and Santa Fe, and a founder of its affiliate, the New Mexico and Southern Pacific Railroad, as well. He was also active in banking and mining. Suffering from ill health, he died suddenly in Las Vegas, New Mexico of complications arising from pneumonia.

FURTHER READING: Gardner, Mark L. "Otero, Miguel Antonio." In *American National Biography*, vol. 16. Edited by John A. Garrity and Mark C. Carnes. New York: Oxford University Press, 1999; Otero, Miguel A., Jr. *My Life on the Frontier, 1864–1882.* New Press of the Pioneers, 1935.

OTERO-WARREN, NINA, 1882–1965. Educator, businesswoman, suffragist. María Adelina Emilia Otero was born in the small central New Mexican town of Los Lunas into a ranching family. After early private education, she attended Marysville College of the Sacred Heart in Missouri briefly and then returned to New Mexico. A decade in the social whirl of Santa Fe, to which the family had moved, led to marriage to Lt. Rawson Warren. The marriage lasted only one year, and after the divorce she became active in local Republican politics. In 1917 she was the New Mexico chairwoman of an early suffragist organization named the Congressional Union and was also elected

Santa Fe County superintendent of schools. Reelected to the latter position, she held it until 1929.

In the following decade she homesteaded a ranch that she named Las Dos, where she wrote a romantic and idealized reminiscence, *Old Spain in Our Southwest*, published in 1936. During these years she also supervised adult education programs, was an inspector in the Indian Service, and worked in the Civilian Conservation Corps as director of education. In 1941 she accepted a similar position in the Works Progress Administration in Puerto Rico. Returning to the mainland during World War II, she became director of the Office of Price Administration in Santa Fe.

In the postwar years Nina Otero-Warren continued to be active in state Republican circles, serving on various committees and commissions. One of the early Nuevomexicanas to become both politically and professionally prominent, in her later years she successfully operated Las Dos Realties and Insurance Agency in Santa Fe.

FURTHER READING: Massman, Ann M. "Adelina 'Nina' Otero-Warren: A Spanish-American Cultural Broker." *Journal of the Southwest* 42:4 (2000) 877–896; "Mrs. Otero-Warren Dies in Home Here." Santa Fe *New Mexican* (4 January 1965); Otero-Warren, Nina. *Old Spain in Our Southwest.* Chicago: Rio Grande Press, 1962 (1936); Perrigo, Lynn I. *Hispanos: Historic Leaders in New Mexico.* Santa Fe: Sunstone Press, 1985; Whaley, Charlotte. *Nina Otero-Warren of Santa Fe.* Albuquerque: University of New Mexico Press, 1994.

PACHECO, ROMUALDO, 1831–1899. Governor, diplomat. Romualdo Pacheco was born in Santa Barbara, the son of an aide to the Mexican governor of Alta California; his father was killed shortly after his birth. Romualdo was sent by his Anglo stepfather to Honolulu to be educated in an English missionary school, and at age fifteen went to work on his stepfather's ships. After the Treaty of **Guadalupe Hidalgo** he devoted his time to overseeing the operation of the family landholdings.

Interested in politics, he won election as county judge in 1853 and then state senator in 1857. At the outbreak of the Civil War he was reelected to the senate, now as a Republican, and was state treasurer from 1863 to 1867. Four years later he was nominated and elected to the lieutenant governorship, and in 1875 became governor for ten months when governor Newton Booth resigned to fill a vacancy in the U.S. Senate. However, in the next election he was not nominated to the governorship by the Republican party. Elected to the U.S. House of Representatives in 1876, he was twice reelected. During this time he also operated a stock brokerage firm in San Francisco.

Although Pacheco was not an energetic congressman, he did serve as chair of the important committee on private land claims. After three terms he decided not to run for reelection, and returned to his widespread business interests in California, Texas, and Mexico. In 1890 he was named minister plenipotentiary to Central America by Republican President Benjamin Harrison. After three years he was removed by Harrison's Democratic successor, President Grover Cleveland, and resumed involvement in his business interests. Semiretired, he died in Oakland at age sixty-seven.

FURTHER READING: Conmy, Peter T. *Romualdo Pacheco, Distinguished Californian of the Mexican and American Periods.* San Francisco: Native Sons of the Golden West, 1957; Garraty, John A., and Mark C. Carnes, eds. *American National Biography,* vol. 16. New York: Oxford University Press, 1999; Genini, Ronald, and Richard Hitchman. *Romualdo Pacheco, A Californio in Two Eras.* San Francisco: Book Club of California, 1985; Melendy, H. Brett, and Benjamin F. Gilbert. *The Governors of California: Peter H. Burnett to Edmund G. Brown.* Georgetown, Calif.: Talisman Press, 1965; Nicholson, Loren. *Romualdo Pacheco's California.* San Luis Obispo: California Heritage Publishing Associates, 1990.

PACHUCO. *Pachuco,* sometimes shortened to 'chuco," is a term of disputed origins used to describe the lifestyle of some barrio youths, some of whom were gang members, had tattoos on the hand, and adopted the zoot suit as a uniform in the 1940s. Nuevomexicano sociologist **George I. Sánchez** believed that pachucos were the by-product of ethnic and racial discrimination that caused them to feel the need to unite in defense of their barrios and culture. Many pachucos viewed themselves as warriors defending the barrio and Chicano culture against the dominating forces in American society. **Edward James Olmos** gave a defining interpretation of the pachuco through his role in **Luis Valdez**'s play *Zoot Suit.* The term can also refer to a non-standard border dialect of Spanish.

FURTHER READING: Luckenbill, Dan. *The Pachuco Era: Catalogue of an Exhibit, University Research Library, September–December 1990.* Los Angeles: Department of Special Collections, University Research Library, University of California, 1990; Madrid-Barela, Arturo. "In Search of the Authentic Pachuco: An Interpretive Essay." *Aztlán.* 4:1 (1973) 31–60; Paz, Octavio. *The Labryinth of Solitude: Life and Thought in Mexico.* New York: Grove Press, 1961; Sánchez, George I. "Pachucos in the Making." Common Ground 4:1 (Autumn 1943) 13–20.

PADRES ASOCIADOS PARA DERECHOS RELIGIOSOS, EDUCATIVOS, Y SOCIALES. PADRES (the acronym) was founded in San Antonio, Texas, in 1969 by a group of about fifty Chicano priests. Early in the following year they met in Tucson, where they incorporated as a national organization. With funding from various sources and the strong support of bishop **Patrick Flores** and Santa Fe archbishop James P. Davis, PADRES pursued concerns of Mexican American Catholics. It was influenced by Alinskyite ideas as well as liberation theology, and sought to make the poor aware of their potential political and economic power. It played an important role in some labor strikes, in getting a number of Mexican Americans appointed bishops by Rome, and in creating community organizations. Its most successful project was the **Mexican American Cultural Center** in San Antonio. Since the 1980s it has been relatively inactive.

FURTHER READING: Romero, Juan. "Charism and Power: An Essay in the History of PADRES." *U.S. Catholic Historian* 9:1-2 (Spring 1990) 147–163; Romero, Juan. "PADRES: Who They Are and Where They Are Going." In *Prophets Denied Honor: An Anthology on the Hispano Church in the United States,* edited by Antonio M. Stevens Arroyo. Maryknoll, N.Y.: Orbis Books, 1980; Tyler, Ron, ed. *The New Handbook of Texas,* vol. 5. Austin: Texas State Historical Association, 1996.

PALOMINO, CARLOS, 1950– . Boxer, actor. Carlos Palomino was born in Sonora, Mexico, and came to southern California as a youth. A good student, during his high school years he worked at two part-time jobs and played semipro baseball in northern Mexico on weekends. Upon graduation from high school he was drafted into the U.S. Army during the Vietnam War. In the army he quickly won a place on the Fort Hood, Texas, boxing team and rapidly moved up to All Army Champion. When he left the army he was World Military Champion with thirty-one wins out of thirty-four fights.

Palomino returned to California and turned professional in 1972. Two years later, with a record of thirty wins out of thirty-one matches, he won the World Welterweight title. In 1977 and 1978 he defended his title against seven contenders, but lost it the following year in a decision bout. When it became evident there would be no rematch, he retired from boxing and began a new career in television and movies.

Meanwhile, in 1976 Palomino had graduated from Long Beach State University. He has made numerous personal appearances, encouraging Chicano high school students not to drop out but to complete their educations. He is considered by many boxing fans to be one of the great twentieth-century welterweights.

FURTHER READING: "Carlos Palomino, Welterweight Champion of the World." *La Luz* 7:11 (November 1978) 20B–20C; Fournier, Carlos. "In the Ring." *Hispanic* (March 1989) 23–26; Putman, Pat. "Staying at the Top of his Class." *Sports Illustrated* 46:5 (31 January 1977).

PALOMINO, ERNIE, 1933– . Teacher, painter, sculptor. Ernesto Palomino was born in Fresno, California, where he grew up in great poverty and attended public schools. Interested in painting from early childhood, in high school he was fortunate to encounter a teacher who encouraged his artistic bent. Upon graduating he served two years in the U.S. Marines during the Korean conflict and then renewed his art studies and work. In 1956 he received a scholarship at the San Francisco Art Institute and had a one-man show at the Legion of Honor Museum. After five years of study, he earned his A.B. degree from San Francisco State in 1965 and then completed an M.A. in the next year. His M.A. thesis project was a short film titled *My Trip in a '52 Ford*, one of the very first Chicano films.

Palomino worked for two years for the Migrant Council in Denver and then took a position as assistant professor at Fresno State College (now University). He was in the vanguard of artists basing their work strongly on the Chicano experience. He has had numerous one-man and group shows, mostly in California.

FURTHER READING: Noriega, Chon A. "Why Chicanos Could Not Be Beat." *Aztlán* 24:2 (Fall 1999) 1–11; Palomino, Ernie. *In Black and White: Evolution of an Artist.* Fresno, Calif.: Academy Library Guild, 1956; Quirarte, Jacinto. *Mexican American Artists.* Austin: University of Texas Press, 1973; *Who's Who in the West, 1980–1981.* Chicago: Marquis, 1980.

PAREDES, AMÉRICO, 1915–1999. Folklorist, teacher. Américo Paredes was born in the border town of Brownsville, Texas, during the troubled times of the **Mexican revolution**. One of eight children, as a lad he worked at various jobs to help with the family finances. While a student in the Brownsville public schools he first encountered discriminatory practices and racism. That ongoing experience led to his lifelong fight against ethnic bias and discrimination.

As a young man Paredes worked as a translator, proofreader, and staff writer on the *Brownsville Herald*. After six years of service during World War II he entered the University of Texas at Austin, where he obtained his B.A., M.A., and finally a Ph.D. in English and folklore studies. A brief teaching stint at Texas Western College in El Paso followed; he then returned to Austin, where he spent the rest of his academic career at the University of Texas. His doctoral thesis on Tejano folk hero **Gregorio Cortez,** brought out in 1958 under the title *"With His Pistol in His Hand!" A Border Ballad and its Hero,* was an immediate publishing success and brought him widespread peer recognition and respect.

In 1967 Paredes helped found the Center for Intercultural Studies of Folklore and Ethnomusicology at the University of Texas. During the 1960s he advocated the creation of a Chicano studies program despite discouraging anti-Mexican attitudes within the university. Persisting in his campaign, he repeatedly challenged the entrenched "old boy" network of his Anglo colleagues. In 1970, with help from other Chicano faculty and graduate students, he finally succeeded in convincing the administration to authorize a center for Mexican American studies. He was named its first director. His struggle for *raza* rights did not end there; he continued to fight against the historically and institutionally ingrained discrimination against Mexicanos widely prevalent in Texas.

At Austin Américo Paredes researched and created a corpus of work that formed the basis of a new school of southwestern folklore. He trained a whole generation of borderland folklorists and imbued them with his strong feelings about ethnic discrimination. His seminal importance was recognized in 1989 when he became the first Mexican American to receive the prestigious Charles Frankel Prize from the National Endowment for the Humanities. In the following year he was awarded the Order of the Aguila Azteca by the Mexican government for his work in preserving **border culture** and for his lifelong defense of human rights. Subsequent to his retirement from teaching in 1985 he continued to write, publishing two novels, a book of poems, a collection of short stories, as well as a scholarly collection, *Folklore and Culture on the Texas-Mexican Border.* After a lengthy illness he died on Cinco de Mayo, 1999.

FURTHER READING: Américo Paredes Papers, 1886-1999. Benson Latin American Collection, General Libraries, University of Texas at Austin; Guerra, Víctor J. "Con su pluma en la mano." *Hopscotch* 2:1 (2000) 86–91; Leal, Luis. "Américo Paredes and Modern Mexican American Scholarship." *Ethnic Affairs* 1 (Fall 1987) 1–11; Limón, José E. "Américo Paredes, a Man From the Border." *Revista Chicano-Riqueña* 8:3 (Fall 1980) 1–5; Martínez, Julio A., and Francisco A. Lomelí, eds. *Chicano Literature: A Reference Guide.* Westport, Conn.: Greenwood Press, 1985; Paredes, Américo. *"With His Pistol in His Hand!" A Border Ballad and Its Hero.* Austin: University of Texas Press, 1958, 1971.

PARSONS, LUCY GONZÁLEZ, ca. 1853–1942. Labor activist, writer, anarchist. Lucía González was born and grew up in Texas near Fort Worth. Although there are contradictory views of her ethnic background, she claimed a mixed Mexicano-American-Indian heritage. While still a teenager she married Albert Parsons, a young socialist newspaperman, and spent the remaining years of her long life in leftist labor movements, advocating and demonstrating for workers' and women's rights.

Spurred by her husband's execution as a result of the 1886 Haymarket Square bombing in Chicago, she redoubled her activities in support of the radical labor movement in the United States. She was a founding member and recruiter for the Industrial Workers of the World, wrote articles for leftist labor journals, raised funds, made speaking tours, led marches, and supported demonstrators. Active and fearless in support of leftist movements all over the United States, she was repeatedly arrested and jailed. Although she worked with the American Communist Party in the 1920s, she did not actually join until 1939. She continued her activities in defense of the rights of labor and women well into her eighties.

FURTHER READING: Ashbaugh, Carolyn. *Lucy Parsons.* Chicago: Kerr, 1976; Mirandé, Alfredo, and Evangelina Enríquez. "Chicanas in the Struggle for Unions." In *Introduction to Chicano Studies,* 2nd ed. Edited by Livie Isauro Durán and H. Russell Bernard. New York: Macmillan, 1982; Palmisano, Joseph M., ed. *Notable Hispanic American Women, Book II.* Detroit: Gale Research, 1998; Salem, Dorothy, ed. *African American Women: A Biographical Dictionary.* New York: Garland, 1993.

PARTIDO DEL PUEBLO UNIDO. This Party of United People arose in New Mexico as part of a populist protest against the fencing in of pueblo lands and corruption in the Republican and Democratic parties. Related to the U.S. populist movement at the end of the nineteenth century, it was successful in electing candidates to local offices in the 1890 and 1892 elections. The party's nomination of an extremist member of the **Gorras Blancas** for the territorial legislature created an internal crisis and split, with many moderate members withholding their electoral support. By the following presidential election its membership had declined drastically and it soon disppeared.

FURTHER READING: Hofstadter, Richard. *The Age of Reform.* New York: Vintage Books, 1955; Meyer, Doris. *Speaking for Themselves: Neomexicano Cultural Identity and the Spanish-Language Press, 1880–1920.* Albuquerque: University of New Mexico Press, 1996.

PATLÁN, JUAN J., 1939– . Political activist. Juan Patlán was an important Texas leader in the Chicano **movimiento** during the late 1960s and the 1970s. A close friend of José Angel Gutiérrez, he was one of the founders of the **Mexican American Youth Organization** as well as of one of its offshoots, the **Mexican American Unity Council** (MAUC). As executive director and president of San Antonio–based MAUC for sixteen years, he switched its emphasis from political activity to the areas of community economic development, social services, and health care. During the mid-1970s he was elected chairman of the board of directors of the National Council of La Raza. In 1978 he was recognized as an outstanding San Antonio civic leader in a Washington, D.C., salute by the National Urban Coalition. During the presidential terms of Ronald Reagan and Jimmy Carter he was appointed to various commissions. His prominence as a businessman in civic affairs led to his nomination in 1995 to the position of president of the governing board of the San Antonio Water System. Currently he is the owner of a real estate firm.

FURTHER READING: *Agenda* 8:2 (March/April 1978) 42; "Regidores se resistan al nombramiento de Juan Patlán." *La Prensa de San Antonio* 8:4 (28 July 1995) 1A; García, Ignacio M. *United We Win: The Rise and Fall of La Raza Unida Party*. Tucson: University of Arizona, Mexican American Studies and Research Center, 1989; Salazar, Verónica. *Dedication Rewarded: Prominent Mexican Americans*. San Antonio: Mexican American Cultural Center, 1976.

PATRÓN, JUAN B., 1855–1884. Political leader. Like many young sons of Nuevomexicano elites of his day, Juan Patrón received his higher education in the United States. After his father was killed in an 1873 racist attack, he operated the family mercantile business and taught in the local school. Assuming a leading role in community politics, he was elected to the territorial legislature three years later. His local leadership often brought him into conflict with Anglos. He played an important part in the Lincoln County War in 1878 and then moved to Puerto de Luna because he feared for his family's safety. He was killed there in a saloon by a stranger, possibly the result of a feud growing out of the Lincoln County War.

FURTHER READING: Ritter, Charles F., and Jon L. Wakelyn, eds. *American Legislative Leaders, 1850–1910*. New York: Greenwood Press, 1989; Simmons, Marc. *New Mexico: An Interpretive History*. Albuquerque: University of New Mexico Press, 1988.

PATRÓN POLITICS. A political practice with deep roots in southwestern history. The patrón, Anglo or Mexican American, through his paternalistic relationship with members of the poorer classes, particularly Mexicanos, was able to assure himself of their votes at election time. In return they could expect to obtain employment in government, on construction projects, and on his and his friends' ranches. During hard economic times the patrón might make food or small loans available to his "dependents." The patrón system declined wherever large-scale irrigated agriculture, with its migrant workforce, replaced the traditional ranching economy.

FURTHER READING: Anders, Evan. *Boss Rule in South Texas: The Progressive Era*. Austin: University of Texas Press, 1982; García, Flaviano Chris. "Manitos and Chicanos in Nuevo México Politics." *Aztlán* 5:1&2 (Spring and Fall 1974) 177–188; Gonzales, Phillip B. "El Jefe: Bronson Cutting and the Politics of Hispano Interests in New Mexico, 1920–1935." *Aztlán* 25:2 (2000) 67–108.

PAZ, OCTAVIO, 1914–1998. Essayist, poet laureate, diplomat. Mexican writer Octavio Paz was one of the major Latin American figures of the twentieth century. Winner of the 1990 Nobel Peace Prize in Literature, he was known for his elegant writing style as well as his insight and erudition. In his most important work, *The Labryinth of Solitude*, 1961, he devoted a thoughtful chapter to the Mexican American. In addition to his literary interests, Paz was a political activist who was critical of Mexico's then-ruling party, the Partido Revolucionario Institucional. In 1968 he resigned from his post as Mexico's ambassador to India in indignation at the Tlatelolco "massacre" of student protesters.

FURTHER READING: Mata, Rodolfo. "Octavio Paz." In *Encyclopedia of Mexican History, Society & Culture*, vol. 2. Edited by Michael Werner. Chicago: Fitzroy Dearborn, 1997; Paz, Octavio. *The Labryinth of Solitude: Life and Thought in Mexico.* New York: Grove Press, 1961; Sefami, Jacobo. "Octavio Paz (Mexico, 1914–1998)." *Mexican Studies/Estudios Mexicanos* 14:2 (Summer 1998) 251–262.

PECAN SHELLERS' STRIKE, 1938. In January 1938, thousands of San Antonio pecan shellers, who had become organized into unions just the previous year, walked out on strike at the news of a 15 percent cut in their already minimal wages. Despite the refusal of pecan shelling contractors to discuss wages, the strikers persisted, under the **leadership** of organizers like radicals **Emma Tenayuca** and Manuela Solís. Police raids, mass arrests, and acts of vigilantism became daily occurrences as the strike went on for weeks. Partly because of its radical leadership, the strike was viewed unfavorably by moderate elements in the community and failed to gain their support.

After two months the strike was settled by arbitration that recognized the strikers' union and reduced the wage cut by one-half. The Fair Labor Standards Act, passed by Congress seven months later, superseded the arbitration by establishing a minimum wage of twenty-five cents an hour. Faced by this new legislation, the pecan shelling industry immediately began mechanizing and eventually about 80 percent of the ten thousand workers lost their jobs.

Shelling pecans by hand, ca. 1938. Courtesy of the Benson Latin American Collection, University of Texas at Austin.

FURTHER READING: Calderón, Roberto, and Emilio Zamora. "Manuela Solís Sager and Emma Tenayuca: A Tribute." In *Chicana Voices: Intersection of Class, Race, and Gender*, edited by Teresa Córdova et al. Austin: Center for Mexican American Studies, University of Texas, 1986; Menefee, Selden C., and Orrin C. Cassmore. *The Pecan Shellers of San Antonio*, reprinted in *Mexican Labor in the United States*. New York: Arno Press, 1974; Vargas, Zaragosa. "Tejana Radical: Emma Tenayuca and the San Antonio Labor Movement during the Great Depression." *Pacific Historical Review* 66:4 (1997) 553–580; Walker, Kenneth P. "The Pecan Shellers of San Antonio and Mechanization." *Southwestern Historical Quarterly* 69:1 (July 1965) 44–58.

PEÑA, ALBERT A., JR., 1917– . Judge, attorney, politician. Tejano Albert Peña was an outstanding member of the World War II Mexican American generation. He served in the U.S. Navy from 1942 to 1946 and then used the G.I. Bill to complete his college education at St. Mary's University in San Antonio. After earning a law degree in 1950, he joined his father's law firm and soon became active in politics. Six years later he was elected a Bexar county commissioner and served sixteen consecutive years. He was appointed a San Antonio municipal court judge in 1977 and remained on the bench until his retirement in 1992. Throughout his life he played a prominent role in San Antonio Democratic politics.

As county commissioner, Peña's two main goals were to end discrimination against Mexican Americans in housing, education, and employment and to develop political activism among Mexican Americans. His efforts caused him to be ridiculed, threatened, and even jailed briefly. At the **Equal Employment Opportunity Commission** meeting in March 1966 he led the "**Albuquerque Walkout**," a crucial step in the Chicano struggle for equal rights and social justice.

Peña was active in various liberal groups, opposed the war in Vietnam, supported marches and boycotts, and expounded his strong civil rights views in several weekly newspapers. He headed the **Political Association of Spanish-Speaking Organizations**, and also had an important part in the founding and early development of the Southwest Council of La Raza, the **Mexican American Unity Council**, and the **Mexican American Legal Defense and Educational Fund.**

Although Peña was quite willing to work collaboratively with Anglo leaders, during the Chicano Movement he preached confrontation as a tactic to achieve raza rights. He quickly acquired a devoted following of youthful Chicanos like **José Angel Gutiérrez** and **Willie Velásquez**, who applauded and strongly supported his crusade for political and social change. In the late 1990s he was still active in electoral politics.

FURTHER READING: Alvarez, Frank. "UTSA Honors Judge Albert Peña, Jr." *La Prensa* (San Antonio) (17 March 1995) 1–A, 3–A; Chacón, José A. *Hispanic Notables in the United States of North America*. Albuquerque: Saguaro Publishing Co., 1978; Pycior, Julie Leininger. *LBJ & Mexican Americans: The Paradox of Power*. Austin: University of Texas Press, 1997.

PEÑA, FEDERICO, 1947– . Politician, lawyer. Federico Peña is best known as mayor of Denver from 1983 to 1991. Born and educated in Texas, he became a staff lawyer in the Denver office of the Mexican American Legal Defense and Educational Fund, after working in an El Paso legal aid office. In 1978 he won election to the Colorado state legislature and quickly became recognized as one of the top lawmakers in the state. Chosen minority Speaker of the House, he supported bilingual education and coauthored a law requiring Colorado schools to offer classes in Hispanic culture. He easily won a second term.

In 1983, at age thirty-six Peña was elected mayor of Denver, becoming the first *raza* mayor of a large city that was not heavily Latino. He served as mayor until 1991. Two years later he was appointed secretary of the Department of Transportation by President Bill Clinton and in 1997 he became secretary of the U.S. Department of Energy, a position he left the following year to take a well-paying position in the private sector.

FURTHER READING: Arias, Anna María. "Federico Peña: A Quick Study." *Hispanic* (June 1993) 16, 18–21; Hero, Rodney. "The Election of Hispanics in City Government: An Examination of the Election of Federico Peña as Mayor of Denver." *Western Political Quarterly* 40 (1987) 93–105. Reprinted in *Land Grants, Housing, and Political Power*, edited by Antoinette Sedillo López. New York: Garland Publishing, 1995; Martínez, Chip. "Federico Peña: Denver's First Hispanic Mayor." *Nuestro* (August 1983) 14-20; *Who's Who in American Politics, 1997–1998*. New York: R. R. Bowker, 1998.

PENITENTES. A lay religious society in New Mexico that probably evolved toward the end of the eighteenth century from the Franciscan Third Order. Its full official name was La Confraternidad de Nuestro Padre Jesús Nazareno. In a frontier area where the number of priests was extremely limited, it was natural for laymen to maintain the church and lead religious observances in the absence of clergy.

After the Treaty of **Guadalupe Hidalgo**, the Southwest was transferred by Rome to the jurisdiction of the U.S. Catholic Church. Many Mexicanos were unhappy with the new bishop **Jean Baptiste Lamy**'s reforms and reorganization of the church, especially his lack of appreciation for Mexican folk Catholicism. Penitente membership expanded rapidly and there was a significant increase in secrecy, as the bishop and his successors tried to gain control of the brotherhood. During the 1890s Penitente secrecy and independence caused the church hierarchy to officially denounce the society, and it was ordered to disband.

In the twentieth century, interest in Penitente membership declined as New Mexico became more a part of mainstream America, and as many young men left the villages for city life. Also village life, which had buttressed the organization, underwent great changes. After years of negotiation, in 1947 Archbishop Edwin V. Byrne officially recognized and reinstated the Penitente brotherhood under ecclesiastical control. However, some *moradas* (chapters) retained their independent stance.

FURTHER READING: Carrol, Michael P. *The Penitente Brotherhood: Patriarchy and Hispano-Catholiciam in New Mexico.* Baltimore: Johns Hopkins University Press, 2002; Henderson, Alice Corbin. *Brothers of Light: The Penitentes of the Southwest.* Las Cruces, New Mexico: Yucca Tree Press, 1998 (1937); Pulido, Alberto L. *The Sacred World of the Penitentes.* Washington, D.C.: Smithsonian Institution Press, 2000; Steele, Thomas J., and Rowena Rivera. *Penitente Self Government: Brotherhoods and Councils, 1797–1947.* Santa Fe: Ancient City Press, 1985; Weigle, Marta. *Brothers of Light, Brothers of Blood: The Penitentes of the Southwest.* Albuquerque: University of New Mexico Press, 1976.

PEOPLE'S CONSTITUTIONAL PARTY. The Partido Constitucional del Pueblo was established at a convention held in Albuquerque in August 1968 by **Reies López Tijerina** and his followers. It nominated a slate of candidates for state offices, including Tijerina as candidate for governor. However, he was disqualified by New Mexico's secretary of state, and the Partido's candidates received fewer than three thousand votes in the 1968 elections. Two years later it again ran a full slate for state offices but had no greater success. In 1971 the Partido was dissolved.

FURTHER READING: Tijerina, Reies López. *Mi lucha por la tierra.* Mexico: Fondo de Cultura Económica, 1978.

PERALES, ALONSO S., 1899–1960. Lawyer, activist. World War I service in the U.S. armed forces helped Alonso Perales focus his life on ways to advance the economic welfare and civil rights of Mexican Americans. Discussions of *raza* concerns with other Tejanos resulted in the founding of the **Order Sons of America** in 1921. At the end of the decade he had a key part in establishing the **League of United Latin American Citizens** (LULAC), which evolved from the Sons. Assuming a principal role in the early development of LULAC, he scrapped the **mutualista** organizational concept for one that was more U.S. mainstream.

Meanwhile, because of his leadership in the Mexican American community and his law degree, Perales began to be called on by Washington during the late 1920s to participate in diplomatic missions to Latin America. As a result of this experience and his early writings, he was selected by President Franklin D. Roosevelt in the next decade as an advisor on Mexican American issues.

In his first book, *El mexicano americano y la política del sur de Texas*, published in 1931, Perales surveyed three decades of Anglo–Mexican American interaction in the border region. In 1936–1937 he issued *En defensa de mi raza*, a two-volume history of the Mexican American struggle for civil rights. Just before America's entrance into World War II he was deeply involved in pushing a racial equality law in the Texas legislature. The bill failed to pass.

During the years of World War II Perales, along with other Mexican American intellectual leaders like **Carlos E. Castañeda** and **George I. Sánchez**, took an important position in the Office of the Coordinator of Inter-American Affairs. In 1945 he participated in the founding conference of the United Nations at San Francisco, acting as legal counsel to the Nicaraguan delegation.

After the war Perales wrote a San Antonio newspaper column that pointed out instances of injustices and civil rights violations. In 1948 he published another important work, *Are We Good Neighbors?* His answer was no. In his writing he strongly advocated legislation and education as ways to combat ethnic discrimination. For a lifetime spent fighting for the social equality and civil rights of Spanish-speaking Americans, he was awarded the Order of Civil Merit by the Spanish government in 1952. He continued to be active in Chicano concerns, serving on numerous civic committees and commissions until his death at the end of the decade.

FURTHER READING: Limón, José E. "Stereotyping and Chicano Resistance: An Historical Dimension." *Aztlán* 4:2 (Fall 1973): 257–270; Orozco, Cynthia E. "The Origins of the League of United Latin American Citizens (LULAC) and the Mexican American Civil Rights Movement in Texas. . . ." Ph.D. diss., University of California, Los Angeles, 1992; Perales, Alonso S., comp. *Are We Good Neighbors?* San Antonio: Artes Gráficas, 1948. Reprint. New York: Arno Press, 1974; Perales, Alonso S. *En defensa de mi raza.* San Antonio: Arte Público Press, 1936–1937; Sloss Vento, Adela. *Alonso S. Perales: His Struggle for the Rights of Mexican-Americans.* San Antonio: Artes Gráficas, 1977.

PICO, ANDRÉS, 1810–1876. Soldier, political leader. Andrés Pico, younger brother of Pío Pico, was born in San Diego into one of the prominent southern Californio families. By his mid-twenties he was active in Mexican territorial politics, supporting the division of Alta California into two sections, northern and southern. As a leader in the southern faction he participated in the sometimes belligerent encounters with the north, headed by the Castro family. Appointed a lieutenant in the San Diego militia in the late 1830s, he was promoted to captain in the mid-1840s with a commission to inventory the property of the recently secularized missions.

Leading resistance to the invading U.S. forces in the **U.S.-Mexican War**, Andrés was promoted to commandant. Initially his forces defeated the Americans at San Pasqual in December 1846, but they lost a month later at Cahuenga and then surrendered to Captain **John Charles Frémont.** After the U.S. takeover he remained a prominent southern Californio leader, being elected to the assembly and later to the state senate. During the Civil War he was offered command of a cavalry battalion but declined because of poor health. In the postwar period he became an ardent railroad and transportation booster. The last two decades of his life were filled with expensive disputes over his two large land grants.

FURTHER READING: Haas, Lisbeth. "War in California, 1846–1848." *California History* 76: 2–3 (1997) 331–355; Pico, Pío. *Don Pío Pico's Historical Narrative.* Glendale, Calif.: Arthur H. Clark, 1973; Pitt, Leonard. *The Decline of the Californios.* Berkeley: University of California Press, 1966.

PICO, PÍO, 1801–1894. Governor, political leader. Pío de Jesús Pico was born at Mission San Gabriel and grew up there and in San Diego, to which the family moved. By his mid-twenties he was active in both business and Alta California politics. He obtained his first land grant while still in his twenties and eventually became one of largest Californio landowners, and then lost it all in his later years. Although he was named administrator of secularized Mission San Luis Rey by the governor appointed by Mexico City, he remained strongly opposed to Mexican centralism and favored separation from Castro-dominated northern California.

Governor for a brief period earlier, Pico took over the job again in 1845. He found it expedient to compromise with the north by appointing José Castro military commander and virtual co-governor headquartered in Monterey. When U.S. forces invaded the following year, he organized resistance until the situation became untenable. Then he and Castro fled into Baja California. After the Guadalupe Hidalgo treaty he returned to his ranches. During the 1850s he served in several local political positions but abstained from state politics. Like his brother Andrés, he strongly supported President Abraham Lincoln during the Civil War. In the postwar era he built and operated Pico House, Los Angeles's largest hotel, but financial success eluded him. In the 1870s and 1880s he lost much of his extensive landholdings because of debts and property mortgages. In the early 1890s he lost his last piece of land in the case *Pico v. Cohn.* He lived with his godchild and friend, John J. Warner, for six decades, and died in poverty.

FURTHER READING: Barrows, Henry D. "Pío Pico." *Annual Publication of the Historical Society of Southern California.* Los Angeles, 1894; Cannon, Marian G. "Pío Pico: The Last Don." *Westways* 73:6 (1981) 49–51+; Pico, Pío. *Don Pío Pico's Historical Narrative.* Glendale, Calif.: Arthur H. Clark Co., 1973.

PLAN DE SAN DIEGO, 1915. Originating with a Mexican national in San Diego, Texas, the Plan was an alleged secret plot calling for the overthrow of U.S. rule in the Southwest, the killing of most male Anglos over sixteen, and the creation of a Mexicano republic. The affair seems to have been largely a reaction to deteriorating conditions along the border because of Mexican revolutionary activity and the frequently brutal conduct of the **Texas Rangers**.

For months the Plan was blamed for raids and bridge destruction in the border region and there were some vigilante reprisals by alarmed Anglos. Secrecy surrounding the Plan and the confusion of the times make it difficult to ascertain the extent of the involvement of Plan adherents in these activities, if any. The question of Plan participation in terrorist acts was further muddled by the border unrest and **banditry** that arose in part from the 1910 Mexican revolution. Because of World War I there were even allegations of a German connection to the Plan. By late 1915 Anglo anxieties about the Plan had died down.

FURTHER READING: Harris, Charles H., III, and Louis R. Sadler. "The Plan of San Diego and the Mexican-United States War Crisis of 1916: A Reexamination." *Hispanic American Historical Review* 58:3 (August 1978) 381–408; Johnson, Benjamin H. "Sedition and Citizenship in South Texas, 1900–1930." Ph.D. Diss. Yale University, 2000; Sandos, James A. *Rebellion in the Borderlands: Anarchism and the Plan of San Diego, 1904–1923.* Norman: University of Oklahoma Press, 1992; Simmons, Ozzie G. *Anglo-Americans and Mexican-Americans in South Texas.* Reprint. New York: Arno Press, 1974.

PLAN DE SANTA BARBARA, 1969. The Plan de Santa Barbara originated in a conference held at the University of California in Santa Barbara. A cultural aspect of the Chicano Movement, the Plan detailed the ideology, organization, and role of the **Movimiento Estudiantil Chicano de Aztlán** (MECHA). It conceived MECHA as an umbrella organization for various college and university groups. By designing special college courses and programs suited to Chicano needs, it hoped to increase and spread knowledge of the Mexican American experience and to develop **leadership.** The Plan had considerable merit and some immediate, as well as long-term, successes in academia. It also helped develop young activist leaders who continued to advance the struggle for Mexican American rights.

FURTHER READING: *El Plan de Santa Barbara.* Santa Barbara, Calif.: La Causa Publications, 1969; Muñoz, Carlos Jr. *Youth, Identity, Power: The Chicano Movement.* New York: Verso, 1989; Nuñez, Rene, and Raoul Contreras. "Principles and Foundations of Chicano Studies: Chicano Organization on University Campuses in California." In *Chicano Discourse: Selected Conference Proceedings of the National Association for Chicano Studies,* ed. by Tatcho Mindiola, Jr., and Emilio Zamora. Houston: Mexican American Studies Program, University of Houston, 1992.

PLAN DEL BARRIO, 1968. The Plan del Barrio was a broad program outlined by **Corky Gonzales** during the **Poor People's March** on Washington, D.C. Among its goals, listed under "Demandas de la Raza," were greater educational opportunity, bilingual education, and better housing. It also called for the return of pueblo lands in the Southwest and financial aid in expanding Chicano-owned barrio businesses. It led directly to the **Plan Espiritual de Aztlán.**

FURTHER READNG: Gómez-Quiñones, Juan. *Chicano Politics: Reality and Promise, 1940–1990.* Albuquerque: University of New Mexico Press, 1990; Gonzales, Rodolfo "Corky." *Message to Aztlán: Selected Writings,* edited by Antonio Esquibel. Houston: Arte Público Press, 2001; Marín, Christine. *A Spokesman for the Mexican American Movement: Rodolfo "Corky" Gonzales and the Fight for Chicano Liberation, 1966–1972.* San Francisco, Calif.: R & E Research Associates, 1977.

PLAN ESPIRITUAL DE AZTLÁN, 1969. In March 1969 at the first annual Youth Liberation Conference in Denver, **Corky Gonzales** elaborated on his earlier **Plan del Barrio** with the Plan Espiritual de Aztlán. The Plan broke sharply with assimilationist goals of most earlier Mexican American organizations. Central to its ideas was a cultural homeland in the Southwest based broadly on the Aztecs' myth of **Aztlán** as the place of their origin. It urged Chicanos to unite in order to create a new political organization that would promote Chicano self-determination and ethnic nationalism.

The Plan led to the formation of the Colorado **La Raza Unida Party** in the following year. The party supported the Plan's concept of an ethnic homeland in the Southwest. In the subsequent struggle within the national Raza Unida Party over its **leadership** and direction, Gonzales lost to **José Angel Gutiérrez**. His defeat was a factor in his decline as one of the foremost Chicano leaders, and essentially marked the end of the Plan.

FURTHER READING: Marín, Christine. *A Spokesman for the Mexican American Movement;:Rodolfo "Corky" Gonzales and the Fight for Chicano Liberation, 1966–1972.* San Francisco: R & E Research Associates, 1977; Pérez-Torres, Rafael. "Refiguring Aztlán." *Aztlán* 22: 2 (Fall 1997) 15–41.

PLESSY v. FERGUSON, **1896.** *Plessy v. Ferguson* concerned the separate school system for African Americans that had been set up in the southern states after emancipation at the end of the Civil War. The court's ruling held that the Fourteenth Amendment was intended to protect only political, not social rights, thereby encouraging continued and expanded segregation and discrimination. It is best known for establishing the "separate but equal" doctrine, which held sway in the U.S. educational system until rejected by the courts in *Brown v. Board of Education of Topeka* in 1954. The U.S. Supreme Court's decision in the case of *Plessy* encouraged the establishment in the Southwest of separate schools for Chicano children.

FURTHER READING: Brook, Thomas, ed. *Plessy v. Ferguson: A Brief History with Documents.* Boston: Bedford Books, 1997; Newby, I. A., ed. *The Development of Segregationist Thought.* Homewood, Ill.: Dorsey Press, 1968.

PLUNKETT, JIM, 1947– . Football great. James Plunkett was born and grew up in San Jose, California. As early as the fifth grade he began developing his natural talent for sports; in high school he led football teams to impressive victories and All-League status. In 1966 he accepted an athletic scholarship to Stanford University, where he majored in political science, maintained a B average, and set new football records. He led the Stanford team to a Rose Bowl victory in his senior year and won the Heisman Trophy for himself.

Plunkett turned professional on graduating from Stanford in 1971, playing for the New England Patriots in Boston. Throwing nineteen touchdown passes in his first year won him the "Rookie of the Year" title. However, coaching staff disagreements and repeated injuries requiring surgery led to his mounting frustration in ensuing years. At his request he was transferred to the San Francisco 49ers, but he found his situation there even worse than in Boston. In 1978 he joined the Oakland Raiders as a free agent and soon rejuvenated his stalled career. In 1981 and 1984 he led the Raiders to Super Bowl victories, but subsequently was once again plagued by injuries that kept him off the field. He retired from football.

During his university years and later as a star quarterback Plunkett worked with young Chicanos, providing them with career counseling and encouraging them to get an education. Since his retirement he has helped raise money for various charities. Today he is a businessman who owns a distributorship for Coors beer and also does sports commentary for the Oakland Raiders weekly show.

FURTHER READING: *Current Biography*, February, 1982. New York: H. W. Wilson Co.; Kalec, William. "Big Game Jitters." *The Times Picayune* (New Orleans) (7 October 2001) Sports, 7; Plunkett, Jim, and Dace Newhouse. *The Jim Plunkett Story*. New York: Dell, 1982; Zimmerman, Paul. "A Runaway for the Raiders." *Sports Illustrated* 60:4 (30 January 1984).

PLYLER v. DOE, 1977–1982. *Plyler v. Doe* was a class action suit filed when the state of Texas passed a law excluding the children of undocumented aliens from free public **education.** Lawyers for the Mexican American Legal Defense and Educational Fund (MALDEF) argued that to deny the children free public education was a violation of their right to equal protection under the Fourteenth Amendment. The court accepted the plaintiffs' contention and ordered the school district to enroll the children.

In 1980 the Fifth District Court of Appeals confirmed the earlier ruling when the Tyler Independent School District appealed the decision. The state of Texas then appealed the case to the U.S. Supreme Court where MALDEF, the League of United Latin American Citizens, and the National Education Association were among groups supporting the original plaintiffs. The Supreme Court, pointing out the vital importance of education in a democratic society, agreed with the lower courts' ruling that the Texas action was a denial of Fourteenth Amendment guarantees.

FURTHER READING: Biegel, Stuart. "Wisdom of Plyler v. Doe." *Chicano-Latino Law Review* 17 (1995) 46–63; Cárdenas, José A. "The Impact of 'Doe v. Plyler' upon Texas Public Schools." *Journal of Law and Education* 15:1 (Winter 1986) 1–17; Carrera, John Willshire. *Immigrant Students: Their Legal Right of Access to Public Schools*, rev. ed. Boston: National Center for Immigrant Students & National Coalition of Advocates for Students, 1992.

POCHO. *Pocho* is a pejorative term for Mexicanos who have become thoroughly Anglicized, who may be unable to understand or speak Spanish. Or they may be so categorized because of their speech, the Anglicizing of Spanish words, and Hispanicizing of English words.

POLITICAL ASSOCIATION OF SPANISH-SPEAKING ORGANIZATIONS.
PASSO arose out of the successful **Viva Kennedy Clubs** organized during the 1960 election campaign. Tejano political leaders converted many of these clubs into a permanent organization they named PASSO. Planned as a national political pressure group, PASSO had a constitution that called for a united effort in seeking political solutions to community social and economic problems. To a degree it challenged the views of some older, more conservative Mexican American politicians by encouraging direct community involvement in politics.

PASSO's considerable success in Texas caused its leaders, most of whom had experience in the League of United Latin American Citizens, to decide to go national. However, efforts to develop branches in nearby Arizona were unsuccessful. PASSO failed to attract Arizonans; instead they decided to create their own separate organization, the **American Coordinating Council of Political Education,** which they considered more closely suited to their needs. Efforts to expand PASSO into other southwestern states encountered a similar lack of success.

Thus PASSO failed to become the nationwide coordinating umbrella organization its organizers had envisioned, remaining essentially a Texas group. Its endorsement of Price Daniel in the 1962 gubernatorial race marked the beginning of its slow decline. It helped get Chicanos elected to the **Crystal City** town council in 1963 and aided black groups during the second half of the 1960s in electing minority candidates to some Texas city offices. Early in the next decade PASSO lost much of its membership to **La Raza Unida Party**, which offered Texas Chicanos a more charismatic and aggressive leadership.

FURTHER READING: Cuellar, Robert. *A Social and Political History of the Mexican American Population of Texas, 1929–1963.* San Francisco: R & E Research Associates, 1974; Pycior, Julie Leininger. *LBJ & Mexican Americans: The Paradox of Power.* Austin: University of Texas Press, 1997; Tirado, Miguel David. "Mexican American Community Political Organization." In *La Causa Política,* edited by F. Chris García. Notre Dame: University of Notre Dame Press, 1974.

POLITICAL PARTICIPATION. Ever since the 1848 Treaty of **Guadalupe Hidalgo**, Mexican Americans have worked to retain their fair share of power in the U.S. political scene. Except in New Mexico and the Texas border region, they quickly found themselves in a position of being almost completely excluded from politics despite the rights guaranteed them by the treaty. Rebuffed in their attempts at political participation, most Mexican Americans outside of New Mexico and south Texas were alienated, became resigned to their impotence, and largely withdrew from politics.

However, World War I marked a turning point. In the 1920s Texas veterans began establishing new organizations through which they hoped to increase *raza* participation in the political arena. In 1929 these groups came together to form the **League of United Latin American Citizens**, which

California Lt. Governor Cruz M. Bustamante takes the oath of office during his swearing in ceremony at the Capitol in Sacramento, California, January 6, 2003. © AP/Wide World Photos.

articulated heretofore largely unvoiced goals of pragmatic political participation. Also, labor union recruiting and organizing in the Southwest during the 1920s began opening political vistas to the fledgling union members.

A quarter century later, World War II veterans brought about a decisive change in Mexican American participation in politics. As Mexican Americans became increasingly an urban people, more intensive community organizing was possible and greater political pressure could be developed. During the 1950s and 1960s the Chicano presence in politics increased at local and state levels, but gross underrepresentation still persisted. Although presidents John F. Kennedy and Lyndon Johnson made Chicano appointments to various federal offices in the 1960s, only a handful of *raza* members were successful as political party candidates.

Animated by the success of the aggressive African American civil rights movement in the early 1960s, Chicanos turned to a confrontational activism as a tool. The Movement of the 1960s and 1970s vociferously demanded a greater share of political power for Chicanos. Post–World War II organizations like the **American G.I. Forum** and the **Mexican American Political Association** used electoral politics to pressure the system. These aggressive tactics resulted in political effectiveness absent from earlier, more restrained efforts.

President Richard Nixon set a new record for the appointment of Mexican Americans to government positions in the early 1970s, despite his negative views about their abilities. A significant number of Chicanos were named to federal offices at various levels by President Jimmy Carter. President Bill Clinton appointed **Henry Cisneros** and **Federico Peña** to his first cabinet in 1993 and later named Nuevomexicano **Bill Richardson** U.S. ambassador to the United Nations. In addition to cabinet appointments, positions at various levels in federal departments and agencies have been opened more widely to Mexican Americans.

The **Voting Rights Act** of 1965 was extremely important to increased Chicano participation in politics, as was the removal of various barriers to **voting** such as poll taxes, literacy tests, and exclusionary residency requirements. These changes smoothed the way for energetic voter registration drives and get-out-the-vote campaigns that enabled Chicano politicians to win more elective positions in the last quarter of the twentieth century. In some smaller towns of the Southwest, particularly along the border, they became the majority on school boards and city councils. In Arizona and New Mexico **Raúl Castro** and **Jerry Apodaca** were elected governors in the 1970s, and in 1982 **Toney Anaya** became governor of New Mexico. These election successes were largely the results of increased *raza* participation in the political process.

At the beginning of the 1970s greater Chicano political activity led to the creation of a national **La Raza Unida Party** (LRUP). Although LRUP was a spectacular effort at participation in politics, it had disappeared by the late 1970s, partly because of divided leadership and bitter internal dissent, leading to internecine power struggles. Since then the Chicano political push has been largely within the Democratic and Republican parties. Between 1984 and 2001 the number of U.S. Latinos elected to government offices nationwide increased a sizable 2,010 from 3,128 to 5,138. It would undoubtedly be more but for the fact that 39 percent of Latinos age eighteen and over are noncitizen immigrants.

Increasingly aspiring Chicano politicians have been appearing on the ballot, and more are winning elections as greater numbers of Mexican Americans vote. In 1987 **Gloria Molina** became the first Chicana to be elected to the Los Angeles city council, the city with the largest Mexicano population in the U.S. In 1990 Dan Morales was elected as the first Chicano state attorney general in Texas history, and six years later Cruz Bustamante became the first Californio to be elected speaker of the state assembly. In 1998 he was elected lieutenant governor and **Antonio Villaraigosa** became the powerful speaker of the Assembly. **Art Torres**, another prominent Chicano politician, is the chairman of the Democratic Party in California. On the other hand, in 1993 **José Angel Gutiérrez** failed in his Texas bid for the U.S. Senate as a Democrat. In California Villaraigosa, the former assembly speaker, was defeated in his bid for the mayoralty of Los Angeles in 2001, and in the following year Tony Sánchez lost his race for the governorship of Texas.

The political representation of the Mexican American community is still not commensurate with its numbers. In 2001 Latinos held 5,138 elected positions. However, in spite of a slow advance and some setbacks, Mexican American political cognizance guarantees continuing efforts to obtain a fairer share of political power through the ballot.

FURTHER READING: Garza, Rudolph O., de la. *The Chicano Political Experience.* North Scituate, Mass.: Duxbury Press, 1977; García, F. Chris, ed. *Pursuing Power: Latinos and the Political System.* Notre Dame: University of Notre Dame Press, 1997; Gómez-Quiñonez, Juan. *Roots of Chicano Politics, 1600–1948.* Albuquerque: University of New Mexico Press, 1994; Guzmán, Ralph C. *The Political Socialization of the Mexican American People,* Reprint. New York: Arno Press, 1976; Maciel, David R., and Isidro D. Ortiz, eds. *Chicanas / Chicanos at the Crossroads: Social, Economic, and Political Change.* Tucson: University of Arizona Press, 1996; Montejano, David, ed. *Chicano Politics and Society in the Late Twentieth Century.* Austin: University of Texas Press, 1999; Vigil, Mauricio. *Chicano Politics.* Washington, D.C.: University Press of America, 1977; Villarreal, Roberto E., and Norma G. Hernández. *Latinos and Political Coalitions: Political Empowerment for the 1990s.* Westport, Conn.: Greenwood Press, 1991.

POLLERO/POLLO. *Pollo* is Spanish for chicken, a word used to refer to an **undocumented** Mexican, and a pollero is a person who leads the pollos across the border. Related terms are *pato,* Spanish for duck, and *patero,* used when the border crossing is across the **Rio Grande.**

PONCE DE LEÓN, MICHAEL, 1922– . Painter, printmaker, teacher. Although born in Miami, Florida, Michael Ponce de León grew up in Mexico City, where he received his education. While he studied architecture at the Universidad Nacional Autónoma de México he also became interested in drawing. He began to publish cartoons in popular magazines like *The New Yorker* after serving in the U.S. Air Force during the 1940s. After World War II his cartoon series titled *Impulses* was syndicated in the United States and Europe. Meanwhile, he also continued his art studies in the United States, Europe, and Mexico. In the 1950s and 1960s he was the recipient of several grants, including a Guggenheim and two Fulbrights.

During the 1960s and 1970s Ponce de León taught art at a number of outstanding universities and institutions in New York and California. In 1964 he was commissioned by the U.S. Post Office to design a stamp celebrating the fine arts, and between 1965 and 1982 he was sent by the State Department to a number of countries in cultural exchange programs. He has exhibited in London, Paris, and Venice as well as in New York and Washington, D.C. His works, especially his collages and intaglios, are represented in permanent collections all over the world. He has won more than sixty-five prestigious medals, awards, and fellowships.

FURTHER READING: Cochrane, Diane. "Michael Ponce de León." *American Artist.* 38 (October 1974) 38-43, 77, 82-83; Cummings, Paul. *Dictionary of Contemporary American Artists,* 6th ed. New York: St. Martin's Press, 1994; Quirarte, Jacinto. *Mexican American Artists.* Austin: University of Texas Press, 1973; *Who's Who in American Art,* 20th ed. New York: R. R. Bowker, 1993.

POOR PEOPLE'S MARCH, 1968. In order to air grievances and to demand enforcement of existing civil rights legislation, Martin Luther King, Jr., and Ralph Abernathy of the Southern Christian Leadership Conference began early in 1968 to organize a protest march on Washington, D.C. King asked **Reies López Tijerina** to put together a Mexican American delegation from the Southwest. During the march Tijerina became a somewhat belligerent subordinate to Abernathy, who had taken over the leadership after King's assassination. He accused Abernathy of ignoring the Chicano contingent. He and coleader **Corky Gonzales** converted the march into an eminently conspicuous and memorable platform for Chicano complaints and demands.

In the U.S. capital Tijerina staged a contentious meeting with Department of State officials, arguing vociferously about loss of Mexican American land grants guaranteed by the Treaty of **Guadalupe Hidalgo**. He also tried to involve the Mexican ambassador in his blustering dispute with State, without success. **Corky Gonzales** seized the opportunity of the march to launch his call for Chicano cultural nationalism. He issued his **Plan del Barrio,** which demanded **bilingual education** and better **housing** for Chicanos, as well as land reforms. All the protest leaders, black, brown, and white, called for increased minority access to jobs, improved housing, and greater educational opportunities.

FURTHER READING: Fager, Charles E. *Uncertain Resurrection: The Poor People's Washington Campaign.* Grand Rapids: Eerdmans, 1969; Tijerina, Reies López. *"They Call Me King Tiger": My Struggle for the Land and Our Rights.* Translated and edited by José Angel Gutiérrez. Houston: Arte Público Press, 1999; Vigil, Ernesto B. *The Crusade for Justice: Chicano Militancy and the Government's War on Dissent.* Madison: University of Wisconsin Press, 1999.

POPULATION, MEXICAN AMERICAN. At the time of the Treaty of Guadalupe Hidalgo there were approximately 80,000 Mexican citizens living in the Southwest. Nearly all of these remained in the new U.S. domain. The largest number, about 60,000, lived in the New Mexico territory; California accounted for some 8,000 and Texas had approximately 5,000. A half century later, the 1900 census indicated that there were 103,000 persons of Mexican birth, nearly all of whom still lived in the Southwest. Adding the number of American-born raised the Chicano total to nearly 200,000.

Between 1900 and 1930 there was a large ingress of Mexican sojourners, perhaps as many as 1,000,000, driven by the great revolution in Mexico and encouraged by the U.S. demand for cheap labor. The census of 1930, based on Mexican origin, indicated that there were 1,509,000, plus a possible undercount of as many as 500,000 according to some authorities. This census also marked the beginning of a movement out of the Southwest as indicated by a record 227,000 living elsewhere. With 684,000, Texas still had nearly half of the Chicano population, but California, with an increase to 368,000, was beginning to rival Texas for the number one position.

Although there was little Mexican immigration during the 1930s, after World War II a rapid influx developed, stimulated in part by the bracero experience. The 1970 census, based on Spanish as the language spoken at home, indicated a total U.S. population of about 6,190,000. This figure must be adjusted for non-Mexican-origin Spanish-speakers included, non-Spanish-speaking Chicanos excluded, and a possible undercount of as much as 2,000,000. The real total may have been as much as 8,000,000. California, with 3,102,000 Latinos, now led Texas, having a million more than the 2,060,000 in that state. In 2000 about a third of California's population was Latino.

The census of 2000 indicated that Mexican Americans would soon become the largest minority group in the United States. It showed that U.S. Latinos, nearly equaling the black American population, numbered 32.8 million, of which Mexican Americans accounted for approximately 21.6 million. Leading the latest immigration wave, some 13 million U.S. Latinos, nearly 40 percent, were foreign-born, of whom 5.6 million had entered the country during the 1990s. Slightly more than half of the Mexican American population had graduated from high school and 6.9 percent had college degrees. Only 14 percent of U.S. Latinos held professional or managerial positions; the majority were employed in service occupations and labor. Almost half lived in a central city within a metropolitan area, and only 8.5 percent lived in nonmetropolitan areas. Nearly 23 percent of all Hispanics were living below the poverty level. Among Hispanics, Mexican Americans had the lowest annual incomes; only 20 percent earned $35,000 or more annually.

FURTHER READING: Brewer, Cynthia A., and Trudy A. Suchan. *Mapping Census 2000: The Geography of U.S. Diversity*. Washington, D.C.: U.S. Census Bureau, 2001; *The Hispanic Population in the United States: March 2000*. Washington, D.C.: U.S. Department of Commerce, Bureau of the Census, 2000; Martínez, Oscar J. "On the Size of the Chicano Population: New Estimates, 1850–1900." *Aztlán* 6 (Spring 1975) 43–59; Teller, Charles H., Leo F. Estrada, and José Hernández, eds. *Cuantos Somos: A Demographic Survey of the Mexican-American Population*. Austin: Center for Mexican American Studies, University of Texas, 1977; U.S., Bureau of the Census. *Persons of Spanish Origin in the United States*. Series P-20:310. Washington, D.C.: Government Printing Office, 1977; Walter, Paul A., Jr. *Population Trends in New Mexico*. Albuquerque: University of New Mexico Press, 1947.

PORTILLO-TRAMBLEY, ESTELA, 1927–1998. Playwright, novelist, poet, teacher. Estela Portillo was born in El Paso, Texas, where she grew up in middle-class comfort, raised by grandparents until their deaths when she was twelve. Her early education in El Paso schools was followed by a 1956 B.A. in English and an M.A. in 1978 at Texas Western College (today the University of Texas, El Paso). Meanwhile she married, taught English at the local high school and drama at El Paso Community College, and worked in radio and television while she raised her six children. Her semiweekly cultural program on television, drama teaching, and involvement in a theater group led her to a serious commitment to writing. Her first play, *Day of the Swallows*, was published in 1971 and won her the Quinto Sol award for literature in the following year.

Day of the Swallows established Portillo-Trambley as a pioneer Chicana writer, and was followed by a collection of her poems titled *Impressions of a Chicana*. In 1975 she published *Rain of Scorpions and Other Writings*, a collection of short fiction that gave clear evidence of her deep feminist concerns. Six years later she received the Writer Recognition Award from the Texas Commission of Arts. Early in 1984 her play *Puente Negro* won the Women's Plays competition at St. Edward's University in Austin, and in the following year her *Blacklight*, first produced in 1979, won second place in the Hispanic American playwrights' competition at the New York Shakespeare Festival.

An outstanding Chicana dramatist, Portillo-Trambley made substantial contributions to Mexican American literature. She opened the field for Chicana writers, who were being ignored by mainstream publishers. She was criticized by some for not writing to promote the political agenda of the Chicano **movimiento,** but she continued on her own path, depicting strong women and holding to her main theme: efforts of Chicanas to achieve autonomous lives. She was visiting professor at a number of universities, occupying the Presidential Chair in Creative Writing at the Davis campus of the University of California in 1995. She was constantly revising her plays, improving on her craftsmanship. In 1993 her revised edition of *Rain of Scorpions* was published by the Bilingual Press in its Clásicos Chicanos series. She was working on another novel when she died of cancer.

FURTHER READING: Bruce-Novoa, Juan. *Chicano Authors: Inquiry by Interview.* Austin: University of Texas Press, 1980; *Fem* 8:34 (June–July 1984) 37–40; Lomelí, Francisco A. "Chicana Novelists in the Process of Creating Fictive Voices." In *A Critical Analysis of Chicana Literature*, edited by María Herrera Sobek. Binghamton, N.Y.: Bilingual Press/Editorial Bilingüe, 1985; Lomelí, Francisco A., and Carl R. Shirley, eds. *Chicano Writers: Third Series.* Detroit: The Gale Group, 1999; Martínez, Julio A., and Francisco A. Lomelí. *Chicano Literature: A Reference Guide.* Westport, Conn.: Greenwood Press, 1985; Ryan, Bryan, ed. *Hispanic Writers.* Detroit: Gale Research, 1991; Vallejo, Tomás. "Estela Portillo Trambley's Fictive Search for Paradise." *Frontiers: A Journal of Women's Studies* 5:2 (Summer 1980) 54–58.

PRECIADO DE BURCIAGA, CECILIA, 1945– . Educational administrator.

Cecilia Preciado began her professional life as a high school Spanish teacher in Chino, California. A subsequent brief and disappointing stint in the U.S. foreign service led her to a staff position in the Interagency Committee for

Mexican American Affairs (ICMAA), on which she had been doing volunteer work. She soon moved from the ICMAA to the U.S. Civil Rights Commission, where she worked as a research analyst on the status of Mexican Americans in education. Her commission experience led to a strong commitment to improving educational opportunities for U.S. Latinos.

When she was appointed Provost for Chicano Affairs and Assistant to the President at Stanford University in 1974, Cecilia returned to California with her husband, Antonio Burciaga. At Stanford her first job was to recruit more Mexican Americans for the student body, faculty, and staff. Three years later she was promoted to assistant provost for Faculty Affairs; here her principal task was to increase the number of minority and women faculty at Stanford. In the second half of the 1980s she was promoted to associate dean of Graduate Studies.

Burciaga acted also as director of the Office of Chicano Affairs and for a time was the university's affirmative action officer as well. In 1991 she was again promoted, this time to associate dean and director of Development. After twenty years at Stanford, Burciaga was dismissed in 1994 by Stanford's new president, Gerhard Casper, in what he described as part of a budget-cutting move. Her dismissal caused campus-wide faculty criticism and student protest. After being dropped by Stanford she was hired as an executive assistant by the newly established California State University at Monterey Bay.

For her dedication to human rights, Preciado de Burciaga was honored by the San Francisco United Nations Association with the Eleanor D. Roosevelt Humanitarian Award. She has served on various national and California boards and commissions, including the president's Advisory Commission on Educational Excellence for Hispanic Americans.

FURTHER READING: "Cecilia Burciaga: A Hispana in Higher Education." *La Luz* 8:8 (October-November 1980) 14 ; Telgen, Diane, and Jim Kamp, eds. *Notable Hispanic American Women*. Detroit: Gale Research, 1993; Treviño, Laramie. "The Hispanic Professional: Cecilia Preciado Burciaga." *Intercambios Femeniles* 3:1 (Spring 1988) 7.

PRESIDENT'S COMMISSION ON MIGRATORY LABOR. The commission was created in 1950 by President Harry Truman to make recommendations for legislation about migrant workers. After holding meetings and public hearings, in the following year the agency issued a report that recommended restructuring the **bracero** program arrangements, outlawing the hiring of **undocumented**s, and making more effective use of American workers.

FURTHER READING: United States. President's Commission on Migratory Labor. *Migratory Labor in American Agriculture: Report*. Washington, D.C.: U.S. Government Printing Office, 1951.

PRIETO, JORGE, 1919–2001. Physician, activist. Jorge Prieto was born in Mexico City and crossed into the United States at age four when his father was forced into exile during the second stage of the 1910 **Mexican revolu-**

tion. After living in Houston, Texas for three years, his parents moved to Los Angeles, where they remained until 1933. When the political climate changed, the family returned to Mexico, and Prieto continued his education there as well as his deep interest in American football.

In 1943 Prieto entered Notre Dame University in Indiana with a partial academic scholarship and dreams of becoming a football hero. While a student, he was influenced to change his prime university goal from football to a medical career by his slender physique and a visit to migrant worker camps in Michigan. He went back to Mexico to complete his medical education at the Universidad Nacional Autónoma de México and then did his year of social service as a physician in an impoverished and isolated area of Zacatecas state.

Returning to the United States to work among Mexicano migrants as he had planned, in 1952 Dr. Prieto started a medical practice in Chicago, Illinois. His clientele was mostly Latino and poor. He was dismayed by the unequal medical services provided minorities and Anglos, and became interested in the early civil rights movement. Inspired by his concern for the voiceless workers, in the spring of 1966 he joined the march to Sacramento by César Chávez and his National Farm Workers Association members and supporters. Taking an increasingly more active part in the Delano strike, he became involved in the grape boycott. During this time he also helped establish the Illinois Migrant Council to make medical care available to migratory agricultural workers.

In 1970 Dr. Prieto was appointed director of community medicine at Chicago's Cabrini Hospital and four years later, after two decades of inner city practice, was named chair of the family practice department at Cook County Hospital. In the latter capacity he became mentor to a generation of family physicians whom he trained and inspired with his ideals of medical service to underserved communities. He set up clinics in Mexicano and black neighborhoods and shifted the training of resident doctors away from the hospital to these areas.

In 1984 Dr. Prieto was appointed president of Chicago's Board of Health by the mayor. In this new position he continued to stress his belief in the importance of close involvement in the community by doctors. In that same year he was awarded an honorary doctorate by Notre Dame University.

FURTHER READING: Prieto, Jorge. *Harvest of Hope: The Pilgrimage of a Mexican-American Physician.* Notre Dame, Indiana: University of Notre Dame Press, 1989; Prieto, Jorge. *The Quarterback Who Almost Wasn't.* Houston: Arte Público Press, 1994; Sotomayor, Frank O. "Dr. Jorge Prieto; Pushed Care for Poor, Migrants." Obituary. *Los Angeles Times* (27 August 2001) II, 14.

PRIMER CONGRESO MEXICANISTA, EL, 1911. The Primer Congreso Mexicanista was one of the early efforts by Mexican Americans to organize in a militant defense of their rights. Inspired largely by Nicasio **Idar**, a rights leader and publisher of the Laredo weekly, *La Crónica*, it was held at Laredo,

Jovita Idar. © Library of Congress.

Texas in 1911. It was in part a response to the often vicious abuse suffered by border Mexicanos at the turn of the twentieth century. The meeting was attended by several hundred Tejano delegates, who discussed what might be done about various concerns, especially discrimination in the schools and official toleration of the **lynching** of Mexicanos. The leaders believed that only by uniting and organizing widely could they successfully assert their rights. They adopted "Por la Raza y Para la Raza" as their motto.

The Congreso was especially notable for inviting Mexicanas to take part in the conference. Led by Nicasio's daughter Jovita, they participated actively in the discussions and later established a women's auxiliary, La Liga Femenil Mexicanista. Jovita Idar presided over the new organization.

To focus continuing attention on the many problems faced daily by Tejanos, the delegates created a statewide organization named La Gran Liga Mexicanista de Beneficencia y Protección. Although the name hinted at mutualism, the league retained little of the **mutualista** concept. The delegates emphasized their rights as American citizens while at the same time supporting language retention and rejecting total assimilation. Ahead of their time, they created a culturally nationalist organization that was protectively militant and nonsexist. The Gran Liga soon faded due to lack of funds and Anglo opposition. Not until the 1960s civil rights movement was there an organization with the advanced ideas put forward by the Congreso.

FURTHER READING: Limón, José E. "El Primer Congreso Mexicanista de 1911: A Precursor to Contemporary Chicanismo." *Aztlán* 5:1&2 (Spring and Fall 1974) 85–117; " 'Por la raza y para la raza': Congreso Mexicanista, 1911." In *Foreigners in Their Native Land: Historical Roots of the Mexican American*, edited by David J. Weber. Albuquerque: University of New Mexico Press, 1973.

PROPOSITION 187, 1994. Proposition 187, approved by nearly 60 percent of California voters in the 1994 elections, made undocumented immigrant children ineligible for public school **education** and denied all **undocumented**s various social services and all nonemergency health care. It also required governmental agencies and schools to report suspected undocumented aliens to the state's Attorney General and to the U.S. Immigration and Naturalization Service. It effectively expired when most of its provisions were declared unconstitutional by the federal district court. Efforts to revive it in 2000 were dropped in the interest of gaining more Latino votes in California for Republican candidates in the presidential election year.

FURTHER READING: Alarcón, Rafael. *Proposition 187: An Effective Measure to Deter Undocumented Migration to California?* San Francisco: Multicultural Education, Training and Advocacy, Inc., 1994; Alvarez, R. Michael, and Tara L. Butterfield. "The Resurgence of Nativism in California? The Case of Proposition 187 and Illegal Immigration." *Social Science Quarterly* 81:1 (2000) 167–179; Delgado, Richard and Jean Stefancic, eds. *The Latino/a Condition: A Critical Reader.* New York: New York University Press, 1998; Gibbs, Jewelle Taylor, and Teiahasha Bankhead. *Preserving Privilege: California Politics, Propositions, and People of Color.* Westport, Conn.: Praeger, 2001.

PROPOSITION 209, 1996. Proposition 209, titled The California Civil Rights Initiative, was passed by California voters in November 1996. It prohibited preferential treatment and discrimination by state or other public entities in employment, education, and contracting. It prohibited the use of preferences, quotas, and set-asides based on gender, color, race, ethnicity, or national origin. Preferences based on other criteria remained unaffected. Supporters claimed it would "level the playing field." In heated discussions, critics and opponents contended that it would unfavorably affect current and future efforts to redress past inequities.

Upon passage, the proposition was immediately challenged in the courts by its critics. They argued that the new law would have the effect of dismantling federal **affirmative action** programs and of devastating efforts to help women and minorities in areas where they have historically been excluded, discriminated against, or grossly underrepresented. Although Judge Thelton Henderson found for the plaintiffs and enjoined implementation or enforcement of the proposition, the strong voter support for Proposition 209 has had a deterring effect on affirmative action programs in the state.

FURTHER READING: Acuña, Rodolfo F. *Sometimes There Is No Other Side: Chicanos and the Myth of Equality.* Notre Dame: University of Notre Dame Press, 1998; Adam, Michelle. "Hopwood/Proposition 209 and Minority Enrollment in Texas and California." *Hispanic Outlook in Higher Education* (18 November 2002) 39–40; Chávez, Lydia. *The Color Bind: California's Battle to End Affirmative Action.* Berkeley: University of California Press, 1998; Gibbs, Jewelle Taylor, and Teiahasha Bankhead. *Preserving Privilege: California Politics, Propositions, and People of Color.* Westport, Conn.: Praeger, 2001; Ong, Paul, ed. *Impacts of Affirmative Action: Policies and Consequences in California.* Walnut Creek, Calif.: Altamira Press, 1999.

PROPOSITION 227, 1998. Proposition 227, called The English Language in the Public Schools Initiative, was passed by California voters in June, 1998. The regulations established by this new legislation essentially required that all public school classes (except foreign language classes) be taught in

English. This mandate primarily affects the teaching of students with limited English-speaking ability. Although the law allows some exceptions, it clearly marks an effort to reduce and bring to an end **bilingual education** practices in the state.

The campaign for Proposition 227 was largely financed by wealthy Silicon Valley businessman Ron Unz and was strongly supported by the conservative Center for Equal Opportunity established by **Linda Chávez,** former head of **U.S. English**, an organization founded to end bilingual education and to establish English as the official language of the United States.

The new legislation was immediately challenged in the courts. Both the **Mexican American Legal Defense and Educational Fund** and the American Civil Liberties Union filed to restrain implementation of the law. They argued that the proposition violated the federal Equal Opportunities Act of 1974 and the Fourteenth Amendment to the U.S. Constitution.

FURTHER READING: Cornejo, Ricardo J. "Bilingual Education: Some Reflections on Proposition 227." *Hispanic Outlook in Higher Education* (9 October 1998) 27–32; Gibbs, Jewelle Taylor, and Teiahasha Bankhead. *Preserving Privilege: California Politics, Propositions, and People of Color.* Westport, Conn.: Praeger, 2001.

PUBLIC LAW 45, 1943. Public Law 45 supplemented the accord reached in 1942 by the United States and Mexico in regard to bringing in Mexican **braceros** during World War II. To a degree it circumvented the agreement by authorizing the Commissioner of Immigration to issue one-year permits to Mexican workers. The Mexican government protested when the commissioner issued permit cards in May 1943, pointing out that the 1942 accord was being violated. As a result, issuance was halted after some 2,000 cards had been given out.

FURTHER READING: Scruggs, Otey M. "Texas and the Bracero Program, 1942–1947." *Pacific Historical Review* 32:3 (1963) 251–264.

PUBLIC LAW 78, 1951. Public Law 78, also called The Migratory Labor Agreement of 1951, was passed by the U.S. Congress during the Korean conflict to regulate the importing of workers from Mexico. In August 1951 it was formalized as a treaty between the two countries. It marked the beginning of the second, post–World War II stage of **bracero** importation. Under it the U.S. Labor Department certified a need for workers and participated in their recruiting, contracting, transporting, and processing. It also guaranteed them minimum conditions of work and pay. P L 78 was limited to two years but was regularly renewed until 1964, when Congress let it lapse because of mounting opposition from Chicano organizations, labor unions, and church groups. It was characterized by a sharp increase in the importation of braceros.

FURTHER READING: Craig, Richard B. *The Bracero Program: Interest Groups and Foreign Policy.* Austin: University of Texas Press, 1971; Meier, Matt S., and Feliciano Ribera. *Mexican Americans/American Mexicans: From Conquistadors to Chicanos.* New York: Hill & Wang, 1993.

QUERÉTARO, PROTOCOL OF, 1948. The Protocol of Querétaro was an assurance given to the government of Mexico after its Congress had approved the **Guadalupe Hidalgo** but before it officially ratified the treaty. The U.S. commissioners verbally assured the Mexican government that Mexicans in the ceded territories would retain all their rights. At the suggestion of Mexico's minister of foreign affairs, these assurances were then restated in writing as a protocol. However, the protocol was never ratified by either government and therefore lacked validity in international law.

FURTHER READING: Bloom, John Porter, ed. *The Treaty of Guadalupe Hidalgo, 1848: Papers of the Sesquicentennial Symposium, 1848–1998.* Las Cruces, N.M.: Yucca Tree Press, 1999; Griswold Del Castillo, Richard. *The Treaty of Guadalupe Hidalgo: A Legacy of Conflict.* Norman: University of Oklahoma Press, 1990. Klein, Julius. *The Making of the Treaty of Guadalupe Hidalgo, February 2, 1848.* Berkeley: University of California Press, 1905.

QUEVEDO, EDUARDO, 1903–1967. Civic leader. Throughout his life, Los Angeleno Eduardo Quevedo was deeply involved in defending the rights of Chicanos. In the late 1930s he was one of the important principals in founding the **Congreso de Los Pueblos de Habla Española** and during World War II he served as chairman of the Coordinating Council for Latin American Youth. In 1943 he vehemently protested the actions of the sheriff's department and the Los Angeles police in the **Zoot Suit Riots**. Later that year he participated energetically in the **Sleepy Lagoon** Defense Committee. His confrontational activities caused him to be singled out for intense federal and local government scrutiny.

In the postwar years Quevedo continued his involvement as a successful community organizer. In 1959 he played an important part in calling the meeting that led to the founding of the **Mexican American Political Association.** He then became its first president, successfully molding the organization in its formative years. As a result of his civil rights interests Quevedo was appointed to various state commissions and boards.

FURTHER READING: Villarreal, José Antonio. "Mexican Americans in Upheaval." In *Readings on La Raza: The Twentieth Century,* edited by Matt S. Meier and

Feliciano Rivera. New York: Hill and Wang, 1974; "Zoot Suit War." *Time* (21 June 1943).

QUINN, ANTHONY, 1916–2001. Actor, artist, writer. Anthony Rudolph Oaxaca Quinn was born in the capital of Chihuahua state during the Mexican revolution and was taken across the border into the United States before his first birthday. When he was four, the family moved from El Paso to Los Angeles, where his father obtained work as property man in a movie studio. Quinn's education in East Los Angeles public schools was adversely affected by the accidental death of his father in 1925, which resulted in his going to work to help support the family. Although his mother's remarriage in 1930 relieved him of family financial responsibilities, he later dropped out of high school in his sophomore year.

During the Great Depression Quinn worked at a variety of menial jobs including custodial work, ditch digging, and migrant farm labor. Acting had for a long time interested him, and for a while he worked in a WPA Federal Theater Project. After an operation to correct a speech defect, he began acting in local theater and played opposite Mae West in a 1936 play, *Clean Beds*. A bit part in a film that same year led to a supporting role as an Indian in Cecil B. DeMille's *The Plainsman*. Acting success led to a decade of roles in Hollywood films as a Latin lover, swarthy villain, and Indian. In 1947

Anthony Quinn as Zorba the Greek, 1964. © The Kobal Collection.

he became a U.S. citizen and also made his Broadway debut, which was a flop. However, he then made a big stage hit replacing Marlon Brando in a two-year run of *A Streetcar Named Desire*. During the 1950s he continued movie work in Hollywood and Italy, winning an international reputation through such films as *Viva Zapata, La Strada*, and *Lust for Life*.

In the 1960s Quinn did some of his best acting, in films like *The Guns of Navaronne, Shoes of the Fisherman*, and *Zorba the Greek*. The astounding popularity of *Zorba* led him back to live theater in an equally successful stage version. However, he had only mixed success in made-for-TV movies and series. During the 1970s and 1980s he continued to turn in sterling performances in films such as *The Children of Sánchez* and *Lion in the Desert*, in which he played strong ethnic characters. Over a period of nearly seven decades he played an entire pantheon of ethnics, including Arab, Chinese, Hawaiian, East Indian, and Eskimo, in an amazing 325 films. He won Academy Awards as Best Supporting Actor in *Viva Zapata* and *Lust for Life*.

A man of great and many talents, Quinn was also a painter and sculptor of some note, as well as playwright, film producer, and author. His paintings have been shown in a number of one-man exhibitions. Fluent in English, Spanish, and Italian, he was a serious reader, with a library of several thousand volumes. Quinn was outspoken on social issues and strongly supported the United Farm Workers union. Like his character Zorba, he believed in living every day to its fullest. He fathered a baker's dozen of children by various wives and lovers; their ages span over half a century. He died of respiratory failure on 3 June 2001.

FURTHER READING: Merill, Alvin H. *The Films of Anthony Quinn*. Secaucus, N.J.: Citadel Press, 1975; Martínez, Julio A., and Francisco A. Lomelí, eds. *Chicano Literature: A Reference Guide*. Westport, Conn.: Greenwood Press, 1985; Quinn, Anthony. *One Man Tango*. New York: HarperCollins, 1995; Quinn, Anthony. *The Original Sin: A Self-Portrait*. Boston: Little, Brown, 1972; Reyes, Luis, and Peter Rubie. *Hispanics in Hollywood: A Celebration of 100 Years in Film and Television*. Hollywood: Lone Eagle, 2000; Silverman, Stephen, et al. "Mighty Quinn." *People* 55:24 (18 June 2001) 92.

QUINTO SOL. Quinto Sol was a publishing organization created in 1967 at Berkeley, California by a group of Mexican American writers, headed by **Octavio I. Romano** and Herminio Ríos. The objective of the group was to provide a forum for Mexican American writers, who at that time had difficulty finding acceptance for their works among mainstream publishers. For seven years Quinto Sol published a literary journal titled *El Grito*, which became a basic part of the Chicano Movement. Quinto Sol also established an annual Quinto Sol award for outstanding Chicano literary works.

FURTHER READING: Paredes, Raymund. "The Evolution of Chicano Literature." In *Three American Literatures: Essays in Chicano, Native American, and Asian-American Literature for Teachers of American Literature*, edited by Houston A. Baker. New York: Modern Language Association of America, 1982; Romano, Octavio Ignacio. "Quinto

Sol and Chicano Publications: The First Five Years, 1967–1972." *El Grito* 5:4 (Summer 1972) 3–11; Romano, Octavio Ignacio, ed. *Voices: Readings from El Grito, a Journal of Contemporary Mexican America Thought.* Berkeley, Calif.: Quinto Sol Publications, 1973 (1971).

RACISM. Racism is an accumulated mixture of habits, attitudes, policies, and actions based on the false assumption that there are innate differences in the three races: Negroid, Mongoloid, and Caucasoid. Racism is usually expressed by policies and acts of domination, segregation, discrimination, prejudice, and persecution. Whether expressed in institutional attitudes and practices or by individual acts, racism commonly serves to rationalize and justify one group's domination over another.

Racism's discrimination and economic exploitation have been important in shaping the Mexicano experience in the United States. Of mixed European and native American ancestry, many Mexican Americans have been excluded from superior social, economic, and political positions because of Indian ancestry. Moreover, discrimination based on race and ethnicity has often denied them even their basic civil rights. The half century delay in statehood for New Mexico because of its Hispano majority is a glaring historical example of political racism.

FURTHER READING: Bonilla-Silva, Eduardo. *White Supremacy and Racism in the Post-Civil Rights Era.* Boulder, Colo.: Lynne Rienner, 2001; Daniels, Roger, and Harry Kitano. *American Racism.* Englewood Cliffs, N.J., Prentice-Hall, 1970; McWilliams, Carey. *North From Mexico: The Spanish-Speaking People of the United States,* New ed. Westport, Conn.: Praeger Publishers, 1990; Martínez, Thomas M. "Advertising and Racism: The Case of the Mexican-American." *El Grito* 2:4 (Summer 1969) 3–13; Stokes, Curtis, Theresa Meléndez, and Genice Rhodes-Reed, eds. *Race in 21st Century America.* East Lansing: Michigan University Press, 2001.

RAILROADS. Mexican Americans have had long-term ties to the U.S. railroads. The building of railway networks in the Southwest in the late 1800s created jobs for thousands of Mexicano workers, most from border areas. Except for **mining,** railroads were the most important early nonagricultural hirer of Mexicanos. In addition, they played a key role in the dispersion of Mexicanos in the U.S. heartland. They also made possible a new integrated economy in the Southwest based on the shipping of mineral and agricultural products, and the new economy, in turn, added more Mexicanos to the labor force.

At the end of the nineteenth century American rail companies began recruiting workers in El Paso, sending them up the Mississippi Valley on six-month contracts. During the first decade of the twentieth century, U.S. railroads were employing Mexicanos throughout the Midwest and Northwest as well as in the Southwest. By the outbreak of World War I, employment or previous employment on the railroads had become a common denominator among male Mexican Americans.

When the United States entered World War I in 1917 the railroads were temporarily allowed to recruit Mexican labor to maintain the rails. Many of these workers came from farther south in Mexico, from Guanajuato, Jalisco, and Michoacán, and went farther north in the midwestern United States. As a result, some of them reached industrial centers like St. Louis, Pittsburgh, and Chicago. A quarter century later, just before U.S. entry into World War II, the railroads again asserted their imperative need to bring in workers from Mexico for track maintenance. The **bracero** program, established in 1942, included workers for the railways, and recruiting in Mexico was an important part of the program. With the aid of some eighty thousand Mexican braceros, the railroads were able to transport crops and domestic goods as well as military supplies with minimal interruption during the war. Recruitment was terminated at the end of the war. When the railroads were refused their requests to be allowed to extend the bracero contracts, they postponed repatriation of the workers until forced to do so by repeated protests from the Mexican government and U.S. labor unions.

FURTHER READING: Craig, Richard B. *The Bracero Program: Interest Groups and Foreign Policy.* Austin: University of Texas Press, 1971; Driscoll, Barbara A. *The Tracks North: The Railroad Bracero Program of World War II.* Austin: Center for Mexican American Studies, University of Texas, 1999; Rosales, Miguel A. "A Mexican Railroad Family in Wyoming." *Annals of Wyoming* 73:2 (2001) 28–32; Smith, Michael M. "Mexicans in Kansas City: The First Generation, 1900–1920." In *Perspectives in Mexican American Studies*, vol. 2. Tucson: Mexican American Studies and Research Center, University of Arizona, 1989.

RAMÍREZ, BLANDINA CÁRDENAS, 1944– . Educational activist. Blandina Ramírez was born and grew up in Del Rio, Texas. After graduation from high school there she spent two years at Texas Woman's University in Denton before completing her undergraduate degree in journalism at the University of Texas, Austin in 1967. Seven years later she earned her Ed.D. at the University of Massachusetts. Meanwhile, she taught in elementary schools in Del Rio and then moved to San Antonio as special assistant to the district superintendent.

Ramírez's training in journalism and public relations secured her a one-year appointment as a Rockefeller fellow in the U.S. Senate in Washington, D.C. in 1974. During the second half of the 1970s she worked for the Department of Health, Education, and Welfare and served on the Texas Advisory Committee to the federal Civil Rights Commission. She also was on the board of directors of the Mexican American Legal Defense and Educational Fund.

In 1983 Blandina Ramírez became a central figure in a civil rights wrangle with President Ronald Reagan. Three years earlier Ramírez had been appointed to the U.S. **Civil Rights Commission** by President Jimmy Carter. In 1983, apparently because she was critical of President Ronald Reagan's (1981–1989) lack of enthusiasm for civil rights, she and two fellow commissioners were replaced by him with three less zealous appointees. When the commission's authorization expired in November 1983, the Democratically controlled Congress reorganized the commission, giving it eight members, four to be appointed by the president and four by Congress. The Congress then appointed Blandina Ramírez as one of its four new appointees.

In 1988 Ramírez accepted a position as a vice president at Our Lady of the Lake University in San Antonio, but returned to Washington, D.C. in the following year as director of the Office of Minorities in Higher Education for the American Council on Education. She then taught in the LBJ Institute of Teaching and Learning, Southwest Texas State University in San Marcos. Currently she is dean of the College of Education and Human Development at the University of Texas, San Antonio. She also continues to be active in various major task forces, committees, and commissions concerning education.

Ramírez has received numerous honors for her pioneering work in **bilingual education** and experimental education: Ford Foundation Fellowship, 1971; Rockefeller Fellowship, 1974; Outstanding Hispanic Woman in Texas and NEA Human Rights Award, 1983; membership on the Board of Governors of the International Union for Child Welfare; and La Raza Award from the National Council of La Raza, 1990. An internationally known educator, she also has been a recipient of the notable Aguila Azteca award from the Mexican government.

FURTHER READING: "Cárdenas Joins Texas-San Antonio." *Hispanic Outlook in Higher Education* 12:9 (11 February 2002) 40; Cerrudo, Margaret. "Blandina Cárdenas Ramírez: On the Forefront of Civil Rights and Education." *Intercambios Femeniles,* 4:1 (Summer 1988) 201; "MALDEF Fights for Rights Commission." *MALDEF* 13:2 (Fall/Winter 1983) 1–2; Tardiff, Joseph C., and L. Mpho Mabunda, eds. *Dictionary of Hispanic Biography.* Detroit: Gale Research, 1996; Telgen, Diane, and Jim Kamp, eds. *Notable Hispanic American Women.* Detroit: Gale Research, 1993.

RAMÍREZ, HENRY M., 1929– . Educator. After studying for the priesthood, Henry Ramírez left the seminary in the mid-1950s to become a teacher. A decade later his innovative ideas involving the community in the education of Mexican American students had earned him a national reputation. Principally because of the "New Horizons" program he had created to reduce Chicano high school dropouts, in 1968 he was named by President Lyndon Johnson to be director of the Mexican American Studies Division in the U.S. Civil Rights Commission.

Three years later Ramírez was appointed by President Richard Nixon chairman of the Council on Opportunities for Spanish-Speaking People, a cabinet level position. In that post he encouraged greater Mexican American involvement in community organizations and in politics. He also made persistent efforts to secure federal policy-making appointments for qualified Chicanos. When the council's mandate expired in 1975, Ramírez retired to private life as an educational consultant.

FURTHER READING: Martínez, Al. *Rising Voices: Profiles of Hispano-American Lives.* New York: New American Library, 1974; Newlon, Clarke. *Famous Mexican Americans.* New York: Dodd, Mead & Co., 1972.

RAMÍREZ, RICARDO, 1936– . Bishop. Ricardo Ramírez was born in Bay City, Texas, where he grew up, attending public grade and high schools there. He earned his B.A. at the University of St. Thomas in Houston in 1959. Four years later, having decided he had a vocation to the priesthood, he began studies at St. Basil's Seminary in Toronto and he was ordained in 1966. After completing a two-year M.A. program at the University of Detroit, he spent five years working in Mexico as chaplain to university students and their families.

During 1973 and 1974 Ramírez studied at the East Asian Pastoral Institute in Manila and then briefly returned to Mexico. In 1976 he was sent to San Antonio, Texas, as executive vice president of the Mexican American Cultural Center, where he taught cultural anthropology. Five years later he was named auxiliary bishop of San Antonio and within the year was appointed the first bishop of the new diocese of Las Cruces, New Mexico. Long active in civic and cultural matters, he has served on many boards and committees; among his numerous activities, he was advisor to the U.S. Bishops Committee on Hispanic Affairs and a board member of the National Catholic Council for Interracial Justice.

FURTHER READING: *American Catholic Who's Who, 1980–1981.* Washington, D.C.: N. C. News Service, 1979; Day, Mark. "Bishop: 'Why Have We Had to Wait So Long for Hispanic Leaders?' " *National Catholic Reporter* 19 (24 December 1982); "Ramírez Named Bishop of Las Cruces." *Nuestro* (October 1982) 43; *Religious Leaders of America,* 2nd ed. Detroit: Gale Research, 1999; *Who's Who in America, 1984–1985.* Chicago: Marquis, 1984.

RAMÍREZ, SARA ESTELA, 1881–1910. Journalist, feminist, teacher, organizer. Born and educated in Coahuila, Mexico, as a young woman Sara Ramírez moved across the Rio Grande to Laredo, Texas after receiving her teaching credential. She soon became deeply involved in the struggle for the rights of Mexicanos on both sides of the border. A staunch liberal in Mexican politics, she recruited for the Partido Liberal Mexicano and acted as **Ricardo Flores Magón**'s official representative in Texas.

At the same time she applied her liberal principles to a Texas career as a border teacher, human rights advocate, poet, and journalist. She published two literary magazines, *La Corregidora* and *Aurora*, between 1904 and her death in 1910. In her writings, all in Spanish, she advocated a society free of racial, class, and gender discrimination. She constantly promoted the liberation of women, whom she urged to take a more active role in the management of their lives. When this precursor in Chicana feminism and early leader in defending the rights of *la raza* died at the age of 29 after a long illness, she was widely eulogized by border journalists as the most knowledgeable Mexicana in Texas.

FURTHER READING: *American National Biography*, vol. 18. New York: Oxford University Press, 1999; Tovar, Inés Hernández. "Sara Estela Ramírez: The Early Twentieth Century Texas-Mexican Poet." Ph.D. diss. University of Houston, 1984; Zamora, Emilio. "Sara Estela Ramírez: Una rosa roja en el movimiento." In *Mexican Women in the United States: Struggles Past and Present*, edited by Magdalena Mora and Adelaida R. Castillo. Los Angeles: University of California, Chicano Studies Research Center, 1980.

RANGEL, IRMA, 1931–2003. Legislator, teacher. Irma Rangel, the first Chicana elected to the Texas House of Representatives, was born to parents who had worked their way from migrant farm workers to middle-class business entrepreneurs. As a young woman she first studied to become a schoolteacher, graduating from Texas A&M University in 1952. After working a decade and a half in education, she reverted to her earlier dream of studying for the law. In 1969 she received her LL.B. from St. Mary's Law School in San Antonio and worked subsequently in several legal positions that gave her firsthand acquaintance with problems faced by Mexican Americans. This newfound awareness eventually led her to seek solutions through politics.

After working in a private law practice, in 1976 Rangel ran for the state legislature, defeating the three-term incumbent and becoming the first Tejana to be elected to that body. As a Texas legislator for the next quarter century, Irma Rangel showed special concern about equality of educational opportunity, particularly for women, which she saw as a vital key to their achieving a satisfying life. She also stressed fair employment practices, voting rights, and equal access to jobs for Chicanas as well as Chicanos. In 1997, after the **Hopwood** case, she was responsible for a law automatically admitting to any Texas college or university all students who graduated in the top 10 percent of their class. Four years later her bill requiring Texas universities to include socioeconomic information as a factor in graduate school admissions passed and became a law. To some extent these laws mitigate the effect of the U.S. court's *Hopwood* case decision prohibiting the use of **affirmative action** in admissions.

Rangel's work in the legislature brought her numerous honors. In 1994 she was inducted into the Texas Women's Hall of Fame and three years later was named Legislator of the Year by the Mexican American Bar Association. In 1998 Texas Young Democrats named her Woman of the Year. Irma Rangel died in March 2003 after a lengthy battle with cancer.

FURTHER READING: Palmisano, Joseph M., ed. *Notable Hispanic American Women, Book II.* Detroit: Gale Research, 1998; Phaup, James D. "Ms. Rangel Goes to Austin: The Education of a Legislator." In *Texas Politics Today,* edited by William Earl Maxwell and Ernest Crain. St. Paul, Minn.: West, 1978; Saavedra-Vela, Pilar. "Irma Rangel–Breaking Down Barriers in Texas." *Agenda* (Jan./Feb. 1978) 34–36; *Who's Who among Hispanic Americans, 1994–1995.* 3rd ed. Detroit: Gale Research, 1994.

RANGERS. The rangers were special police forces established in a number of western states and territories in the latter 1800s. Usually they were created for a specific task and often were authorized for a limited time period; both of these conditions were set for the California ranger force that sought the Five Joaquíns. The **Texas Rangers**, on the other hand, had no such limitations.

FURTHER READING: Bernal, Joe, Julian Samora, and Albert Peña, *Gunpowder Justice: A Reassessment of the Texas Rangers.* Notre Dame, Ind.: University of Notre Dame Press, 1979; Jackson, Joseph Henry. *Bad Company.* New York: Harcourt, Brace and Co., 1939; Lynch, Michael J., III. "The Role of J. T. Canales in the Development of Tejano Identity and Mexican American Integration in Twentieth Century South Texas." *Journal of South Texas* 13:2 (2000) 220–239.

RAZA, LA. The Spanish term *raza* literally means race or lineage. As used by Chicanos in a cultural sense, it connotes brotherhood and unity. In its widest application it includes all Latinos, but is often used in the United States to refer to Mexican Americans. Although the term dates back to the nineteenth century at least, it gained extensive currency duing the Chicano Movement in the 1960s and 1970s.

RAZA UNIDA PARTY, LA. The concept and term La Raza Unida has had a long history, dating from 1848 when it was first used by **Juan N. Cortina.** La Raza Unida Party (LRUP) was formally established in January 1970 at a meeting of young Texas Chicano leaders headed by **José Angel Gutiérrez.** It had its genesis in the **Mexican American Youth Organization** (MAYO) and the second Crystal City electoral revolt in 1969. Several months after its founding, **Corky Gonzales** announced the creation of a Raza Unida party in Colorado.

The new political party was conceived not as a single unified organization, but rather as an umbrella structure that would include a variety of Chicano organizations. It quickly spread from Texas and Colorado to the rest of the Southwest and even to the Midwest, where chapters were established in Mexican American communities in Illinois, Indiana, Michigan, and Ohio.

LRUP planned to use its political clout to bring Chicano concerns forcefully to the attention of U.S. society. Its immediate goal was to register

Chicanos and organize them into a unified voting bloc. This bloc could elect candidates to local and state offices or at least might act as a balance of power, or swing vote, between major party candidates. LRUP had both successes and failures.

LRUP victories in local Texas elections in 1970 and 1971 greatly heartened party leaders. The party was persuaded to accept the arguments of Corky Gonzales and his followers to form a nationwide third party, and a national LRUP was established at a convention held in El Paso in September 1972. However, a bitter and divisive leadership struggle between Gonzales and Gutiérrez ensued immediately. Gutiérrez, a pragmatic politician with a largely rural and semirural constituency that stressed local issues and generally opposed fielding national candidates, was elected the first national LRUP president.

In the November elections **Ramsey Muñiz,** the LRUP candidate for the Texas governorship, received over six percent of the votes, resulting in the first election of a Texas governor by a less-than-majority vote. Other LRUP candidates were successful in school district and other local elections; some were even elected to minor statewide offices. However, outside of Texas LRUP was unable to develop broad grassroots support. Its failure to qualify for the statewide ballot in Arizona and California was a major political setback.

Although LRUP won some local political victories in the mid-1970s, its political charisma declined. Between 1972 and 1974 LRUP voters dropped by about 50 percent and in the latter year Gonzales took the Colorado LRUP out of the national party. In 1976 the organizing of the **Mexican American Democrats** group by liberal Chicano activists in south Texas cut further into the LRUP vote. Two years later **Mario Compeán,** running for the governorship of Texas on the LRUP ticket, received less than 2 percent of the vote in a humiliating defeat. His failure to get the required minimum vote caused LRUP to be dropped from future ballots. Personality conflicts and power struggles within LRUP further weakened the organization. The arrest and indictment of Muñiz on drug charges gave the party the coup de grace by the end of the decade.

Although less than a resounding success, LRUP did have a substantial role in advancing the political empowerment of Chicanos. The ideas it put forward had real impact on the community's concept of ethnic politics. Further, it forced Democratic and Republican leaders to take raza concerns more seriously and to field more Chicano candidates at local and state levels. Lastly, it caused many Mexican Americans to scrutinize the local, state, and national political scene with active concern and deeper interest.

FURTHER READING: Compeán, Mario, and José Angel Gutiérrez. *La Raza Unida Party in Texas.* New York: Pathfinder Press, 1970; García, Ignacio M. *United We Win: The Rise and Fall of La Raza Unida Party.* Tucson: University of Arizona, Mexican American Studies and Research Center, 1989; Gutiérrez, José Angel. *La Raza and*

Revolution. San Francisco, Calif.: R & E Research Associates, 1972; Muñoz, Carlos, Jr. and María Barrera. "La Raza Unida Party and the Chicano Student Movement in California." In *Latinos and the Political System,* edited by F. Chris García. Notre Dame: University of Notre Dame Press, 1988; Navarro, Armando. *La Raza Unida Party: A Chicano Challenge to the U.S. Two-Party Dictatorship.* Philadelphia: Temple University Press, 2000; Pendas, Miguel, and Harry Ring. *Toward Chicano Power: Building La Raza Unida Party.* New York: Pathfinder Press, 1974; Santillán, Richard A. *Chicano Politics: La Raza Unida.* Los Angeles: Tlaquilo Publications, 1973.

RECHY, JOHN F., 1934– . Novelist, playwright. John Rechy was born and grew up in El Paso, Texas. From childhood he wanted to write and be an actor. Encouraged by some of his teachers, he wrote his first novelette while still in high school. In 1952 he entered what is today the University of Texas at El Paso on a scholarship; after graduation he served in the U.S. armed forces in Germany, all the time continuing to write, particularly short stories. Out of the army, he traveled widely in the United States, visiting cities with extensive gay populations.

Rechy's first full-length novel, *City of Night,* published in 1963, was an immediate best-seller and established him as an important new young American writer. He followed it with *Numbers,* 1967; *This Day's Death,* 1969; *The Fourth Angel,* 1972; a nonfiction work, *The Sexual Outlaw,* 1977; *Rushes,* 1979; *Bodies and Souls,* 1983; *Marilyn's Daughter,* 1988; *Our Lady of Babylon,* 1996; *The Coming of the Night,* 1999; and others. His novels often deal with urban homosexual life and some are partly autobiographical, according to Rechy. His works have been published in nearly two dozen countries in more than a dozen languages. In addition to his novels, he has written two plays and numerous articles, short stories, and essays. In the early 1970s Rechy began teaching creative writing, serving as a visiting scholar at several southern California universities. He taught writing at Columbia University at the beginning of the 1980s and from 1983 to 1999 was an adjunct professor in the graduate school of the University of Southern California.

Rechy has been the recipient of many awards, honors, and prizes, among them the Longview Foundation fiction prize, 1961; National Endowment for the Arts grant, 1976; *Los Angeles Times* Book Award nomination, 1984; PEN-USA-West Lifetime Achievement award, 1997; and Lifetime Achievement Award, University of Southern California, 2001. He was elected to the El Paso Hall of Fame in Writing, and in 2000 his novel *City of Night* was included in the Publishing Triangle's list of twenty-five all-time best novels.

FURTHER READING: Casillo, Charles. *Outlaw: The Lives and Careers of John Rechy.* Los Angeles: Advocate Books/Allyson Publications, 2002; Castillo, Debra. "Interview with John Rechy." *Diacritics: A Review of Contemporary Criticism* 25:1 (1995) 113–125; Lomelí, Francisco A., and Carl R. Shirley, eds. *Chicano Writers: Second Series.* Detroit: Gale Research, 1992; Martínez Julio A., and Francisco A. Lomelí. *Chicano Literature: A Reference Guide.* Westport, Conn.: Greenwood Press, 1985; Tatum, Charles M. *Chicano Literature.* Boston: Twayne, 1982.

RELIGION. Nearly all Mexican immigrants coming to the United States have been at least nominally Catholic. However, many who consider themselves Catholic conform in only a limited way to the accepted norms of the U.S. church. There is a lower than average level of Sunday mass attendance, particularly among males; and many, like their fellow Anglo Catholics, ignore the Vatican's stand on birth control, abortion, and other personal issues. For many, Catholicism is as much cultural as religious; some have therefore, consciously or unconsciously, viewed conversion to Protestantism as a way to social acceptance and upward social mobility in the United States.

In the nineteenth century Mexicanos in the Southwest practiced a Catholicism that was to a large extent untutored and centered strongly on devotion to the **Virgin of Guadalupe**. Partly because of their isolation, the folk religion they practiced had only limited connections with the institutional church and its hierarchy. The French clerics whom Bishop Lamy brought to the Southwest after the Treaty of Guadalupe Hidalgo generally viewed them as uninstructed and in dire need of missionary work. So did early Protestant missionaries.

Both Protestant and Catholic clergy included Americanization as well as religious education in their roles, especially during the nineteenth century. As Mexican Americans became a larger presence in the Catholic church in the twentieth century, they pushed to have their religious presence as Mexicanos acknowledged by the appointment of more Latino pastors and members of the hierarchy. Another important result was greater attention by the church to Mexican traditional worship, especially an expanded devotion to Mary as La Virgen de Guadalupe.

Meanwhile, the pressure of mere numbers of Mexicanos in the U.S. Catholic church led to greater participation in church governance. In 1970 Rome appointed **Patrick Flores** the first Mexican American bishop, and later he was consecrated archbishop of San Antonio. By the end of the decade, eight more Mexican American priests had been raised to the episcopacy. Today there are approximately three dozen Hispanic bishops; the majority of them, with names like Ochoa, Peña, and Soto, are Mexican Americans.

FURTHER READING: Barton, Paul. "In Both Worlds: A History of Hispanic Protestantism in the U. S. Southwest." Ph. D. diss., Southern Methodist University, 1999; Brackenridge, R. Douglas, and Francisco O. García-Treto. *Iglesia Presbiteriana: A History of Presbyterians and Mexican Americans in the Southwest.* San Antonio: Trinity University Press, 1987; Dolan, Jay P., and Gilberto M. Hinojosa. *Mexican Americans and the Catholic Church, 1900–1965.* Notre Dame: University of Notre Dame Press, 1994; Guerrero, Andrés G. *A Chicano Theology.* Maryknoll, NY: Orbis Books, 1987; Sandoval, Moisés. *Fronteras: A History of the Latin American Church in the USA since 1513.* San Antonio: Mexican American Cultural Center, 1983; Steele, Thomas J., Paul Rhetts, and Barbe Await, eds. *Seeds of Struggle, Harvest of Faith: A History of the Catholic Church in New Mexico.* Albuquerque: LPD Press, 1999.

REPATRIATION. The term repatriation is usually used to refer specifically to the massive movements of the early 1930s and the mid-1950s. However, repatriation has taken place formally and informally from the time of the Treaty of **Guadalupe Hidalgo**, when Mexicans who wanted to remain under the Mexican government were assisted by Mexico in moving southward across the new treaty border. In the mid-1850s and again in the 1870s Mexico offered various incentives to encourage repatriation, but elicited little response. During the second half of the nineteenth century perhaps 2 percent of the Mexican population in the area acquired by the United States repatriated.

In 1921 the post–World War I recession forced nearly a quarter of a million unemployed Mexican workers to move southward across the border, from which the government of Mexico then transported them to their hometowns and villages. The decade-long **Great Depression** that began at the end of the 1920s fueled Anglo hostility and the next surge in Mexican repatriation. Statistics on the volume of this movement are mostly educated guesses, but an idea of the numbers can be obtained from census figures. Between 1930 and 1940 the number of Mexican-born living in the United States decreased by 263,000. Some recent estimates suggest that as many as half a million Mexican nationals, some accompanied by their American-born wives and children, were repatriated in the early 1930s as the result of deportation and the fear thereof. Few deportees received court hearings, and most who did received a summary hearing that lasted only a few minutes.

Operation Wetback was the next extensive repatriation drive. In June 1954, U.S. Attorney General Herbert Brownell, Jr. ordered a mass roundup and deportation of undocumented Mexican workers, citing possible entry of communist subversives as the reason. Behind this "red scare" excuse, nativism was clearly visible. Brownell's massive deportation was preceded by an extensive publicity campaign aimed at encouraging voluntary return to Mexico. As in the 1930s, the rights of deportees and their families were often callously ignored. Over 1 million Mexican nationals were forcibly repatriated in 1954. Between 1950 and 1955 about 3.7 million deportations occurred; only 63,500 were preceded by formal court hearings.

FURTHER READING: Balderrama, Francisco E. *Decade of Betrayal: Mexican Repatriation in the 1930s.* Albuquerque: University of New Mexico Press, 1995; García, Juan Ramón. *Operation Wetback: The Mass Deportation of Undocumented Workers in 1954.* Westport, Conn.: Greenwood Press, 1980; Guerin-Gonzales, Camille. *Mexican Workers and American Dreams: Immigration, Repatriation, and California Farm Labor, 1900–1939.* New Brunswick, N.J.: Rutgers University Press, 1994; Hoffman, Abraham. *Unwanted Mexican Americans in the Great Depression: Repatriation Pressures, 1929–1939.* Tucson: University of Arizona Press, 1974; Kiser, George C. and David Silverman. "Mexican Repatriation During the Great Depression." *Journal of Mexican American History* 3 (1973) 139–164.

REYNOSO, CRUZ, 1931– . Lawyer, judge. After graduating from Pomoma College in 1953, Cruz Reynoso went into the army for two years. He studied for the law at the University of California, Berkeley, obtained his law degree in 1958, and entered private practice for several years. He quickly became notable as an activist in the **California Rural Legal Assistance** (CRLA) program—which led to a position as assistant chief in California's Division of Fair Employment Practices. In 1967 he was appointed general counsel in the federal **Equal Employment Opportunity Commission** in Washington, D.C., by President Lyndon Johnson.

In the following year Reynoso returned to California to become deputy director of the CRLA and then was appointed to the directorship. In 1972 he stepped down from that position to teach law at the University of New Mexico. Four years later he was appointed an associate justice in the California Court of Appeals, and in 1982 became the first Mexican American appointed to the California Supreme Court. As the result of a venomous conservative attack on his liberal interpretation of the law he was denied reconfirmation by the voters in the 1986 elections. He retired to private practice in Los Angeles and in 1991 joined the law faculty there at the University of California. In 1999 he was named the Distinguished Visiting Professor at the University of California law school in Davis.

Reynoso's legal stature has been attested to by his appointment to various federal and state commissions and to the United Nations Commission on Human Rights. President Jimmy Carter also appointed him to the Select Commission on Immigration and Refugee Policy. He is vice chairman of the U.S. Commission on Civil Rights and a board member of several civil rights and educational organizations. In August 2000 he was awarded the Presidential Medal of Freedom by President Bill Clinton.

FURTHER READING: "Cruz Reynoso, A Distinguished Career," *Caminos* 5:2 (February 1984) 36; *Who's Who among Hispanic Americans, 1994–1995*. Detroit: Gale Research, 1994; *Martindale-Hubbell Law Directory*. Los Angeles: Reed Elsevier Inc., 2001.

RICHARDSON, BILL, 1947– . Ambassador, legislator, governor. Bill Richardson was born in Pasadena, California, but lived in Mexico City from age one to thirteen. He entered Tufts University in 1966, graduating with a B.A. in 1970. In the following year he earned a masters degree from Tufts Fletcher School of Law and Diplomacy. For the next three years he worked as a staff member in the House of Representatives and from 1976 to 1978 served as a staff member in the U.S. Senate. He then moved to New Mexico and for the next four years he was self-employed there.

In 1982 Richardson was elected U.S. congressman from New Mexico and was reelected seven times to the House, where he served for a time as deputy whip. A strong advocate of the North American Free Trade Agreement, he helped President Bill Clinton with negotiations on the NAFTA in 1993. Meanwhile, as a result of obtaining the freedom of U.S. hostages in Iraq,

Cuba, and elsewhere he gained a wide national reputation as a diplomatic troubleshooter. In late 1996 he was nominated by President Clinton to be the U.S. ambassador to the United Nations, the first Mexican American to hold that office. Confirmed in the following January, he did an excellent job as ambassador. In 1998 he was nominated and confirmed as the Clinton administration's Secretary of Energy, becoming the highest-ranking Latino in the U.S. government. After leaving office when Republican George W. Bush was declared president, he was named senior managing director of Washington-based Kissinger McLarty Associates. In early January 2002 he announced he would seek the Democratic nomination for governor of New Mexico. He was elected and took office in January 2003.

Richardson is the author of articles and essays, most dealing with foreign affairs and international trade. He has been a board member on various organizations, foundations, and councils, including the Congressional Hispanic Caucus Institute. As result of his congressional and UN service he has received numerous awards and commendations, including the Hispanic Heritage Leadership Award in 1997. For his successful hostage negotiations he was twice nominated for a Nobel peace prize, in 1995 and 1997.

FURTHER READING: Lewis, Neil A. "Man in the News: William Blaine Richardson: Derring-Do at Energy." *The New York Times* (19 June 1998) A 26; "The Most Influential Latinos." *Hispanic* (Sept. 2000) 28; United States. Congress. Senate. Committee on Energy and Natural Resources. *Bill Richardson Nomination: Hearing before the Committee on Energy and Natural Resources.* Washington, D.C.: Government Printing Office, 1998; United States. Congress. Senate. Committee on Foreign Relations. *Nomination of Hon. Bill Richardson of New Mexico to be the Representative to the United Nations with the Rank of Ambassador and the U.S. Representative in the Security Council of the United Nations: Hearing before the Committee on Foreign Relations.* Washington, D.C.: Government Printing Office, 1997.

RIO GRANDE. The Rio Grande, or Rio Bravo as it was known earlier and still is in Mexico, has its source in Colorado, flows south through New Mexico, and then turns eastward, emptying into the Gulf of Mexico. The eastward segment forms the boundary between the state of Texas and Mexico, the border set by the Treaty of **Guadalupe Hidalgo**. An important waterway, in the second half of the nineteenth century this eastward section was especially useful as a route for the export of cotton from Texas. It also provided egress for slaves fleeing their bondage and ready ingress for Mexican migrants who came to pick the cotton beginning in the last decades of the century. In the twentieth century, as both Mexico and the United States built dams on it and its tributaries, the division and use of its water became an important concern of both countries. The lower Rio Grande provides irrigation to a rich Texas agricultural region known as the winter garden area, in which many Mexicanos find employment. Water allocation continues to be a source of discussion and conflict between the United States and Mexico.

FURTHER READING: Eaton, David J., and David Hurlbut. *Challenges in the Binational Management of Water Resources in the Rio Grande/Río Bravo.* Austin: LBJ School of Public Affairs, University of Texas at Austin, 1994; Horgan, Paul. *Great River: The Rio Grande in North American History,* 2 vols. New York: Holt Rinehart & Winston, 1954; Hundley, Norris. *Dividing the Waters: A Century of Controversy between the United States and Mexico.* Berkeley: University of California Press, 1966.

RÍOS, TONY P., 1914–1999. Activist, labor organizer. Anthony Ríos was born in the border town of Calexico, California, but moved to Los Angeles in the early 1930s. While still in his teens he helped his fellow lemon pickers organize and negotiate with the growers. He spent a decade as a labor unionist in agriculture and steel mills, but his most important contribution to the betterment of *la raza* was his work as a community organizer.

In 1949 Ríos was one of the leaders, along with **Fred Ross, Sr.**, in founding the **Community Service Organization** (CSO) in Los Angeles to help elect Edward Roybal to the city council. A strong believer in using the ballot to develop what he referred to as "barrio power," as head of the CSO in Los Angeles he promoted and led citizenship classes, voter registration drives, and get-out-the-vote campaigns. During his long life he also helped establish and was active in numerous other community organizations. In the late 1960s he supported the Chicano Movement although he disagreed somewhat with confrontational militants who, he felt, were not fully aware of their predecessors' efforts and gave them little credit. He remained steadfastly devoted to his goal of bettering the lives of all Mexican Americans, until his death from pneumonia in May 1999.

FURTHER READING: Woo, Elaine. "Anthony Rios Dies: Helped Latinos 'Find Their Political Voice.' " *Los Angeles Times* (22 May 1999) A17.

RIVERA, TOMÁS, 1935–1984. Writer, teacher, educational administrator. Tomás Rivera was born in Crystal City, Texas, to immigrant parents who earned their livelihood on the migrant agricultural circuit. The family placed a high value on education and as a result, despite the difficulties arising from migrant life, Tomás was able to graduate from Crystal City high school and, after working for a few years, enter college. In 1958 he received his B.S. degree in English education and began teaching. Six years later he earned his M.Ed., and in 1969 completed his doctorate in Romance languages and literature at the University of Oklahoma. He continued to teach and in 1971 accepted a professorship at the University of Texas, San Antonio (UTSA), chairing the Romance language department and teaching Spanish.

Rivera's administrative abilities were quickly recognized, and he soon was promoted to associate dean and then to vice-president for administration. In 1978 he left UTSA to become executive vice president for academic affairs at the University of Texas, El Paso and in the following year accepted an offer to become the first Mexican American chancellor in the University of California system, at the Riverside campus. Despite the many duties his administrative and academic position entailed, Rivera also found time to write.

Encouraged by his family, Rivera had begun writing at an early age but began to publish only at the end of the 1960s. In 1970 his —*y no se lo tragó la tierra*, a novel about migrant life, won the first Quinto Sol National Literary Prize and was published in a bilingual edition in the following year. It is widely regarded as a benchmark in Chicano literature, and was followed a few years later by a collection of his poetry in *Always and Other Poems*. He also published some short stories and essays on **education** and literature as well as more poetry.

Rivera received various honors and accolades in his all-too-short academic life. In addition to several honorary doctoral degrees, he received recognition by appointment to the boards of the prestigious Ford Foundation and the Carnegie Foundation for the Advancement of Teaching. Presidents Jimmy Carter and Ronald Reagan both appointed him to commissions on higher education.

FURTHER READING: *American National Biography*, vol. 18. New York: Oxford University Press, 1999; Hinojosa-Smith, Rolando, et al. *Tomás Rivera, 1935–1984: The Man and His Work*. Tempe, Arizona: Bilingual Review / Press, 1988; Lomelí, Francisco and Carl R. Shirley, eds. *Chicano Writers: First Series*. Detroit: Gale Research, 1989; Olivares, Julian. *Tomás Rivera: The Complete Works*. Houston, Texas: Arte Público Press, 1992; Rivera, Tomás. —*Y no se lo tragó la tierra*, 2nd ed. Houston: Arte Público Press, 1992 (1970); *Revista Chicano-Riqueña* 13:3–4 (Fall–Winter 1985) entire issue.

RODRÍGUEZ, CHIPITA, ?–1863. Chipita (Josefa?) Rodríguez was arrested in August 1863 because the body of a man murdered with an axe was found near her cabin northwest of Corpus Christi, Texas. In spite of the absence of any real evidence, she was indicted by the grand jury, tried, and convicted of murder. Judge Benjamin F. Neal ignored the limited circumstantial evidence as well as the trial jury's recommendation for mercy and sentenced her to death. She was hanged at San Patricio on November 13, 1863. In 1985 the Texas legislature passed a resolution absolving her of the murder.

FURTHER READING: Guthrie, Keith. *The Legend of Chipita: The Only Woman Hanged in Texas*. Austin: Eakin Press, 1990; Smylie, Vernon. *A Noose for Chipita*. Corpus Christi: Texas News Syndicate Press, 1970; Tyler, Ron, ed. *The New Handbook of Texas*, vol. 4. Austin: Texas State Historical Association, 1996.

RODRÍGUEZ, PAUL, 1955– . Stand-up comic, actor, director. Paul Rodríguez was born in the Mexican west coast town of Culiacán, the youngest of five children in the family. When he was three, the Rodríguezes immigrated to the United States and settled in East Los Angeles. His father worked in a steel plant until an injury he suffered caused the family to enter the migrant agricultural stream, working as farmhands in California, Texas, and Michigan. In his early teen years Paul spent much time on the streets of East L.A., especially after he dropped out of high school. At eighteen he enlisted in the U.S. Air Force, where he served four years.

When he returned to civilian life he obtained a high school diploma equivalency and used the G.I. Bill to enroll in Long Beach City College. Afer completing two years there he entered the state university at Long Beach, where he began studies he hoped would lead to his becoming a lawyer. However, he took a class in theater, and the professor introduced him to stand-up comedy at L.A.'s Comedy Store. He perfected his comedic talents by performing there, in nightclubs, and on college campuses.

Rodríguez's first break in show business came when he was doing comedy warm-ups for TV producer Norman Lear's audiences. At the end of the 1970s his acquaintance with producer Lear led to the lead in a short-lived television sitcom with a U.S. Latino theme, *a.k.a. Pablo*, the first TV show about a Mexican American family. It received heavy criticism from some members of *la raza* who accused him of perpetuating Latino stereotypes. It also attracted the attention of Hollywood. His career as an actor in films began in 1983 with a part in *D.C. Cab*, which was followed by comedic parts in a number of films. In 1987 he got his first substantial movie role in *Born in East L.A.*, directed by Cheech Marín. It marked a milestone in his acting career. After a decade of acting in films, in 1994 he added directing to his repertoire in *A Million to Juan*, a highly successful lighthearted comedy about a Mexican immigrant in Los Angeles. Altogether he has appeared in over twenty-five films; between 1999 and 2001 he had roles in eight movies in less than two years. His most recent role was that of a boxing physician in *Ali*, a 2002 film about the ring career of Muhammed Ali.

Today Rodríguez remains busy not only as a comedian; he also is involved in various projects with Warner Brothers, HBO, Virgin Records, and the restaurant chain El Pollo Loco. His success has not caused him to forget his roots and he strongly believes in giving something back to the community. He is seriously concerned about his position as a role model for young Mexican Americans. He has made substantial financial and personal contributions to *la raza*, serves on various boards, and supports Project Literacy and other groups. He was a pallbearer at César Chávez's funeral in 1993.

FURTHER READING: Cano-Murillo, Kathy. "Acting Role Helps Comic Fill Seats." *The Arizona Republic* (7 June 2001); "Paul Rodríguez Meets the Press." *Nuestro* (June/July 1984) 37–38; Tardiff, Joseph C., and L. Mpho Mabunda, eds. *Dictionary of Hispanic Biography*. Detroit: Gale Research, 1996.

RODRÍGUEZ, PETER, 1926– . Painter, museum director. Peter Rodríguez was born and grew up mostly in Stockton and Jackson, California. At a very early age he was attracted to art, and in high school began to work seriously to become an artist. Although basically self-taught, he studied art at Stockton Community College and much later was a student of museum management at the University of California.

At the ripe age of thirteen Rodríguez had his first exhibition, in New York, and in 1940 exhibited at the San Francisco World Fair. During the 1950s he had seven one-man shows and participated in thirteen group exhibitions in the United States and Mexico. In the early 1950s he made his first visit to Mexico, which so captivated him that he remained for six months, painting, and then went back in 1956. When he returned to California, he settled in San Francisco, where he began carrying out his idea of a museum for Mexican and Chicano art.

In 1970, with a group of younger Chicano artists, Rodríguez founded La Galería de la Raza. Three years later a disagreement about the concept of the gallery as museum resulted in his leaving and in 1975 establishing the Mexican Museum, which he headed for its critical formative decade. He set the museum's goal to collect, interpret, and present the artistic culture of the Mexican people. In 1985 Rodríguez gave up the executive directorship of the museum but remained active as a consultant. After stepping down as director he resumed the production and exhibition of his collages and other visual art works. In 1987 his "Milagros" was part of the Ceremony of Memory exhibition at the Centro Cultural de la Raza in San Francisco. His pioneering work as founder of the Mexican Museum was commemorated when the museum celebrated its twenty-fifth anniversary in 2000.

FURTHER READING: Aguirre, Rosaines. "San Francisco's Mexican Museum." *Lector* 5:2 (1988) 9–10; Brezezinski, Jamey. "Gentle Advocacy: The Art of Peter Rodríguez." *Artweek* (21 January 1993) back cover; "Peter Rodríguez." *La Luz* 4:4–5 (July–August 1975) 4; Quirarte, Jacinto. *Mexican American Artists.* Austin: University of Texas Press, 1973.

RODRÍGUEZ, RICHARD, 1944– . Author, commentator. Richard Rodríguez was born in San Francisco, California, the son of middle-class Mexican immigrants. He grew up in Sacramento, California, where he received his early education. An outstanding student, after high school he entered Stanford University in 1963. With an A.B. from Stanford he went to Columbia University for his M.A. and then returned to California to enter a doctoral program in English literature and language at the University of California in Berkeley.

During the five years Rodríguez worked on his Ph.D. he was increasingly beset with feelings of alienation from his family and his cultural roots. He also began to feel guilty about the advantages he had enjoyed as a result of affirmative action. Over the years he came to reject **bilingual education** as well as **affirmative action**, which had earlier served him so well, and pointedly turned down several prestigious university positions offered to him. He published his ideas and concerns in journal articles and in his first book, *Hunger of Memory: The Education of Richard Rodríguez, An Autobiography*, 1981.

Rodríguez's criticism of affirmative action and bilingual education in *Hunger of Memory* made him an instant celebrity as well as the center of acrimonious controversy. The book won him the 1982 Anisfield-Wolf Award for Race Relations from the Cleveland Foundation for its defense of civil rights. *Hunger of Memory* argued that affirmative action principally benefitted middle-class Mexican Americans rather than barrio youths, who remained in greatest need of assistance. It suggested that class rather than ethnicity should be the basis of affirmative action.

Rodríguez's second book, *Days of Obligation: An Argument with My Mexican Father*, 1993, was somewhat less controversial; it received critical acclaim and nomination for the Pulitzer Prize. In it he lamented the loss of ethnic cultures in the United States and worldwide, while reiterating his firm belief in the need to learn English as the "public language." Rodríguez still characterized most bilingual and bicultural programs as ill-conceived and advocated that everyone should be taught English. His most recent work, *Brown: The Last Discovery of America*, 2002, celebrates racial amalgamation in a series of essays and meditations.

Among Rodríguez's honors are the Frankel Medal from the National Endowment for the Humanities, the International Journalism Award from the World Affairs Council of California, and the 1997 Peabody Award. He continues to express his strongly held views through essays in the press, in journals, on radio, and on television. He is currently an editor at Pacific News Service and contributing editor to *Harper's Magazine* and *U.S. News.*

FURTHER READING: *Hispanic Writers: A Selection of Sketches from Contemporary Authors*, 2nd ed. Detroit: Gale Research, 1999; Holt, Patricia. "Richard Rodríguez." *Publishers Weekly* (26 March 1982) 6–8; Rodríguez, Richard. *Hunger of Memory: The Education of Richard Rodríguez, An Autobiography*. Boston: David R. Godine, 1981; Tardiff, Joseph C., and L. Mpho Mabunda, eds. *Dictionary of Hispanic Biography*. Detroit: Gale Research, 1996; Zweig, Paul. "The Child of Two Cultures." *New York Times Book Review* (28 February 1982).

ROLAND, GILBERT, 1905–1994. Actor. Gilbert Roland was born Luis Antonio Alonso in the Mexican border town of Ciudad Juárez. When Francisco Villa attacked the town in 1911, the Alonso family joined the general exodus across the Rio Grande to El Paso, Texas, where most of its members remained as the revolution continued year after year. In El Paso Luis began his education and became acquainted with Hollywood movies. Infatuated with the cinema, at age thirteen he hopped a train to California to become a movie star.

Years of walk-ons and bit parts followed, but Luis persisted and graduated to supporting roles. At this time he adopted a professional name from his two favorite stars: John Gilbert and Ruth Roland. In 1927 his role opposite Norma Talmadge in *Camille* finally brought him stardom, and he became much in demand as a leading man in the Hollywood studios. However, the advent of talking pictures at the end of the 1920s brought him a temporary setback. For several years he was forced to take whatever roles he could get. In 1937 his performance in *The Last Train from Madrid* received high praise from critics and revived his career. In the following years he made some of his best films.

During World War II Roland became an American citizen and enlisted in the U.S. Army Air Corps. When he was mustered out of the service he returned to Hollywood and resumed his film career. In the 1950s and 1960s he was again in great demand and made numerous films: *The Bullfighter and the Lady, Beneath the Twelve Mile Reef, Thunderbay, Cheyenne Autumn,* and *The Treasure of Pancho Villa* among them. In addition to his big screen career he had roles in various TV series and also became an author of some note, particularly for his short stories. During the 1970s and early 1980s he had no difficulty in finding supporting roles in a large number of films as well as work in television. After nearly seventy years in the cinema, he died just before his eighty-ninth birthday.

FURTHER READING: "Gilbert Roland." *Hollywood Close-Up* 2:26 (16 July 1959); Keller, Gary. *A Biographical Handbook of Hispanics and United States Films.* Tempe, Arizona: Bilingual Press, 1997; Reyes, Luis, and Peter Rubie. *Hispanics in Hollywood: A Celebration of 100 Years in Film and Television.* Hollywood: Lone Eagle Pub., 2000; *Who's Who in America, 1980–1981.* Chicago: Marquis, 1980.

ROMANO, OCTAVIO I., 1932– . Teacher, publisher, editor, writer. A high school dropout, Octavio Romano served in the U.S. Army and then entered college. With an undergraduate degree from the University of New Mexico, he earned his Ph.D. in social anthropology at the University of California, Berkeley. As a professor at the university, he was one of the early prominent activists in the Chicano movement. In the many talks and lectures that he gave in the late 1960s and early 1970s, he spoke out vigorously against demeaning stereotypes of Mexican Americans.

In addition to his lectures, most made at colleges and universities, Octavio Romano's important contribution to the Chicano Movement was in establishing Quinto Sol Publications in 1967 and in being the founding editor of *El Grito: A Journal of Contemporary Mexican-American Thought.* Through Quinto Sol he provided publishing possibilities for Chicano authors when most Anglo literary mavens argued that there was no such a thing as Chicano literature. In *El Grito* he made available a forum for essays expounding and defending Chicanos' social and civil rights at a time when arenas in which such discussion could reach print were extremely limited. His publication of *El Espejo—The Mirror* in 1969 further helped to provide Chicano writers with a forum and to acquaint American readers with their work. In 1995 he was awarded recognition by the National Hispanic Employees association for his quarter century of "National Educational Excellence and Service to the Community."

FURTHER READING: Martínez, Julio A. *Chicano Scholars and Writers: A Bio-Bibliographical Directory.* Metuchen, N.J.: Scarecrow Press, 1979; Lomelí, Francisco A., and Carl R. Shirley, eds. *Chicano Writers: Second Series.* Detroit: Gale Research, 1992; Romano, Octavio I. *Geriatric Fu: My First Sixty-five Years in the United States.* Berkeley:

TQS, 1990; Ryan, Bryan, ed. *Hispanic Writers: A Selection of Sketches from Contemporary Authors.* Detroit: Gale Research, 1991.

RONSTADT, LINDA, 1946–. Singer. Linda Ronstadt was born into an upper-middle-class Mexican American family in Tucson, Arizona, where she received her education. She grew up in a lively musical milieu; both her father and her paternal grandfather were active Mexicano musicians of some note. As a teenager she became completely involved in music, even singing semiprofessionally. At age eighteen she left Tucson for Los Angeles, California, to make her mark in the music world.

In Los Angeles Linda joined two other young musicians to form a group they called The Stone Poneys. The group had some success, but finally broke up over the issue of the kind of music the members wanted to make. In the last years of the 1960s Linda began nearly a decade of traveling on the road, opening concerts for established musicians. The hectic road show life took its toll and in the early 1970s she underwent psychiatric counseling for the lack of self-worth she felt.

In the mid-1970s, with Peter Asher as her manager and producer, Ronstadt began to find herself musically. Her 1974 album, "Heart Like a Wheel," was her first to go "platinum," to sell over a million copies. It was followed in the second half of the 1970s by eight consecutive platinum albums. In 1978 she made her film debut in *FM*, a rock and roll comedy. In spite of her undeniable success and a Grammy award, she remained insecure about her musical ability.

In 1980 Ronstadt moved to New York to star in *The Pirates of Penzance*. It was an immense success, and her singing received a Tony Award nomination. *Penzance* was followed in 1984 by a pop version of *La Boheme* that also won her high praise from the critics. In the first half of the 1980s her singing was deeply influenced by Nelson Riddle, who did many of her song arrangements. She sang with her friends Dolly Parton and Emmylou Harris and did a duet in Spanish with Rubén Blades. Her revived interest in Spanish led in 1987 to an album "Canciones de mi Padre," which was followed by a second album of Mexican folk songs. Her folk songs became the basis for a long concert tour and a television production with Luis Valdez.

In 1996 Ronstadt issued "Dedicated to the One I Love," a collection of rock favorites sung as lullabies to her first adopted child, Mary Clementine. Later she adopted a second child, named Carlos, to complete her family. Although linked romantically to several men over the years, she has never married. At the end of the 1990s she left San Francisco, which she had made her home, to return to Tucson and her extended family there.

FURTHER READING: Bego, Mark. *Linda Ronstadt: It's So Easy.* Austin: Eakin Publications, 1990; Berman, Connie. *Linda Ronstadt.* Carson City, Nev.: Proteus, 1980; Burciaga, José Antonio. "Linda Ronstadt: My Mexican Soul." *Vista* 2:10 (July

1987) 6–8; Claire, Vivian. *Ronstadt*. New York: Flash Books, 1978; Moore, Mary Ellen. *The Linda Ronstadt Scrapbook*. New York: Sunridge Press, 1978; Tardiff, Joseph C., and L. Mpho Mabunda, eds. *Dictionary of Hispanic Biography*. Detroit: Gale Research, 1996.

ROSS, FRED, SR., 1910–1992. Labor organizer, activist. When he graduated from the University of Southern California in 1936, Fred Ross was unable to obtain a teaching position as he wished, so he opted for social work, getting employment with the California state relief agency. Toward the end of the Great Depression he was employed by the U.S. Farm Security Administration to manage a migrant worker camp, and during World War II worked for the War Relocation Authority as an official in a Japanese American internment camp in Idaho.

In 1946 Ross returned to southern California, where he began organizing **Unity Leagues** for the American Council on Race Relations. His acquaintance with Saul Alinsky led to his becoming involved in forming **Community Service Organization** (CSO) groups in southern California raza barrios. As business manager for the CSO, Ross made the acquaintance of **César Chávez,** whom he persuaded Alinsky to hire as a CSO organizer in 1954. Nearly a decade later Ross joined Chávez in his effort to develop an agricultural workers union. He immediately became an important aide to Chávez in what eventually became the **United Farm Workers** union (UFW). Throughout the **Delano grape strike,** 1965–1970, and beyond into the mid-1970s, Ross was in charge of training recruiters and organizers for the UFW. In his later years he was working with his son, Fred Jr., in an organization called Neighbor to Neighbor. He also was writing a personal account of his longtime experience as a labor organizer. He died in 1992 of natural causes after a lifetime spent defending and furthering the rights of poor and powerless workers.

FURTHER READING: Ferris, Susan, and Ricardo Sandoval. "Remembering Fred Ross." In *The Fight in the Fields: César Chávez and the Farmworkers Movement*, edited by Susan Ferris and Ricardo Sandoval. New York: Harcourt Brace, 1997; Folkart, Burt A. "Fred Ross: Worked Quietly for Downtrodden Laborers." *Los Angeles Times* (1 October 1992) Metro A26; Rodríguez, Roberto. "Fred Ross: Unsung Hero." *Caminos* 5:8 (September–October 1985) 40; Ross, Fred W. (Sr.) *Community Organization in Mexican-American Communities*. Los Angeles: American Council on Race Relations, 1947.

ROYBAL, EDWARD R., 1916– . Congressman, educator. Edward Roybal was born February 10, 1916 in Albuquerque, New Mexico, the eldest of eight children of a railroad worker. The family moved to California and he grew up there, attending public schools in Boyle Heights, an East Los Angeles barrio. After graduating in 1933 from Roosevelt High and a stint in the Civilian Conservation Corps, he enrolled in the University of California in Los Angeles.

Edward R. Roybal. © Library of Congress.

Roybal graduated with a degree in accounting and obtained a position with 20th Century Fox Studios. At this time he became aware of the high incidence of tuberculosis among Mexican Americans and the importance of testing children for the disease. As a result of his volunteer work testing schoolchildren, he was appointed a public health educator in the Los Angeles County Tuberculosis and Health Association. Roybal's job with the association was interrupted by service in World War II.

Upon his discharge from the U.S. army Roybal resumed his career in public health as director of health education for the tuberculosis association. In his new position Roybal quickly became aware of the politics of public health service and decided to file for political office. Unsuccessful in seeking a seat on the Los Angeles City Council in 1947, he won two years later with the support of the **Community Service Organization**. He was the first Mexican American on the city council in the twentieth century and regularly won reelection. As a councilman his principal emphasis was on community health care.

After thirteen years on the council, in 1962 Roybal was elected to the U.S. House of Representatives in Washington, D.C. For the next thirty years he was routinely reelected every two years. In Congress he continued to demonstrate his concern for health care and social reform. He strongly supported bilingual education and introduced a bill to create a cabinet-level Committee on Opportunities for Spanish Speaking People.

In 1975 Edward Roybal led in the creation of the **National Association of Latino Elected and Appointed Officials**, and two years later was an important participant in establishing the **Congressional Hispanic Caucus**. In addition to his vigorous leadership in these groups and his service on congressional committees, he was also active in a wide variety of nongovernmental organizations with broad humanitarian goals. During his half century of public service he constantly advocated greater citizen participation in the political process.

An energetic but moderate, nonconfrontational activist, Congressman Roybal retired in January 1993 after thirty years in the U.S. House of Representatives and a lifetime of public service. Roybal's moderate activism made it easier for other Latinos to follow in his footsteps of public service. In retirement he continued to champion the rights of all Americans to health care.

FURTHER READING: Cantú, Héctor. "Roybal: A Long-Distance Runner Who Made a Difference." *Hispanic Business* 14:5 (May 1992) 50, 52; Díaz, Katherine A. "Congressman Edward Roybal: Los Angeles before the 1960s." *Caminos* 4:7 (July–August 1983) 15–17, 38; Padilla, Steve. "Stories That Shaped the Century: The Seeds of Latino Leadership Are Sown." *Los Angeles Times* (19 November 1999) Metro B6; Rodríguez, Roberto. "Congressman Edward Roybal: Elder Statesman." *Américas 2001* 1:1 (June–July 1987) 23–25; Roybal, Edward R. "Hispanics: A Political Perspective. *Social Education* 43 (February 1979) 101–103; Vigil, Maurilio E. *Hispanics in Congress: A Historical and Political Survey.* Lanham, N.Y.: University Press of America, 1996.

ROYBAL-ALLARD, LUCILLE, 1941– . Politician. Lucille Roybal was born in Boyle Heights, a Hispanic barrio of Los Angeles, into the politically active family of Edward Roybal. She remembers having a somewhat unusual childhood stuffing envelopes, registering voters, and avoiding police harassment. Her experiences led to a determination to never become or marry a politician. After high school she enrolled in Los Angeles State University, where she earned her degree in bilingual speech therapy in 1965. After graduation she became a fund-raising and public relations executive.

When **Gloria Molina** vacated her state assembly seat in 1986, Roybal-Allard was persuaded to run for her 56th District Assembly post after serious consideration and with full support from her husband and parents. She won the election. In the assembly she followed in her father's liberal footsteps, supporting the rights of the poor and powerless and espousing environmental concerns. At the beginning of her third term in office the Sierra Club recognized her work, with the Legislative Environmental Award.

In 1992 Roybal-Allard won a seat in the U.S. House of Representatives with more than 60 percent of the votes cast. In the House she has followed her father's example of hard work and support of liberal causes. The first Latina and the first woman selected to chair the California Democratic Congressional Delegation, she also became the first woman to chair the **Congressional Hispanic Caucus.** She serves as a member of the powerful House Appropriations Committee and on the floor of the House supports health care, bilingual education, and immigration reform including a fair guest-worker program. Easily reelected every two years like her father, she both pushes Chicano empowerment through the ballot and supports coalition-building. Like her father, with whom she is often compared, she strongly believes her job in Congress is to serve her constituents by opening doors and expanding economic and political opportunities. In December 2001 she was honored by the National Farmworker Partnership Conference for her work on behalf of farm workers. She is no longer just "Roybal's daughter."

FURTHER READING: Ralston, Tyler. "Lucille Roybal-Allard." *Latino Leaders* (February–March 2001) 56–62; Telgen, Diane, and Jim Kamp, eds. *Notable Hispanic American Women*, Detroit: Gale Research, 1993.

S

SACRAMENTO MARCH, 1966. The march to Sacramento, California, was an important episode in the **Delano grape strike.** By early 1966 the first bloom of the strikers' enthusiasm was beginning to fade. Strikebreakers had been brought into the vineyards; finances needed to support the strike had not yet been developed. Recognizing the need for something dramatic to raise the strikers' lagging spirits, as well as the importance of publicity, César Chávez announced a march from Delano to the state capitol steps, where the marchers would demand help from Governor "Pat" Brown.

Heralded by flags with the union's black eagle and large banners bearing the image of the Virgin of Guadalupe, the march attracted Catholics, Protestants, Jews, agnostics, atheists, and clerics, Protestant as well as Catholic. The three-hundred-mile, twenty-five-day march began in Delano with some sixty marchers, grew at times to nearly a thousand, and swept into Sacramento on Easter Sunday only to find that the governor had opted to spend the weekend in Palm Springs with his friend Frank Sinatra, rather than meet the farm workers.

Chávez was able to offset the disappointment of the governor's absence by announcing the heartwarming news that the Schenley liquor company, which owned several vineyards in California's central valley, had agreed to recognize and negotiate with the union. The march served to draw nationwide attention to the Delano strike, to arouse widespread sympathy, and to bring the strikers thousands of new supporters.

FURTHER READING: "From Delano to Sacramento." *America* 114 (2 April 1966) 430; "March of the Migrants." *Life* 60:17 (29 April 1966) 94–95; Matthiesen, Peter. *Sal si puedes: César Chávez and the New American Revolution.* New York: Random House, 1969; Rodríguez, Rosa María, and Arturo Villarreal. "The UFW Strategies." *San Jose Studies* 20:2 (1994) 63–70.

SÁENZ, JOSÉ DE LA LUZ, 1888–1953. Teacher, activist. Luz Sáenz played an important part in the early days of the Mexican American civil rights struggle. The first Mexican American male to graduate from the Alice, Texas, public high school, he enjoyed a long career as a teacher and south Texas community leader.

Strongly believing that Mexican Americans' service in World War I should assure them all citizen rights, Sáenz renewed his prewar efforts to advance the cause of equal treatment after he was mustered out. In the late 1920s along with **Alonso Perales, J. T. Canales,** and others, he took an active part in establishing the **League of United Latin American Citizens** (LULAC) and was important in developing its first constitution. From 1930 to 1932 he served on its board of trustees, and throughout the 1930s and 1940s he promoted and refined LULAC's point of view through numerous articles in south Texas newspapers. His long leadership in the fight for equality for all citizens was fueled by a staunch belief in democracy.

FURTHER READING: Sáenz, José de la Luz. *Los méxico-americanos en la Gran Guerra: su contingente en pro de la democracia, la humanidad y la justicia.* San Antonio: Artes Gráficas, 1933; Zamora, Emilio. "Fighting on Two Fronts: The World War I Diary of José de la Luz Sáenz and the Language of the Mexican American Civil Rights Movement." Paper presented at the Fifth Conference of Recovering the U.S. Hispanic Literary Heritage. Houston, Texas, 4–5 December 1998.

SAGER, MANUELA SOLÍS, 1912–1996. Labor organizer, activist. While still a teenager Manuela Solís began organizing workers. Her sustained energetic efforts in forming unions among Texas agricultural and garment workers led to her appointment, with her husband James Sager, as official organizers for the South Texas Agricultural Workers Union when it was founded in 1935. Three years later she and her husband took active roles in the San Antonio **pecan shellers'** strike.

Sager was aggressively involved in all the major struggles against discrimination that took place in Texas during her lifetime. She was a vigorous defender of immigrants' rights, an advocate of electoral politics, and a leader in promoting the early feminist movement in Texas. A member of the Communist Party for sixty years, she supported various leftist and liberal causes and welcomed the Chicano **movimiento.** At the beginning of the 1970s she spoke out forcefully for **La Raza Unida Party** as part of her long fight for civil rights.

Manuela Solis Sager spent seven decades in support of the struggle for human dignity.

FURTHER READING: Calderón, Roberto R. and Emilio Zamora. "Manuela Solis Sager and Emma Tenayuca: A Tribute." In *Between Borders: Essays in Mexicana/Chicana History*, edited by Adelaida R. Del Castillo. Albuquerque: Floricanto Press, 1990; *Las Mujeres: Mexican American/Chicana Women.* Windsor, Calif.: National Women's History Project, 1991.

SALAZAR, RUBÉN, 1928–1970. Journalist. Although Rubén Salazar was born in Mexico, he grew up in El Paso, Texas. After high school he attended what is today the University of Texas at El Paso and graduated with a degree in journalism. He got his early newspaper experience as a reporter on the *El Paso Herald Post*, the *Press Democrat* in Santa Rosa, California, and the *San*

Francisco News. In 1959 he went to work for the *Los Angeles Times.* During his years in the *Times* city room he voiced concerns for *la raza* in a series of articles that he wrote about the Los Angeles Latino community. His investigative journalism earned him an award as well as a reputation for conscientious and objective reporting.

In 1965 Salazar was sent to Vietnam to report on the escalating American involvement there, and two years later he was named Mexico City bureau chief by the *Times.* At the end of 1968 Salazar was brought back to Los Angeles with an assignment to cover the Mexican American community. A year later he accepted a position as news director of TV station KMEX, but continued to write a weekly column in the *Times* explicating the Chicano community. Always a moderate, he wrote in a responsible professional manner condemning racism and the denial of civil rights. Abuse of Mexicanos by the police became an area of his special concern. As a result he soon became the target of local police investigation and federal surveillance.

In late August 1970 Salazar covered the Los Angeles **National Chicano Moratorium** march, organized to protest U.S. involvement in Vietnam. While relaxing with friends in the Silver Dollar Café toward the end of the march, he was killed by a high-velocity tear gas projectile that hit him in the head. The subsequent sixteen-day coroner's inquest failed to indict the deputy sheriff who fired the projectile. Many Anglos and Chicanos felt that the inquest was seriously bungled.

Salazar's unfortunate death and the coroner's flawed actions almost inevitably made him a symbol of police abuse and the failure of the American justice system to uphold the rights of Mexican Americans. The tragic and never adequately explained killing of the prominent and popular Salazar transformed him into an instant martyr of the Chicano movement. Without dispute, he was the most prominent twentieth century casualty of the Chicano struggle for justice.

FURTHER READING: Drummond, William J. "The Death of a Man in the Middle: Requiem for Rubén Salazar." *Esquire* (April 1972) 74, 76+; Gómez, David F. "The Story of Rubén Salazar." In *Introduction to Chicano Studies,* 2nd ed. Edited by Livie I. Durán and H. Russell Bernard. New York: Macmillan, 1982; Salazar, Rubén. *Border Correspondent: Selected Writings, 1955–1970.* Edited by Mario T. García. Berkeley: University of California Press, 1995.

SALINAS, PORFIRIO, JR., 1910–1973. Painter. Porfirio Salinas was born in Bastrop County, Texas and grew up in San Antonio. In school he showed an aptitude for art and began painting at an early age. As a hobby he first painted scenes connected with bullfighting. Without formal art training, he developed a particular interest in Texas landscapes and became famous later in life for his "bluebonnet scenes." By the 1960s he had become one of most popular artists in Texas. During President Lyndon B. Johnson's administration five of his paintings hung in the White House.

FURTHER READING: Goddard, Ruth. *Porfirio Salinas.* Austin: Rock House Press, 1975; Quirarte, Jacinto. *Mexican American Artists.* Austin: University of Texas Press, 1973; Salinas, Porfirio. *Bluebonnet and Cactus: An Album of Southwestern Paintings.* Austin: Pemberton Press, 1967.

SALPOINTE, JEAN BAPTISTE, 1825–1898. Archbishop. In 1859 Jean Baptiste Salpointe arrived in the Southwest, one of the French priests recruited by Bishop Lamy. After seven years of missionary work he was appointed bishop of the newly created Arizona Territory. Despite some early friction with Hispano parishioners, he showed himself to be an outstanding administrator, organizing parishes and building churches in his sparsely inhabited diocese. When Lamy retired in 1885, he was named archbishop of Santa Fe. More than any other person, he was responsible for the successful political career of Octaviano Larrazolo (1859–1930). After serving as archbishop for nine years he retired to Tucson.

FURTHER READING: Lamar, Howard R., ed. *The New Encyclopedia of the American West.* New Haven: Yale University Press, 1998; Zerwekh, Sister Edward Mary. "Jean Baptiste Salpointe, 1825–1894." *New Mexico Historical Review* 37:1 (1962) 1–19; 37:2 (1962) 132–154; 37:3 (1962) 214–229.

SALT WAR, 1877. The Salt War of 1877 was the result of a decade-long smouldering conflict over access to salt beds near San Elizario, Texas. The salt deposits, long known among Mexicanos as Guadalupe lakes, had traditionally been used by people from both sides of the border. Beginning in the mid-1860s various entrepreneurs including Samuel Maverick tried to monopolize the salt beds. In a very complex and confusing political and economic situation, plus intense personal rivalries and personality conflicts, they demanded payment for any salt taken out. In September 1877 the arrest of two Mexican Americans for taking salt incited a riot, followed temporarily by free access to the salt beds again.

Three months later the resumption of efforts to charge fees for the salt led to a second riot by about five hundred Mexicanos. Mob violence, looting, robbery, rape, and murder were interspersed with vigilante justice. A congressional investigation of the affair led to the re-stationing of troops at Fort Bliss, and after months of rapine full order was finally restored. Ultimately those who took salt had to pay a fee to the Anglo who was confirmed as owner of the salt beds.

FURTHER READING: Romero, Mary. "El Paso Salt War." *Aztlán* 16:1–2 (1985) 119–143; Sonnichsen, Charles L. *The El Paso Salt War, 1877.* El Paso: C. Hertzog, 1961; Tyler, Ron, ed. *The New Handbook of Texas, vol. 5.* Austin: Texas State Historical Association, 1996.

***SALVATIERRA v. DEL RIO INDEPENDENT SCHOOL DISTRICT*, 1930.** Also sometimes cited as *DEL RIO INDEPENDENT SCHOOL DISTRICT v. SALVATIERRA.* *Salvatierra v. Del Rio* was a class action suit by Mexican American parents against school officials in the Texas border town of Del Rio. The parents, with help from the newly formed **League of United Latin American Citizens,** argued that the school placed their children in a separate facility because of their ethnicity, thereby violating U.S. constitutional guarantees. They did not contest the content or quality of the education; their only complaint was the placing of their children in a building separate from other students. The school superintendent denied that the school was discriminating on the basis of ethnicity or race, alleging that the reasons for separation were language problems, late enrollments, and irregular attendance.

In this early legal challenge to ethnic segregation the court ruled that, although racial or ethnic discrimination was illegal, separation based on educational grounds was permissible and did not violate the U.S. Constitution. It found that the school district's policies were based on reasonable educational practices and that there was no evidence of intent to discriminate. Until the Delgado case in 1948, the court's decision in Salvatierra set the basis for negative judicial response to Mexican American challenges to segregation in public schools.

FURTHER READING: San Miguel, Guadalupe. *"Let All of Them Take Heed": Mexican Americans and the Campaign for Educational Equality in Texas, 1910–1981.* Austin: University of Texas Press, 1987; Tyler, Ron, ed. *The New Handbook of Texas*, vol. 5. Austin: Texas State Historical Association, 1996.

SAMANIEGO, MARIANO G., 1844–1907. Political leader, businessman. Mariano Samaniego was a member of a well-to-do Sonoran mercantile family located in Mesilla, in southwestern New Mexico, at the beginning of the 1850s. As a result of the **Gadsden Purchase** he became a U.S. national at age ten. After graduating from St. Louis University in Missouri, he settled in Tucson and soon became one of its leading businessmen. In the post–Civil War era he was very successful in freighting and merchandising, hauling supplies for civilians as well as the army. Even before the arrival of the railroad to Tucson in 1880 he sold his freighting interest and began diversifying, investing in stage lines, ranching properties, and urban real estate. He was also involved in water and irrigation companies and some mining ventures. His adaptability and diverse investments enabled him to retain his position as a leading businessman and political leader in Arizona.

In the last three decades of the century Samaniego held more public offices than any other Arizona Mexican American. From 1869 to 1877 he was advisor to Governor Anson Safford and then was elected, and reelected three times, to the territorial assembly. He also served multiple terms on the Tucson city council and on the county board of supervisors. An ardent advocate of public education, in 1886 he became a member of the state university's first board of regents. He was the founding president of the Alianza Hispano-Americana and was also a leading figure in the Arizona Pioneers Historical Society.

FURTHER READING: Gonzales, Manuel G. "Mariano G. Samaniego." *Journal of Arizona History* 31:2 (1990) 141–160; Sheridan, Thomas E. *Los Tucsonenses: The Mexican Community in Tucson, 1854–1941.* Tucson: University of Arizona Press, 1986; Sheridan, Thomas E. "Peacock in the Parlor: Frontier Tucson's Mexican Elite." *Journal of Arizona History* 25:3 (1984) 245–264.

SAMORA, JULIAN, 1921–1996. Educator, author, activist. Julian Samora was the first Mexican American to earn a Ph.D. in sociology and anthropology. Born in Pagosa Springs, Colorado, he grew up and received his early education there. In school he frequently encountered prejudice and discrimination, experiences that prompted a lifelong commitment to fight for civil and societal rights. His 1953 doctoral degree from Washington University in St. Louis led to a pioneering role as a university professor specializing in the sociology of the Chicano.

Samora was a prominent leader in the first generation of Mexican American scholars, spending almost all of his twenty-eight-year academic career teaching at Notre Dame University. As head of its sociology department, he made Notre Dame into an early center for research and publishing about the Mexican American experience. He researched and wrote extensively; he was the author or coauthor of various works, the best-known of which were *La Raza: Forgotten Americans*, 1966 and *Gunpowder Justice: A Reassessment of the Texas Rangers*, 1979, the latter a revisionist history of the **Texas Rangers.** In addition, he attracted numerous graduate students who formed a "school" of Samora's protegés.

Samora also had a long career as an activist. He was a founder of two outstanding advocacy organizations for Chicano rights: the Southwest Council of La Raza and the **Mexican American Legal Defense and Educational Fund.** In addition, he played a role in the Chicano Movement that began in the 1960s. In his efforts to reduce societal barriers he was indefatigable in pressuring government agencies to adopt and practice policies that would help Mexican Americans. His important contributions as an energetic activist and a leading Mexican American scholar were recognized by a presidential Hispanic Heritage Award as well as by an Aguila Azteca, Mexico's highest award to a foreigner.

FURTHER READING: Rodríguez, Roberto. "Chicano Studies Pioneer Praised." *Black Issues in Higher Education* 12 (5 October 1995) 34–37; Ryan, Bryan, ed. *Hispanic Writers: A Selection of Sketches from Contemporary Authors.* Detroit: Gale Research, 1991; Thomas, Robert M., Jr. "Julian Samora, 75, a Pioneering Sociologist." *New York Times* (6 February 1996) B11.

SAN ANTONIO. The San Antonio pueblo grew out of the San Antonio de Béjar presidio, established in 1718. Half a century later, with a population of about two thousand, it was named the capital of Spanish Texas. The town declared for Mexican independence from Spain in 1813, and saw its population greatly reduced when it was retaken by royalist forces. During the

Texas revolt from Mexico it was the site of several battles, the most notable being the siege of the **Alamo** and the Battle of San Jacinto. After Texas established de facto independence, Mexican forces captured the town twice in their unsuccessful efforts to subdue the Texas rebels. In the years immediately before the outbreak of war between the United States and Mexico the population had dwindled to about eight hundred, but growth was rapid after Texas became a state in 1845. By the beginning of the 1860s it had over eight thousand inhabitants, a majority of them Mexicanos.

After the Civil War, San Antonio became the hub and outfitter for the long cattle drives northward. Adding to its importance was its location as a distribution center serving merchants and the military in the border regions of the Southwest. The advent of the **railroads,** beginning in 1877, marked the city's entrance into the national economy and a new era of growth. A heavy in-migration of Anglos from the Old South pushed the population to more than 20,000 by 1880, and exiles from the Mexican revolution of 1910 help to account for a population of 161,000 in 1920. Many Mexicanos were employed in the rapidly expanding service and border industries.

During both World War I and World War II San Antonio served as an important military center, a status that it retains. World War II led to the establishment of several Air Force bases, which, along with tourism and educational and research institutions, helped form a viable economic base for the city. Also, it became a favorite retirement area, especially for the military who had been stationed there. By 2000 its Mexicano population had reached 671,000, almost half of the city's total.

FURTHER READING: Fehrenbach, T. R. *The San Antonio Story.* Tulsa: Continental Heritage Press, 1978; Garcia, Richard A. *Rise of the Mexican American Middle Class: San Antonio, 1929–1941.* College Station: Texas A&M University Press, 1991; Rosales, Rodolfo. *The Illusion of Inclusion: The Untold Political Story of San Antonio.* Austin: University of Texas, 2000.

SÁNCHEZ, GEORGE I., 1906–1972. Teacher, author. Jorge Isidro Sánchez y Sánchez, son of a miner, grew up and received his early education in Jerome, Arizona, and began teaching in a one-room school after his graduation at age sixteen from New Mexico's Albuquerque High School. By the end of the 1920s he had earned his bachelor of arts degree at the University of New Mexico. A Rockefeller Foundation fellowship then enabled him to continue his studies at the University of Texas under educational psychologist Herschel T. Manuel. In 1934 he completed his doctorate in education at the University of California, Berkeley; his dissertation was titled "The Education of Bilinguals in a State School System."

After three years spent surveying rural schools in the Southwest for the Julius Rosenwald Fund and one year in Venezuela as director of the National Teaching Institute, Sánchez returned to the Southwest as associate professor at the University of New Mexico. In 1940 he moved to the University of Texas at Austin, which remained his academic home for the rest of his life.

However, he left Austin frequently to share his educational and sociological expertise with various government agencies and U.S. presidents.

During World War II Sánchez took a leave of absence from the university to work in the Office of Coordinator of Inter-American Affairs. After returning to Austin he spent the next quarter of a century deeply involved with the educational and social needs of Spanish-speaking children. In addition to carrying a full teaching load at the university he remained active in Mexican American organizations. For several years Sánchez served as director of education in the **League of United Latin American Citizens** and was its president in 1941–1942. In 1951 he took a prominent part in founding and subsequently directing the **American Council of Spanish-Speaking People**.

During the 1960s Sánchez strongly supported the Chicano Movement, which he saw as important in righting historical wrongs suffered by Mexican Americans. Nevertheless, some young activists criticized him for not supporting Chicano nationalism and for not being sufficiently confrontational. On the other hand, his clearly articulated views in support of the **movimiento** may have hurt him professionally and financially. Author of over one hundred journal articles, bulletins, and reports, as well as a number of important books, George I. Sánchez is best known for his seminal work, *Forgotten People: A Study of New Mexicans*, 1940.

For more than forty years George I. Sánchez, outstanding scholar and grand old man of the Mexican American rights struggle, was a spokesman for *la raza*. Both as an individual and as a professional he spent a lifetime persistently advocating greater social justice for *la raza* and demanding equality of opportunity for all Americans. Deeply concerned with Chicanos' educational rights, he insistently condemned their educational and social segregation. He viewed **education** as the key to effecting social change and was an early champion of **bilingual education** as a way to achieve greater equality of opportunity for Spanish-speaking children.

FURTHER READING: García, Mario T. *Mexican Americans: Leadership, Ideology, and Identity, 1930–1960*. New Haven, Conn.: Yale University Press, 1989; George I. Sánchez Papers, 1892–1972. Benson Latin American Collection, General Libraries, University of Texas at Austin; *Humanidad: Essays in Honor of George I. Sánchez*. Edited by Américo Paredes. Los Angeles: University of California, Chicano Studies Center, 1977; Leff, Gladys R. "George I. Sánchez: Don Quijote of the Southwest," Thesis. Denton: North Texas State University, 1976; Romo, Ricardo. "George I. Sánchez and the Civil Rights Movement: 1940–1960." *La Raza Law Journal* 1:3 (Fall 1986) 342–362; Welsh, Michael. "A Prophet without Honor: George I. Sánchez and Bilingualism in New Mexico." *New Mexico Historical Review* 69:1 (January 1994) 19–34.

SÁNCHEZ, PHILLIP VICTOR, 1929– . Ambassador, businessman. Phillip Sánchez was born in the small central California town of Pinedale and received his early education there. He attended Coalinga Junior College and then Fresno State, where he received his A.B. in 1953. After working as an analyst in the county government for nine years, he was appointed Fresno County manager in 1962. Two years later he was named one of California's five outstanding young men.

In 1971 Sánchez's administrative skills were recognized by President Richard Nixon, who appointed him assistant director and then director of the **Office of Economic Opportunity**. His success as director there led to his appointment as ambassador to Honduras, and in 1976 President Gerald Ford named him ambassador to Colombia, a position he held until the Jimmy Carter presidency.

Returning to California, Sánchez turned to consulting work and then became the founding president of the Woodside Consulting Group. In 1987 he was named publisher of *Noticias del Mundo*, a chain of Spanish language daily newspapers with which he was affiliated. He was a founder of the National Hispanic University and served as its chairman. A member of the University of Bridgeport's board of trustees, he also serves on several corporate boards and makes presentations at conferences for Causa U.S.A. and Causa International, which he strongly supports. In 2002 he was named as one of the "Hispanic Media 100."

FURTHER READING: Alverio, Diane. "No, Thank You, Mr. President." *Nuestro* (April 1981) 56; Martínez, Al. *Rising Voices: Profiles of Hispano American Lives.* New York: New American Library, 1974; U.S. Department of State, *Biographic Register.* Washington, D.C. (July 1974); *Who's Who in American Politics, 1995–1996.* New Providence, N.J.: R. R. Bowker, 1995.

SÁNCHEZ, RICARDO, 1941–1995. Poet, author, teacher. Born and raised in El Paso, Ricardo Sánchez began writing poetry while still in grade school. Despite a lack of encouragement from the educational system, he persisted in his studies but later dropped out of high school to enlist in the army, where he earned a general equivalency diploma. Out of the army, he was nearly destroyed by a series of deaths in the family and committed a string of felonies that landed him in prison in Texas. He was paroled in 1963, soon married, and two years later, devastated by his inability to pay the costs of his first child's birth, found himself back in prison in California for armed robbery and parole violation. He was paroled again in 1969 but continued to be consumed with a deep-seated bitterness and resentment at society, emotions that he expressed in his poetry.

With the support of a Frederick Douglass fellowship Sánchez spent the years 1968–1970 at Virginia Commonwealth University and then got a teaching job at the University of Massachusetts. He gradually became aware that he was limited professionally by his lack of a doctorate. Aided by a Ford Foundation grant, he was able to complete his Ph.D. in American studies at the Union Graduate School in Yellow Springs, Ohio, in 1974. In the following year he was the National Endowment for the Arts poet in residence at the El Paso Community College. Up until his death in 1995 from cancer he taught at various universities in Texas, New Mexico, Utah, and Wisconsin and gave lectures and readings of his poetry at many more. Throughout his life he participated actively in a variety of community-related organizations; from 1979 to 1981 he served as vice president of the Utah *American G.I. Forum.*

One of the foremost early Chicano poets along with **Abelardo** and **Alurista,** Sánchez published a dozen books and had his poems and other works published in various journals and a number of anthologies. He is perhaps best known for his first work, *Canto y grito mi liberación,* 1971, a blast of humiliation, frustration, anger, and fear. His last published work was *Amerikan Journeys: Jornadas Americanas,* issued the year before his death. He was an editor of *Quetzal* and *La Luz* and was a founder of Mictla Publications, on whose board he served. He also wrote columns for several Texas newspapers.

FURTHER READING: Bruce-Novoa, Juan. *Chicano Authors: Inquiry by Interview.* Austin: University of Texas Press, 1980; Christensen, Paul. *West of the American Dream: An Encounter with Texas.* College Station: Texas A&M University Press, 2001; Lomelí, Francisco A., and Carl R. Shirley, eds. *Chicano Writers: First Series.* Detroit: Gale Research, 1989; López, Miguel R. *Chicano Timespace: The Poetry and Politics of Ricardo Sánchez.* College Station: Texas A&M University Press, 2001.

SÁNCHEZ, ROBERT F., 1934– . Archbishop, teacher. Robert Sánchez was born and received his early education in Socorro, a town on the Rio Grande River in southern New Mexico. In 1950 he began studying for the priesthood in Santa Fe and from there entered the North American College in Rome. Nine years later he was ordained and in 1960 began teaching at St. Pius High School in Albuquerque.

While he served as pastor in two parishes, Sánchez also earned a certificate in counseling at the University of New Mexico and for a year studied canon law at the Catholic University in Washington, D.C. In the early 1970s he was elected by his fellow priests to the archdiocesan priests' senate and later to the National Federation of Priests Councils. In 1974 he was appointed the first Mexican American archbishop of Santa Fe by Pope Paul VI. As archbishop he continued to stress a closeness to his flock of Anglos, Indians, and Mexican Americans. In 1993 he resigned after a sexual scandal.

FURTHER READING: *American Catholic Who's Who, 1980–1981.* Washington, D.C.: N.C. News Service, 1980; Nelson, Jay. "Secrets of Archbishop Sánchez." *Missing Link* (Fall 1996–Winter 1997); "Pope Accepts Resignation of Bishop." *Los Angeles Times.* (7 April 1993) A20; Steiner, Stan. "Archbishop of All the People." *Nuestro* (April 1977) 50–52.

SANTA ANNA, ANTONIO LÓPEZ DE, 1794–1876. Mexican president, soldier. Santa Anna entered the Spanish army in Mexico on the eve of the war for independence in 1810. Joining in Agustín de Iturbide's movement for independence a decade later, he was promoted to brigadier general in 1822.

Santa Anna dominated Mexico politically for three decades, serving as president eleven times between 1833 and 1855. During his first presidency Texas revolted and successfully established its de facto independence in spite of his efforts at reconquest. In 1846 he unsuccessfully resisted the U.S. invasion of Mexico, and during his last presidency he sold the Mesilla valley to the U.S. for ten million dollars.

FURTHER READING: Jones, Oakah. *Santa Anna*. New York: Twayne, 1968; Lynch, John. *Caudillos in Spanish America*. New York: Oxford University Press, 1992; Miller, Robert Ryal. *Mexico: A History*. Norman: University of Oklahoma Press, 1985; Santa Anna, Antonio López de. *The Eagle: The Autobiography of Santa Anna*, edited by Ann Fears Crawford. Austin: State House Press, 1988 (1967).

SANTA FE. Santa Fe, the capital of New Mexico, was established in 1609. A century and a half later it had become an important trade link between Chihuahua and the Mississippi valley. After 1820 it became one of the southern termini of the trade with Missouri. The acquisition of the Southwest by the United States led to the creation of a stage line in 1849 connecting it more intimately with Independence, Missouri and the rest of the United States. Thirty years later the arrival of the railroad had mixed results. It brought a new prosperity to Santa Fe, but also resulted in the decline and ultimate demise of its premier role in freighting and stagecoaching.

After decades of seeking statehood, in 1912 New Mexico became the forty-seventh state and Santa Fe began a new chapter in its history. Its Mexican American elite increasingly identified with the Anglo minority leadership, but a substantial influx of refugees fleeing the Mexican revolution created a new element in the Hispanic element of the tri-ethnic makeup of Santa Fe. The city also began to attract painters, writers, and other artists from eastern parts of the United States and even overseas. Its population of about six thousand at statehood had doubled by 1930 to some twelve thousand. By the end of the century it reached over sixty-seven thousand.

During World War II Los Alamos, where the atom bomb was developed, was the recipient of enormous U.S. government research funds but they led to little development in Santa Fe until the last two decades of the twentieth century. The importance of mining in the state's economy has declined considerably in recent years. Its place has been taken by tourism, thanks to a resurgence in traditional crafts, and there has been an accompanying increase in service industries' jobs.

FURTHER READING: González, Deena J. *Refusing the Favor: The Spanish-Mexican Women of Santa Fe, 1820–1880*. New York: Oxford University Press, 1999; Simmons, Marc. *New Mexico: An Interpretive History*. Albuquerque: University of New Mexico Press, 1988; Vigil, Maurilio E. *The Hispanics of New Mexico: Essays on History and Culture*. Bristol, Ind.: Wyndham Hall Press, 1984; Wilson, Chris. *The Myth of Santa Fe: Creating a Modern Regional Tradition*. Albuquerque: University of New Mexico Press, 1997.

SANTA FE RING. The Santa Fe Ring was a shifting informal alliance of Nuevomexicano elites and Anglos who manipulated and exploited New Mexico's resources in the last quarter of the nineteenth century. Formed in the 1870s, the Ring used Anglo control of the territorial government to dominate the economy, especially the sale of lands. Thomas B. Catron, who headed the territorial Republican Party, was its most prominent leader. The Ring's powerful control was weakened and ultimately broken by **Bronson Cutting,** who was later elected U.S. senator from New Mexico.

FURTHER READING: Rasch, Philip J. "The People of the Territory of New Mexico vs. the Santa Fe Ring." *New Mexico Historical Review* 47:2 (1972) 185–202; Simmons, Marc. *New Mexico: An Interpretive History.* Albuquerque: University of New Mexico Press, 1988; Zeleny, Carolyn. *Relations between the Spanish-Americans and Anglo-Americans in New Mexico.* Reprint. New York: Arno Press, 1974.

SANTA FE TRADE. The Santa Fe trade developed between that north Mexican outpost and the Missouri frontier of the United States. With Mexican independence from Spain in 1821 the trade blossomed and by the end of the decade it had become well defined, reaching about $250,000 annually. The trade brought avidly desired manufactured goods to Nuevo México and also a settlement of Anglo traders who influenced Nuevomexicano attitudes toward takeover by the United States. As Nuevo México became increasingly more dependent on the trade, the Mexican government's fear of U.S. manifest destiny increased. After the war between the United States and Mexico, the trade expanded greatly. At the peak of the California gold rush era it amounted to about $5,000,000 a year. The arrival of the **railroads** at the beginning of the 1880s meant the death knell of the trade's decades-long history.

FURTHER READING: Boyle, Susan Calafate. *Los Capitalistas: Hispanic Merchants and the Santa Fe Trade.* Albuquerque: University of New Mexico Press, 1997; Duffus, Robert L. *The Santa Fe Trail.* Albuquerque: University of New Mexico Press, 1971; Hyslop, Stephen G. *Bound for Santa Fe: The Road to New Mexico and the American Conquest, 1806–1848.* Norman: University of Oklahoma Press, 2002.

SANTERO. A *santero* is a carver of wooden effigies of the saints and Jesus, typically in a primitive style. From the colonial period to the present, *santeros* have been particularly noted in New Mexico. In the late twentieth century there was renewed interest in *santero* art, in part arising out of the Chicano **movimiento** and the earlier folk art revival in the 1930s.

FURTHER READING: Boyd, E. *Saints and Saint Makers of New Mexico,* revised and edited by Robin Farwell Gavin. Santa Fe: Western Edge, 1998; Rosenack, Chuck. *The Saint Makers: Contemporary Santeras and Santeros.* Flagstaff, Ariz.: Northland, 1998; Steele, Thomas J. *Santos and Saints: The Religious Folk Art of Hispanic New Mexico,* rev. ed. Santa Fe: Ancient City Press, 1994.

SCHECHTER, HOPE MENDOZA, 1921– . Labor organizer, activist. Esperanza Mendoza dropped out of high school at age seventeen to go to work in a Los Angeles garment factory. After World War II she returned to the clothing industry to help organize workers. During the late 1940s and early 1950s she began to interest herself in community affairs and helped establish the **Community Service Organization** (CSO) in southern California. For seven years she served on the CSO board of directors. After her marriage to Harvey Schechter in 1955, she turned increasingly to Democratic politics while retaining her basic concerns for her fellow Mexican Americans. Her continuing interest in *raza* community problems resulted in positions on the board of directors in the Mexican American Youth Opportunities Foundation and in the Council of Mexican American Affairs, and her deeper involvement in the Democratic party led to offices in various Democratic party organizations. The driving forces in her life were shaped by her concerns for her fellow working-class Mexican Americans.

FURTHER READING: "Hope Mendoza Schechter: Activist in the Labor Movement, the Democratic Party, and the Mexican-American Community." Berkeley: Regional Oral History Office, Bancroft Library, University of California, 1980; Telgen, Dianne, and Jim Kamp, eds. *Notable Hispanic American Women.* Detroit: Gale Research, 1993.

SECRETARIAT FOR THE SPANISH SPEAKING. The Secretariat for the Spanish Speaking evolved from the Bishops Committee for the Spanish Speaking, created in 1945 under the leadership of **Robert E. Lucey**, archbishop of San Antonio. Its objective was to develop social as well as spiritual programs for improving the lives of Mexican Americans. In addition to various pastoral concerns, it became seriously involved in community self-help development. It made available to Mexican Americans a variety of social services, including voter registration, citizenship classes, youth programs, and leadership training. In 1970 the Bishops Committee had an important role in bringing César Chávez's **Delano grape strike** to a successful conclusion.

In 1975, as the Secretariat, it became an agency of the National Conference of Catholic Bishops. From its Washington, D.C., headquarters the Secretariat acts as a concept and planning center and an organizing tool for programs in housing, health, employment, education, and civil rights.

FURTHER READING: Dolan, Jay P., and Gilberto M. Hinojosa. *Mexican Americans and the Catholic Church, 1900–1965.* Notre Dame: University of Notre Dame Press, 1994; Sandoval, Moisés. "The Organization of a Hispanic Church." In *Hispanic Catholic Culture in the U.S.: Issues and Concerns,* edited by Jay P. Nolan and Allan Figueroa Deck. Notre Dame: University of Notre Dame Press, 1994; Walsh, Albeus. "Work of the Catholic Bishops Committee for the Spanish Speaking in the U.S." M.A. Thesis, University of Texas at Austin, 1952.

SEGREGATION. Segregation is the forcing of ethnic or racial groups by law or custom to live, go to school, use public facilities, and so on apart from other citizens. Segregation may be de jure (based on legislation) or de facto (without any legal basis). Most segregation suffered by Mexicanos, with widespread exception in the area of education, has been de facto. De jure segregation has been declared unconstitutional by the courts and has largely ended, but de facto segregation of Mexican Americans continues.

Segregation of Mexican Americans has been particularly notable in three areas: schools, housing, and public and semipublic facilities. They have been denied hotel accommodation, refused service in restaurants, restricted in use of swimming pools, forced to sit in certain seats in theaters and even churches, and refused personal services. These discriminatory practices, once commonplace, have greatly attenuated since the 1960s. During the 1950s and 1960s campaigns by the **American G.I. Forum** in Texas, by **Ignacio López** in his southern California newspaper *El Espectador,* and by the **Alianza Hispano-Americana** in Arizona against such customary discrimination helped to focus attention on Mexicano segregation.

In **housing,** Mexican Americans historically have been forced to live in barrios, apart from mainstream American town-dwellers. This segregation is the result of income levels as well as restrictive housing covenants and some real estate firms' policies of ethnic and racist discrimination. Although conditions have improved in recent decades, these widely employed covenants have often forced Mexican Americans to accept inferior housing in the past. Nearly all housing discrimination has its basis in custom, not law. However, in the matter of school segregation law has had a more influential role.

School segregation was widespread until the past few decades, with separate schools or classrooms often being justified on the basis of language problems and attendance. Education codes and school board policies in the Southwest firmly fixed separation of Mexican American children in school systems. At the end of the 1920s, Chicano parents began fighting such school segregation policies. In the 1930 case of *Salvatierra v. Del Rio Independent School District* (Texas), the court found that Mexicano children were being segregated without regard for individual language ability, and ruled that separate classes might be used only for legitimate educational goals. In the Méndez, or Westminster, case fifteen years later in California, a federal court held that the school board's segregation of Mexicano children violated the constitutional guarantee of equal protection under the law. On appeal, the court's decision was upheld as also violating California statute law. The **League of United Latin American Citizens**, whose attorneys fought this important case, has been notable for its leadership in fighting school segregation since the 1930s.

FURTHER READING: Donato, Rubén. *The Other Struggle for Equal Schools: Mexican Americans during the Civil Rights Era.* Albany: State University of New York Press, 1997; González, Gilbert G. *Chicano Education in the Era of Segregation.* Philadelphia: Balch Institute Press, 1990; Guzmán, Ralph. "The Hand of Esau: Words Change, Practices Remain in Racial Covenants." *Frontier* 7: 8 (June 1956) 7, 16; López, Manuel Mariano. "Su casa no es mi casa: Hispanic Housing Conditions in Contemporary America, 1949–1980." In *Race, Ethnicity, and Minority Housing in the United States,* edited by Janshid A. Momeni. Westport, Conn.: Greenwood Press, 1986;

Menchaca, Martha. *The Mexican Outsiders: A Community History of Marginalization and Discrimination in California.* Austin: University of Texas Press, 1995; Montejano, David. "The Demise of Jim Crow." In *Land Grants, Housing, and Political Power,* edited by Antoinette Sedillo López. New York: Garland, 1995; Rangel, Jorge C. and Carlos C. Alcalá. "Project Report: De Jure Segregation of Chicanos in Texas Schools." *Harvard Civil Rights-Civil Liberties Law Review* 7 (March 1972) 307–391; "Residential Segregation." In *The Mexican American People: The Nation's Second Largest Minority,* edited by Leo Grebler, Joan W. Moore, and Ralph C. Guzmán. New York: The Free Press, 1970; Sánchez, George I. *Concerning Segregation of Spanish-Speaking Children in the Public Schools.* Austin: University of Texas Press, 1951.

SEGUÍN, JUAN NEPOMUCENO, 1806–1889. Juan Seguín was born in San Antonio, Texas, of a prominent, politically involved father. Before he reached twenty-one he was elected to the San Antonio city council as an alcalde. In the 1830s his opposition to the centralizing government of Mexican president Antonio López de Santa Anna led him to join the revolt against Mexican control. At the Alamo he was the leader of a small Tejano contingent. He served Texas faithfully and well as a soldier and officer and then after the war as a senator and mayor of San Antonio.

As mayor of San Antonio, Seguín strongly defended Tejano rights and in return earned the undying enmity of the many Anglo adventurers who had descended on Texas after independence. Their intense and unremitting hatred and harrying followed him for the rest of his life. He was unjustly accused of traitorous sentiments and of being favorably disposed toward Mexican attempts to reconquer Texas in the late 1830s. Repeated threats against his life and increasing danger to his family finally forced him to move his family out of Texas.

Across the Rio Grande, Seguín was jailed by local Mexican military officials and, on direct orders from President Santa Anna, given the choice of army service or imprisonment. With a large family to provide for, the impoverished Seguín felt he had little choice. After the Mexican-U.S. War and the 1848 Treaty of **Guadalupe Hidalgo** he was allowed to return to his native Texas with his family, despite acrimonious vocal opposition.

Seguín lived quietly on a family ranch near San Antonio after his return but continued his interest in Texas politics. During the 1850s and 1860s he wrote his memoirs, in which he defended his conduct and described the hounding by his enemies. Sometime in the 1870s Seguín once again crossed the Rio Grande, and in 1889 he died at the home of one of his sons in the Mexican border state of Nuevo León.

FURTHER READING: Seguín, Juan. *Personal Memoirs of John N. Seguín from 1834 to . . . 1842.* San Antonio: The Ledger Book and Job Office, 1858; Seguín, Juan. *A Revolution Remembered: The Memoirs and Selected Correspondence of Juan N. Seguín.* Edited by Jesús F. de la Teja. Austin: State House Press, 1991; Tyler, Ron, ed. *New Handbook of Texas,* vol 5. Austin: Texas State Historical Association, 1996. Vernon, Ida S. "Activities of the Seguins in Early Texas History." *West Texas Historical Association Year Book* 25 (Oct. 1949) 11–38.

SELENA

Selena singing to schoolchildren in Corpus Christi, Texas, in 1994. © AP/Wide World Photos.

SELENA, 1971–1995. Singer. Selena Quintanilla was born in Lake Jackson, Texas, where she began singing with the family's musical group, Los Dinos, at age nine. Her entire life was greatly influenced by her father, a singer who had formed Los Dinos and later also managed her career, coaching her to sing phonetically in Spanish. At age eight she recorded her first song. Two years later Selena and the other family members began touring the towns of south Texas as the band "Selena y Los Dinos," playing at roadhouses, *quinceañeras*, and weddings. While still in high school she cut her first albums and began winning music awards. In 1987, at fifteen, she was named the female vocalist of the year at the Tejano Music Awards. Several years after completing high school, in 1992 she married Christopher Pérez, the lead guitarist in Los Dinos.

Between 1984 and 1994 Selena made a dozen albums, singing ballads, blues, pop, rock, rhythm, Tejano, mariachi, and cumbia. On the advice of her father she began taking Spanish lessons in the early 1990s in order to sound more genuinely Mexicana. In the 1993 *Billboard* Premio Lo Nuestro ratings she dominated the Regional Mexican category, walking off with the song, album, and female singer-of-the-year awards. In 1994 her *Selena Live* album won a Grammy; in the following year her *Amor Prohibido* CD, which sold over 500,000 copies (and after her death an amazing 1,000,000 copies) was nominated for a Grammy; and she signed a tour sponsorship contract with Coca-Cola. By the beginning of 1995 her albums had sold a total of 3,000,000 copies, placing her in the select company of Gloria Estefan, Jon Secada, and Luis Miguel. In 1995 she won a Grammy, swept the Annual Tejano Music Awards, taking six awards, and was poised for even wider acceptance as she began work on her first album in English for SBK Records.

On 31 March 1995 the fashion-conscious singer was shot in a Corpus Christi motel by Yolanda Saldívar, founder of the Selena Fan Club and her personal assistant. Selena, who suspected Saldívar of financial mismanagement and embezzlement in connection with the Selena, Etc. boutiques in Corpus Christi and San Antonio, was in the process of firing her. Selena's death cut short an extremely promising career and occasioned an unprecedented outpouring of popular emotion and grief. Her funeral attracted fifty thousand tearful fans, who saw her buried beneath a canopy of eight thousand white roses. Saldívar, whose motivation was never completely clarified, was later tried, found guilty, and given life imprisonment. Selena's grave continues to attract thousands of her admirers, à la Elvis Presley.

A singer of contagious energy, on stage she exuded warmth, passion, and sexuality, while maintaining an offstage down-to-earth persona of the wholesome young girl next door. In October 2001 she was posthumously named to the Tejano Walk of Fame.

FURTHER READING: Castillo, Ana. "Selena Aside," obit. *Nation* 260:21 (1995) 764; Hewitt, Bill, Joseph Harmes, and Bob Stewart. "Before Her Time." *People* (17 April 1995) 49–53; Limón, José E. "Selena: Sexuality, Performance, and the Problematic of Hegemony." In *Reflexiones 1997*, edited by Neil Foley. Austin: Center for Mexican American Studies, University of Texas, 1997; Patoski, Joe Nick. *Selena, como la flor*. Boston: Little Brown, 1996; Sánchez, Sandra. "8,000 Roses, in Remembrance." *USA Today* (4 April 1995) 3A; Terry-Azios, Diana A. "Tejano Music Queen." *Hispanic* (March 2000) 28.

***SERRANO v. PRIEST*, 1968–1976.** In 1968 John Serrano filed a suit against the California state treasurer, arguing that his son was receiving an inferior education as the result of the system of school financing by property taxes. He held that this was a violation of his son's right to equal protection under the law. The California courts, up to and including the state supreme court, agreed with Serrano. Basing its decision on the California constitution, the U.S. Supreme Court upheld the decision of the California courts but limited its finding of unequal protection of the law to that state. The decision was an important step in shifting school financing away from a local property tax base, a system that operated against poorer Chicano districts.

FURTHER READING: Browning, R. Stephen. "School Finance Reform: The Role of the Courts." *Civil Rights Digest/Perspectives*. 5:3 (October 1972) 12–19; Domínguez, John F. "School Finance: The Issues of Equity and Efficiency." *Aztlán* 8:1 (1977) 175–199; Wickert, Donald M. "Some School Finance Issues Related to the Implementation of Serrano and Proposition 13." *Journal of Education Finance* 10 (Spring 1985) 535–542.

SILEX, HUMBERTO, 1903–2002. Labor organizer. Nicaraguan immigrant Humberto Silex came to the United States via Mexico and spent most of his life organizing Mexicano workers along the Mexico-U.S. border. After serving as a volunteer in the U.S. Army at the end of World War I and then working at a variety of jobs, at the end of the 1920s he settled in El Paso, working for American Smelting and Refining Company (ASARCO). By 1937 he had become seriously involved in union organizing at ASARCO for the International Union of Mine, Mill and Smelter Workers, a Congress of Industrial Organizations affiliate.

Silex strongly supported the union's policy of unqualified opposition to discrimination, and as president of Local 509 helped bring about an end to discriminatory practices at ASARCO. At the end of World War II he was given an award for his union's wartime stabilizing efforts and then was one of the leaders in a successful four-month 1946 strike against ASARCO and Dodge-Phelps by over one thousand workers, mostly Mexicanos. While the strike was in progress, the Immigration and Naturalization Service began an attempt to arrest and deport Silex, despite his completely legal status. The deportation effort lasted nearly a year; his blacklisting lasted much longer.

In 1947 Silex's application for citizenship was at first approved, then denied by the government in the mounting anti-communist frenzy of the Cold War era. Labeled as a subversive, he was able to fight the efforts to deport him but was not allowed to continue his union organizing work. For the rest of his long life he earned his living repairing vending machines, and finally received his citizenship at age eighty-eight. Eleven years later he died of complications resulting from pneumonia.

FURTHER READING: "Humberto Silex: CIO Organizer from Nicaragua." *Southwest Economy and Society* 4 (Fall 1978) 3–18; Martínez, Oscar J. *Border People: Life and Society in the U.S.-Mexico Borderlands.* Tucson: University of Arizona Press, 1994.

SINARQUISTA MOVEMENT. *Sinarquismo* was an extremely conservative Mexican sociopolitical movement begun in the 1930s. With European fascist support, it advocated a national regeneration that would reject materialism and return to traditional values of an earlier Mexico. The Sinarquistas strongly opposed Mexico's collaboration with the United States during World War II and attempted to spread their ideas among Mexican Americans in the Southwest. They promoted various rumors to discourage active Chicano participation in the war effort. The movement was taken with some seriousness by the U.S. and Mexican governments, both of which infiltrated the organization. However, *sinarquismo* was never widely accepted in either country and disappeared after the war.

FURTHER READING: Prado, Enrique L. "Sinarquism in the United States." *New Republic* 109 (26 July 1943) 97–102.

SLEEPY LAGOON, 1942–1944. Sleepy Lagoon was the name given by the media to a notorious Los Angeles murder case. In late 1942 some twenty-four members of a Chicano street gang were indicted by a grand jury for the death by beating of one José Díaz. There followed a lengthy trial in which no direct evidence was ever brought forward to link the accused gang members to Díaz's death. During the trial there was repeated evidence of strong anti-Mexican bias on the part of the prosecution and the judge; seventeen of the indicted youths were found guilty of murder or assault.

A campaign to appeal the court's decision was organized by **Josefina Fierro de Bright,** with a Sleepy Lagoon Defense Committee headed by **Carey**

McWilliams. In October 1944 by unanimous vote the California District Court of Appeals voided the lower court's verdicts for lack of evidence. It also criticized the prosecutor and Judge Charles W. Fricke for their biased and racist conduct of the trial.

The flagrant and systematic violation of the accused youths' civil rights in the Sleepy Lagoon affair aroused widespread indignation that led to a limited and temporary decline in civil rights abuses in the Los Angeles area.

FURTHER READING: Day, Mark. "The Pertinence of the 'Sleepy Lagoon' Case." *Journal of Mexican American History* 4:1 (1974) 71–98; Endore, S. Guy. *The Sleepy Lagoon Mystery*. Los Angeles: Sleepy Lagoon Defense Committee, 1944. Reprinted by R & E Research Associates. San Francisco, 1972; Eulau, Heinz H. "Sleepy Lagoon Case: Court of Appeals Reverses Judgements." *New Republic* 111 (11 December 1944) 795–796; McWilliams, Carey. *North from Mexico: The Spanish-Speaking People of the United States*, rev. ed. New York: Praeger, 1990; *The Sleepy Lagoon Case*. Los Angeles: Sleepy Lagoon Defense Committee, 1943. Reprinted in *The Mexican American and the Law*. New York: Arno Press, 1974.

SOLÍS, HILDA, 1957–. Lawmaker. After completing her master's degree at the University of Southern California, Hilda Solís obtained an internship in Washington from the Jimmy Carter White House. Her internship turned into a two-year position in the Office of Management and Budget. She returned to California in 1985 and six years later was appointed to the Los Angeles County Insurance Commission. In 1992 she won a seat in the California lower house and later became the first Chicana elected to the state senate. In the March 2000 primary elections she defeated her incumbent Democratic opponent for a seat in the U.S. House of Representatives by a two-to-one vote. With no Republican opponent in the general election, she was guaranteed her position in the House. On May 22 she was presented with the John F. Kennedy Profile in Courage Award at the John F. Kennedy Library in Boston.

FURTHER READING: Barone, Michael, Richard E. Cohen, and Chas. E. Cook, Jr., eds. *Almanac of American Politics*, 2002 ed. Washington, D.C.: Washington National Journal, 2001; Radelat, Ana. "Hilda Solís." *Hispanic* (June 2000) 26; Walton, Anthony. "Hilda Solís." In *Profiles in Courage for Our Time*, edited by Caroline Kennedy. New York: Hyperion, 2002.

SOUTHWEST. In its narrowest definition the Southwest might include only New Mexico, Arizona, and the El Paso region of Texas. In a broader and widely accepted definition it encompasses all of Texas, New Mexico, Arizona, California, and southern parts of Nevada, Utah, and Colorado. First settled by Hispanics at the end of the sixteenth century, it ultimately became the homeland of a new culture, a blend of Mexican, Native American, and later Anglo contributions. After U.S. acquisition in 1848 by the Treaty of **Guadalupe Hidalgo**, the isolation that characterized it slowly began to lessen. As **railroads** created new economic ties and greater interaction with the

Midwest and the East Coast, it was gradually integrated into the national economy. Until the beginning of the twentieth century it was the Mexican American homeland. It is still the Mexican American heartland.

FURTHER READING: Chávez, John R. *The Lost Land: The Chicano Image of the Southwest.* Albuquerque: University of New Mexico Press, 1984; Kessell, John L. *Spain in the Southwest: A Narrative History of Colonial New Mexico, Arizona, Texas, and California.* Norman: University of Oklahoma Press, 2002; Meléndez, Gabriel, et al., eds. *The Multicultural Southwest: A Reader.* Tucson: University of Arizona Press, 2001; Nostrand, Richard L. *The Hispano Homeland.* Norman: University of Oklahoma Press, 1992; Rosenbaum, Robert J. *Mexicano Resistance in the Southwest.* Dallas: Southern Methodist University Press, 1981; Vélez-Ibáñez, Carlos G. *Border Visions: Mexican Cultures of the Southwest United States.* Tucson: University of Arizona Press, 1996; Weber, David J. *Myth and the History of the Hispanic Southwest: Essays.* Albuquerque: University of New Mexico Press, 1998.

SOUTHWEST VOTER REGISTRATION EDUCATION PROJECT. The SVREP was founded in San Antonio in 1974 by **Willie Velásquez** with the help of a small grant. Based on the Voter Education Project organized by black Americans in the 1960s, it proposed to work with existing agencies. It has closely allied itself with the **Mexican American Legal Defense and Educational Fund** and other Chicano civic organizations and community groups. With a small staff and many volunteers, it centers its activities on voter registration drives and also files suits over discriminatory voting restrictions. It also conducts studies on political matters of concern to the Mexican American community.

Between the mid-1970s and 1985 the SVREP registered over half a million new Mexican American voters in the Midwest and Southwest, an achievement made possible by the dedication of volunteers and by amendments to the 1965 **Voting Rights Act**. Its activities in voter registration, elections, and the courts have been a significant factor in the larger number of Chicanos elected to public office in recent years. Although less successful in the Midwest and the rest of the Southwest than in Texas, the SVREP is still the principal agency in putting Mexican Americans on the election rolls and helping to elect more Mexican Americans to political office.

FURTHER READING: Pycior, Julie Leininger. *LBJ and Mexican Americans: The Paradox of Power.* Austin: University of Texas Press, 1997; Scuros, Mariana. "The Southwest Voter Registration Education Project." *Church and Society* 74:5 (May–June 1984) 26–35; Skerry, Peter. *Mexican Americans: The Ambivalent Minority.* New York: Free Press, 1993; Treviño, Jesse. "The Political Game." *Vista* (15 January 1989) 6–7, 13.

SPANISH AMERICAN. The term *Spanish American* was once widely used in the United States to refer to all Spanish speakers in the country. However, it can also apply to all Spanish-speakers in the western hemisphere. In New Mexico the terms Spanish, Hispanic, and **Hispano** American are often used by Mexican American elites to refer to themselves. This practice may connote an implicit denial of any Native American roots. In Texas the term has been used as a euphemism for Mexican because of the derogation commonly attached to the latter term in that state.

SPANISH SURNAME. *Spanish surname* is a term used for persons with a Spanish family name. Not all Spanish-surnamed persons speak Spanish, nor do all necessarily identify with Hispanic culture. Likewise, the term clearly does not include all persons of Spanish cultural background. Like Spanish American, it is sometimes used as a euphemism for Mexican or Mexican American.

STEREOTYPING. Stereotyping is the ascribing to all persons of a group an identical pattern of characteristics, attitudes, or abilities. Mexican Americans have often been characterized over the years by two somewhat antithetical negative stereotypes: the violent, knife-wielding urban criminal and the indolent, ignorant peasant. There are also the contradictory stereotypes of Mexican immigrants as people who take jobs from American citizens and who come to the United States just to get welfare payments and other social benefits. Denigrating epithets like "greaser," "wetback," "beaner," and "spic" add negative implications of uncleanliness and inferior status to the stereotype.

American literature, radio, films, the print media, and television have all served to spread negative stereotypes of Mexicanos. Beginning in the late 1800s individual Mexican Americans spoke out against stereotyping, protesting its unfairness. During the early post–World War II period, Chicanos made concerted efforts to end this offensive disregard and infringement of their social rights, with some success. Of course, not all stereotyping has ended.

FURTHER READING: Anderson, Mark C. "What's to Be Done with 'Em? Images of Mexican Cultural Backwardness, Racial Limitations, and Moral Decrepitude in the United States Press, 1913–1915." *Mexican Studies/Estudios Mexicanos* 14:1 (Winter 1998) 23–70; Berg, Charles Ramírez. *Latino Images in Film: Stereotypes, Subversion, & Resistance.* Austin: University of Texas Press, 2002; Limón, José E. "Stereotyping and the Chicano Resistance: An Historical Dimension." *Aztlán* 4:2 (Fall 1973) 257–270; Martínez, Thomas M. "Advertising and Racism: The Case of the Mexican American." *El Grito* 2:4 (Summer 1969) 3–13; Pettit, Arthur G. *Images of the Mexican American in Fiction and Film.* College Station: Texas A&M University Press, 1980. Robinson, Cecil. *With the Ears of Strangers: The Mexican in American Literature.* Tucson: University of Arizona Press, 1971.

STUDENT ACTIVISM. Denial of educational rights and widespread stereotyping of Mexican American students combined in the post–World War II era to unleash a powerful student protest movement in the United States. To a degree Chicano student activism was also a part of the worldwide youth rebellion of the 1960s. The greatly enlarged Mexican American classroom population of this period called for changes in the U.S. educational system, rejecting the passive role usually assigned to young people by the Mexican culture of their elders as well as by Anglo educators.

Predominantly youths from working-class families, Chicano students aggressively demanded reforms at high school, college, and university levels. They created militant organizations to channel their demands. In high schools all over the Southwest they boycotted classes and staged school walkouts, demanding Latino teachers and counselors as well as classes oriented toward their ethnic educational needs. At colleges and universities students organized demonstrations, sit-ins, and teach-ins, and called for Chicano professors, courses in Chicano history and culture, the creation of Chicano studies programs, and admission of more Chicano students. At all levels student activists demanded that their voices be heard in the entire academic process.

Texas and California Chicano students led the movement for educational reform. In the spring of 1968 the latter walked out of five East Los Angeles high schools when their earlier demands for educational reform were completely ignored. Prompted by this example, students in New Mexico, Colorado, and the rest of the Southwest also initiated protests. The initial reaction of school administrators was overwhelmingly negative. Despite harassment by school authorities and police as well as a lack of enthusiasm on the part of some elders in the Chicano community, the protesters persisted in their demands. Overcoming apathy and opposition, eventually they were able to achieve many of their objectives despite a spate of popular anti-Mexican education legislation. However, continuing high dropout rates in high school, the small numbers attending colleges and universities, and occasional outbursts of student dissatisfaction in the 1980s and 1990s indicate that the battle for quality and equality in education has yet to be won.

Along the way the students created organizations to provide continuity to their protest. However, by the mid-1970s student activism declined, as the drive of these groups was blunted by partial success and beset by internal conflicts. Moreover, the overall student movement itself became less aggressive as Chicano professors and students moved towards the mainstream. On the positive side, the lessons that Chicano youths learned on college and university campuses made them aware of the potential effectiveness of active participation in community affairs and the political arena.

FURTHER READING: Acuña, Rodolfo. *Occupied America: A History of Chicanos*, 3rd ed. New York: Harper & Row, 1988; Briegel, Kaye. "Chicano Student Militancy: The Los Angeles High School Strike of 1968." In *An Awakened Minority: The Mexican-Americans*, 2nd ed. Edited by Manuel P. Servín. Beverly Hills: Glencoe Press, 1974; Frisbie, Parker. "Militancy among Mexican American High School Students." *Social Science Quarterly* 53:4 (March 1973) 865–883; Gómez-Quiñones, Juan. *Mexican Students Por La Raza: The Chicano Student Movement in Southern California 1967–1977*. Santa Barbara, Calif.: Editorial La Causa, 1978; Muñoz, Carlos Jr. *Youth, Identity, Power: The Chicano Movement*. New York: Verso, 1989; Pizarro, Marc. "Power, Borders, and Identity Formation: Understanding the World of Chicana/o Students." *Perspectives in Mexican American Studies* 6 (1997) 142–167; San Miguel, Guadalupe Jr. "Actors Not Victims: Chicanas/os and the Struggle for Educational Equality." In *Chicanas / Chicanos at the Crossroads*, edited by David R. Maciel and Isidro D. Ortiz. Tucson: University of Arizona Press, 1996; San Miguel, Guadalupe Jr. "*Let All of Them Take Heed*": *Mexican Americans and the Campaign for Educational Equality in Texas, 1910–1981*. Austin: University of Texas Press, 1987.

STUDENT ORGANIZATIONS. During the second half of the 1960s Chicano student activists, often with help from community leaders, created organizations all over the Southwest to give support and continuity to their protests and to the Chicano Movement. Although the primary concentration of these organizations was on the quality of education and other student concerns, civil rights on campus and in the community also became major issues.

By the second half of the 1960s student activists were seriously involved in the formation of Chicano groups on college campuses; a large number of student organizations were established from California to Texas, the two states in the forefront of the movement. In southern California the **Mexican American Student Association** (MASA) was organized at the East Los Angeles Community College early in 1967 and was followed in May by the **United Mexican American Students** (UMAS), which developed from a meeting at Loyola University in Los Angeles and which soon incorporated MASA groups as chapters. UMAS supplied much of the leadership and organization during the Los Angeles **student walkouts** of 1968. By the end of the following year UMAS had spread over the entire Southwest and even appeared in Indiana at Notre Dame University.

In northern California Chicano students at San Jose State College (now University) started the organizing movement a bit earlier, in 1964, with a group they named Student Initiative. Student Initiative tended to be less community oriented than its southern counterparts, and more political. It was later reorganized as the Mexican American Student Confederation. Nearly all these groups at first stressed advancement through education and looked forward to a generation of university-trained Chicano professionals and leaders. Later most of them became committed to broader political goals.

In Texas **José Angel Gutiérrez** and other Texas student leaders at St. Mary's University created the **Mexican American Youth Organization** (MAYO) with the aid of a eight thousand dollar Ford Foundation grant. From its 1967 beginnings, MAYO was aggressively political in support of both community and student concerns. It quickly spread to other Texas colleges and high schools, dominating the entire student movement in that state.

In New Mexico Hispanic college and high school students seemed less actively engaged in the student movement that was sweeping the Southwest. New Mexico Highlands University students did form a Spanish American

Students Organization, only later replacing the term *Spanish American* with the word *Chicano.* Following their lead, high school students in Albuquerque created the Chicano Youth Association.

In California the explosion of Chicano student groups led in 1969 to a unifying conference at the University of California in Santa Barbara. The representatives chose **Movimiento Estudiantil Chicano de Aztlán** (MEChA) as the name of their new umbrella organization and then drew up a declaration of goals and detailed plans for developing college programs. Later this was issued as the **Plan de Santa Bárbara**. Most earlier student organizations, particularly in California, ultimately became MEChA chapters.

By the beginning of the 1970s student organizations succeeded in achieving some educational reforms. Protests by student organizations forced teachers and professors to become more sensitive to ethnic denigration, to add Chicano cultural and historical materials to their courses, and to develop new courses in the history, culture, sociology, literature, and art of the Mexican American. School administrations hired more Chicano teachers, counselors, and administrators and provided new or improved school buildings and other accommodations. Student involvement provided an example that boosted community spirit and pride, helping lead to more active participation by their elders in education and politics.

Although the decline of the Chicano Movement from the mid-1970s onward led to the atrophying of some student groups, the 1990s saw an increase in Latino organizations oriented toward specific careers in engineering, the sciences, and business. In some colleges and universities fraternities and sororities geared to Mexican Americans also made their appearance.

FURTHER READING: Gómez-Quiñones, Juan. *Mexican Students por La Raza: The Chicano Student Movement in Southern California, 1967–1977.* Santa Barbara, Calif.: Editorial La Causa, 1978; Martínez, Douglas R. "El Movimiento Estudiantil: From the Sixties to the Seventies." *Agenda* 8:3 (May–June 1978) 19–21; Muñoz, Carlos Jr. *Youth, Identity, Power: The Chicano Movement.* New York: Verso, 1989; Navarro, Armando. *Mexican American Youth Organization: Avant-Garde of the Chicano Movement in Texas.* Austin: University of Texas Press, 1995; Puente, Teresa. "Getting Organized." *Hispanic* (March 1992) 32, 34; Valle, María Eva. "MEChA and the Transformation of Chicano Student Activism: Generational Change, Conflict, and Continuity." Ph.D. diss. University of California, San Diego, 1996.

STUDENT WALKOUTS, 1968–1969. Thousands of Chicano students walked out of East Los Angeles high schools in March 1968, asserting that complaints about the quality of their education were being ignored and their educational rights abused. Influenced generally by a worldwide climate of youthful unrest and more directly by high school teacher **Sal Castro,** they set in motion a chain reaction of similar protests in urban centers in California, throughout the Southwest, and even in the Midwest. The walkouts were in protest against overcrowding, poor educational facilities, an inadequate curriculum, poorly trained and often racist teachers, and a dropout rate of over 50 percent. The students demanded more Chicano teachers, counselors, and administrators as well as courses in the Mexican American experience and Mexican culture.

These high school "blowouts " led to comparable actions by Chicano college and university students, who used demonstrations, sit-ins, and abstention from graduation ceremonies to emphasize their demands for Chicano faculty, courses, departments, and administrators, as well as the admission of more Chicano students. Most Chicano community organizations supported the students and their leaders. A dozen of the more militant leaders of the Los Angeles walkouts were arrested for criminal conspiracy; on appeal the charge was held unconstitutional and then was dropped in 1970.

Although Chicano efforts for educational change were diffuse because of the absence of a central organization, by 1970 student walkouts had achieved a degree of success in California and Texas. They were less successful in Arizona and New Mexico. Since the early 1970s the walkout technique has continued to be used sporadically by Chicano students to persuade school administrators to give serious consideration to their educational grievances.

FURTHER READING: Acuña, Rodolfo. *A Community under Siege: A Chronicle of Chicanos East of the Los Angeles River, 1945–1975*. Los Angeles: Chicano Studies Research Center, University of California, 1984; Briegel, Kaye. "Chicano Student Militancy: The Los Angeles High School Strike of 1968." In *The Mexican Americans: An Awakening Minority*, 2nd ed.Edited by Manuel P. Servín. Beverly Hills: Glencoe Press, 1974; Carter, Thomas P. *Mexican Americans in School: A History of Educational Neglect*. New York: College Entrance Examinations Board, 1970; Fields, Rona Marcia. "The Brown Berets: A Participant Observation Study of Social Action in the Schools of Los Angeles." Ph.D. diss., University of Southern California, 1970; Frisbie, Parker. "Militancy among Mexican American High School Students." *Social Science Quarterly* 53:4 (March 1973) 865–883; Inda, Juan Javier. *La comunidad en lucha: The Development of the East Los Angeles High School Blowouts*. Stanford: Stanford University Center for Chicano Research, 1990.

SUTTER, JOHN A., 1803–1880. Land grantee, entrepreneur. John Sutter arrived in California from Europe in 1839. After becoming a Mexican citizen, he obtained a large land grant in the Sacramento valley from Governor Juan Bautista Alvarado. Hoping to establish for himself a baronial European lifestyle, he created his New Helvetia colony in which he encouraged in-migrating Anglos to settle. Sutter supported the Bear Flag revolt in 1846 and three years later served in California's constitutional convention. The discovery of gold on his land resulted in the desertion of his employees and widespread influx of squatters in 1849. His efforts to oust them and to obtain U.S. confirmation of his grant bankrupted Sutter. Although he ultimately received confirmation for most of his property, he died virtually a pauper.

FURTHER READING: Holden, William. "The Rise and Fall of 'Captain' John Sutter." *American History* 32:6 (1998) 30–34, 64, 66; Owens, Kenneth N., ed. *John Sutter and a Wider West.* Lincoln: University of Nebraska Press, 1994; Sutter, Johann A. *New Helvetia Diary: A Record of Events Kept by John A. Sutter and His Clerks at New Helvetia, California from September 9, 1845 to May 25, 1848.* San Francisco: Grabhorn Press, 1939; Zollinger, James P. *Sutter: The Man and His Empire.* New York: Oxford University Press, 1939.

TAOS REBELLION, 1846–1847. In reality there were two Taos rebellions. After the Missouri Volunteers under Colonel Stephen Kearny took over Nuevo México in 1846 and then departed for California, a group of Nuevo-mexicanos began to plot the overthrow of the small U.S. force left behind. Leading the conspiracy were disgruntled influential Nuevomexicanos including **Diego Archuleta,** Tomás Ortiz, the Reverend **Antonio José Martínez,** and Reverend Juan Felipe Ortiz. The American authorities became aware of the plot in December and ended the affair by arresting most of the instigators except the two clergymen.

In January 1847 a new set of revolutionaries, made up of Mexicans and Indians of the Taos pueblo, murdered the American governor and killed a number of Anglos and Nuevomexicano elites. There is no evidence to connect this second Taos uprising to the first intrigue; it seems to have been largely spontaneous. With some difficulty the American authorities suppressed the rebellion by midsummer, tried the surviving ringleaders for treason (despite their noncitizen status) and murder, and hanged fifteen of them. Their execution perturbed many Nuevomexicanos and left a legacy of animosity and suspicion.

FURTHER READING: Beck, Warren A. *New Mexico: A History of Four Centuries.* Norman: University of Oklahoma Press, 1962; Chávez, Angélico. *But Time and Chance: The Story of Padre Martínez of Taos, 1793–1867.* Santa Fe: Sunstone Press, 1981; Simmons, Marc. *True Tales of Hispanic New Mexico.* Santa Fe: Ancient City Press, 1978; Sunseri, Alvin R. "Revolt in Taos, 1846–1847." *Palacio* 96:1 (1990) 38–47.

TAYLOR, PAUL S., 1895–1984. Labor economist, educator. Paul Taylor began his research on Mexican immigration and labor in 1927. One of the earliest students of the Mexican worker experience in the United States, he undertook studies and involvement in this area that dominated the rest of his long career. In addition to numerous articles in professional journals, he researched and published thirteen pioneering volumes on the condition of Mexicano labor in the United States. He taught classes at the University of California in Berkeley his entire academic life and also served on various committees and government agencies concerned with land reform and labor issues.

Retired from the classroom after nearly forty years, during the 1960s and early 1970s Taylor participated in many Chicano Movement conferences and symposia. He was highly regarded as one of the first Anglo battlers in the Mexican American workers' struggle for their rights and a better life. Among his honors were a Guggenheim fellowship in 1931, a Doctor of Laws from the University of California in 1965, a Henry Wagner Award from the California Historical Society in 1977, and the U.S. Department of Interior's highest honor, the Conservation Service Award, in 1980.

FURTHER READING: *The International Who's Who*. 46th ed. London: Europa Publications, Ltd., 1982; Street, Richard. "The Economist as Humanist—The Career of Paul S. Taylor." *California History* 58:4 (Winter 1979–1980) 350–361; Taylor, Paul S. *On the Ground in the Thirties*. Salt Lake City: G. M. Smith, 1983.

TEATRO CAMPESINO. The Teatro Campesino was established by **Luis Valdez** in 1965 as part of the **Delano grape strike.** During the two years it was active in the strike it served to publicize the goals of the strikers and to educate both the strikers and the general public. In short skits, called *actos*, it dramatized and explained in simple terms the social and economic problems facing the strikers in their struggle to gain recognition of their union from agribusiness.

In 1967 Luis Valdez established the Teatro as a theater collective and cultural center in Del Rey, California and later moved it to a permanent base in San Juan Bautista. After the successful conclusion of the strike, he broadened its scope by moving from a limited concern for farm workers to involvement in all aspects of Mexicano culture. While still pursuing politicizing goals, the Teatro also used the stage and cinema to inform Chicanos more thoroughly about their long and rich heritage and thereby to instill a sense of pride. The success of the play and films *Zoot Suit* and *La Bamba* led to a number of television specials like the 1987 *Corridos! Tales of Passion and Revolution*. The Teatro company has toured extensively in Europe as well as in the United States and Mexico.

The Teatro Campesino, now a production company, has been the recipient of an Emmy, an Off-Broadway Obie award, and three Los Angeles Drama Critics' Circle awards. Its considerable success led to the formation of over one hundred similar Chicano theatrical groups throughout the United States.

FURTHER READING: Broyles-González, Yolanda. *El Teatro Campesino: Theater in the Chicano Movement*. Austin: University of Texas Press, 1994; Delucchi, Mary Phelan. "El Teatro Campesino de Aztlán: Chicano Protest through Drama." *Pacific Historian* 16:1 (1972) 15–27; Xavier, Roy Eric. *Politics of Chicano Culture: A Perspective on El Teatro Campesino*. Berkeley: Chicano Studies Library Publications, University of California, 1983.

TEJANO. In its narrowest sense *Tejano* is used to refer to Mexicanos living in Texas at the time of its separation from Mexico and to their descendants. More broadly used, it may refer to all Texans of Mexican cultural ancestry.

TELLES, RAYMOND L., JR., 1915– . Politician, businessman. Raymond Telles was born in El Paso into a family that was politically very active. He graduated from high school into a Works Progress Administration job that enabled him to get a business school education. During World War II he served in the armed forces, returning to El Paso with the rank of major in the Air Force. Persuaded to run for El Paso county clerk in 1948, he won that election and subsequent reelections until 1957. His nine-year administration in that position served as a model that helped pave the way for other Tejanos in local and state politics.

Telles's success also convinced El Paso's Mexican American leaders that as a well-known border politician he would be an ideal candidate for the office of mayor. In 1967 he won handily as Mexican Americans voted in record numbers. The election of Raymond Telles as the first Mexican American mayor of El Paso in the twentieth century was an important step in the long struggle of Tejanos for political rights. A major advance in itself, his election also stimulated broader participation in Texas politics by Chicanos, renewing and increasing their sense of self-worth and self-confidence.

In 1969 Telles was reelected to a second term as mayor of El Paso. Not a radical social crusader, he sought and gained limited socioeconomic change. While advancing the Chicano struggle for justice and equality, he used an incremental approach in addressing the problems of the Chicano community. His temperate approach enabled him to pursue a moderately success-ful reform program and still keep the Anglo establishment reasonably happy. As in the county clerk's office, his able administration as mayor opened wider the doors of opportunity for following generations of Texas Chicanos.

In 1961 Telles was appointed ambassador to Costa Rica by President John F. Kennedy, the first Mexican American to hold the post of ambassador. During the Lyndon Johnson administration he became an appointee to the new U.S.-Mexican Border Commission, a position he filled until Richard M. Nixon took over the presidency in 1969. His subsequent campaign for the U.S. Congress ended in ignominious defeat, in part because many young Chicano militants viewed him as virtually a Tío Taco. After serving on the **Equal Employment Opportunity Commission** in Washington during the Nixon administration, he left government service for the private sector.

FURTHER READING: García, Mario T. *The Making of a Mexican American Mayor: Raymond L. Telles of El Paso.* El Paso: Texas Western Press, 1998; García, Mario T. *Mexican Americans: Leadership, Ideology, & Identity, 1930–1960.* New Haven, Conn.: Yale University Press, 1989.

TENAYUCA, EMMA, 1917–1999. Activist, labor organizer. Growing up in a middle-class San Antonio home, Emma Tenayuca was exposed from early youth to a wide spectrum of broadly leftist economic and political ideas by her father and maternal grandfather. In the evenings the family often sat around the kitchen table discussing politics. In school she was a serious and inquisitive as well as excellent student, reading Charles Darwin, Thomas Paine, and later Karl Marx while still in the elementary grades.

In high school Emma adopted an active stance and began speaking out publically for *raza* rights. While still in her first year, she helped organize and lead a march of unemployed to the Austin capitol in 1931. At age seventeen she was jailed with the San Antonio strikers at one of the city's largest employers, the Finck Cigar Company. After graduation from high school she spent much of her free time helping to organize Mexicana garment industry workers in the International Ladies Garment Workers Union and the radical Workers Alliance, an offshoot of the communist-dominated Trade Union Unity League.

Convinced that confrontational tactics were essential to bring about real societal change, Emma Tenayuca had become a spokesperson for the unorganized workers by the second half of the 1930s. She joined the Communist Party because she felt that it alone seemed concerned about Mexican American rights. Her strong activist role inevitably led to a reputation as a labor agitator, and to frequent arrests. Often jailed as a result of labor dispute involvements, she emerged from brief incarcerations only more determined to continue demanding civil rights and social justice for the poor and powerless.

In late 1937 Emma married Homer Brooks, a Communist Party organizer. She remained a party member until the 1939 Soviet-German rapprochement, eighteen months later. She and Homer continued to call for an end to economic, political, and social discrimination against Mexicanos.

In January 1938 Tenayuca took a leading role in the strike of several thousand San Antonio **pecan shellers** who demanded higher pay and better working conditions. Her enthusiasm and energy made her an effective organizer, but her known communist affiliation caused her to be replaced as strike leader. Nevertheless, she was named honorary representative by the strikers in a declaration of their trust in her. The strike was later settled by arbitration, and the debacle of her post-strike rally in early 1939 ended her career as a political activist and Texas labor organizer.

In post–World War II Emma Tenayuca was blacklisted by the House Un-American Activities Committee and found she could not obtain employment in San Antonio. In 1948 she left for Los Angeles, California, where she worked as a recruiter for the American Federation of Labor, but was unable to find her place in the California labor movement. She subsequently returned to Texas, enrolled in college, and obtained her A.B. degree. After completing her M.A. at St. Mary's University, she taught in a San Antonio elementary school until her retirement in 1982. Although she shunned the limelight, after retiring she continued to participate in community civil rights groups like **Citizens Organized for Public Service**.

FURTHER READING: Blackwelder, Julia Kirk. " Emma Tenayuca: Vision and Courage." In *The Human Tradition in Texas*, edited by Ty Cashion and Jesús F. de la Teja. Wilmington, Del.: Scholarly Resources, 2001; Calderón, Roberto, and Emilio Zamora. "Manuela Solís Sager and Emma Tenayuca: A Tribute." In *Chicana Voices*, edited by Teresa Córdova et al. Austin: Center for Mexican American Studies, University of Texas, 1986; Hardy, Gayle J., ed. *American Women Civil Rights Activists*. Jefferson, N.C.: McFarland, 1993; Rips, Geoffrey, and Emma Tenayuca. "Living History: Emma Tenayuca Tells Her Story." *Texas Observer* (28 October 1983) 7–15; Vargas, Zaragosa. "Tejana Radical: Emma Tenayuca and the San Antonio Labor Movement during the Great Depression." *Pacific Historical Review* 66:4 (1997) 553–580; Zophy, Angela H., ed. *Handbook of American Women's History*. New York: Garland Publishing, 1990.

TEXAS. When Texas became part of the United States at the end of 1845 it had about four thousand Tejanos and approximately thirty thousand Anglos as a result of a considerable influx of immigrants from the cotton-growing slave states of the Old South. Anti-Mexican feelings ran high, partly because of the Texas fight for independence from Mexico a decade earlier. By 1860 the population numbers had changed to six hundred thousand Anglos and twelve thousand Mexicanos, a greatly increased fifty-to-one ratio. The arrival of ever-larger numbers of Anglos in the 1870s and 1880s led to a further increase in the imbalance of the two groups.

Greatly outnumbered in the new society, Tejanos were often denied the basic guarantees of the Treaty of **Guadalupe Hidalgo** and the U.S. Constitution despite their efforts to participate in the new political system. During the years of the Texas republic (1836–1845) Tejano elites sought to integrate themselves into the new system that some of them had helped bring about. However, even before the 1846–1848 invasion of Mexico by the United States, as a group Mexicanos were treated as a conquered people without rights, and most were soon reduced to positions of economic and social inferiority. After the war many of the Anglo veterans who settled in Texas took the view that Spanish-speakers had been the enemy and therefore deserved ill-treatment. This attitude, based on racist and nativist rationalization, in their minds justified all mistreatment of Mexicans.

Land ownership soon began shifting from Tejanos to Anglos. Through loss of their lands, many of the Tejano elite began to suffer economically, losing social status and often becoming victims of racism. The poorer classes suffered from the not uncommon frontier violence of Anglos, in which Mexican-bashing was widely acceptable. Laws as well as societal traditions of the Old South frequently denied Mexican Americans their minimal rights. In the **Cart War** of 1857 some Mexicano freighters suffered the ultimate denial of their civil rights—death at the hands of Anglo competitors.

Constant denial of liberties guaranteed by the Treaty of Guadalupe Hidalgo sometimes led to social **banditry** and occasionally to more widespread civil disorder. The so-called El Paso **Salt War** of 1877, for example, was largely a response to denial of traditional rights long enjoyed by Mexicanos. The negative experiences of **Juan N. Cortina**, **Gregorio Cortez**, and others with American justice were unexceptional, and in the second half of the nineteenth century the **lynching** of Mexicanos was common. Ethnic and racial stereotyping were used to justify the **Texas Rangers'** use of summary violence and complete denial of civil liberties to rural Mexicanos.

Toward the end of the nineteenth century the Indian ancestry of Mexican immigrants became the basis of efforts to deny them the right to become citizens. In the 1890s this movement, using nativist arguments in an effort to disenfranchise all Mexican Americans, found considerable support in south Texas politics. Urban Mexicanos along the border suffered less than their rural cohorts, and continued to participate in local politics. Early in the 1900s a San Antonio organization, La Agrupación Protectora Mexicana, was formed to protect Mexicanos' civil rights. It condemned police brutality and protested the widespread lynchings and other abuses of Mexicanos.

During World War I a "brown" scare, brought on in part by heavy immigration to provide wartime workers, led to large numbers, hundreds at least, of Mexicanos in Texas being hunted down and murdered in cold blood by vigilantes and Texas Rangers. The 1915 **Plan de San Diego** became a convenient excuse for the heightened repression of Mexicanos by Texas Rangers.

Beginning in the 1900s the older, usually somewhat paternalistic, relations between Anglos and Mexicanos in a traditional ranching culture tended to become less personal. The "factories in the fields" of the Winter Garden area turned increasingly to the use of **migratory laborers,** many from Mexico, who often worked under extremely oppressive conditions. As more Mexican Americans became urbanized, relations between them and Anglo Texans underwent further changes. Union organizing among Mexicanos in meatpacking, the maritime industry, and smelters met with considerable resistance from Texans with roots in the Old South.

In the twentieth century, Texas Mexican Americans found their position in American society continuing to erode. In the 1920s concern for the ill-treatment of *la raza* led to the creation of civil rights groups, culminating in the establishment of the **League of United Latin American Citizens** at the end of the decade. During the **Great Depression** years of the early 1930s thousands of **undocumented** Mexicans, and some Mexican Americans, were "repatriated" with little regard for their rights. In the next decade World War II served to arouse Texas Mexicanos to greater awareness of their rights; nevertheless these often continued to be denied them, sometimes even in death, as the case of **Félix Longoria** clearly showed. However, the war did beget a new generation of Chicano leaders and the **organizations** that they created.

In the postwar years Texas, and California, led in the development of local and regional groups to fight for *raza* rights. Political participation by Mexican Americans greatly increased as the postwar generation provided younger, more aggressive leadership. By the late 1960s a full range of social, political, and civil rights organizations had been developed in Texas, and in 1970 a new political force, **La Raza Unida Party** (LRUP), was created by **José Angel Gutiérrez** and others. Solutions to many political, social, and educational problems appeared to be achievable, particularly as the state's economy boomed in the last quarter of the twentieth century.

The demise of LRUP in the second half of the 1970s was a serious blow to the political hopes of many Texas Chicanos. However, conditions for Mexican Americans in Texas have improved over the years; more have entered middle-class ranks. New goals continue to seem attainable, but police brutality and denial of civil rights have by no means completely disappeared. Although there is some evidence of greater mutual respect, the repression of civil rights, especially in rural areas and among agricultural workers, has continued, often supported by local sheriffs and the Texas Rangers. In times of business downturn Mexicanos frequently continue to be blamed for poor economic conditions and high levels of unemployment. Moreover, Tejano social and economic problems often continue to be ascribed to a stereotype of cultural and ethnic inferiority.

Census 2000 indicates Texas is now the second largest state in population, with 20.8 million, of whom 32 percent, over 6.5 million, are Latino, about two-thirds of them Mexican. The Southwest Voter Registration Project estimates that about 2 million Latinos are currently registered in Texas and that 1 million of them voted in the 2000 elections. With a Latino population younger than the national average and increasingly using its political clout, Tejano leaders have high hopes for the future. In 2002 Tejano Democrat Tony Sánchez was a candidate to become the first Latino governor of Texas, but lost in the statewide sweep by Republicans.

FURTHER READING: Arreola, Daniel D. *Tejano South Texas: A Mexican American Cultural Province.* Austin: University of Texas Press, 2002; Clinchy, Everett Ross, Jr. *Equality of Opportunity for Latin-Americans in Texas.* Reprint. New York: Arno Press, 1974; Coronado, Roberto, and Lucinda Vargas. "Economic Update on El Paso del Norte (Part 1)." *Business Frontier.* 2 (2001) Federal Reserve Bank of Dallas, El Paso Branch, 2001; Cortés, Carlos. *The Mexican Experience in Texas.* New York: Arno Press, 1976; De León, Arnoldo. *Mexican Americans in Texas: A Brief History,* 2nd ed. Wheeling, Ill.: Harlan Davidson, 1999; Fehrenbach, T. R. *Lone Star: A History of Texas and Texans.* New York: Macmillan Publishing, 1968; Foley, Douglas F., et al. *From Peones to Politicos: Ethnic Relations in a South Texas Town, 1900–1987,* rev. ed. Austin: University of Texas Press, 1988; Kibbe, Pauline R. *Latin-Americans in Texas.* Albuquerque: University of New Mexico Press, 1946. Reprint, New York: Arno Press, 1974; Montejano, David. *Anglos and Mexicans in the Making of Texas, 1836–1986.* Austin: University of Texas Press, 1987; Perales, Alonso S. *El Mexicano Americano y la política del sur de Texas.* San Antonio: Artes Gráficas, 1931; Poyo, Gerald E., ed. *Tejano Jour-*

ney, 1770–1850. Austin: University of Texas Press, 1996; San Miguel, Guadalupe. *"Let All of Them Take Heed": Mexican Americans and the Campaign for Educational Equality in Texas, 1910–1981.* Austin: University of Texas Press, 1987; Shelton, Edgar. *Political Conditions among Texas Mexicans.* San Francisco: R & E Research, 1974; Simmons, Ozzie G. *Anglo-Americans and Mexican-Americans in South Texas.* Reprint. New York: Arno Press, 1974; Stewart, Kenneth L., and Arnoldo de León. *Not Room Enough: Mexicans, Anglos and Socioeconomic Change in Texas, 1650–1900.* Albuquerque: University of New Mexico Press, 1993; Zamora, Emilio, Cynthia Orozco, and Rodolfo Rocha, eds. *Mexican Americans in Texas History: Selected Essays.* Austin: Texas State Historical Association, 2000.

TEXAS GOOD NEIGHBOR COMMISSION. The Good Neighbor Commission was established in 1943 by Governor Coke Stevenson in an attempt to mollify the Mexican government, which refused to supply Texas with **bracero**s during World War II because of severe discrimination and exploitation in the state. After the war it was made a permanent state agency. In 1965 it took over the duties of the Council on Migrant Labor, established in the late 1950s to foster better working and living conditions for migrant workers.

Funded by the Texas government but made up largely of volunteers, the commission's objective was to promote goodwill, understanding, and mutual respect between Anglos and Mexicans. It fostered cultural and educational exchanges and promoted measures to reduce discrimination against Mexican Americans and to eradicate ethnic conflict. However, from its inception the commission was viewed by many Texas politicians as merely a public relations gimmick. When **Pauline Kibbe,** its first head, criticized farm labor conditions experienced by Mexicanos in Texas in 1947, she was forced to resign by Texas Governor Beauford Jester.

Later the commission concerned itself primarily with border diplomacy at the visiting dignitary level rather than with the rights of Mexicano workers. Nevertheless, it had a useful, though limited, role in promoting unofficial channels of communication between the two sides of the Texas-Mexican border. The commission was abolished in 1987.

FURTHER READING: Kibbe, Pauline R. *Latin-Americans in Texas.* Albuquerque: University of New Mexico Press, 1946; Kingrea, Nellie Ward. *History of the First Ten Years of the Texas Good Neighbor Commission.* Fort Worth: Texas Christian University Press, 1954; Perales, Alonso. *Are We Good Neighbors?* San Antonio: Artes Gráficas, 1948. Reprint. New York: Arno Press, 1974; Stevenson, Coke R. and Ezequiel Padilla. *The Good Neighbor Policy and Mexicans in Texas.* Mexico City, 1943. Reprinted in *The Mexican American and the Law.* New York: Arno Press, 1974.

TEXAS RANGERS. The first Texas Rangers were a mounted militia originally created by **Stephen Austin** in 1823 because of unstable frontier conditions. During and after the 1836 Texas revolt against Mexico the rangers became a force whose stated purpose was to deter marauders on the southern border and the northwestern Texas frontier. During the **U.S.-Mexican**

War, an expanded ranger force fought under the commands of generals Zachary Taylor and Winfield Scott. After the war the rangers resumed their earlier tasks of policing border bandits, cattle rustlers, and Indians. Like a majority in the larger society of the Southwest, the rangers considered Mexicans and Indians as "natural" enemies, as hindrances to Anglo frontier expansion and economic development.

During the post–Civil War reconstruction era the rangers were replaced with a state police force, but in 1874 they were reestablished by the Texas legislature. The new Texas Rangers concerned themselves with cattle rustling, border banditry, and cattlemen's feuds. Despite a "law and order" mentality, many rangers felt themselves little constrained by legal concepts or citizen rights. Holding that violence was the only tool to pacify the Texas frontier, they adopted an attitude often described as "shoot first and ask questions later." As a result, the rights of many innocent Mexicanos were ignored, often fatally.

Early in the twentieth century the highly controversial Texas Rangers became a force largely at the service of Anglo landowners, enforcing vagrancy legislation, pass systems, and other restraints on Mexicano liberties, particularly in rural areas. During World War I the agency, expanded to about one thousand, terrorized Mexicanos in the border region and was responsible for numerous deaths along the border. As the result of widespread complaints, in 1919 Texas representative José T. Canales introduced and secured passage of legislation that reduced the force to fewer than one hundred men.

In 1935 ranger embroilment in state politics caused the agency to be brought under a newly created Department of Public Safety. Used to enforce the virtual serfdom of Mexicanos in rural Texas, after World War II rangers were frequently employed to combat agricultural unionism and Mexican American participation in politics. During the Chicano Movement the rangers continued in the traditions of their nineteenth century predecessors. In the 1963 **Crystal City** elections Captain Alfred Y. Allee used the rangers to actively harass the Chicano candidates. Three years later in the Rio Grande Valley melon strike, verbal abuse, harassment, threats, and mass arrests were among ranger techniques criticized by the press as well as by civil rights activists. In 1974 the U.S. Supreme Court ruled against the rangers in *Medrano v. Allee,* a lawsuit arising out of the 1966–1967 melon strike. To Mexican Americans in Texas the rangers, *los rinches,* from their inception have been viewed as being the enemy.

FURTHER READING: Bailey, Richard. "The Starr County Strike." *Red River Valley Historical Review* 4:1 (1979) 42–61; Coles, Robert. "Our Hands Belong to the Valley: Texas Americans." *Atlantic* 235 (March 1975) 72–78; Lynch, Michael J., III. "The Role of J. T. Canales in the Development of Tejano Identity and Mexican American Integration in Twentieth Century South Texas." *Journal of South Texas* 13:2 (2000) 220–239; Proctor, Ben H. "The Modern Texas Rangers: A Law Enforcement Dilemma in the Rio Grande Valley." In *The Mexican Americans: An Awakening Minority,* edited by Manuel P. Servín. Beverly Hills: Glencoe Press, 1970; Samora, Julian, Joe

Bernal, and Albert Peña. *Gunpowder Justice: A Reassessment of the Texas Rangers.* Notre Dame: University of Notre Dame Press, 1979; Webb, Walter Prescott. *The Texas Rangers: A Century of Frontier Defense.* Boston: Houghton Mifflin, 1935.

TIERRA AMARILLA, 1967. Tierra Amarilla is a small village, the county seat of Rio Arriba County in northwestern New Mexico. In mid-1967 it leaped into national headlines and consciousness as the result of an ongoing conflict between members of Reies López Tijerina's **Alianza Federal de Pueblos Libres** and the district attorney, Alfonso Sánchez.

In June Tijerina and some members of his Alianza descended on the Tierra Amarilla courthouse to make a citizens' arrest. In the ensuing confrontation there was gunplay between Alianza members and law officers. The *aliancistas* fled, only to be pursued subsequently by helicopters, airplanes, and tanks. The event attracted national media coverage. Many Anglo Americans, and even some Chicanos, believed or feared that the Tierra Amarilla incident signaled the beginning of a serious revolutionary movement, or at least of guerrilla warfare.

Tijerina was quickly apprehended and charged with various crimes in both state and federal courts. He was acquitted of federal charges arising out of the courthouse shootout; however, in 1970 he was convicted in New Mexico courts on state complaints arising from the raid.

FURTHER READING: García, Robert G. "The Alianza: A Hope and a Dream." In *Aztlán: An Anthology of Mexican American Literature,* edited by Luis Valdez and Stan Steiner. New York: Vintage, 1972; Knowlton, Clark S. "Tijerina, Hero of the Militants." In *An Awakened Minority: The Mexican-Americans,* 2nd ed. Edited by Manuel P. Servín. Beverly Hills: Glencoe Press, 1974; Meier, Matt S. "'King Tiger': Reies López Tijerina." *Journal of the West* 27:2 (April 1988) 60–68; Nabokov, Peter. *Tijerina and the Courthouse Raid,* 2nd ed. Berkeley, Calif.: Ramparts Press, 1970.

TIJERINA, PETE, 1922–2003. Activist, judge, lawyer. As a young man, San Antonio native Pete Tijerina became involved in the Mexican American struggle for civil rights through his participation in the League of United Latin American Citizens (LULAC). The almost complete exclusion of Chicanos from Texas juries, despite the U.S. Supreme Court's ruling in *Hernández v. The State of Texas,* was a major factor in his active involvement in the civil rights struggle. After studying law at St. Mary's University in 1951, he passed the bar exam. Then he led a "traveling squad" of LULAC members who were available to investigate and take action against denial of rights anywhere in Texas.

Tijerina's most important contribution to the fight for raza rights was his leading role in founding the **Mexican American Legal Defense and Educational Fund** (MALDEF). In 1967 he applied to the Ford Foundation for a grant to create a Texas organization to monitor court rulings on the civil rights of Chicanos; he was successful beyond his most sanguine expectations. His proposal resulted in a five-year, $2.2 million grant that would enable

MALDEF to cover the entire Southwest. In the following year he established its headquarters in San Antonio. As the agency's first executive director, he organized committees in California, Arizona, Colorado, and New Mexico, as well as Texas. He resigned as director when MALDEF's headquarters were moved to San Francisco, California in 1970, because the Ford Foundation wanted to create a more national organization and image.

Tijerina continued to be an active leader in LULAC, serving for years as national civil rights chairman. With a special interest in equality of educational opportunity for Mexican Americans, Pete Tijerina took a leading role in several important civil rights lawsuits. Until shortly before his death in May 2003 Tijerina was in private practice in San Antonio.

FURTHER READING: Beyette, Beverly. "A Time of Transition for MALDEF." *California Lawyer* 2:5 (May 1982) 28–32; Luther, Claudia. "Pedro Tijerina, 80: Founder of the Civil Rights Group MALDEF." *Los Angeles Times*, California Metro, 21; Oliviera, Annette. *MALDEF: Diez Años*. San Francisco: MALDEF, 1978; Salazar, Veronica. *Dedication Rewarded: Prominent Mexican Americans*. San Antonio: Mexican American Cultural Center, 1976; San Miguel, Guadalupe. *"Let All of Them Take Heed": Mexican Americans and the Campaign for Educational Equality in Texas, 1910–1981.* Austin: University of Texas Press, 1987.

TIJERINA, REIES LÓPEZ, 1926– . Activist, clergyman. Reies López Tijerina was one of ten children born into a poor sharecropping family in southern Texas. He grew up in dire poverty as the family was forced into migrant agricultural work. After sporadic formal education in Texas schools, at age eighteen Tijerina entered an Assembly of God Bible school, having earlier abandoned his Catholicism. His Bible studies ultimately led him to the life of an itinerant nondenominational preacher along the Mexican border.

Tijerina gradually moved from religious interests to a pragmatic concern for social justice. After a disastrous experience as the leader of a utopian community in southern Arizona, he traveled in Mexico and California. Finally he settled in northern New Mexico, where the complex history of Spanish and Mexican land grants soon became his consuming passion. To work for the return of land to the heirs of the grantees, in 1963 he organized the Alianza Federal de Mercedes (Federal Alliance of [Land] Grants) and began to recruit supporters.

In their struggle to regain grant lands Tijerina and his followers drew attention to their demands by a variety of aggressive actions. *Aliancistas* filed lawsuits for the return of pueblo and private lands, marched on the state capitol at Santa Fe, and asserted their claims to part of the **Kit Carson National Forest.** Confrontation with and citizens' arrest of forest rangers at Kit Carson and the later raid on the Tierra Amarilla courthouse resulted in criminal charges being filed against Tijerina. Freed on bail, he continued to promote the goals of the Alianza, now called the **Alianza Federal de Pueblos Libres** (Federal Alliance of Free Towns). As a leader in the 1968 **Poor**

People's March he was able to publicize his demands in Washington. D.C. as well as in New Mexico.

Eventually Tijerina was convicted on various state and federal indictments. In mid-1971 he was released from prison on a parole that included the provision that he not be active in the Alianza for five years. His conviction and subsequent absence from the public forum unquestionably diminished his earlier charismatic leadership. At the end of his five-year parole he resumed the presidency of a greatly diminished Alianza. As the Chicano movement languished in the late 1970s, he took less confrontational positions but remained in the struggle, assuming the role of elder statesman. A 1987 interview in Mexico City quoted him as vowing to continue his fight against ethnic discrimination. However, his sphere of influence had clearly been dramatically reduced from the national to the local, principally the Tierra Amarilla region.

Tijerina occupies a unique position in the Mexican American experience. He gave voice to widespread but diffuse and unarticulated feelings of Nuevomexicano outrage at loss of their lands and of mistrust in the U.S. government. For a time during the 1960s he seemed to have the answer to Chicano demands for vigorous action. Supported by both conservative older rural Nuevomexicanos and radical young urban Chicanos, he never wavered in his fight to end discriminatory treatment of Mexican Americans.

FURTHER READING: Blawis, Patricia Bell. *Tijerina and the Land Grants.* New York: International, 1971; Cummings, Richard. *Grito! Reies Tijerina and the New Mexico Land Grant War of 1967.* New York: Harper & Row, 1971; Knowlton, Clark S. "Tijerina, Hero of the Militants." In *An Awakened Minority: The Mexican-Americans*, 2nd ed. Edited by Manuel P. Servín. Beverly Hills: Glencoe Press, 1974; Meier, Matt S. "`King Tiger': Reies López Tijerina." *Journal of the West*, 27:2 (April 1988) 60–68; Tijerina, Reies López. "From Prison." In *The Chicanos: Mexican American Voices*, edited by Edward W. Ludwig and James Santibáñez. Baltimore: Penguin Books, 1971; Tijerina, Reies López. *They Called Me "King Tiger:" My Struggle for the Land and Our Rights.* Houston: Arte Público Press, 2000; Valdez, Armando. "Insurrection in New Mexico–Land of Enchantment." *El Grito* 1:1 (Fall 1967) 15–24.

TÍO TACO. Tío Taco (Uncle Taco) is a phrase used to describe a Mexican American who rejects his ethnic heritage and tries to assimilate completely. The pejorative term was widely used during the Chicano Movement by militants to demean conservatives within the Mexican American community. For example, Texas congressman **Henry B. González** was frequently denounced as a Tio Taco by youthful Texas movimiento activists. Related expressions are coconut (brown on the outside but white inside) and the more intemperate *vendido* (sellout).

FURTHER READING: Martínez, Thomas M. "Advertising and Racism: The Case of the Mexican American." *El Grito* 2:4 (Summer 1969) 3–13; Steiner, Stan. *La Raza: The Mexican American.* New York: Harper & Row, 1969.

TIREMAN, LOYD S., 1896–1959. Educator. Loyd Tireman was one of the pioneers in researching the educational disadvantages suffered by Mexicano children in the Southwest. A complex and sometimes difficult man, he consistently failed to recognize his own cultural biases. As a result, his research on the education of Spanish-speaking children was marred by his tacit assumption that Anglo culture was inherently superior to Mexican culture. Although he was an early advocate and promoter of **bilingual education,** he saw it almost solely as a technique to Anglicize Mexican American students through the acquisition of English. In his work he came to realize that the real key to success in improving the education of Mexicano children was parental and community involvement in their schooling.

FURTHER READING: Bachelor, Davis L. *Educational Reform in New Mexico: Tireman, San José, and Nambe.* Albuquerque: University of New Mexico Press, 1991; Getz, Lynne Marie. *Schools of Their Own: The Education of Hispanos in New Mexico, 1850–1940.* Albuquerque: University of New Mexico Press, 1997.

TORRES, ART, 1946– . Politician. Art Torres was born in Los Angeles, California, and received his early education there. In 1966 he earned his A.A. at East Los Angeles City College, two years later was granted his B.A. at the University of California, Santa Cruz, and in 1971 was awarded his J.D. from the University of California law school at Davis. He served as a John F. Kennedy teaching fellow at Harvard University.

In 1974 Torres won election to the state assembly, where he served four terms and then was elected to the California senate, in which he served until 1994. Energetic and action-oriented, during his twenty years in Sacramento he was a charismatic and often fiery orator of the old style. In the senate years his primary concern was education, especially the high school dropout rate among Mexican American students. In 1994 he became the first U.S. Latino nominated for a statewide office, running unsuccessfully for California Insurance Commissioner.

In December 1994 Torres moved to the private sector to work in a Los Angeles engineering consultant firm, Cordoba International, Inc., from which he resigned two years later after being elected to the chairmanship of the California Democratic party. Shortly thereafter he was accused of improperly receiving federal payments, or at least being overpaid, while at Cordoba International.

The first Latino elected to head the Democratic party in a major state, in 2000 he became the first Latino head of the Walter Kaitz Foundation, a national organization dedicated to expanding minority management job opportunities in the TV cable industry. He was also the head of Torres Consulting in San Francisco, which he founded.

FURTHER READING: "Dem Boss under Fire." *Human Events* 52:35 (20 September 1996) 18; Fritz, Sara. "Torres Resigns Post at Firm Targeted by Probes." *Los Angeles Times.* (9 May 1996) A3; Heines, Vivienne. "Torres' Next Campaign." *Hispanic Business* (December 2000) 64–66.

TORRES, ESTEBAN E., 1930– . Ambassador, labor organizer. Esteban Torres was born in Miami, Arizona, where his Mexico-born father worked in the copper mines and was a union organizer. When his father was deported, the family moved to East Los Angeles, where he began his schooling. Upon graduating from James A. Garfield high school, he entered the armed services and served in the Corps of Engineers during the Korean war. After his army discharge in 1953 he took an assembly line welder job with the Chrysler Corporation and became active in union organizing. He also attended night classes at East Los Angeles College and in 1963 earned his B.A. degree from the University of California, Los Angeles. From 1965 to 1968 he was the United Auto Workers' (UAW) inter-American representative in Washington, D.C., a position in which he gained further experience in Latin America as a labor organizer.

Torres returned to Los Angeles in 1968 with a charge from Walter Reuther, head of the United Auto Workers union (UAW), to organize a community action program. The highly successful **East Los Angeles Community Union** (TELACU) resulted. While heading TELACU, he served in various organizations and gradually became active in California politics. In 1974 he unsuccessfully sought the Democratic nomination for the U.S. House of Representatives and then returned to Washington, D.C. as assistant director of the UAW's International Affairs Department.

In 1977 Torres was named Permanent Representative to UNESCO with rank of ambassador by President Jimmy Carter, and two years later became a special assistant to the president. When Ronald Reagan entered the White House in 1981, Torres left the public sector and established a foreign trade company, International Enterprise and Development Corporation. In the following year he was elected to the House of Representatives and was subsequently reelected for seven terms. As a Representative he showed concern for Latin American and ecological topics; he retired in 1998. A former member of the House Banking Committee, he was appointed to the board of the Federal National Mortgage Association by President Bill Clinton. In the year 1999 he was honored with a Distinguished Leadership award by the Los Angeles Intercommunity Blind Center. He acts as spokesman for the National Hispanic Media Coalition.

FURTHER READING: Ehrenhalt, Alan, ed. *Politics in America*. Washington, D.C.: *Congressional Quarterly*, 1983; "Inside Washington." *National Journal* 33:2 (13 January 2001) 71; Morán, Julio "Esteban Torres. Our Hot Line to the President." *Nuestro* (March 1980) 29–31.

TORTILLA CURTAIN. The so-called Tortilla Curtain refers to various U.S. efforts to establish fences along the border with Mexico. One instance occurred in the late 1970s over proposed fences at Tijuana and Ciudad Juárez. As originally described, the fence design was viewed by border Mexicans as a barbarous and life-threatening way of enforcing immigration control.

Opposition to the proposed expanded metal and barbed wire construction flared up on both sides of the border and led to a demonstration in El Paso by indignant Mexicanos. Hostile criticism from nearly all local leaders caused a reconsideration of the fence and ultimately led to a scaling down of its length, height, and composition acceptable to the Mexican government.

FURTHER READING: Stoddard, Ellwyn R., Oscar J. Martínez, and Miguel Angel Martínez Lasso. *El Paso—Ciudad Juárez Relations and the "Tortilla Curtain": A Study of Local Adaptation to Federal Border Policies.* El Paso, Tex.: El Paso Council on the Arts and Humanities, 1979.

TREVIÑO, LEE, 1939– . Golfer, philanthropist. Lee Treviño was born in Dallas, Texas, where he grew up next door to a golf course. During the eighth grade he dropped out of school in order to contribute his bit to the family's meager finances. A longtime observer and imitator of the golfers he could see from his yard, he got work as a caddy and continued to practice his golf game. At fifteen he entered his first tournament; he shot a 77. Two years later he enlisted in the Marine Corps, where he spent a good deal of his (peacetime) enlistment representing the Marines in golf tournaments. Upon his return to civilian life in 1960 he resumed his life as a golf gofer in a small Dallas club.

As Treviño's game continued to improve, he began to consider the possibility of joining the professional golf tour. After missing third place by just a few strokes in the 1962 Dallas Open, he won a number of victories in non–Class A tournaments. In 1967, having finally obtained his Class A card, he qualified for the U.S. Open, where he took fifth place and six thousand dollars in prize money. Now joining the tour full time, he finished in the money in eleven of the thirteen tournaments he entered, and was named Rookie of 1967. In the following year he continued to cut a wide swath in tournament golf and represented the United States at the World Cup Tournament in Italy. The year 1971 saw Treviño at his peak. After winning virtually every open in sight, he was named PGA (Professional Golf Association) Player of the Year, *Sports Illustrated* Sportsman of the Year, and BBC International Sports Personality of the Year.

During the rest of the 1970s and the 1980s Treviño continued to play spectacular golf. In 1990 he began playing on the PGA senior circuit, where he chalked up twenty impressive wins in four years. Two years later his lifetime earnings surpassed ten million dollars. A generous person, he often donated a sizable part of his winnings to charity and was known to host impromptu hot dog and soft drink galas for youngsters attending the tournaments. He continues his successful golfing career, playing in the PGA senior circuit.

FURTHER READING: Garrity, John. "Lee Treviño." *Sports Illustrated* 80:16 (25 April 1994) 46–47; Newlon, Clark. *Famous Mexican Americans.* New York: Dodd, Mead, 1972; Treviño, Lee. *The Snake in the Sand Trap.* New York: Holt, Rinehart, & Winston, 1985; Treviño, Lee. *They Call Me Supermex.* New York: Random House, 1982.

TUCSON. Although there was missionary activity and a military presence in the area many decades earlier, 1775 is commonly accepted as the founding date for Tucson. In that year the establishment of a presidio made Tucson one of the important anchors of the northern frontier of New Spain. After 1821, independent Mexico did its best to maintain the presidio, which often served as a refuge for Sonorans during Apache raiding in the 1830s and 1840s. At the time of the California gold rush a decade later the town became an important stopover for easterners heading for the mines. In 1853 the **Gadsden Purchase Treaty** brought Tucson into the United States. As a prominent trade center it attracted Mexicano entrepreneurs during the 1850s and beyond. Elite businessmen like **Esteban Ochoa**, **Mariano Samaniego**, Federico Ronstadt, Leopoldo Carrillo, and others prospered under the new economic and political system, becoming leading citizens of the town. Other Tucsonenses operated small restaurants, general stores, groceries, butcher shops, bakeries, barbershops, and similar establishments requiring only limited capital.

A pattern of intermarriage between Anglo males and the daughters of Mexicano elites like the Oteros, Pachecos, Ochoas, and Elíases soon developed into a distinguishing aspect of Tucson society. However, intermarriage did not prevent ethnic strife and discrimination from some of the recent arrivals. After the 1870s the railroad brought to Tucson its share of rascals and undesirables as well as solid citizens. To defend Mexicano rights, Samaniego and other leaders, at the end of the nineteenth century, established the **Alianza Hispano-Americano**, the earliest Arizona urban protective association. Tucson remained essentially a frontier village into the 1890s despite some law and order movement a decade earlier. As it became linked more closely to the national economy, the earlier Mexicano village was on its way to becoming an Anglo city.

The 1910 **Mexican revolution** brought a variety of refugees, many of them middle-class, into the Tucson area, and the World War I demand for workers in the copper mines added many Sonoran workers. Continuing turbulent fighting and unrest in Mexico during the latter 1920s added further to Tucson's Mexicano population. This more recent immigration has resulted in a strong stamp of Sonoran culture in the city. At the same time, the Sunbelt reputation of Tucson also brought more Anglos from the Midwest and East Coast, as did economic activities resulting from World War II a decade later. During the war years Tucson Chicanas, with their men away in the armed services, developed organizing skills that later served them well in the Chicano movimiento.

In the immediate postwar era Tucson boasted a population of 45,000; it grew rapidly to 213,000 by 1960 and to 331,000 in 1980. According to the 2000 census, Tucson has a population of 487,000. During the twentieth century Mexicanos have regularly formed between 20 and 25 percent of Tucson's population. By the end of World War II they owned over one hundred businesses and were beginning to enter the professions in larger numbers. They continue to take important roles in city and state governments, serving on school boards, on the city council, and in the state legislature. Today the Sonoran heritage and Mexican presence remains strong in the city.

FURTHER READING: Martin, Patricia Preciado. *Images and Conversations: Mexican Americans Recall a Southwestern Past.* Tucson: University of Arizona Press, 1983; Sheridan, Thomas E. *Los Tucsonenses: The Mexican Community in Tucson, 1854–1941.* Tucson: University of Arizona Press, 1986; Sonnichsen, Charles L. *Tucson: The Life and Times of an American City.* Norman: University of Oklahoma Press, 1982.

U

ULIBARRÍ, SABINE R., 1919–2003. Author, poet, educator. Sabine Ulibarrí was born of highly educated "old family" parents in Tierra Amarilla, New Mexico, and grew up in its rural environment of subsistence agriculture and sheep and cattle raising. After high school he attended the University of New Mexico (UNM) and taught in county schools from 1939 to 1942, when he went into the U.S. Army Air Force. After thirty-five missions during three years of service in the European theater he was given his discharge.

Ulibarrí returned to New Mexico, and used the G.I. Bill to complete his A.B. and get his M.A. degree at UNM. He then enrolled in a Ph.D. program at the University of California at Los Angeles. In 1958, with his doctorate completed, he returned to UNM to become a full-time faculty member and subsequently the longtime chairman of the Classical and Modern Languages Department. He became widely known as a writer and teacher. In the mid-sixties he directed a language institute in Quito, Ecuador and returned there in 1968 to establish the UNM Andean Center. During the 1970s he made lecture tours in Latin America and Spain under the State Department's auspices.

Ulibarrí has been a very prolific writer of poetry and short stories recalling New Mexico's pastoral past. He is most widely known for his second collection of short stories based on his childhood years, *Mi abuela fumaba puros: y otros cuentos de Tierra Amarilla; My Grandma Smoked Cigars: and Other Tales of Tierra Amarilla*, published bilingually in 1977 by Quinto Sol. Two books of his poems, *Amor y Ecuador* and *Al cielo se sube a pie*, were published in Spain in 1966. He is also the author of textbooks, essays, and other scholarly works. Ulibarrí is somewhat unusual among Chicano authors in that he writes mostly in Spanish or bilingually. Professor emeritus at UNM, he has been the recipient of numerous honors. In 1989 he was given the White House Hispanic Heritage Award. In January of 2003 he died of the cancer he had suffered from for some time.

FURTHER READING: Duke dos Santos, María I., and Patricia de la Fuente, eds. *Sabine R. Ulibarrí: Critical Essays.* Albuquerque: University of New Mexico Press, 1995; Tatum, Charles M. *Chicano Literature.* Boston: Twayne, 1982; Tatum, Charles M. "Sabine Ulibarrí: Another Look at a Chicano Literary Master." In *Pasó por aquí:*

Critical Essays on the New Mexican Literary Tradition, edited by Erlinda Gonzales-Berry. Albuquerque: University of New Mexico Press, 1989; Montaño, Mary. *Tradiciones Nuevomexicanas; Hispanic Arts and Culture of New Mexico.* Albuquerque: University of New Mexico Press, 2001.

UNDOCUMENTED. Undocumented is the term preferred by most Mexican Americans as well as others to describe a person who is in the United States without proper legal papers. Unlike the term *illegal,* it does not imply criminality. A person may become an undocumented by overstaying the time limits of a legal entrance, by entering the country surreptitiously, or by ignoring limitations of an immigration document.

Historically, the border between the United States and Mexico has been relatively porous. In the second half of the nineteenth century casual border crossing in both directions took place regularly without regard for the generally unmarked and unguarded boundary. A dramatic increase in Mexican immigration, most of it without documents, resulted from the 1910 revolution in Mexico and U.S. labor demands in the 1920s. Only at the end of the 1920s was undocumented entry made a punishable offense.

After World War II there was a rapid increase in undocumented immigration from Mexico as U.S. demand for unskilled labor soared. In 1954 the greater number of undocumented Mexican sojourners in the country resulted in **Operation Wetback**, in which more than one million undocumenteds were apprehended and returned to Mexico. A decade later the termination of the **bracero** program led to a rapid rise in the number of undocumented entries; by the end of the 1970s there were a million apprehensions and deportations annually. In the 1970s and 1980s barrio sweeps and factory raids by the INS, while often harassing Mexican Americans, seemed to have little effect on diminishing the number of undocumenteds entering the country.

No one knows how many undocumenteds there are in the United States; reliable estimates at the beginning of the twenty-first century indicate that there might be fewer than two million, about half of them Mexican. Immigration and Naturalization Service estimates run about 35 percent higher. Among the notable trends in undocumented Mexican immigration in recent decades is the increase in female and family migration, the growing number of skilled and semiskilled workers, and the wider dispersal of the immigrants in the United States.

FURTHER READING: Bean, Frank D., et al., eds. *At the Crossroads: Mexican Migration and U.S. Policy.* Lanham, MD.: Rowman and Littlefield, 1997; Grebler, Leo. *Mexican Immigration to the United States: The Record and Its Implication.* Los Angeles: University of California, 1966; Heer, David M. *Undocumented Mexicans in the United States.* New York: Cambridge University Press, 1990; Lorey, David. *The U.S.-Mexican Border in the Twentieth Century.* Los Angeles: Latin American Center, University of California, 1992; Massey, Douglas S., Jorge Durand, and Nolan J. Malone. *Beyond Smoke and Mirrors: Mexican Immigration in an Era of Economic Integration.* New York:

Russell Sage Foundation, 2002; Samora, Julian. *Los Mojados: The Wetback Story*. Notre Dame: The University of Notre Dame Press, 1971; Vogel, Walter. *Mexican Illegal Alien Workers in the United States*. Los Angeles: University of California Press, 1978.

UNITED CANNERY, AGRICULTURAL, PACKING, AND ALLIED WORKERS OF AMERICA. The UCAPAWA was organized in 1937 by the Congress of Industrial Organizations (CIO) to compete with the American Federation of Labor, particularly in agriculture. Mexicanos played a major role in its early organizing activities, and a number of Mexicano unions affiliated with it. In 1944 it was renamed the Food, Tobacco, and Agricultural Workers International. As the result of communist infiltration and increasing influence in the union, it was later expelled from the CIO.

FURTHER READING: Nelson-Cisneros, Victor B. "UCAPAWA Organizing Activities in Texas, 1935–1950." *Aztlán* 9 (1978) 71–84; Ruiz, Vicki L. "A Promise Fulfilled: Mexican Cannery Workers in Southern California." In *Unequal Sisters: A Multicultural Reader in U.S. Women's History*, 3rd ed. Edited by Vicki Ruiz and Ellen Carol Dubois. New York: Routledge, 2000.

UNITED FARM WORKERS. The UFW was originally begun in 1962 by **Cêsar Chávez** as the National Farm Workers Association (NFWA). When it became a full-fledged AFL-CIO union ten years later, the organization's name was changed to the United Farm Workers. More than just a labor union, from its early days it had as its goals social justice and human dignity for workers in agriculture. In its push to ameliorate conditions in the fields, the NFWA soon developed into a cooperative that included a credit union, health clinic, pharmacy, grocery, and gasoline station.

In 1965 the NFWA undertook its first strike, by rose grafters, and later that year followed with the famous **Delano grape strike,** which continued for five years before it was successfully concluded. Following a policy prescribed by Chávez of strict nonviolence, the NFWA was aided financially by other unions and received widespread support from college students, clergymen of various faiths, and finally the Catholic Bishops Committee. The union's long struggle was punctuated by a number of dramatic events: the 1966 march to Sacramento, the interposition of the Teamsters union, Chávez's twenty-five-day fast in 1967, the national **boycott** of table grapes in the next year, and in 1969 its extension to Europe.

After its success in the grape strike, the NFWA moved its main unionizing efforts to the lettuce fields of the Salinas Valley. Here a long, drawn-out conflict developed and full success eluded the union. Organizing farm labor outside of California also proved extremely difficult for the union. In 1972 the NFWA became an AFL-CIO union, changing its name to the United Farm Workers. When its 1970 grape contracts expired in 1973, the UFW lost most of them to the teamsters. Growers failed to renew, citing the union's inability to supply needed workers at peak harvesting times and other administrative weaknesses in the UFW.

The UFW was instrumental in the 1975 passage of the **California Agricultural Labor Relations Act,** which raised great hopes by mandating secret ballot union elections. Union membership, which had reached nearly eighty thousand in 1970 and plummeted to five thousand by 1973, now rebounded sharply. However, when the state legislature failed to adequately fund the act and the appointed agricultural labor board failed to enforce it, UFW membership again began a long decline. Efforts to use the union's political clout to obtain fulfillment of the law were unsuccessful.

Sadly acknowledging the failure of the legislative approach, in the 1980s the UFW returned to the boycott, now using computers, mailing lists, and TV spots. Meanwhile, the union was weakened further by a variey of factors: an antiunion trend in the country, the greatly increased urbanization of Mexicanos, and internal union dissent, intense personality clashes, and a degree of paranoia. Chávez's personal and nearly absolute control of the union had earlier resulted in a number of co-workers leaving, and continued to be criticized and to weaken the UFW's struggle. In an effort to recapture the early dream, in the 1980s the UFW shifted its stress from field organizing to broader goals like the reduction of pesticide use.

By the 1990s UFW boycotts had become so institutionalized that few consumers seemed aware of them; however, the union remained the symbolic leader in the fight for farm worker rights. When César Chávez died in 1993, his son-in-law, Arturo Rodríguez, became head of the UFW. One of Rodríguez's principal tasks was to rebuild the union by gaining new members. Chávez's death helped revive the early spirit of the UFW, and the union obtained twenty-two new contracts and won eighteen elections between 1993 and 1998. By the year 2000 membership had pushed over the twenty-five thousand mark. However, despite the UFW's long struggle and some successes, today most farm workers continue to live near or below the poverty level.

FURTHER READING: Ferriss, Susan, and Ricardo Sandoval. *The Fight in the Fields: César Chávez and the Farmworkers Movement.* New York: Harcourt Brace, 1997; Fusco, Paul and George Horwitz. *La Causa: The California Grape Strike.* New York: Macmillan, 1970; Jenkins, J. Craig. *The Politics of Insurgency: The Farm Worker Movement in the 1960s.* New York: Columbia University Press, 1985; Levy, Jacques E. *César Chávez: Autobiography of La Causa.* New York: Norton, 1975; Rodríguez, Rosa María, and Arturo Villarreal. "The UFW Strategies." *San Jose Studies* 20:2 (1994) 63–70; Rose, Margaret. "From the Fields to the Picket Line: Huelga Women and the Boycott, 1965–1975." *Labor History* 31:3 (1990) 271–293. www.ufw.org

UNITED MEXICAN AMERICAN STUDENTS. UMAS, a Chicano youth organization, arose out of a conference held in May 1967 at Loyola University in Los Angeles. Its ten Los Angeles chapters attracted a considerable membership and support, and in the following year it had a vital role in the Los Angeles student walkouts led by **Sal Castro**. It articulated frustrations in the community and particularly concerns about the quality of public education. It also was active in local politics. In 1969 it joined other area Chicano youth groups to form the **Movimiento Estudiantil Chicano de Aztlán**.

FURTHER READING: Muñoz, Carlos, Jr. *Youth, Identity, Power: The Chicano Movement.* New York: Verso, 1989; Rosen, Gerald. "The Development of the Chicano Movement in Los Angeles from 1967 to 1969." *Aztlán* 4:1 (1973) 155–183.

UNITED NEIGHBORHOODS ORGANIZATION. The first UNO was established in Los Angeles, California, in 1975 with the help of auxiliary Catholic bishop Juan Arzube after a visit he made to San Antonio, Texas where he witnessed the community work being done by **Communities for Public Service** (COPS). UNO was based on the COPS organizational model and its early leaders received the benefit of advice and training from the principal founder of COPS, **Ernesto Cortés**; nevertheless, UNO was unable to duplicate the COPS success story.

UNO concerned itself primarily with housing, segregation, nongovernmental services, and economic issues in the community rather than with a political approach. This difference seems to have been dictated by the large nonvoting undocumented population and other differences between the Los Angeles and San Antonio Mexicano population. Lack of support from Los Angeles Cardinal James Francis McIntyre and only limited help from his successor, Cardinal Timothy Manning, also undercut UNO's early successes and by the late 1980s it had become moribund.

FURTHER READING: Grimond, John. "Reconquista Begins." *Economist* (3 April 1982) 12–17; Martínez, Douglas. "Tomorrow: The Growing Campaign to Conquer Injustice." *Nuestro* (August 1979) 62–63; Skerry, Peter. *Mexican Americans: The Ambivalent Minority.* New York: Free Press, 1993; Ventriss, Curtis. "Community Participation and Modernization: A Reexamination of Political Chores." *Public Administration Review,* 44:3 (May–June 1984) 224–231.

UNITY LEAGUES. The Los Angeles area Unity Leagues were begun in 1947 principally by **Ignacio López,** editor of the San Bernardino weekly *El Espectador,* and **Fred Ross, Sr.,** a Saul Alinsky disciple. Unlike pre–World War II middle-class Mexican American organizations, the Unity Leagues were grassroots groups that recruited membership largely among poorer Mexicanos. They were made possible by the greater urbanization of Chicanos and were part of the postwar explosion of organizations created by activists to involve various segments of la raza.

The Unity Leagues' overall objective was to end discrimination against Mexican Americans by using a variety of approaches. Following López's skillful leadership, they filed suits in the courts, publicized incidents of flagrant racism, and engaged in voter registration and get-out-the-vote campaigns. Using community organizations and political pressure tactics, the leagues achieved some success in the late 1940s and in the 1950s. They won several segregation lawsuits and elected some Mexican Americans to local offices, including Edward Roybal to a Los Angeles city council seat in 1949.

FURTHER READING: García, Mario T. *Mexican Americans: Leadership, Ideology, and Identity, 1930–1960.* New Haven, Conn.: Yale University Press, 1989; Tirado, David. "Mexican American Community Political Organization: 'The Key to Chicano Political Power'" *Aztlán* 1:1 (1970) 53–78; Tuck, Ruth. "Sprinkling the Grass Roots." *Common Ground* 7 (Spring 1947) 80–83; Ross, Fred W. *Community Organization in Mexican-American Communities.* Los Angeles: American Council on Race Relations, 1947.

UNZUETA, MANUEL, 1949– . Artist, muralist. Manuel Unzueta was born and spent his early years in Ciudad Juárez, across the border from El Paso. He early developed an interest in art and music, playing in a local band at age eleven. In 1963 he moved to Santa Barbara, California, where he studied art and music in high school and junior college. A summer art scholarship took him to Europe to study, an experience that, along with the Chicano movimiento, aroused his social consciousness, and in 1971 he went to Mexico to study the works of the great Mexican muralists, particularly David Alfaro Siquieros. Greatly impressed by their works, he began following in the footsteps of the Mexican masters.

During the next two decades Unzueta painted over twenty murals in California, the Southwest, and Mexico, most in the style of Mexican realism. In addition, he paints acrylics depicting childhood memories and his ecological concerns. He has had exhibitions of his paintings in several states and in Mexico. In addition to his painting, which has gained him a reputation as one of the top muralists in America, he also teaches at the University of California at Santa Barbara and at Santa Barbara City College. In the 1990s he was the recipient of an Outstanding Teacher of Culture and an Outstanding Hispanic of Santa Barbara award.

FURTHER READING: Lewis, William. "Mexico and U.S. Influence Muralist's Work." *Nuestro* (December 1984) 58-59; *Who's Who among Hispanic Americans, 1994–1995.* Detroit: Gale Research, 1994.

URBANIZATION. Following the old Roman pattern, Spanish settlement in the New World was generally based on the town. Although Mexico's northern frontier was characterized by extensive land grants and a pastoral economy, the three prongs of settlement were essentially urban: pueblos, presidios, and missions.

After Mexico's independence from Spain in 1821, the new country's more liberal trade policies encouraged the development of its northern frontier towns into populous centers of trade with the United States. Mexicans, especially Sonorans, and Anglos moved into these towns to take advantage of the rapidly expanding international trade. After the Treaty of **Guadalupe Hidalgo** in 1848, incorporation of the Southwest into the U.S. national economy encouraged further urbanization.

Early in the twentieth century the Mexican revolution and the lure of jobs on the railroads, in the mines, and in agriculture drew over one million Mexican workers into the Southwest. Most settled in the "old towns" already existing throughout the Southwest or formed new barrios. The **Great Depression** of the 1930s greatly expanded the trend toward urbanization as many rural Mexican Americans tried to solve their economic problems by turning to the city for employment, help from family or friends, and federal relief programs.

As U.S. industry geared up for World War II, the increased demand for workers pulled more Mexicanos into urban areas and by 1940 over 50 percent lived in cities or towns. In the postwar era urbanization trends continued and even accelerated. Typically, many undocumented Mexicans headed for the cities where they could readily achieve anonymity. As Mexicanos moved out of the Southwest in search of more remunerative employment, they settled in many mid-western towns as well as in industrial centers like Detroit, Chicago, and Omaha.

Today Mexican Americans are overwhelmingly an urban people. Well over 90 percent of Chicanos lead a typically urban existence.

FURTHER READING: Arciniega, Tomás A. *The Urban Mexican American.* Las Cruces: New Mexico State University, 1971; Cruz, Gilbert R. *"Let There Be Towns": Spanish Municipal Origins in the American Southwest, 1610–1810.* College Station: Texas A&M University Press, 1988; Garr, Daniel J., ed. *Hispanic Urban Planning in North America.* New York: Garland, 1991; Martínez, Oscar J. "Chicanos and the Border Cities: An Interpretive Essay." *Pacific Historical Review* 46 (February 1977) 85–106; Romo, Ricardo. "The Urbanization of the Southwestern Chicanos in the Early Twentieth Century." *New Scholar* 6 (1977) 183–207.

URREA, TERESA, 1873–1906. *Curandera.* Teresa Urrea was the offspring of the casual mating of a Sinaloa *hacendado* and a fifteen-year-old Indian servant. When her politically involved father was forced to flee Sinaloa to his properties in adjacent Sonora, seven-year-old Teresa and her mother were among the servants who went with him. After her mother disappeared a few years later, she was raised by an aunt and then her father took her into the ranche household at his Cabora hacienda, where she received an education along with her half-siblings. She also helped an elderly Indian *curandera* on the ranche, learning herbal remedies in the process.

As a teenager Teresa began to experience epileptic fits and later suffered cataleptic seizures. During one of her catalepsies she remained unconscious for several days, and after a long, slow recovery decided she had a mission in life to help others. When the old *curandera* died, she took over her work and quickly acquired a reputation, particularly among the Indians, as a miraculous healer. Soon the teenage *curandera* had become widely known among the Indians as La Santa de Cabora.

Because of her influence among the Tarahumara and Yaqui Indians who were strongly resisting Mexican governmental efforts to control them at the time, president Porfirio Díaz had her and her father arrested in 1892. Briefly jailed, they were sent into exile in Arizona, where Teresa continued her healing mission. After several moves, including to El Paso, Texas, Teresa and her father settled in Clifton, Arizona where, before long, she became a southwestern cult figure rumored to have preternatural powers. In 1900 she was prevailed upon to help the ill daughter of a friend in San Jose, California. Here she came to the attention of a group of San Francisco entrepreneurs who persuaded her to lend her healing skills to a medical "crusade."

The crusade, featuring her curative powers, began in San Francisco toward the end of 1900, and moved to St. Louis and then New York in lengthy sojourns. By late 1902, when the crusade headed to Los Angeles, a disillusioned Teresa had begun to seriously question the professed altruism of her partners, and she terminated her agreement with them a little over a year later.

Teresa returned to Arizona and resumed her work of healing the physically and mentally ill in Clifton. About this time she seems to have undergone sharp personality changes. She frequently appeared moody and preoccupied, and her health soon began to deteriorate. In December 1905 she contracted a severe bronchial infection and died a month later.

FURTHER READING: Aguirre, Lauro. *La Santa de Cabora.* El Paso, Tex.: El Progresista, 1902; Holden, William C. *Teresita.* Owings Mill, Md.: Stemmer House, 1978; Putnam, Frank Bishop. "Teresa Urrea, 'the Saint of Cabora.'" *Southern California Quarterly* 45:3 (Sept. 1963) 245–264; Vanderwood, Paul J. *The Power of God against the Guns of Government: Religious Upheaval in Mexico at the Turn of the Nineteenth Century.* Stanford: Stanford University Press, 1998.

U.S. ENGLISH. U.S. English is a Washington, D.C.–based organization, cofounded in 1983 by senator and linguistic scientist S. I. Hayakawa and ophthalmologist and anti-immigration guru John Stanton. It proposes to preserve the unifying role of English by establishing it as the official language of the United States, and is strongly opposed to **bilingual education** programs. It has spent millions pushing for state and federal legislation to make English officially the U.S. language. While unsuccessful at the national level, U.S. English has achieved some success in more than a score of states and a number of cities. Although the laws have had little practical effect thus far, they do have negative potentialities.

Critics of U.S. English charge that, like Stanton's other organization, **Federation for American Immigration Reform**, it is racist, white supremacist, anti-Latino, and anti-Catholic and promotes fear of foreigners and intolerance of ethnic minorities.

FURTHER READING: Barfield, Chet. "Immigration Perils U.S., Group Fears; Critics Charge Lobbyists Breed Fear, Racism." *The San Diego Union-Tribune* (3 March 1989) A–1; Crawford, James, ed. *Language Loyalties: A Source Book on the Official English Controversy.* Chicago: University of Chicago Press, 1992; Imhoff, Gary. "The Position of U.S. English on Bilingual Education." *Annals of the American Academy of*

Political and Social Science (March 1990) 48–61; Pugh, Kristin. "Official English Is an Empty Symbol." *St. Louis Post Dispatch* (4 February 1996) 3B; Ramos, Leo Jonathan. "English First Legislation: Potential National Origin Discrimination." *Chicano-Latino Law Review* 11:1 (Spring 1991) 77–99. www.us-english.org

U.S.-MEXICAN WAR, 1846–1848. The invasion of Mexico by the United States in 1846 was a result in part of the U.S. conviction that it was manifestly destined to extend the benefits of American democracy to the Pacific shores and, some extremists would have it, from the polar cap to the Isthmus of Panama. Repeated efforts by the United States from the 1830s onward to purchase part or all of the Southwest aroused the concern of the Mexican government. In 1845 Texas, having earlier separated from Mexico, was annexed, and the United States declared war against Mexico in the following year. New Mexico was now taken without opposition by fifteen hundred Americans under Colonel Stephen W. Kearny. In California, U.S. forces, with orchestrated help from **John Charles Frémont** and the Bear Flaggers, successfully overcame the local opposition in pitched battle.

American soldiers were landed at Veracruz in the spring of 1847 and captured Mexico City seven months later. The Treaty of **Guadalupe Hidalgo**, ratified by Mexico in May of the following year, ceded to the United States nearly half of Mexico's territory, albeit sparsely inhabited by about eighty thousand of her citizens, the majority in New Mexico. Mexico received from the United States a compensation of fifteen million dollars.

The Treaty of Guadalupe Hidalgo, which made the southwest region part of the United States, stipulated that the Mexicans living in the area had the choice of remaining Mexican citizens or of becoming nationals, and eventually citizens, of the United States. Whichever choice they made, the treaty guaranteed their property rights and religious liberty. Those who opted to become U.S. nationals were to enjoy "all the rights of citizens of the United States according to the principles of the Constitution." About 97 percent of the *norteños* became U.S. nationals by choice or default. The property rights guaranteed by the treaty, particularly in the matter of land ownership, were later often ignored or violated by "reinterpretation" of the treaty's intent.

FURTHER READING: Christensen, Carol, and Thomas Christensen. *The U.S.-Mexican War.* San Francisco, Calif.: Bay Books, 1998; Clarke, Dwight L. *Stephen Watts Kearny: Soldier of the West.* Norman: University of Oklahoma Press, 1961; Crawford, Mark. *Encyclopedia of the Mexican-American War.* Santa Barbara, Calif.: ABC-CLIO, 1999; Engstrand, Iris H. W., Richard Griswold del Castillo, and Elena Poniatowska. *Culture y cultura: Consequences of the U.S.-Mexican War, 1846–1848.* Los Angeles: Autry Museum of Western Heritage, 1998; Francaviglia, Richard V., and Douglas W. Richmond, eds. *Dueling Eagles: Reinterpreting the U.S.-Mexican War, 1846–1848.* Fort Worth: Texas Christian University Press, 2000.

V

VALDEZ, LUIS, 1940– . Dramatist, theatrical producer, social activist. Luis Valdez was born in the tiny California town of Delano to parents who, like many others, were forced into the migrant agricultural stream in the post–World War II era by the loss of their small farm. The family settled in San Jose, California, where Luis received his education, graduating from San Jose State University in 1964 with an A.B. in English and an abiding interest in the theater. After college he worked briefly with the San Francisco Mime Troupe.

During the first year of the **Delano grape strike**, Valdez used his theatrical skills in support of **César Chávez** and the struggle for farm worker rights. As founder and director of the **Teatro Campesino**, he created a series of one-act plays that were simple but effective tools to educate strikers and the general public about the problems of Mexicanos and the goals of Chávez's "La Causa."

After 1967 Valdez expanded his field of interest, creating and staging his highly successful play *Zoot Suit*, which called national attention to the World War II trial and denial of rights to twenty-three Chicano youths. *Zoot Suit* was later taken to Broadway and then in 1981 converted into a film. His second film, *La Bamba*, 1987, based on the life of early Chicano rock star Ritchie Valens, was even more widely successful as a movie than *Zoot Suit*.

During the late 1960s and 1970s Valdez took his Teatro Campesino on several European tours as well as regular tours in the United States. In 1973 he established a permanent home for his theatrical group in San Juan Bautista, a small California mission town south of San Jose. During the 1980s he turned to Mexican *corridos* for inspiration and in 1987 produced *Corridos: Tales of Passion and Revolution*, a highly successful TV film featuring singer Linda Ronstadt. A decade later he did a PBS documentary on Chávez and the United Farm Workers union titled *Fight in the Fields*. In 2000 *The Mummified Deer*, his most recent and first new play in fourteen years, opened at the Repertory Theater in San Diego.

Valdez, almost singlehandedly, created a nationwide grassroots Chicano theatrical movement. A prolific author, between 1964 and 2000 he wrote two dozen plays and short theatrical skits. In addition to his direct contributions as founder of the Teatro Campesino, a playwright, and a theatrical director, he has also been the inspiration behind the creation of more than one hundred Chicano theater groups throughout the United States.

FURTHER READING: Elam, Harry J., Jr. *Taking It to the Streets: The Social Protest Theater of Luis Valdez and Amiri Baraka*. Ann Arbor: University of Michigan Press, 1997; Lomelí, Francisco A., and Carl R. Shirley, eds. *Chicano Writers: Second Series*. Detroit: Gale Research, 1992; Gross, Terry. "Interviews with Daniel Valdez and Luis Valdez." *San Jose Studies* 19:1 (1993) 53–59; Mendoza, Sylvia. "Luis Valdez: A Trailblazer." *Hispanic* (October 2000) 84–86.

VALLEJO, MARIANO GUADALUPE, 1808–1890. At age twenty-three, Mariano Vallejo became the Mexican commander of the San Francisco presidio and two years later was appointed military commander of northern California. A prominent member of the Vallejo family, he became an outstanding Californio political and civic leader. Although he was mildly favorable to a takeover of California by the Americans, he was imprisoned by them at Sutter's fort during the **Bear Flag revolt** of 1846.

Three years later Vallejo was the leading figure among the eight Californios who participated in writing California's first constitution. He spoke out for raza concerns and was able to get some minimal protection for Californios written into the document by active participation in committee work. His notable failure was in the matter of participation in elections; California's first constitution limited the franchise to white males, despite the guarantees of the **Guadalupe Hidalgo treaty**.

Vallejo spent his declining years as a patriarchal figure devoted to his orchardist concerns, to writing his memoirs, and to enjoying his family and friends.

FURTHER READING: Gonzales, Manuel G. *Hispanic Elite of the Southwest*. El Paso: University of Texas, 1989; McKittrick, Myrtle M. *Vallejo, Son of California*. Portland, Oregon: Binfords & Mort, 1944; Rosenus, Alan. *General M. G. Vallejo and the Advent of the Americans: A Biography*. Albuquerque: University of New Mexico Press, 1995.

VARELA, MARÍA, 1940– . Social activist. From 1963 to 1967 María Varela developed her civil rights skills as a worker in the Student Non-Violent Coordinating Committee. After her experience organizing African Americans in Mississippi, she joined **Reies López Tijerina**'s staff in Albuquerque. Turning her attention to the economic problems of Nuevomexicanos in the **Tierra Amarilla** area, in 1973 she helped organize a farm cooperative. Next came a clinic and a law clinic to improve the health and defend the rights of poor **Hispanos**. In 1983 there followed Ganados del Valle, a successful wool-growing and weaving cooperative. It soon became the largest year-round employer in the Chama valley, with revenues exceeding $440,000 in 1994.

At the end of the 1970s Varela began working in Albuquerque to develop a political coalition between the black and Chicano communities. In 1990 she received a MacArthur Foundation fellowship, the "genius award," primarily because of her work in community economic development in the Tierra Amarilla region. She has also been honored by the Smithsonian Institution and the New York Public Library, which have held exhibitions of her outstanding photographs documenting the black and Chicano civil rights movements.

FURTHER READING: Chu, Dan and Leslie Linthicum. "McArthur Grant Winner María Varela . . ." *People* (14 January 1991) 115; Jackson, D. D. "Around Los Ojos, Sheep and Land Are Fighting Words." *Smithsonian* (April 1991) 36+; "María Varela." *New America* 4:3 (1982) 111–113; *Las Mujeres: Mexican American/Chicana Women*. Windsor, Calif.: National Women's History Project, 1991; Ryan, Michael. "The Village That Came Back to Life." *Parade Magazine* (3 May 1992) 8, 11.

VÁSQUEZ, TIBURCIO, 1835–1875. Social bandit. Tiburcio Vásquez belongs to that group of Mexicanos who were thrust into a life outside the law by the discrimination they suffered. To avoid being lynched because of the death of an Anglo constable in 1852, he fled into a life of brigandage. He soon began to be viewed as an avenger of their wrongs by many Californios, who were distressed at the loss of their lands and the decline in their economic and social position.

Vásquez was arrested and jailed several times on horse stealing and cattle rustling charges. Upon his release from San Quentin in 1870, he assembled a small band that soon became noted for stage robberies and daring payroll holdups. In 1874 a posted reward of six thousand dollars dead and eight thousand alive brought him into the hands of the law, betrayed by Abdón Leiva, one of his own men. While awaiting trial in San Jose, California he justified his actions to newsmen as a defense of Mexicano rights in the face of great Anglo injustice. He was found guilty on a murder charge and on 19 March 1875 was executed by hanging.

FURTHER READING: Castillo, Pedro, and Alberto Camarillo, eds. *Furia y muerte: los bandidos chicanos*. Los Angeles: Aztlán Publications/Chicano Studies Center, University of California, 1973; López, Rubén E. "The Legend of Tiburcio Vásquez." *Pacific Historian* 15:2 (1971) 20–30; Sawyer, Eugene T. *The Life and Career of Tiburcio Vásquez*. Oakland, Calif.: Biobooks, 1944 (1875).

VELASCO, CARLOS I., 1837–1914. Journalist, community leader. Carlos Velasco was born and grew up in Hermosillo, Sonora. After his early education he studied for the law and became active in local and state politics. His support of Ignacio Pesqueira, Sonora's Liberal leader, forced him to flee across the border into Arizona in 1865. He remained in Tucson for five years, returning to Mexico when conditions there became more friendly. He quickly resumed political and journalistic activity in the pro-Pesqueira faction. When the Pesqueira political power structure was overthrown in 1877, he again fled to Tucson.

After a brief try at mercantile activity, Velasco turned again to journalism. As founding publisher and editor of *El Fronterizo*, which became a daily in the early 1890s, he helped mold public opinion on both sides of the border. He used his paper to defend Mexicanos from Anglo discrimination and mistreatment, while advocating the order and progress goals of Positivism. In 1894 he led in founding the **Alianza Hispano-Americana** and was selected as its first president. His continuing support of President Porfirio Díaz at the beginning of the twentieth century and his strong positivist beliefs led to a rift with most Alianza members. Despite this latter-day divergence from the majority political sentiment among border Mexicanos, for a quarter century Velasco was a leading Mexicano voice in border journalism.

FURTHER READING: *Frontier Tucson: Hispanic Contributions*. Tucson: Arizona Historical Society, 1987; Gonzales, Manuel G. "Carlos I. Velasco." *Journal of Arizona History* 25:3 (Autumn 1984) 265–284.

VELÁSQUEZ, BALDEMAR, 1947– . Labor organizer. Although primarily a labor organizer, Texas-born Baldemar Velásquez has devoted his adult years to the general goal of improving the lives of farm workers in the Midwest. In both his goals and the ways to attain them he was deeply influenced by the ideas of Mohandas K. Gandhi and Martin Luther King, Jr., as well as of **César Chávez.**

Velásquez's concerns for Mexican Americans evolved naturally from his early life as a migrant farm worker encountering racial slurs and maltreatment from field supervisors and growers. While still in college he gained further valuable insight into working-class problems through volunteer work with the Congress of Racial Equality. His experiences led to deep convictions about social justice and agricultural workers' rights. As a result, with the help of his father and several other farm workers, he began organizing the **Farm Labor Organizing Committee** (FLOC) in 1967. As longtime president of FLOC Velásquez has pursued broad goals of social justice as well as improved treatment of farm laborers. Under his leadership FLOC has focused on farm worker education and the establishment of law clinics. Also, he has committed FLOC to public stands supporting various civil rights organizations and alliances with them.

Among the many honors recognizing his accomplishments, in 1990 Velásquez was named a fellow of the prestigious McArthur Foundation and in the following year received the Hispanic Leadership Award from the **National Council of La Raza**. In 1994 he was honored with Mexico's highest award to a foreigner, the Aguila Azteca.

FURTHER READING: Barger, W. K., and Ernesto M. Reza. *The Farm Labor Movement in the Midwest*. Austin: University of Texas Press, 1994; Valdés, Dennis N. *Al norte: Agricultural Workers in the Great Lakes Region, 1917–1970*. Austin: University of Texas Press, 1991.

VELÁSQUEZ, WILLIE, 1944–1988. Activist. Tejano Willie Velásquez was one of Los Cinco who led in founding the **Mexican American Youth Organization** (MAYO) in 1967. In the following year he obtained funding for an economic development organization, the Mexican American Unity Council, which became an important source of MAYO financing. He also wrote a proposal for funding the Southwest Council of La Raza and helped found the **Southwest Voter Registration Education Project** (SVREP) to implement his views on the importance of Mexican American participation in the political process.

Velásquez viewed organization and legislation as the principal routes for *la raza*'s achievement of greater equality, particularly in the latter years of the **movimiento.** Although a leader in MAYO, he resigned from the organization in 1969 because of its increasingly militant stance, internal bickering, and particularly the third-party concept adopted by La Raza Unida. He believed that the more effective course of political action lay in working through the Democratic Party in the U.S. two-party system.

Perhaps Velásquez's most important contribution to the Mexican American experience was his 1974 creation of the SVREP, of which he remained director until his death. During the last decade of his life he traveled extensively throughout the Southwest, but particularly in Texas, persuading Mexican Americans that the route to greater equality was to register and vote, and then urging them to do so. Widely recognized as one of the most important organizers in the Chicano fight for political representation, in 1995 he was posthumously awarded the nation's highest civilian honor, the Presidential Medal of Freedom, by President Bill Clinton.

FURTHER READING: "Hispanic Activist." *Newsweek* (16 March 1987) 30; "Loss of a Leader." *Newsweek* (11 July 1988) 5; Navarro, Armando. *Mexican American Youth Organization: Avant-Garde of the Chicano Movement in Texas.* Austin: University of Texas Press, 1995; Pycior, Julie Leininger. *LBJ and Mexican Americans: The Paradox of Power.* Austin: University of Texas Press, 1997; Rosales, F. Arturo. *Chicano!: The History of the Mexican American Civil Rights Movement,* 2nd ed. Houston: Arte Público Press, 1997.

VENDIDO. *Vendido* literally means sold or betrayed, or more loosely, a sell-out. It was an epithet widely used during the **movimiento** to characterize a Mexican American who had become completely integrated into Anglo society and ignored his or her *raza* roots. Related terms were coconut (brown on the outside but white inside) and Tío Taco (after Uncle Tom).

VIETNAM CONFLICT, 1954–1975. United States involvement in the Vietnam War began with its aid to the government of South Vietnam in its efforts to suppress communist insurgency. After the Gulf of Tonkin resolution in 1964, the U.S. military support rapidly escalated; by 1969 over five hundred thousand troops were involved, of whom an estimated eighty-three thousand were Latinos. They suffered a casualty rate of approximately 50 percent; giving little credence to the U.S. rationale for the war, they suffered from low morale. The patriotism and machismo of their fathers' generation was replaced with a pragmatic ambivalence. As the guerrilla fighting went on year after year, their overriding concern soon became survival, simply getting through another day without getting killed or wounded.

On the home front, the Chicano community was early divided by the issues raised by the U.S. involvement in Vietnam. Issues of class, generation, gender, and individual experience divided the community. The burgeoning Chicano **movimiento** served to politicize segments of the community, but its dominant institutions yielded only slowly to the changing popular sentiment. By the end of the 1960s, the **National Chicano Moratorium** committee had been created in southern California and in December 1969 it organized its first demonstration and march. Draft counseling, draft resistance, and antiwar demonstrations soon became the order of the day. The climax came with the 29 August 1970 antiwar demonstration at Laguna Park in Los Angeles that attracted about twenty-five thousand persons and was converted into a riot by police action. In the following months there were lesser demonstrations against the war all over the Southwest, but especially in California. By the end of 1972 issues of the draft and Vietnam slowly subsided and Moratorium leaders were turning to other concerns like police brutality, education, and housing.

Many Chicanos were changed by the Vietnam War experience. One of the very few positive results of the Mexican American involvement in the war was the heightened political awareness of many veterans. Many were not yet twenty-one, and the war was a maturing experience for them. On the negative side, the returning vets found jobs scarce and the unemployment rate for Chicanos was higher than the 12 percent average.

FURTHER READING: Appy, Christian G. *Working Class War: American Combat Soldiers and Vietnam.* Chapel Hill: University of North Carolina Press, 1993; Mariscal, George, ed. *Aztlán and Viet Nam: Chicano and Chicana Experiences of the War.* Berkeley: University of California Press, 1999; Oropeza, Lorena. "¡La batalla esta aquí! Chicanos Oppose the War in Vietnam." Ph. D. dissertation, Cornell University, 1996; Ramírez, Juan. *A Patriot After All: The Story of a Vietnam Vet.* Albuquerque: University of New Mexico Press, 1999; Trujillo, Charley, ed. *Soldados: Chicanos in Viet Nam.* San Jose, Calif.: Chusma House, 1990.

VIGIL, DONACIANO, 1802–1877. Soldier, political leader. Donaciano Vigil, the scion of an old Nuevoméxicano family, was born and grew up in Santa Fe. Since no formal schools existed on the north Mexican frontier during his childhood, he and his siblings were tutored by their father, a minor public official. Throughout his life Vigil read extensively. Although without formal scholastic training, he was considered one of the best educated Nuevomexicanos of his day.

At age twenty-one, Donaciano became a soldier in the Santa Fe presidio and soon got to be widely known as a result of his courageous actions in campaigns against raiding Navahos. Supported by governor **Manuel Armijo**, he won election to the territorial legislature in 1838 and then became Armijo's secretary. In 1846 he led in the military preparations to oppose the U.S. invasion, but decided not to resist when the governor fled to Chihuahua.

Vigil was appointed territorial secretary in the new government established by U.S. general Stephen Kearny. Then as a result of governor Charles Bent's assassination during the Taos revolt he became acting governor, and at the end of 1847 was appointed civil governor. Subsequently he served in both the territorial assembly and council established by the United States. In 1855 he became an important participant in the U.S. Surveyor General's investigation of New Mexico land claims, and apparently used his position to legally enrich his friends and himself. During the Civil War he was a forthright supporter of the Union and President Abraham Lincoln's policies. When he died at age seventy-five, he was widely respected for his wise and moderate leadership during a time of considerable political turmoil and difficult cultural transition.

FURTHER READING: Crocchiola, Stanley F. *Giant in Lilliput: The Story of Donaciano Vigil.* Pampa, Tex.: Pampa Print Shop, 1963; Hall, G. Emlen. "Giant before the Surveyor General: The Land Career of Donaciano Vigil." *Journal of the West* 19:3 (1980) 64–73; Salazar, J. Richard. *The Military Career of Donaciano Vigil.* Guadalupita, N.M.: Center for Land Grant Studies, 1994; Weber, David J., ed. *Arms, Indians, and the Mismanagement of New Mexico: Donaciano Vigil.* El Paso: Texas Western Press, 1986.

VIGILANTISM. *Vigilantism* is the assumption of governmental functions, particularly law enforcement, by an extralegal group, frequently self-appointed. Vigilante activity was widespread in the American West during the second half of the 1800s, and Mexicanos were often its victims in the Southwest. Because most were mestizos, they were first stereotyped as guilty of crimes in California gold fields and Texas plains, and then given over to vigilante "justice," which often meant being hanged immediately from the nearest tree. While theoretically invoked to create law and order in an area where there was little or none, vigilantism in the Southwest often was merely "lynch law" for Mexicanos.

FURTHER READING: Blew, Robert W. "Vigilantism in Los Angeles, 1835–1874." *Southern California Quarterly* 54:1 (Spring 1972) 11–30; Hollon, W. Eugene. *Frontier Violence.* New York: Oxford University Press, 1974; Johnson, David A. "Vigilance and the Law: The Moral Authority of Popular Justice in the Far West." *American Quarterly* 33:5 (1981) 558–586.

VILLA, PANCHO (FRANCISCO), 1878–1923. Mexican revolutionary. Pancho Villa (Doroteo Arango) was one of the charismatic leaders of the 1910 **Mexican revolution** in the north. Originally a peon on a northern hacienda and at various times a peddler, miner, construction worker, small-time bandit, and cattle rustler, he joined the Mexican revolution in support of Francisco Madero. As head of a guerrilla band that fought the "*federales*," he came to symbolize the spirit of revolt among Mexico's poorest classes in the north. Given this background, it was perhaps inevitable that, like **Emiliano Zapata**, he became a revolutionary symbol for many Chicano activists during the movimiento.

FURTHER READING: Katz, Friedrich. *The Life and Times of Pancho Villa.* Stanford: Stanford University Press, 1998; Krauze, Enrique. *Mexico: Biography of Power: A History of Modern Mexico, 1810–1996.* New York: HarperCollins, 1997; McLynn, Frank. *Villa and Zapata: A History of the Mexican Revolution.* New York: Carroll & Graf, 2001.

VILLALPANDO, CATHI (CATALINA) V., 1940– . Businesswoman. Cathi Villalpando was born and grew up in San Marcos, Texas, where she attended parochial grade school and public high school. After high school she worked in a jewelry store and then as a secretary at Southwest Texas State College, where she continued her studies. Influenced by her father, she then enrolled in the Austin College of Business while working part-time at the regional Republican headquarters. In 1969 she became assistant to the local director of the Community Service Administration, the first of several appointments having to do with minorities and small businessmen. A decade later she organized V. P. Promotions, a firm with a government contract to provide advice and assistance to minority-owned savings and loan companies.

With Ronald Reagan's win in 1980, Republican Villalpando went to Washington briefly but then returned to the business world, where she soon became a senior vice president in Communications International. In 1983 she returned to Washington as special assistant to president Ronald Reagan for Hispanic affairs, and six years later was appointed U.S. Treasurer by president George Bush. In September 1994 she was convicted of tax fraud, obstructing justice, and conspiracy and was sentenced to four months in prison and three years of probation, during which she would spend four months in house arrest and perform two hundred hours of community service.

FURTHER READING: "Catalina Villalpando." *U.S. News & World Report* 117: 12 (26 September 1994) 32; "Former Treasurer Villalpando Jailed for Federal Tax Evasion." *Financial Times* (London) (14 September 1994) 4; Goode, Stephen. "Cathi Villalpando, Special Assistant to the President." *Nuestro* (January–February 1985) 16–19.

VILLANUEVA, DANNY, 1937– . Football great, businessman. Daniel Villanueva was born of migrant missionary workers at Tucumcari in eastern New Mexico. While he was still quite small, the family moved, first to Arizona and then to the Imperial Valley in California, where he attended grade and high schools. In high school and college he showed considerable skill in sports, especially in football. After attending Reedly College in California and then graduating from New Mexico State University at Las

Cruces with an A.B. in English, he played four years for the Los Angeles Rams and then three years with the Dallas Cowboys. In 1968 he retired from football, becoming a sports broadcaster for KMEX-TV, a Los Angeles Spanish language station. Within a year he had been promoted to news director, station manager, and in 1971 to general manager and vice president. In the following year he organized Spanish International Network-West, in which he was vice president and general manager, and then became president of KMEX-TV. For years he hosted Navidad en el Barrio, a Christmas telethon to raise money for the poor. In 1985 he helped launch a telethon that raised fifteen million dollars for victims of the 1985 earthquake in Mexico.

In all of his positions Villanueva has pursued a policy of social commitment. In 1989 he established the Villanueva Foundation to provide an annual one hundred thousand dollars in scholarships for promising Latino students. His commitment and philanthropy have brought him appointments to a dozen committees and boards and numerous awards for his community involvement.

FURTHER READING: Kirk, Robin. "Where Charity Begins." *Vista* (20 January 1990) 5–6. Longoria, Mario. *Athletes Remembered: Mexicano/Latino Professional Football Players*. Tempe, Arizona: Bilingual Press, 1997; Márquez, Pauline. "Doing What Comes Naturally." *Caminos* 5:7 (July–August 1984) 26–27, 28; Martínez, Al. *Rising Voices: Profiles of Hispano American Lives*. New York: New American Library, 1974.

VILLANUEVA, TINO, 1941– . Poet, critic, short story writer, painter. Tino Villanueva was born of immigrant parents in San Marcos, Texas, where he grew up. In high school he was more interested in sport activities than academic pursuits and on graduation went to work in a furniture factory. In 1964 he was drafted into the U.S. Army and spent two years in the Panama Canal Zone. Out of the service, he enrolled in Southwest Texas State at San Marcos and received his B.A. in 1969. Two years later he earned his M.A. in Romance languages at State University of New York, Buffalo. He has taught at the State University of New York, Boston University, and Wellesley College.

In 1972 Villanueva published the first book of his poetry, *Hay otra voz: Poems*, which won high praise from the critics. It was followed by works of literary criticism and more poetry. In 1993 he published what was to become his most widely and highly acclaimed work, *Scene from the Movie GIANT*. His poems have been published in various literary collections and journals. Considered one of the top Chicano poets, he is also editor of *Imagine: International Chicano Poetry Journal* as well as a painter of some note.

FURTHER READING: Binder, Wolfgang, ed. *Partial Autobiographies: Interviews with Twenty Chicano Poets*. Erlangen, Germany: Palm & Enke, 1985; Bruce-Novoa, Juan. *Chicano Authors: Inquiry by Interview*. Austin: University of Texas Press, 1980; Villanueva, Tino. *Scene from the Movie GIANT*. Willimantic, Conn.: Curbstone Press, 1993.

VILLARAIGOSA, ANTONIO R., 1953– . Assembly speaker. Antonio Villaraigosa was born in the City Terrace barrio of East Los Angeles and grew up there. He had a difficult childhood, defined early by the alcoholism and domestic violence of his Mexican immigrant father, who abandoned the family. After age five he was raised solely by his mother. As a boy he sold newspapers, shined shoes, and swept barbershop floors to help the family finances. He played football in high school and joined his teammates in the Black Student Union; he helped found the United Mexican American Students organization and chaired a chapter of the **Movimiento Estudiantil Chicano de Aztlán**. A rebellious leader of student protests and an indifferent student, in 1969 he was expelled from Cathedral High School in his junior year.

Although Villaraigosa dropped out of school, because of **affirmative action** he was later able to enter the University of California at Los Angeles and its law school. After graduation he went to work in the labor movement as a union organizer.

In 1994 Villaraigosa won election to the California Assembly, where he focused on educational opportunity and helping the state's most disadvantaged citizens. A coalition builder, he soon became widely respected as one of the assembly's hardest workers and most diplomatic persuaders. He declared that his priority was to hammer out a compromise with Republicans on a statewide school bond proposal. The high point of his work in the assembly was passage of the $9.2 billion bond measure to modernize California's public education system. In 1998 he was elected speaker of the assembly, which made him an ex officio member of the University of California's board of regents. After the demise of affirmative action, he persuaded the members of the board to make possible increased eligibility and access to the university.

In 1999 Cathedral High School held a celebration in his honor in which he was given his diploma, a class ring, and a school jacket. The next year Villaraigosa was the recipient of the César Chávez Acción Y Compromiso Human and Civil Rights Award from the National Education Association for his commitment to helping workers achieve dignity as well as better working conditions and wages. In March 2001 he was named Humanitarian of the Year by the Israel Humanitarian Foundation for his concern and efforts on behalf of California's most vulnerable residents.

Having left the assembly because of term limits, Villaraigosa ran for mayor of Los Angeles in 2001. In the April primary he led the aspirants for the office, with 30 percent of the vote. After a campaign characterized by anti-Mexican attacks, considerable mudslinging, and a poor turnout (41 percent) of registered Latino voters, the board member of the American Civil Liberties Union and unapologetic liberal lost his bid for the mayor's office in the June runoff to Anglo James Hahn.

FURTHER READING: Franco, Chris. "Antonio Villaraigosa: Dedicated to Bringing L.A. Together." *Latin Style* 39 (May/June 2001) 38–43; Radelat, Ana. " Why Latinos Lost in L.A." *Hispanic* (July/August 2001) 22-23.

VILLARREAL, JOSÉ ANTONIO, 1924– . Novelist, professor. José Antonio Villarreal was born in Los Angeles of immigrant Mexican parents but grew up and received his early education in Santa Clara, California, where the family settled out of the migrant stream. As a youth he was an avid reader and frequent patron of the town library. Certain that he wanted to become a writer, during his high school years he began writing short stories and sending them off for publication. When the United States entered World War II in 1941, the seventeen-year-old high school graduate enlisted in the U.S. Navy.

Mustered out of the service, Villarreal enrolled in the University of California at Berkeley to fulfill his dream of becoming a writer. He graduated in 1950 with an B.A. in English literature and began writing what was to become his first novel, *Pocho*. During the 1950s he married, started a family, and worked at various jobs while he continued revising *Pocho* and submitting it for publication. Finally in 1959 he succeeded in getting it published, but the work attracted little interest and was soon allowed to go out of print. The rise of the Chicano Movement in the 1960s aroused considerable interest in his broadly autobiographical book, and it quickly became the premier, if somewhat controversial, novel of the Chicano literary renaissance.

Meanwhile, Villarreal began work on a loose tetralogy, of which *Pocho* was to be a part, while he taught at various universities, visited Mexico, and freelanced as a writer. A steadfast individualist and a romantic, in the early 1970s he decided to move permanently to Mexico. While retaining his U.S. citizenship, he became a Mexican citizen and continued to teach at universities in both countries. In 1974 *The Fifth Horseman*, the second volume of the tetralogy, was published, and ten years later the Bilingual Press issued volume three, *Clemente Chacón*. Volume four, on which Villarreal continues to work, has yet to appear.

In 1992 Villarreal brought his family back to the United States and settled in a small north California town, where he continues his vocation as a writer.

FURTHER READING: Bruce-Novoa, Juan. *Chicano Authors: Inquiry by Interview.* Austin: University of Texas Press, 1980; Jiménez, Francisco. "An Interview with José Antonio Villarreal." *Bilingual Review* 3:1 (Spring 1976) 66–72; Lomelí, Francisco A., and Carl R. Shirley, eds. *Chicano Writers: First Series.* Detroit: Gale Research, 1989; Martínez, Julio A., and Francisco A. Lomelí, eds. *Chicano Literature: A Reference Guide.* Westport, Conn.: Greenwood Press, 1985; Ryan, Bryan, ed. *Hispanic Writers: A Selection of Sketches from Contemporary Authors.* Detroit: Gale Research, 1991.

VIVA KENNEDY CLUBS. During the 1960 presidential campaign the Viva Kennedy clubs were created by Dr. **Héctor Pérez García** and Carlos

McCormick of the **American G.I. Forum** to organize Chicano support for the Democratic candidate, John F. Kennedy. Viewed as sympathetic to their aspirations, Kennedy captured the imagination of Mexican Americans, and the clubs quickly spread over the entire Southwest. The enthusiastic support of the clubs was important in Kennedy's narrow victory over his Republican opponent, Richard Nixon. Kennedy's win also increased realization among Mexican Americans of the potential in their political participation. After the election many of the clubs were converted to more enduring organizations, including Mexican Americans for Political Action and the **Political Association of Spanish-Speaking Organizations**.

FURTHER READING: García, Ignacio M. *Viva Kennedy: Mexican Americans in Search of Camelot*. College Station: Texas A & M University Press, 2000; Pycior, Julie Leininger. *LBJ and Mexican Americans: The Paradox of Power*. Austin: University of Texas Press, 1997.

VIZZARD, JAMES L., 1916–1988. Social activist. James Vizzard was a student and disciple of Paul S. Taylor, longtime researcher in Mexicano labor, and a friend of Chicago-based rights activist Saul Alinsky. After becoming a Jesuit priest in 1946, Vizzard spent the rest of his life as a vocal defender of farm workers' rights. He did graduate study in agricultural economics at several universities and in 1955 began thirteen years working for the National Catholic Rural Life Conference. During this time he became acquainted with and a close friend of **César Chávez.** Persistent health problems forced him to resign from the Conference, but he soon was appointed director of the Jesuit social apostolate in California.

In 1972, at Chávez's urging, Vizzard agreed to become the Washington, D.C. spokesman and lobbyist for the **United Farm Workers**. In that position he testified before numerous congressional committees as an expert witness on agricultural economics and the rights of labor. During his forty years of speaking out for unorganized labor he was influential in the passage of legislation to improve the lot of farm workers. He helped secure the passage of the Farm Labor Contractor Registration Act Amendment of 1974 and the Child Labor Law Amendment of the same year. Three years later he had to resign because of his seriously deteriorating health, and spent the last years of his life at Santa Clara University. He was the author of over two hundred articles, most related to farm labor.

FURTHER READING: Aiello, Louise. "Fr. Vizzard: Outspoken Witness." *Lines and Spaces* (Santa Clara University) 1:1 (September 1971); Vizzard, James L. "The Extraordinary César Chávez. *Progressive* 30 (July 1966) 16–20. James L. Vizzard Papers, 1942-1983 (M0324), Special Collections and University Archives, Green Library, Stanford University.

VOTING. Low levels of voter registration and voter turnout continue to be serious problems in the Chicano struggle for political power and greater equality. Historically, Mexican American voting has been severely obstructed by many factors, principally legal or de facto disenfranchisement and constant, as well as sometimes violent, discouragement by Anglos. Long-standing discriminatory political practices clearly continue to affect Mexican American voting even today.

California's first constitution denied many darker-skinned Californios the vote by limiting the privilege to white males, despite guarantees of the **Guadalupe Hidalgo treaty**. In Texas, intimidation, threats, and physical abuse were widely used for over a century, in addition to the grandfather clause, to discourage Mexican Americans from registering and from going to the polls. Some states used interpretation of English language passages and literacy tests, which could be applied selectively with ease, to deny Mexican Americans the ballot. At-large elections and gerrymandering are two other devices frequently employed to dilute the Mexican American vote.

A further variety of stratagems has clearly helped discourage Mexican American participation in electoral politics. Residency requirements as well as limited and inconvenient access to registration kept many migrant workers from being able to vote. In some states a requirement of annual re-registration to retain eligibility was one more technique that deterred Mexican American voting. In addition, until fairly recently poll taxes were used to further discourage participation in the political process. The almost complete domination of politics in the Southwest by Anglos, with the partial exception of New Mexico and to a lesser extent south Texas, has further intimidated *raza* voters.

Voting also responds to cultural factors, especially among naturalized citizens, many of whom may feel cynical about elections and government in general, from past experience in both Mexico and the United States. Finally, poverty and low levels of education are widely accepted as having a negative effect on registration and voting. Some experts believe that the levels of education are the single most important factor in registration and election turnout.

After the mid-twentieth century, court challenges to gerrymandering and at-large elections enabled more Mexican Americans to register and vote, and in the 1960s a series of federal civil rights acts, aimed primarily to help African Americans, made it possible for many Mexican Americans to take part in the electoral process for the first time. The **Voting Rights Act** of 1965 and amendments in 1975 and 1982 led to widespread voter registration drives among Chicanos. Between 1976 and 1980 the number of Mexican Americans registered to vote increased by 25 percent and the number who voted was up by 20 percent. During the 1980s continuing registration drives led to further registration increases; however, the number actually voting remained unsatisfactorily low, as is true of the general population.

In 1996 the **Southwest Voter Registration Education Project**, the Midwest Voter Registration Education Project, and the Hispanic Education and Legal Fund joined forces to form Latino Vote USA '96, which registered over one million new *raza* voters in Texas and California. During the 1990s the number of Latino voters doubled.

Impelled by anti-immigrant propositions on the California ballot and the immigrant-bashing of Republican governor Pete Wilson, more than a million California Latinos voted in the 1996 election for the first time. After lagging badly in the past two decades, when only 25 to 30 percent of those registered actually voted, in the 1996 presidential election about 50 percent cast their ballots. In the non-presidential elections two years later, a California newspaper headline proclaimed: "Latinos prove powerful at polls." Cruz Bustamante was elected lieutenant governor, the first Latino elected to statewide office in over a hundred years, and Latinos won six additional seats in the legislature at Sacramento. In New Mexico's 1998 political contests voters elected four Mexican Americans to state offices: secretary of state, attorney general, treasurer, and auditor. In Colorado Denver attorney Ken Salazar became the state's first Mexican American attorney general.

Today Mexican American voters have awakened more fully to the power of the ballot and their voting record has become respectable. Further, population projections and electoral statistics clearly indicate the potential of their political power in the twenty-first century.

FURTHER READING: Avila, Joaquín G. "Access to the Political Process and the Development of Leadership." *La Raza Law Journal* 11:2 (1999–2000) 91–97; Camarillo, Lydia. "Counting Our Election Returns." *Hispanic* (January/February 1997) 108; De Sipio, Louis. *Counting on the Latino Vote: Latinos as a New Electorate.* Charlottesville: University Press of Virginia, 1996; García, F. Chris and Rudolph O. de la Garza. *The Chicano Political Experience: Three Perspectives.* North Scituate, Mass.: Duxbury Press, 1977; García, F. Chris, ed. *Pursuing Power: Latinos and the Political System.* Notre Dame: University of Notre Dame Press, 1997; Gonzales, Raymond J. "Why Chicanos Don't Vote." *California Journal* 6:7 (July 1975) 245–246; Vigil, Maurilio E. "The Hispanic Vote." *Hispanics in American Politics.* Lanham, Md.: University Press of America, 1987; Yáñez-Chávez, Anibal, ed. *Latino Politics in California.* San Diego: Center for U.S.-Mexican Studies, University of California, San Diego, 1996.

VOTING RIGHTS ACT, 1965. The Voting Rights Act, also known as the Civil Rights Act of 1965, was initially advanced by President Lyndon Johnson to protect the civil rights of African Americans. It made possible direct federal intervention, where necessary, to enable citizens to register and vote. The law specifically rejected the inability of some citizens to speak English as a basis for denying them the franchise, and it limited the use of literacy tests to disqualify citizens from voting. Although written basically to protect the voting rights of black Americans in the South, the act also served to encourage accelerated Chicano voter registration and get-out-the-vote drives.

In 1970 the Voting Rights Act was extended by Congress for five years with an added provision to prevent the erection of new barriers to political participation. In 1975 the act was again renewed with important additions for

Mexican Americans. New provisions included a requirement for bilingual ballots in certain language-dominated areas, and the ban on literacy tests was made permanent. Another provision allowed individuals to file suit against local jurisdictions for denial of their voting rights. Seven years later the act was extended to the year 2007, and included an absolute abolition of discriminatory practices such as at-large elections. The 1975 and 1982 acts specifically aimed at language minority groups like Mexican Americans. The success of the voting rights acts for Mexican Americans is attested to by both the much larger numbers voting and the growing number elected to public office.

FURTHER READING: Davidson, Chandler. "The Voting Rights Act: Protecting the Rights of Racial and Language Minorities in the Electoral Process." *Chicano-Latino Law Review* (Summer 1993) 1–14; De la Garza, Rodolfo O. and Louis DeSipio. "Save the Baby, Change the Bathwater, and Scrub the Tub: Latino Electoral Participation after Twenty Years of Voting Rights Act Coverage." In *Pursuing Power: Latinos and the Political System,* edited by F. Chris García. Notre Dame: University of Notre Dame Press, 1997; García, John A. "The Voting Rights Act and Hispanic Political Representation in the Southwest." *The Journal of Federalism* 16 (Fall 1986) 49–66; Graham, Hugh Davis. *The Civil Rights Era, 1960–1972.* New York: Oxford University Press, 1990; Polinard, J. L. et al. *Electoral Structure and Urban Policy: The Impact on Mexican American Communities.* Armonk, N.Y.: M. E. Sharpe, 1994.

WASHINGTON MARCH, 1996. The 1996 march on Washington, D.C., was a rally by Latino civil rights advocates and other activists to voice their demands for equality of treatment in the United States. The march was a result of broad Chicano concerns, especially the increasing attacks on **affirmative action** programs in the 1990s.

Led by Los Angeles activist Juan José Gutiérrez, the march assembled at the Ellipse, where the participants listened to various speakers describe a platform listing seven demands centered on human and constitutional rights for all and including a simplified citizenship process. The crowd of attendees, estimated at between twenty and thirty thousand, was notable for the large number of grassroots workers from communities all over the country.

FURTHER READING: Gage, Julienne. "Latino March on Washington." *Sojourners* (January–February 1996) 15; *Hispanic Link Weekly Report* (23 September 1996) 1; Ramos, George. "Thousands of Latinos March in Washington." *Los Angeles Times* (13 October 1996) A1, A39.

WESTERN FEDERATION OF MINERS. The WFM was established in 1893 by the merger of several Rocky Mountain miners' unions. A radical anticapitalist labor organization, it battled against employers throughout the 1890s in a series of violent conflicts and in the following decade was important in establishing the Industrial Workers of the World. In 1916 it became the International Union of Mine, Mill, and Smelter Workers after rejoining the American Federation of Labor (to which it had briefly belonged in the 1990s) five years earlier. Because of atrocious conditions in the western coal and copper mines, many Mexicanos joined the WFM; some learned organizing skills that they later found useful in developing their own unions.

FURTHER READING: Jensen, Vernon H. *Heritage of Conflict.* Ithaca, N.Y.: Cornell University Press, 1950; Mellinger, Philip J. *Race and Labor in Western Copper: The Fight for Equality, 1896–1918.* Tucson: University of Arizona Press, 1995.

WETBACK. *Wetback* is a pejorative term for an undocumented entrant to the United States from Mexico. It derives from the assumption that entrance was made by crossing the **Rio Grande.** A dry land border-crosser is known as an *alambrista,* one who climbs over a wire fence. It does not have the strong pejorative connotation of wetback.

WHEATLAND RIOT, 1913. The Wheatland riot was a significant incident in a major agricultural strike in 1913 near Wheatland, California. Landowner Ralph Durst's advertisement for workers brought nearly three thousand applicants, many of whom were Mexicanos, to his hop ranch. Once there, they were offered low pay and dehumanizing unsanitary housing conditions. Under the leadership of Industrial Workers of the World organizers they formed a committee to demand better conditions. A warning shot fired by a sheriff's deputy during a rally touched off a riot in which four people died and many more were injured. The arrival of four companies of the National Guard brought about the arrest of about a hundred workers and an end to the violence.

The Wheatland riot created a greater awareness of the inhumane conditions under which **migratory labor** often worked, and led to state inspection of California farm labor camps.

FURTHER READING: Jamieson, Stuart M. *Labor Unionism in American Agriculture.* Washington, D.C.: Government Printing Office, 1945; Street, Richard Steven. "'We Are Not Slaves:' The Photographic Records of the Wheatland Hop Riot: the First Images of Protesting Farm Workers in America." *Southern California Quarterly* 64;3 (1982) 205–226.

WILLIAMS, TED, 1918–2002. In February 2001 Ted Williams was installed as the first Latino to be inducted into the Hispanic Heritage Baseball Museum Hall of Fame in San Francisco, California. The fact that he was of Mexican American heritage surprised many, even dedicated baseball fans, a surprise that arose because of his feeling that family matters were private matters. Throughout his career he seemed to take a rather dim view of everything that the press wrote about his exploits and him, especially about his private life.

Williams was born and grew up in San Diego, California, the son of May Venzor, a first-generation Mexican American, and Samuel Williams. As a youth he was strongly interested in sports, especially handball and baseball. His mother's brother, Saul Venzor, who played semipro ball and managed a local team, had a decisive influence on the boy. Ted seemed determined to prove himself to his uncle as a ballplayer. That resolve was nurtured in the frequent lessons from Uncle Saul and formed the basis for his later exploits as a professional baseball player. An outfielder, he was one of the greatest hitters in the game, with a batting average of over 400. Twice he interrupted his very successful baseball career to serve as a fighter pilot in the U.S. Air Force, during World War II and the Korean conflict.

Williams spoke no Spanish and never thought of himself as anything other than an American. His Mexican heritage, which he neither denied nor trumpeted, was simply not a part of his life as a baseball icon.

FURTHER READING: Barra, Allen. "A Legend, Plain and Simple." *San Jose Mercury News* (14 July 2002) 2C; Nowlin, Bill. "El Splinter Esplendido." *Boston Globe Magazine* (2 June 2002) 15–19; Nowlin, Bill. *Ted Williams: The Pursuit of Perfection.* Sports Publishing, 2002; Seidel, Michael. *Ted Williams: A Baseball Life.* Chicago: Contemporary Books, 1991; Williams, Ted. *My Turn at Bat.* New York: Simon and Schuster, 1969.

WORLD WAR I, 1914–1919. World War I saw thousands of Mexican Americans, proportionately more than members of any other ethnic group, voluntarily enlisting in the U.S. armed services. In the service they continued to experience much of the discrimination earlier encountered in civilian life, but many broadened their horizons and raised levels of expectations. Some achieved distinguished military records and most developed a fuller awareness of themselves as American citizens. Their experiences in the military also lessened their long-standing rural southwestern isolation, pushed them further into the American mainstream, and provided organizational training for some. Newly acquired leadership skills furnished much of the basis for the Mexican American organizational development that followed in the 1920s.

At home, the war's industrial needs became a major factor in enabling more Mexicanos to move out of their traditional rural southwestern isolation, to urban environments and especially to better-paying jobs in the growing industrial centers of the Midwest. At the same time wartime labor demands in southwestern agriculture, mining, and railroading attracted perhaps as many as 150,000 workers from Mexico.

FURTHER READING: Christian, Carole E. "Joining the American Mainstream: Texas Mexican Americans during World War I." *Southwestern Historical Quarterly* 92:4 (April 1989) 559–595; García, Mario T. "Americans All: The Mexican American Generation and the Politics of Wartime Los Angeles, 1914–1945." *Social Science Quarterly* 65:2 (1984) 278–285; Meier, Matt S., and Feliciano Ribera. *Mexican Americans/American Mexicans: From Conquistadors to Chicanos.* New York: Hill and Wang, 1993; Sáenz, José de la Luz. *Los México-americanos en la gran guerra: y su contingente en pro de la democracia, la humanidad y la justicia.* San Antonio: Artes Gráficas, 1933.

WORLD WAR II, 1939–1945. World War II was a definite benchmark in the Mexican American experience. As a result of their service in the armed forces during the war, more than 300,000 Chicanos gained access to a variety of opportunities to improve the quality of their lives and their position in American society. Through the G.I. Bill that came out of the war many were enabled to obtain employment training and university educations. World War II also exposed many born in the 1920s and early 1930s to possibilities outside the confines of urban barrios or the rural Southwest for the first time. It helped engender greater self-confidence and fostered higher aspirations. It created a greater political awareness that promoted greater participation in American life, fueled vigorous protests in the postwar against discriminatory practices, and led to the founding of a large number of dynamic **organizations**—local, regional, and national.

On the home front during the war, the proliferation of military bases and the expansion of industry in the Southwest brought to the city large numbers of Mexican Americans, whose children were then afforded better educational opportunities than their rural parents had experienced. During the war Chicanos increasingly demanded equality in the workplace, and the federal government created the **Fair Employment Practices Committee** to enforce the prohibition on worker discrimination in defense industries holding government contracts. The committee's investigations of discriminatory labor practices encouraged Mexicano workers to speak out more freely in defense of their rights, and righted some obvious wrongs. Mexican American women were able to get jobs in the defense industry and participated in various war-related activities including war bond drives.

World War II also brought into sharper focus the social and educational problems faced by Mexican Americans. State and federal agencies mounted efforts to lessen prejudice against them and to end discrimination. In the interest of greater mutual respect, some public schools began programs to reduce **segregation** and to develop appreciation of Mexican culture. Institutes and workshops were organized to implement these objectives, to sensitize teachers, and to develop more understanding attitudes toward Mexicano children and their educational rights. These partially successful efforts in turn created some minimal awareness of other social problems.

Wartime experiences helped Chicano veterans develop energetic self-help organizations: the **American G.I. Forum**, **Community Service Organization**, **Mexican American Political Association**, **Political Association of Spanish-Speaking Organizations**, and other regional and national groups whose leaders vigorously spearheaded a renewed drive for Chicano rights. Explicitly political in their objectives, these groups challenged racism and discriminatory practices and demanded full civic rights for all Mexican Americans. Also, many prewar organizations like the **League of United Latin American Citizens,** now having many veterans in their enlarged membership, moved with the times and gave greater emphasis to civil rights issues in their agendas.

Clearly, World War II set in motion increased Chicano participation in all aspects of American life. The veterans of World War II, overwhelmingly native-born, felt less culturally Mexican and experienced a deeper sense of American citizenship than did their parents. Using political pressure and the ballot, they reinvigorated and expanded the fight against discrimination and racism. Their children, brought up in this heady, energizing postwar atmosphere, went further, creating a medley of student groups, and **La Raza Unida Party**.

FURTHER READING: García, Mario T. "Americans All: The Mexican American Generation and the Politics of Wartime Los Angeles, 1914–1945." *Social Science Quarterly* 65:2 (1984) 278–285; Gonzalez, Larry. "Hero Street USA." *Hispanic* (March

1990) 23–24; Marín, Christine. " Mexican Americans on the Home Front: Community Organizations in Arizona during World War II." *Perspectives in Mexican American Studies* 4 (1993) 75–92; Morín, Raúl. *Among the Valiant: Mexican Americans in World War II and Korea.* Los Angeles: Borden, 1963; *Narratives: Stories of U.S. Latinos and Latinas and World War II.* 2:1 (Fall 2000), 2:2 (Spring 2001), 3:1 (Fall 2001). U. S. Latino and Latina WWII Oral History Project, School of Journalism, University of Texas at Austin; Santillán, Richard. "Rosita the Riveter: Midwest Mexican American Women During World War II, 1941–1945." *Perspectives in Mexican American Studies* (1989) 115–147; *Spanish Speaking Americans in the War: The Southwest.* Washington, D.C.: Office of the Coordinator of Inter-American Affairs, 1940–1949.

XIMENES, VICENTE TREVIÑO, 1919– . Economist, government official, social activist. Born in Floresville, Texas, southeast of San Antonio, Vicente Ximenes attended the University of Texas at Austin after high school and a year in the Civilian Conservation Corps. Having completed three semesters at Austin in 1940, he took a job as the principal of a two-room Texas elementary school. He served in the Army Air Force from 1941 to 1947, retiring as a major, and completed his B.A. at the University of New Mexico in 1950. In the following year he earned an M.A. in economics. Between 1952 and 1964 he was involved in doing research, teaching economics, and working for the federal Agency for International Development in Ecuador and Panama.

An energetic participant in various activities of the **American G.I. Forum**, of which he was national chairman in 1950, Ximenes became campaign director of the Viva Johnson movement for the Democratic National Committee in 1964. Three years later he was named by President Lyndon B. Johnson to a four-year term on the **Equal Employment Opportunity Commission** (EEOC). As a commissioner, Ximenes used his position to introduce **affirmative action** as an approach to further the struggle for the rights of disadvantaged minorities. In the fall of 1967 he programmed the first National Conference on Mexican American Affairs, held in El Paso, Texas. He organized EEOC hearings and conferences in several southwestern cities to secure the support of business in the elimination of workplace discrimination.

As a result of his leadership, Ximenes was later selected by President Johnson to head the new **Inter-Agency Committee on Mexican American Affairs**. As its chairman he was instrumental in securing some four thousand federal positions for Mexican Americans. In 1982 Ximenes returned to Albuquerque, where he subsequently founded a human rights group. From 1988 to 1990 he was the executive director of the New Mexico State Democratic Party. Active in Common Cause, he was recently involved in New Mexico's governorship race. For his efforts to secure greater social justice for the disadvantaged he was given the United Nations' human rights award and various other honors, including the Order of Vasco Nuñez de Balboa by the government of Panama.

FURTHER READING: Alford, Harold J. *The Proud Peoples*. New York: David McKay Co., 1972; Chacón, José A. *Hispanic Notables in the United States of North America*. Albuquerque: Saguaro Press, 1978; Martínez, Erika Liliana. "Man Fought to Eliminate Segregation He Grew Up With." *Narratives: Stories of U.S. Latinos and Latinas and World War II*. 3:1 (Fall Semester 2001) 4; Pycior, Julie Leininger. *LBJ and Mexican Americans: Paradox of Power*. Austin: University of Texas Press, 1997.

Y

YZAGUIRRE, RAÚL, 1939– . Activist, organizer. While still a teenager in the Rio Grande valley of south Texas, Raúl Yzaguirre became involved in improving educational opportunities for Mexican American students. With this objective in mind and inspired by Dr. **Héctor Pérez García**, he was active in high school, organizing youth chapters of the **American G.I. Forum**. After high school and service in the U.S. Air Force from 1958 to 1962 he entered George Washington University, where he created a Chicano umbrella group named the National Organization for Mexican American Services. With his university degree, in 1966 he went to work as a program analyst in the Migrant Division of the Office of Economic Opportunity (OEO).

With the goal of addressing Mexican American problems, Yzaguirre left the OEO in 1969 to organize a research and consulting firm, Interstate Research Associates. Five years later he agreed to take over the directorship of the **National Council of La Raza** (NCLR), the former Southwest Council of La Raza, which had recently moved from Texas to Washington, D.C. As its executive director for over a quarter of a century he was responsible, more than anyone else, for making the council an effective and highly respected Hispanic umbrella organization. His leadership has made the NCLR the preeminent U.S. Latino think tank and the largest federation of Latino organizations in the United States, with nearly three hundred formally affiliated groups and an annual budget of over five million dollars.

For his outstanding leadership Yzaguirre has been the recipient of numerous honors and awards. Chair of the Smithsonian Task Force on Latino Issues, he has served and serves on numerous private and governmental boards and commissions. In 1979 he became the first Mexican American to receive the Rockefeller Public Service Award from Princeton University. Seven years later he was honored with the Common Cause Award for Public Service. In 1989 he was named Hispanic Fellow at Harvard University's John F. Kennedy School of Government and four years later he was the recipient of the Aguila Azteca, Mexico's highest award to a noncitizen. For his contributions to the human and civil rights struggle he was also awarded the Martin Luther King, Jr. Medallion.

FURTHER READING: Frase-Blunt, Martha. "Committed to Unity." Hispanic (July 1992) 11–14; Gonzales, Sylvia A. *Hispanic American Voluntary Organizations.* Westport, Conn.: Greenwood Press, 1985; "Interview with Raúl Yzaguirre." *La Luz* 1:11 (March 1973) 26–28, 30; Martínez, Douglas. "Yzaguirre at the Helm." *Américas* 32:6–7 (June–July 1980) 49; Mora, Sabine. "In Recognition of Raúl Yzaguirre: President, National Council of La Raza." *Texas Hispanic Journal of Law and Policy* 7:1 (Fall 2001) 3–11; "The Movement's Organization Man." *Nuestro* (March 1982) 22–24, 62; "Profile of Leadership: Raúl Yzaguirre." *Hispanic Journal* (NCLR Special Edition, July 2–3, 2000) 15.

Z

ZAMORA, BERNICE, 1938– . Poet, teacher, writer. Bernice Ortiz was born in the town of Aguilar in southern Colorado of parents whose families had settled there during the 1700s. She grew up and received her early education in Denver and Pueblo, demonstrating considerable scholastic aptitude. In high school she became deeply interested in writing. Upon graduation she married at age nineteen, worked in a Pueblo bank, and continued her education through evening classes. At twenty-eight, with two children, she enrolled in Southern Colorado State and received her B.A. in 1969. Three years later she earned her M.A. in English and French literature at Colorado State University in Fort Collins.

Zamora then started a Ph.D. program, but interrupted it as her marriage began to flounder. In 1974 she moved to California with her two daughters. In California she began a doctoral program at Stanford University, where she organized small monthly social gatherings of Chicano writers. While a graduate student she published in various Chicano journals and also taught part-time. In 1976 she and **José Antonio Burciaga** published a collection of their poems titled *Restless Serpents*. It was greeted with great enthusiasm and was subsequently translated into five languages, including Chinese. The book made her a seminal poet in the Chicano literary renaissance. Three years later she again interrupted her graduate studies to accept the editorship of the magazine *De Colores* in Albuquerque.

After Albuquerque and a sojourn in Texas Zamora returned to California, completed her doctorate, and accepted a teaching position at Santa Clara University. In 1994 her most recent collection of poems, *Releasing Serpents*, was published by Bilingual Press. Although she does not consider herself a feminist, in her poetry Zamora explores feminist issues. Her poems express concern, indignation, and censure at all forms of exploitation and oppression.

FURTHER READING: Binder, Wolfgang, ed. *Partial Autobiographies: Interviews with Twenty Chicano Poets.* Erlangen, Germany: Palm & Enke, 1985; Bruce-Novoa, Juan. "Bernice Zamora and Lorna Dee Cervantes: Una estética feminista." *Revista Iberoamericana* 50 (July–December 1985) 565–573; Bruce-Novoa, Juan. *Chicano Authors: Inquiry by Interview.* Austin: University of Texas Press, 1980. Li, Gloria Elsa. "Bernice

Zamora: Interview." In *Chicana (W)rites on Word and Film*, edited by María Herrera Sobek and Helena María Viramontes. Berkeley: Third Woman Press, 1995.

ZAPATA, CARMEN, 1927– . Actress, producer, social activist. Carmen Zapata was born in New York City and grew up in Spanish Harlem. As a child she played the violin and piano in family musical evenings; at school she was active in dramatic presentations and sang in the choir. Later studies at the Actors Studio and work under famous drama coach Uta Hagen led to parts in Broadway musical plays. For two decades she appeared in outstanding musicals like *Oklahoma, Stop the World. I Want to Get Off,* and *Guys and Dolls.*

In 1967, after a Broadway flop, her mother's death, and a divorce, Zapata left New York for southern California, where she soon developed a highly successful movie and television career despite the stereotyping she frequently encountered. Two years later she was one of the cofounders, along with **Ricardo Montalbán**, of Nosotros, the Latino actors' rights group. For nine years she was Doña Luz, the mainstay of the Public Broadcasting System's bilingual program *Villa Alegre.* In 1970 she began what was to become the renowned Bilingual Foundation of the Arts, dedicated to bringing Spanish language theater to Los Angeles Latinos and, in translation, to Anglos. In 1993 she retired from the foundation.

Zapata, first lady of Latino cinema, has appeared in numerous films and television programs. Ever a hard-working activist, she has served on the boards of various groups, including the National Conference of Christians and Jews, the Mexican American Opportunities Foundation, and the California Arts Council Ethnic Advisory Minority Panel. For her unflagging efforts in social activism she has been the recipient of numerous awards at local, national, and international levels.

FURTHER READING: "Carmen Zapata." *Nuestro* (July 1978) 13–14; Hadley-García, George. *Hispanic Hollywood.* New York: Carol, 1990; Mejías-Rentería, Antonio. "The Coming Home of Carmen Zapata." *Vista* (12 March 1989) 5+; Telgen, Dianne, and Jim Kamp, eds. *Latinas! Women of Achievement.* Detroit: Visible Ink Press, 1996.

ZAPATA, EMILIANO, 1879–1919. Mexican revolutionary. Emiliano Zapata was the principal leader of peasant guerrilla fighters in central Mexico during the 1910 revolution. Probably the most unpretentious, selfless, and honest of the 1910 revolutionary leaders, he became the symbol of the Mexican peons' land hunger with his slogan "*Tierra y Libertad.*" It was almost foreordained that in the 1960s he would become a leading symbol for the Chicano Movement and especially for those militants who advocated a Chicano homeland in the Southwest.

FURTHER READING: Brunk, Samuel. *Emiliano Zapata: Revolution and Betrayal in Mexico.* Albuquerque: University of New Mexico, 1995; Krauze, Enrique. *Mexico: Biography of Power: A History of Modern Mexico, 1810–1996.* New York: HarperCollins, 1997; McLynn, Frank. *Villa and Zapata: A History of the Mexican Revolution.* New York:

Carroll & Graf, 2001; Womack, John, Jr. *Zapata and the Mexican Revolution.* New York: Alfred A. Knopf, 1969.

ZARAGOZA SEGUÍN, IGNACIO, 1829–1862. Tejano general. Ignacio Zaragoza was born in Texas and educated in Monterrey in the state of Nuevo León, to which his father moved when Texas gained its independence from Mexico. After studying for the priesthood, he followed in his father's footsteps, entered the Mexican army, and fought on the liberal side during Mexico's conservative-liberal conflict of the 1850s and 1860s. The crowning achievement of his military career was his repelling of the formidable invading French army at Puebla on May 5, 1862. This accomplishment is recalled every year by the Mexican American celebration of Cinco de Mayo as a cultural holiday. In the 1960s General Zaragoza State Historic Site was established to commemorate his birthplace near Goliad, Texas.

FURTHER READING: Berrueto Ramón, Federico. *Ignacio Zaragoza.* Mexico, D.F.: Secretaría de Educación Pública, Subsecretaría de Asuntos Culturales, 1966; Tyler, Ron, ed. *New Handbook of Texas*, vol. 6. Austin: Texas State Historical Association, 1996.

ZAVALA, ADINA EMILIA DE, 1861–1955. Civic leader. Adina de Zavala, the granddaughter of empresario grantee Lorenzo de Zavala, was born near Houston. Having completed her college education in Texas and Missouri, she taught school and soon became interested in preserving historical sites. About 1889 she and other San Antonio women established a preservationist society that later affiliated with the Daughters of the Republic of Texas. Her outstanding achievement was preventing a part of the Alamo complex from being razed in the first decade of the twentieth century in the mistaken belief that it dated from after the famous siege. She even barricaded herself in the building for three days in her resolute stand against its destruction.

Adina de Zavala was outstanding in stirring up interest in the preservation of sites from the Spanish and Mexican eras. She was a charter member of the Texas State Historical Association, and in 1912 she organized the Texas Historical and Landmarks Association. She was an active member of numerous organizations including the Texas Women's Press Association and was the author of *History and Legends of the Alamo and Other Missions in and Around San Antonio* as well as some historical pamphlets.

FURTHER READING: Ables, Robert L. "The Second Battle for the Alamo." *Southwestern Historical Quarterly* 70:3 (1976) 372–413; Tyler, Ron, ed. *New Handbook of Texas, vol 6.* Austin: Texas State Historical Association, 1996; Zavala, Adina de. *History and Legends of the Alamo and Other Missions in and around San Antonio.* Edited and introduced by Richard R. Flores. Houston: Arte Público Press, 1996.

ZOOT SUIT RIOTS, 1943. Following the **Sleepy Lagoon** case, tensions between Anglos and Mexican American youths remained high in Los Angeles. The city had a large second-generation Mexican American population whose teenage members had adopted as a kind of badge the zoot suit out-fit then all the rage among urban American youths. A number of small alter-cations occurred in the early spring of 1943, when sailors and soldiers attacked zoot-suiters, removing their baggy pants. When Chicano youths retaliated they were subjected to harsh repression by the authorities and many were arrested. At the beginning of June there were serious clashes in which restive armed forces personnel attacked Chicano youths on the streets of Los Angeles. Zoot-suiters were dragged off streetcars and out of buses and cinemas; many were assaulted with sticks, clubs, and chains, and had their clothes ripped off, and some had their longish hair cut. A virtual war on Chicano youths rapidly ensued.

Fueled by sensationalist press coverage, a series of street brawls quickly turned into full-scale race riots. Sheriff's deputies and police followed the action, usually ignoring the military aggressors and arresting the victims for disturbing the peace. The Los Angeles violence triggered similar racial at-tacks on Chicano youths in a number of U.S. cities with sizeable Mexican American populations. Finally, as a result of pressure from Washington the military police cracked down and military leaves were canceled. By mid-June the attacks tapered off and order was restored.

California governor Earl Warren appointed a citizens' committee to in-vestigate the causes of the Zoot Suit rioting and to make recommendations. Its damning report on the way the riots were handled led to the inaugura-tion of a few programs to improve communication between Los Angeles officials and the Mexican American community. Overall, however, there were few long-term achievements in improving conditions in the barrio or enforc-ing civil rights. In the Los Angeles Chicano community the handling of this outrageous attack by the authorities left a residue of mistrust and great bit-terness. This hostile feeling was strongly reinforced and renewed by the death of **Rubén Salazar** during the Chicano Moratorium a quarter of a cen-tury later.

FURTHER READING: California, Governor. *Citizens Committee Report on the Zoot Suit Riots.* Sacramento: State Printing Office, 1943; Griswold del Castillo, Richard. "The Los Angeles 'Zoot Suit Riots' Revisited: Mexican and Latin American Perspec-tives." *Mexican Studies* 16:2 (Summer 2000) 367–391; McWilliams, Carey. *North from Mexico: The Spanish-Speaking People of the United States,* rev. ed. Westport, Conn.: Praeger, 1990; McWilliams, Carey. "Zoot Suit Riots." *New Republic* 108 (21 June 1943) 818–820; Mazón, Mauricio. *The Zoot Suit Riots: The Psychology of Symbolic Annihilation.* Austin: University of Texas Press, 1994; Sánchez, George I. "Pachucos in the Mak-ing." *Common Ground.* 4:1 (Fall 1943) 13–20; Tuck, Ruth. "Behind the Zoot Suit Riots." *Survey Graphic* 32 (August 1943) 313–316, 335–336.

ZOOT-SUITER. The term zoot-suiter described a Chicano youth who took up a form of dress and lifestyle adopted by many urban American youths during the 1940s. He was characterized by wearing loose-fitting pegged trousers, a jacket heavily padded in the shoulders and reaching almost to the knees, and a wide-brimmed, low-crowned hat. The term was at least mildly pejorative.

FURTHER READING: Luckenbill, Don. *The Pachuco Era: Catalogue of an Exhibit, University Research Library, September–December 1990*. Los Angeles: University of California, University Research Library, Department of Special Collections, 1990.

Index

About the Authors

MATT S. MEIER (deceased) was Patrick A. Donohoe, S.J. Professor Emeritus at Santa Clara University. He was a pioneer in researching and teaching the history of Mexican Americans. His most recent books include the *Encyclopedia of the Mexican American Civil Rights Movement* (2000, with Margo Gutiérrez) and *Notable Latino Americans: A Biographical Dictionary* (1997).

MARGO GUTIÉRREZ is Assistant Head Librarian at the Nettie Lee Benson Latin American Collection at the University of Texas, Austin. She is the coauthor of the *Encyclopedia of the Mexican American Civil Rights Movement* (2000, with Matt Meier) and *The Border Guide* (1992).